STREET Aberdeenshire

Aberdeen, Ellon, Fraserburgh, Inverurie, Peterhead, Stonehaven

www.philips-maps.co.uk

First published in 2004 by

Philip's, a division of
Octopus Publishing Group Ltd
www.octopusbooks.co.uk
2-4 Heron Quays, London E14 4JP
An Hachette Livre UK Company
www.hachettelivre.co.uk

Second edition 2008
First impression 2008
ABDBA

ISBN 978-0-540-09291-8 (pocket)

Printed and bound in China by Toppan

Contents

II **List of mobile speed cameras**

III **Key to map symbols**

IV **Key to map pages**

VI **Route planning**

X **Administrative and Postcode boundaries**

1 **Street maps** at 1⅓ inches to 1 mile

139 **Street maps** at 2⅔ inches to 1 mile

190 **Street map of Aberdeen city centre** at 5⅓ inches to 1 mile

191 **Index** of towns, villages, streets, hospitals, industrial estates, railway stations, schools, shopping centres, universities and places of interest

Digital Data

The exceptionally high-quality mapping found in this atlas is available as digital data in TIFF format, which is easily convertible to other bitmapped (raster) image formats.

The index is also available in digital form as a standard database table. It contains all the details found in the printed index together with the National Grid reference for the map square in which each entry is named.

For further information and to discuss your requirements, please contact james.mann@philips-maps.co.uk

On-line route planner

For detailed driving directions and estimated driving times visit our free route planner at www.philips-maps.co.uk

Mobile speed cameras

The vast majority of speed cameras used on Britain's roads are operated by safety camera partnerships. These comprise local authorities, the police, Her Majesty's Court Service (HMCS) and the Highways Agency.

This table lists the sites where each safety camera partnership may enforce speed limits through the use of mobile cameras or detectors. These are usually set up on the roadside or a bridge spanning the road and operated by a police or civilian enforcement officer. The speed limit at each site (if available) is shown in red type, followed by the approximate location in black type.

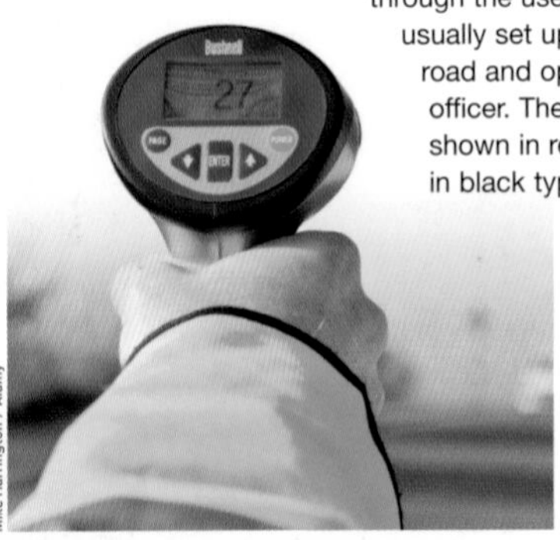

Mike Harrington / Alamy

A90
- 40 Aberdeen, Midstocket Rd to Whitestripes Rdbt
- 60 btwn bend at South of Leys and Bogbrae
- 60 btwn Bogbrae and north of Bridgend
- 70 btwn Candy and Upper Criggie
- 70 btwn Laurencekirk and north of Fourdon
- 70 btwn Mill of Barnes and Laurencekirk
- 70 Dundee to Aberdeen Rd at Jct with B9120 Laurencekirk
- 70 north of Newtonhill Jct to South of Schoolhill Rd
- 60 Peterhead, btwn north of Bridgend and Blackhills
- 70 south of Schoolhill Rd, Portlethen to South Damhead (northbound)

A92
- NSL btwn Johnshaven and Inverbervie
- NSL btwn rdside of Kinneff and Mill of Uras

A93
- 30 Aboyne
- 40 at Banchory eastbound from Caravan Site
- 30 at Banchory westbound from Church
- NSL btwn Cambus O'May and Dinnet
- NSL btwn Dinnet to Aboyne
- NSL btwn Kincardine O'Neil and Haugh of Sluie

A95
- 30 Cornhill

A96
- NSL btwn north of Pitmachie and Jct with A920 at Kirton of Culsalmond
- NSL Keith to Huntly Rd betwn Auchairn and Coachford
- 30 Btwn Haudagain and Chapel of Stoneywood
- NSL Huntly btwn A920 Dufftown and B9022 Portsey jcns
- 70 Inverurie btwn Thainstone Agricultural Centre and Port Elphinstone
- 60 Inverurie btwn Inveramsey and Conglass

A98
- 30 Banff

A933
- NSL Arbroath to Brechin, Redford

A935
- NSL Brechin to Montrose, Gilrivie
- NSL Brechin to Montrose, House of Dun
- NSL Brechin to Montrose, Tayock

A944
- 30,40,60 Westhill Rd btwn Gairloch and Westhill Rdbt

A947
- NSL btwn Mains of Tulloch Jct and Fyvie
- NSL btwn Newmachar and Whiterashes

A948
- NSL btwn Ellon to Auchnagatt

A952
- NSL btwn New Leeds and Jct with A90 at Cortes

A956
- 30 Aberdeen, Ellon Rd
- 30 Aberdeen, King St near St Ninian's
- 30 Aberdeen, North Esplanade West
- 40 Aberdeen, Wellington Rd

A978
- NSL Aberdeen, St Machar Drive

B9040
- NSL btwn Silver Sands Caravan Park to Jct with B9012

B9077
- 30 Aberdeen, Great Southern Rd

B9089
- NSL from Kinloss and crossroads at Roseisle Maltings

Unclassified
- 30 Aberdeen, Beach Boulevard to Links Rd
- 30 Aberdeen, Beach Boulevard to Wales St
- 30 Aberdeen, Ellon, Craigs Rd
- 30 Aberdeen, Springhill Rd
- 40 Aberdeen, Wellington Rd
- 40 Aberdeen, West Tullos Rd

Key to map symbols

Motorway with junction number
Primary route – dual/single carriageway
A road – dual/single carriageway
B road – dual/single carriageway
Minor road – dual/single carriageway
Other minor road – dual/single carriageway
Road under construction
Tunnel, covered road
Speed cameras - single, multiple
Rural track, private road or narrow road in urban area
Gate or obstruction to traffic (restrictions may not apply at all times or to all vehicles)
Path, bridleway, byway open to all traffic, restricted byway
Pedestrianised area
DY7 Postcode boundaries
County and unitary authority boundaries
Railway, tunnel, railway under construction
Tramway, tramway under construction
Miniature railway
Walsall Railway station
Private railway station
South Shields Metro station
Tram stop, tram stop under construction
Bus, coach station

Ambulance station
Coastguard station
Fire station
Police station
Accident and Emergency entrance to hospital
Hospital
Place of worship
Information Centre (open all year)
Shopping Centre
Parking, Park and Ride
Post Office
Camping site, caravan site
Golf course, picnic site
Prim Sch Important buildings, schools, colleges, universities and hospitals
Built up area
Woods
River Ouse Tidal water, water name
Non-tidal water – lake, river, canal or stream
Lock, weir, tunnel
Church Non-Roman antiquity
ROMAN FORT Roman antiquity
87 237 Adjoining page indicators and overlap bands
The colour of the arrow and the band indicates the scale of the adjoining or overlapping page (see scales below)

Acad	Academy	Inst	Institute	Recn Gd	Recreation Ground
Allot Gdns	Allotments	Ct	Law Court	Resr	Reservoir
Cemy	Cemetery	L Ctr	Leisure Centre	Ret Pk	Retail Park
C Ctr	Civic Centre	LC	Level Crossing	Sch	School
CH	Club House	Liby	Library	Sh Ctr	Shopping Centre
Coll	College	Mkt	Market	TH	Town Hall/House
Crem	Crematorium	Meml	Memorial	Trad Est	Trading Estate
Ent	Enterprise	Mon	Monument	Univ	University
Ex H	Exhibition Hall	Mus	Museum	W Twr	Water Tower
Ind Est	Industrial Estate	Obsy	Observatory	Wks	Works
IRB Sta	Inshore Rescue Boat Station	Pal	Royal Palace	YH	Youth Hostel
		PH	Public House		

Enlarged mapping only

Railway or bus station building
Place of interest
Parkland

■ The small numbers around the edges of the maps identify the 1 kilometre National Grid lines ■ The dark grey border on the inside edge of some pages indicates that the mapping does not continue onto the adjacent page

The scale of the maps on the pages numbered in blue is 4.2 cm to 1 km • 2⅔ inches to 1 mile • 1: 23810

0 ¼ ½ ¾ 1 mile
0 250m 500m 750m 1 kilometre

The scale of the maps on pages numbered in green is 2.1 cm to 1 km • 1⅓ inches to 1 mile • 1: 47620

0 ¼ ½ ¾ 1 mile
0 250m 500m 750m 1 kilometre

The scale of the maps on pages numbered in red is 8.4 cm to 1 km • 5⅓ inches to 1 mile • 1: 11900

0 220 yards 440 yards 660 yards ½ mile
0 125m 250m 375m ½ kilometre

Key to map pages

190	Map pages at 5⅓ inches to 1 mile
180	Map pages at 2⅔ inches to 1 mile
138	Map pages at 1⅓ inches to 1 mile

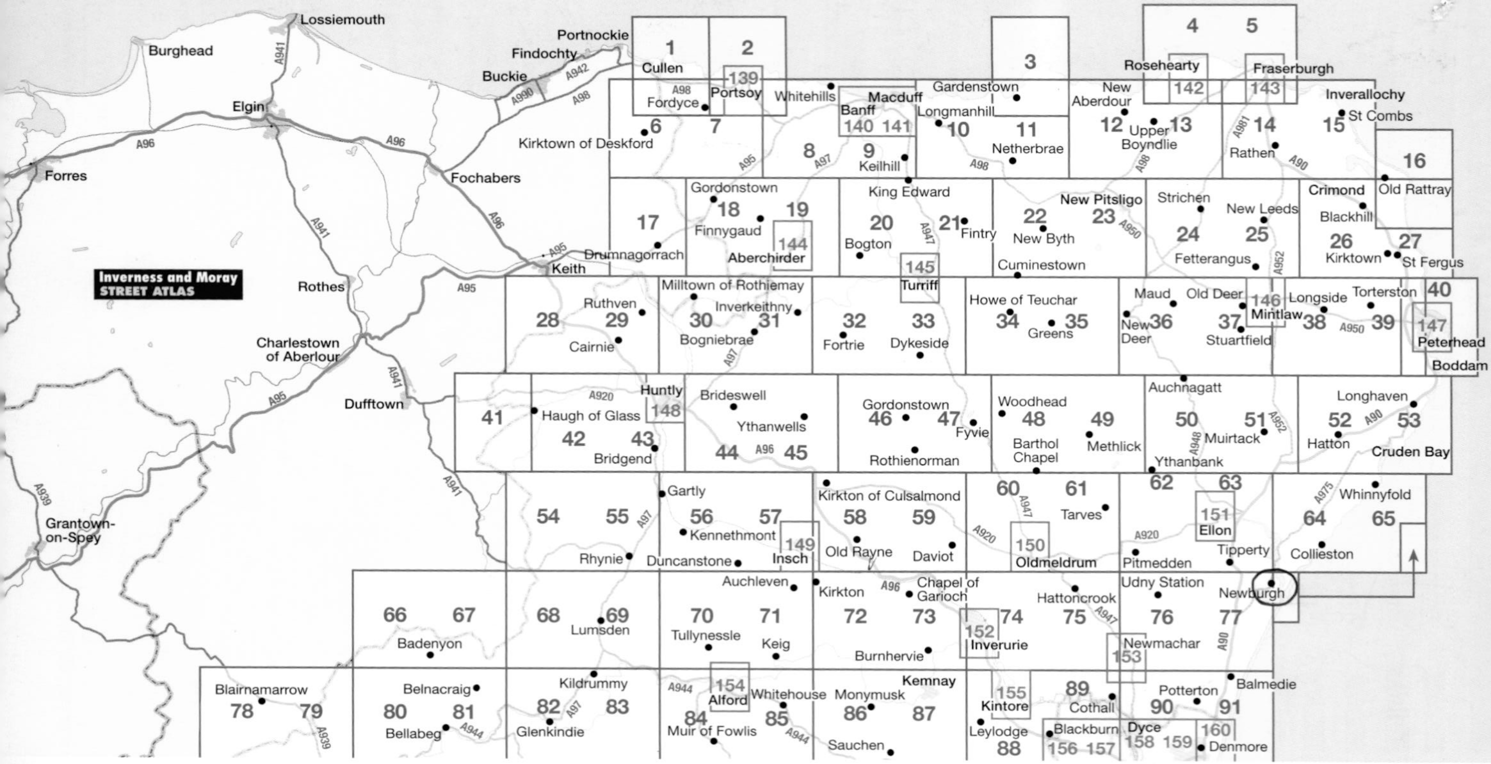

Inverness and Moray STREET ATLAS

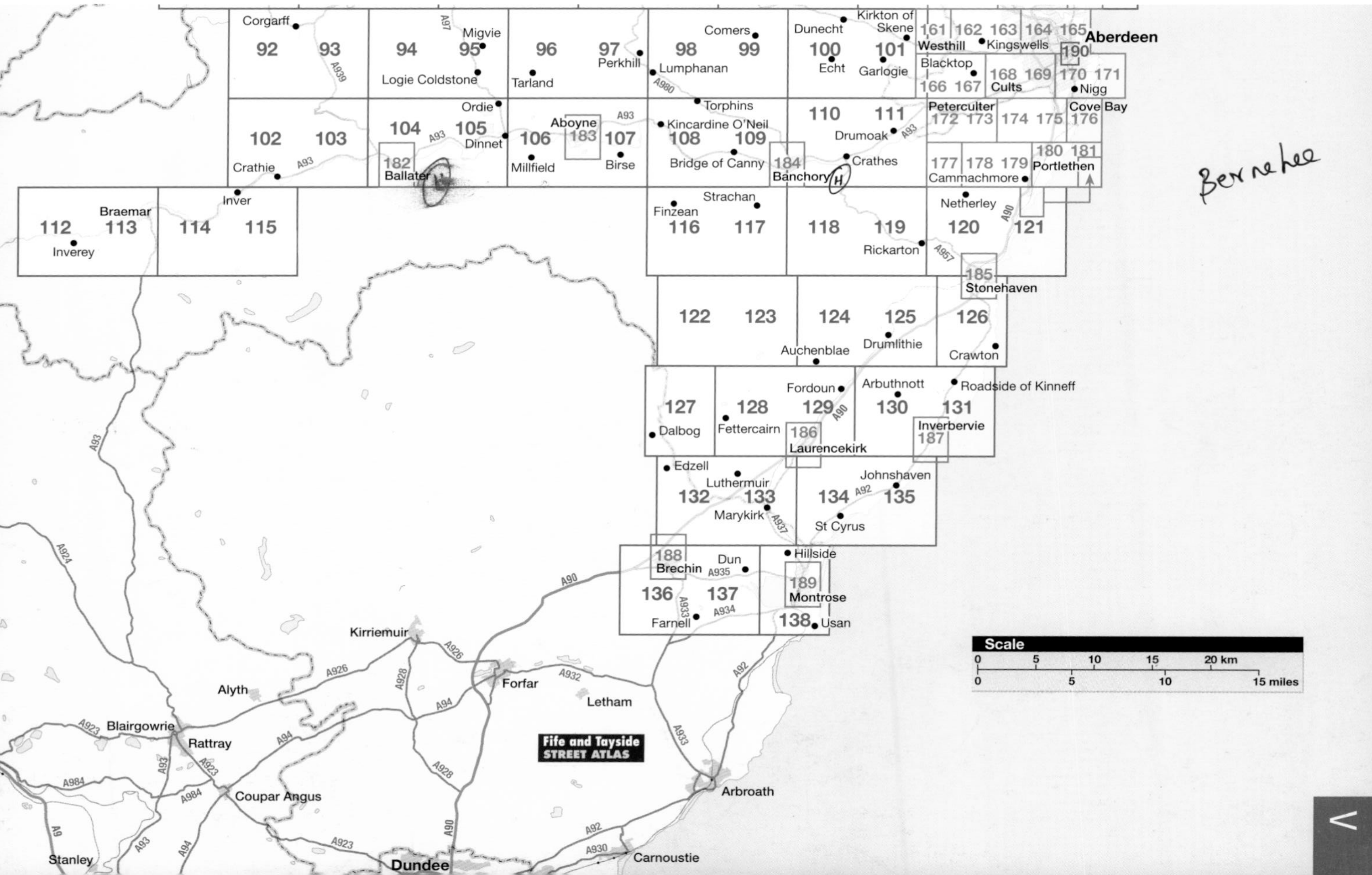
Aberdeen
Westhill
Kingswells
Kirkton of Skene
Dunecht
Echt
Garlogie
Blacktop
Cults
Nigg
Cove Bay
Peterculter
Portlethen
Cammachmore
Corgarff
Migvie
Logie Coldstone
Tarland
Perkhill
Comers
Lumphanan
Torphins
Kincardine O'Neil
Bridge of Canny
Drumoak
Crathes
Banchory
Ordie
Dinnet
Aboyne
Birse
Millfield
Crathie
Ballater
Inver
Braemar
Inverey
Finzean
Strachan
Netherley
Rickarton
Stonehaven
Auchenblae
Drumlithie
Crawton
Fordoun
Arbuthnott
Roadside of Kinneff
Fettercairn
Dalbog
Laurencekirk
Inverbervie
Edzell
Luthermuir
Marykirk
Johnshaven
St Cyrus
Hillside
Brechin
Dun
Montrose
Farnell
Usan
Kirriemuir
Forfar
Letham
Alyth
Blairgowrie
Rattray
Coupar Angus
Arbroath
Carnoustie
Stanley
Dundee
Fife and Tayside STREET ATLAS
Scale
0 5 10 15 20 km
0 5 10 15 miles
92 93 94 95 96 97 98 99 100 101
161 162 163 164 165 166 167 168 169 170 171 172 173 174 175 176 177 178 179 180 181
190
102 103 104 105 106 107 108 109 110 111
182 183 184
112 113 114 115 116 117 118 119 120 121
185
122 123 124 125 126
127 128 129 130 131
186 187
132 133 134 135
188 189
136 137 138
A97 A939 A93 A980 A90 A957 A92 A937 A935 A934 A933 A926 A928 A932 A94 A923 A984 A924 A9 A930

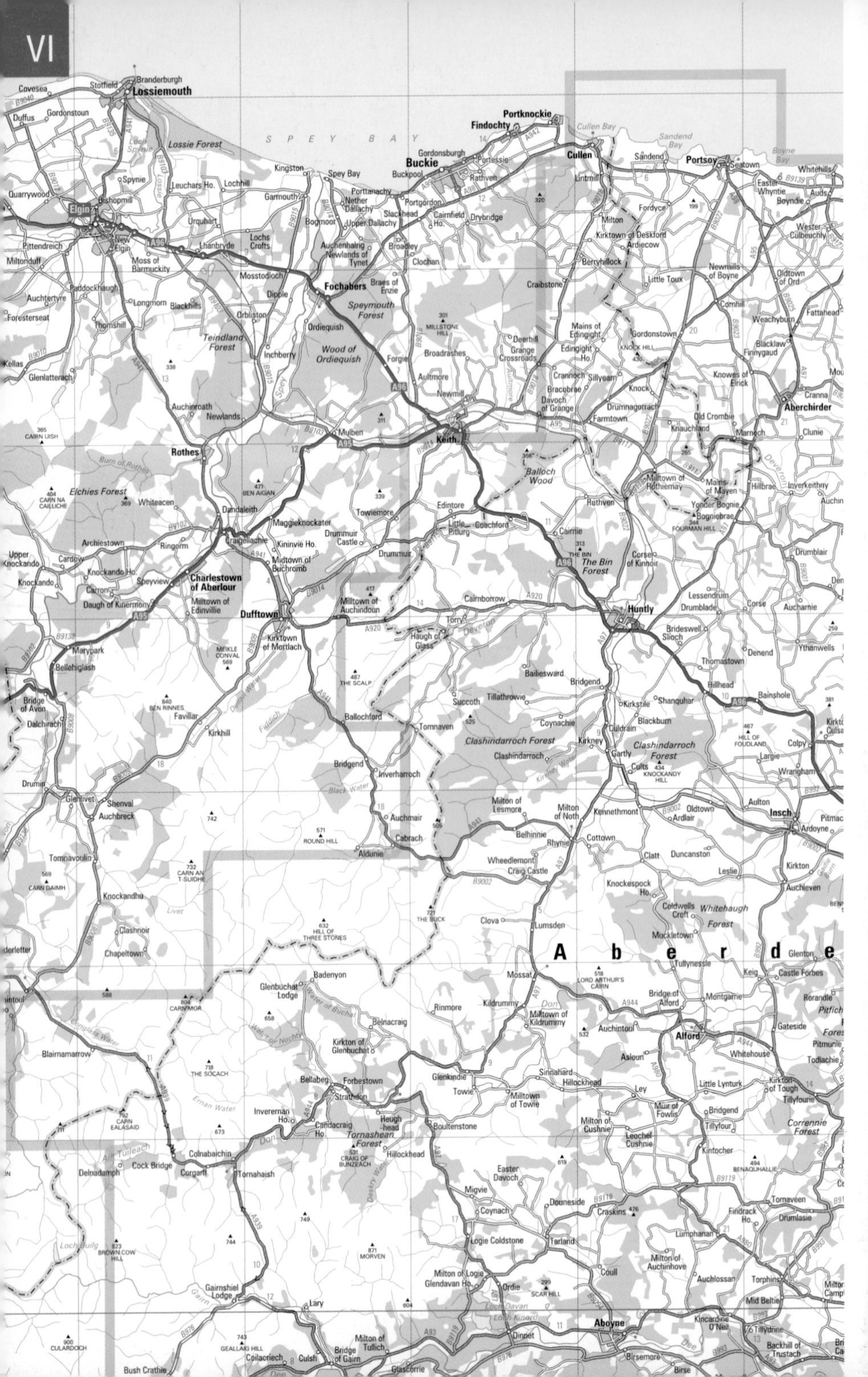
Covesea
Stotfield
Branderburgh
Lossiemouth
Duffus
Gordonstoun
Lossie Forest
SPEY BAY
Findochty
Portknockie
Cullen Bay
Sandend Bay
Boyne Bay
Cullen
Sandend
Portsoy
Seatown
Whitehills
Kingston
Spey Bay
Gordonsburgh
Buckie
Buckpool
Portessie
Rathven
Spynie
Leuchars Ho.
Lochhill
Garmouth
Porttannachy
Nether Dallachy
Portgordon
Linmill
Fordyce
Easter Whyntie
Boyndie
Quarrywood
Bishopmill
Elgin
Urquhart
Slackhead
Cairnfield Ho.
Drybridge
Milton
Bogmoor
Upper Dallachy
Kirktown of Deskford
Ardiecow
Wester Culbeuchly
Pittendreich
New Elgin
Lhanbryde
Lochs Crofts
Auchenhalrig
Newlands of Tynet
Broadley
Miltonduff
Moss of Barmuckity
Clochan
Berryhillock
Newmills of Boyne
Oldtown of Ord
Mosstodloch
Braes of Enzie
Little Toux
Paddockhaugh
Fochabers
Craibstone
Auchtertyre
Longmorn
Blackhills
Dipple
Speymouth Forest
Cornhill
Fattahead
Foresterseat
Thomshill
Orbliston
Ordiequish
Millstone Hill
Mains of Edingight
Gordonstown
Weachyburn
Teindland Forest
Deerhill
Grange Crossroads
Edingight Ho.
Knock Hill
Blacklaw
Finnygaud
Kellas
Inchberry
Wood of Ordiequish
Forgie
Broadrashes
Glenlatterach
Spey
Aultmore
Crannoch
Sillyearn
Knowes of Elrick
Newmill
Bracobrae
Knock
Cranna
Davoch of Grange
Drumnagorrach
Aberchirder
Auchinroath
Newlands
Old Crombie
Farmtown
Cairn Uish
Mulben
Keith
Knauchland
Marnoch
Clunie
Rothes
Burn of Rothes
Balloch Wood
Milltown of Rothiemay
Mains of Mayen
Hillbrae
Inverkeithny
Elchies Forest
Carn na Cailliche
Ben Aigan
Ruthven
Yonder Bognie
Bogniebrae
Fourman Hill
Whiteacen
Dandaleith
Edintore
Towiemore
Maggieknockater
Little Pitlurg
Coachford
Cairnie
Archiestown
Ringorm
Craigellachie
Kininvie Ho.
Drummuir Castle
Upper Knockando
Cardow
Midtown of Buchromb
Drummuir
The Bin
The Bin Forest
Corse of Kinnoir
Drumblair
Knockando
Knockando Ho.
Charlestown of Aberlour
Speyview
Carron
Daugh of Kinermony
Milltown of Edinvillie
Dufftown
Milltown of Auchindoun
Cairnborrow
Torry
Lessendrum
Drumblade
Corse
Auchamie
Huntly
Haugh of Glass
Deveron
Brideswell
Slioch
Marypark
Belleheiglash
Kirktown of Mortlach
Meikle Conval
Ythanwells
Denend
Thomastown
The Scalp
Bailiesward
Bridgend
Hillhead
Bainshole
Bridge of Avon
Ben Rinnes
Favillar
Succoth
Tillathrowie
Kirkstile
Shanquhar
Dalchirach
Kirkhill
Dullan Water
Fiddich
Ballochford
Tomnaven
Coynachie
Blackburn
Culdrain
Hill of Foudland
Colpy
Clashindarroch Forest
Clashindarroch
Kirkney
Gartly
Cults
Knockandy Hill
Largie
Wrangham
Drumin
Bridgend
Inverharroch
Glenlivet
Shenval
Auchbreck
Black Water
Milton of Lesmore
Milton of Noth
Kennethmont
Oldtown
Ardlair
Aulton
Insch
Auchmair
Belhinnie
Rhynie
Cottown
Ardoyne
Round Hill
Cabrach
Aldunie
Tomnavoulin
Wheedlemont
Craig Castle
Clatt
Duncanston
Leslie
Kirkton
Carn an t-Suidhe
Carn Daimh
Knockandhu
Livet
Knockespock Ho.
Auchleven
The Buck
Clova
Lumsden
Coldwells Croft
Whitehaugh Forest
Clashnoir
Hill of Three Stones
Muckletown
Chapeltown
Aberdeen
Glenton
Badenyon
Mossat
Lord Arthur's Cairn
Tullynessle
Keig
Castle Forbes
Glenbuchat Lodge
Water of Buchat
Carn Mor
Rinmore
Kildrummy
Milltown of Kildrummy
Don
Bridge of Alford
Montgarrie
Rorandle
Belnacraig
Auchintoul
Alford
Gateside
Pitmunie
Conglass Water
Water of Nochty
Kirkton of Glenbuchat
Blairnamarrow
Asloun
Whitehouse
Todlachie
The Socach
Glenkindie
Sinnahard
Hillockhead
Bellabeg
Forbestown
Towie
Milltown of Towie
Ley
Little Lynturk
Kirkton of Tough
Tillyfourie
Strathdon
Ernan Water
Muir of Fowlis
Bridgend
Carn Ealasaid
Inverernan Ho.
Candacraig Ho.
Heugh-head
Boultenstone
Milton of Cushnie
Leochel Cushnie
Tillyfour
Corrennie Forest
Tornashean Forest
Allt Tuileach
Colnabaichin
Craig of Bunzeach
Hillockhead
Kintocher
Benaquhallie
Cock Bridge
Delnadamph
Corgarff
Tornahaish
Deskry Water
Easter Davoch
Migvie
Douneside
Craskins
Tornaveen
Coynach
Findrack Ho.
Drumlasie
Loch Builg
Brown Cow Hill
Logie Coldstone
Tarland
Lumphanan
Morven
Milton of Auchinhove
Milton of Logie
Glendavan Ho.
Ordie
Scar Hill
Coull
Auchlossan
Torphins
Gairnshiel Lodge
Gairn
Lary
Loch Davan
Loch Kinord
Mid Beltie
Aboyne
Kincardine O'Neil
Tillydrine
Culardoch
Geallaig Hill
Coilacriech
Culsh
Bridge of Gairn
Milton of Tullich
Dinnet
Dee
Birsemore
Birse
Backhill of Trustach
Bush Crathie
Glascorrie

Route Planning
Scale
0 5 10 km
0 1 2 3 4 5 6 miles
KIRKWALL 6:00
LERWICK 14:00
Aberdeen City
enshire
Fraserburgh
Peterhead
Aberdeen
Macduff
Banff
Rosehearty
Inverallochy
Crimond
New Pitsligo
Turriff
Mintlaw
Boddam
Cruden Bay
Ellon
Oldmeldrum
Inverurie
Newmachar
Kemnay
Kintore
Dyce
Westhill
Bridge of Don
Cults
Peterculter
Cove Bay
Gardenstown
Pennan
New Aberdour
Strichen
Maud
New Deer
Fyvie
Methlick
Newburgh
Balmedie
Blackdog
Stonehaven
St Fergus
St Combs
Cairnbulg Castle
Port Erroll
Collieston
Forest of Deer
Midmar Forest
Loch of Strathbeg
Fraserburgh Bay
Peterhead Bay
Sandford Bay
Bay of Cruden
Nigg Bay
Loch of Skene

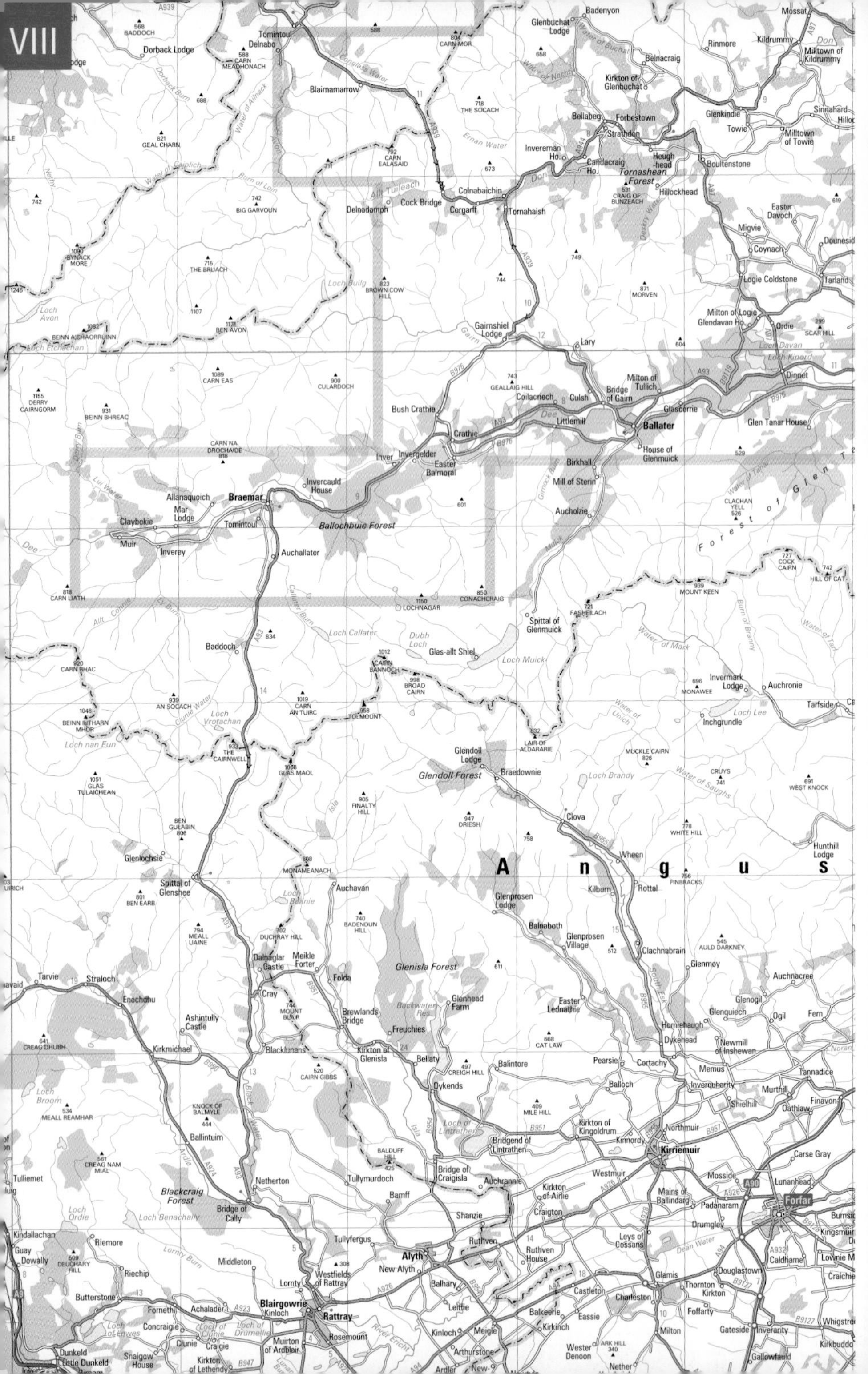

Tomintoul
Delnabo
Dorback Lodge
588 BADDOCH
588 CARN MEADHONACH
806 CARN MOR
Blairnamarrow
Conglass Water
688
718 THE SOCACH
821 GEAL CHARN
792 CARN EALASAID
673
Ernan Water
Glenbuchat Lodge
Badenyon
Water of Buchat
658
Water of Nochty
Belnacraig
Kirkton of Glenbuchat
Bellabeg
Forbestown
Strathdon
Invererman Ho.
Candacraig Ho.
Heugh-head
Tornashean Forest
531 CRAIG OF BUNZEACH
Hillockhead
Rinmore
Kildrummy
Mossat
Milltown of Kildrummy
Glenkindie
Towie
Sinnahard
Milltown of Towie
Boultenstone
Colnabaichin
Cock Bridge
Corgarff
Tornahaish
Delnadamph
Allt Tuileach
742 BIG GARVOUN
742
1090 BYNACK MORE
715 THE BRUIACH
1107
1171 BEN AVON
1082 BEINN A'CHAORRUINN
Loch Avon
Loch Etchachan
Loch Builg
823 BROWN COW HILL
744
749
871 MORVEN
Easter Davoch
Migvie
Coynach
Logie Coldstone
Tarland
Milton of Logie
Glendavan Ho.
Ordie
299 SCAR HILL
Loch Davan
Loch Kinord
Dinnet
Gairnshiel Lodge
Lary
604
1089 CARN EAS
900 CULARDOCH
743 GEALLAIG HILL
1155 DERRY CAIRNGORM
931 BEINN BHREAC
Bush Crathie
Coilacriech
Culsh
Bridge of Gairn
Milton of Tullich
Glascorrie
Ballater
Glen Tanar House
Crathie
Littlemill
Dee
House of Glenmuick
CARN NA DROCHAIDE 818
Inver
Invergelder
Easter Balmoral
Birkhall
Mill of Sterin
529
Invercauld House
Allanaquoich
Braemar
Mar Lodge
Claybokie
Tomintoul
Muir
Inverey
Ballochbuie Forest
601
Aucholzie
Water of Tanar
CLACHAN YELL 526
Forest of Glen Tanar
Auchallater
818 CARN LIATH
1150 LOCHNAGAR
850 CONACHCRAIG
727 COCK CAIRN
742 HILL OF CAT
939 MOUNT KEEN
721 FASHEILACH
Spittal of Glenmuick
Loch Callater
Dubh Loch
Glas-allt Shiel
Loch Muick
Water of Mark
Baddoch
834
1012 CARN BANNOCH
998 BROAD CAIRN
920 CARN BHAC
939 AN SOCACH
1019 CARN AN TUIRC
958 TOLMOUNT
Loch Vrotachan
1048 BEINN IUTHARN MHOR
Loch nan Eun
933 THE CAIRNWELL
1068 GLAS MAOL
832 LAIR OF ALDARARIE
696 MONAWEE
Invermark Lodge
Auchronie
Tarfside
Loch Lee
Inchgrundle
Glendoll Lodge
Braedownie
Glendoll Forest
MUCKLE CAIRN 826
CRUYS 741
691 WEST KNOCK
Loch Brandy
Water of Saughs
1051 GLAS TULAICHEAN
905 FINALTY HILL
947 DRIESH
Clova
778 WHITE HILL
BEN GULABIN 806
758
Glenlochsie
868 MONAMEANACH
Wheen
Hunthill Lodge
Angus
Spittal of Glenshee
801 BEN EARB
Auchavan
Loch Beanie
Glenprosen Lodge
Kilburn
Rottal
756 FINBRACKS
740 BADENDUN HILL
794 MEALL UAINE
702 DUCHRAY HILL
Balnaboth
Glenprosen Village
512
Clachnabrain
545 AULD DARKNEY
Dalnaglar Castle
Meikle Forter
Glenisla Forest
611
Glenmoy
Tarvie
Straloch
Enochdhu
Folda
Cray
744 MOUNT BLAIR
Brewlands Bridge
Backwater Res.
Glenhead Farm
Easter Lednathie
Auchnacree
Glenogil
Glenquiech
Ogil
Fern
Ashintully Castle
Freuchies
Horniehaugh
Dykehead
Newmill of Inshewan
641 CREAG DHUBH
Kirkmichael
Blacklunans
Kirkton of Glenisla
Bellaty
668 CAT LAW
Pearsie
Cortachy
Memus
Tannadice
520 CAIRN GIBBS
497 CREIGH HILL
Balintore
Dykends
Balloch
Inverquharity
Murthill
Loch Broom
534 MEALL REAMHAR
KNOCK OF BALMYLE 444
409 MILE HILL
Shielhill
Finavon
Oathlaw
Loch of Lintrathen
Bridgend of Lintrathen
Kirkton of Kingoldrum
Kinnordy
Northmuir
Kirriemuir
Ballintuim
561 CREAG NAM MIAL
BALDUFF HILL 425
Bridge of Craigisla
Auchrannie
Westmuir
Mosside
Lunanhead
Carse Gray
Tulliemet
Blackcraig Forest
Netherton
Tullymurdoch
Bamff
Kirkton of Airlie
Craigton
Mains of Ballindarg
Padanaram
Forfar
Drumgley
Loch Ordie
Loch Benachally
Bridge of Cally
Shanzie
Ruthven
Leys of Cossans
Kindallachan
Guay
Dowally
509 DEUCHARY HILL
Riemore
Riechip
Middleton
Tullyfergus
308
Alyth
New Alyth
Ruthven House
Dean Water
Caldhame
Lownie
Douglastown
Burnside
Kingsmuir
Westfields of Rattray
Lornty
Balhary
Glamis
Thornton
Kirkton
Castleton
Charleston
Crichie
Butterstone
Forneth
Achalader
Blairgowrie
Kinloch
Rattray
Leitfie
Balkeerie
Eassie
Foffarty
Loch of Lowes
Concraigie
Loch of Clunie
Loch of Drumellie
Rosemount
Kirkinch
Milton
Gateside
Inverarity
Whigstreet
Clunie
Craigie
Muirton of Ardblair
River Ericht
Kinloch
Meigle
Arthurstone
Wester Denoon
ARK HILL 340
Dunkeld
Little Dunkeld
Snaigow House
Kirkton of Lethendy
Gallowfauld
Kirkbuddo
Nether

IX
Aberdeen City
Aberdeen
Alford
Kemnay
Kintore
Newmachar
Dyce
Westhill
Cults
Peterculter
Bridge of Don
Old Aberdeen
Torry
Nigg Bay
Cove Bay
Portlethen
Newtonhill
Muchalls
Stonehaven
Cowie
Castle Haven
Thornyhive Bay
Crawton
Crawton Bay
Catterline
Braidon Bay
Kinneff
Little John's Haven
Inverbervie
Bervie Bay
Gourdon
Johnshaven
St Cyrus
Laurencekirk
Fettercairn
Edzell
Brechin
Montrose
Montrose Basin
Ferryden
Fishtown of Usan
Lunan Bay
Inverkeilor
Letham
Friockheim
Auchmithie
Banchory
Aboyne
Torphins
Lumphanan
Echt
Midmar Forest
Blackhall Forest
Durris Forest
Fetteresso Forest
Drumtochty Forest
Montreathmont Forest
Corrennie Forest
Pitfichie Forest
Mount Battock
Hill of Wirren
Kerloch
Mongour
Cairn Mon Earn
Hill of Fare
Benachallie
Mount Shade
Meluncart
Carnferg
Tom's Cairn
Glendye Lodge
Bridge of Dye
Clatterin Bridge
Auchenblae
Fordoun
Marykirk
North Water Bridge
Drumoak
Crathes
Skene
Loch of Skene
Kirkton of Skene
Blackburn
Kingswells
Mastrick
Bucksburn
Stoneywood
Portlethen
A90
A96
A93
A92
A944
A980
A957
A935
A933
A934
A932
B9077
B966
B974
B979
B9119
B9125
B993
B976
Scale
0 5 10 km
0 1 2 3 4 5 6 miles

Administrative and Postcode boundaries

County and unitary authority boundaries

Postcode boundaries

Area covered by this atlas

Scale: 1⅓ inches to 1 mile
0 ¼ ½ mile
0 250m 500m 750m 1 km

2

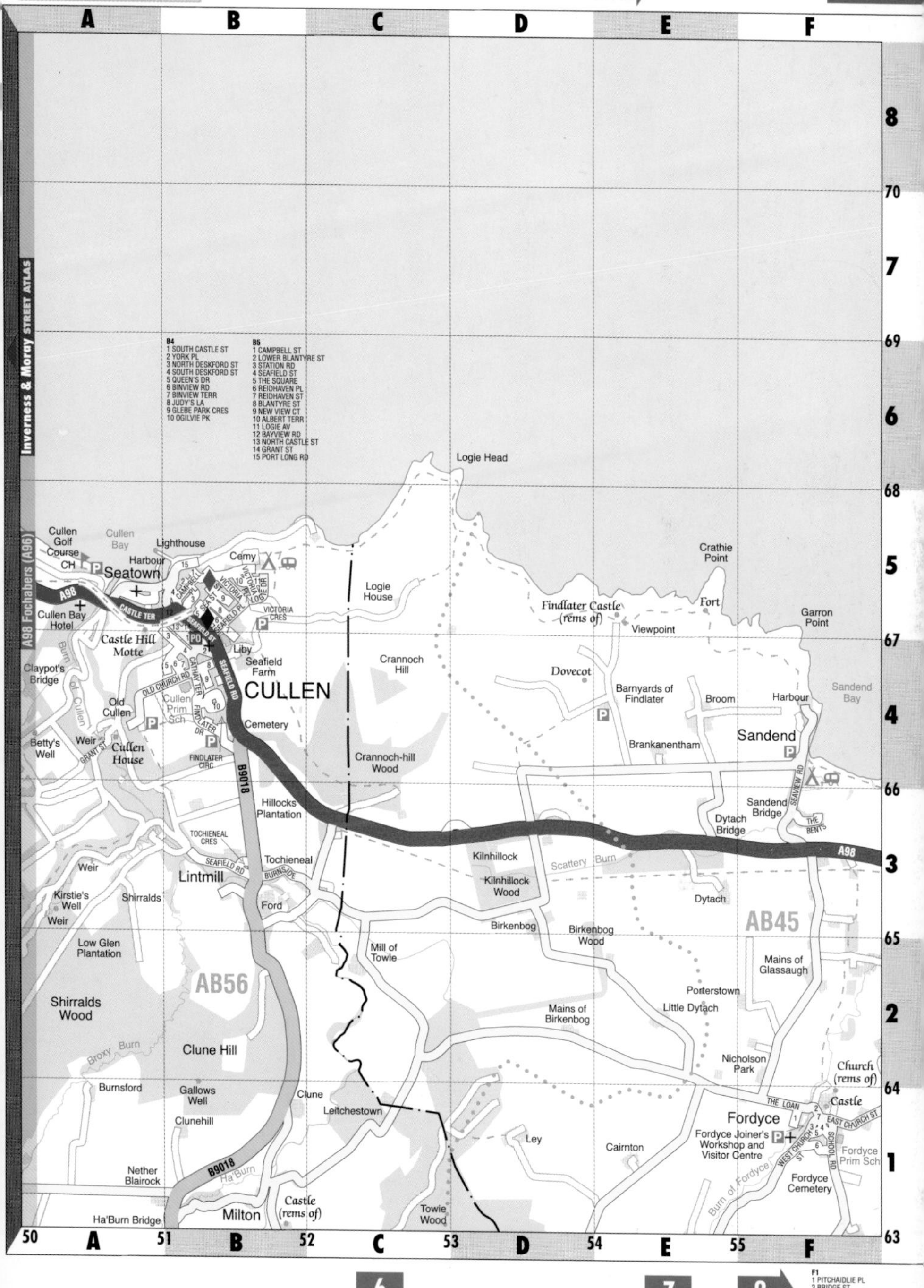

6
7
2

F1
1 PITCHAIDLIE PL
2 BRIDGE ST
3 CHURCH ST
4 CASTLE LA
5 BACK ST
6 ST TARQUINS PL
7 THE SQUARE

1

For full street detail of the highlighted area see page 139.

Scale: 1⅓ inches to 1 mile

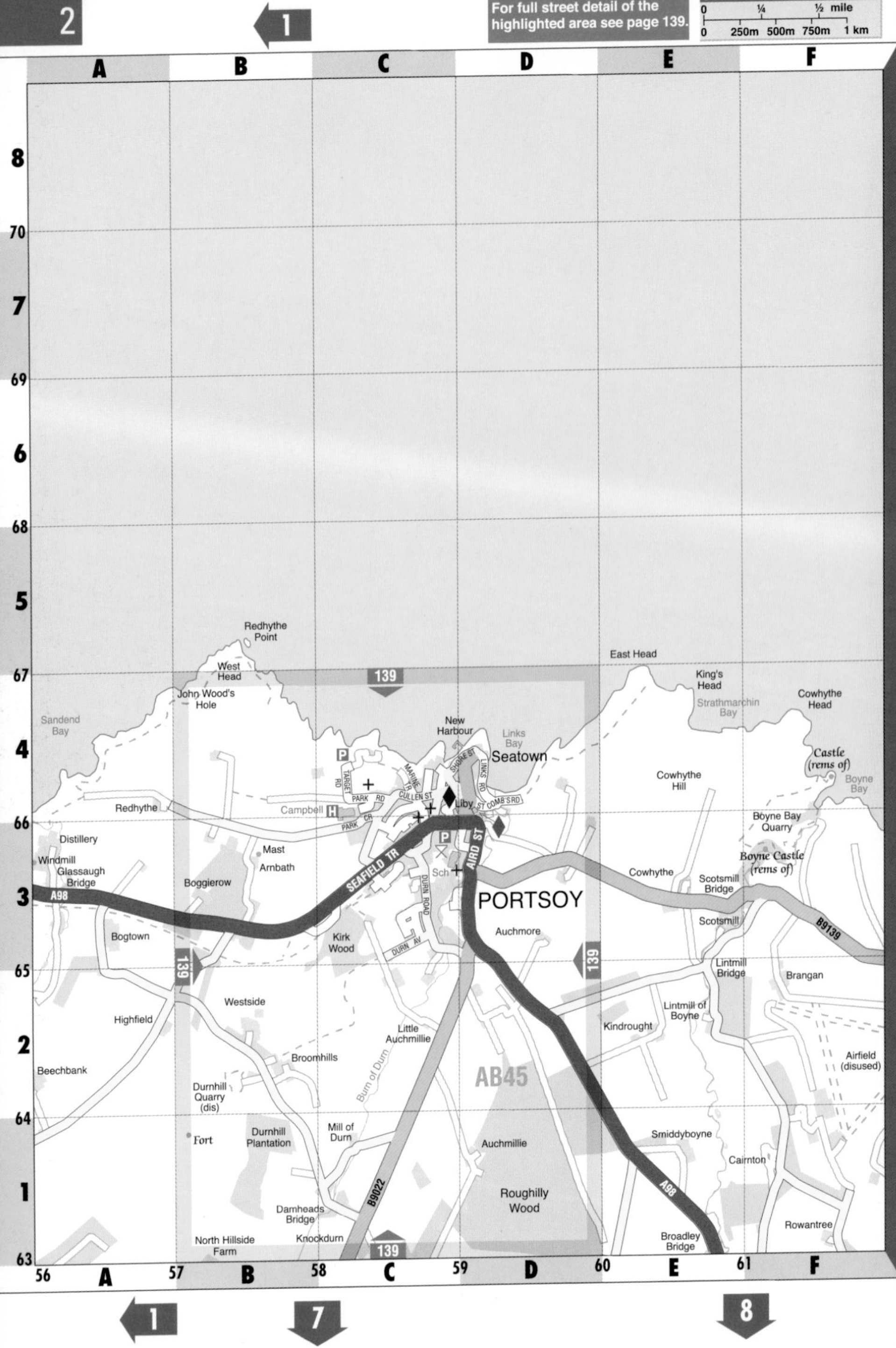

1
7
8

Scale: 1⅓ inches to 1 mile
0 ¼ ½ mile
0 250m 500m 750m 1 km

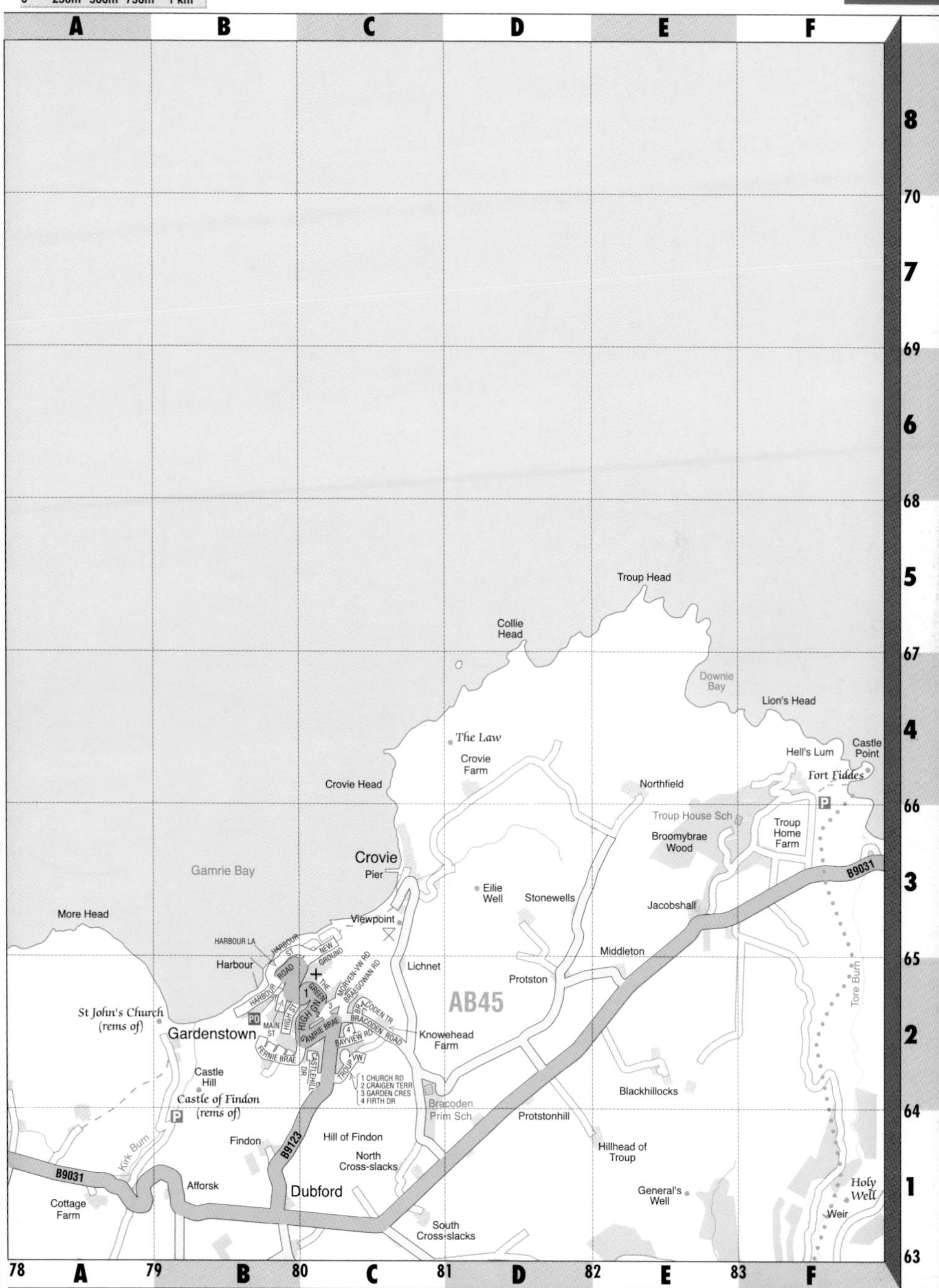

10
11
12

Scale: 1⅓ inches to 1 mile

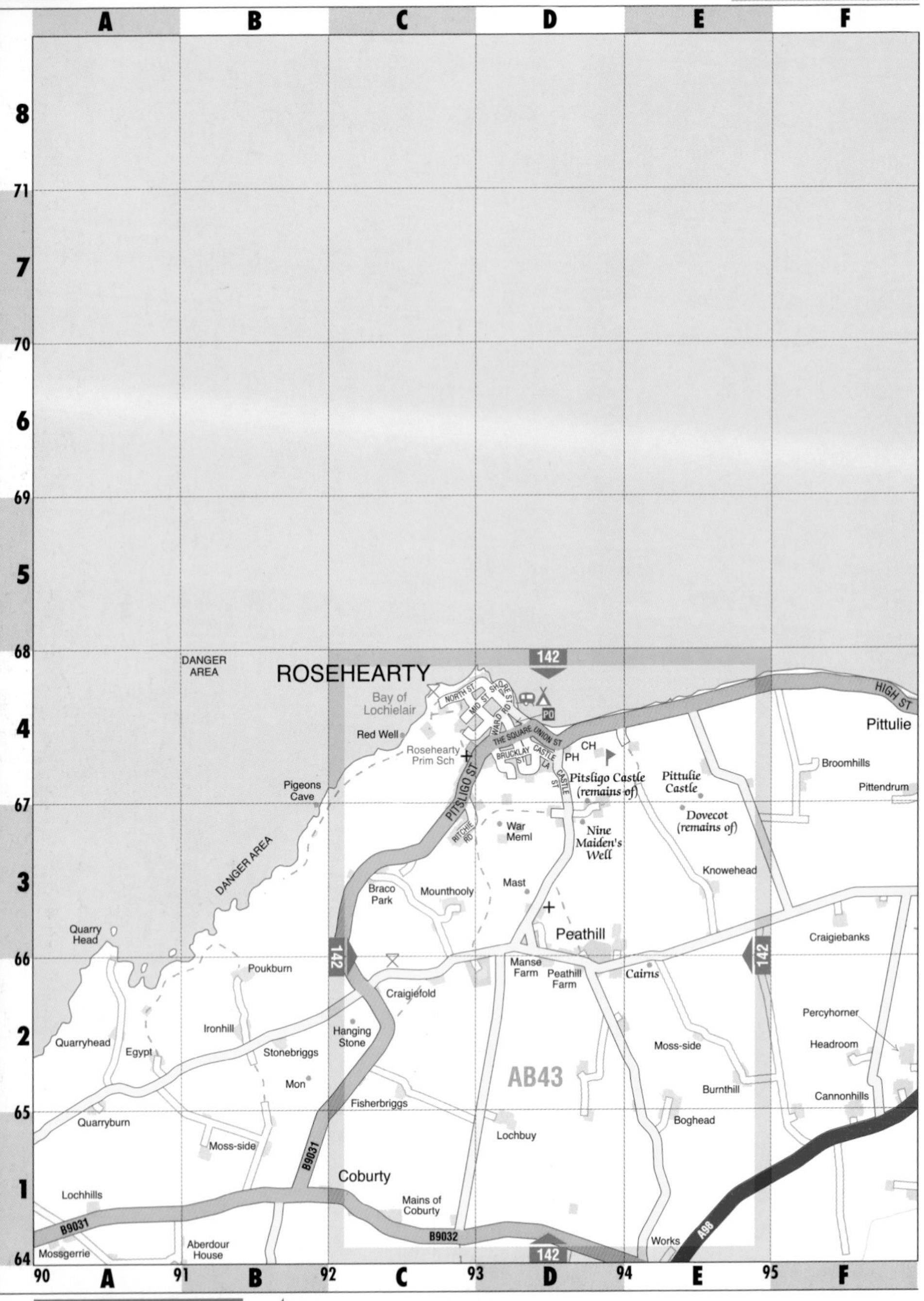

For full street detail of the highlighted area see page 142.

12

13

Scale: 1⅓ inches to 1 mile

14
15
For full street detail of the highlighted area see page 143.

1

Scale: 1⅓ inches to 1 mile

0 ¼ ½ mile

0 250m 500m 750m 1 km

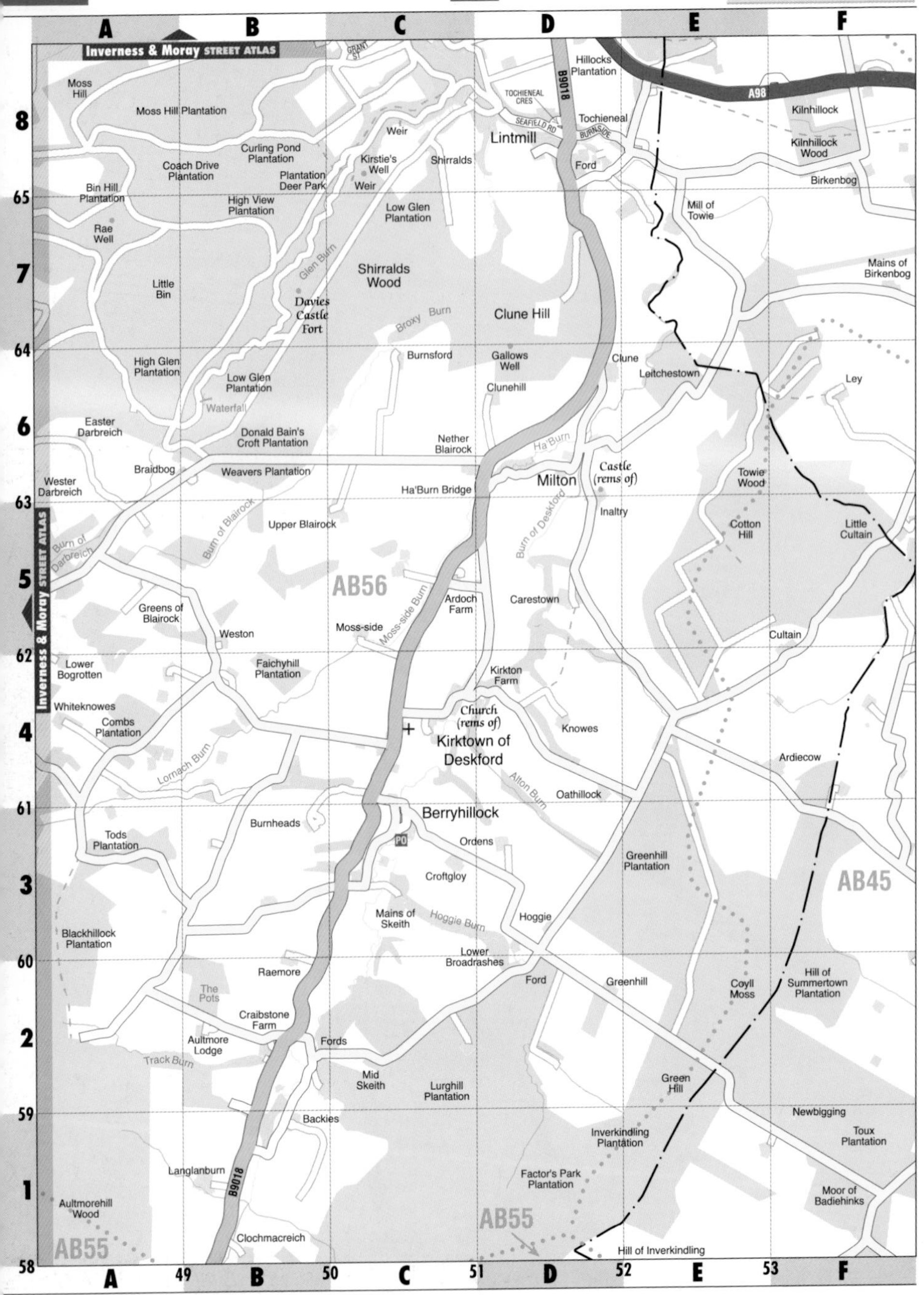

17

Scale: 1⅓ inches to 1 mile

For full street detail of the highlighted area see page 139.

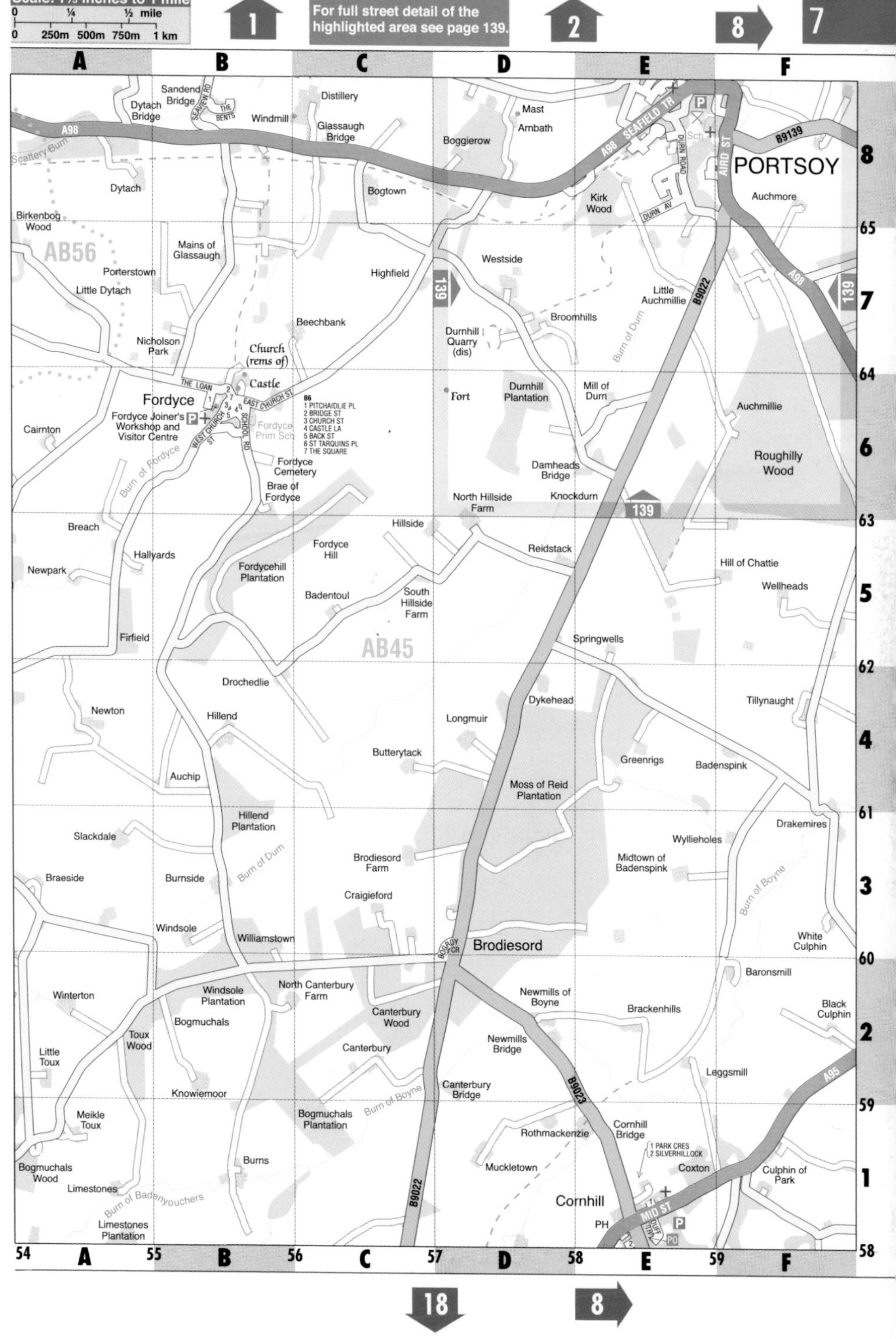

1 2 8 18 8 139

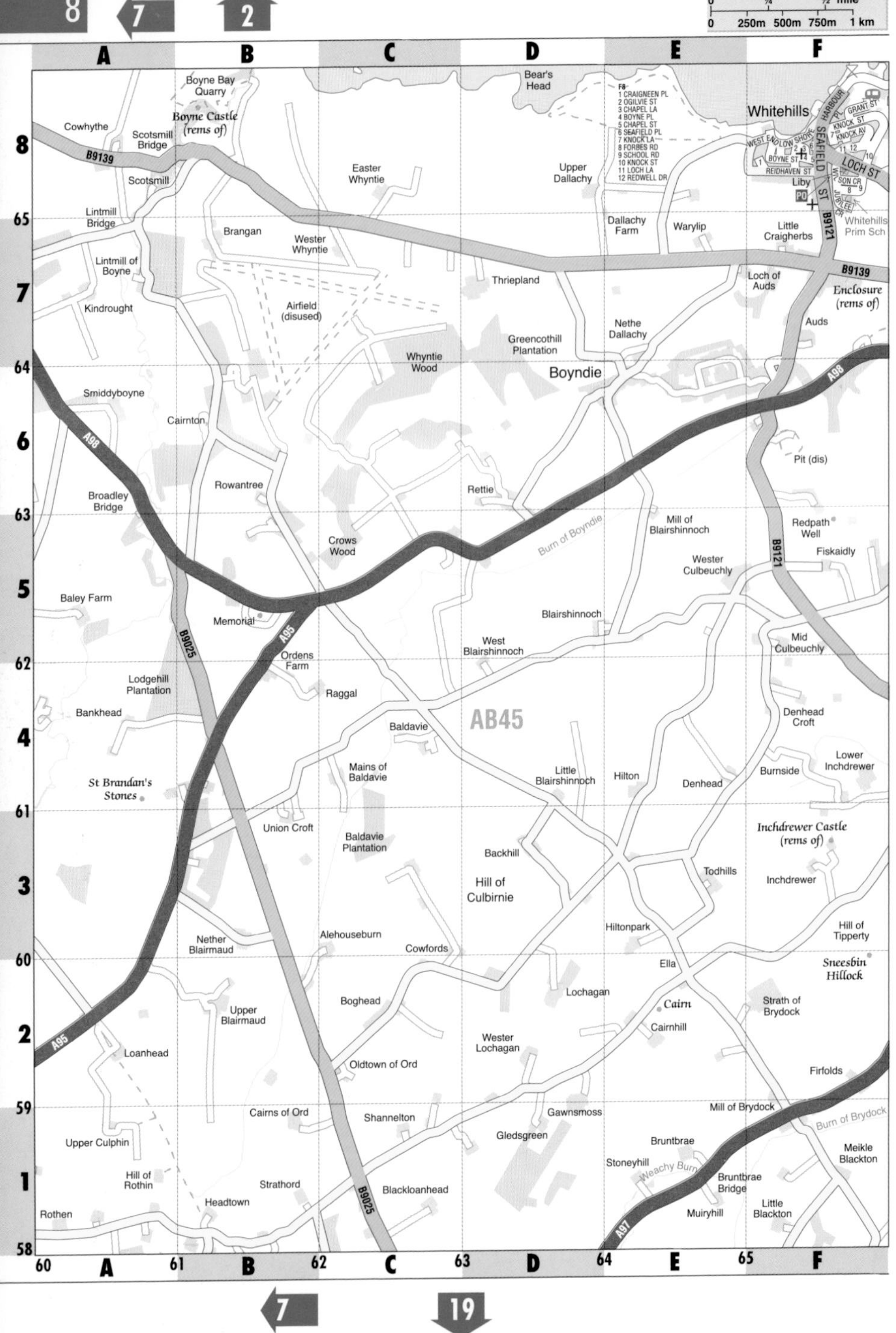

7
2
Scale: 1⅓ inches to 1 mile
Boyne Bay Quarry
Boyne Castle (rems of)
Bear's Head
Cowhythe
Scotsmill Bridge
Scotsmill
Whitehills
Easter Whyntie
Upper Dallachy
Lintmill Bridge
Brangan
Wester Whyntie
Dallachy Farm
Warylip
Little Craigherbs
Whitehills Prim Sch
Lintmill of Boyne
Kindrought
Airfield (disused)
Thriepland
Loch of Auds
Enclosure (rems of)
Auds
Nethe Dallachy
Greencothill Plantation
Whyntie Wood
Boyndie
Smiddyboyne
Cairnton
Rowantree
Rettie
Pit (dis)
Broadley Bridge
Crows Wood
Mill of Blairshinnoch
Redpath Well
Fiskaidly
Burn of Boyndie
Wester Culbeuchly
Baley Farm
Memorial
Blairshinnoch
West Blairshinnoch
Mid Culbeuchly
Ordens Farm
Lodgehill Plantation
Raggal
Bankhead
Baldavie
AB45
Denhead Croft
Mains of Baldavie
Little Blairshinnoch
Hilton
Denhead
Burnside
Lower Inchdrewer
St Brandan's Stones
Union Croft
Baldavie Plantation
Inchdrewer Castle (rems of)
Backhill
Hill of Culbirnie
Todhills
Inchdrewer
Nether Blairmaud
Alehouseburn
Cowfords
Hiltonpark
Hill of Tipperty
Ella
Sneesbin Hillock
Lochagan
Upper Blairmaud
Boghead
Cairn
Strath of Brydock
Cairnhill
Wester Lochagan
Loanhead
Oldtown of Ord
Firfolds
Cairns of Ord
Shannelton
Gawnsmoss
Mill of Brydock
Burn of Brydock
Upper Culphin
Gledsgreen
Bruntbrae
Meikle Blackton
Stoneyhill
Weachy Burn
Hill of Rothin
Strathord
Blackloanhead
Bruntbrae Bridge
Headtown
Little Blackton
Muiryhill
Rothen
B9139
A98
A95
B9025
B9121
A97
F8
1 CRAIGNEEN PL
2 OGILVIE ST
3 CHAPEL LA
4 BOYNE PL
5 CHAPEL ST
6 SEAFIELD PL
7 KNOCK LA
8 FORBES RD
9 SCHOOL RD
10 KNOCK ST
11 LOCH LA
12 REDWELL DR
HARBOUR PL
GRANT ST
KNOCK ST
KNOCK AV
SEAFIELD ST
LOCH ST
WEST END
LOW SHORE
BOYNE ST
REIDHAVEN ST
Liby
PO
A B C D E F
60 61 62 63 64 65
58 59 60 61 62 63 64 65
1 2 3 4 5 6 7 8
7
19

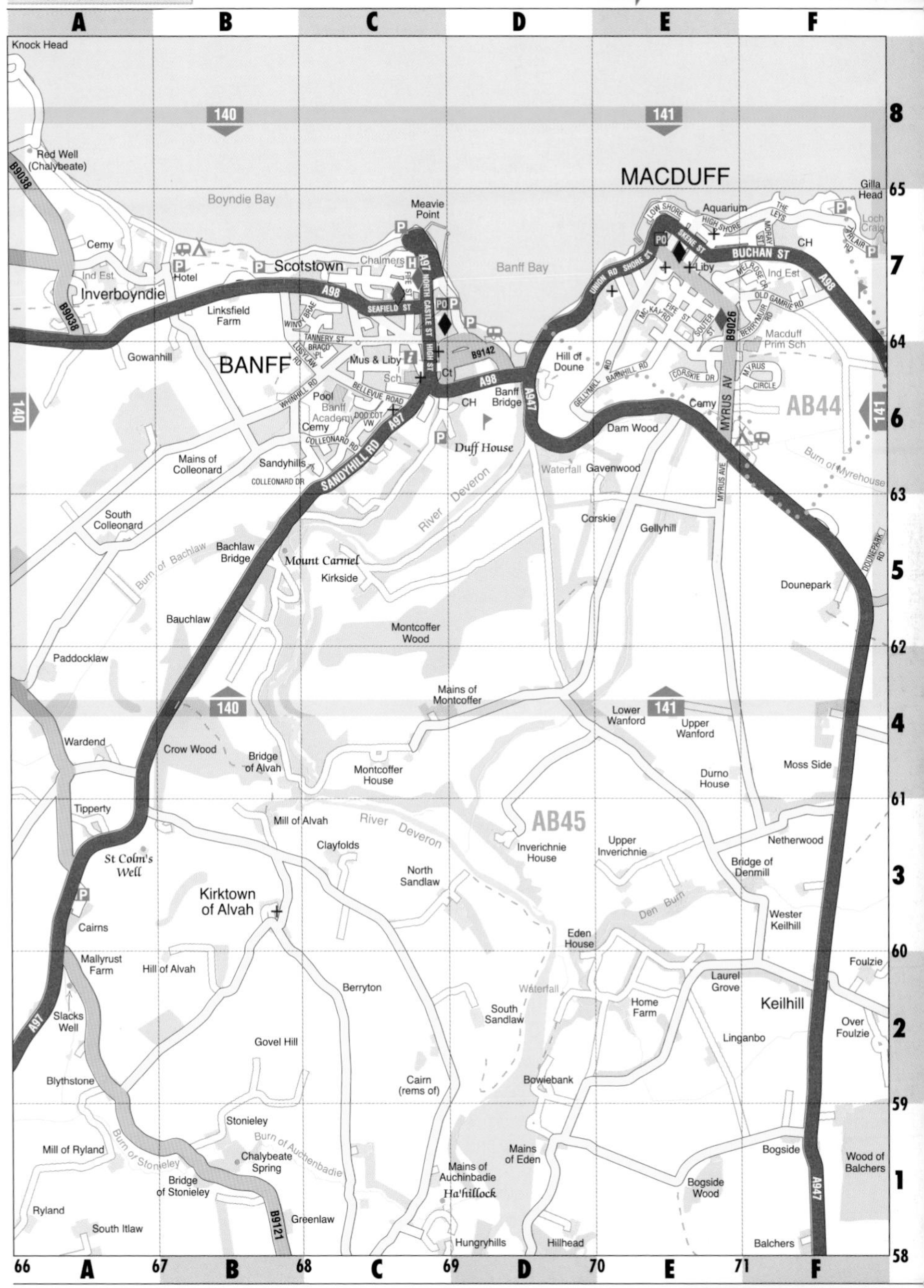

For full street detail of the highlighted area see pages 140 & 141.

9

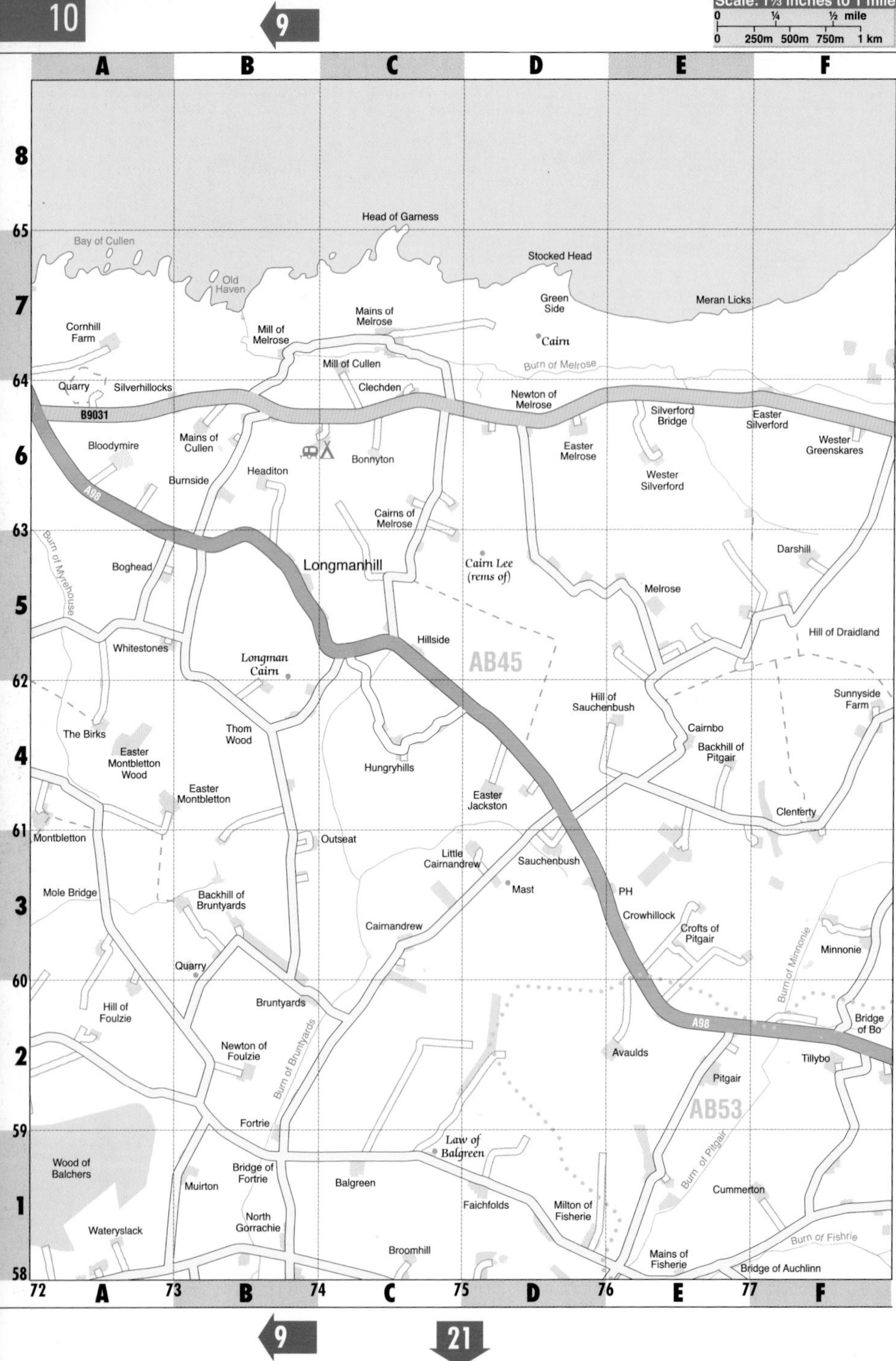

Scale: 1⅓ inches to 1 mile
0 ¼ ½ mile
0 250m 500m 750m 1 km
A B C D E F
8 7 6 5 4 3 2 1
65 64 63 62 61 60 59 58
72 73 74 75 76 77
Head of Garness
Bay of Cullen
Stocked Head
Old Haven
Green Side
Meran Licks
Cornhill Farm
Mill of Melrose
Mains of Melrose
Cairn
Burn of Melrose
Mill of Cullen
Quarry
Silverhillocks
Clechden
Newton of Melrose
Silverford Bridge
Easter Silverford
B9031
Mains of Cullen
Bloodymire
Easter Melrose
Wester Greenskares
Bonnyton
Headiton
Wester Silverford
Burnside
A98
Cairns of Melrose
Burn of Myrehouse
Darshill
Boghead
Longmanhill
Cairn Lee (rems of)
Melrose
Hillside
Hill of Draidland
Whitestones
Longman Cairn
AB45
Hill of Sauchenbush
Sunnyside Farm
The Birks
Thom Wood
Cairnbo
Easter Montbletton Wood
Backhill of Pitgair
Hungryhills
Easter Montbletton
Easter Jackston
Clenterty
Montbletton
Outseat
Little Cairnandrew
Sauchenbush
Mole Bridge
Backhill of Bruntyards
Mast
PH
Crowhillock
Cairnandrew
Crofts of Pitgair
Burn of Minnonie
Minnonie
Quarry
Hill of Foulzie
Bruntyards
Bridge of Bo
Newton of Foulzie
Burn of Bruntyards
Avaulds
Tillybo
Pitgair
AB53
Fortrie
Wood of Balchers
Law of Balgreen
Bridge of Fortrie
Burn of Pitgair
Muirton
Balgreen
Cummerton
Faichfolds
Milton of Fisherie
North Gorrachie
Wateryslack
Burn of Fishrie
Broomhill
Mains of Fisherie
Bridge of Auchlinn

9
21

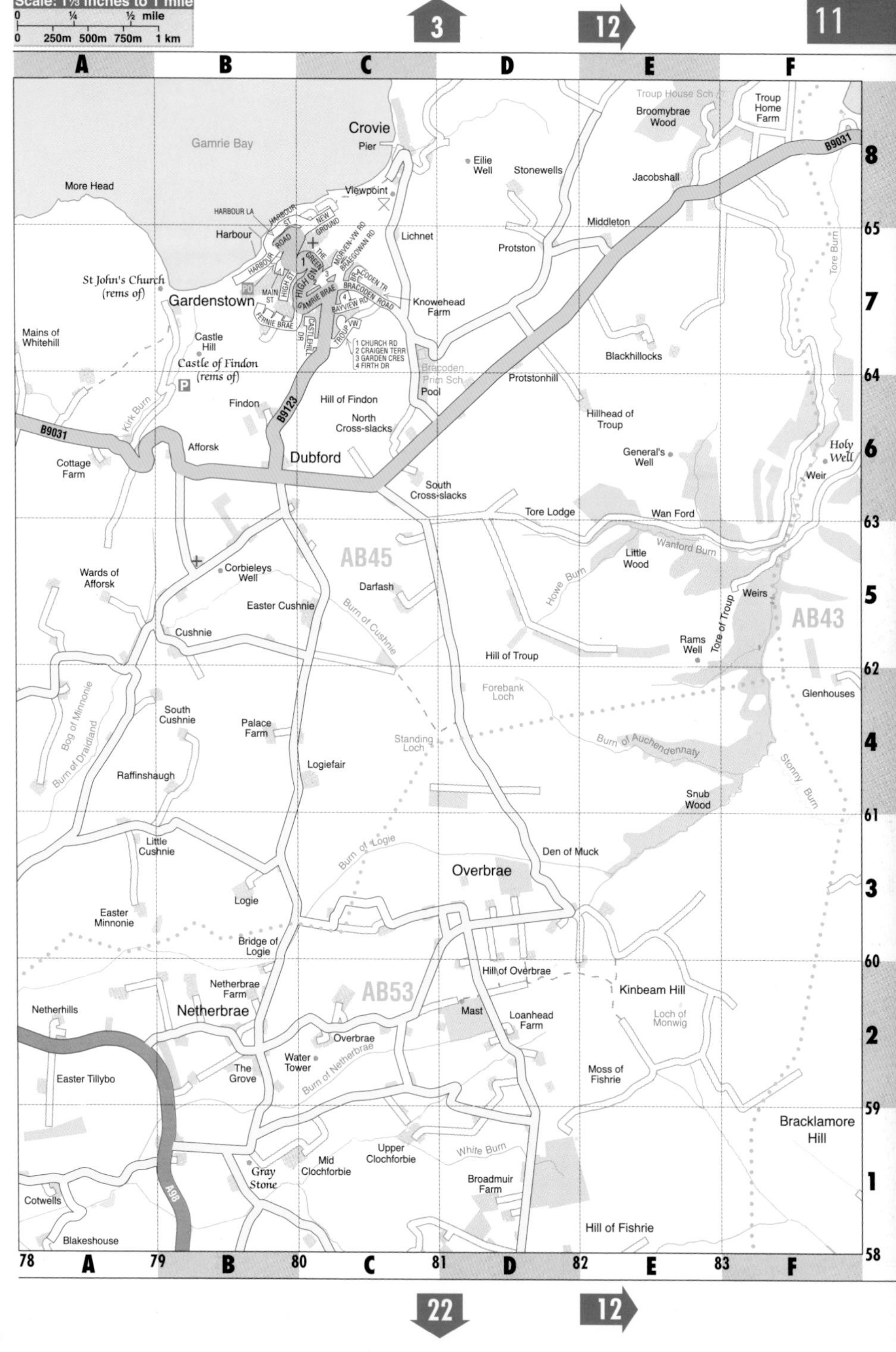

Scale: 1⅓ inches to 1 mile
0 ¼ ½ mile
0 250m 500m 750m 1 km
3
12
A B C D E F
Crovie
Pier
Gamrie Bay
More Head
Viewpoint
Harbour
St John's Church (rems of)
Gardenstown
Mains of Whitehill
Castle Hill
Castle of Findon (rems of)
Findon
Hill of Findon
North Cross-slacks
Dubford
Afforsk
Cottage Farm
B9031
B9123
Kirk Burn
Lichnet
Knowehead Farm
Bracoden Prim Sch
Pool
1 CHURCH RD
2 CRAIGEN TERR
3 GARDEN CRES
4 FIRTH DR
Eilie Well
Stonewells
Protston
Protstonhill
Troup House Sch
Broomybrae Wood
Troup Home Farm
Jacobshall
Middleton
Blackhillocks
Hillhead of Troup
General's Well
Holy Well
Weir
Tore Burn
South Cross-slacks
Tore Lodge
Wan Ford
Wanford Burn
Little Wood
Howe Burn
AB45
Darfash
Wards of Afforsk
Corbieleys Well
Easter Cushnie
Cushnie
Burn of Cushnie
Hill of Troup
Rams Well
Tore of Troup
Weirs
AB43
Glenhouses
Forebank Loch
South Cushnie
Palace Farm
Standing Loch
Burn of Auchendennaty
Stonny Burn
Bog of Minnonie
Burn of Draidland
Raffinshaugh
Logiefair
Snub Wood
Little Cushnie
Burn of Logie
Den of Muck
Overbrae
Logie
Easter Minnonie
Bridge of Logie
Hill of Overbrae
Kinbeam Hill
Loch of Monwig
Netherbrae Farm
Netherbrae
Netherhills
AB53
Mast
Loanhead Farm
Overbrae
Water Tower
Burn of Netherbrae
The Grove
Easter Tillybo
Moss of Fishrie
Bracklamore Hill
Gray Stone
Mid Clochforbie
Upper Clochforbie
White Burn
Broadmuir Farm
A98
Cotwells
Blakeshouse
Hill of Fishrie
8 65 7 64 6 63 5 62 4 61 3 60 2 59 1 58
78 79 80 81 82 83
22
12

11

Scale: 1⅓ inches to 1 mile
0 ¼ ½ mile
0 250m 500m 750m 1 km

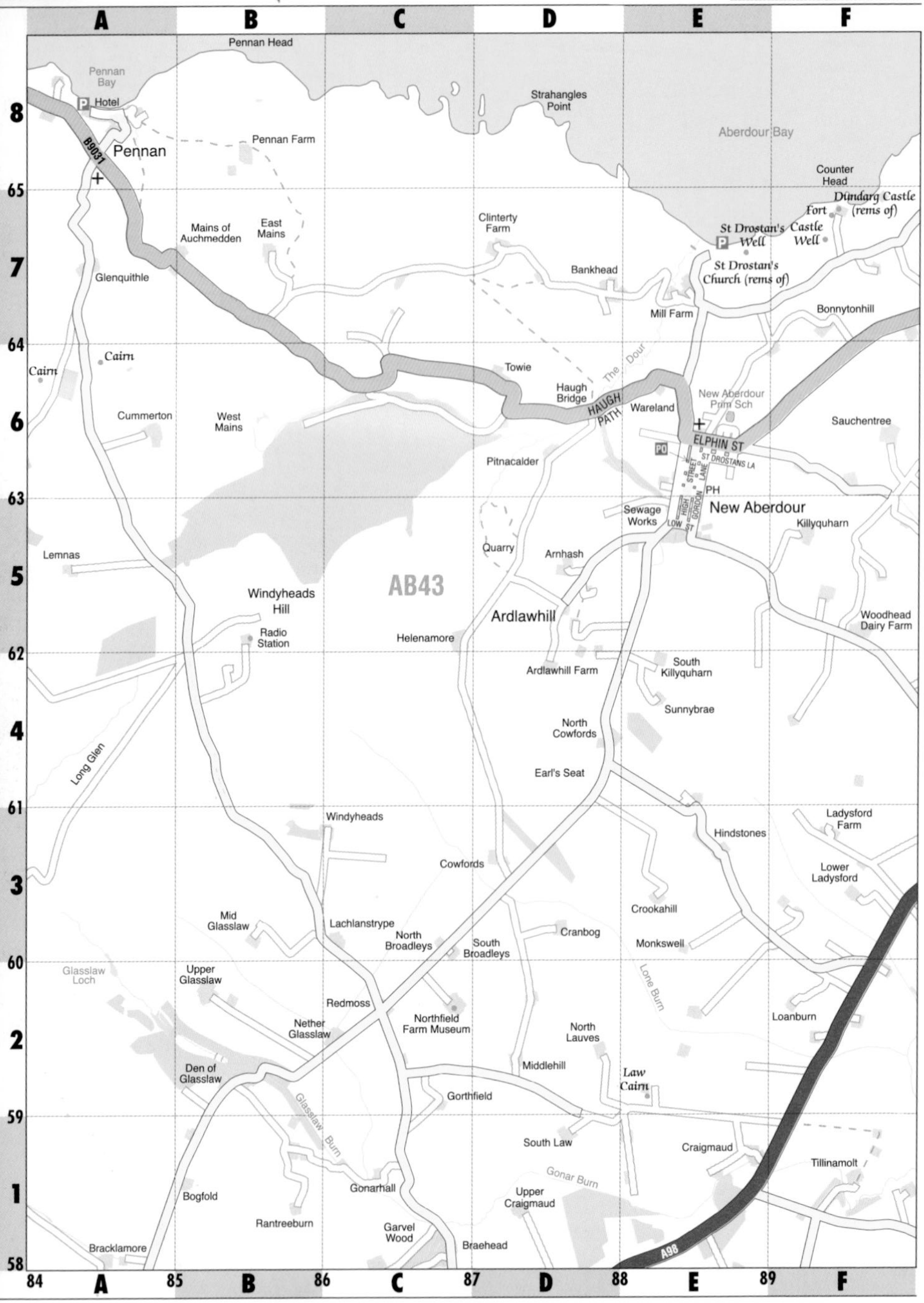

11

23

Scale: 1⅓ inches to 1 mile
0 ¼ ½ mile
0 250m 500m 750m 1 km

4
14

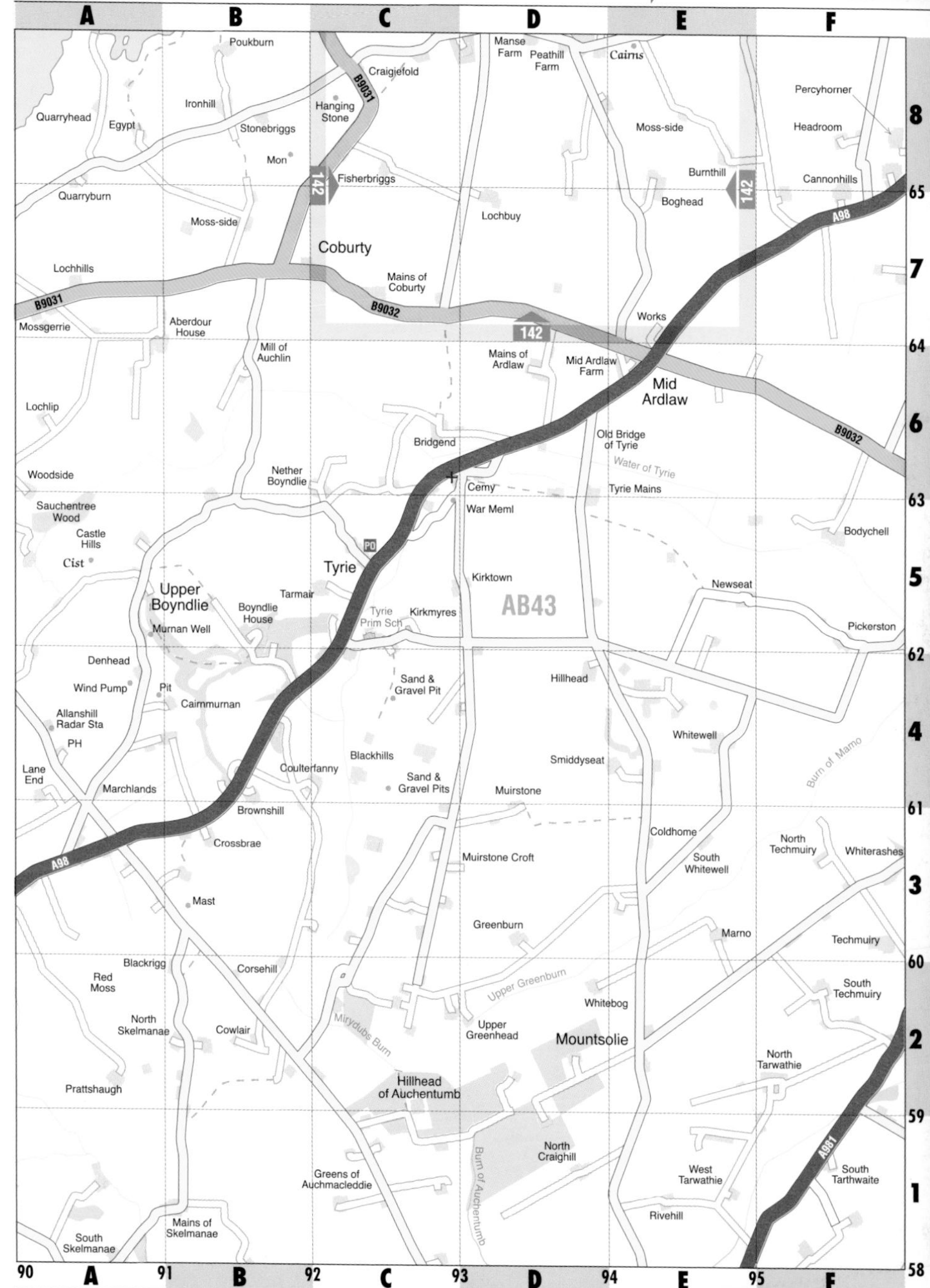

24
14
For full street detail of the highlighted area see page 142.

13
5

Scale: 1⅓ inches to 1 mile
0 ¼ ½ mile
0 250m 500m 750m 1 km

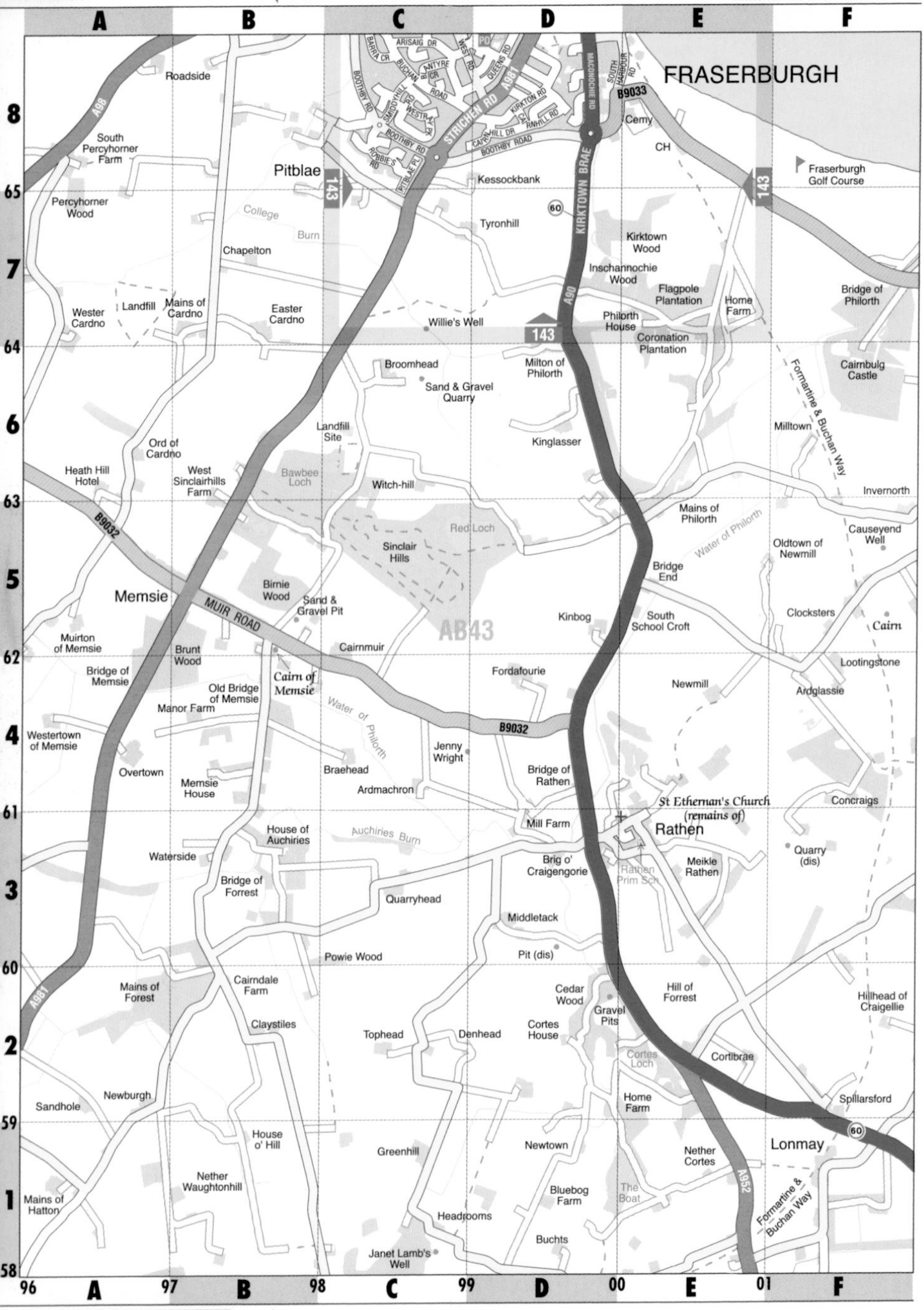

A B C D E F

8 65 7 64 6 63 5 62 4 61 3 60 2 59 1 58

FRASERBURGH

A98 A981 A90 A952 B9033 B9032 MUIR ROAD KIRKTOWN BRAE STRICHEN RD MACONOCHIE RD SOUTH HARBOUR RD BOOTHBY ROAD BOOTHBY RD ARISAIG DR BARRA CR BUCHAN KINTYRE CR ROAD WEST RD QUEENS RD SMIDDYHILL RD WESTRAY CR KIRKTON RD CAIRNHILL DR CAIRNHILL RD ROBBIE'S RD PITBLAE PL PO

Roadside
South Percyhorner Farm
Pitblae
Kessockbank
Cemy
CH
Fraserburgh Golf Course
Percyhorner Wood
College Burn
Tyronhill
Kirktown Wood
Chapelton
Inschannochie Wood
Flagpole Plantation
Home Farm
Bridge of Philorth
Wester Cardno
Landfill
Mains of Cardno
Easter Cardno
Willie's Well
Philorth House
Coronation Plantation
143
Broomhead
Sand & Gravel Quarry
Milton of Philorth
Cairnbulg Castle
Formartine & Buchan Way
Landfill Site
Milltown
Ord of Cardno
Kinglasser
Heath Hill Hotel
West Sinclairhills Farm
Bawbee Loch
Witch-hill
Invernorth
Mains of Philorth
Red Loch
Water of Philorth
Causeyend Well
Sinclair Hills
Oldtown of Newmill
Bridge End
Memsie
Birnie Wood
Sand & Gravel Pit
Kinbog
South School Croft
Clocksters
Cairn
AB43
Muirton of Memsie
Brunt Wood
Cairnmuir
Lootingstone
Bridge of Memsie
Cairn of Memsie
Fordafourie
Newmill
Ardglassie
Old Bridge of Memsie
Manor Farm
Water of Philorth
Westertown of Memsie
Jenny Wright
Overtown
Memsie House
Braehead
Bridge of Rathen
Ardmachron
Concraigs
St Ethernan's Church (remains of)
House of Auchiries
Auchiries Burn
Mill Farm
Rathen
Quarry (dis)
Waterside
Brig o' Craigengorie
Rathen Prim Sch
Meikle Rathen
Bridge of Forrest
Quarryhead
Middletack
Powie Wood
Pit (dis)
Mains of Forest
Cairndale Farm
Cedar Wood
Hill of Forrest
Hillhead of Craigellie
Gravel Pits
Claystiles
Tophead
Denhead
Cortes House
Cortes Loch
Cortlbrae
Sandhole
Newburgh
Home Farm
Spillarsford
House o' Hill
Greenhill
Newtown
Lonmay
Nether Cortes
Nether Waughtonhill
Bluebog Farm
The Boat
Formartine & Buchan Way
Mains of Hatton
Headrooms
Buchts
Janet Lamb's Well

60

96 A 97 B 98 C 99 D 00 E 01 F

For full street detail of the highlighted area see page 143.

13
25

Scale: 1⅓ inches to 1 mile

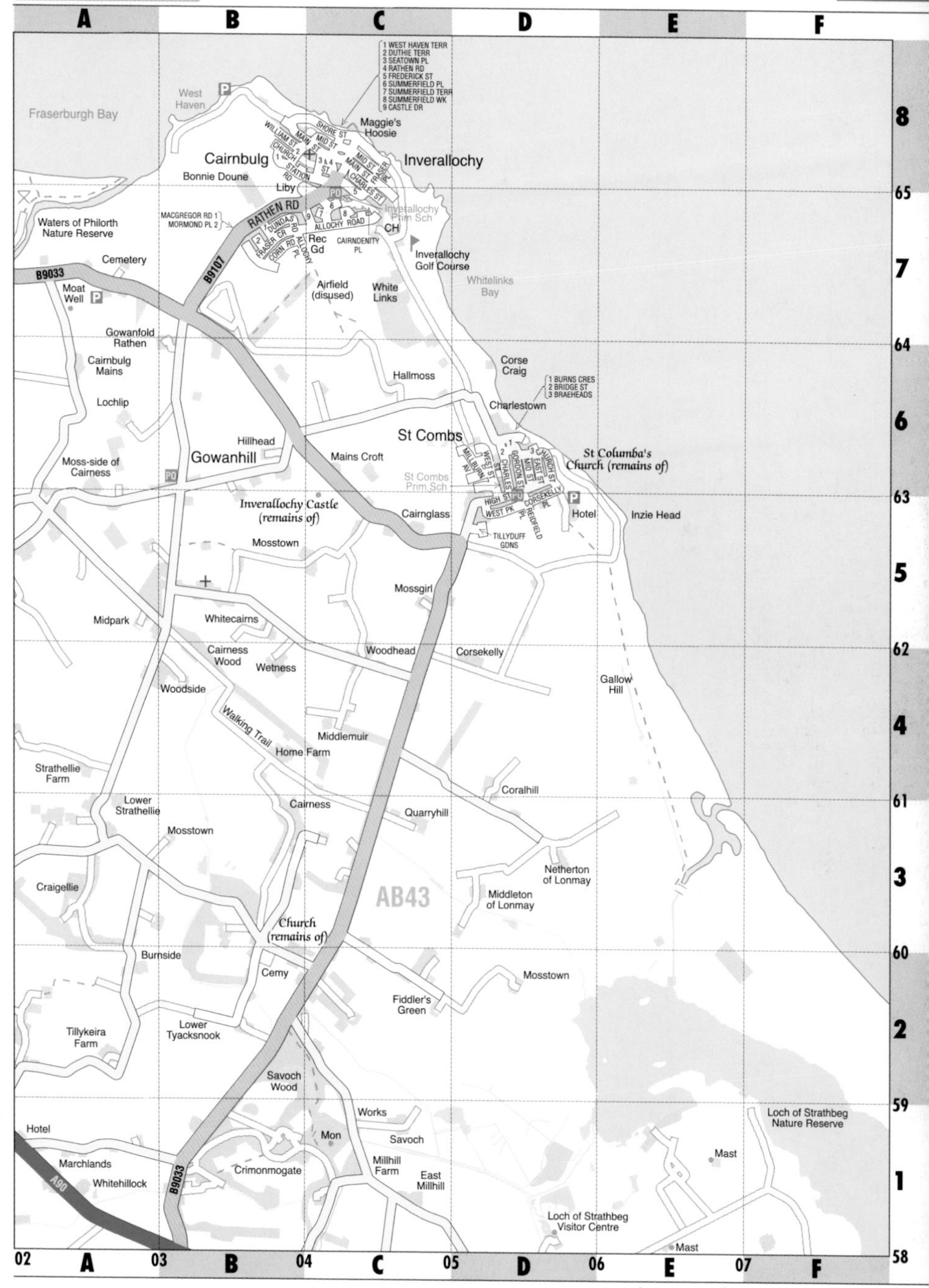

26
16

15

Scale: 1⅓ inches to 1 mile

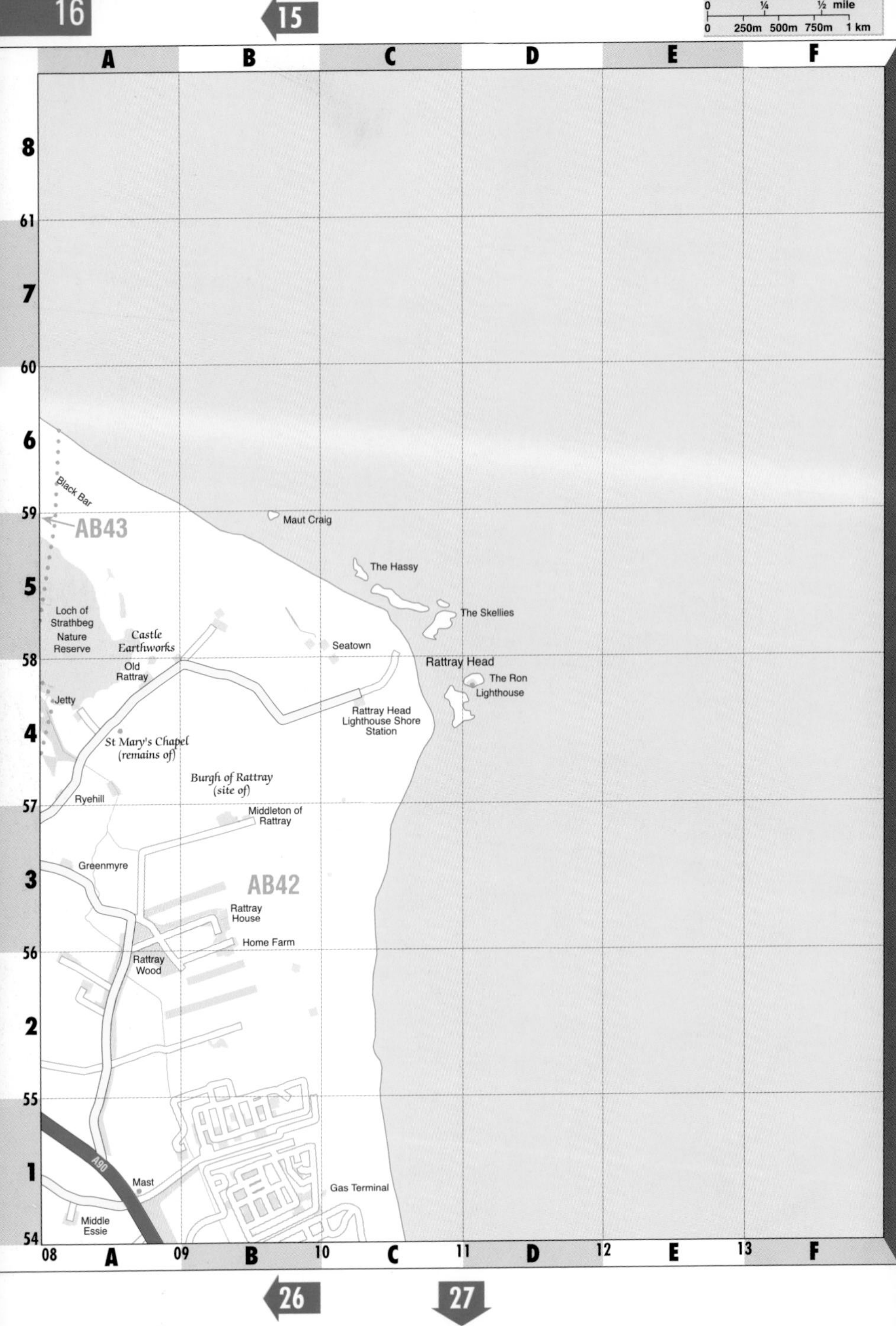

26

27

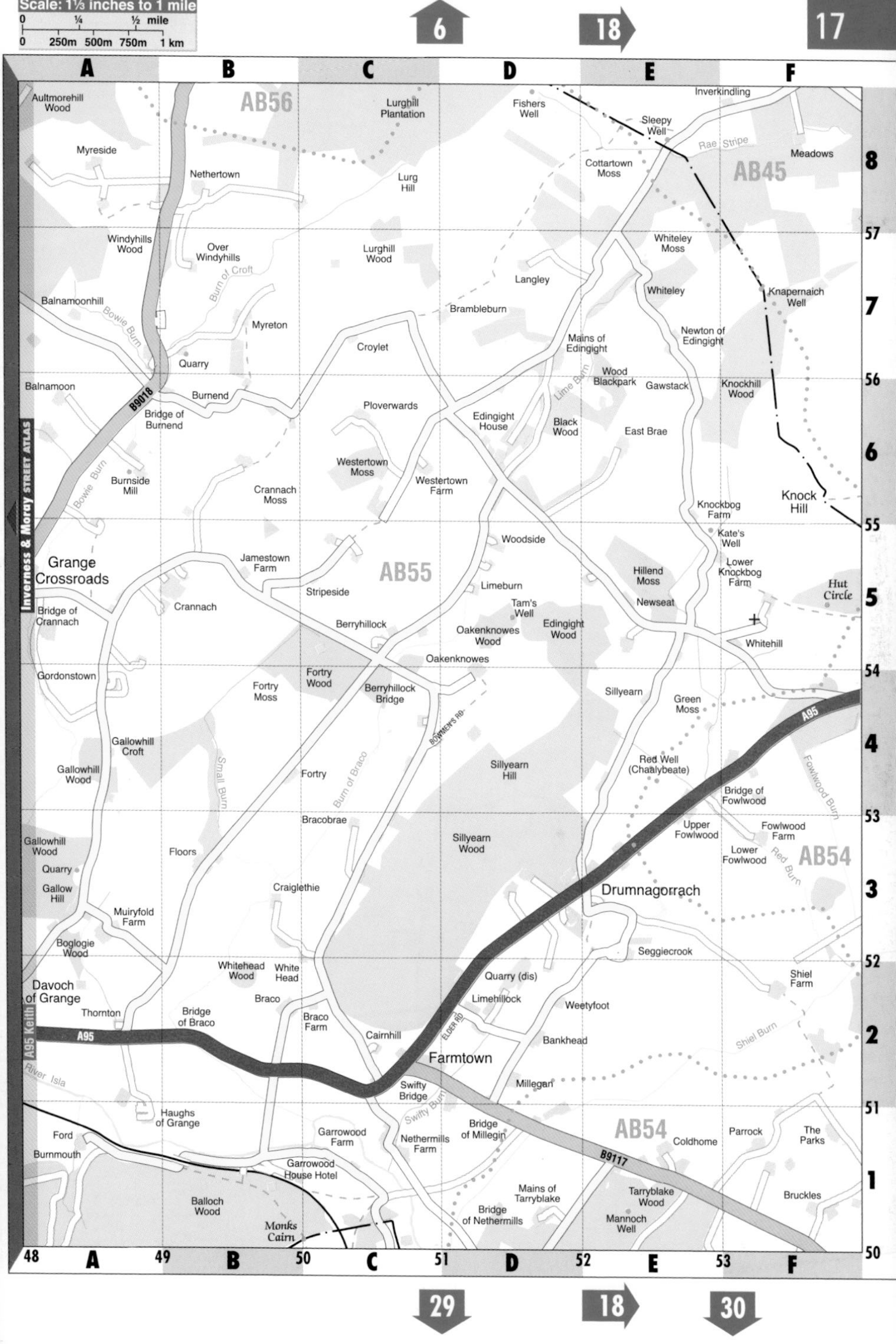
Scale: 1⅓ inches to 1 mile
0 ¼ ½ mile
0 250m 500m 750m 1 km
6
18
A B C D E F
Aultmorehill Wood
AB56
Lurghill Plantation
Fishers Well
Inverkindling
Sleepy Well
Rae Stripe
Myreside
Meadows
Cottartown Moss
AB45
Nethertown
Lurg Hill
Windyhills Wood
Over Windyhills
Lurghill Wood
Whiteley Moss
Burn of Croft
Langley
Whiteley
Knapernaich Well
Balnamoonhill
Bowie Burn
Myreton
Brambleburn
Newton of Edingight
Croylet
Mains of Edingight
Quarry
Wood Blackpark
Gawstack
Knockhill Wood
Balnamoon
Burnend
Lime Burn
B9018
Bridge of Burnend
Ploverwards
Edingight House
Black Wood
East Brae
Inverness & Moray STREET ATLAS
Westertown Moss
Westertown Farm
Burnside Mill
Bowie Burn
Crannach Moss
Knock Hill
Knockbog Farm
Woodside
Kate's Well
Grange Crossroads
Jamestown Farm
AB55
Lower Knockbog Farm
Hillend Moss
Hut Circle
Limeburn
Stripeside
Bridge of Crannach
Crannach
Tam's Well
Newseat
Berryhillock
Oakenknowes Wood
Edingight Wood
Whitehill
Oakenknowes
Gordonstown
Fortry Wood
Fortry Moss
Berryhillock Bridge
Sillyearn
Green Moss
BOWMEN'S RD
A95
Gallowhill Croft
Small Burn
Red Well (Chaalybeate)
Gallowhill Wood
Sillyearn Hill
Fortry
Fowlwood Burn
Burn of Braco
Bridge of Fowlwood
Bracobrae
Upper Fowlwood
Fowlwood Farm
Gallowhill Wood
Sillyearn Wood
Floors
Lower Fowlwood
AB54
Quarry
Red Burn
Gallow Hill
Craiglethie
Drumnagorrach
Muiryfold Farm
Boglogie Wood
Seggiecrook
Whitehead Wood
White Head
Quarry (dis)
Shiel Farm
Davoch of Grange
Braco
Limehillock
Weetyfoot
Thornton
Bridge of Braco
Braco Farm
ELDER RD
A95 Keith
A95
Cairnhill
Bankhead
Shiel Burn
Farmtown
River Isla
Swifty Bridge
Millegan
Haughs of Grange
Swifty Burn
Bridge of Millegin
AB54
Ford
Garrowood Farm
Nethermills Farm
Coldhome
Parrock
The Parks
Burnmouth
B9117
Garrowood House Hotel
Mains of Tarryblake
Tarryblake Wood
Bruckles
Balloch Wood
Bridge of Nethermills
Mannoch Well
Monks Cairn
8 57 7 56 6 55 5 54 4 53 3 52 2 51 1 50
48 49 50 51 52 53
29
18
30

Scale: 1⅓ inches to 1 mile
0 ¼ ½ mile
0 250m 500m 750m 1 km

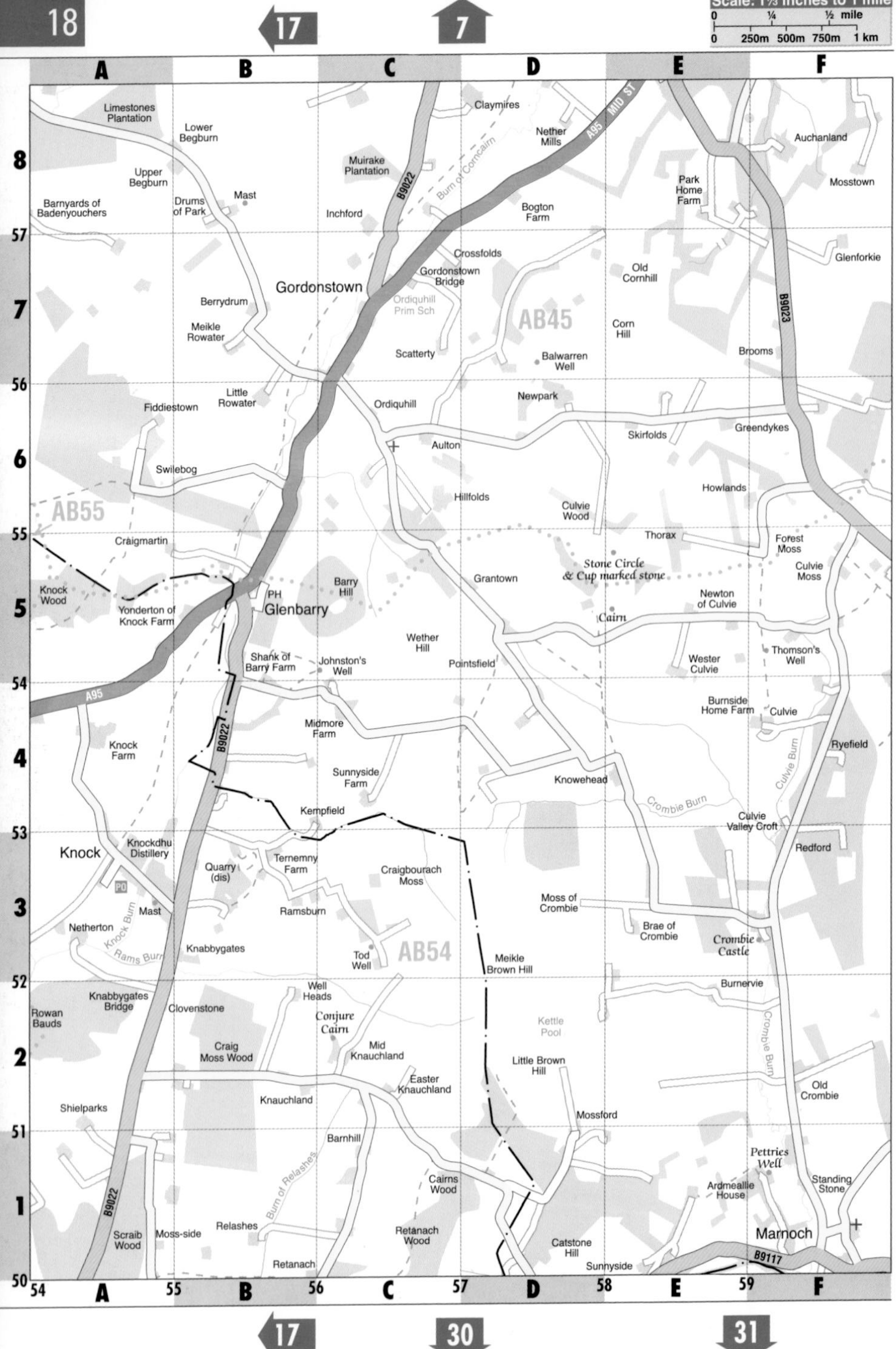

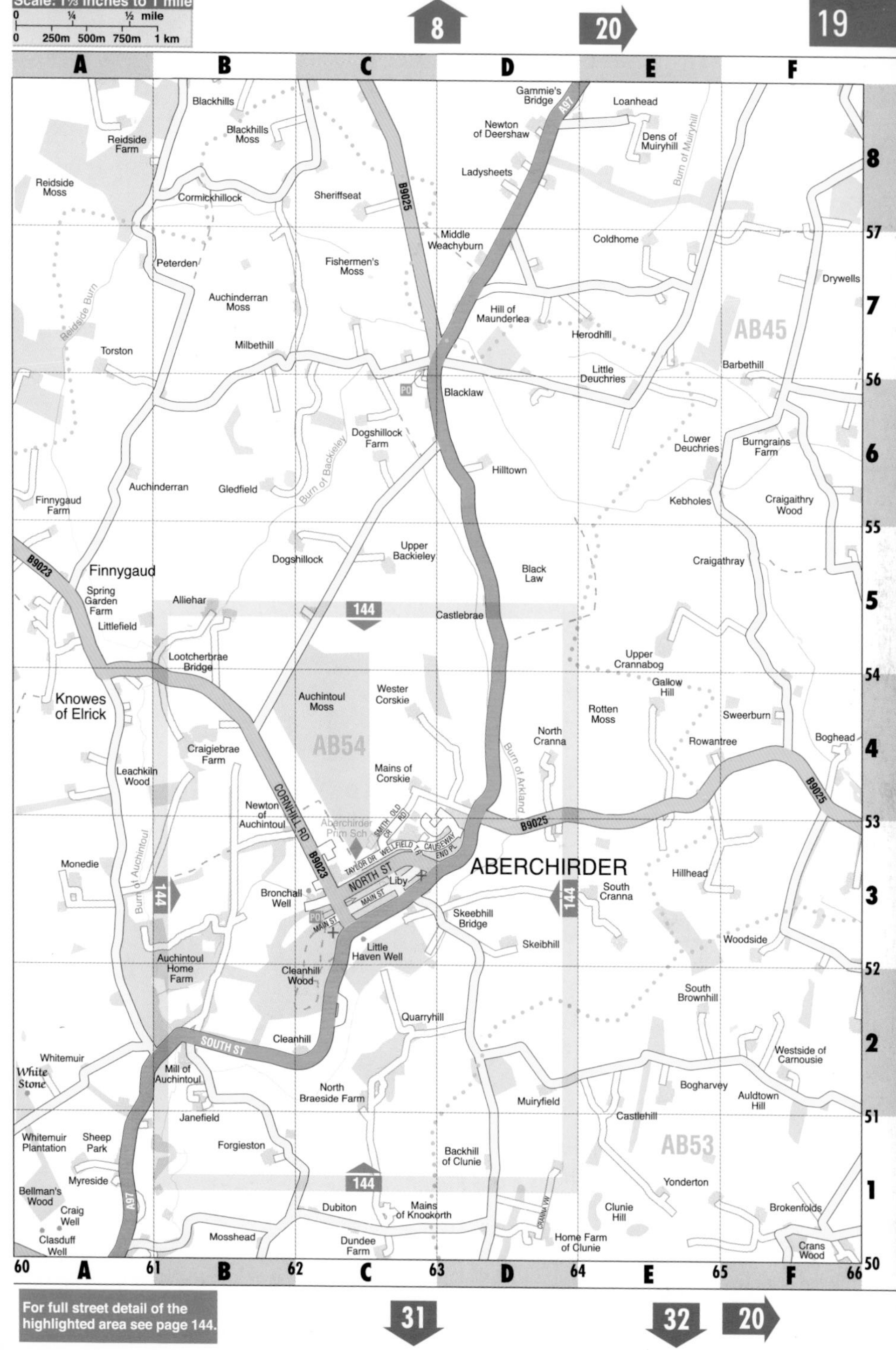

For full street detail of the highlighted area see page 144.

31 32 20

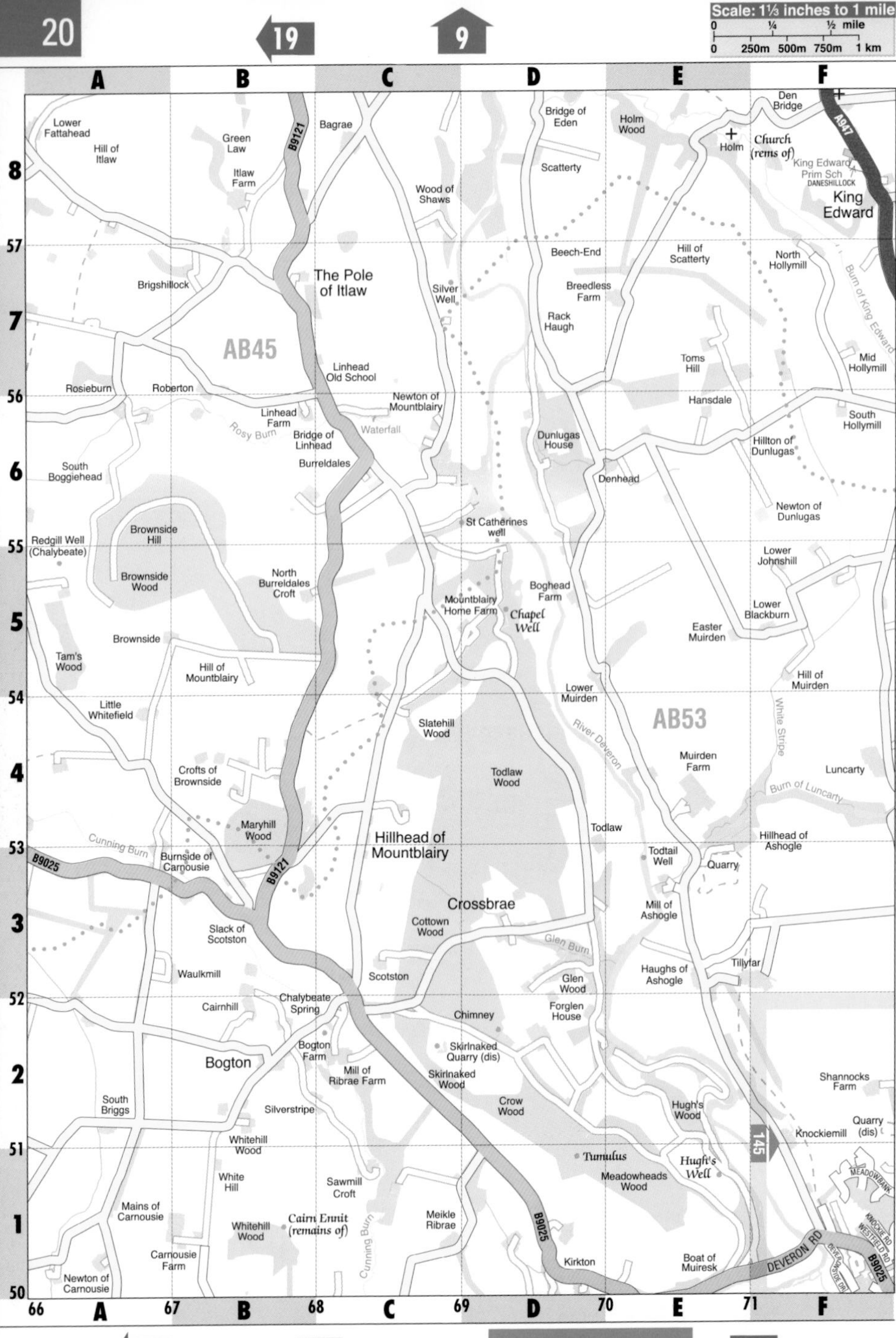

19
32
For full street detail of the highlighted area see page 145.
33

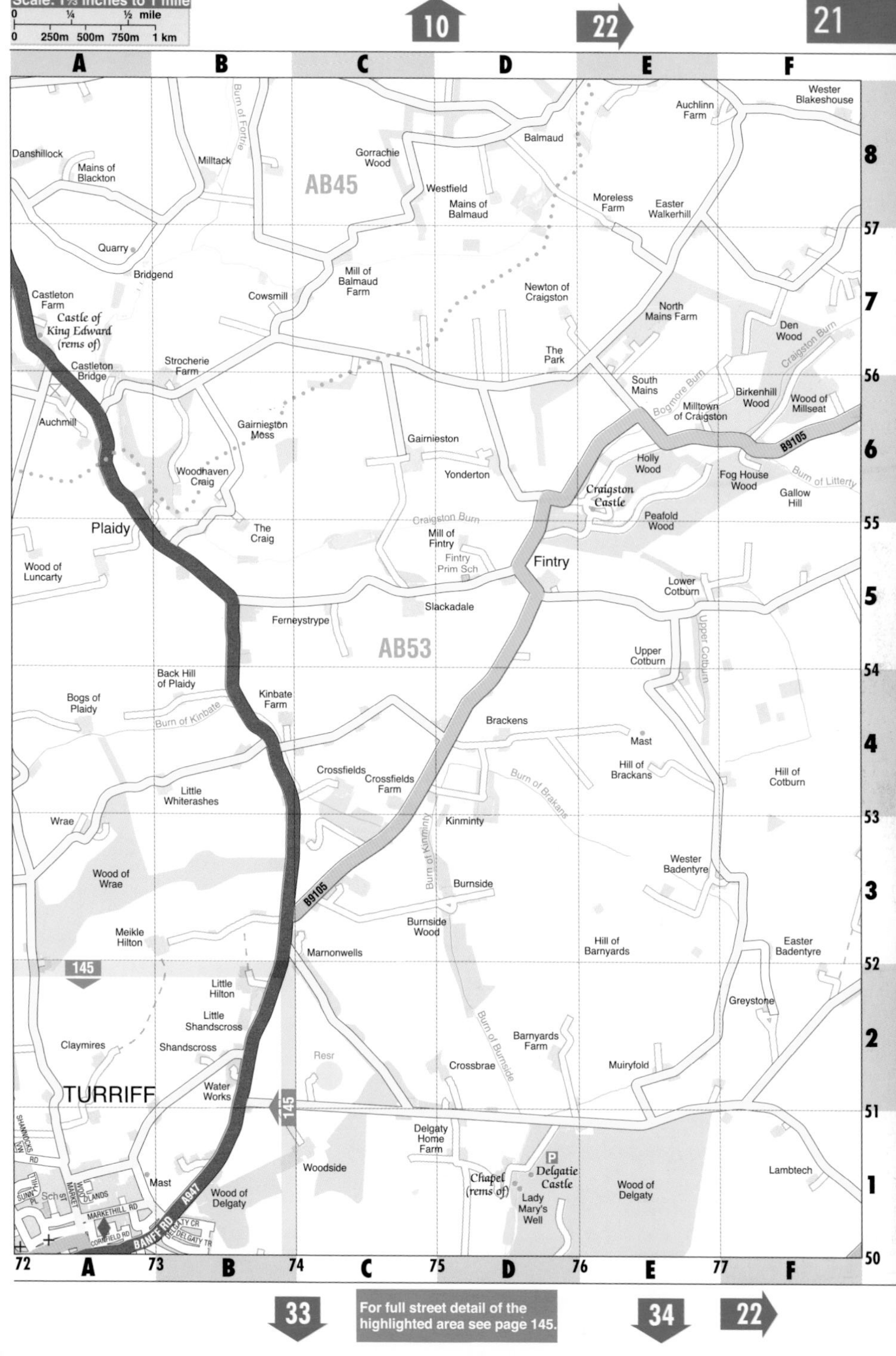

For full street detail of the highlighted area see page 145.

21
11

Scale: 1⅓ inches to 1 mile

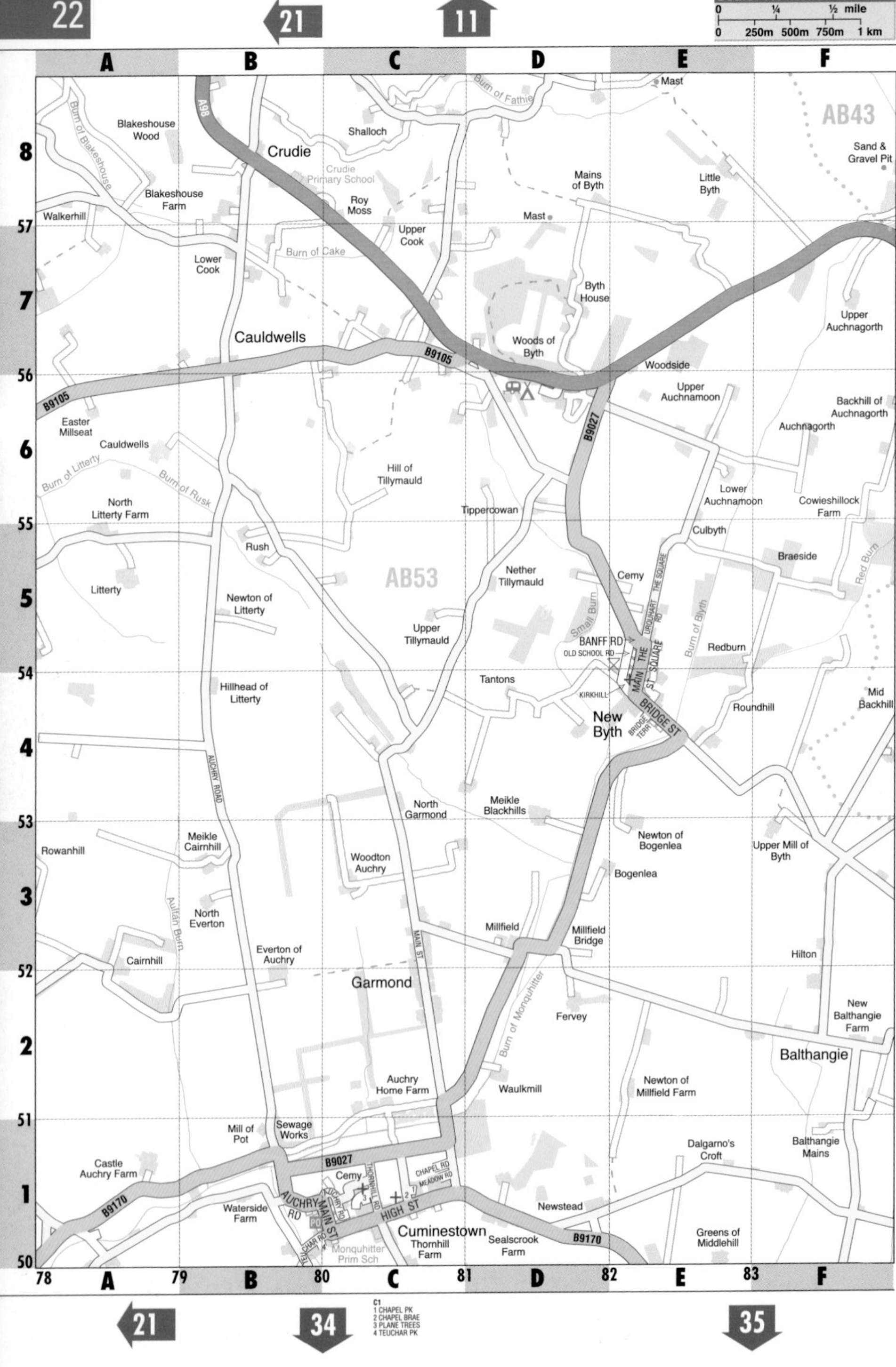

C1
1 CHAPEL PK
2 CHAPEL BRAE
3 PLANE TREES
4 TEUCHAR PK

21
34
35

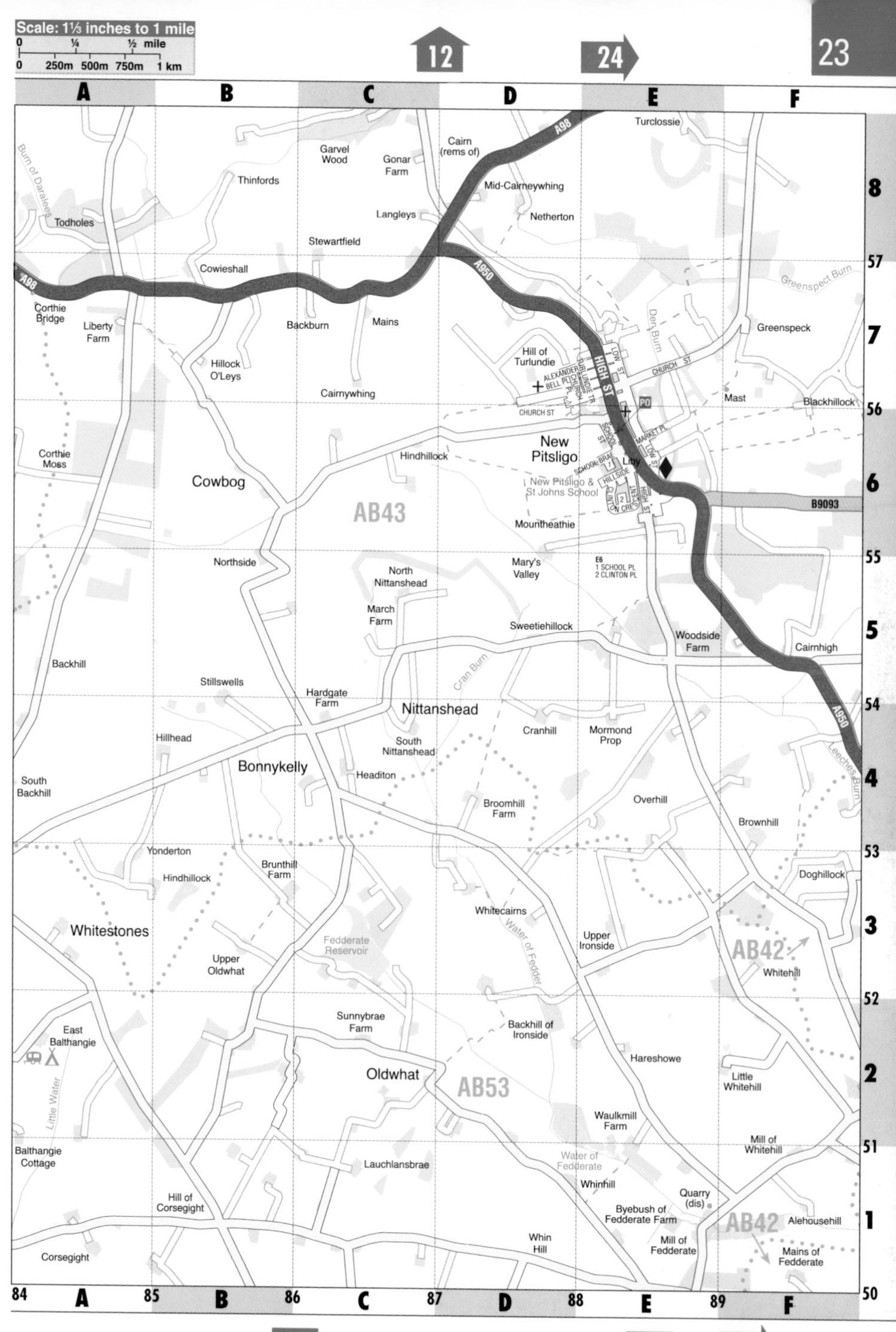
Scale: 1⅓ inches to 1 mile
0 ¼ ½ mile
0 250m 500m 750m 1 km
12
24
A B C D E F
Turclossie
Cairn (rems of)
Garvel Wood
Gonar Farm
A98
Thinfords
Mid-Cairneywhing
Burn of Daralees
Langleys
Netherton
Todholes
Stewartfield
Cowieshall
A950
Greenspect Burn
Corthie Bridge
Liberty Farm
Backburn
Mains
Greenspeck
Hill of Turlundie
Hillock O'Leys
Cairnywhing
HIGH ST
LOW ST
CHURCH ST
ALEXANDER BELL PL
TURLUNDIE TR
CHURCH PL
Mast
PO
Blackhillock
Corthie Moss
Hindhillock
New Pitsligo
SCHOOL ST
MARKET PL
SCHOOL BRAE
Liby
HILLSIDE
CLINTON CRES
Cowbog
New Pitsligo & St Johns School
B9093
AB43
Mountheathie
Northside
North Nittanshead
Mary's Valley
E6
1 SCHOOL PL
2 CLINTON PL
March Farm
Sweetiehillock
Woodside Farm
Cairnhigh
Backhill
Stillswells
Cran Burn
Hardgate Farm
Nittanshead
Cranhill
Mormond Prop
Hillhead
South Nittanshead
Bonnykelly
Headiton
Leeches Burn
South Backhill
Broomhill Farm
Overhill
Brownhill
Yonderton
Brunthill Farm
Hindhillock
Doghillock
Whitecairns
Whitestones
Fedderate Reservoir
Water of Fedder
Upper Ironside
AB42
Upper Oldwhat
Whitehill
Sunnybrae Farm
Backhill of Ironside
East Balthangie
Hareshowe
Oldwhat
AB53
Little Whitehill
Little Water
Waulkmill Farm
Mill of Whitehill
Balthangie Cottage
Water of Fedderate
Lauchlansbrae
Whinhill
Hill of Corsegight
Quarry (dis)
Byebush of Fedderate Farm
AB42
Alehousehill
Mill of Fedderate
Whin Hill
Mains of Fedderate
Corsegight
57
56
55
54
53
52
51
50
8
7
6
5
4
3
2
1
84 85 86 87 88 89
35
36
24

23
13

E6
1 UGIE VW
2 WHITE SHIP CT
3 RECTORY DR
4 POLICE LA
5 SCHOOL PK
6 SLEIGH CRES
7 BURNSHANGIE RD
8 HILLVIEW
9 MARKET TERR
10 MARKET LA
11 SMITHY LA
12 LIBRARY GDNS
13 BRIDGE ST
14 CHURCH VW

Scale: 1⅓ inches to 1 mile

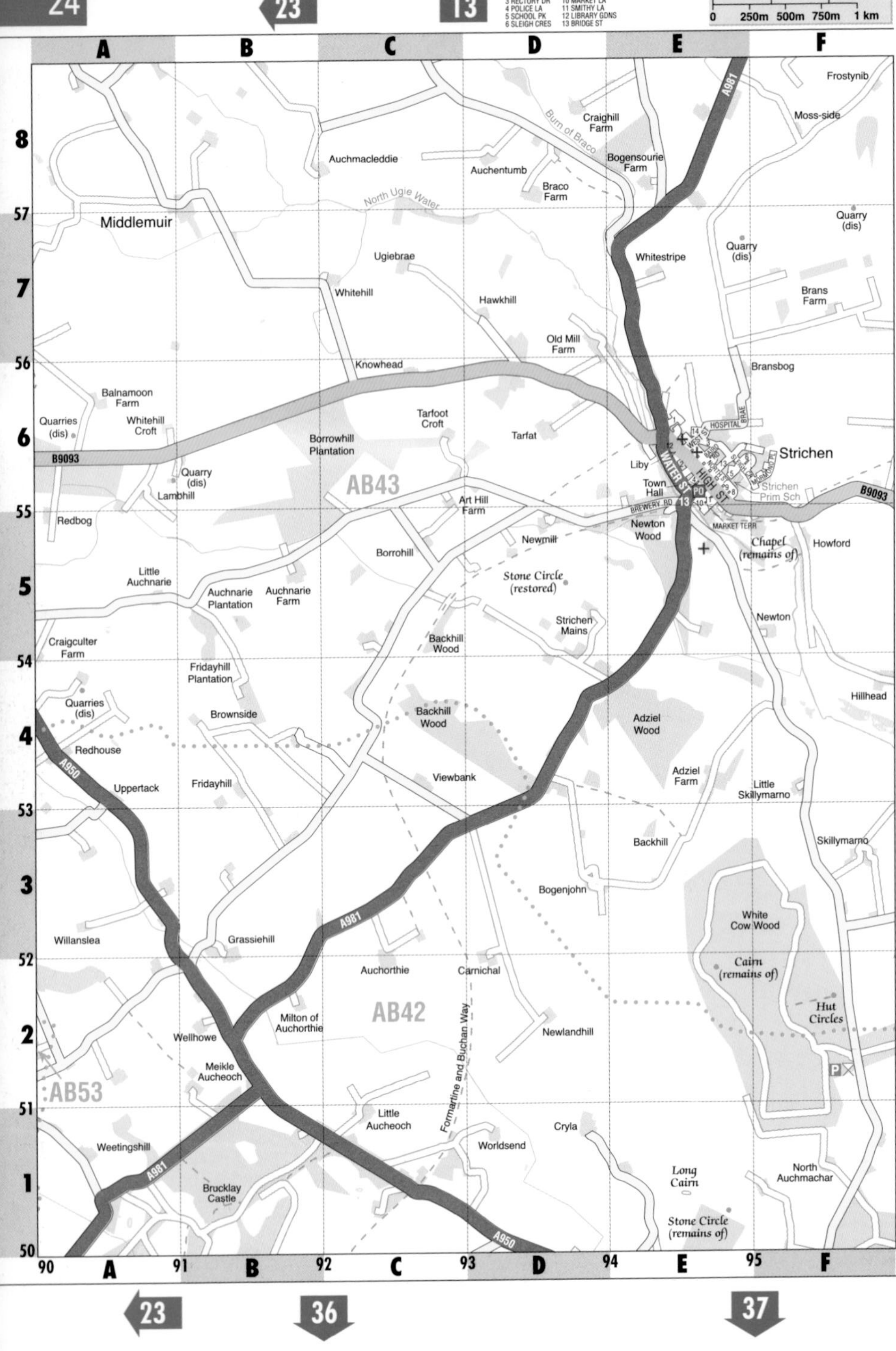

23
36
37

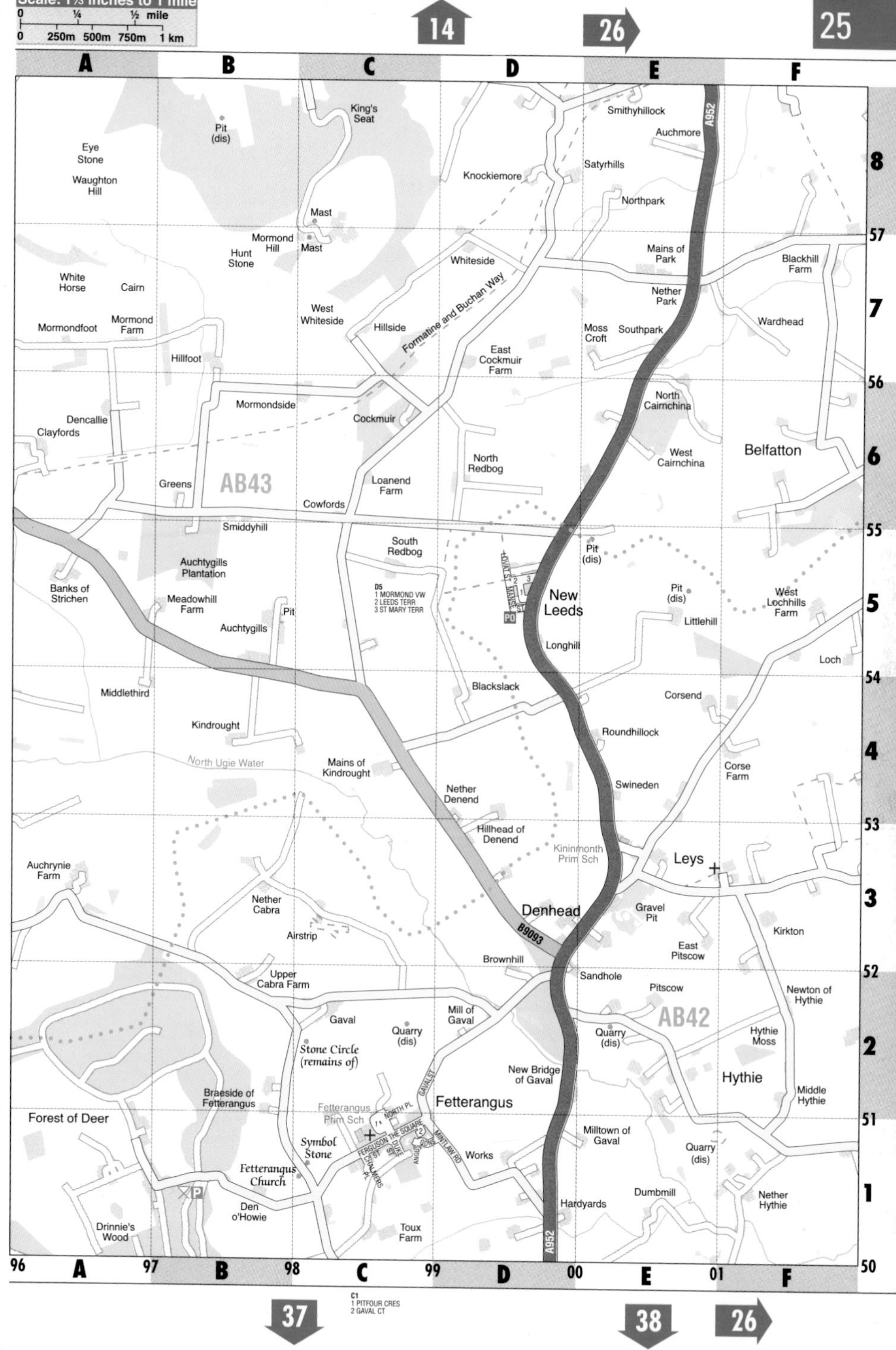
Scale: 1⅓ inches to 1 mile
0 ¼ ½ mile
0 250m 500m 750m 1 km
14
26
37
38
26
A B C D E F
8 57 7 56 6 55 5 54 4 53 3 52 2 51 1 50
96 97 98 99 00 01
King's Seat
Pit (dis)
Eye Stone
Waughton Hill
Smithyhillock
Auchmore
Satyrhills
Knockiemore
Northpark
Mast
Mormond Hill
Hunt Stone
White Horse
Cairn
Whiteside
Mains of Park
Blackhill Farm
Nether Park
West Whiteside
Mormondfoot
Mormond Farm
Hillside
Formatine and Buchan Way
Moss Croft
Southpark
Wardhead
Hillfoot
East Cockmuir Farm
Mormondside
Cockmuir
North Cairnchina
Dencallie
Clayfords
West Cairnchina
Belfatton
North Redbog
Greens
AB43
Loanend Farm
Cowfords
Smiddyhill
South Redbog
Pit (dis)
Auchtygills Plantation
Banks of Strichen
D5
1 MORMOND VW
2 LEEDS TERR
3 ST MARY TERR
New Leeds
Pit (dis)
West Lochhills Farm
Meadowhill Farm
Pit
Auchtygills
PO
Littlehill
Longhill
Loch
Middlethird
Blackslack
Corsend
Kindrought
Roundhillock
North Ugie Water
Mains of Kindrought
Corse Farm
Swineden
Nether Denend
Hillhead of Denend
Kininmonth Prim Sch
Leys
Auchrynie Farm
Nether Cabra
Denhead
Gravel Pit
Kirkton
Airstrip
B9093
East Pitscow
Brownhill
Upper Cabra Farm
Sandhole
Pitscow
Newton of Hythie
Gaval
Mill of Gaval
AB42
Quarry (dis)
Quarry (dis)
Hythie Moss
Stone Circle (remains of)
New Bridge of Gaval
Hythie
Braeside of Fetterangus
Fetterangus
Middle Hythie
Forest of Deer
Fetterangus Prim Sch
NORTH PL
GAVAL ST
THE SQUARE
FERGUSON ST
DUKE ST
ANGUS RD
MINTLAW RD
CHALMERS PL
Milltown of Gaval
Symbol Stone
Works
Quarry (dis)
Fetterangus Church
P
Hardyards
Dumbmill
Nether Hythie
Den o'Howie
Drinnie's Wood
Toux Farm
A952
C1
1 PITFOUR CRES
2 GAVAL CT

25 15

Scale: 1⅓ inches to 1 mile

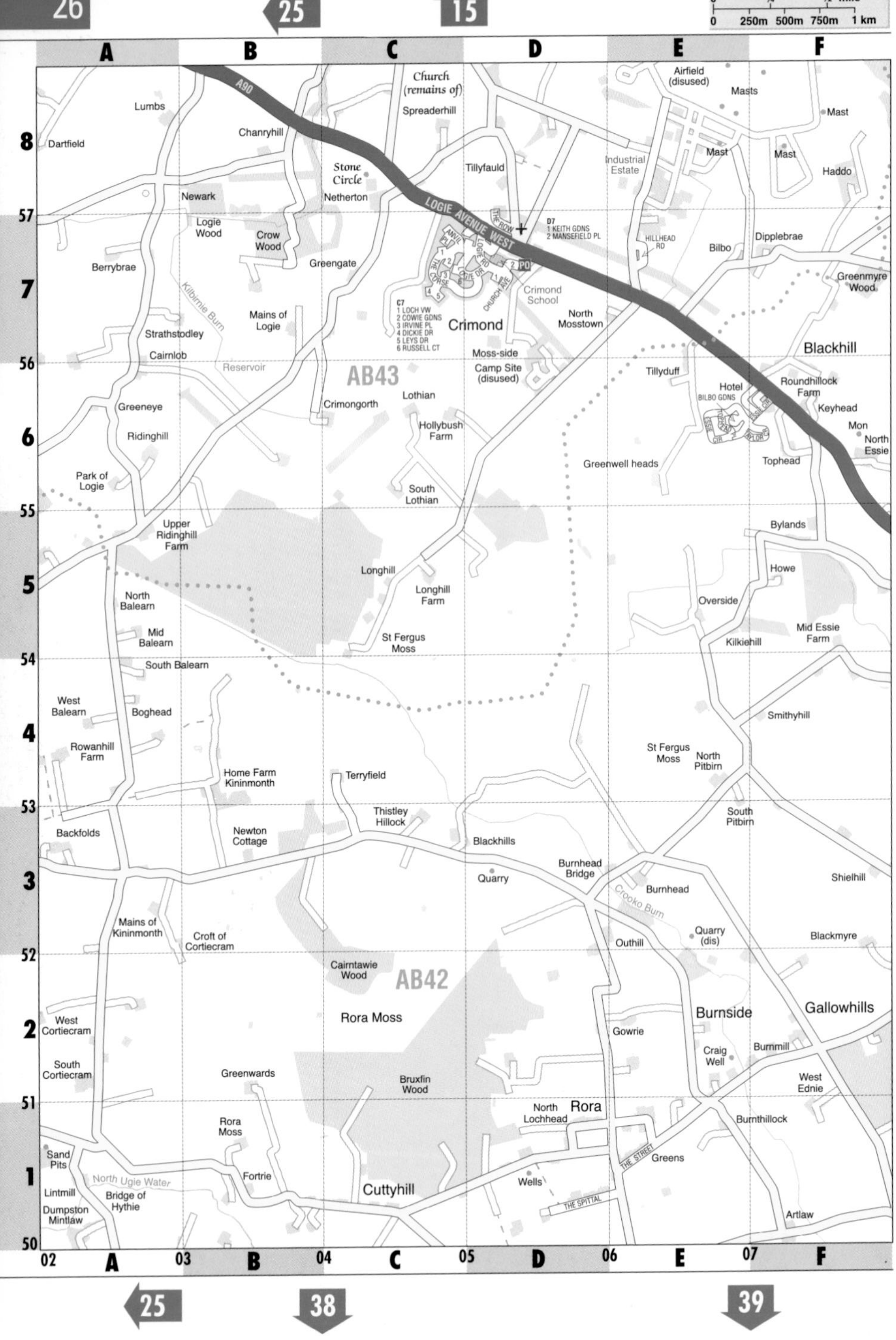

25 38 39

16

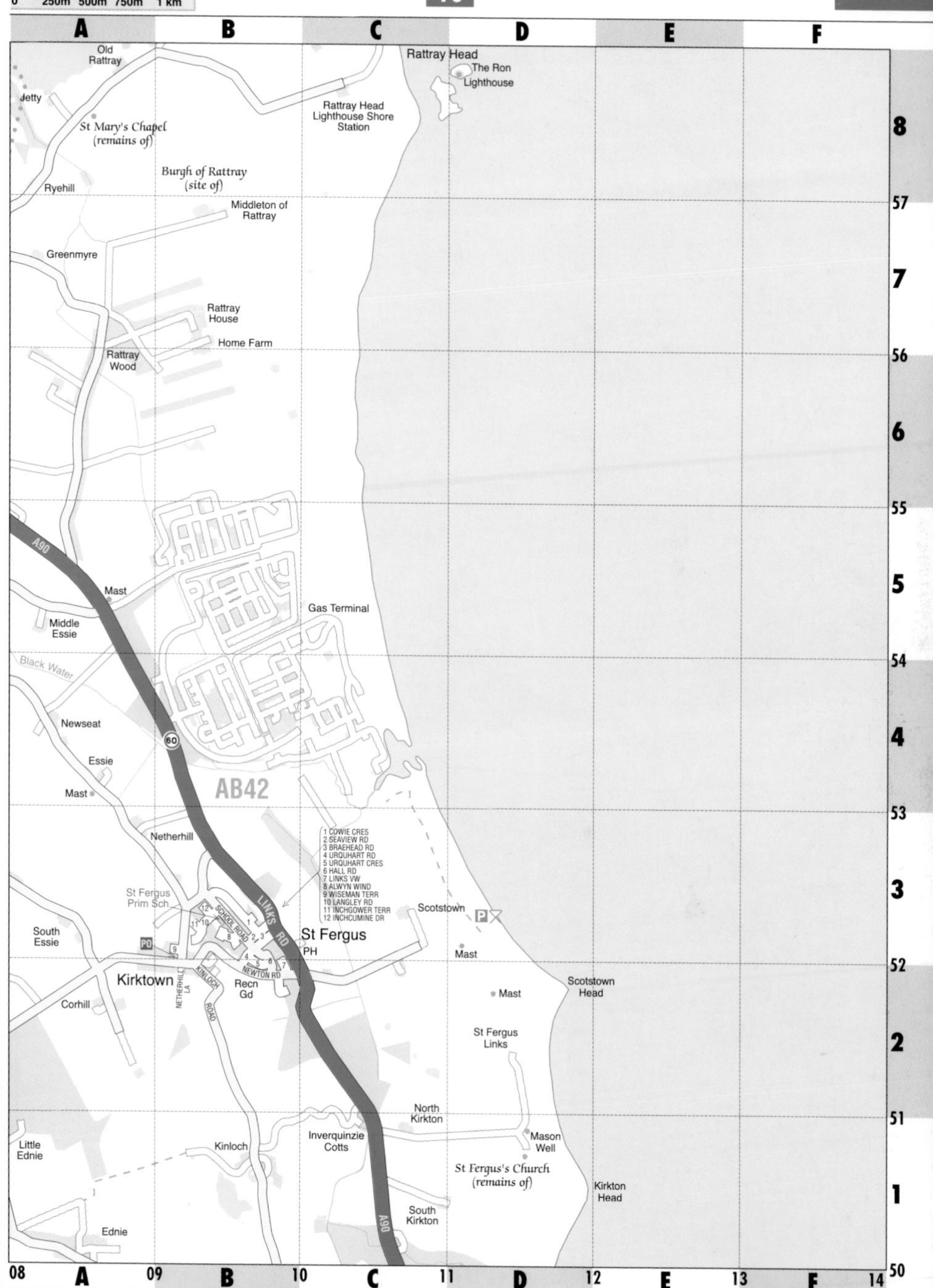
A
B
C
D
E
F
Old Rattray
Jetty
St Mary's Chapel (remains of)
Rattray Head
The Ron
Lighthouse
Rattray Head Lighthouse Shore Station
Burgh of Rattray (site of)
Ryehill
Middleton of Rattray
Greenmyre
Rattray House
Home Farm
Rattray Wood
A90
Mast
Middle Essie
Gas Terminal
Black Water
Newseat
60
Essie
Mast
AB42
Netherhill
1 COWIE CRES
2 SEAVIEW RD
3 BRAEHEAD RD
4 URQUHART RD
5 URQUHART CRES
6 HALL RD
7 LINKS VW
8 ALWYN WIND
9 WISEMAN TERR
10 LANGLEY RD
11 INCHGOWER TERR
12 INCHCUMINE DR
St Fergus Prim Sch
SCHOOL ROAD
LINKS RD
St Fergus
PH
Scotstown
P
Mast
South Essie
PO
NEWTON RD
Kirktown
KINLOCH ROAD
NETHERHILL LA
Recn Gd
Corhill
Mast
Scotstown Head
St Fergus Links
North Kirkton
Mason Well
Little Ednie
Kinloch
Inverquinzie Cotts
St Fergus's Church (remains of)
Kirkton Head
South Kirkton
A90
Ednie
8
57
7
56
6
55
5
54
4
53
3
52
2
51
1
50
08
09
10
11
12
13
14

39

40

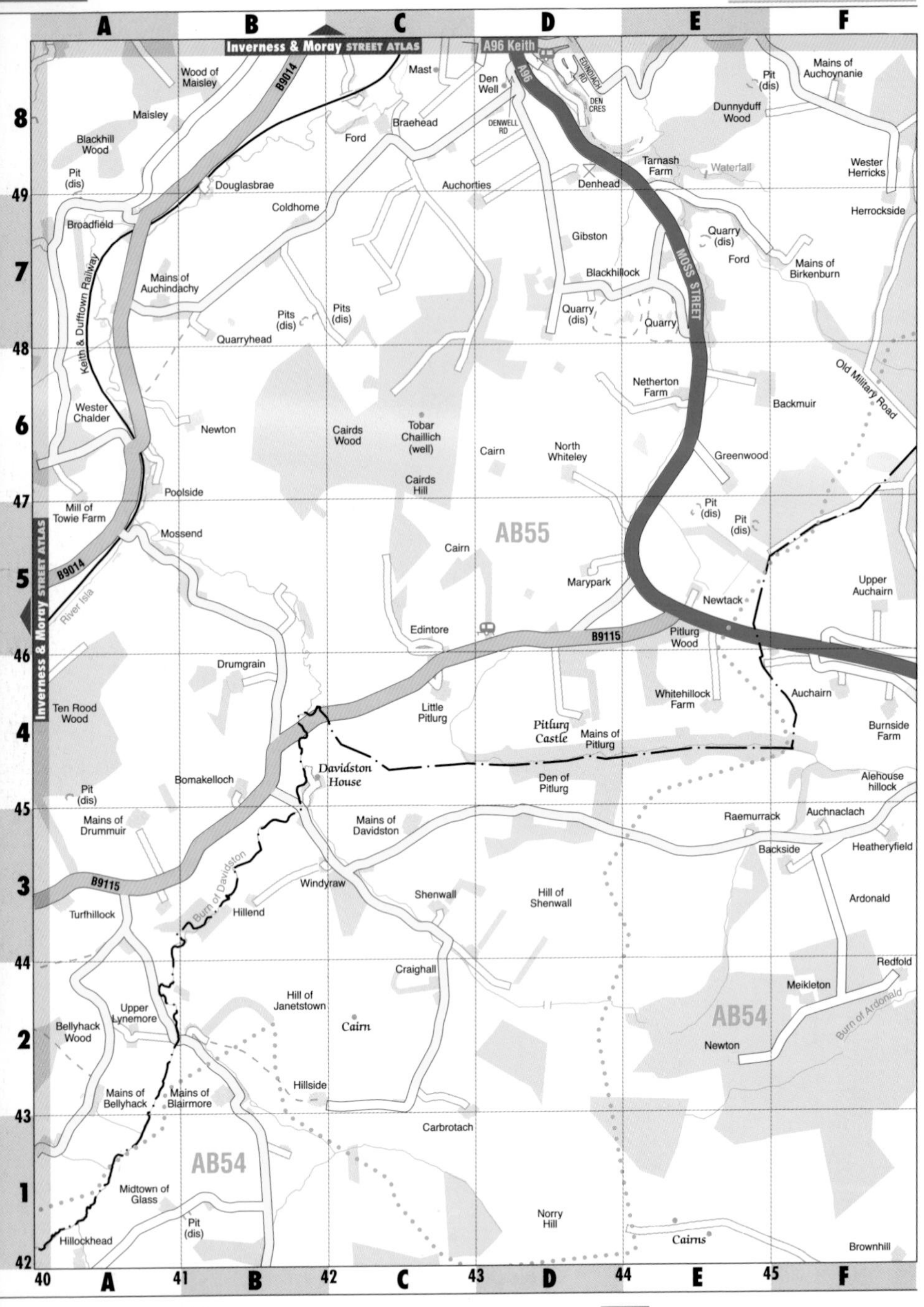
Scale: 1⅓ inches to 1 mile
0 ¼ ½ mile
0 250m 500m 750m 1 km
A B C D E F
Inverness & Moray STREET ATLAS
A96 Keith
Wood of Maisley
Maisley
Blackhill Wood
Pit (dis)
Broadfield
Douglasbrae
Coldhome
Ford
Braehead
Mast
Den Well
DENWELL RD
EDINDIACH RD
DEN CRES
Auchorties
Denhead
Tarnash Farm
Waterfall
Pit (dis)
Mains of Auchoynanie
Dunnyduff Wood
Wester Herricks
Herrockside
Gibston
Quarry (dis)
Ford
Mains of Birkenburn
Blackhillock
MOSS STREET
Keith & Dufftown Railway
Mains of Auchindachy
Pits (dis)
Pits (dis)
Quarry (dis)
Quarry
Quarryhead
Netherton Farm
Old Military Road
Backmuir
Wester Chalder
Newton
Cairds Wood
Tobar Chaillich (well)
Cairn
North Whiteley
Greenwood
Cairds Hill
Poolside
Mill of Towie Farm
Mossend
Pit (dis)
Pit (dis)
AB55
Cairn
B9014
Marypark
Newtack
Upper Auchairn
River Isla
Edintore
B9115
Pitlurg Wood
Drumgrain
Whitehillock Farm
Auchairn
Ten Rood Wood
Little Pitlurg
Pitlurg Castle
Mains of Pitlurg
Burnside Farm
Davidston House
Bomakelloch
Den of Pitlurg
Alehouse hillock
Pit (dis)
Mains of Drummuir
Mains of Davidston
Raemurrack
Auchnaclach
Backside
Heatheryfield
Burn of Davidston
B9115
Windyraw
Shenwall
Hill of Shenwall
Ardonald
Turfhillock
Hillend
Craighall
Redfold
Meikleton
Hill of Janetstown
Upper Lynemore
AB54
Bellyhack Wood
Cairn
Newton
Burn of Ardonald
Hillside
Mains of Bellyhack
Mains of Blairmore
Carbrotach
AB54
Midtown of Glass
Norry Hill
Pit (dis)
Hillockhead
Cairns
Brownhill
8 49 7 48 6 47 5 46 4 45 3 44 2 43 1 42
40 41 42 43 44 45

41
42

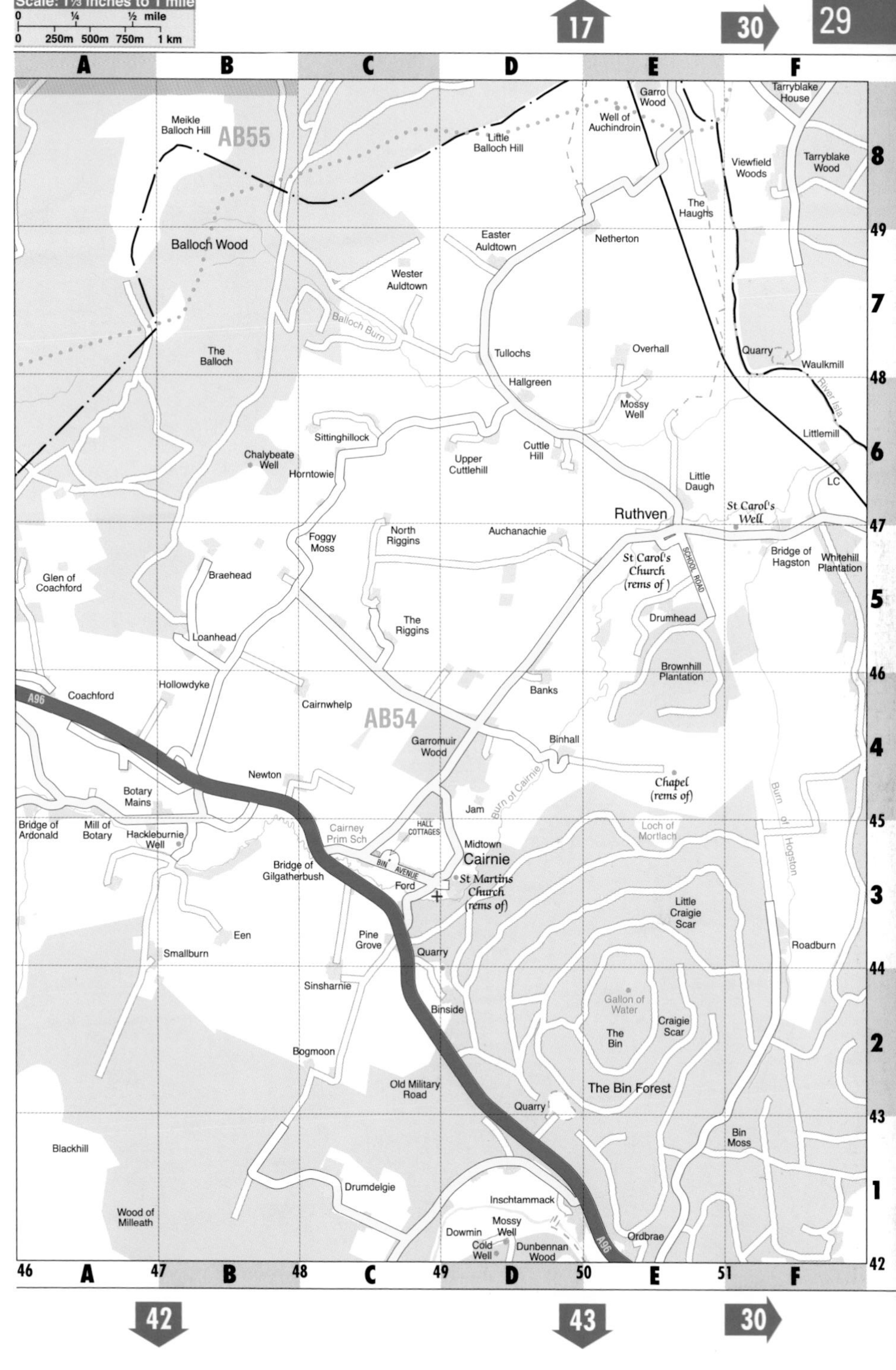
Scale: 1⅓ inches to 1 mile
0 ¼ ½ mile
0 250m 500m 750m 1 km
17
30
A B C D E F
Meikle Balloch Hill
AB55
Little Balloch Hill
Garro Wood
Well of Auchindroin
Tarryblake House
Viewfield Woods
Tarryblake Wood
The Haughs
Balloch Wood
Easter Auldtown
Netherton
Wester Auldtown
Balloch Burn
The Balloch
Tullochs
Overhall
Quarry
Waulkmill
Hallgreen
Mossy Well
River Isla
Littlemill
Sittinghillock
Chalybeate Well
Horntowie
Upper Cuttlehill
Cuttle Hill
Little Daugh
LC
Ruthven
St Carol's Well
Foggy Moss
North Riggins
Auchanachie
St Carol's Church (rems of)
SCHOOL ROAD
Bridge of Hagston
Whitehill Plantation
Glen of Coachford
Braehead
The Riggins
Drumhead
Loanhead
Brownhill Plantation
Hollowdyke
Coachford
A96
Cairnwhelp
AB54
Banks
Garromuir Wood
Binhall
Newton
Burn of Cairnie
Chapel (rems of)
Botary Mains
Jam
Burn of Hogston
Bridge of Ardonald
Mill of Botary
Hackleburnie Well
Cairney Prim Sch
HALL COTTAGES
Loch of Mortlach
Midtown
Cairnie
Bridge of Gilgatherbush
BIN AVENUE
St Martins Church (rems of)
Ford
Little Craigie Scar
Een
Pine Grove
Smallburn
Quarry
Roadburn
Sinsharnie
Gallon of Water
Binside
The Bin
Craigie Scar
Bogmoon
Old Military Road
The Bin Forest
Quarry
Blackhill
Bin Moss
Drumdelgie
Inschtammack
Wood of Milleath
Mossy Well
Dowmin
Cold Well
Dunbennan Wood
Ordbrae
A96
8
49
7
48
6
47
5
46
4
45
3
44
2
43
1
42
46 A 47 B 48 C 49 D 50 E 51 F
42
43
30

29 17 18

Scale: 1⅓ inches to 1 mile

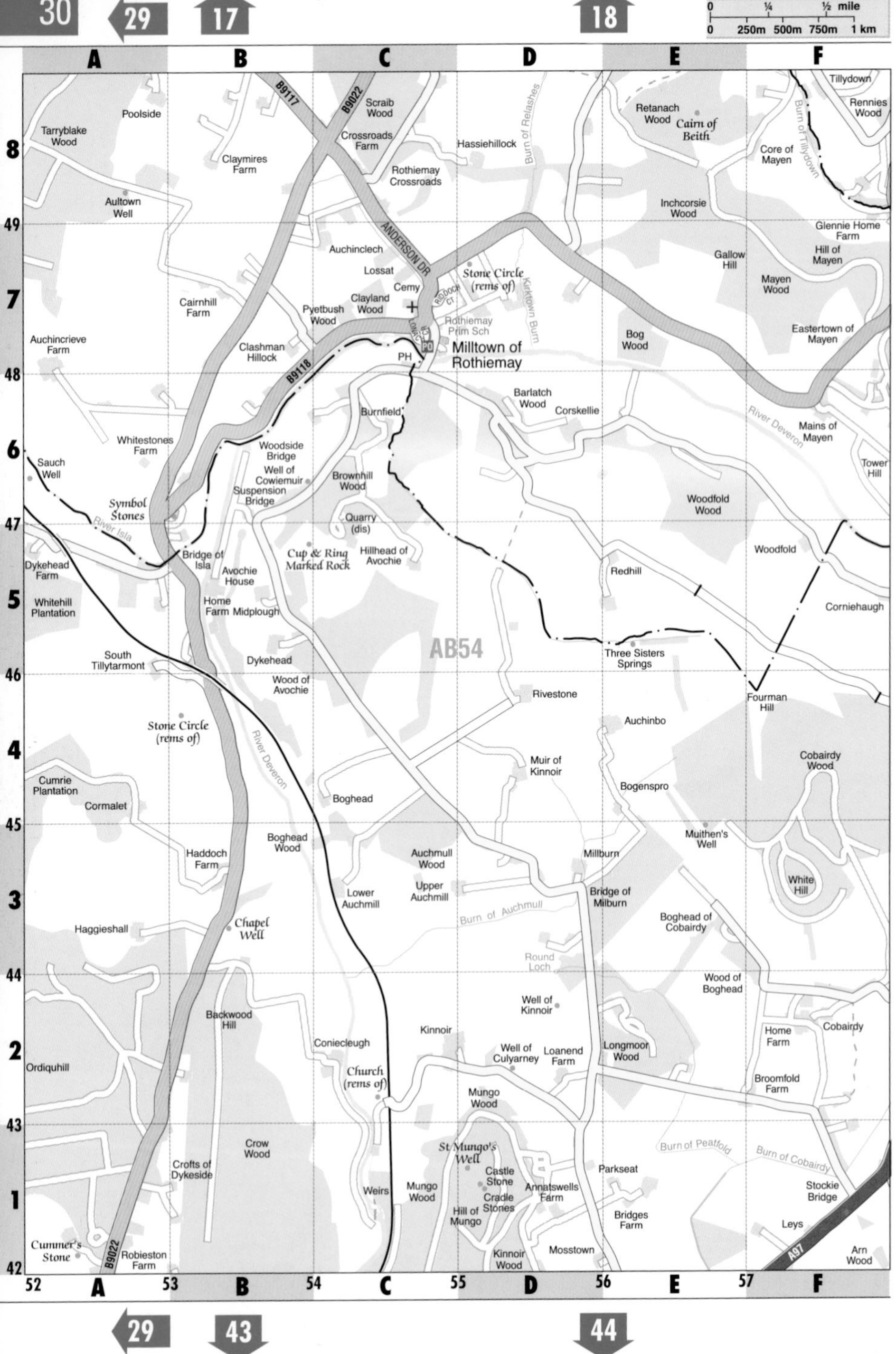

29 43 44

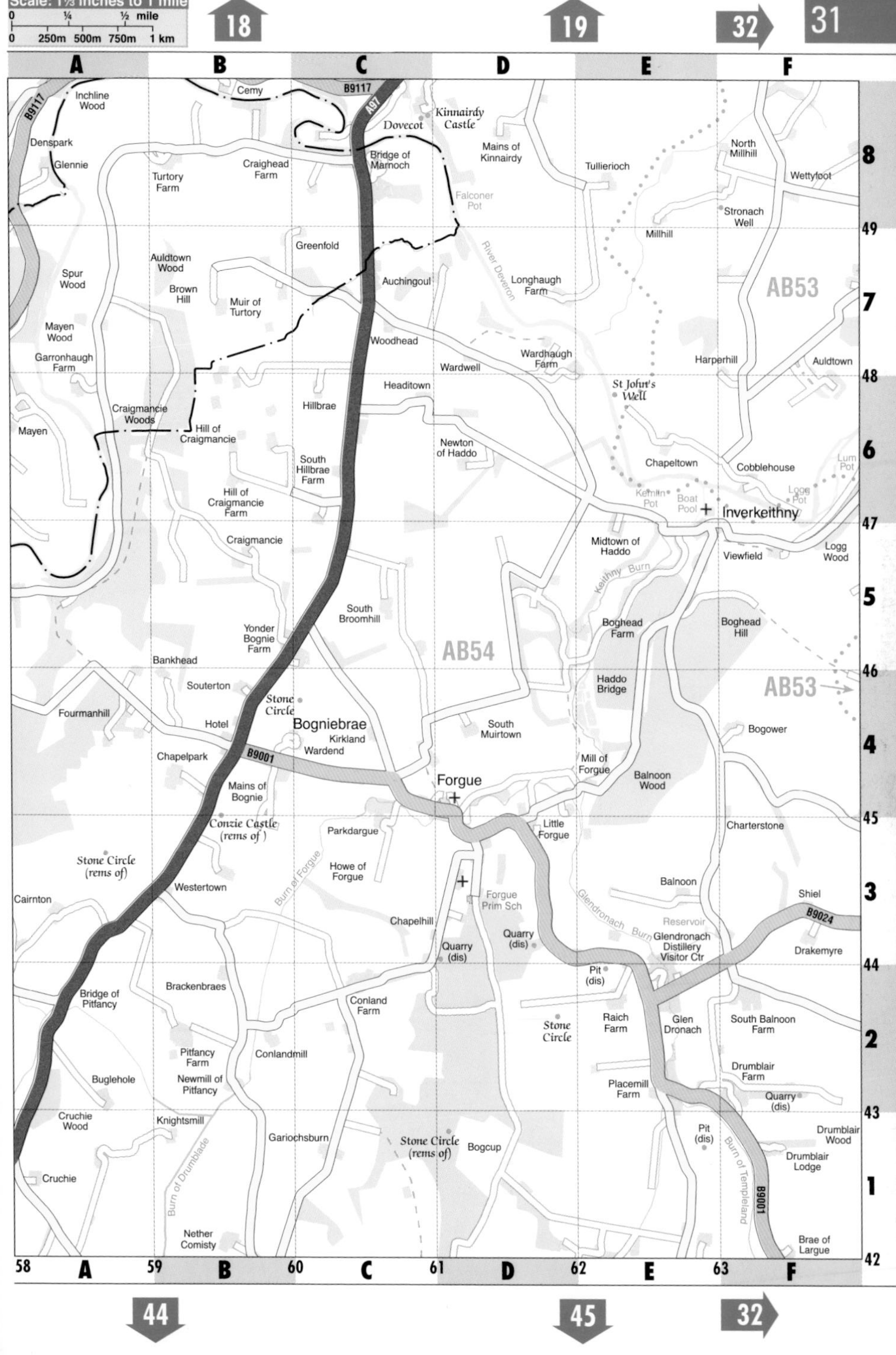
Scale: 1⅓ inches to 1 mile
0 ¼ ½ mile
0 250m 500m 750m 1 km
18
19
32
A B C D E F
B9117
Inchline Wood
Cemy
A97
Kinnairdy Castle
Dovecot
Denspark
Glennie
Turtory Farm
Craighead Farm
Bridge of Marnoch
Mains of Kinnairdy
Tullierioch
North Millhill
Wettyfoot
Falconer Pot
Stronach Well
Millhill
Greenfold
River Deveron
Spur Wood
Auldtown Wood
Brown Hill
Muir of Turtory
Auchingoul
Longhaugh Farm
AB53
Mayen Wood
Garronhaugh Farm
Woodhead
Wardwell
Wardhaugh Farm
Harperhill
Auldtown
Headitown
St John's Well
Mayen
Craigmancie Woods
Hill of Craigmancie
Hillbrae
Newton of Haddo
South Hillbrae Farm
Chapeltown
Cobblehouse
Lum Pot
Hill of Craigmancie Farm
Kelmin Pot
Boat Pool
Inverkeithny
Logg Pot
Craigmancie
Midtown of Haddo
Viewfield
Logg Wood
Keithny Burn
South Broomhill
Yonder Bognie Farm
AB54
Boghead Farm
Boghead Hill
Bankhead
Souterton
Stone Circle
Haddo Bridge
AB53
Fourmanhill
Hotel
Bogniebrae
Kirkland
Wardend
South Muirtown
Bogower
Chapelpark
B9001
Mill of Forgue
Mains of Bognie
Forgue
Balnoon Wood
Conzie Castle (rems of)
Parkdargue
Little Forgue
Charterstone
Stone Circle (rems of)
Burn of Forgue
Howe of Forgue
Forgue Prim Sch
Balnoon
Cairnton
Westertown
Glendronach Burn
Shiel
Reservoir
B9024
Chapelhill
Quarry (dis)
Glendronach Distillery Visitor Ctr
Drakemyre
Pit (dis)
Brackenbraes
Bridge of Pitfancy
Conland Farm
Raich Farm
Glen Dronach
South Balnoon Farm
Stone Circle
Pitfancy Farm
Conlandmill
Buglehole
Newmill of Pitfancy
Placemill Farm
Drumblair Farm
Quarry (dis)
Cruchie Wood
Knightsmill
Gariochsburn
Stone Circle (rems of)
Bogcup
Pit (dis)
Drumblair Wood
Drumblair Lodge
Cruchie
Burn of Drumblade
Burn of Templeland
Nether Comisty
Brae of Largue
8
49
7
48
6
47
5
46
4
45
3
44
2
43
1
42
58 59 60 61 62 63
44
45
32

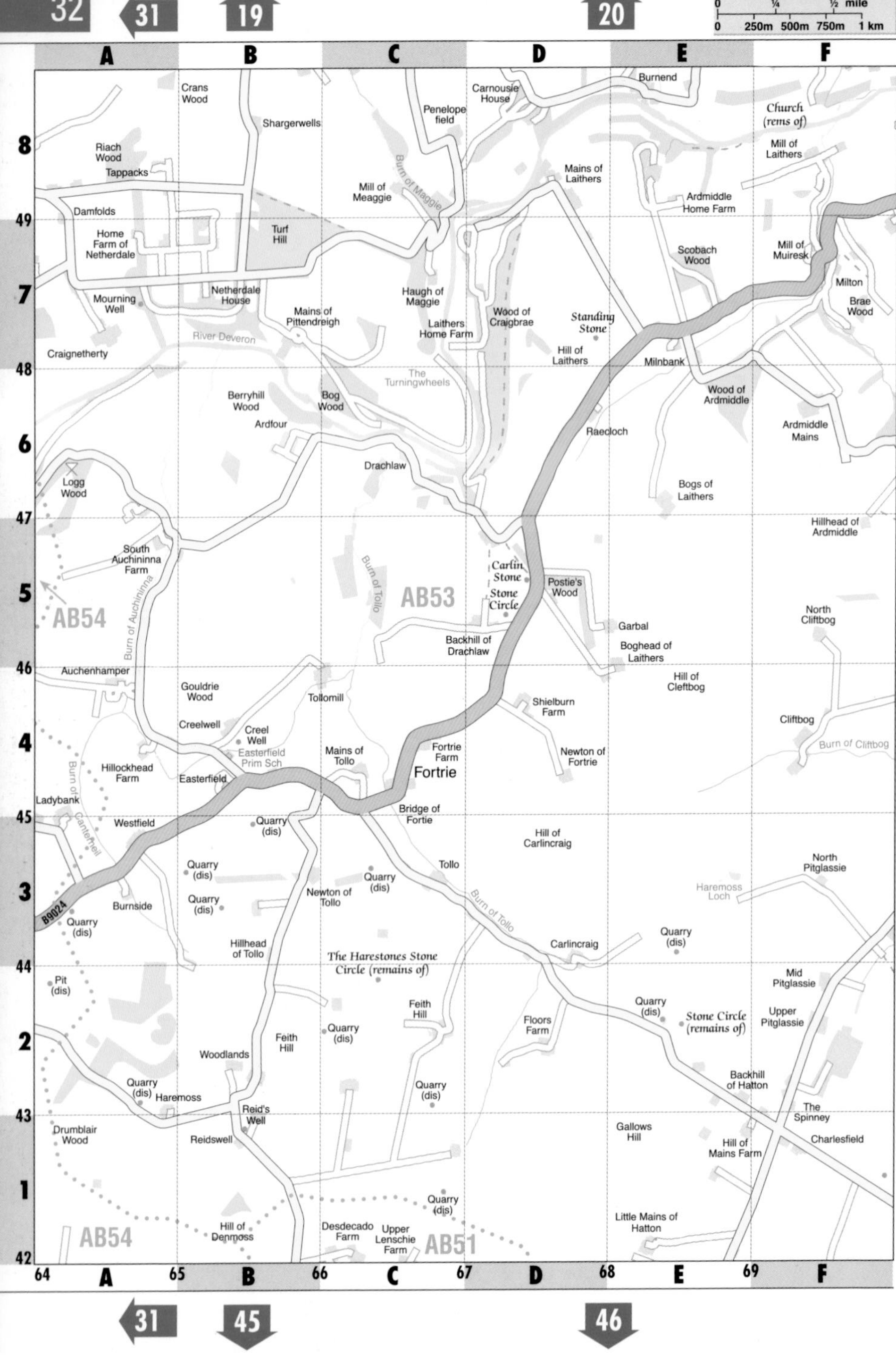
31
19
20
Scale: 1⅓ inches to 1 mile
0 ¼ ½ mile
0 250m 500m 750m 1 km
A B C D E F
8 49 7 48 6 47 5 46 4 45 3 44 2 43 1 42
64 65 66 67 68 69
Crans Wood
Riach Wood
Tappacks
Damfolds
Home Farm of Netherdale
Shargerwells
Turf Hill
Netherdale House
Mourning Well
Craignetherty
River Deveron
Mains of Pittendreigh
Penelope field
Carnousie House
Burnend
Mill of Meaggie
Burn of Maggie
Haugh of Maggie
Laithers Home Farm
Wood of Craigbrae
Mains of Laithers
Standing Stone
Hill of Laithers
Church (rems of)
Mill of Laithers
Ardmiddle Home Farm
Scobach Wood
Mill of Muiresk
Milton
Brae Wood
Milnbank
Wood of Ardmiddle
Ardmiddle Mains
Raecloch
Bogs of Laithers
Hillhead of Ardmiddle
The Turningwheels
Berryhill Wood
Bog Wood
Ardfour
Drachlaw
Logg Wood
South Auchininna Farm
Burn of Auchininna
AB54
Burn of Tollo
AB53
Carlin Stone
Stone Circle
Postie's Wood
Garbal
Boghead of Laithers
Backhill of Drachlaw
North Cliftbog
Hill of Cleftbog
Cliftbog
Burn of Cliftbog
Auchenhamper
Gouldrie Wood
Tollomill
Shielburn Farm
Creelwell
Creel Well
Easterfield Prim Sch
Mains of Tollo
Fortrie Farm
Fortrie
Newton of Fortrie
Hillockhead Farm
Easterfield
Burn of Cantenell
Ladybank
Westfield
Quarry (dis)
Bridge of Fortie
Hill of Carlincraig
Tollo
North Pitglassie
Haremoss Loch
Burnside
Newton of Tollo
B9024
Hillhead of Tollo
Carlincraig
The Harestones Stone Circle (remains of)
Mid Pitglassie
Pit (dis)
Feith Hill
Floors Farm
Stone Circle (remains of)
Upper Pitglassie
Woodlands
Haremoss
Reid's Well
Backhill of Hatton
The Spinney
Charlesfield
Drumblair Wood
Reidswell
Gallows Hill
Hill of Mains Farm
Hill of Denmoss
Desdecado Farm
Upper Lenschie Farm
AB51
Little Mains of Hatton
31
45
46

Scale: 1⅓ inches to 1 mile

20
21
34

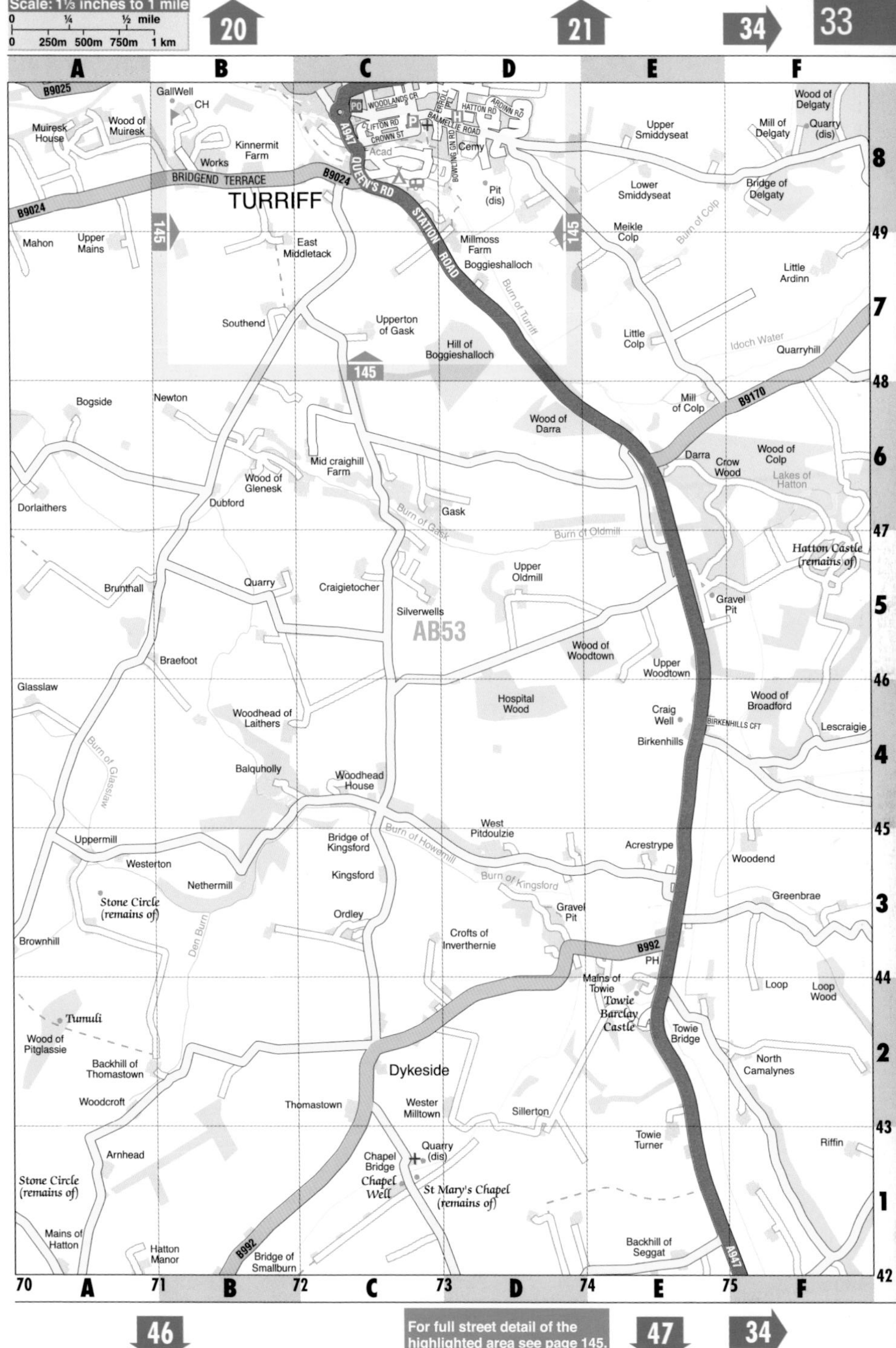

46
For full street detail of the highlighted area see page 145.
47
34

Scale: 1⅓ inches to 1 mile

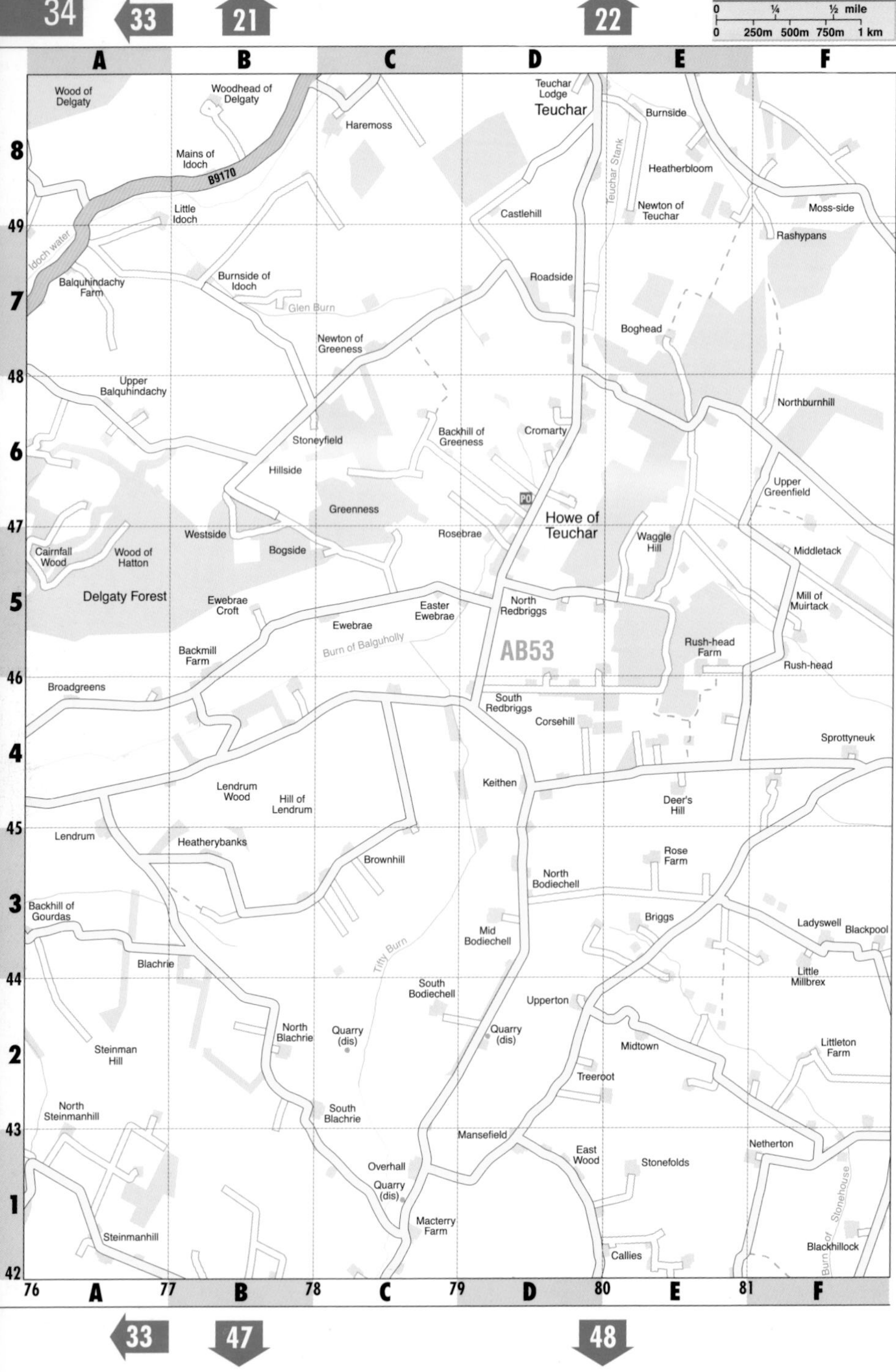

Scale: 1⅓ inches to 1 mile

22 23 36

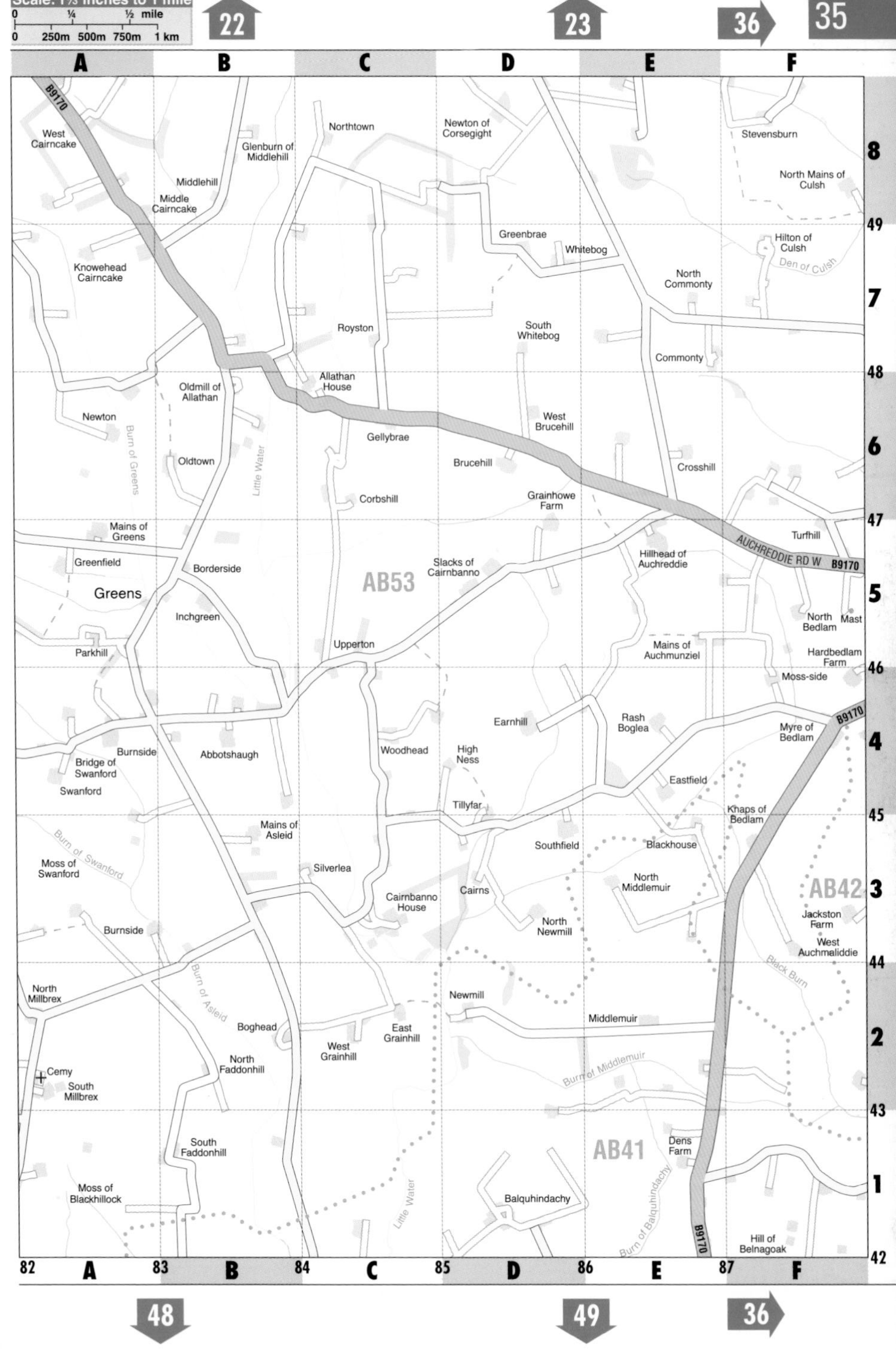

48 49 36

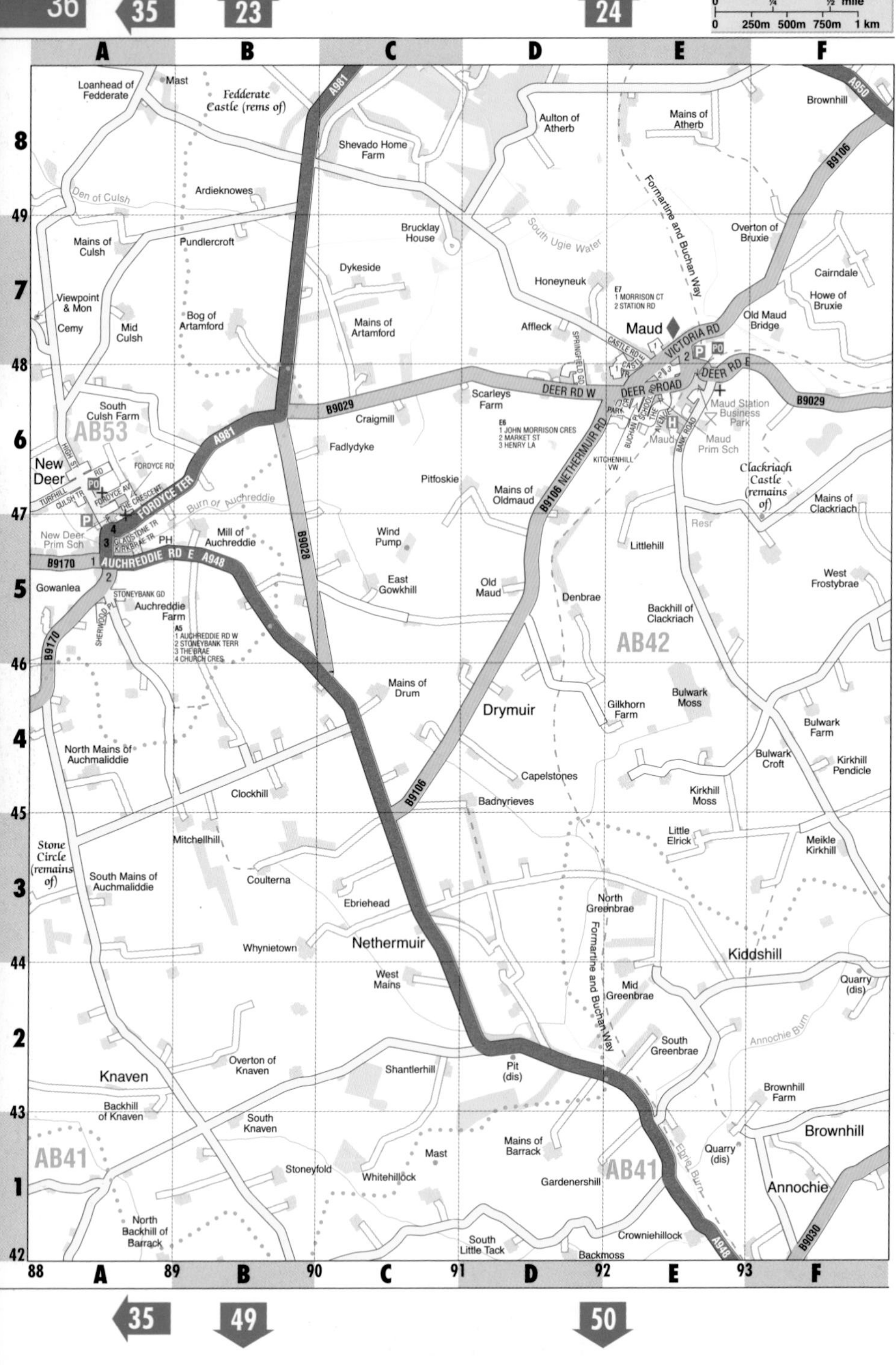
35
23
24
Scale: 1⅓ inches to 1 mile
0 ¼ ½ mile
0 250m 500m 750m 1 km
A B C D E F
Loanhead of Fedderate
Mast
Fedderate Castle (rems of)
Shevado Home Farm
Aulton of Atherb
Mains of Atherb
Brownhill
Den of Culsh
Ardieknowes
Formartine and Buchan Way
Brucklay House
South Ugie Water
Overton of Bruxie
Mains of Culsh
Pundlercroft
Dykeside
Honeyneuk
Cairndale
Viewpoint & Mon
Cemy
Mid Culsh
Bog of Artamford
Mains of Artamford
E7
1 MORRISON CT
2 STATION RD
Howe of Bruxie
Affleck
Maud
Old Maud Bridge
VICTORIA RD
CASTLE RD
SPRINGFIELD GD
DEER RD E
DEER RD W
DEER ROAD
Scarleys Farm
B9029
Craigmill
South Culsh Farm
AB53
A981
Maud Station Business Park
E6
1 JOHN MORRISON CRES
2 MARKET ST
3 HENRY LA
Maud
Maud Prim Sch
BANK ROAD
NETHERMUIR RD
Fadlydyke
New Deer
FORDYCE RD
KITCHENHILL VW
Clackriach Castle (remains of)
Pitfoskie
Mains of Oldmaud
Mains of Clackriach
FORDYCE TER
Burn of Auchreddie
Resr
New Deer Prim Sch
GLADSTONE TR
KIRKBRAE TR
PH
Mill of Auchreddie
Wind Pump
Littlehill
B9170
AUCHREDDIE RD E
A948
B9028
B9106
West Frostybrae
Gowanlea
STONEYBANK GD
East Gowkhill
Old Maud
Denbrae
Auchreddie Farm
Backhill of Clackriach
A5
1 AUCHREDDIE RD W
2 STONEYBANK TERR
3 THE BRAE
4 CHURCH CRES
AB42
Mains of Drum
Drymuir
Gilkhorn Farm
Bulwark Moss
Bulwark Farm
North Mains of Auchmaliddie
Bulwark Croft
Kirkhill Pendicle
Capelstones
Clockhill
Kirkhill Moss
Badnyrieves
Little Elrick
Meikle Kirkhill
Stone Circle (remains of)
Mitchellhill
South Mains of Auchmaliddie
Coulterna
North Greenbrae
Ebriehead
Whynietown
Nethermuir
Kiddshill
West Mains
Mid Greenbrae
Quarry (dis)
Annochie Burn
South Greenbrae
Overton of Knaven
Shantlerhill
Pit (dis)
Knaven
Brownhill Farm
Backhill of Knaven
South Knaven
Brownhill
Mains of Barrack
Quarry (dis)
Ebrie Burn
AB41
Mast
Stoneyfold
Whitehillock
Gardenershill
Annochie
North Backhill of Barrack
South Little Tack
Crowniehillock
Backmoss
B9030
A950
B9106
88 89 90 91 92 93
8 49 7 48 6 47 5 46 4 45 3 44 2 43 1 42
35
49
50

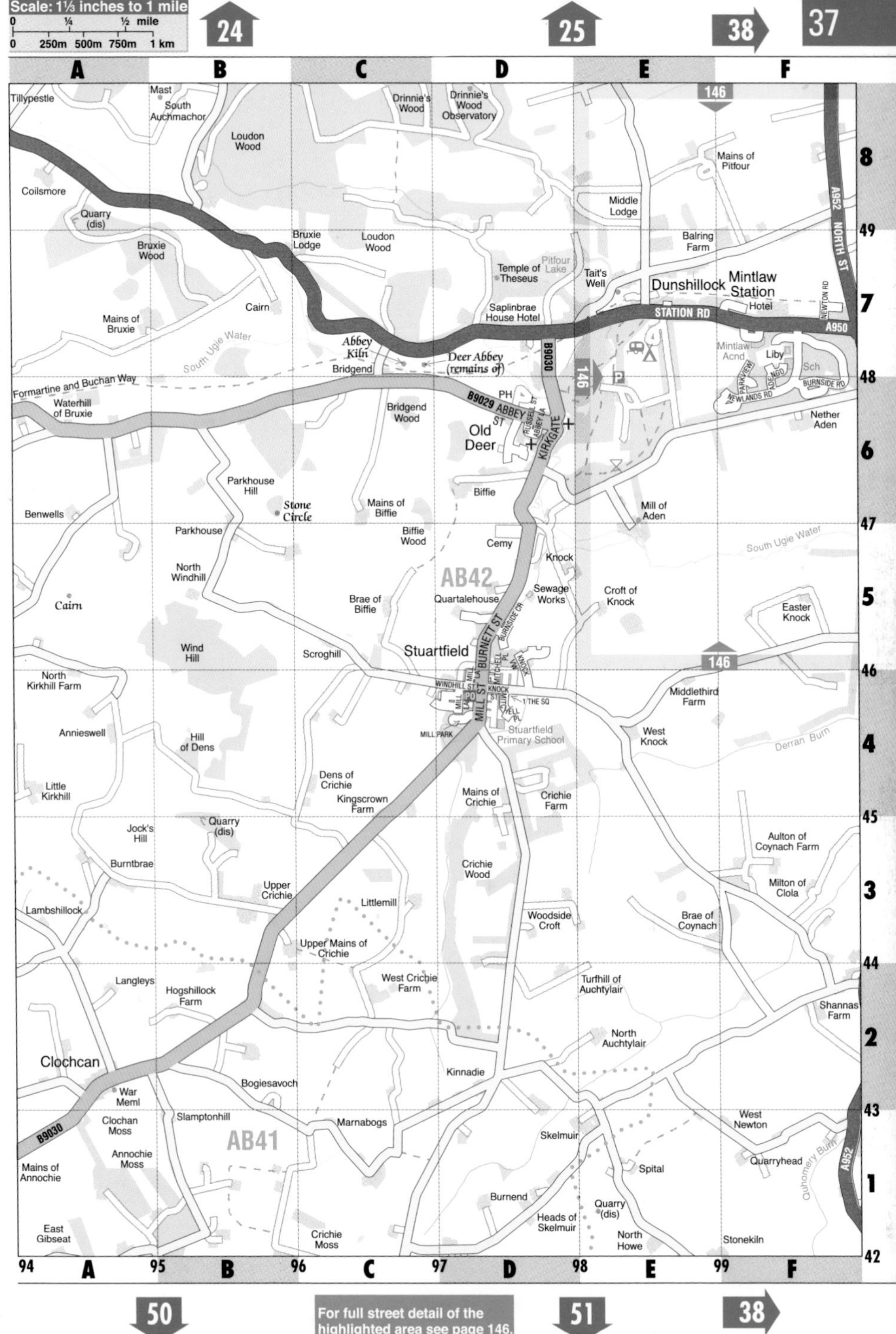

For full street detail of the highlighted area see page 146.

37 25 26

D6
1 BRUCE BRAE
2 TULLOCHGORUM GDNS
3 MARKET HILL
4 INVERQUHOMERY RD
5 PARKVALE
6 WINDING BRAE
7 SMITHY LA
8 ARMOURY LA
9 THE RIGGS
10 COOPER'S BRAE
11 LABURNUM LA
12 GLEBEFIELD
13 BRAEHEAD PL
14 CHEVES Cl
15 FLEEMAN WY

Scale: 1⅓ inches to 1 mile
0 ¼ ½ mile
0 250m 500m 750m 1 km

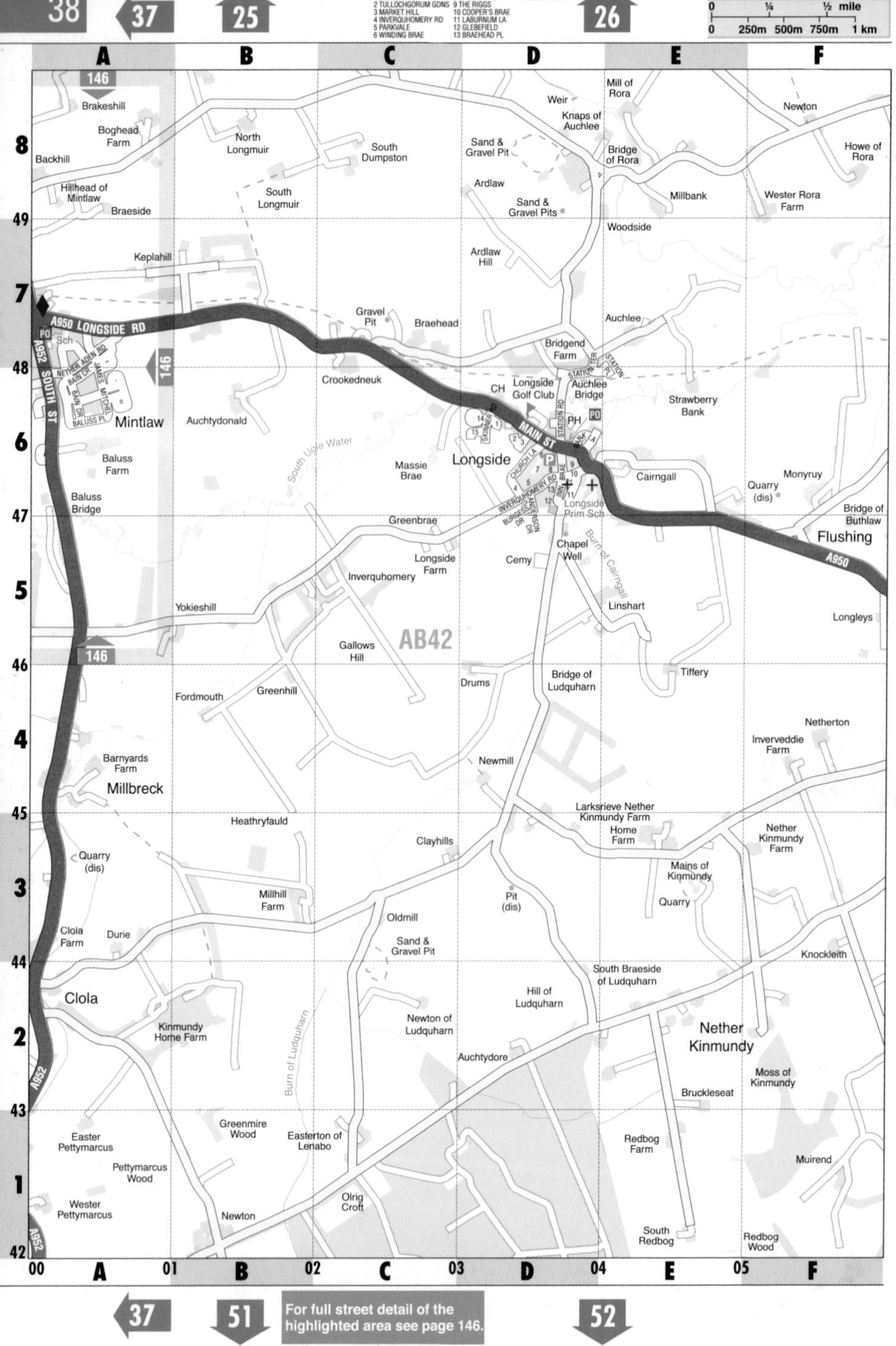

37 51 52

For full street detail of the highlighted area see page 146.

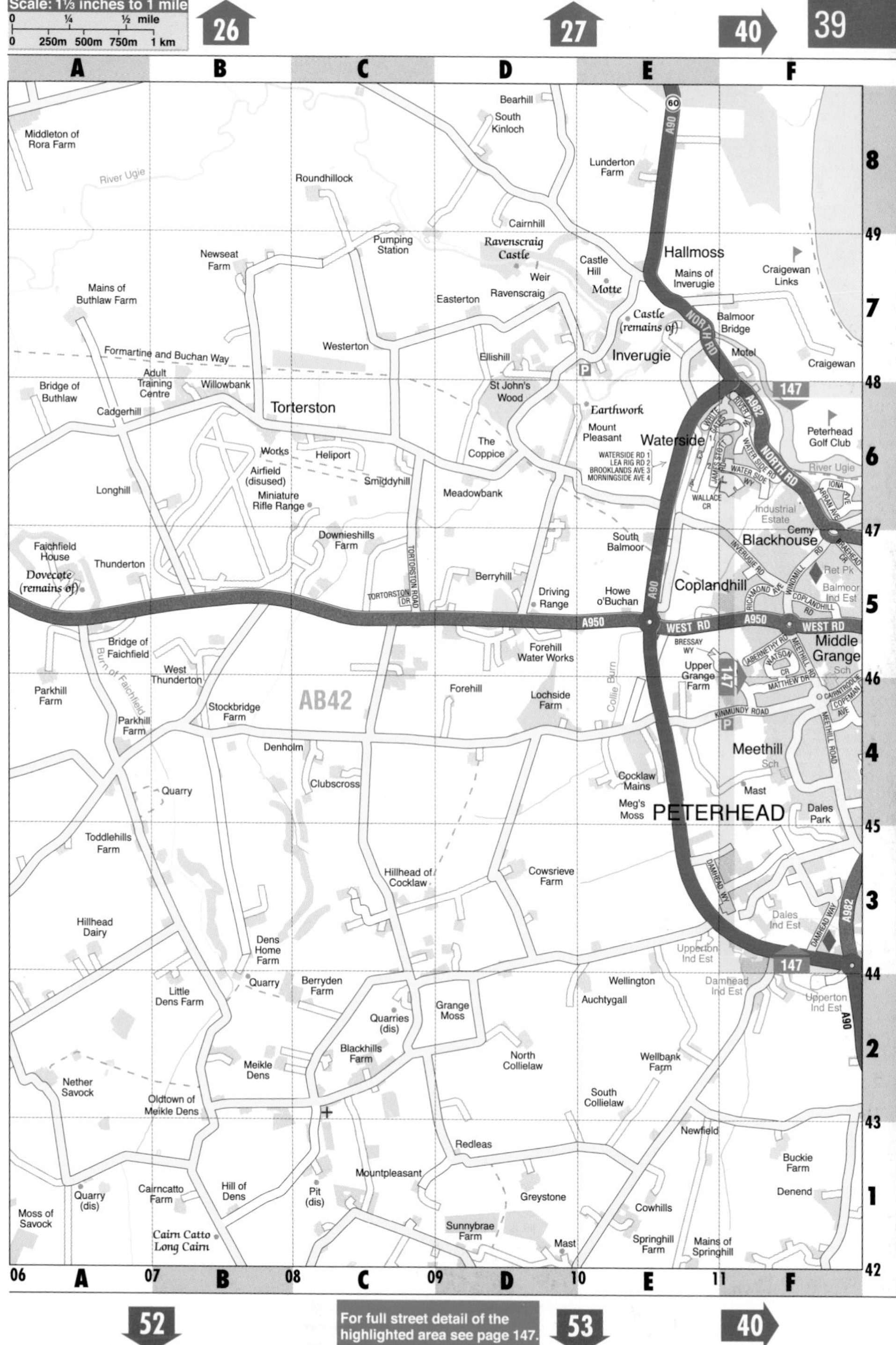
A
B
C
D
E
F
8
49
7
48
6
47
5
46
4
45
3
44
2
43
1
42
06
07
08
09
10
11
Bearhill
South Kinloch
60
A90
Middleton of Rora Farm
River Ugie
Roundhillock
Lunderton Farm
Cairnhill
Pumping Station
Ravenscraig Castle
Newseat Farm
Castle Hill
Motte
Hallmoss
Mains of Inverugie
Craigewan Links
Mains of Buthlaw Farm
Weir
Ravenscraig
Easterton
Castle (remains of)
NORTH RD
Balmoor Bridge
Westerton
Formartine and Buchan Way
Ellishill
Inverugie
Motel
Craigewan
Adult Training Centre
Willowbank
Bridge of Buthlaw
Cadgerhill
Torterston
St John's Wood
Earthwork
147
A982
Mount Pleasant
Waterside
Peterhead Golf Club
Works
Heliport
The Coppice
WATERSIDE RD 1
LEA RIG RD 2
BROOKLANDS AVE 3
MORNINGSIDE AVE 4
WATER SIDE RD
WATER SIDE WY
River Ugie
Airfield (disused)
Smiddyhill
Longhill
Meadowbank
Miniature Rifle Range
WALLACE CR
IONA AVE
ARRAN AVE
Industrial Estate
Cemy
Downieshills Farm
Faichfield House
South Balmoor
Blackhouse
INVERUGIE RD
Thunderton
TORTORSTON ROAD
Berryhill
WINDMILL
Ret Pk
Dovecote (remains of)
Coplandhill
Balmoor Ind Est
TORTORSTON DR
Driving Range
Howe o'Buchan
RICHMOND AVE
COPLANDHILL RD
A950
WEST RD
Bridge of Faichfield
BRESSAY WY
Forehill Water Works
Middle Grange
Upper Grange Farm
ABERNETHY RD
MEETHILL RD
WATSON CR
Sch
West Thunderton
Collie Burn
MATTHEW DR
CAIRNTRODLIE
COPEMAN AVE
Parkhill Farm
Burn of Faichfield
AB42
Forehill
Lochside Farm
Stockbridge Farm
KINMUNDY ROAD
Parkhill Farm
P
Denholm
Meethill
MEETHILL ROAD
Sch
Quarry
Clubscross
Cocklaw Mains
Mast
Meg's Moss
PETERHEAD
Dales Park
Toddlehills Farm
Hillhead of Cocklaw
Cowsrieve Farm
DAMHEAD WY
Hillhead Dairy
Dales Ind Est
DAMHEAD WAY
Dens Home Farm
Upperton Ind Est
Quarry
Berryden Farm
Little Dens Farm
Wellington
Damhead Ind Est
Grange Moss
Auchtygall
Upperton Ind Est
Quarries (dis)
Blackhills Farm
North Collielaw
Wellbank Farm
Meikle Dens
Nether Savock
Oldtown of Meikle Dens
South Collielaw
Newfield
Redleas
Buckie Farm
Mountpleasant
Denend
Cairncatto Farm
Hill of Dens
Quarry (dis)
Pit (dis)
Greystone
Cowhills
Moss of Savock
Sunnybrae Farm
Cairn Catto Long Cairn
Mast
Springhill Farm
Mains of Springhill

For full street detail of the highlighted area see page 147.

D1
1 HARBOUR ST
2 VIEW GDNS
3 DUNDONNIE ST
4 BUCHANNESS DR
5 SANDFORD PL
6 EARL'S CT
7 QUEEN'S CRES
8 QUEEN'S LA
9 QUEEN'S WK
10 CASTLE DR
11 GORDON CL
12 CHURCH PL
13 GORDON ST
14 SKERRY PK
15 BUCHANNESS PL
16 BRAE ST
17 NEW ST
18 ST HELENA CT
19 ROCKSLEY DR
20 BRIDGE ST
21 BIRNIE PL
22 QUEEN'S RD
23 MANSE TERR
24 SEAVIEW RD

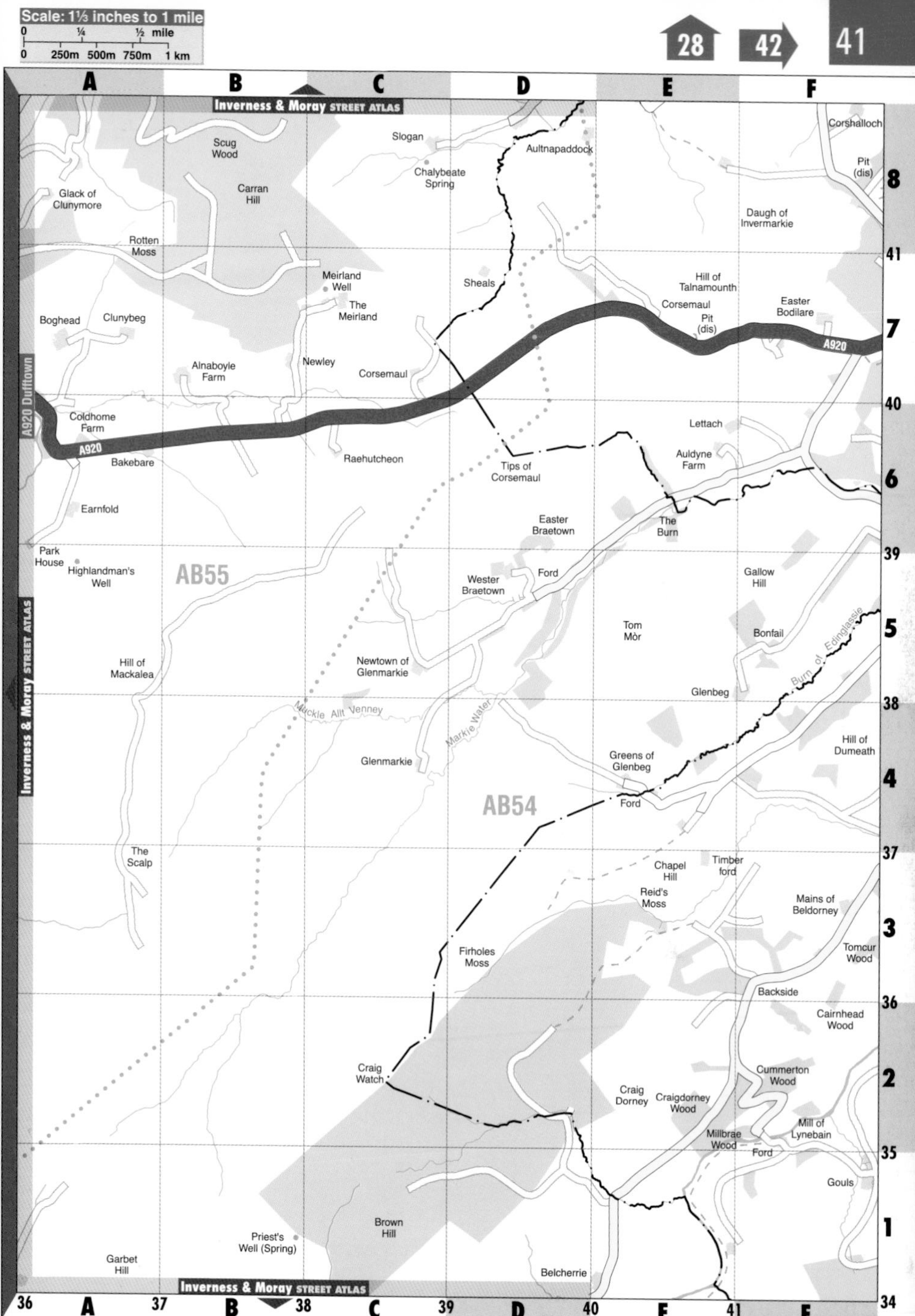
Scale: 1⅓ inches to 1 mile
0 ¼ ½ mile
0 250m 500m 750m 1 km
28
42
A
B
C
D
E
F
Inverness & Moray STREET ATLAS
Slogan
Aultnapaddock
Corshalloch
Pit (dis)
Scug Wood
Chalybeate Spring
Carran Hill
Glack of Clunymore
Daugh of Invermarkie
Rotten Moss
Meirland Well
Hill of Talnamounth
Sheals
The Meirland
Corsemaul
Easter Bodilare
Boghead
Clunybeg
Pit (dis)
A920
Alnaboyle Farm
Newley
Corsemaul
A920 Dufftown
Coldhome Farm
Lettach
A920
Bakebare
Raehutcheon
Auldyne Farm
Tips of Corsemaul
Earnfold
Easter Braetown
The Burn
Park House
Highlandman's Well
AB55
Wester Braetown
Ford
Gallow Hill
Tom Mòr
Bonfail
Hill of Mackalea
Newtown of Glenmarkie
Burn of Edinglassie
Glenbeg
Muckle Allt Venney
Markie Water
Glenmarkie
Greens of Glenbeg
Hill of Dumeath
AB54
Ford
The Scalp
Chapel Hill
Timber ford
Reid's Moss
Mains of Beldorney
Firholes Moss
Tomcur Wood
Backside
Cairnhead Wood
Craig Watch
Cummerton Wood
Craig Dorney
Craigdorney Wood
Mill of Lynebain
Millbrae Wood
Ford
Gouls
Brown Hill
Priest's Well (Spring)
Garbet Hill
Belcherrie
8
41
7
40
6
39
5
38
4
37
3
36
2
35
1
34
36
37
38
39
40
41
Inverness & Moray STREET ATLAS

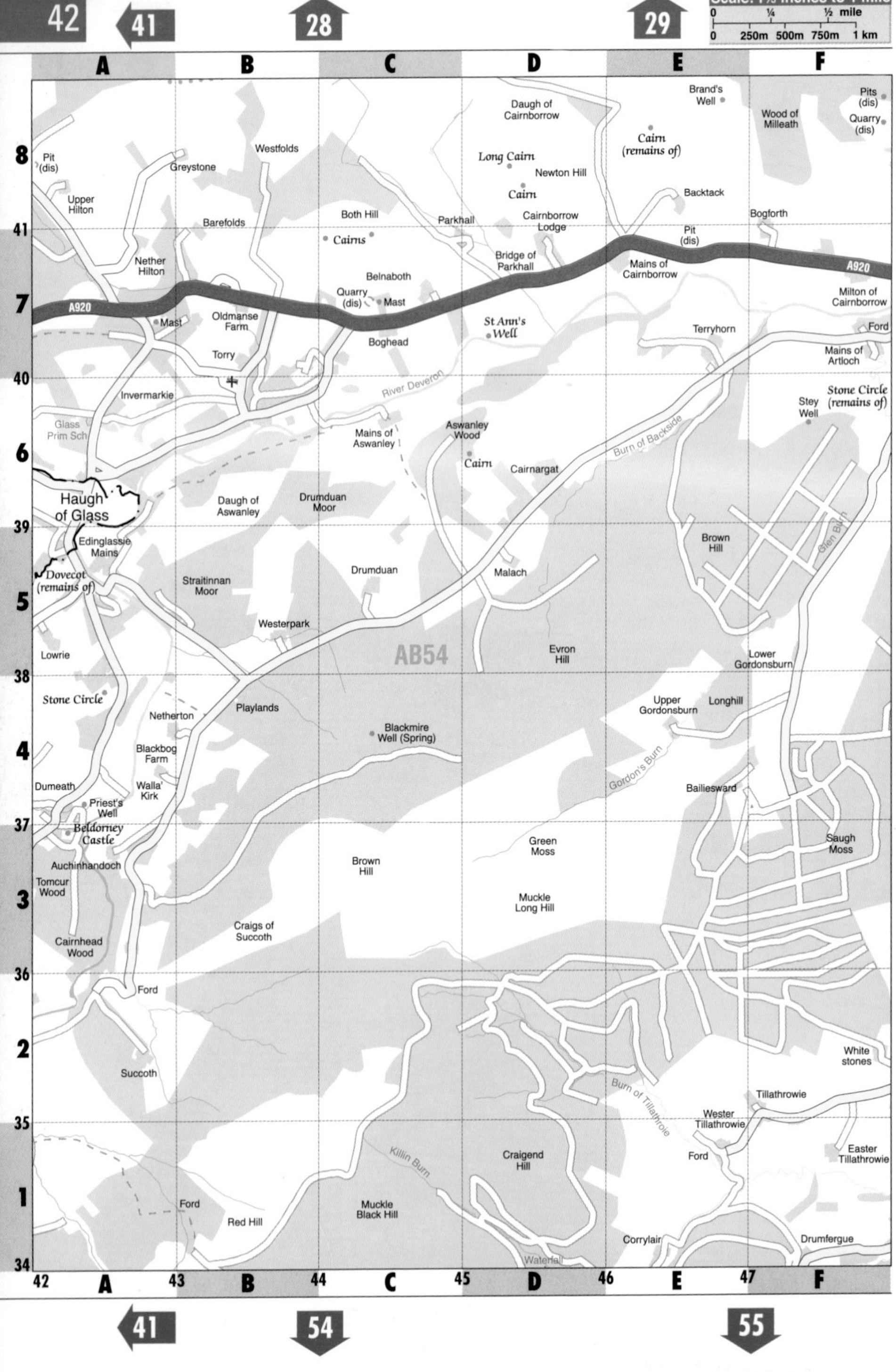
41
28
29
Scale: 1⅓ inches to 1 mile
0 ¼ ½ mile
0 250m 500m 750m 1 km
A B C D E F
8 41 7 40 6 39 5 38 4 37 3 36 2 35 1 34
42 43 44 45 46 47
Pit (dis)
Upper Hilton
Greystone
Westfolds
Barefolds
Nether Hilton
Both Hill
Cairns
Parkhall
Daugh of Cairnborrow
Long Cairn
Newton Hill
Cairn
Cairnborrow Lodge
Bridge of Parkhall
Brand's Well
Cairn (remains of)
Backtack
Pit (dis)
Mains of Cairnborrow
Wood of Milleath
Pits (dis)
Quarry (dis)
Bogforth
A920
Milton of Cairnborrow
Belnaboth
Quarry (dis)
Mast
Mast
Oldmanse Farm
Torry
Boghead
St Ann's Well
Terryhorn
Ford
Mains of Artloch
Invermarkie
Glass Prim Sch
River Deveron
Mains of Aswanley
Aswanley Wood
Cairn
Cairnargat
Burn of Backside
Stone Circle (remains of)
Stey Well
Haugh of Glass
Daugh of Aswanley
Drumduan Moor
Brown Hill
Glen Burn
Edinglassie Mains
Dovecot (remains of)
Straitinnan Moor
Drumduan
Malach
Westerpark
AB54
Evron Hill
Lowrie
Lower Gordonsburn
Stone Circle
Playlands
Netherton
Blackmire Well (Spring)
Upper Gordonsburn
Longhill
Blackbog Farm
Gordon's Burn
Dumeath
Walla' Kirk
Priest's Well
Bailiesward
Beldorney Castle
Green Moss
Saugh Moss
Auchinhandoch
Tomcur Wood
Brown Hill
Muckle Long Hill
Craigs of Succoth
Cairnhead Wood
Ford
Succoth
White stones
Burn of Tillathroie
Tillathrowie
Wester Tillathrowie
Easter Tillathrowie
Ford
Killin Burn
Craigend Hill
Ford
Red Hill
Muckle Black Hill
Corrylair
Drumfergue
Waterfall
41
54
55

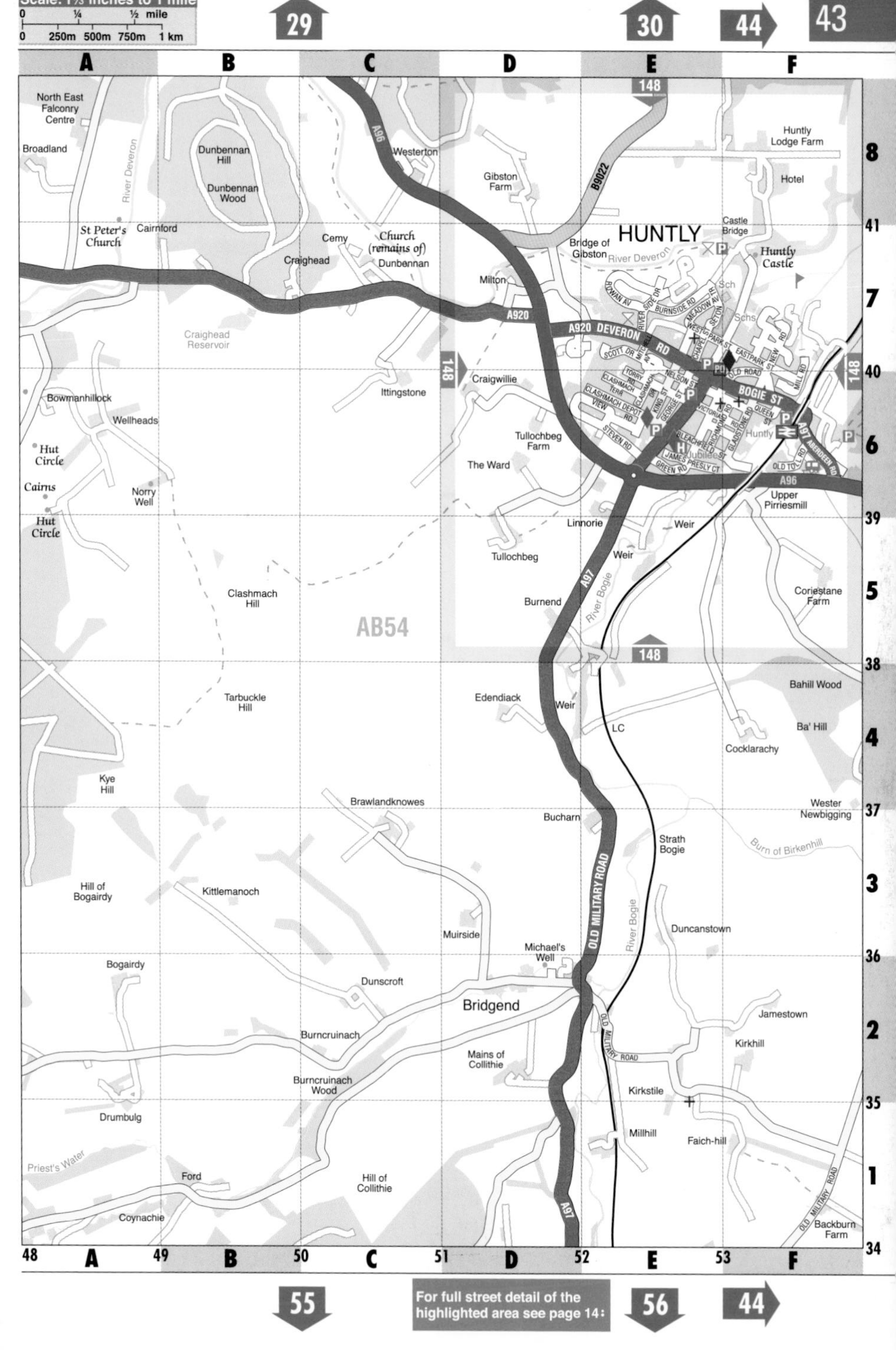

55
For full street detail of the highlighted area see page 14:
56
44

Scale: 1⅓ inches to 1 mile

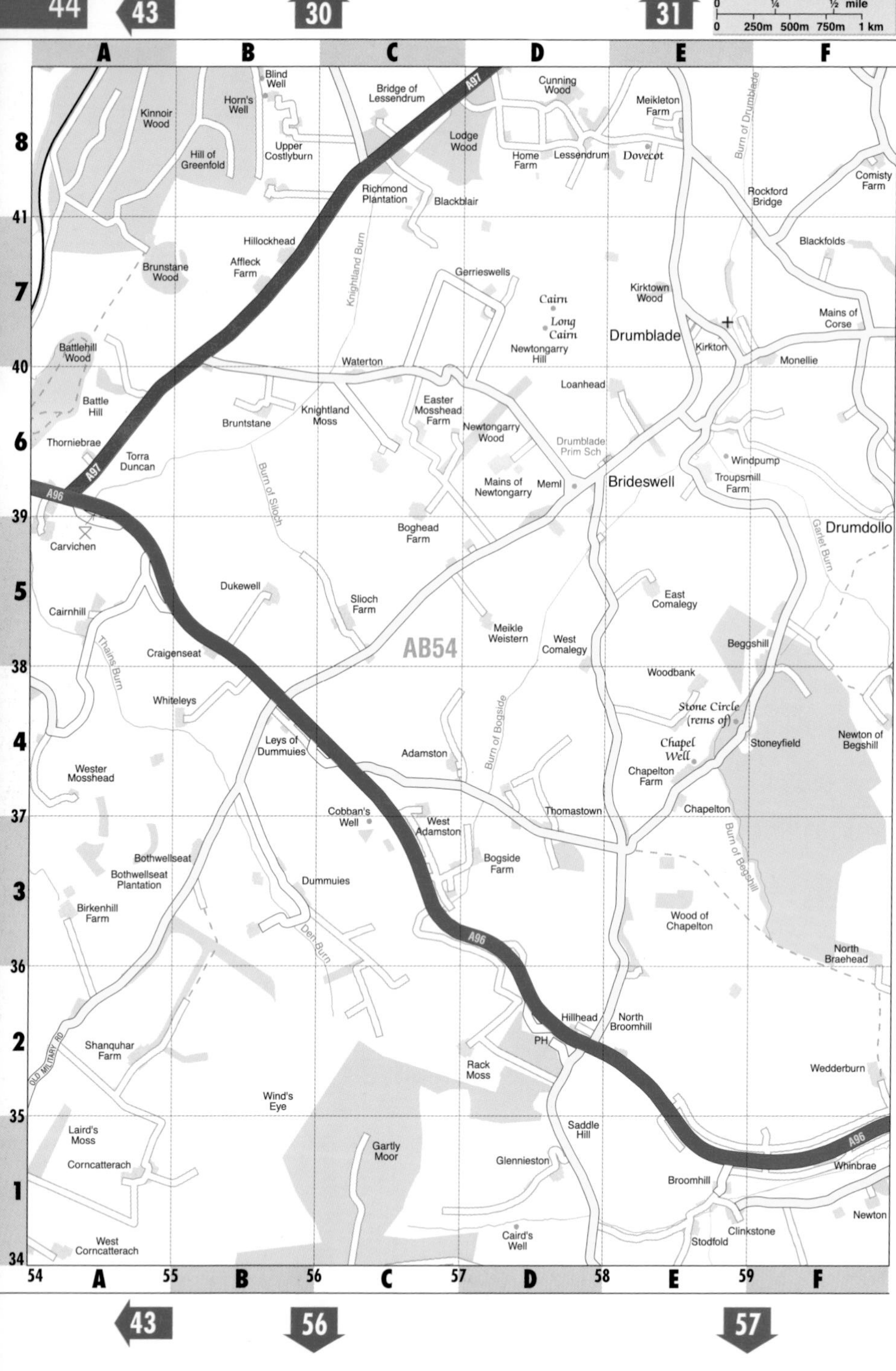

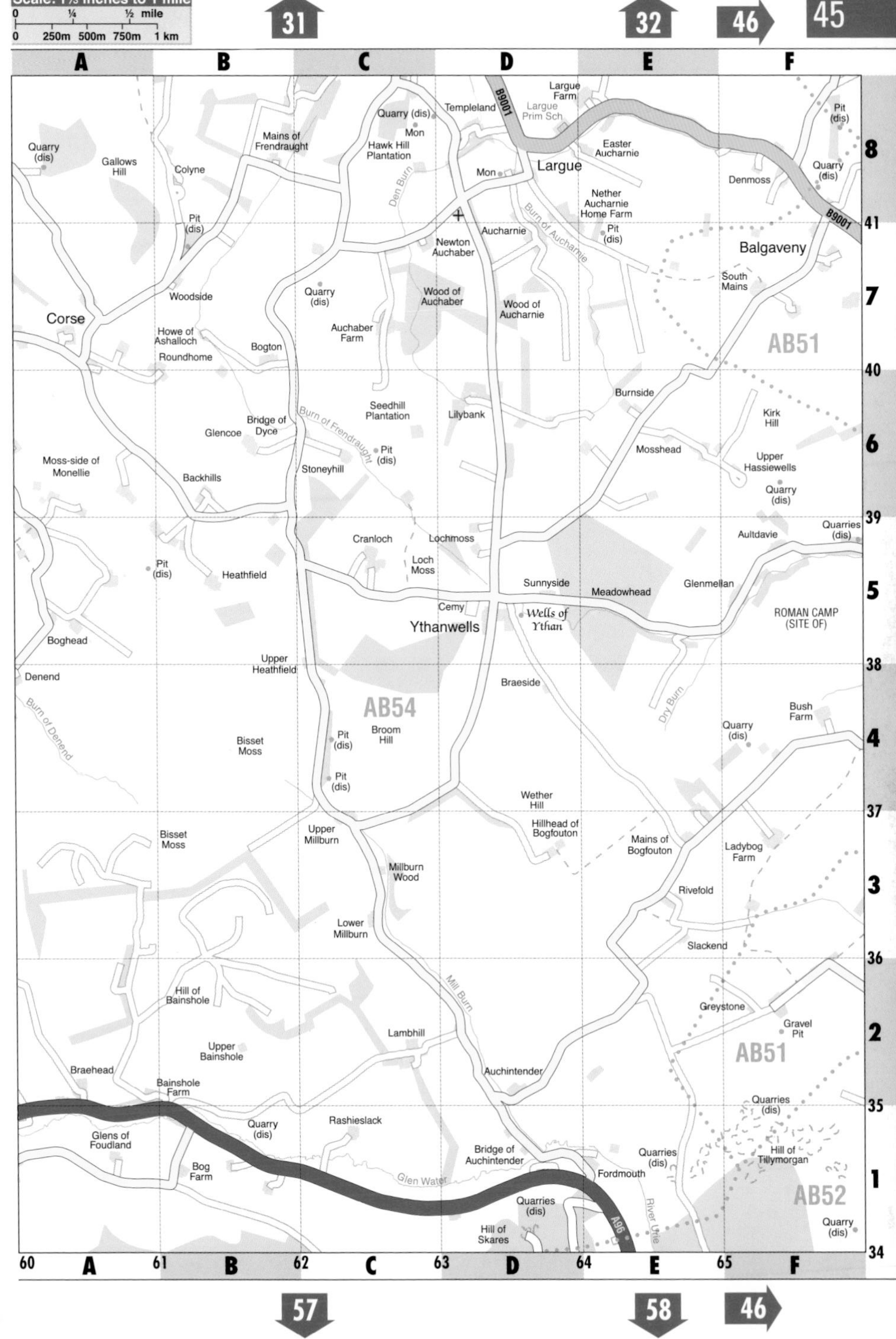
Scale: 1⅓ inches to 1 mile
31
32
46
A
B
C
D
E
F
Largue Farm
Templeland
Quarry (dis)
Mon
Hawk Hill Plantation
Mains of Frendraught
Quarry (dis)
Gallows Hill
Colyne
Largue Prim Sch
Easter Aucharnie
Largue
Mon
Denmoss
Pit (dis)
Quarry (dis)
B9001
Nether Aucharnie Home Farm
Pit (dis)
Aucharnie
Newton Auchaber
Burn of Aucharnie
Den Burn
Balgaveny
South Mains
Woodside
Corse
Quarry (dis)
Wood of Auchaber
Wood of Aucharnie
Howe of Ashalloch
Roundhome
Bogton
Auchaber Farm
AB51
Burnside
Seedhill Plantation
Lilybank
Kirk Hill
Bridge of Dyce
Glencoe
Burn of Frendraught
Pit (dis)
Mosshead
Upper Hassiewells
Moss-side of Monellie
Backhills
Stoneyhill
Quarry (dis)
Aultdavie
Quarries (dis)
Cranloch
Lochmoss
Loch Moss
Pit (dis)
Heathfield
Sunnyside
Meadowhead
Glenmellan
Cemy
Wells of Ythan
Ythanwells
ROMAN CAMP (SITE OF)
Boghead
Upper Heathfield
Denend
Braeside
Burn of Denend
Dry Burn
AB54
Bush Farm
Quarry (dis)
Broom Hill
Pit (dis)
Bisset Moss
Pit (dis)
Wether Hill
Hillhead of Bogfouton
Upper Millburn
Bisset Moss
Mains of Bogfouton
Ladybog Farm
Millburn Wood
Rivefold
Lower Millburn
Slackend
Hill of Bainshole
Mill Burn
Greystone
Gravel Pit
Lambhill
Upper Bainshole
AB51
Braehead
Auchintender
Bainshole Farm
Quarries (dis)
Quarry (dis)
Rashieslack
Glens of Foudland
Bridge of Auchintender
Quarries (dis)
Hill of Tillymorgan
Bog Farm
Fordmouth
Glen Water
AB52
Quarries (dis)
A96
River Urie
Hill of Skares
Quarry (dis)
8
41
7
40
6
39
5
38
4
37
3
36
2
35
1
34
60
61
62
63
64
65
57
58
46

Scale: 1⅓ inches to 1 mile

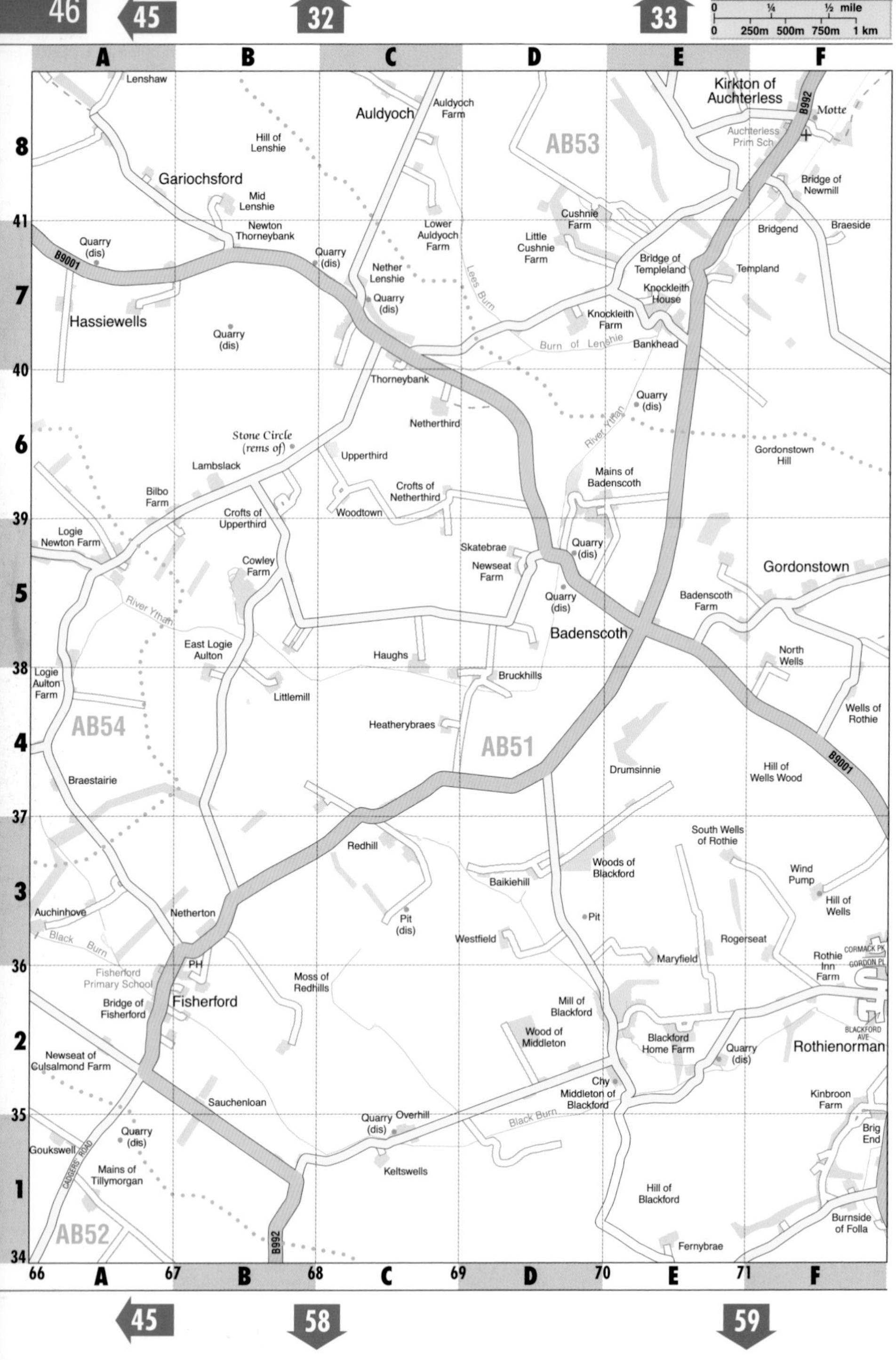

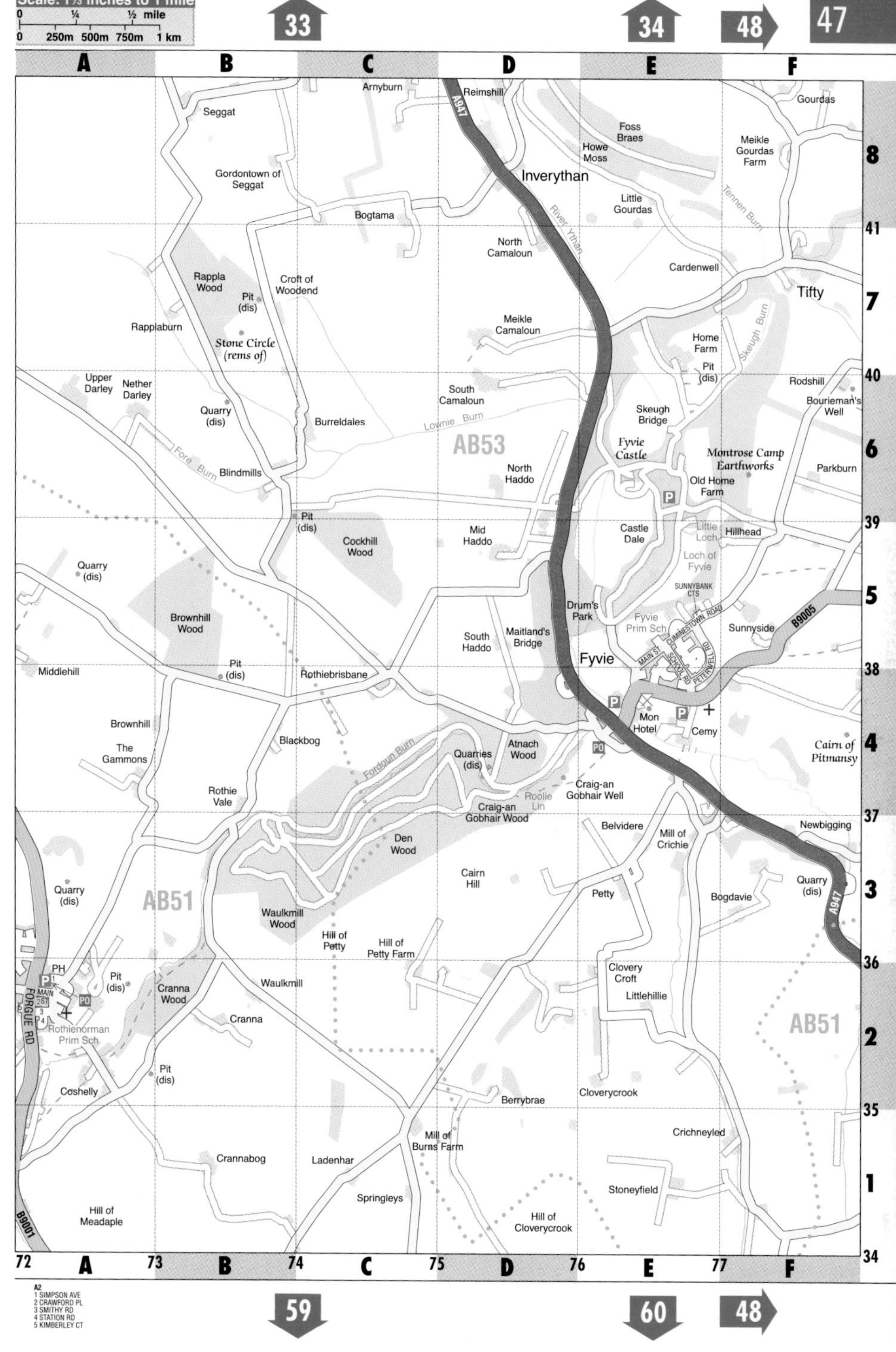

A2
1 SIMPSON AVE
2 CRAWFORD PL
3 SMITHY RD
4 STATION RD
5 KIMBERLEY CT

59 60 48

47
34
35

Scale: 1⅓ inches to 1 mile
0 ¼ ½ mile
0 250m 500m 750m 1 km

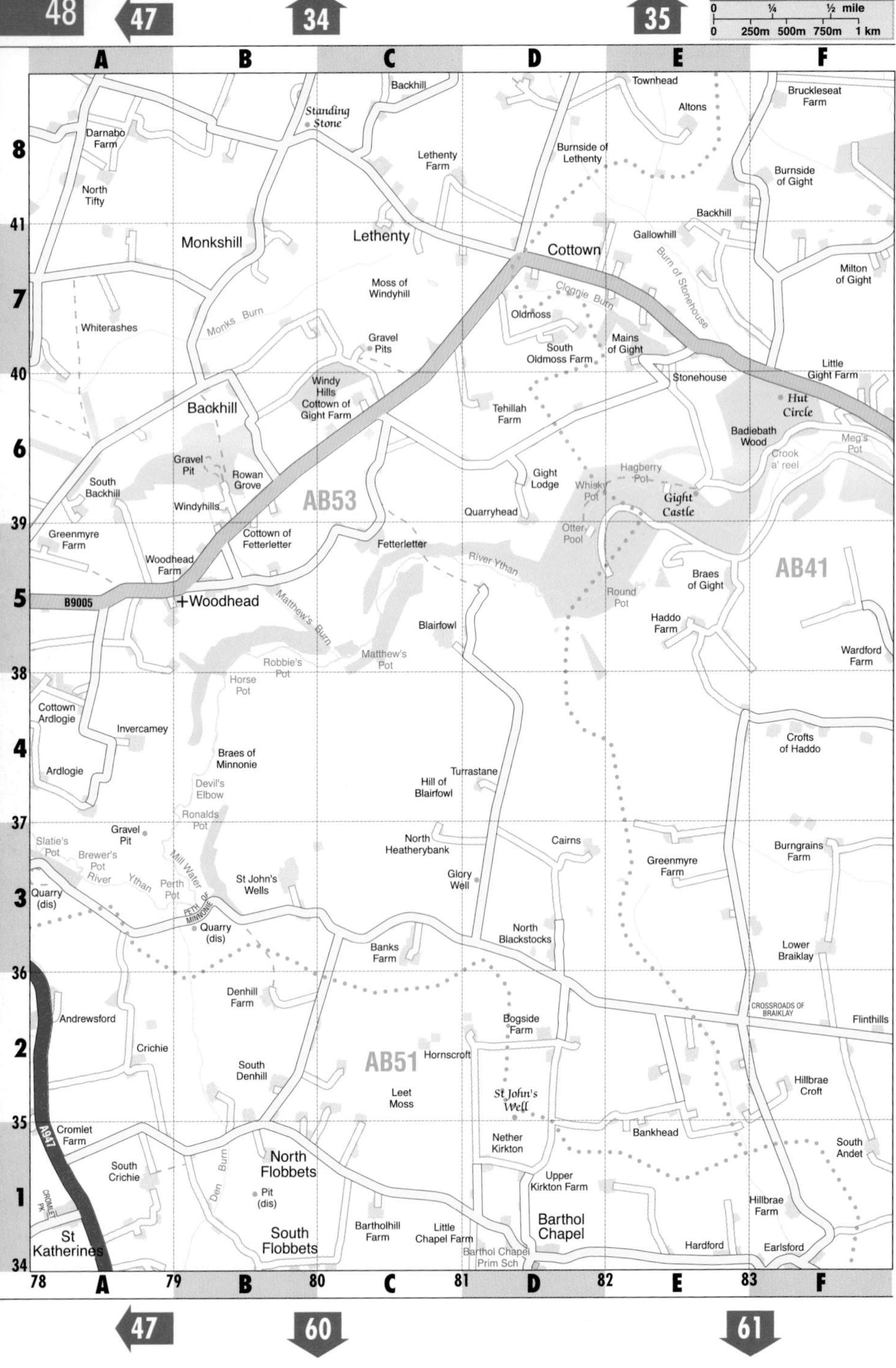

47
60
61

Scale: 1⅓ inches to 1 mile

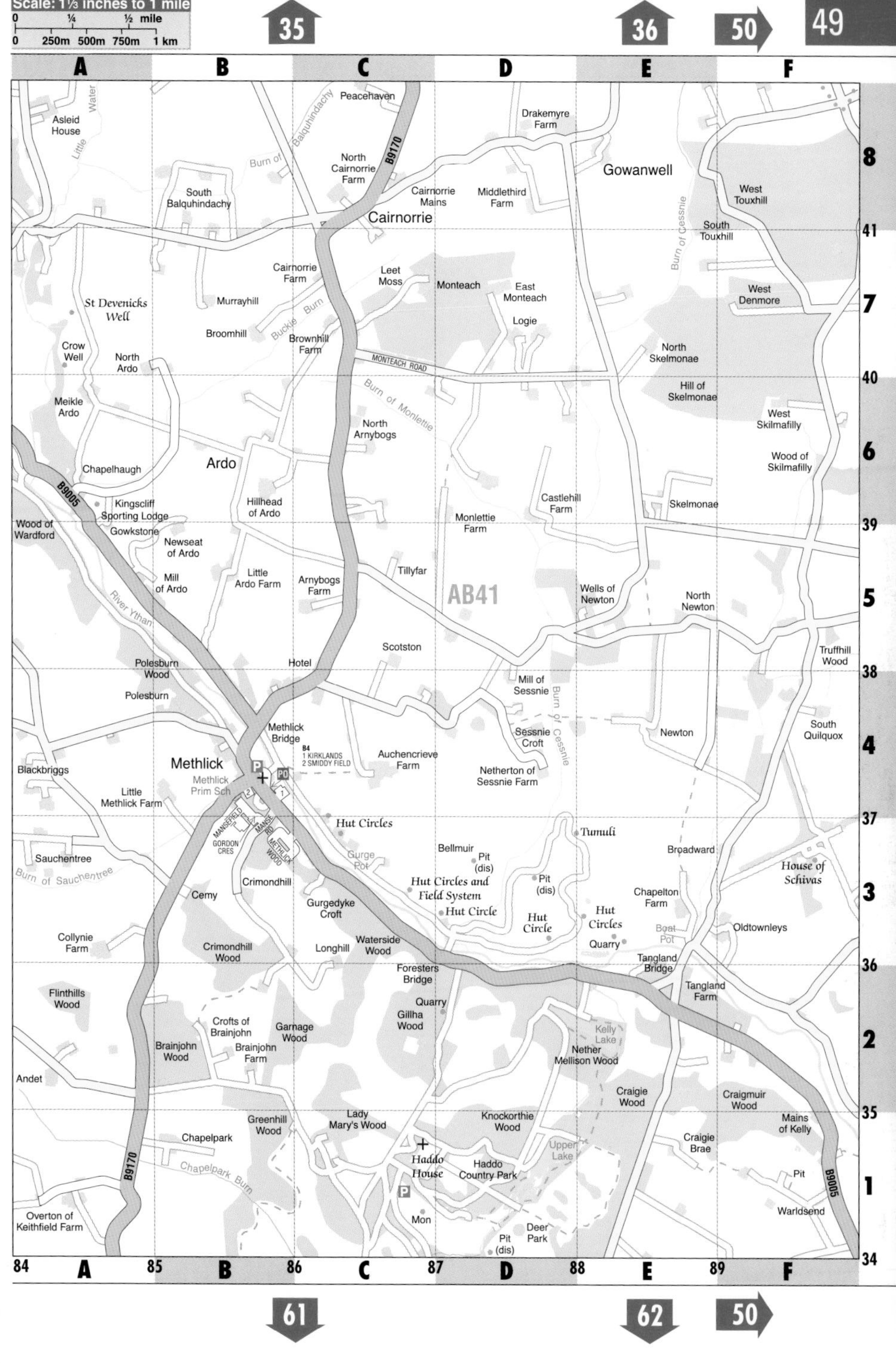

49
36
37

Scale: 1⅓ inches to 1 mile

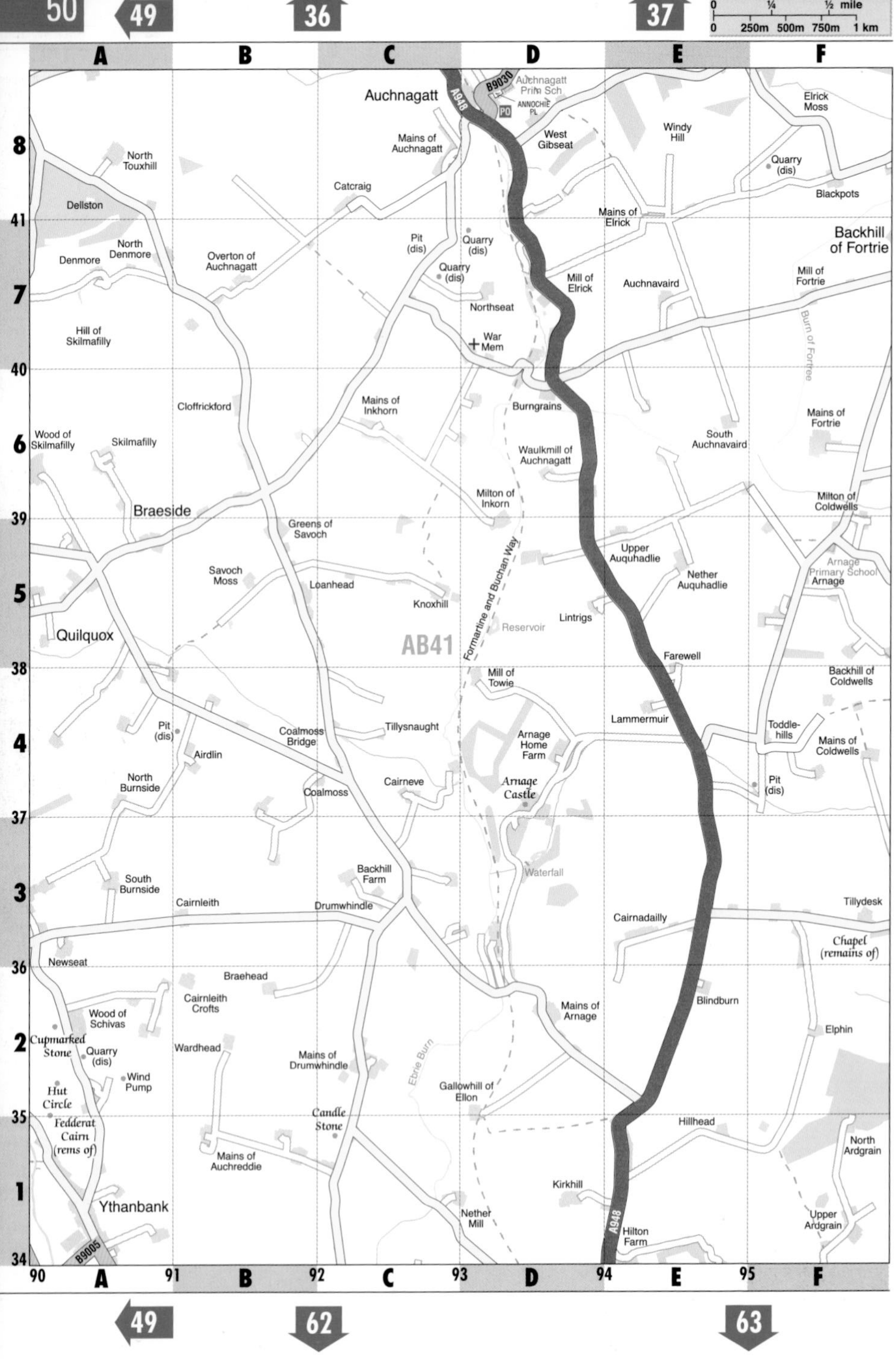

49
62
63

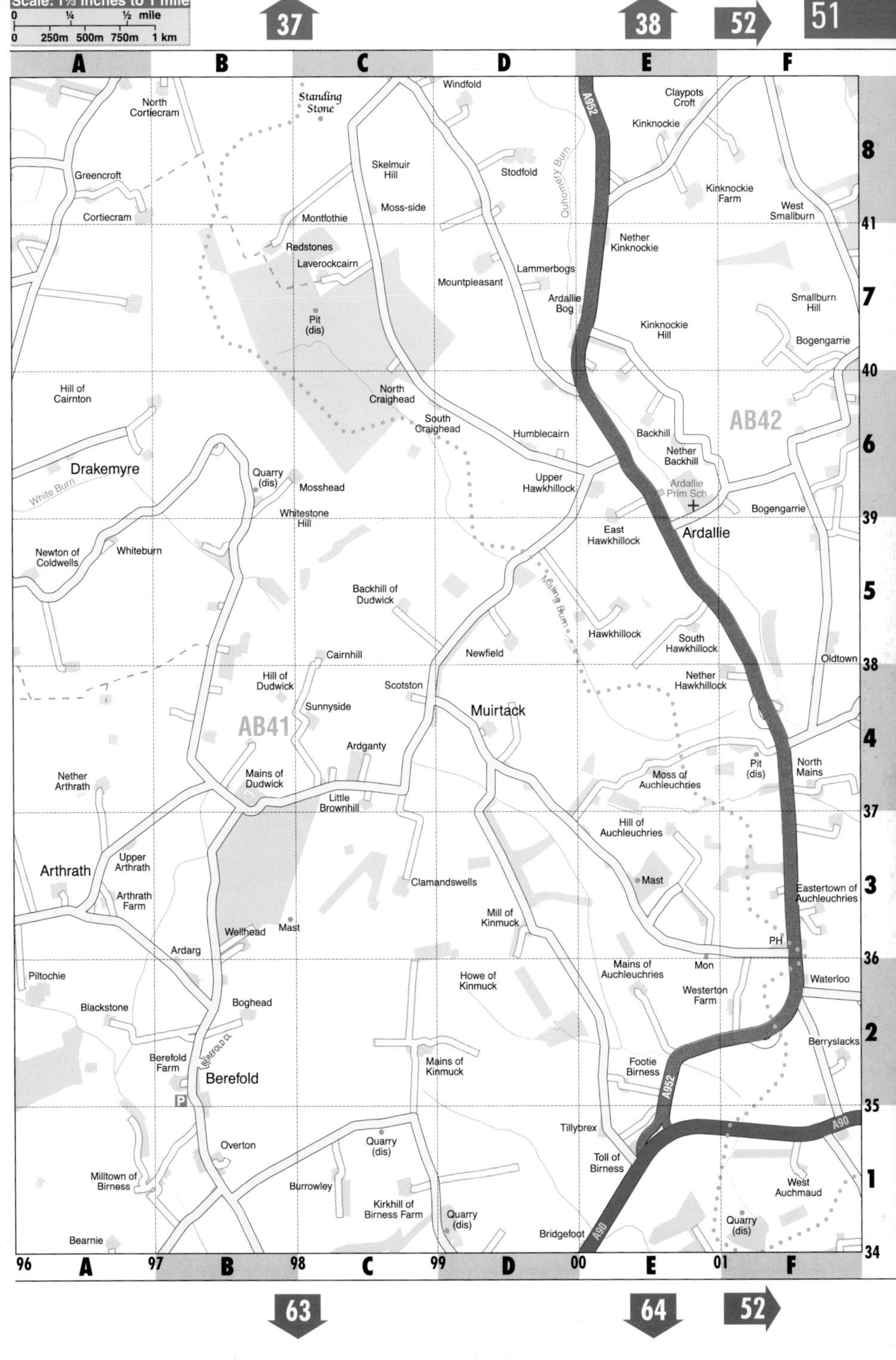

Scale: 1⅓ inches to 1 mile
0 ¼ ½ mile
0 250m 500m 750m 1 km
37
38
52
A B C D E F
Windfold
Standing Stone
North Cortiecram
Claypots Croft
Kinknockie
Skelmuir Hill
Stodfold
Greencroft
Quhomery Burn
Kinknockie Farm
West Smallburn
Cortiecram
Montfothie
Moss-side
Redstones
Nether Kinknockie
Laverockcairn
Lammerbogs
Mountpleasant
Smallburn Hill
Ardallie Bog
Pit (dis)
Kinknockie Hill
Bogengarrie
Hill of Cairnton
North Craighead
South Craighead
AB42
Humblecairn
Backhill
Nether Backhill
Drakemyre
Quarry (dis)
Mosshead
Upper Hawkhillock
Ardallie Prim Sch
White Burn
Whitestone Hill
Bogengarrie
East Hawkhillock
Ardallie
Newton of Coldwells
Whiteburn
Backhill of Dudwick
Maling Burn
Hawkhillock
South Hawkhillock
Cairnhill
Newfield
Oldtown
Hill of Dudwick
Scotston
Nether Hawkhillock
Sunnyside
Muirtack
AB41
Ardganty
Pit (dis)
North Mains
Nether Arthrath
Mains of Dudwick
Moss of Auchleuchries
Little Brownhill
Hill of Auchleuchries
Upper Arthrath
Arthrath
Clamandswells
Mast
Eastertown of Auchleuchries
Arthrath Farm
Mill of Kinmuck
Wellhead
Mast
PH
Ardarg
Mon
Piltochie
Howe of Kinmuck
Mains of Auchleuchries
Waterloo
Westerton Farm
Blackstone
Boghead
Berryslacks
Berefold Farm
BEREFOLD CL
Mains of Kinmuck
Footie Birness
Berefold
P
A952
Tillybrex
A90
Overton
Quarry (dis)
Toll of Birness
Milltown of Birness
Burrowley
West Auchmaud
Kirkhill of Birness Farm
Quarry (dis)
Quarry (dis)
Bearnie
Bridgefoot
8
41
7
40
6
39
5
38
4
37
3
36
2
35
1
34
96 A 97 B 98 C 99 D 00 E 01 F
63
64
52

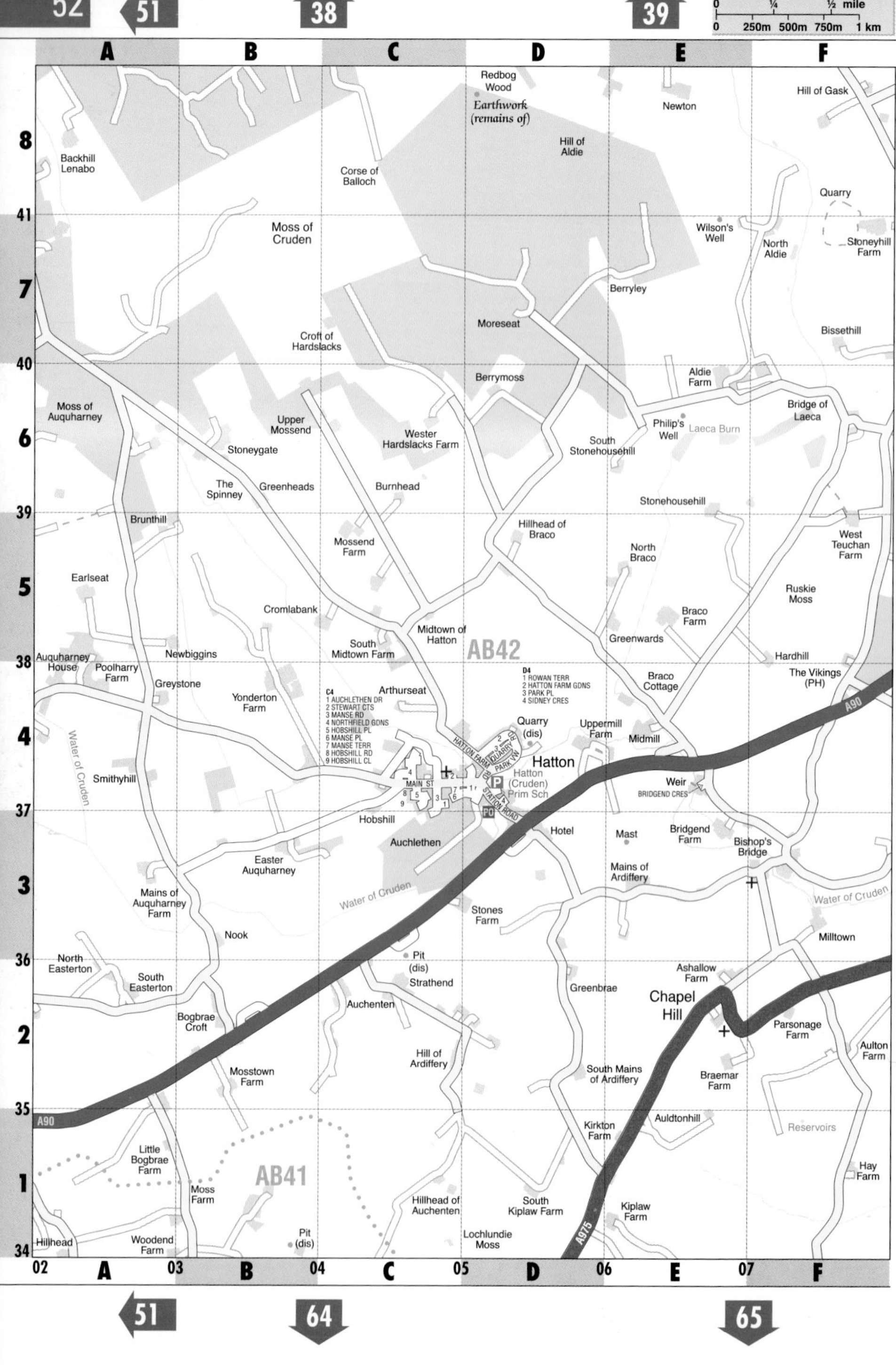

51
38
39
Scale: 1⅓ inches to 1 mile
0 ¼ ½ mile
0 250m 500m 750m 1 km
A
B
C
D
E
F
8
41
7
40
6
39
5
38
4
37
3
36
2
35
1
34
02
03
04
05
06
07
Redbog Wood
Earthwork (remains of)
Newton
Hill of Gask
Backhill Lenabo
Hill of Aldie
Corse of Balloch
Quarry
Moss of Cruden
Wilson's Well
North Aldie
Stoneyhill Farm
Berryley
Moreseat
Bissethill
Croft of Hardslacks
Berrymoss
Aldie Farm
Moss of Auquharney
Upper Mossend
Wester Hardslacks Farm
Philip's Well
Laeca Burn
Bridge of Laeca
South Stonehousehill
Stoneygate
The Spinney
Greenheads
Burnhead
Stonehousehill
Brunthill
Hillhead of Braco
North Braco
West Teuchan Farm
Mossend Farm
Earlseat
Ruskie Moss
Cromlabank
Braco Farm
Midtown of Hatton
AB42
Greenwards
Newbiggins
South Midtown Farm
Hardhill
Auquharney House
Poolharry Farm
The Vikings (PH)
Greystone
Arthurseat
Braco Cottage
Yonderton Farm
D4
1 ROWAN TERR
2 HATTON FARM GDNS
3 PARK PL
4 SIDNEY CRES
C4
1 AUCHLETHEN DR
2 STEWART CTS
3 MANSE RD
4 NORTHFIELD GDNS
5 HOBSHILL PL
6 MANSE PL
7 MANSE TERR
8 HOBSHILL RD
9 HOBSHILL CL
Quarry (dis)
Uppermill Farm
Midmill
A90
Water of Cruden
HATTON FARM RD
QUARRY RD
PARK VW
Hatton
Smithyhill
MAIN ST
Hatton (Cruden) Prim Sch
Weir
BRIDGEND CRES
STATION ROAD
PO
Hobshill
Hotel
Mast
Bridgend Farm
Bishop's Bridge
Auchlethen
Easter Auquharney
Mains of Ardiffery
Mains of Auquharney Farm
Water of Cruden
Stones Farm
Water of Cruden
Nook
Milltown
Pit (dis)
North Easterton
South Easterton
Ashallow Farm
Strathend
Greenbrae
Chapel Hill
Auchenten
Bogbrae Croft
Parsonage Farm
Aulton Farm
Hill of Ardiffery
Mosstown Farm
South Mains of Ardiffery
Braemar Farm
A90
Auldtonhill
Kirkton Farm
Reservoirs
Little Bogbrae Farm
AB41
Hay Farm
Moss Farm
Hillhead of Auchenten
South Kiplaw Farm
Kiplaw Farm
A975
Pit (dis)
Lochlundie Moss
Hillhead
Woodend Farm
51
64
65

A3
1 GOLF PK
2 STATION PL
3 CANTLAY CT
4 ST OLAVE PL
5 KILMARNOCK DR
6 BOWNESS RD

41
42

Scale: 1⅓ inches to 1 mile

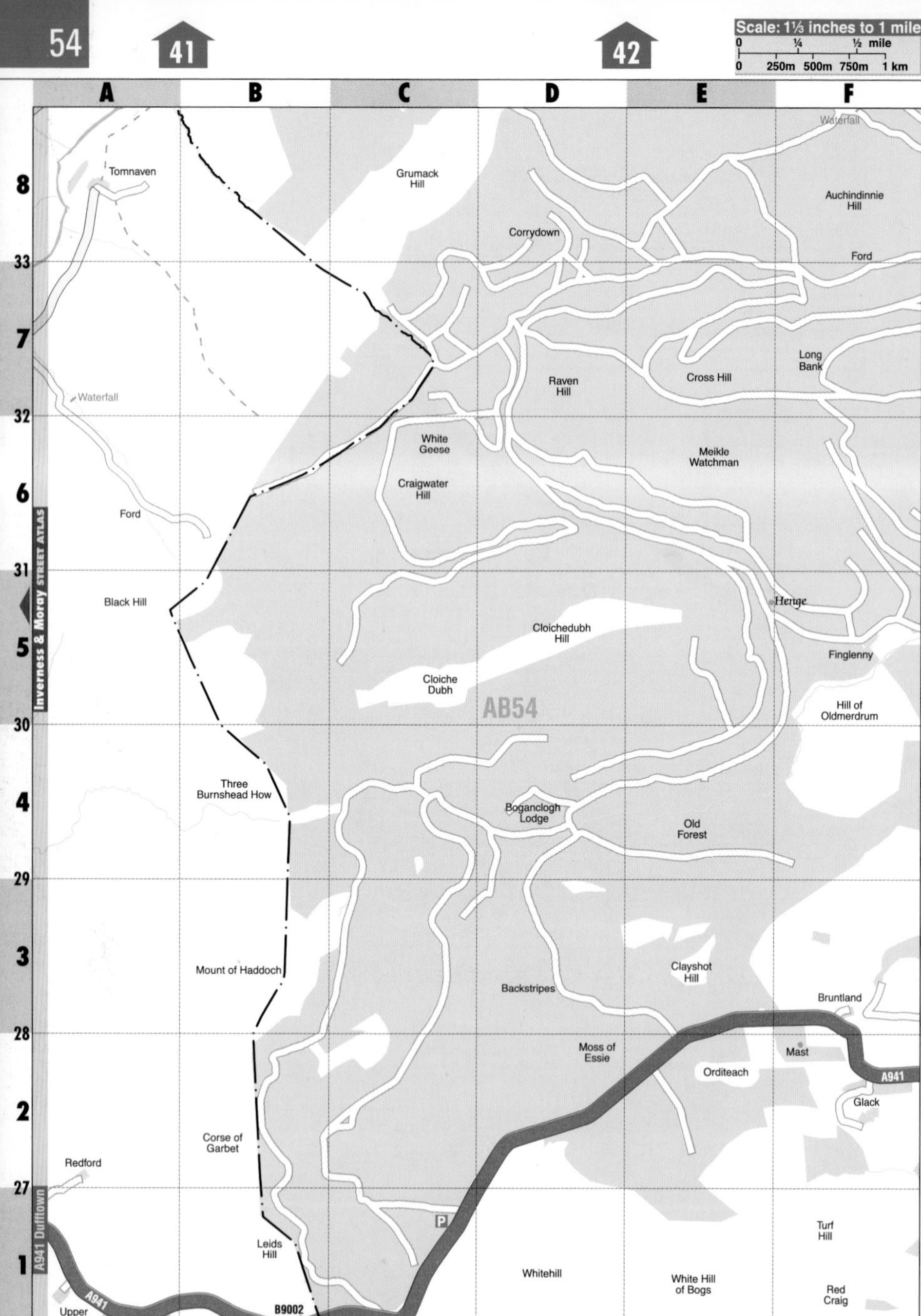

68

Scale: 1⅓ inches to 1 mile

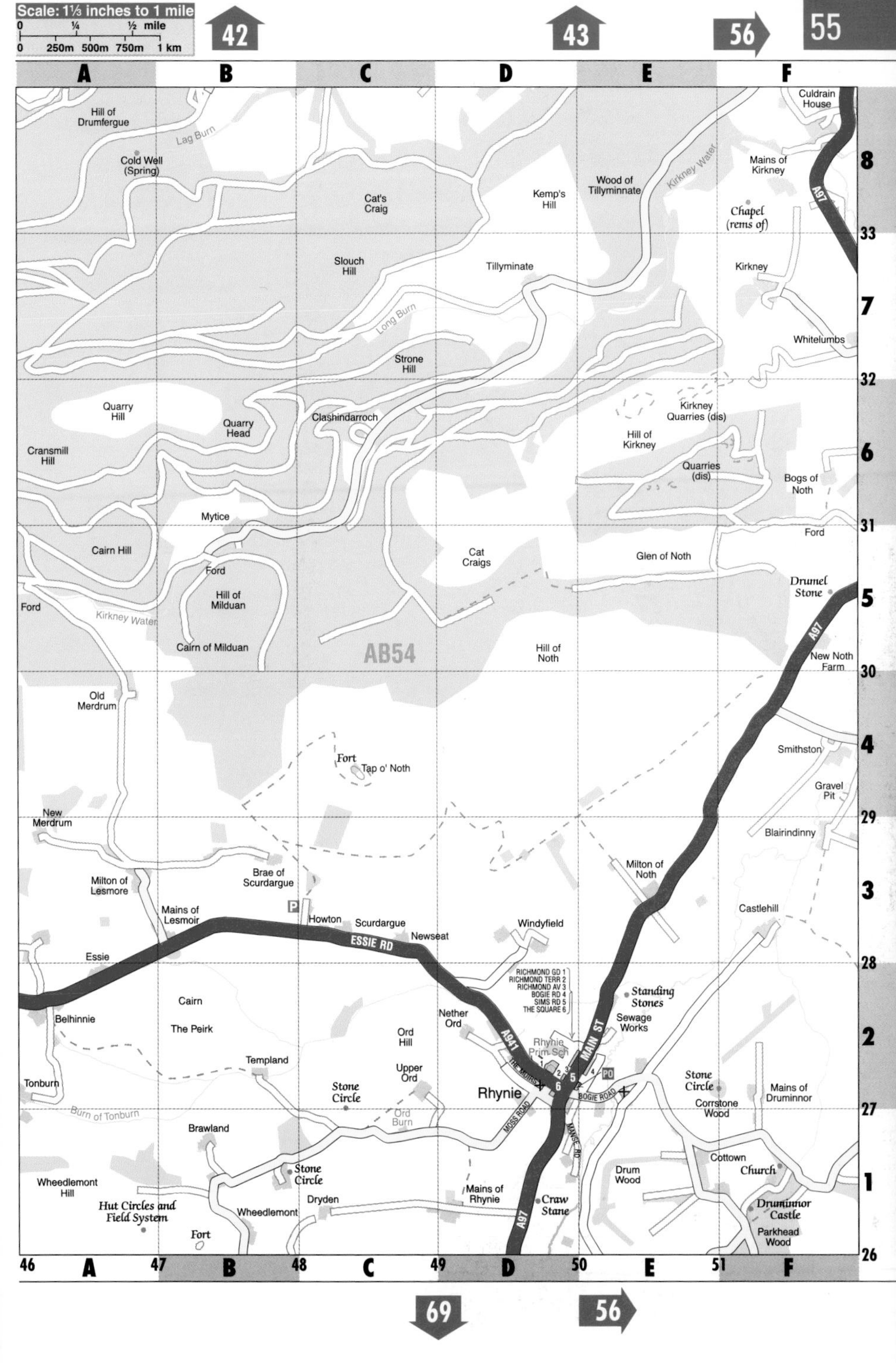

69
56

55
43
44
Scale: 1⅓ inches to 1 mile

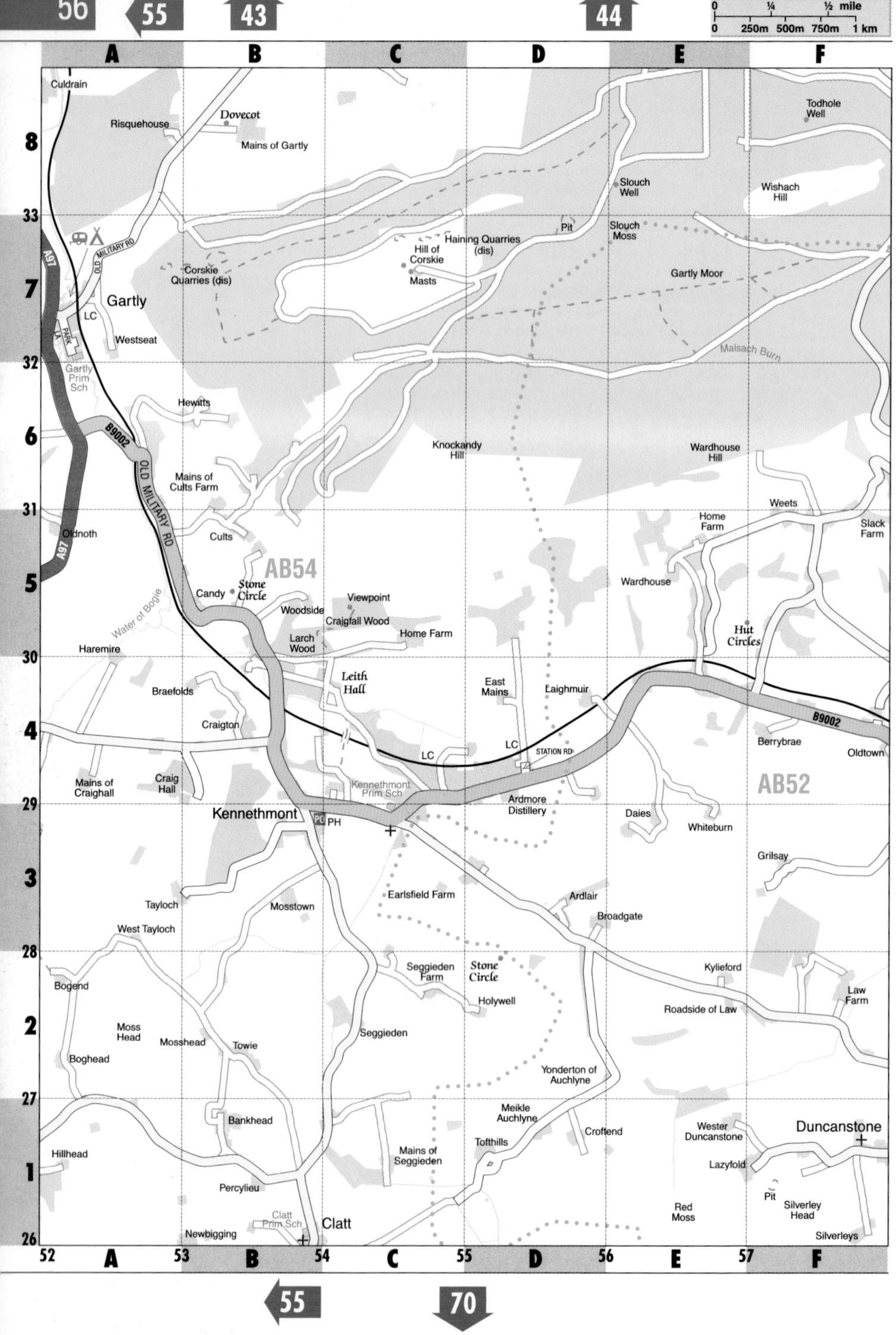

55
70

Scale: 1⅓ inches to 1 mile

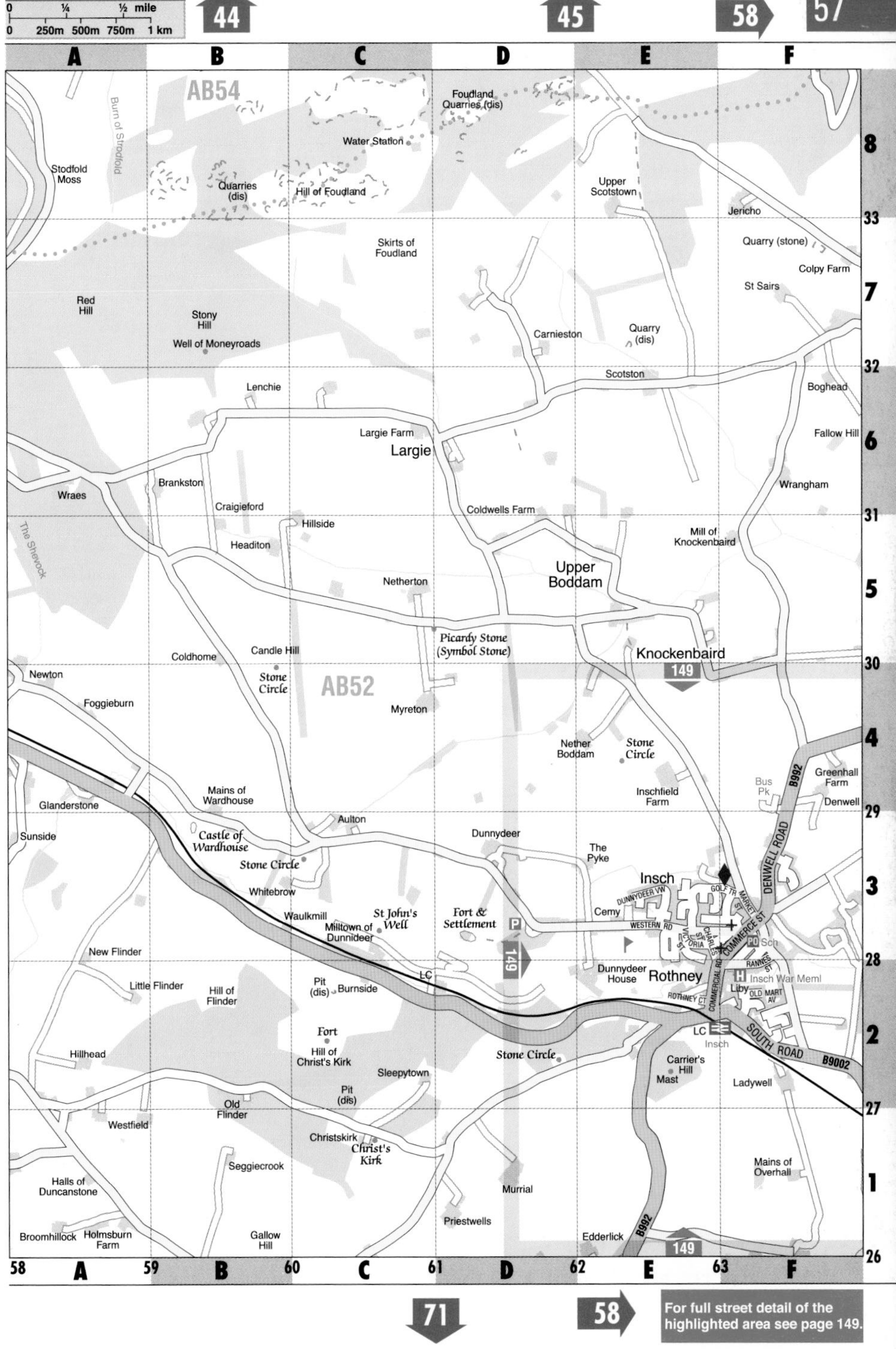

For full street detail of the highlighted area see page 149.

Scale: 1⅓ inches to 1 mile
0 ¼ ½ mile
0 250m 500m 750m 1 km

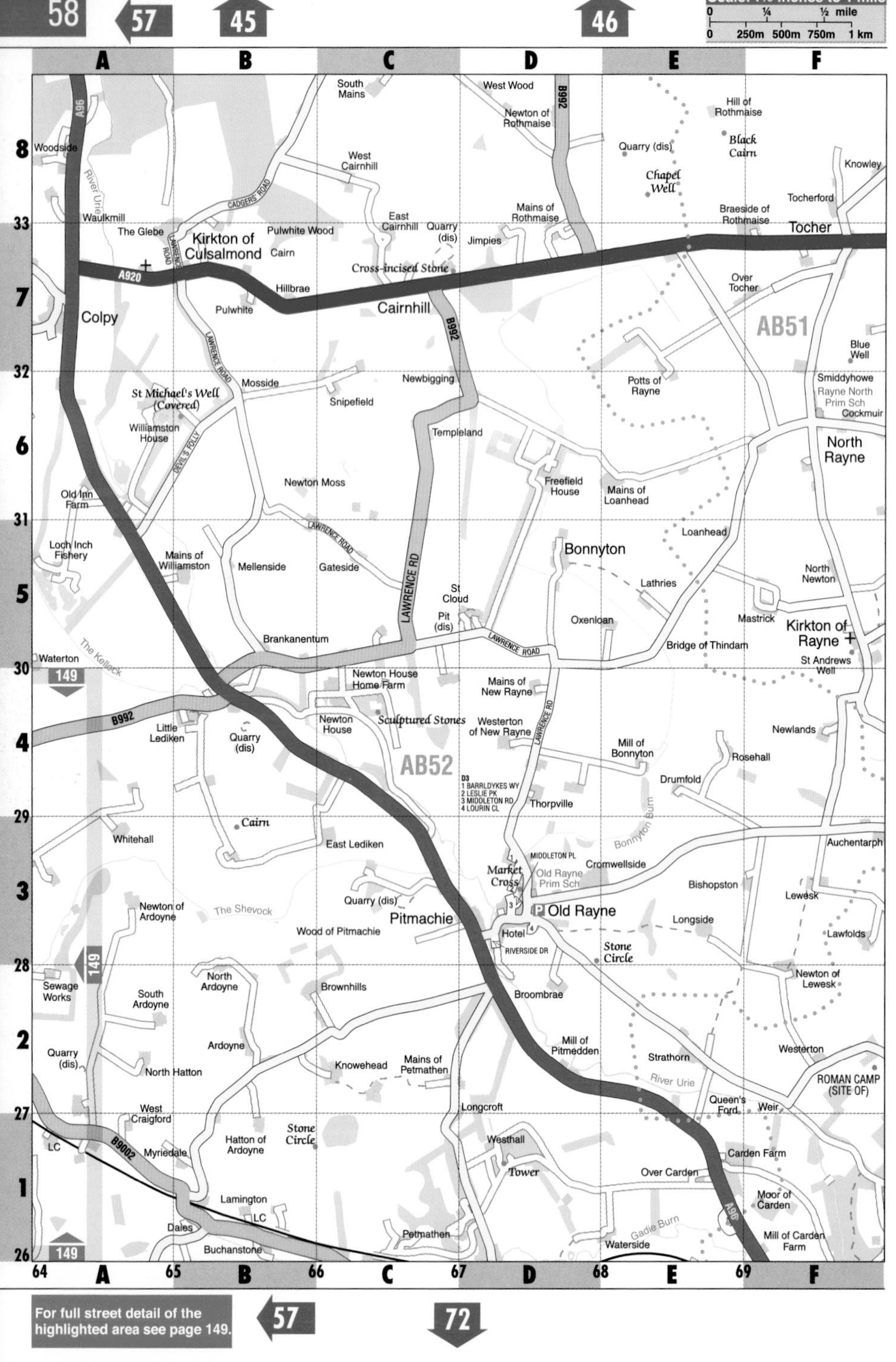

For full street detail of the highlighted area see page 149.

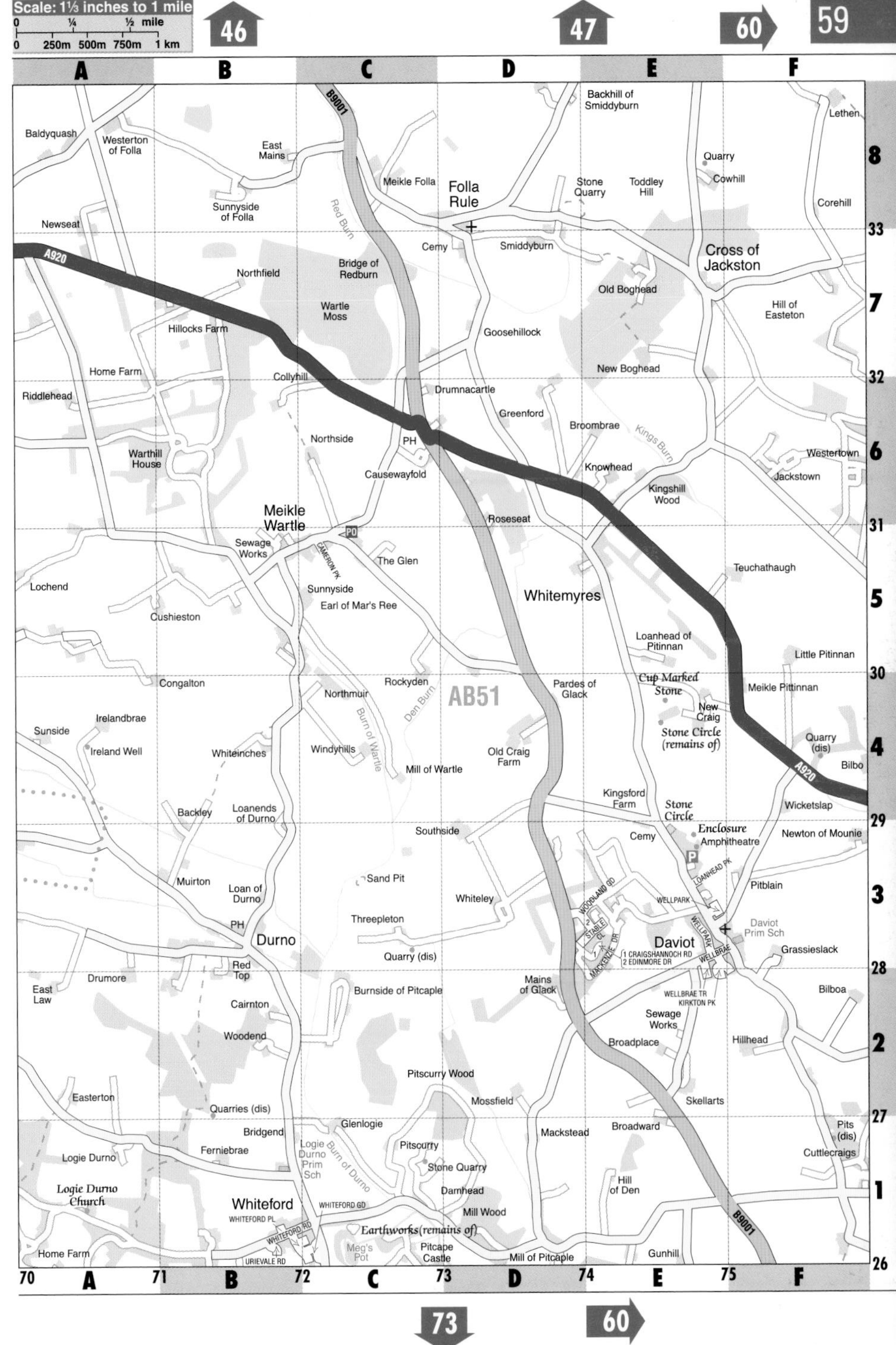
Scale: 1⅓ inches to 1 mile
0 ¼ ½ mile
0 250m 500m 750m 1 km
46
47
60
A
B
C
D
E
F
B9001
Backhill of Smiddyburn
Lethen
Baldyquash
Westerton of Folla
East Mains
Quarry
Cowhill
Meikle Folla
Folla Rule
Stone Quarry
Toddley Hill
Corehill
Sunnyside of Folla
Red Burn
Newseat
Cemy
Smiddyburn
Cross of Jackston
A920
Northfield
Bridge of Redburn
Old Boghead
Wartle Moss
Hill of Easteton
Hillocks Farm
Goosehillock
Home Farm
New Boghead
Collyhill
Riddlehead
Drumnacartle
Greenford
Broombrae
Kings Burn
Northside
PH
Westertown
Warthill House
Knowhead
Jackstown
Causewayfold
Kingshill Wood
Meikle Wartle
Roseseat
PO
Sewage Works
CAMERON PK
The Glen
Teuchathaugh
Lochend
Sunnyside
Whitemyres
Earl of Mar's Ree
Cushieston
Loanhead of Pitinnan
Little Pitinnan
Congalton
Rockyden
Pardes of Glack
Cup Marked Stone
Meikle Pittinnan
Northmuir
Den Burn
AB51
New Craig
Irelandbrae
Burn of Wartle
Stone Circle (remains of)
Sunside
Ireland Well
Whiteinches
Windyhills
Old Craig Farm
Quarry (dis)
Mill of Wartle
Bilbo
Kingsford Farm
Stone Circle
Wicketslap
Backley
Loanends of Durno
Southside
Enclosure
Cemy
Amphitheatre
Newton of Mounie
P
Sand Pit
LOANHEAD PK
Muirton
Loan of Durno
Whiteley
WOODLAND GD
WELLPARK
Pitblain
Threepleton
STABLE CL
Daviot Prim Sch
PH
Durno
MACKENZIE DR
Daviot
1 CRAIGSHANNOCH RD
2 EDINMORE DR
WELLBRAE
Grassieslack
Quarry (dis)
Red Top
Drumore
East Law
Mains of Glack
Bilboa
Burnside of Pitcaple
WELLBRAE TR
KIRKTON PK
Cairnton
Sewage Works
Woodend
Broadplace
Hillhead
Pitscurry Wood
Easterton
Mossfield
Skellarts
Quarries (dis)
Glenlogie
Bridgend
Mackstead
Broadward
Pits (dis)
Logie Durno Prim Sch
Burn of Durno
Pitscurry
Cuttlecraigs
Ferniebrae
Logie Durno
Stone Quarry
Hill of Den
Logie Durno Church
Damhead
Whiteford
WHITEFORD GD
Mill Wood
WHITEFORD PL
WHITEFORD RD
Earthworks (remains of)
Meg's Pot
Pitcape Castle
Home Farm
URIEVALE RD
Mill of Pitcaple
Gunhill
B9001
8
33
7
32
6
31
5
30
4
29
3
28
2
27
1
26
70
71
72
73
74
75

Scale: 1⅓ inches to 1 mile

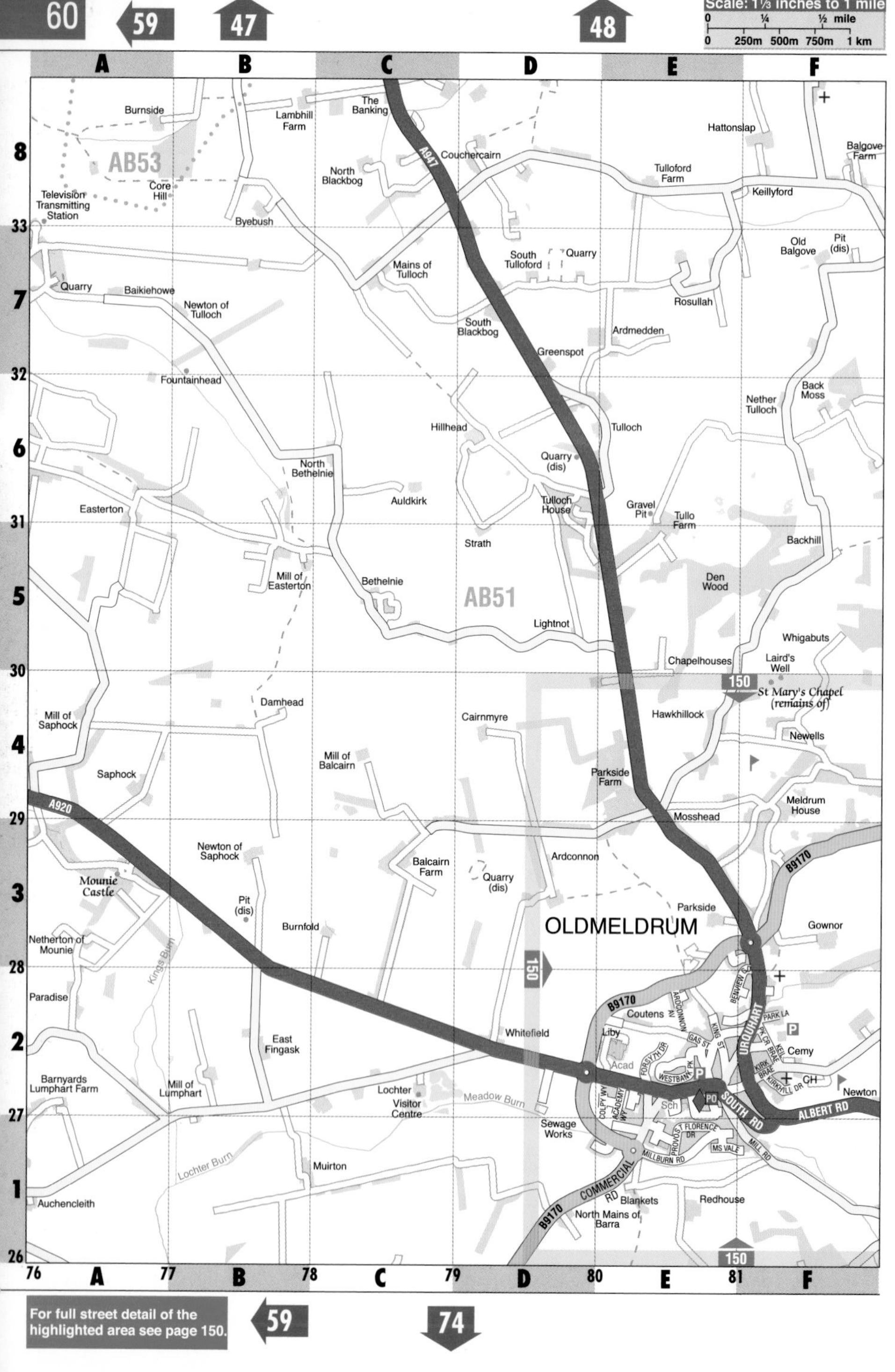

Scale: 1⅓ inches to 1 mile

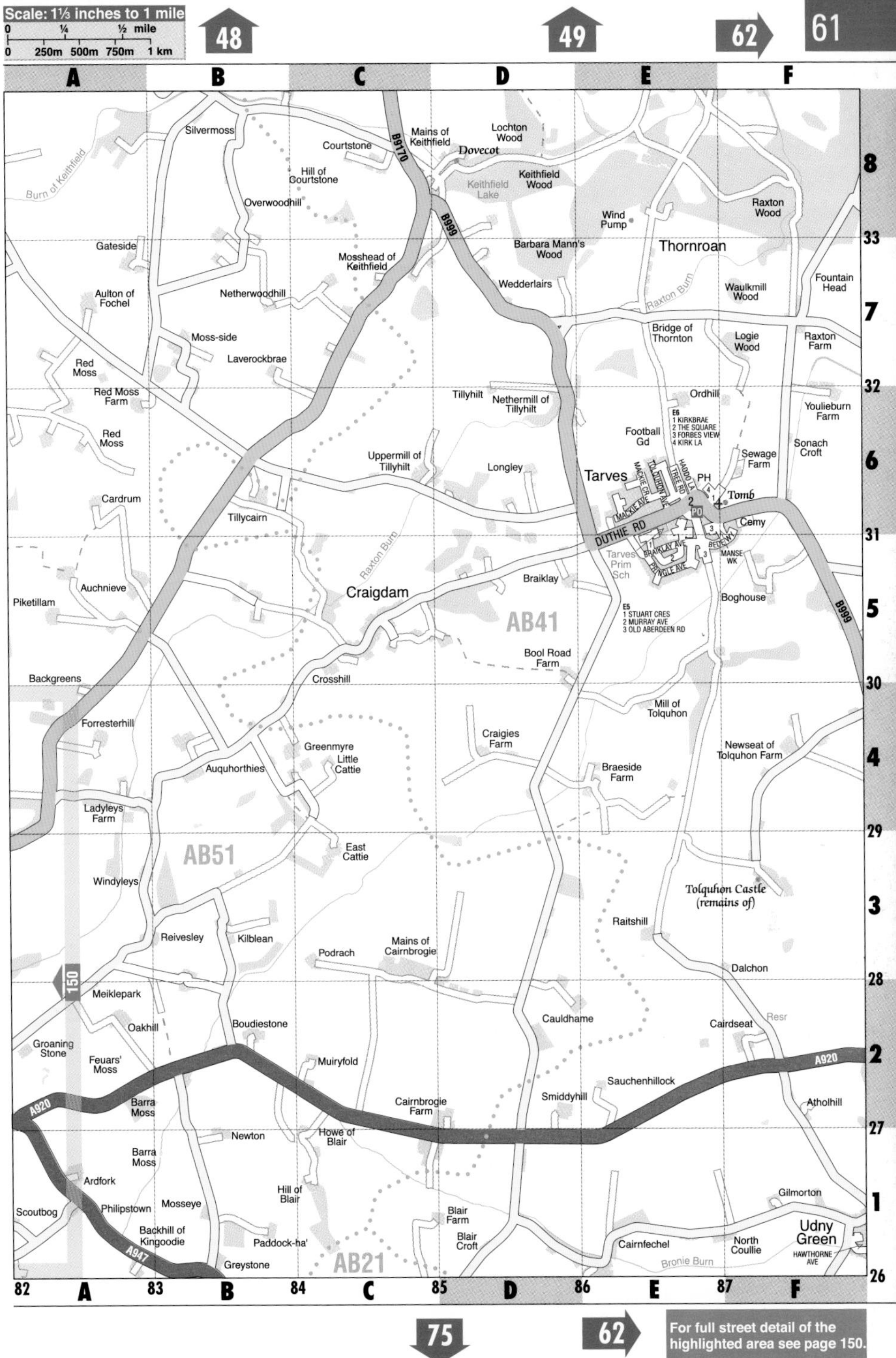

For full street detail of the highlighted area see page 150.

Scale: 1⅓ inches to 1 mile

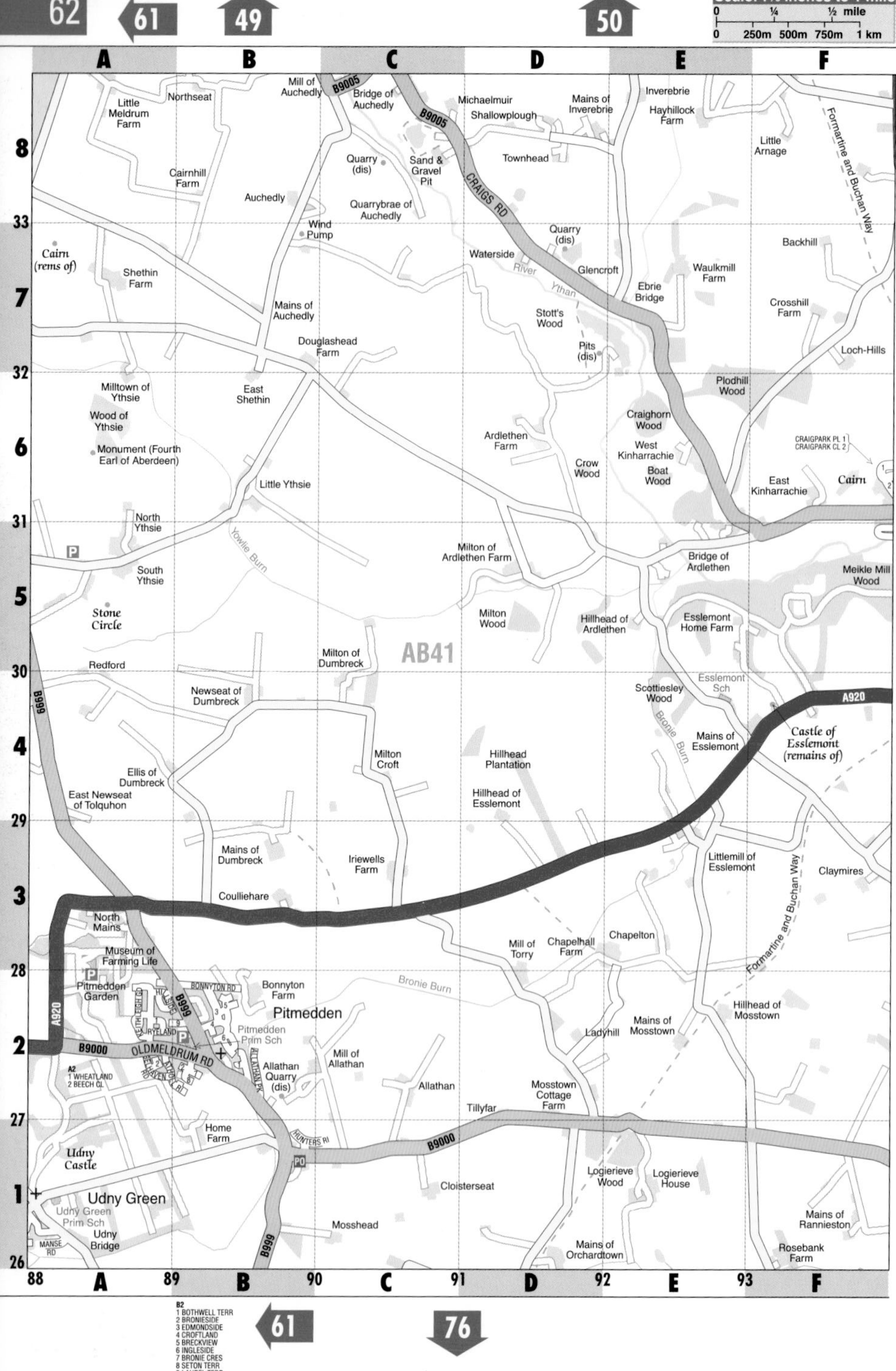

B2
1 BOTHWELL TERR
2 BRONIESIDE
3 EDMONDSIDE
4 CROFTLAND
5 BRECKVIEW
6 INGLESIDE
7 BRONIE CRES
8 SETON TERR
9 LAUREL TERR

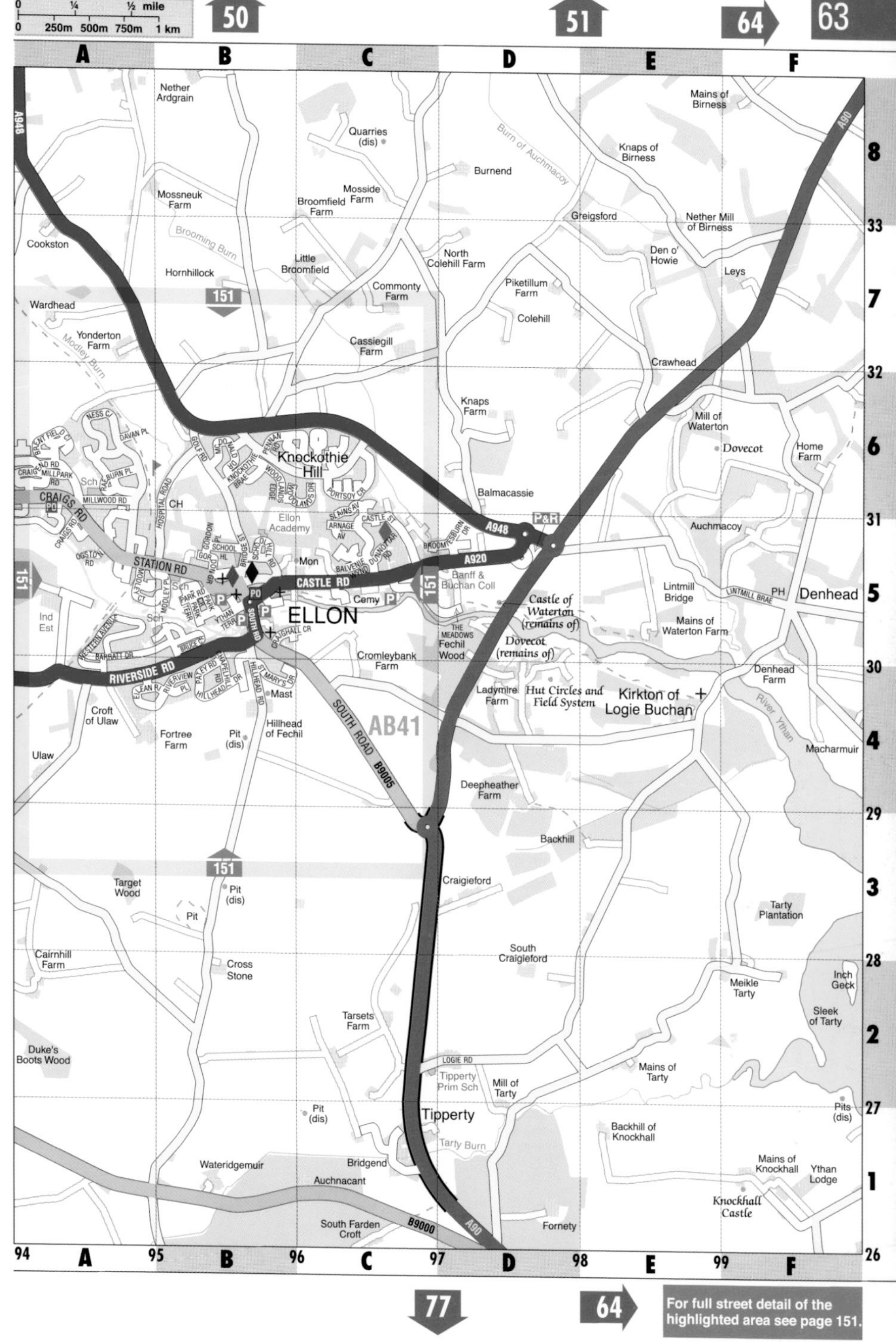
Scale: 1⅓ inches to 1 mile
0 ¼ ½ mile
0 250m 500m 750m 1 km
50
51
64
A B C D E F
Nether Ardgrain
Quarries (dis)
Mains of Birness
Burn of Auchmacoy
Knaps of Birness
Burnend
Mosside Farm
Mossneuk Farm
Broomfield Farm
Greigsford
Nether Mill of Birness
Brooming Burn
Cookston
North Colehill Farm
Den o' Howie
Little Broomfield
Hornhillock
Leys
Piketillum Farm
Commonty Farm
151
Wardhead
Colehill
Yonderton Farm
Cassiegill Farm
Modley Burn
Crawhead
Knaps Farm
Mill of Waterton
Dovecot
Home Farm
Knockothie Hill
Balmacassie
CH
Ellon Academy
A948
P&R
Auchmacoy
A920
Mon
CRAIGS RD
STATION RD
CASTLE RD
Banff & Buchan Coll
Lintmill Bridge
LINTMILL BRAE
PH
Denhead
Cemy
ELLON
Castle of Waterton (remains of)
Ind Est
Mains of Waterton Farm
THE MEADOWS
Fechil Wood
Dovecot (remains of)
Cromleybank Farm
RIVERSIDE RD
Denhead Farm
Ladymire Farm
Hut Circles and Field System
Kirkton of Logie Buchan
Mast
River Ythan
Croft of Ulaw
Hillhead of Fechil
AB41
Fortree Farm
Pit (dis)
SOUTH ROAD
B9005
Ulaw
Macharmuir
Deepheather Farm
Backhill
Craigieford
Target Wood
Pit (dis)
Pit
Tarty Plantation
South Craigieford
Cairnhill Farm
Cross Stone
Inch Geck
Meikle Tarty
Tarsets Farm
Sleek of Tarty
Duke's Boots Wood
LOGIE RD
Mains of Tarty
Tipperty Prim Sch
Mill of Tarty
Pit (dis)
Tipperty
Pits (dis)
Backhill of Knockhall
Tarty Burn
Wateridgemuir
Bridgend
Mains of Knockhall
Ythan Lodge
Auchnacant
Knockhall Castle
South Farden Croft
B9000
A90
Fornety
8
33
7
32
6
31
5
30
4
29
3
28
2
27
1
26
94 95 96 97 98 99
77
64
For full street detail of the highlighted area see page 151.

63
51
52

Scale: 1⅓ inches to 1 mile
0 ¼ ½ mile
0 250m 500m 750m 1 km

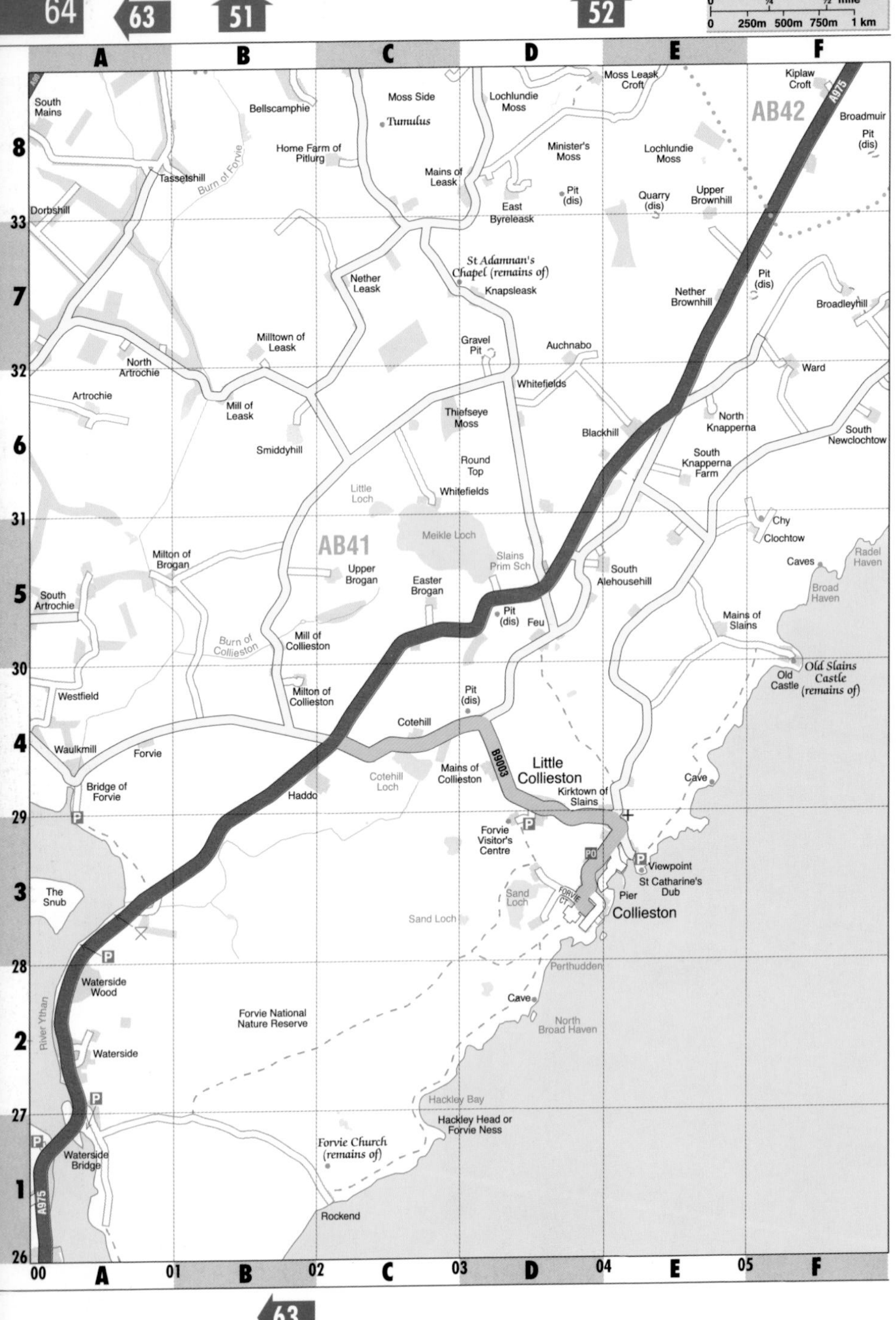

63

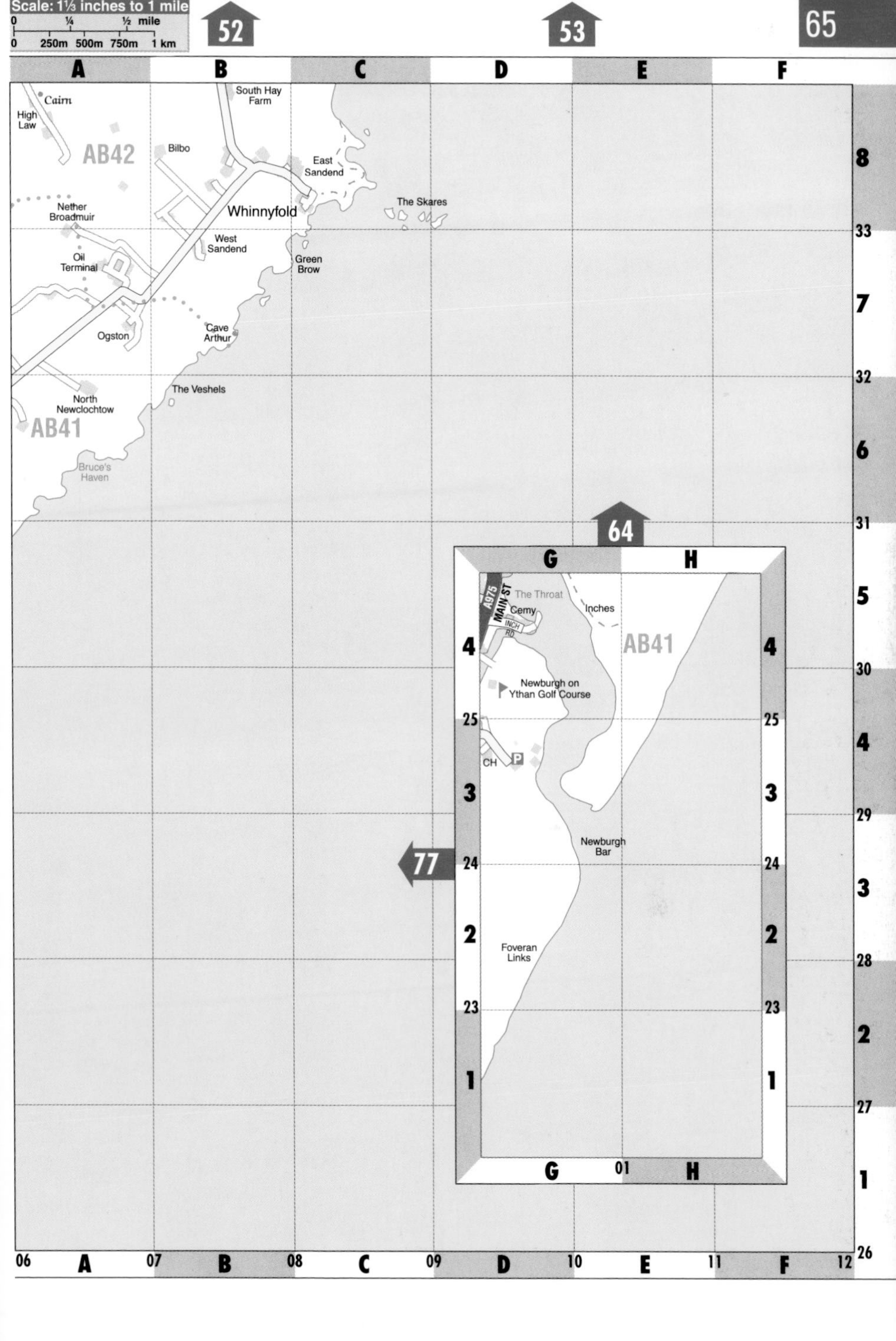

Scale: 1⅓ inches to 1 mile
0 ¼ ½ mile
0 250m 500m 750m 1 km
52
53
A
B
C
D
E
F
Cairn
High Law
AB42
South Hay Farm
Bilbo
East Sandend
The Skares
Nether Broadmuir
Whinnyfold
West Sandend
Oil Terminal
Green Brow
Ogston
Cave Arthur
The Veshels
North Newclochtow
AB41
Bruce's Haven
64
G
H
A975
MAIN ST
The Throat
Cemy
INCH RD
Inches
AB41
Newburgh on Ythan Golf Course
CH
P
Newburgh Bar
77
Foveran Links
01
06
07
08
09
10
11
12
33
32
31
30
29
28
27
26
25
24
23
8
7
6
5
4
3
2
1

Scale: 1⅓ inches to 1 mile

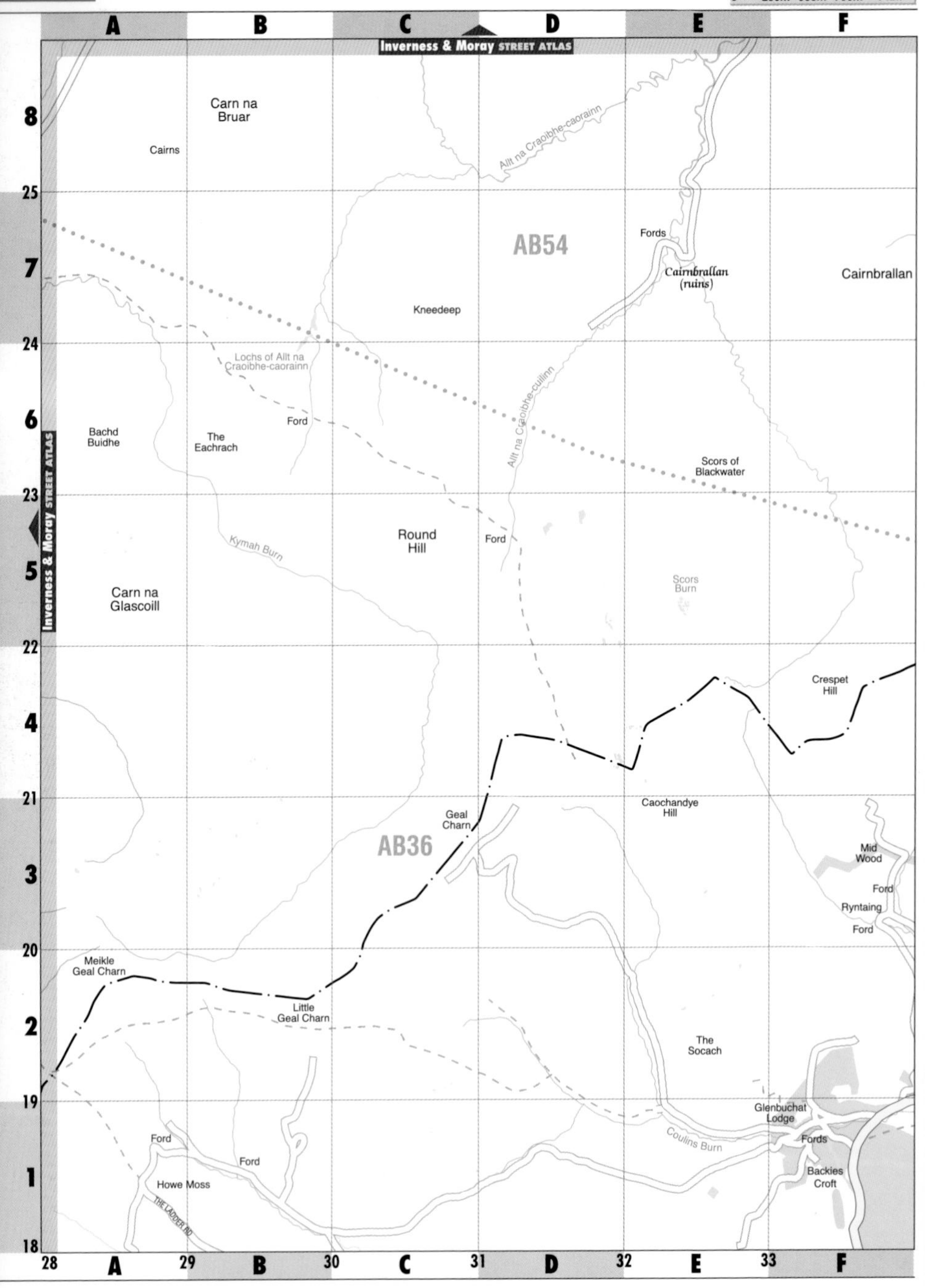

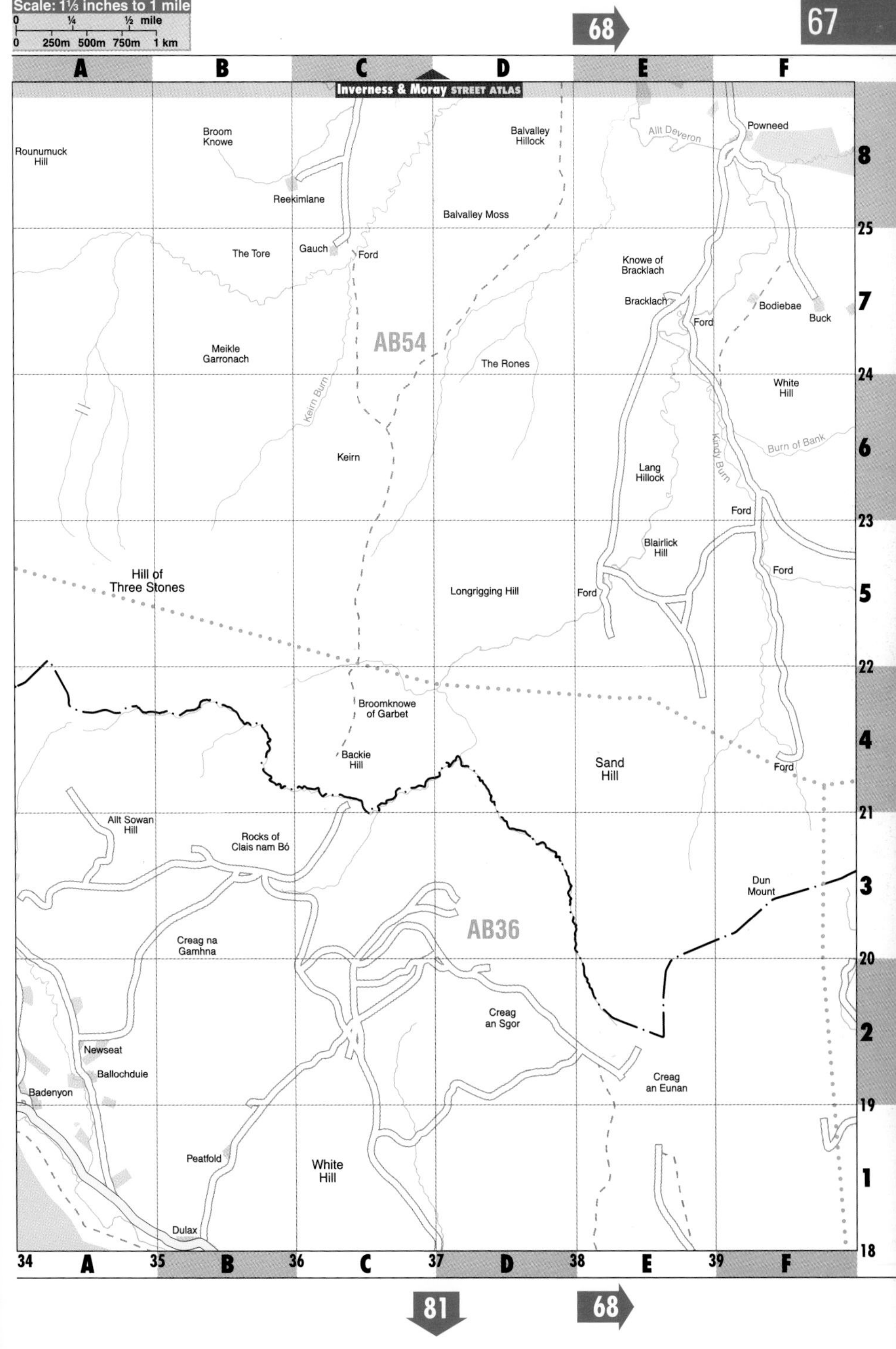
Scale: 1⅓ inches to 1 mile
0 ¼ ½ mile
0 250m 500m 750m 1 km
68
A B C D E F
Inverness & Moray STREET ATLAS
Rounumuck Hill
Broom Knowe
Reekimlane
Balvalley Hillock
Balvalley Moss
Allt Deveron
Powneed
8
25
The Tore
Gauch
Ford
Knowe of Bracklach
Bracklach
Ford
Bodiebae
Buck
7
Meikle Garronach
AB54
The Rones
24
White Hill
Keirn Burn
Keirn
Kindy Burn
Burn of Bank
6
Lang Hillock
Ford
23
Blairlick Hill
Hill of Three Stones
Longrigging Hill
Ford
Ford
5
22
Broomknowe of Garbet
Backie Hill
Sand Hill
Ford
4
21
Allt Sowan Hill
Rocks of Clais nam Bó
Dun Mount
3
AB36
Creag na Gamhna
20
Creag an Sgor
2
Newseat
Ballochduie
Creag an Eunan
Badenyon
19
Peatfold
White Hill
1
Dulax
18
34 A 35 B 36 C 37 D 38 E 39 F
81
68

67
54

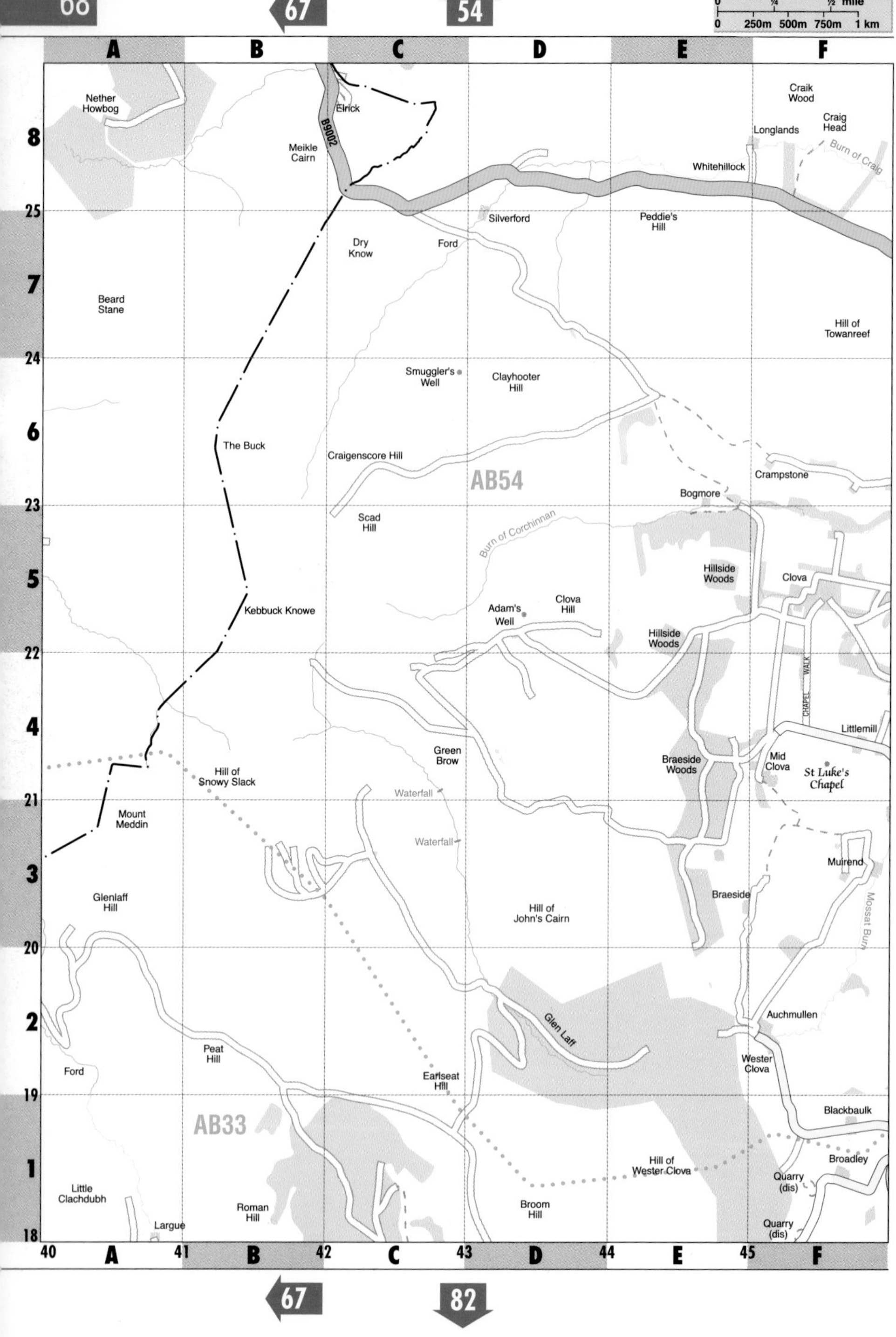
Scale: 1⅓ inches to 1 mile
0 ¼ ½ mile
0 250m 500m 750m 1 km
A B C D E F
8
7
6
5
4
3
2
1
25
24
23
22
21
20
19
18
40 41 42 43 44 45
Nether Howbog
Elrick
B9002
Meikle Cairn
Craik Wood
Craig Head
Longlands
Burn of Craig
Whitehillock
Silverford
Peddie's Hill
Dry Know
Ford
Beard Stane
Hill of Towanreef
Smuggler's Well
Clayhooter Hill
The Buck
Craigenscore Hill
AB54
Crampstone
Bogmore
Scad Hill
Burn of Corchinnan
Hillside Woods
Clova
Adam's Well
Clova Hill
Kebbuck Knowe
Hillside Woods
CHAPEL WALK
Littlemill
Green Brow
Braeside Woods
Mid Clova
St Luke's Chapel
Hill of Snowy Slack
Waterfall
Mount Meddin
Waterfall
Muirend
Braeside
Glenlaff Hill
Hill of John's Cairn
Mossat Burn
Auchmullen
Glen Laff
Wester Clova
Peat Hill
Ford
Earlseat Hill
Blackbaulk
AB33
Hill of Wester Clova
Broadley
Quarry (dis)
Little Clachdubh
Roman Hill
Broom Hill
Largue
Quarry (dis)

67
82

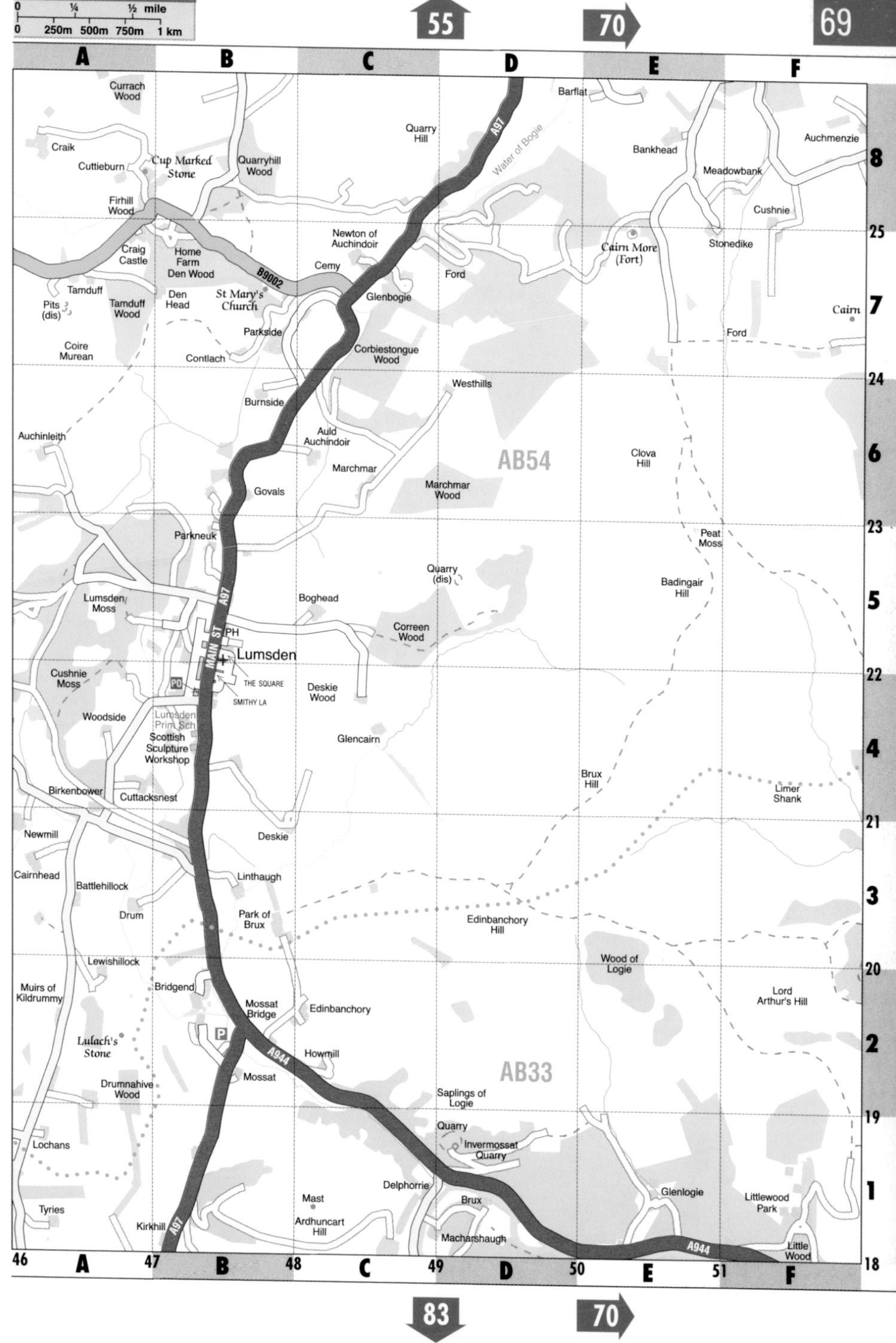
Scale: 1⅓ inches to 1 mile
0 ¼ ½ mile
0 250m 500m 750m 1 km
55
70
A B C D E F
Currach Wood
Barflat
Quarry Hill
A97
Water of Bogie
Auchmenzie
Craik
Bankhead
Cuttieburn
Cup Marked Stone
Quarryhill Wood
Meadowbank
Firhill Wood
Cushnie
Newton of Auchindoir
Cairn More (Fort)
Stonedike
Craig Castle
Home Farm
Den Wood
B9002
Cemy
Ford
Tamduff
Pits (dis)
Tamduff Wood
Den Head
St Mary's Church
Glenbogie
Cairn
Parkside
Ford
Coire Murean
Contlach
Corbiestongue Wood
Westhills
Burnside
Auchinleith
Auld Auchindoir
Clova Hill
AB54
Marchmar
Govals
Marchmar Wood
Parkneuk
Peat Moss
Quarry (dis)
Badingair Hill
Lumsden Moss
Boghead
MAIN ST
PH
Correen Wood
Lumsden
Cushnie Moss
PO
THE SQUARE
Deskie Wood
SMITHY LA
Woodside
Lumsden Prim Sch
Scottish Sculpture Workshop
Glencairn
Brux Hill
Birkenbower
Cuttacksnest
Limer Shank
Newmill
Deskie
Cairnhead
Linthaugh
Battlehillock
Drum
Park of Brux
Edinbanchory Hill
Lewishillock
Wood of Logie
Muirs of Kildrummy
Bridgend
Lord Arthur's Hill
Mossat Bridge
Edinbanchory
P
Lulach's Stone
A944
Howmill
Mossat
AB33
Drumnahive Wood
Saplings of Logie
Quarry
Lochans
Invermossat Quarry
Delphorrie
Glenlogie
Littlewood Park
Mast
Brux
Tyries
Ardhuncart Hill
Kirkhill
Macharshaugh
Little Wood
25
24
23
22
21
20
19
18
8 7 6 5 4 3 2 1
46 47 48 49 50 51
83
70

Scale: 1⅓ inches to 1 mile

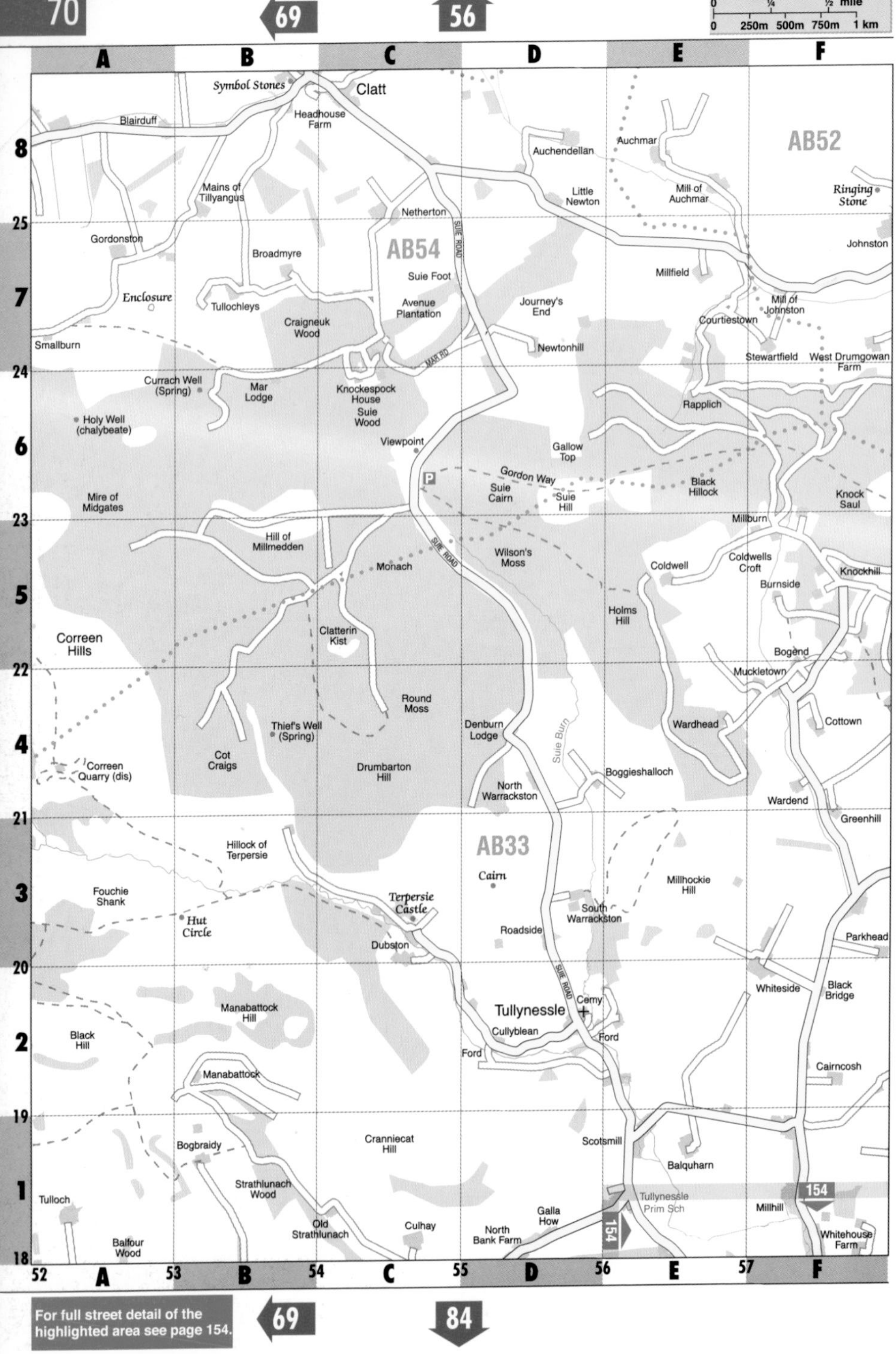

For full street detail of the highlighted area see page 154.

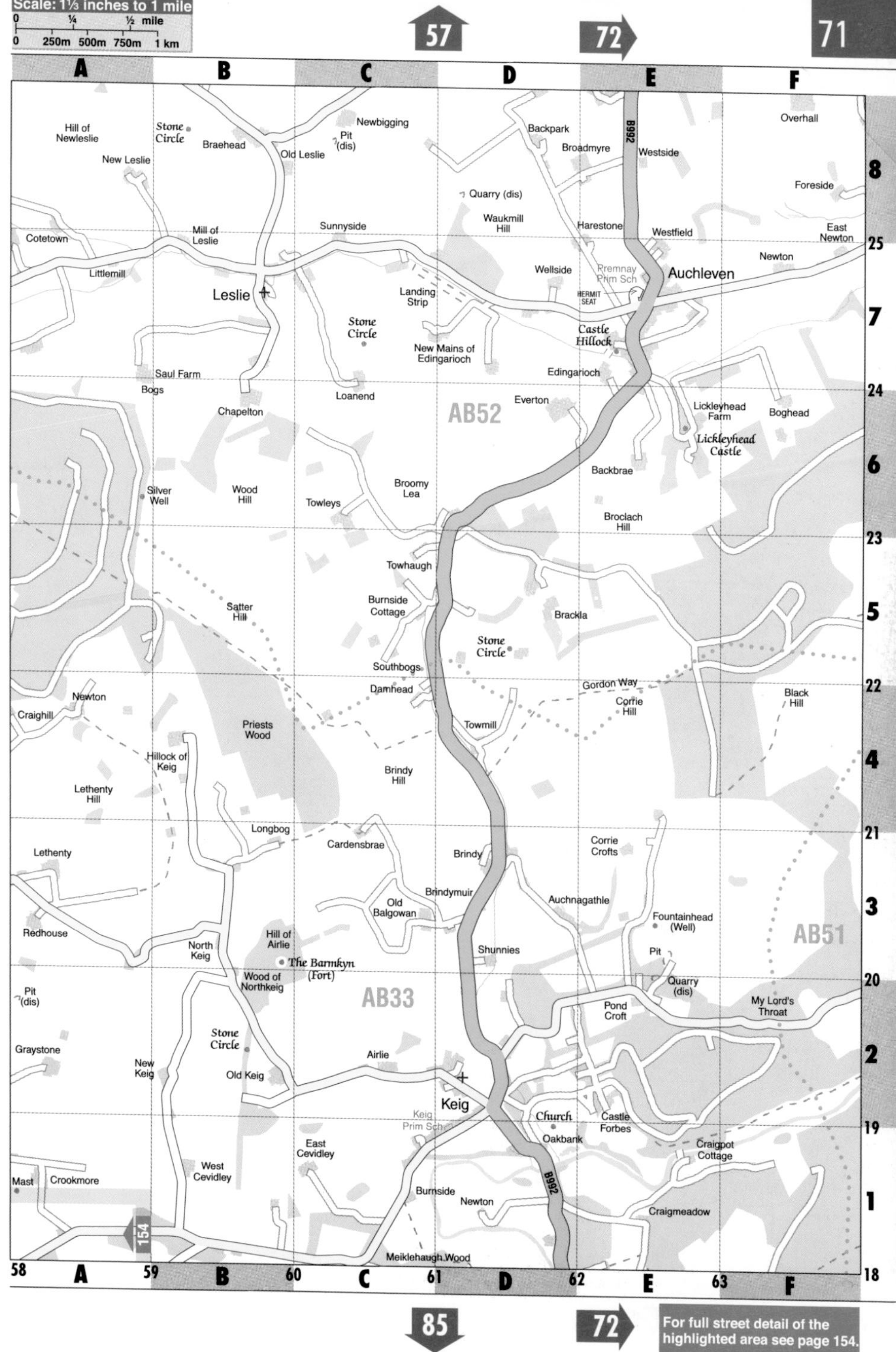

For full street detail of the highlighted area see page 154.

71 58

Scale: 1⅓ inches to 1 mile
0 ¼ ½ mile
0 250m 500m 750m 1 km

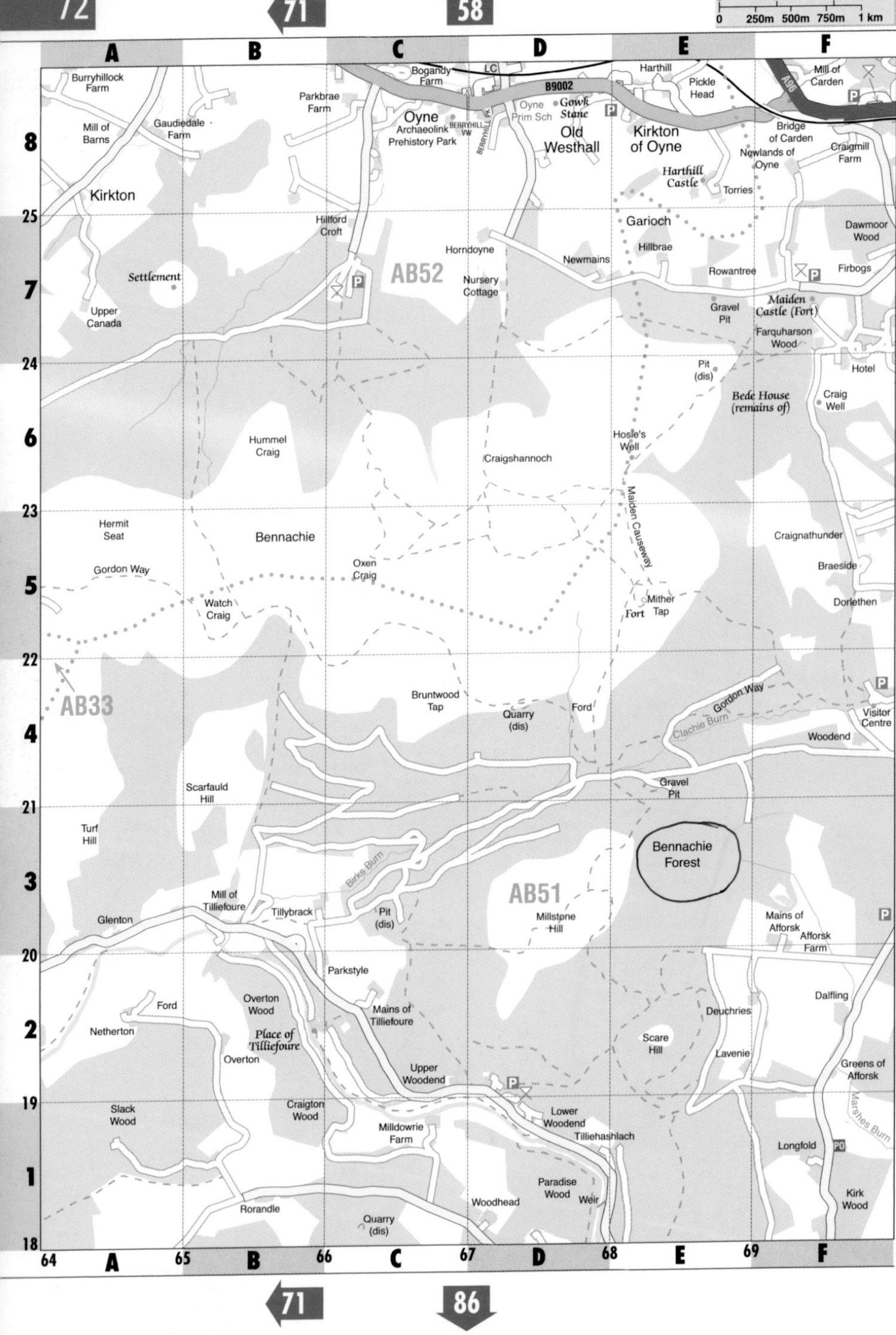

71 86

Scale: 1⅓ inches to 1 mile
0 ¼ ½ mile
0 250m 500m 750m 1 km

59
74

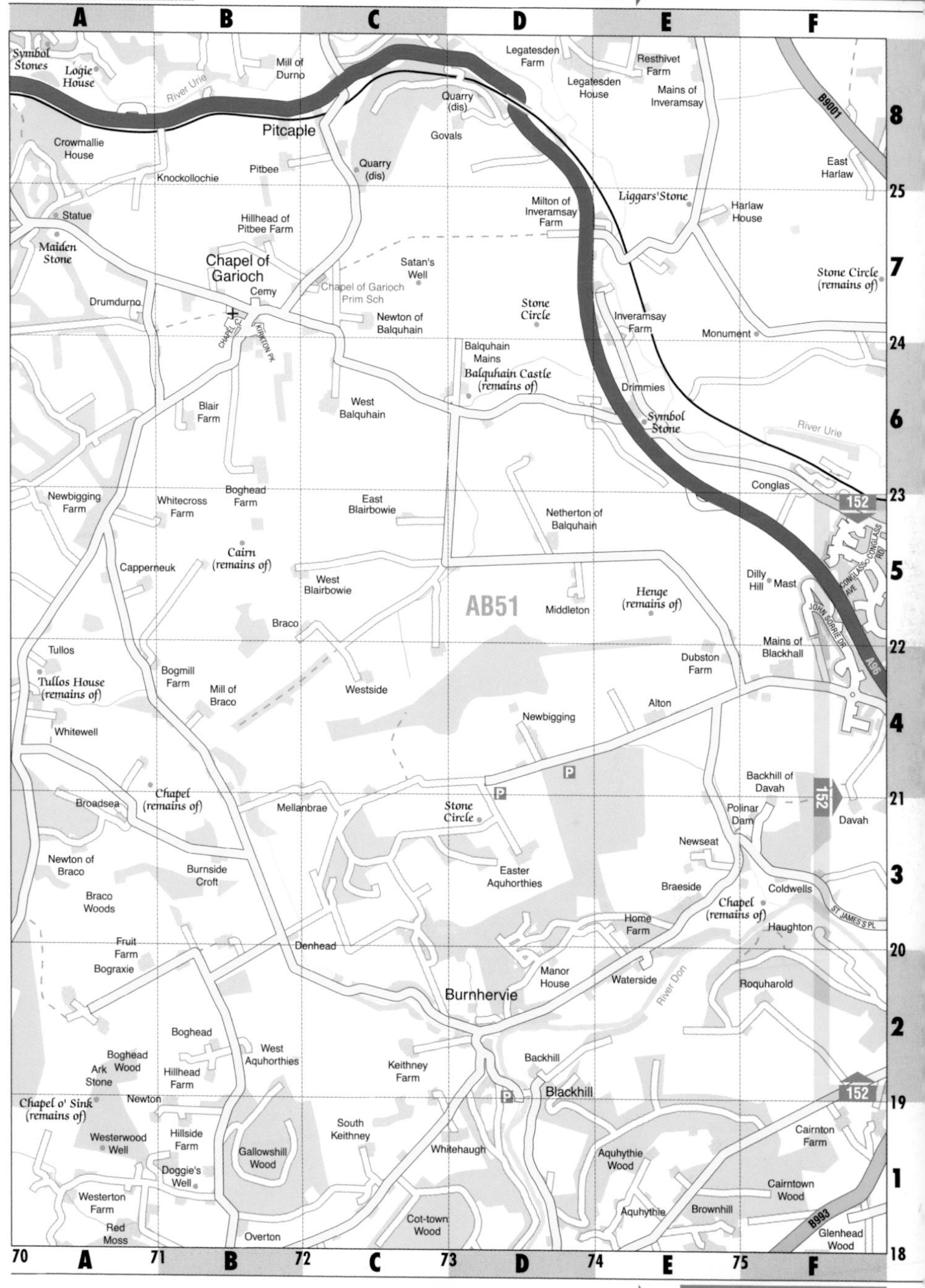

87
74

For full street detail of the highlighted area see page 152.

Scale: 1⅓ inches to 1 mile
0 ¼ ½ mile
0 250m 500m 750m 1 km

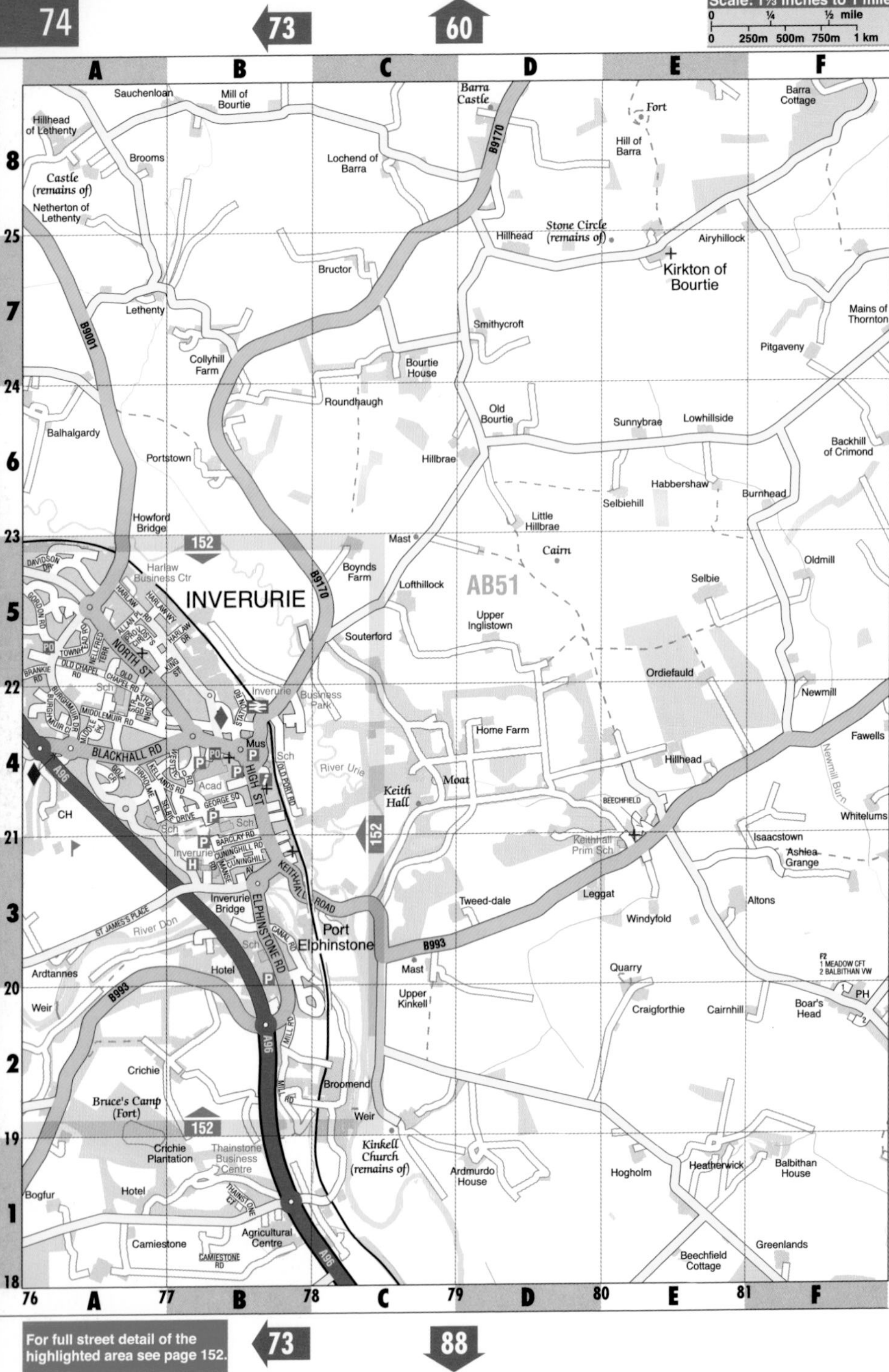

For full street detail of the highlighted area see page 152.

61
76

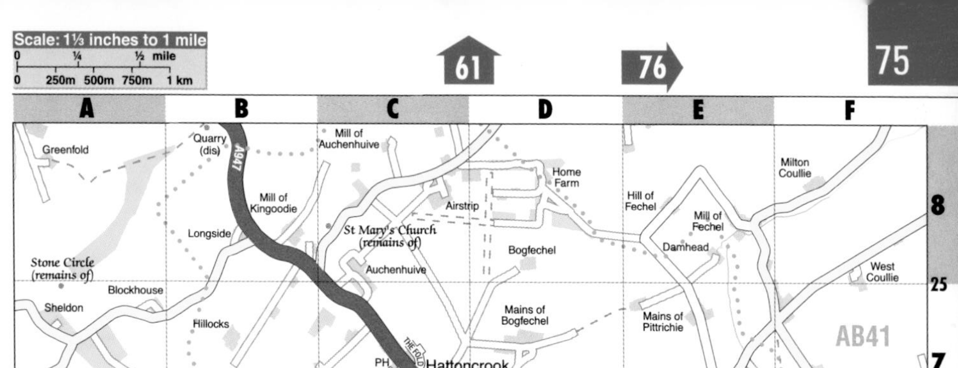

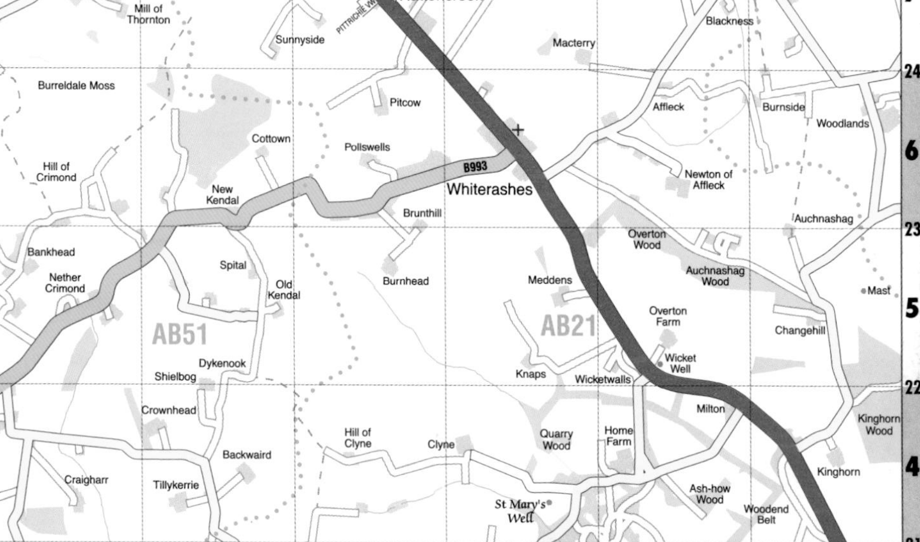

89
76
For full street detail of the highlighted area see page 153.

75
62

Scale: 1⅓ inches to 1 mile

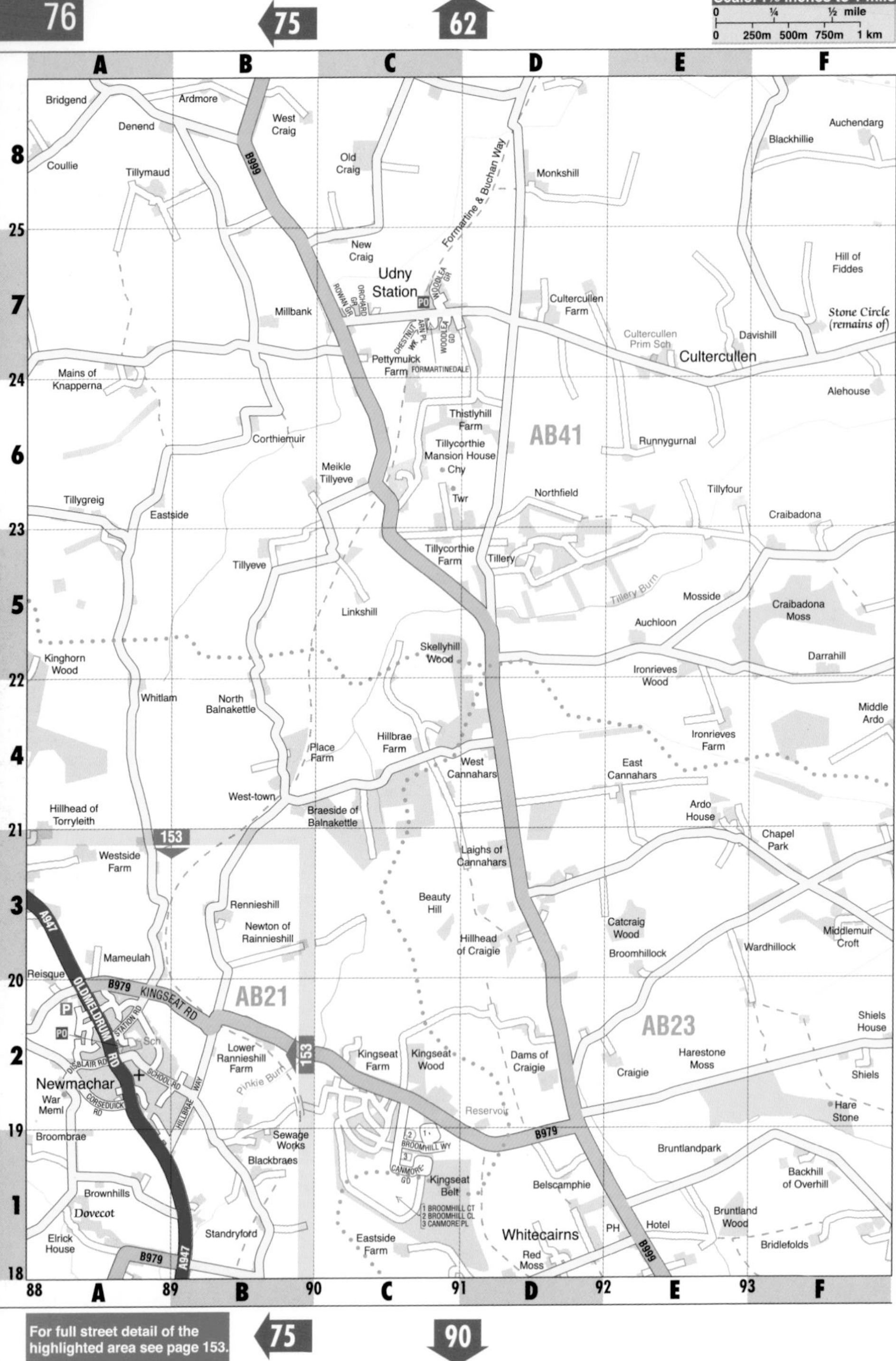

For full street detail of the highlighted area see page 153.

75
90

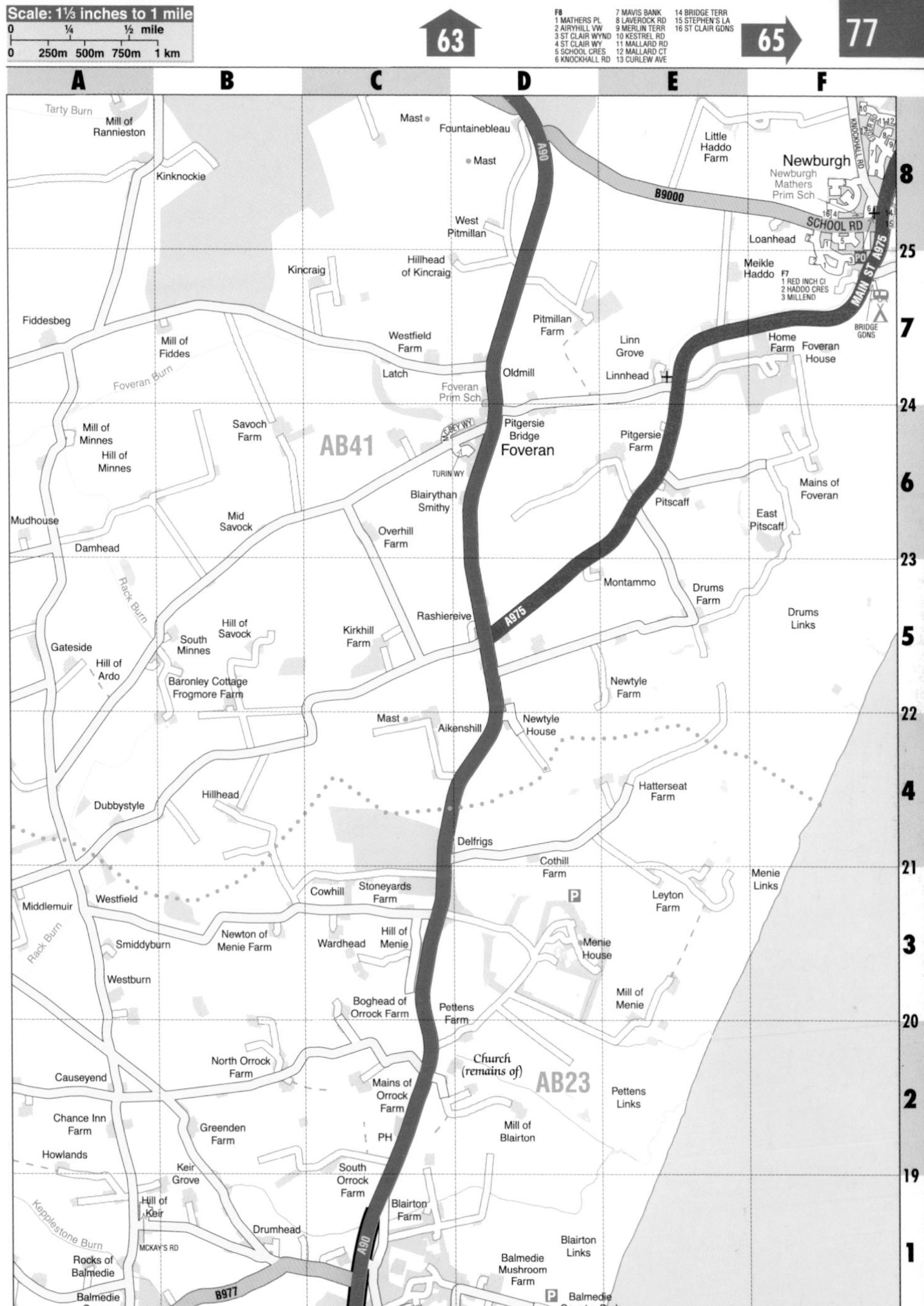

Scale: 1⅓ inches to 1 mile
0 ¼ ½ mile
0 250m 500m 750m 1 km
63
65
77
F8
1 MATHERS PL
2 AIRYHILL VW
3 ST CLAIR WYND
4 ST CLAIR WY
5 SCHOOL CRES
6 KNOCKHALL RD
7 MAVIS BANK
8 LAVEROCK RD
9 MERLIN TERR
10 KESTREL RD
11 MALLARD RD
12 MALLARD CT
13 CURLEW AVE
14 BRIDGE TERR
15 STEPHEN'S LA
16 ST CLAIR GDNS
F7
1 RED INCH CI
2 HADDO CRES
3 MILLEND
A B C D E F
8 25 7 24 6 23 5 22 4 21 3 20 2 19 1 18
94 95 96 97 98 99
Tarty Burn
Mill of Rannieston
Kinknockie
Mast
Fountainebleau
Mast
A90
B9000
Little Haddo Farm
Newburgh
Newburgh Mathers Prim Sch
KNOCKHALL RD
SCHOOL RD
Loanhead
Meikle Haddo
MAIN ST A975
PO
BRIDGE GDNS
West Pitmillan
Hillhead of Kincraig
Kincraig
Fiddesbeg
Mill of Fiddes
Westfield Farm
Pitmillan Farm
Linn Grove
Home Farm
Foveran House
Foveran Burn
Latch
Oldmill
Linnhead
Foveran Prim Sch
Mill of Minnes
Hill of Minnes
Savoch Farm
AB41
Pitgersie Bridge
Foveran
Pitgersie Farm
TURIN WY
Blairythan Smithy
Mains of Foveran
Pitscaff
East Pitscaff
Mudhouse
Mid Savock
Overhill Farm
Damhead
Rack Burn
Montammo
Drums Farm
Drums Links
Rashiereive
A975
Hill of Savock
Kirkhill Farm
South Minnes
Gateside
Hill of Ardo
Baronley Cottage
Frogmore Farm
Newtyle Farm
Mast
Aikenshill
Newtyle House
Hatterseat Farm
Hillhead
Dubbystyle
Delfrigs
Cothill Farm
Menie Links
Cowhill
Stoneyards Farm
Leyton Farm
Middlemuir
Westfield
Rack Burn
Newton of Menie Farm
Wardhead
Hill of Menie
Menie House
Smiddyburn
Westburn
Mill of Menie
Boghead of Orrock Farm
Pettens Farm
North Orrock Farm
Church (remains of)
AB23
Causeyend
Mains of Orrock Farm
Pettens Links
Chance Inn Farm
Greenden Farm
PH
Mill of Blairton
Howlands
Keir Grove
South Orrock Farm
Kepplestone Burn
Hill of Keir
Blairton Farm
Drumhead
MCKAY'S RD
A90
Blairton Links
Rocks of Balmedie
Balmedie Mushroom Farm
B977
Balmedie Quarry (disused)
LUMSDEN WY
Balmedie Country Park Visitor Centre

91

Scale: 1⅓ inches to 1 mile

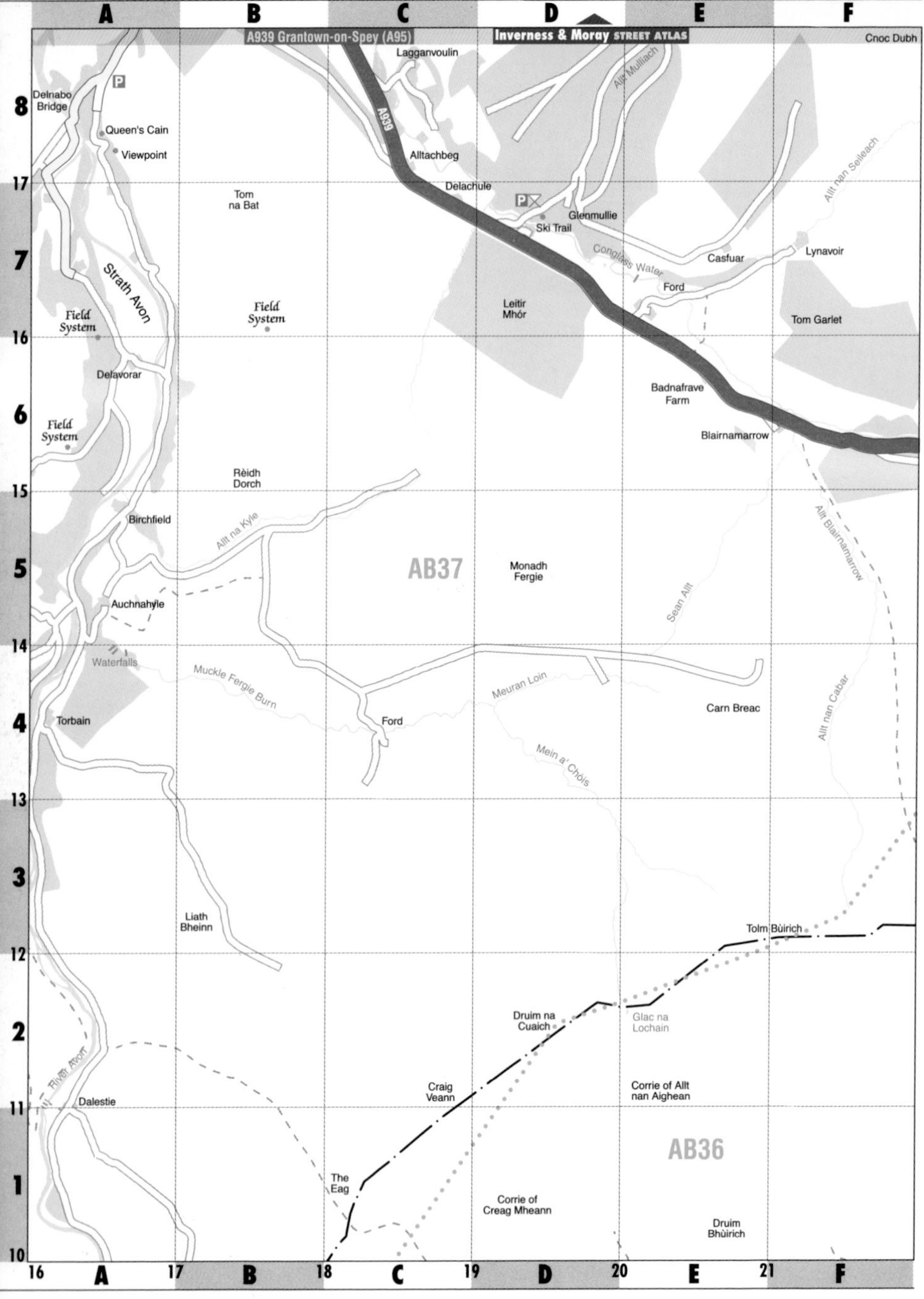

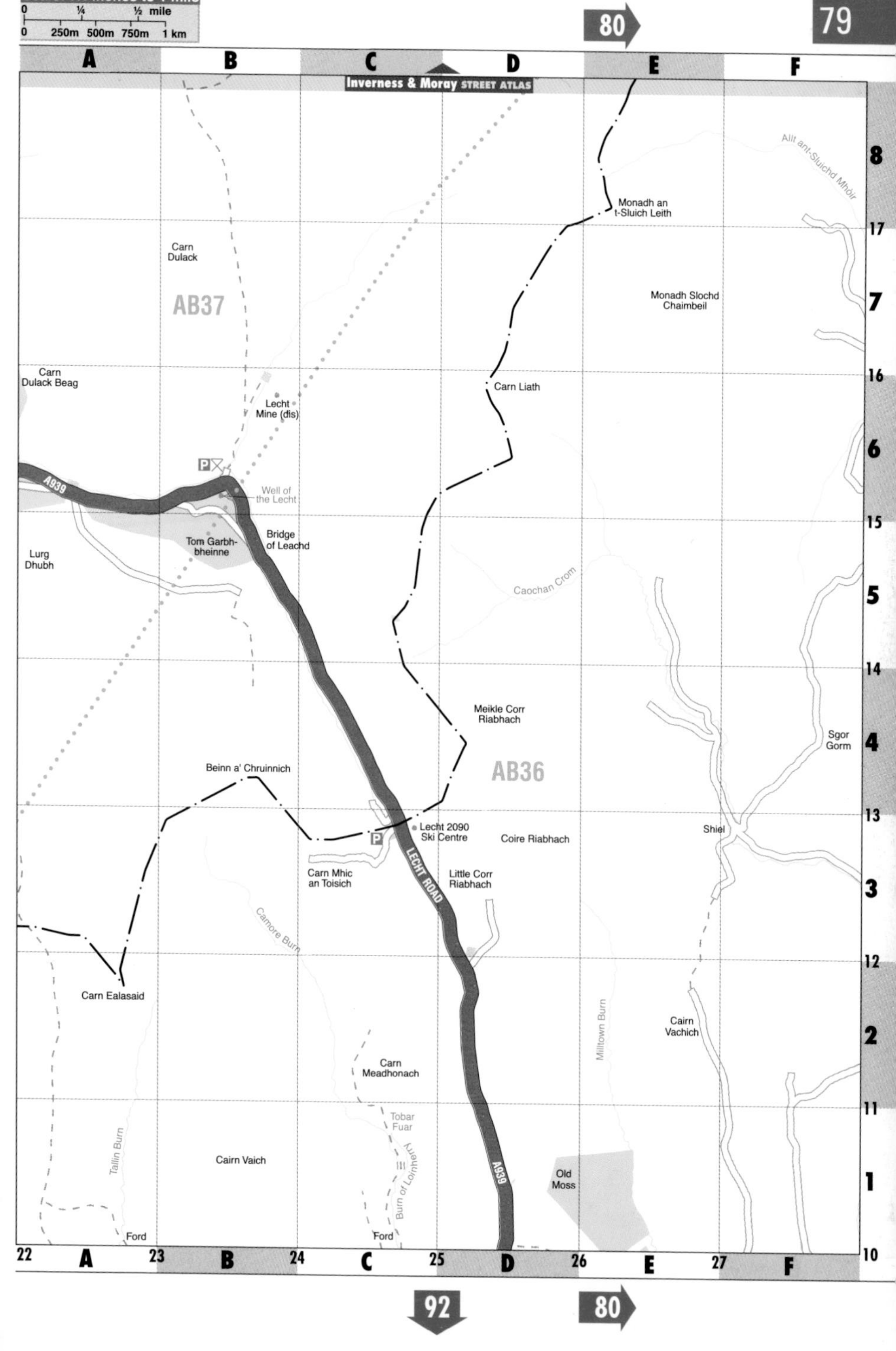

Scale: 1⅓ inches to 1 mile
0
¼
½ mile
0
250m
500m
750m
1 km
80
A
B
C
D
E
F
Inverness & Moray STREET ATLAS
Allt ant-Sluichd Mhòir
Monadh an t-Sluich Leith
Carn Dulack
AB37
Monadh Slochd Chaimbeil
Carn Dulack Beag
Lecht Mine (dis)
Carn Liath
A939
Well of the Lecht
Bridge of Leachd
Tom Garbh-bheinne
Lurg Dhubh
Caochan Crom
Meikle Corr Riabhach
Sgor Gorm
Beinn a' Chruinnich
AB36
Lecht 2090 Ski Centre
Coire Riabhach
Shiel
Carn Mhic an Toisich
LECHT ROAD
Little Corr Riabhach
Camore Burn
Carn Ealasaid
Cairn Vachich
Milltown Burn
Carn Meadhonach
Tobar Fuar
Tallin Burn
Cairn Vaich
Burn of Loinherry
A939
Old Moss
Ford
Ford
8
17
7
16
6
15
5
14
4
13
3
12
2
11
1
10
22
A
23
B
24
C
25
D
26
E
27
F
92
80

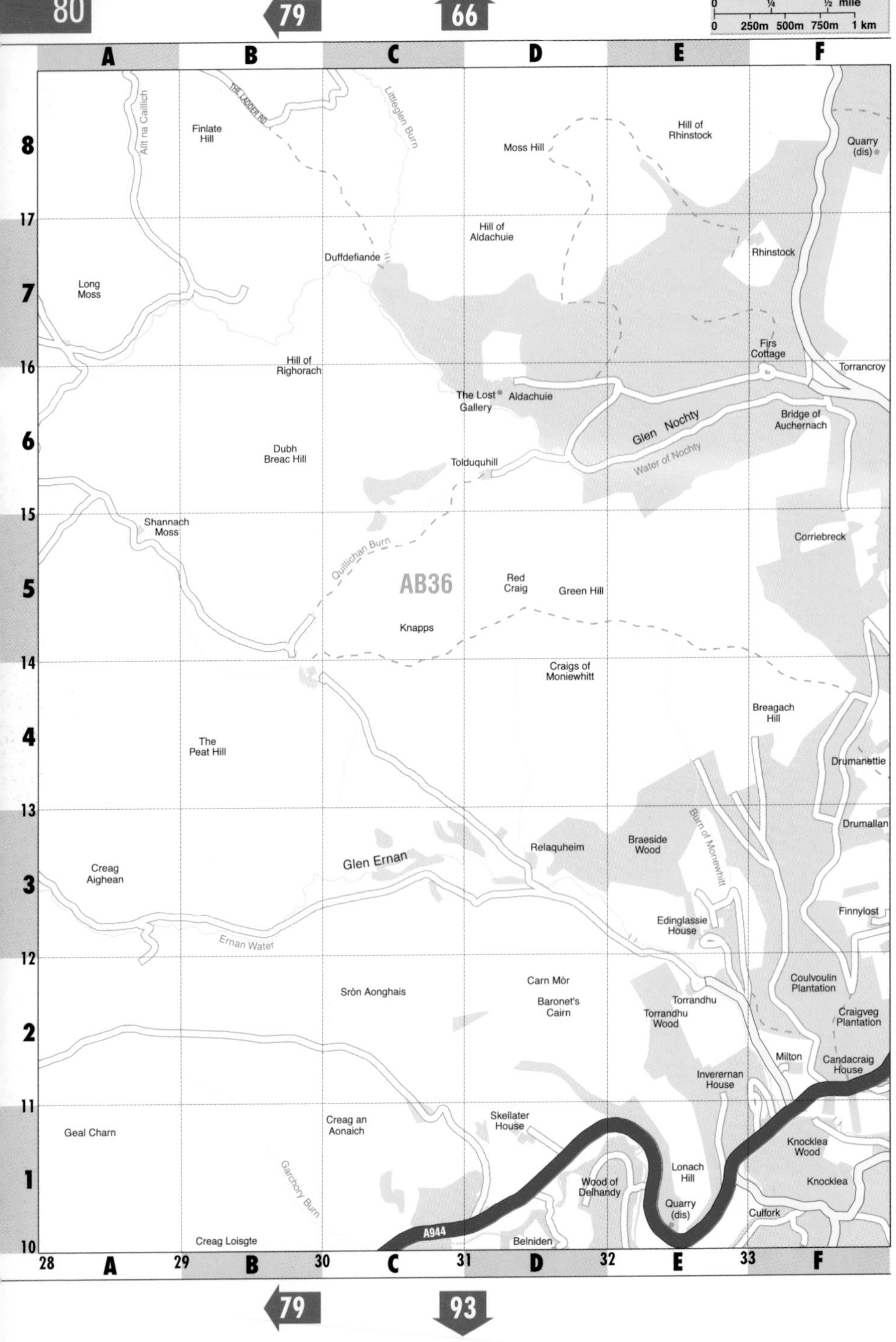
79
66
Scale: 1⅓ inches to 1 mile
0 ¼ ½ mile
0 250m 500m 750m 1 km
A B C D E F
8
17
7
16
6
15
5
14
4
13
3
12
2
11
1
10
THE LADDER RD
Allt na Caillich
Finlate Hill
Littleglen Burn
Moss Hill
Hill of Rhinstock
Quarry (dis)
Hill of Aldachuie
Duffdefiance
Rhinstock
Long Moss
Firs Cottage
Hill of Righorach
Torrancroy
The Lost Gallery
Aldachuie
Bridge of Auchernach
Glen Nochty
Dubh Breac Hill
Tolduquhill
Water of Nochty
Shannach Moss
Corriebreck
Quillichan Burn
AB36
Red Craig
Green Hill
Knapps
Craigs of Moniewhitt
Breagach Hill
The Peat Hill
Drumanettie
Drumallan
Burn of Moniewhitt
Braeside Wood
Relaquheim
Creag Aighean
Glen Ernan
Finnylost
Edinglassie House
Ernan Water
Coulvoulin Plantation
Carn Mòr
Sròn Aonghais
Torrandhu
Baronet's Cairn
Torrandhu Wood
Craigveg Plantation
Milton
Candacraig House
Inverernan House
Geal Charn
Creag an Aonaich
Skellater House
Knocklea Wood
Lonach Hill
Wood of Delhandy
Knocklea
Garchory Burn
Quarry (dis)
Culfork
A944
Creag Loisgte
Belniden
28 29 30 31 32 33
79
93

Scale: 1⅓ inches to 1 mile

67
82

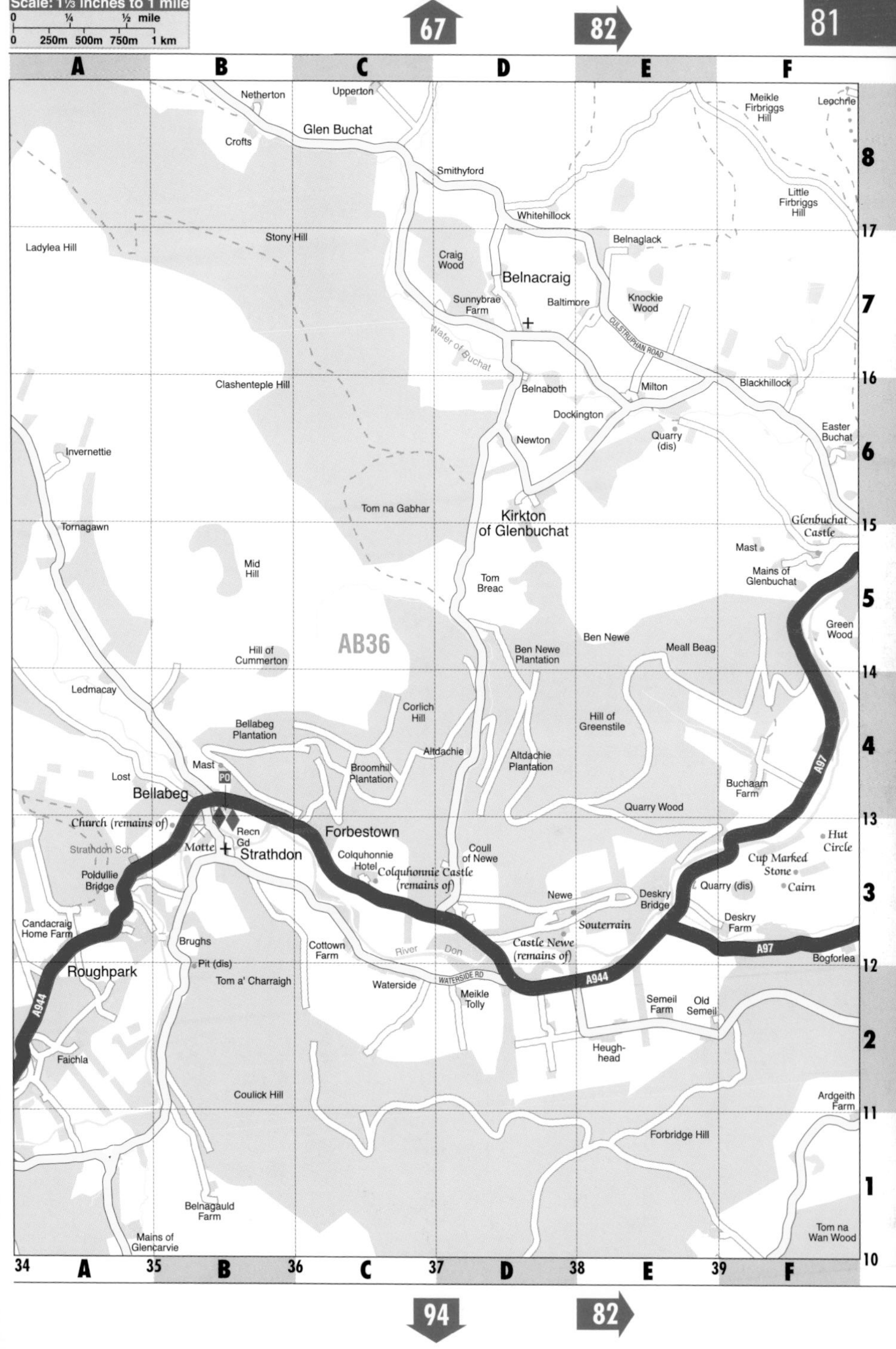

94
82

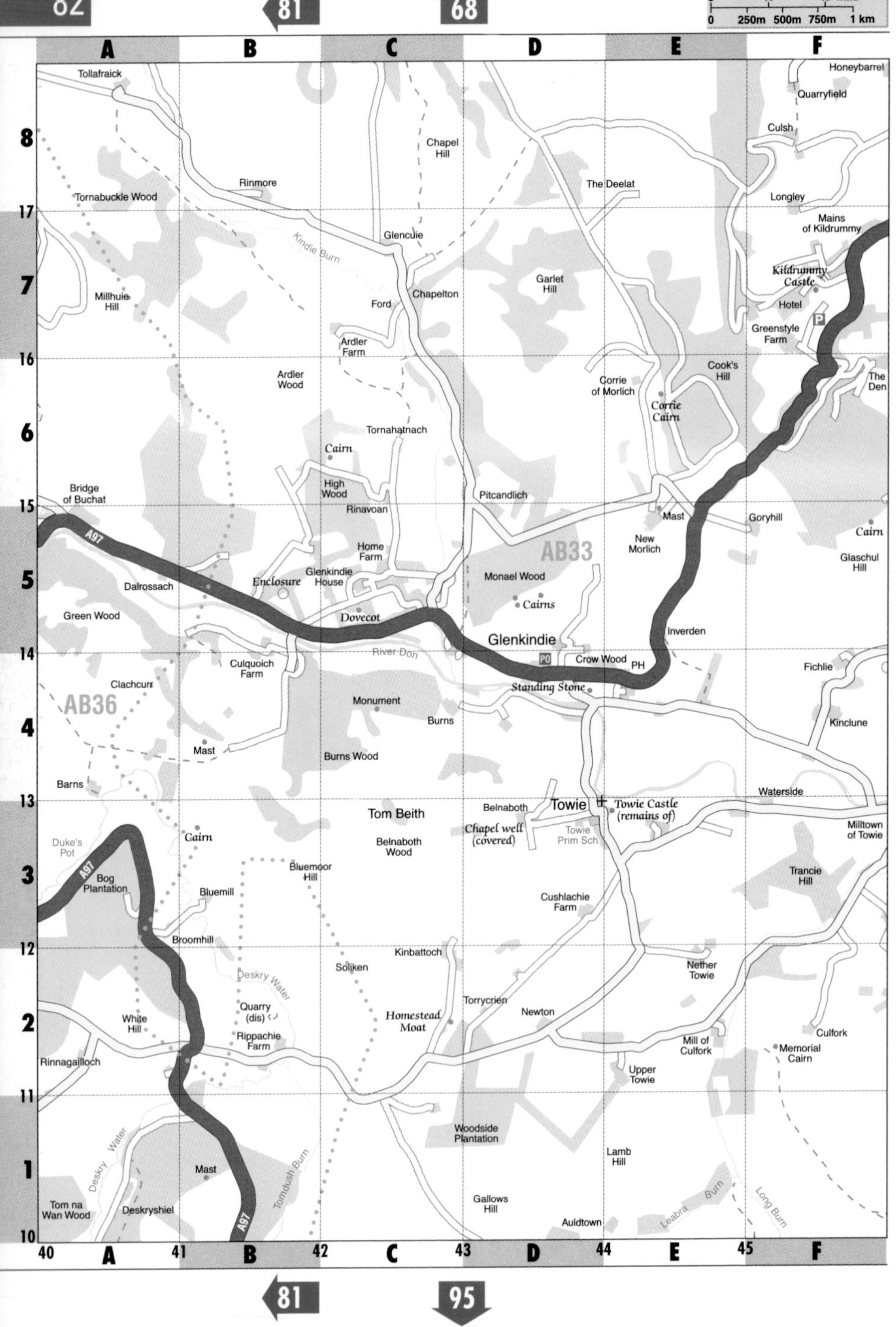
81
68
Scale: 1⅓ inches to 1 mile
0 ¼ ½ mile
0 250m 500m 750m 1 km
A B C D E F
Tollafraick
Honeybarrel
Quarryfield
Culsh
Chapel Hill
Rinmore
The Deelat
Longley
Tornabuckle Wood
Mains of Kildrummy
Glencuie
Kindie Burn
Kildrummy Castle
Hotel
Garlet Hill
Chapelton
Millhuie Hill
Ford
Greenstyle Farm
Ardler Farm
Cook's Hill
Ardler Wood
Corrie of Morlich
Corrie Cairn
The Den
Tornahatnach
Cairn
High Wood
Bridge of Buchat
Pitcandlich
Rinavoan
Mast
Goryhill
New Morlich
AB33
Cairn
A97
Home Farm
Glaschul Hill
Dalrossach
Enclosure
Glenkindie House
Monael Wood
Cairns
Green Wood
Dovecot
Inverden
Glenkindie
River Don
PO
Crow Wood
PH
Fichlie
Clachcurr
Culquoich Farm
Standing Stone
AB36
Monument
Burns
Kinclune
Mast
Burns Wood
Barns
Waterside
Belnaboth
Towie
Towie Castle (remains of)
Tom Beith
Milltown of Towie
Duke's Pot
Cairn
Chapel well (covered)
Towie Prim Sch
Belnaboth Wood
A97
Bluemoor Hill
Trancie Hill
Bog Plantation
Bluemill
Cushlachie Farm
Broomhill
Kinbattoch
Soliken
Nether Towie
Deskry Water
Torrycrien
Newton
Quarry (dis)
Homestead Moat
White Hill
Culfork
Mill of Culfork
Rippachie Farm
Memorial Cairn
Rinnagalloch
Upper Towie
Woodside Plantation
Deskry Water
Mast
Tomdush Burn
Lamb Hill
Tom na Wan Wood
Deskryshiel
Gallows Hill
Leabra Burn
Long Burn
Auldtown
A97
8
17
7
16
6
15
5
14
4
13
3
12
2
11
1
10
40 41 42 43 44 45
81
95

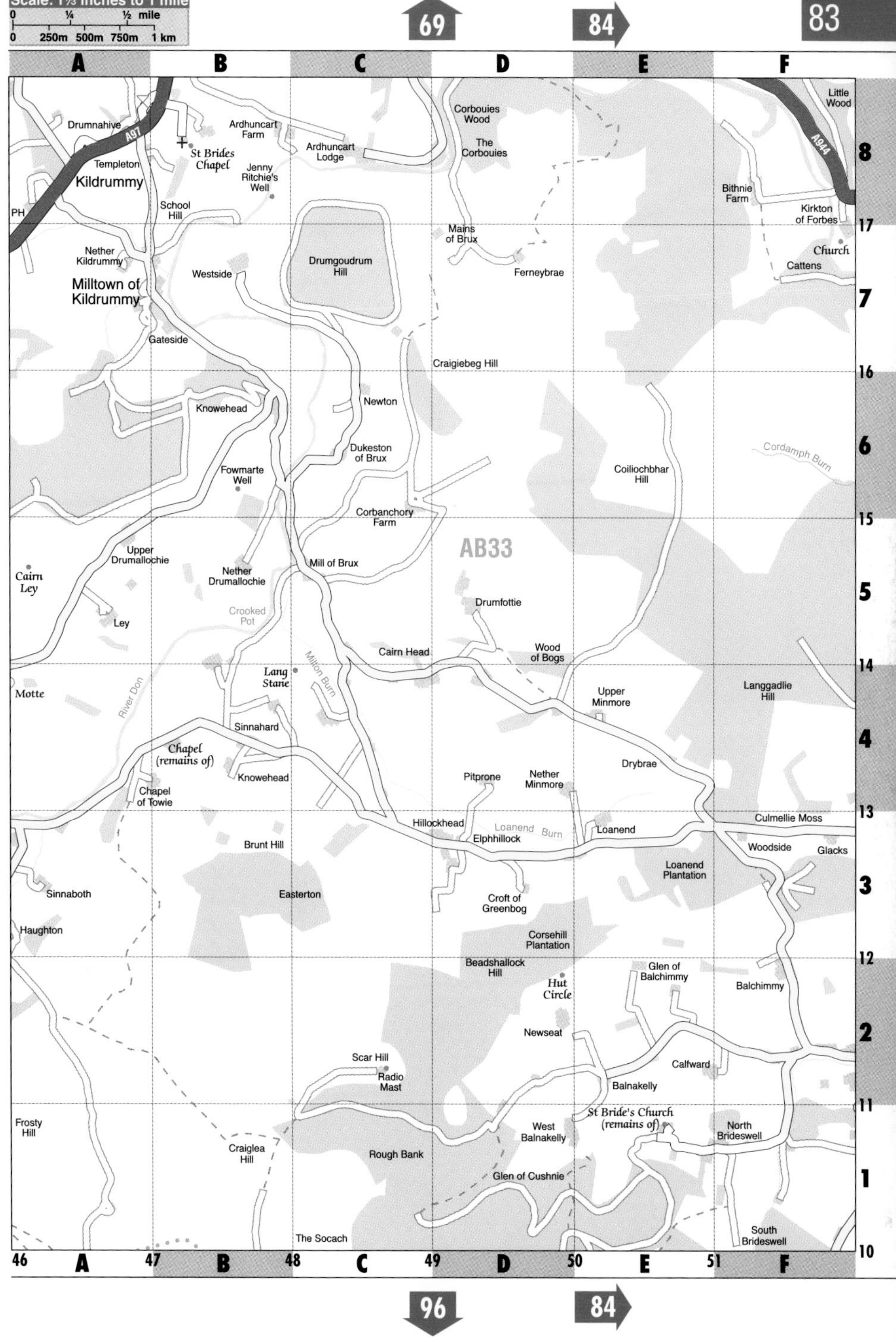
Scale: 1⅓ inches to 1 mile
0
¼
½ mile
0
250m
500m
750m
1 km
69
84
A
B
C
D
E
F
Drumnahive
A97
Ardhuncart Farm
St Brides Chapel
Ardhuncart Lodge
Corbouies Wood
The Corbouies
Little Wood
A944
Templeton
Kildrummy
Jenny Ritchie's Well
PH
School Hill
Bithnie Farm
Kirkton of Forbes
Mains of Brux
Nether Kildrummy
Drumgoudrum Hill
Church
Cattens
Westside
Ferneybrae
Milltown of Kildrummy
Gateside
Craigiebeg Hill
Knowehead
Newton
Dukeston of Brux
Cordamph Burn
Fowmarte Well
Coiliochbhar Hill
Corbanchory Farm
AB33
Upper Drumallochie
Mill of Brux
Cairn Ley
Nether Drumallochie
Drumfottie
Crooked Pot
Ley
Cairn Head
Wood of Bogs
Lang Stane
Milton Burn
Motte
River Don
Upper Minmore
Langgadlie Hill
Sinnahard
Chapel (remains of)
Drybrae
Knowehead
Pitprone
Nether Minmore
Chapel of Towie
Hillockhead
Culmellie Moss
Loanend Burn
Loanend
Elphhillock
Brunt Hill
Woodside
Glacks
Loanend Plantation
Sinnaboth
Easterton
Croft of Greenbog
Haughton
Corsehill Plantation
Beadshallock Hill
Glen of Balchimmy
Hut Circle
Balchimmy
Newseat
Scar Hill
Radio Mast
Calfward
Balnakelly
Frosty Hill
West Balnakelly
St Bride's Church (remains of)
North Brideswell
Craiglea Hill
Rough Bank
Glen of Cushnie
South Brideswell
The Socach
8
17
7
16
6
15
5
14
4
13
3
12
2
11
1
10
46
47
48
49
50
51
96
84

Scale: 1⅓ inches to 1 mile
0 ¼ ½ mile
0 250m 500m 750m 1 km

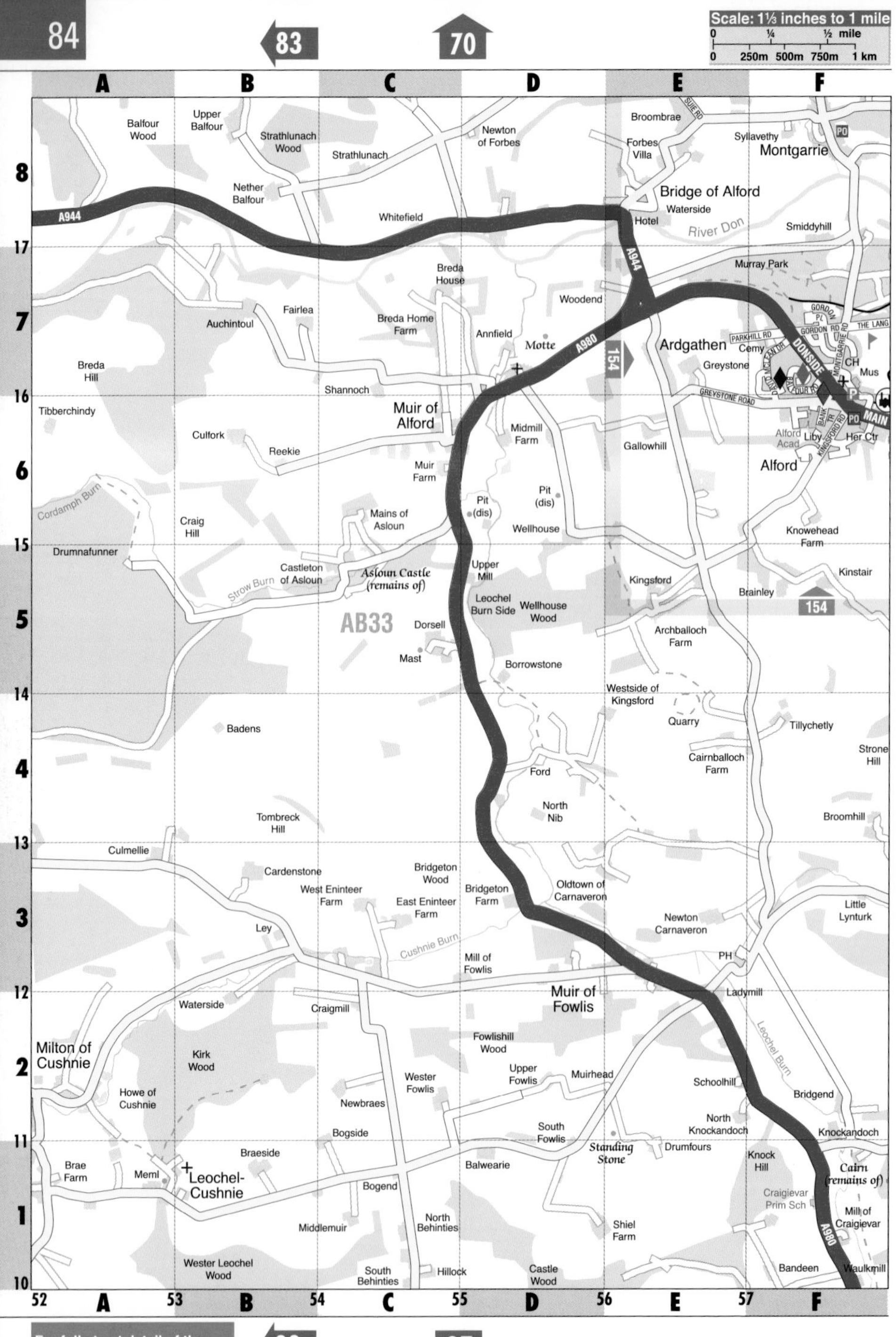

For full street detail of the highlighted area see page 154.

Scale: 1⅓ inches to 1 mile

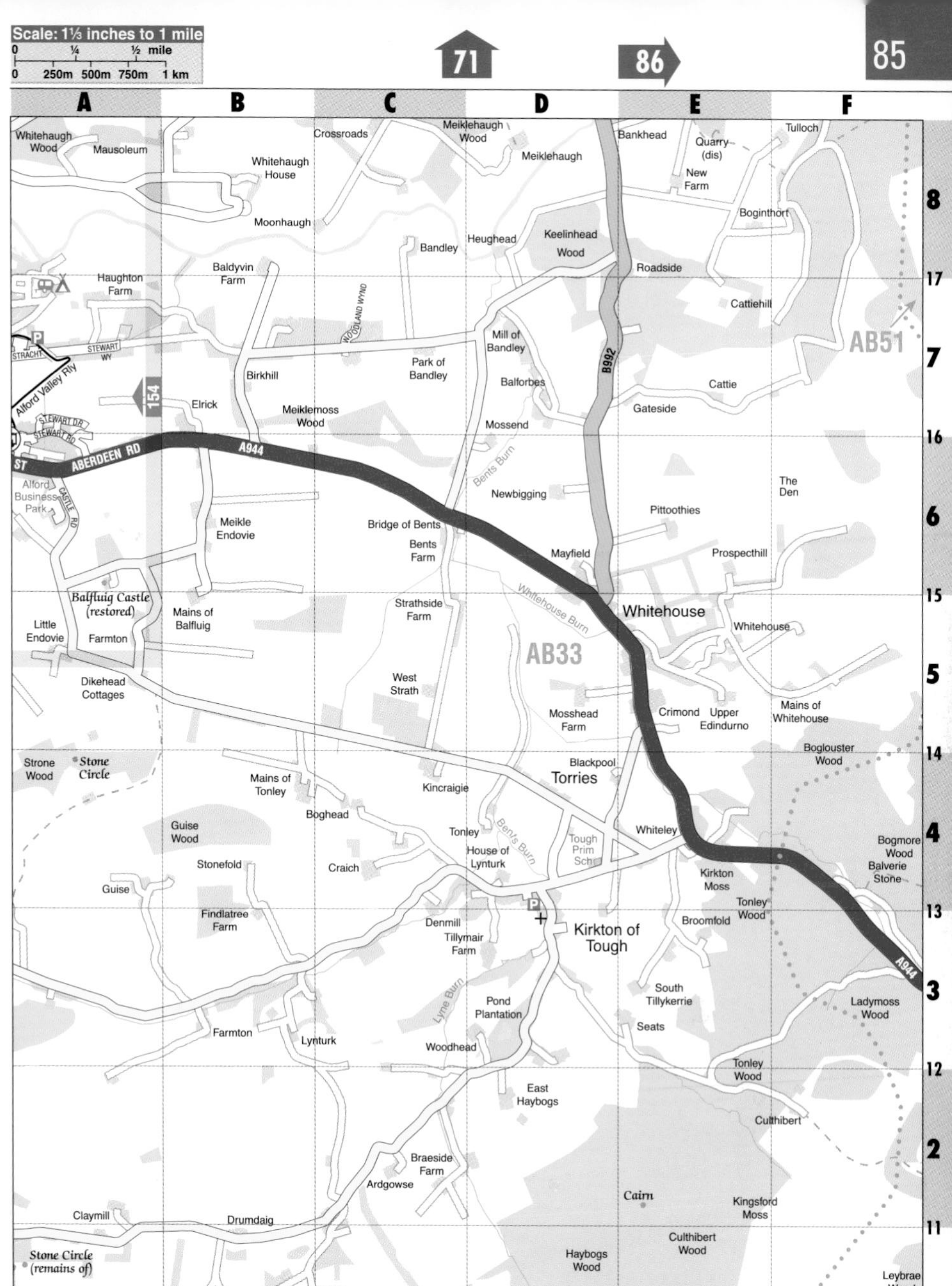

For full street detail of the highlighted area see page 154.

85
72

Scale: 1⅓ inches to 1 mile

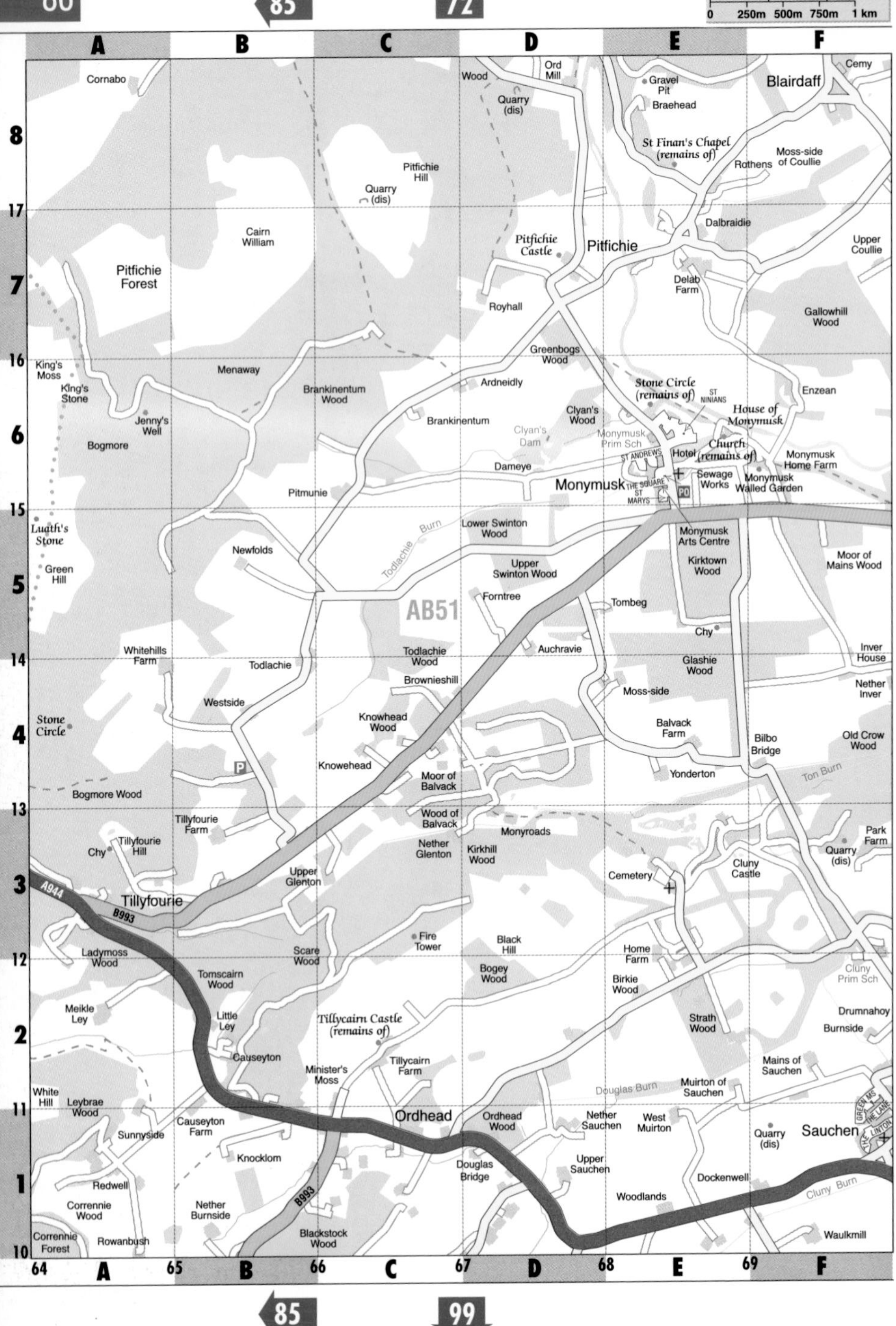

85
99

Scale: 1⅓ inches to 1 mile
0 ¼ ½ mile
0 250m 500m 750m 1 km

73
88

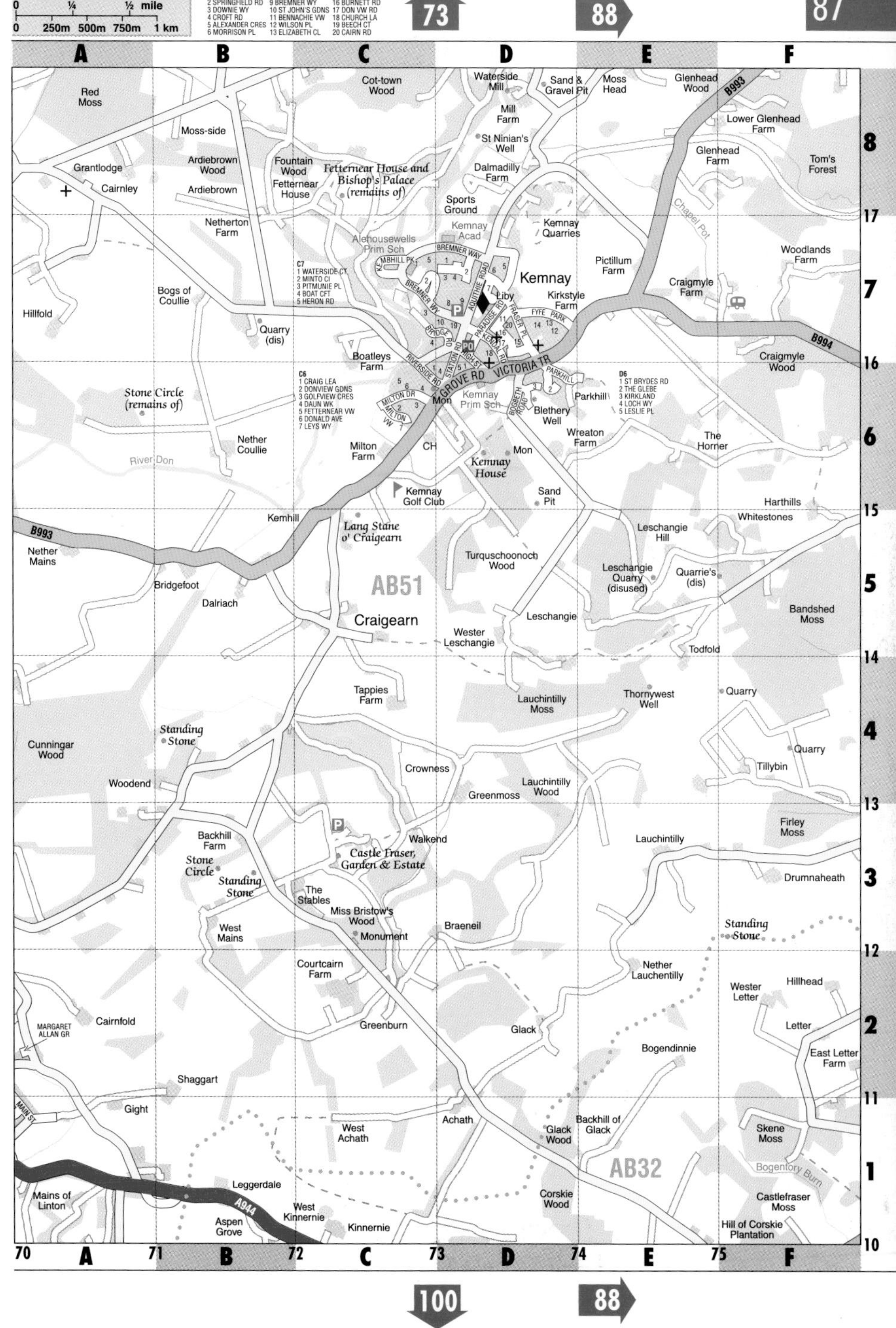

100
88

87
74

Scale: 1⅓ inches to 1 mile
0 ¼ ½ mile
0 250m 500m 750m 1 km

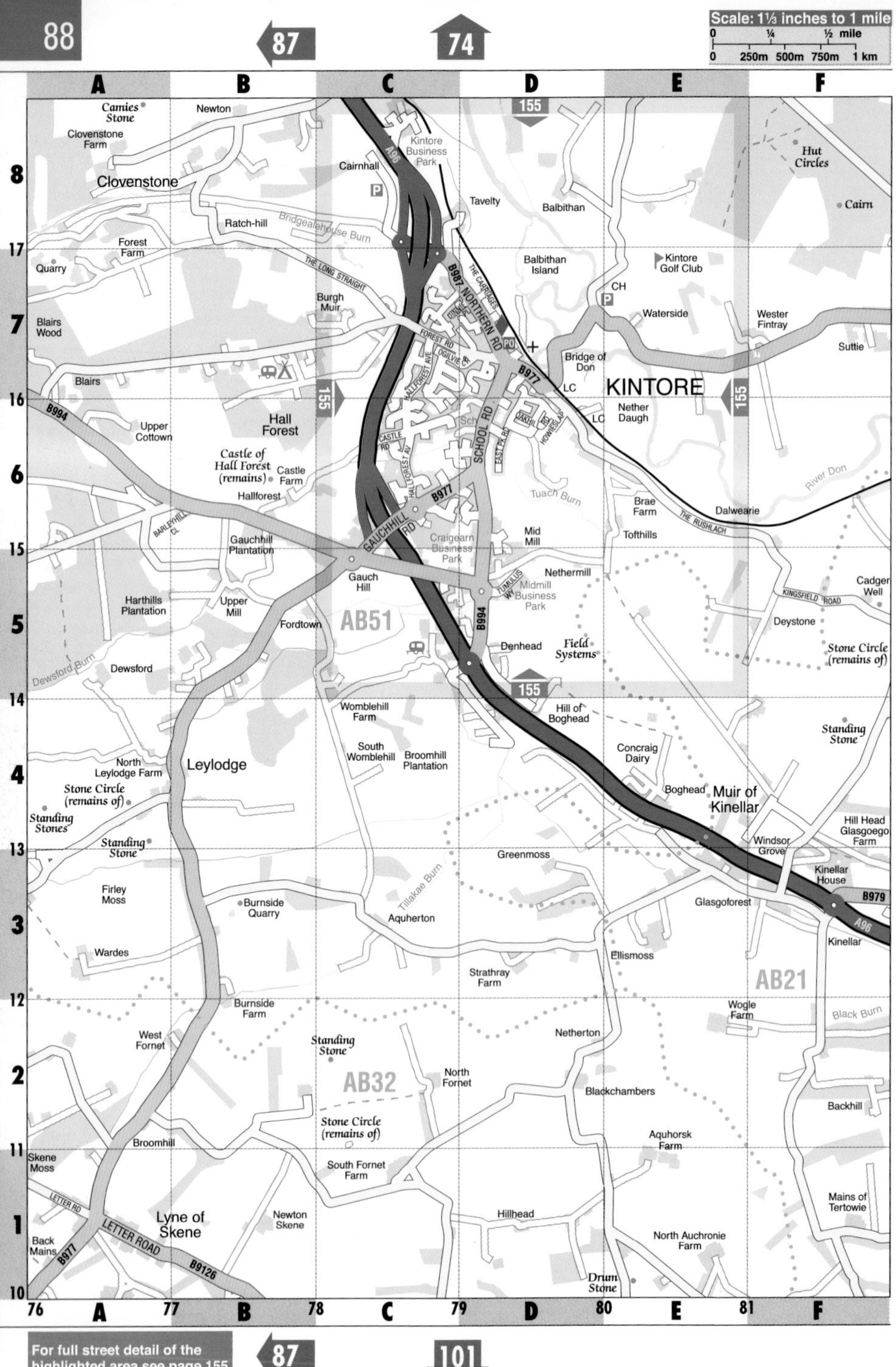

A B C D E F
8 17 7 16 6 15 5 14 4 13 3 12 2 11 1 10
76 77 78 79 80 81

For full street detail of the highlighted area see page 155.
87
101

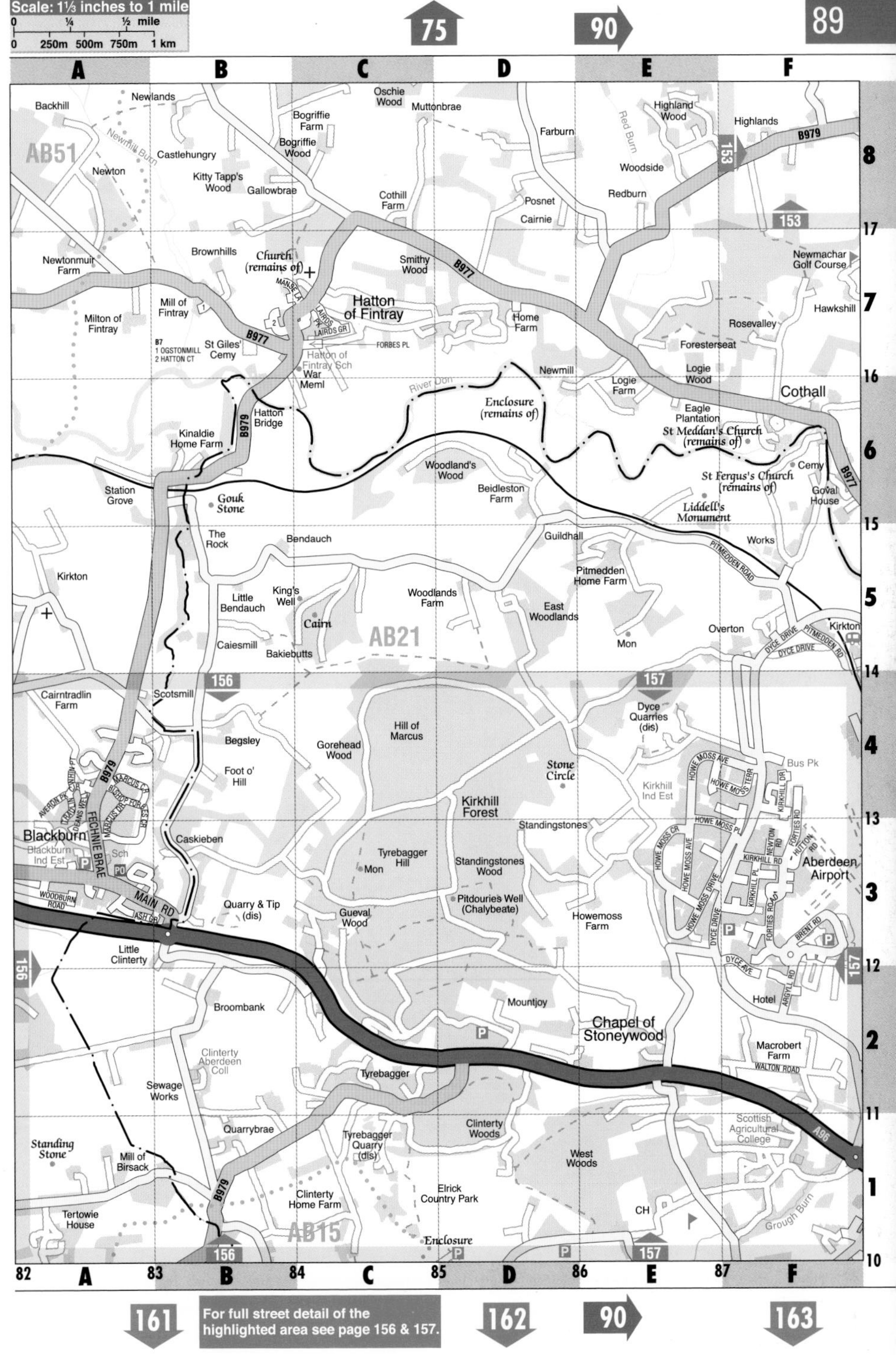

161
For full street detail of the highlighted area see page 156 & 157.
162
90
163

For full street detail of the highlighted area see page 153.

89

76

Scale: 1⅓ inches to 1 mile

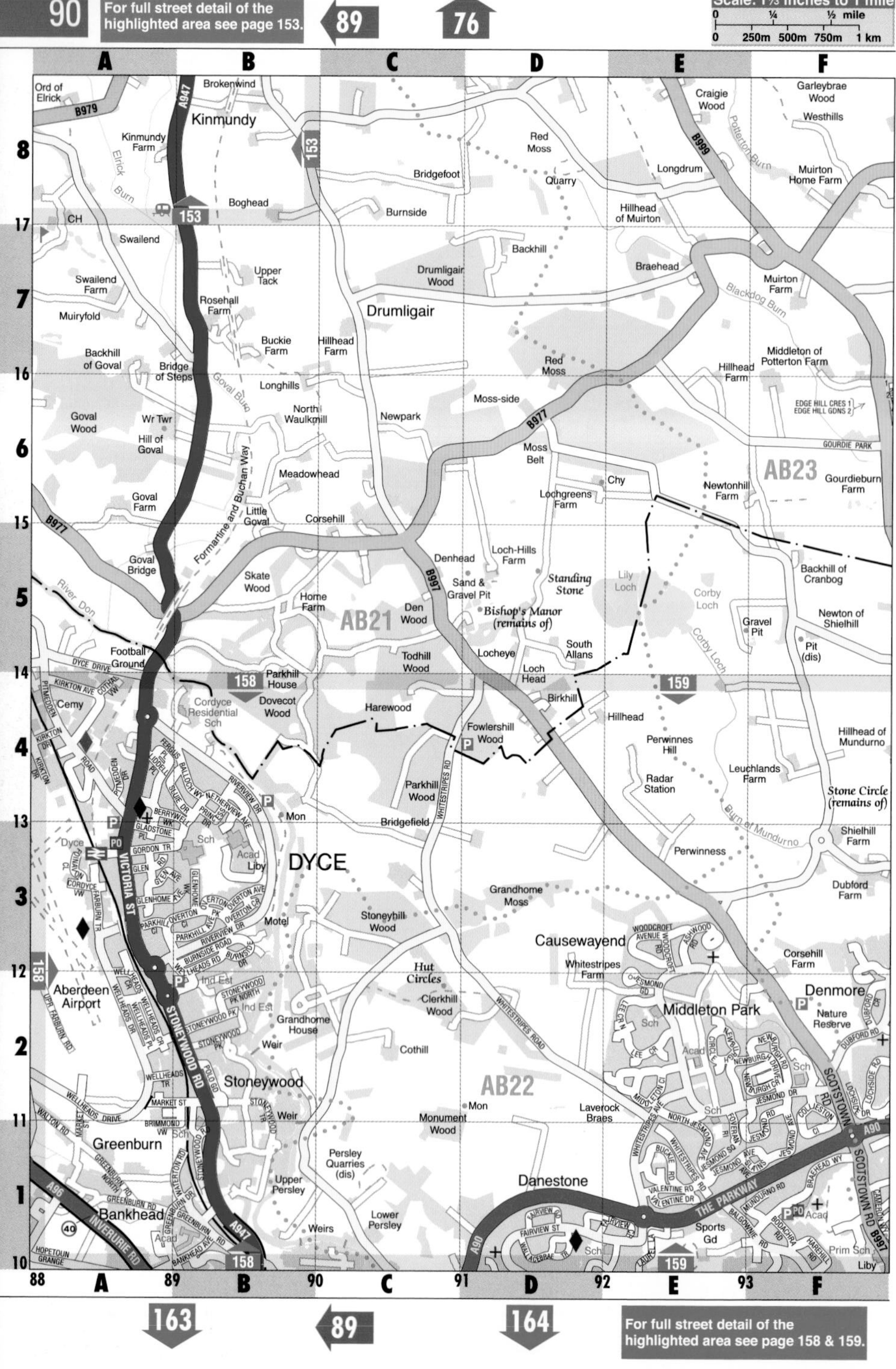

163

89

164

For full street detail of the highlighted area see page 158 & 159.

165

For full street detail of the highlighted area see page 160.

79

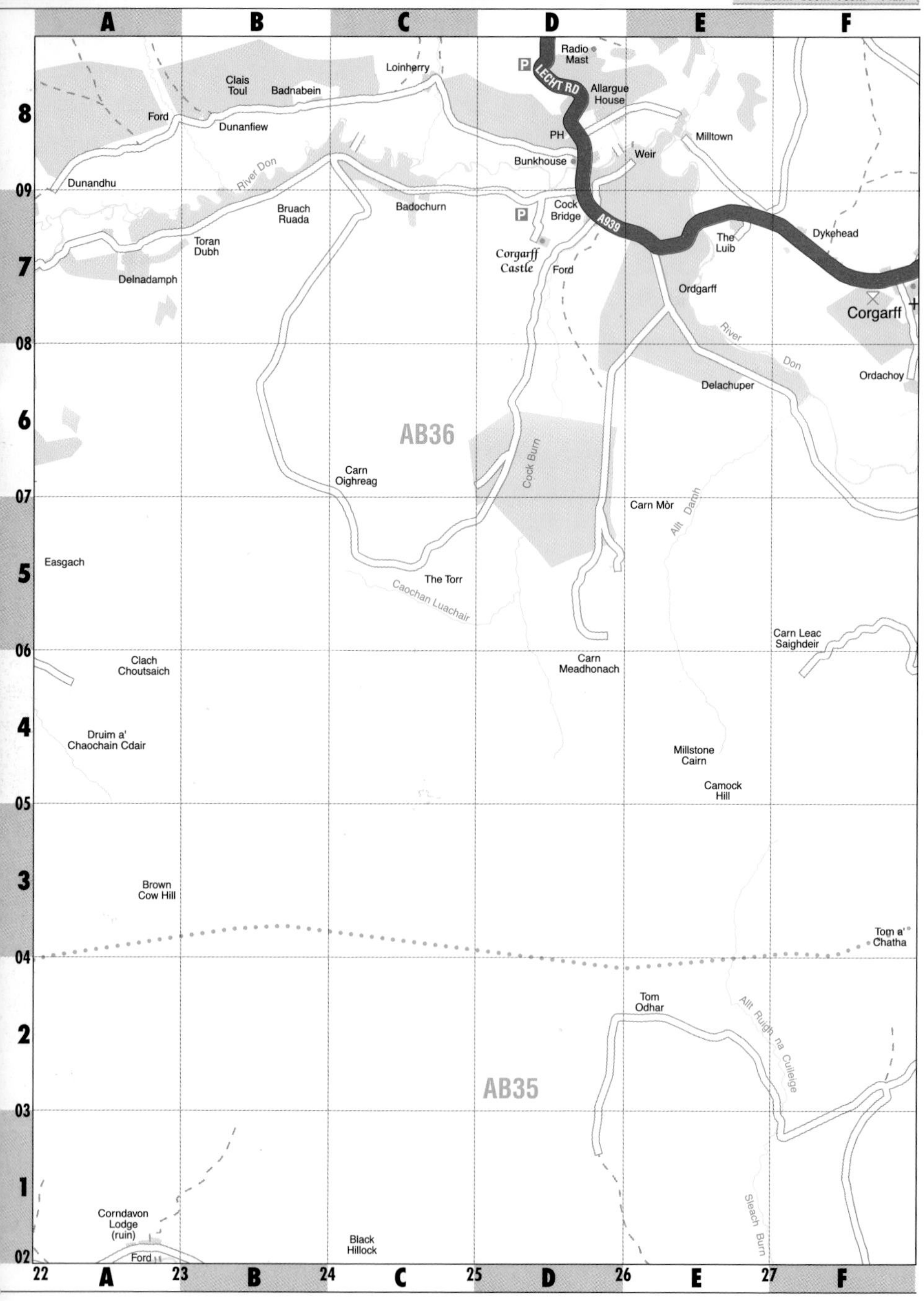
Scale: 1⅓ inches to 1 mile
0 ¼ ½ mile
0 250m 500m 750m 1 km
A B C D E F
Radio Mast
Loinherry
Clais Toul
Badnabein
LECHT RD
Allargue House
Ford
Dunanfiew
PH
Milltown
Bunkhouse
Weir
River Don
Dunandhu
Bruach Ruada
Badochurn
Cock Bridge
A939
Toran Dubh
The Luib
Dykehead
Corgarff Castle
Ford
Delnadamph
Ordgarff
Corgarff
River Don
Ordachoy
Delachuper
AB36
Cock Burn
Carn Oighreag
Carn Mòr
Allt Damh
Easgach
The Torr
Caochan Luachair
Carn Leac Saighdeir
Carn Meadhonach
Clach Choutsaich
Druim a' Chaochain Cdair
Millstone Cairn
Camock Hill
Brown Cow Hill
Tom a' Chatha
Tom Odhar
Allt Ruigh na Cuileige
AB35
Corndavon Lodge (ruin)
Black Hillock
Sleach Burn
Ford
8 09 7 08 6 07 5 06 4 05 3 04 2 03 1 02
22 23 24 25 26 27

102

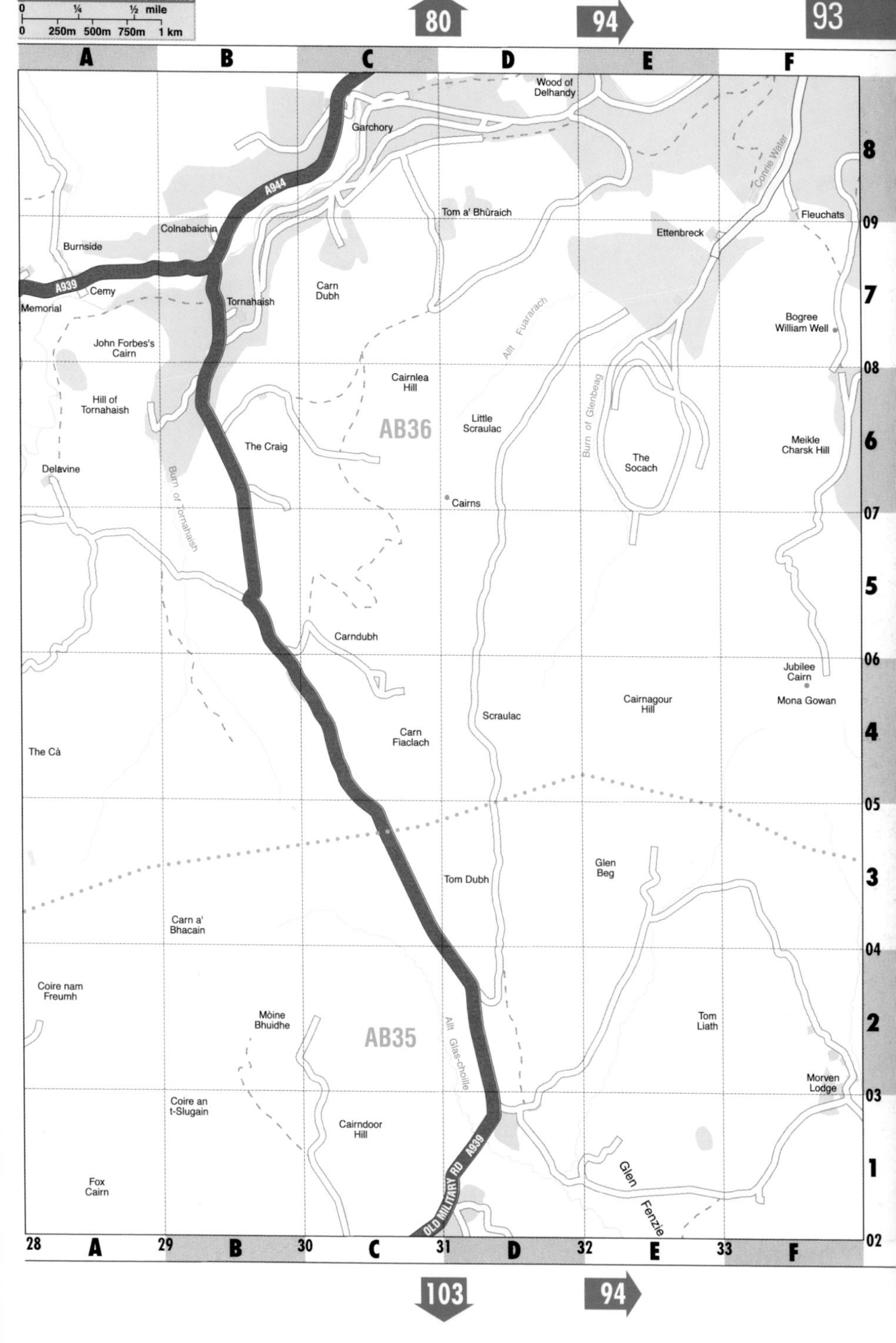
Scale: 1⅓ inches to 1 mile
0 ¼ ½ mile
0 250m 500m 750m 1 km
80
94
A B C D E F
Wood of Delhandy
Garchory
A944
Connie Water
Tom a' Bhùraich
Fleuchats
Colnabaichin
Burnside
Ettenbreck
A939
Cemy
Memorial
Tornahaish
Carn Dubh
Allt Fuararach
Bogree William Well
John Forbes's Cairn
Cairnlea Hill
Burn of Glenbeag
Hill of Tornahaish
AB36
Little Scraulac
The Craig
The Socach
Meikle Charsk Hill
Delavine
Burn of Tornahaish
Cairns
Carndubh
Jubilee Cairn
Cairnagour Hill
Mona Gowan
Scraulac
Carn Fiaclach
The Cà
Glen Beg
Tom Dubh
Carn a' Bhacain
Coire nam Freumh
Mòine Bhuidhe
Tom Liath
AB35
Allt Glas-choille
Morven Lodge
Coire an t-Slugain
Cairndoor Hill
A939
OLD MILITARY RD
Glen Fenzie
Fox Cairn
8 09 7 08 6 07 5 06 4 05 3 04 2 03 1 02
28 29 30 31 32 33
103
94

93
81

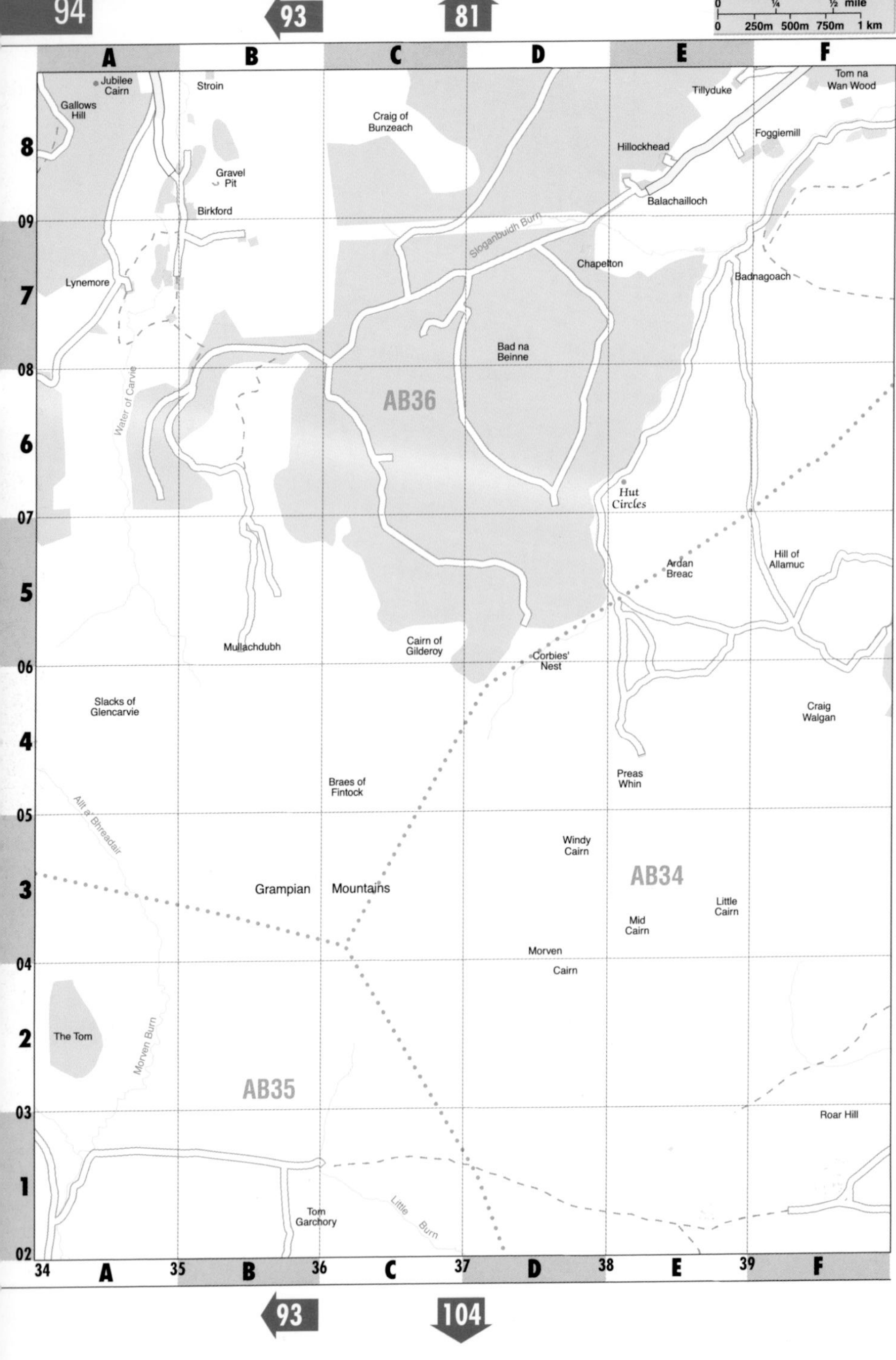
Scale: 1⅓ inches to 1 mile
0 ¼ ½ mile
0 250m 500m 750m 1 km
A B C D E F
Jubilee Cairn
Gallows Hill
Stroin
Craig of Bunzeach
Tillyduke
Tom na Wan Wood
Foggiemill
Hillockhead
Gravel Pit
Birkford
Balachailloch
Sloganbuidh Burn
Chapelton
Lynemore
Badnagoach
Bad na Beinne
Water of Carvie
AB36
Hut Circles
Ardan Breac
Hill of Allamuc
Mullachdubh
Cairn of Gilderoy
Corbies' Nest
Slacks of Glencarvie
Craig Walgan
Braes of Fintock
Preas Whin
Allt a' Bhreadair
Windy Cairn
AB34
Grampian Mountains
Little Cairn
Mid Cairn
Morven
Cairn
The Tom
Morven Burn
AB35
Roar Hill
Tom Garchory
Little Burn
8
09
7
08
6
07
5
06
4
05
3
04
2
03
1
02
34 35 36 37 38 39

93
104

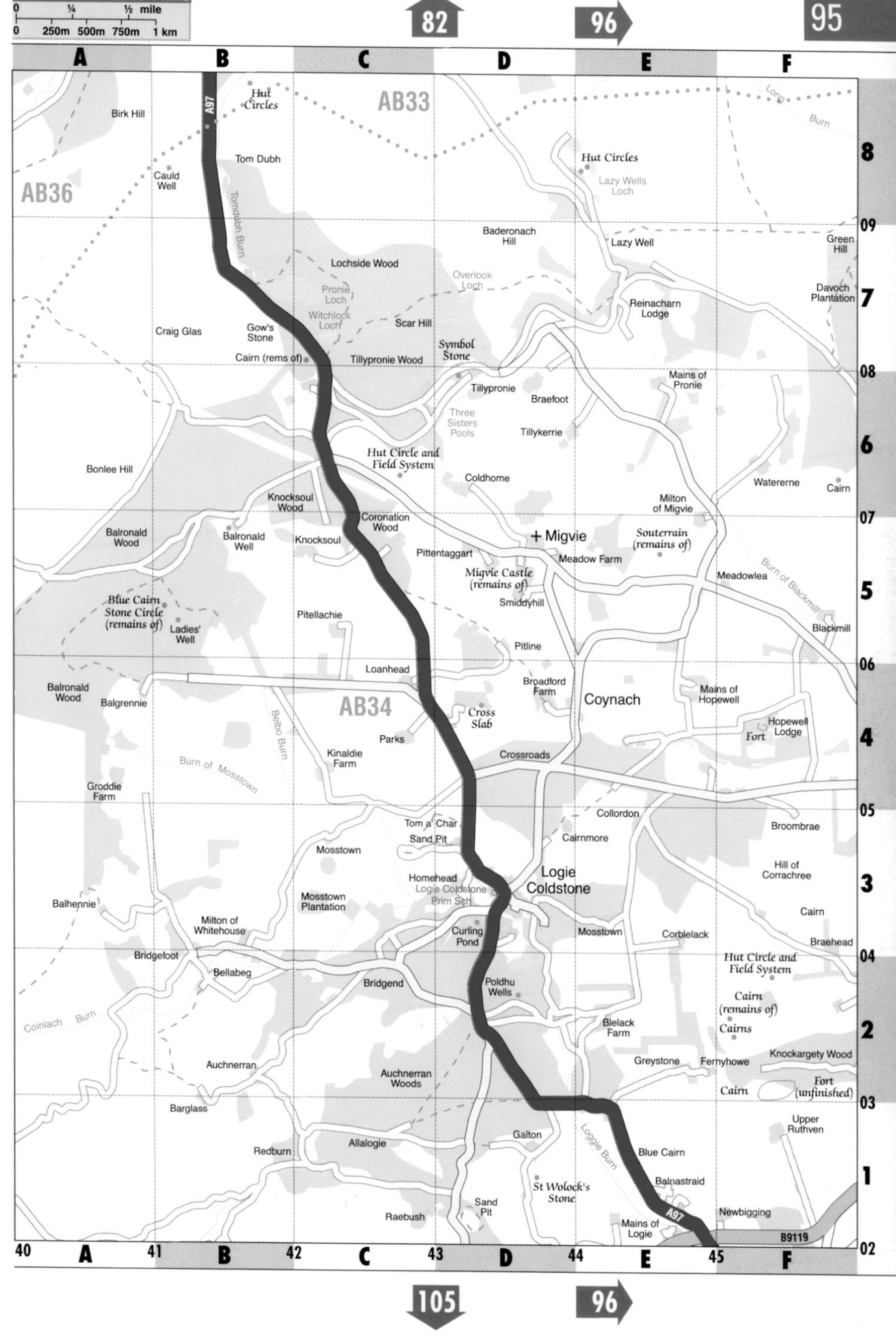
Scale: 1⅓ inches to 1 mile
82
96
A
B
C
D
E
F
A97
Hut Circles
AB33
Birk Hill
Tom Dubh
Cauld Well
AB36
Tomdubh Burn
Hut Circles
Lazy Wells Loch
Baderonach Hill
Lazy Well
Green Hill
Lochside Wood
Overlook Loch
Pronie Loch
Witchlock Loch
Reinacharn Lodge
Davoch Plantation
Craig Glas
Gow's Stone
Scar Hill
Symbol Stone
Cairn (rems of)
Tillypronie Wood
Tillypronie
Braefoot
Mains of Pronie
Three Sisters Pools
Tillykerrie
Hut Circle and Field System
Bonlee Hill
Coldhome
Watererne
Cairn
Knocksoul Wood
Coronation Wood
Milton of Migvie
Balronald Wood
Balronald Well
Knocksoul
Migvie
Souterrain (remains of)
Pittentaggart
Meadow Farm
Migvie Castle (remains of)
Meadowlea
Burn of Blackmill
Smiddyhill
Blue Cairn Stone Circle (remains of)
Ladies' Well
Pitellachie
Blackmill
Pitline
Loanhead
Balronald Wood
Balgrennie
Broadford Farm
Coynach
Mains of Hopewell
AB34
Cross Slab
Hopewell Lodge
Fort
Belbo Burn
Parks
Kinaldie Farm
Crossroads
Burn of Mosstown
Groddie Farm
Collordon
Tom a' Char
Broombrae
Sand Pit
Cairnmore
Mosstown
Hill of Corrachree
Homehead
Logie Coldstone
Logie Coldstone Prim Sch
Mosstown Plantation
Balhennie
Cairn
Milton of Whitehouse
Curling Pond
Mosstown
Corblelack
Braehead
Bridgefoot
Hut Circle and Field System
Bellabeg
Bridgend
Poldhu Wells
Cairn (remains of)
Coinlach Burn
Cairns
Bleack Farm
Auchnerran
Greystone
Fernyhowe
Knockargety Wood
Auchnerran Woods
Fort (unfinished)
Cairn
Barglass
Upper Ruthven
Galton
Loggie Burn
Redburn
Allalogie
Blue Cairn
Balnastraid
St Wolock's Stone
Sand Pit
Raebush
Newbigging
Mains of Logie
B9119
8
09
7
08
6
07
5
06
4
05
3
04
2
03
1
02
40
41
42
43
44
45
105
96

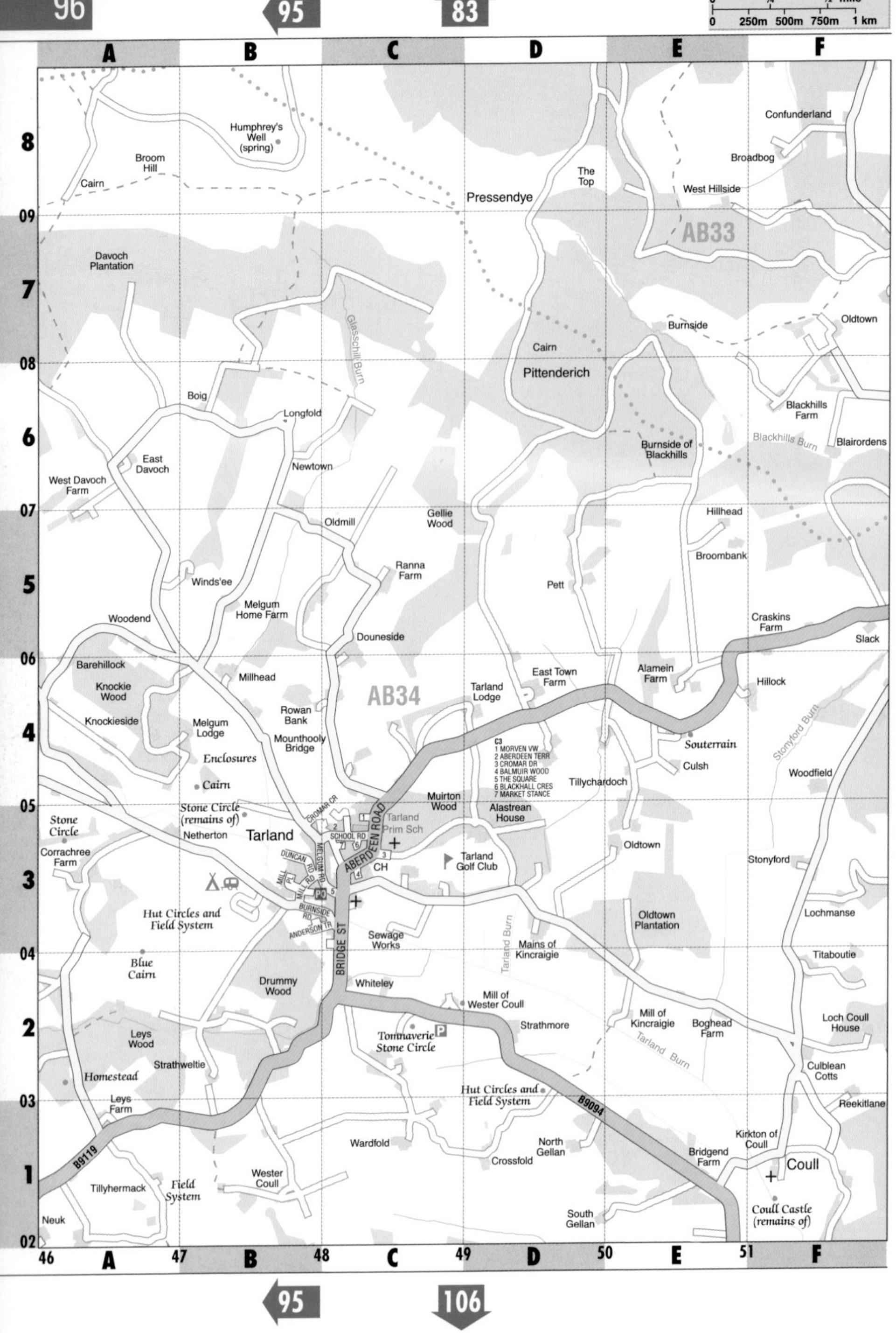
95
83
Scale: 1⅓ inches to 1 mile
0 ¼ ½ mile
0 250m 500m 750m 1 km
A B C D E F
Humphrey's Well (spring)
Broom Hill
Cairn
Pressendye
The Top
Confunderland
Broadbog
West Hillside
AB33
Davoch Plantation
Glasschill Burn
Burnside
Oldtown
Cairn
Pittenderich
Boig
Longfold
Blackhills Farm
Blairordens
Blackhills Burn
Burnside of Blackhills
East Davoch
West Davoch Farm
Newtown
Oldmill
Gellie Wood
Hillhead
Broombank
Ranna Farm
Winds'ee
Pett
Melgum Home Farm
Woodend
Douneside
Craskins Farm
Slack
Barehillock
Knockie Wood
Millhead
East Town Farm
Alamein Farm
Hillock
Tarland Lodge
AB34
Rowan Bank
Knockieside
Melgum Lodge
Mounthooly Bridge
Souterrain
Culsh
Stonyford Burn
Enclosures
Woodfield
C3
1 MORVEN VW
2 ABERDEEN TERR
3 CROMAR DR
4 BALMUIR WOOD
5 THE SQUARE
6 BLACKHALL CRES
7 MARKET STANCE
Tillychardoch
Cairn
Stone Circle (remains of)
Muirton Wood
Alastrean House
Stone Circle
CROMAR CR
Tarland Prim Sch
ABERDEEN ROAD
Netherton
Tarland
SCHOOL RD
Corrachree Farm
DUNCAN RD
MELGUM RD
Tarland Golf Club
Oldtown
Stonyford
CH
MILL PL
MILL RD
BURNSIDE RD
ANDERSON TR
Hut Circles and Field System
Lochmanse
Oldtown Plantation
Sewage Works
BRIDGE ST
Tarland Burn
Mains of Kincraigie
Titaboutie
Blue Cairn
Drummy Wood
Whiteley
Mill of Wester Coull
Strathmore
Mill of Kincraigie
Boghead Farm
Loch Coull House
Leys Wood
Tomnaverie Stone Circle
Tarland Burn
Strathweltie
Culblean Cotts
Homestead
Hut Circles and Field System
Leys Farm
B9094
Reekitlane
Wardfold
North Gellan
Kirkton of Coull
B9119
Crossfold
Bridgend Farm
Coull
Tillyhermack
Field System
Wester Coull
Coull Castle (remains of)
Neuk
South Gellan
8 09 7 08 6 07 5 06 4 05 3 04 2 03 1 02
46 47 48 49 50 51
95
106

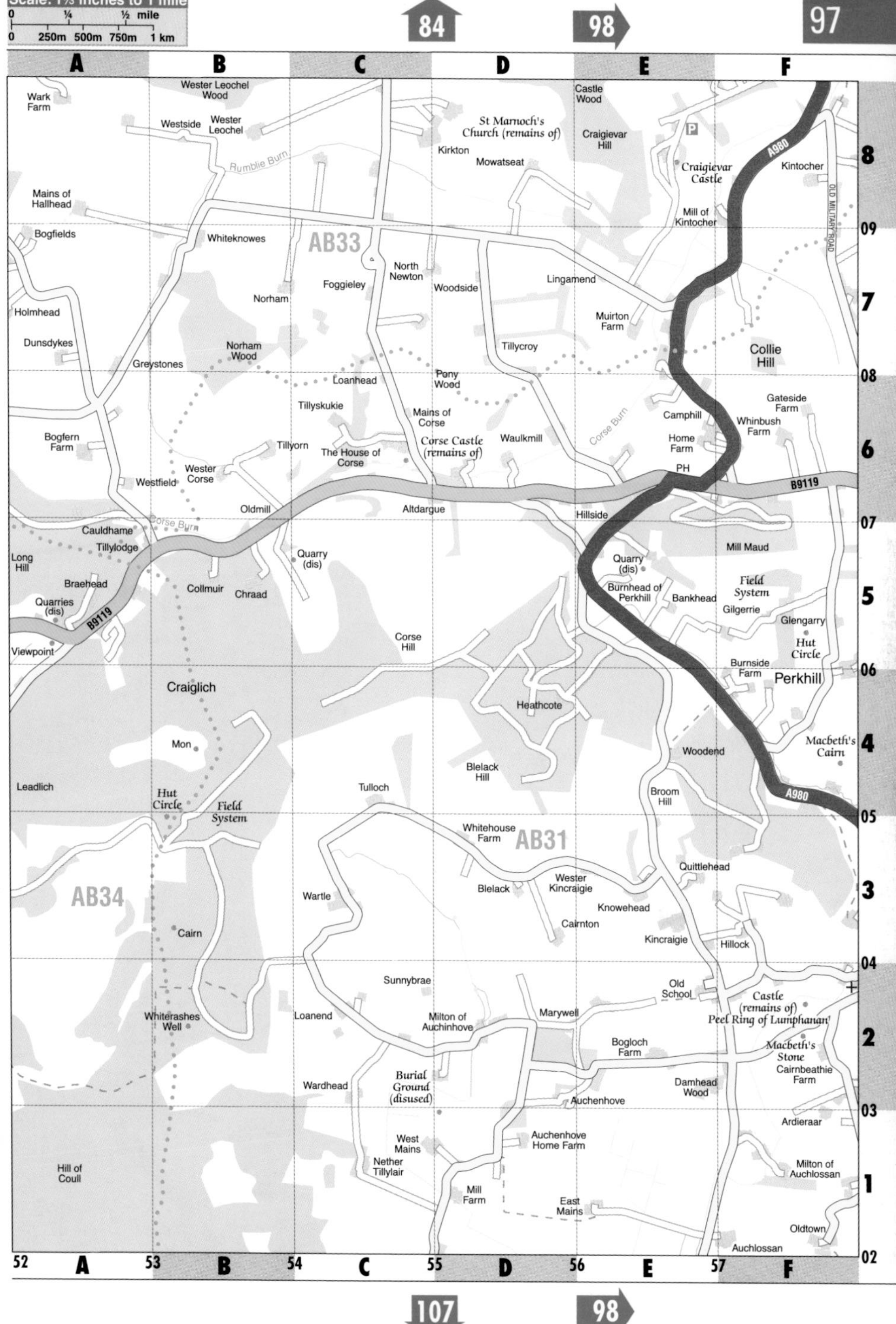
Scale: 1⅓ inches to 1 mile
0 ¼ ½ mile
0 250m 500m 750m 1 km
84
98
A B C D E F
Wark Farm
Wester Leochel Wood
Westside
Wester Leochel
Rumblie Burn
Castle Wood
St Marnoch's Church (remains of)
Craigievar Hill
Kirkton
Mowatseat
Craigievar Castle
Kintocher
A980
OLD MILITARY ROAD
Mains of Hallhead
Mill of Kintocher
Bogfields
Whiteknowes
AB33
North Newton
Foggieley
Woodside
Lingamend
Norham
Holmhead
Muirton Farm
Dunsdykes
Norham Wood
Tillycroy
Collie Hill
Greystones
Loanhead
Pony Wood
Tillyskukie
Mains of Corse
Gateside Farm
Camphill
Whinbush Farm
Bogfern Farm
Corse Castle (remains of)
Waulkmill
Corse Burn
Home Farm
Tillyorn
The House of Corse
Wester Corse
Westfield
PH
B9119
Oldmill
Altdargue
Hillside
Corse Burn
Cauldhame
Tillylodge
Quarry (dis)
Mill Maud
Long Hill
Quarry (dis)
Braehead
Collmuir
Chraad
Burnhead of Perkhill
Bankhead
Field System
Quarries (dis)
Gilgerrie
Glengarry
B9119
Viewpoint
Corse Hill
Hut Circle
Burnside Farm
Perkhill
Craiglich
Heathcote
Mon
Macbeth's Cairn
Woodend
Blelack Hill
Leadlich
Tulloch
Broom Hill
Hut Circle
Field System
A980
Whitehouse Farm
AB31
Quittlehead
Wester Kincraigie
Blelack
AB34
Wartle
Knowehead
Cairnton
Cairn
Kincraigie
Hillock
Sunnybrae
Old School
Castle (remains of)
Peel Ring of Lumphanan
Whiterashes Well
Loanend
Milton of Auchinhove
Marywell
Bogloch Farm
Macbeth's Stone
Cairnbeathie Farm
Burial Ground (disused)
Wardhead
Damhead Wood
Auchenhove
Ardieraar
West Mains
Auchenhove Home Farm
Nether Tillylair
Milton of Auchlossan
Hill of Coull
Mill Farm
East Mains
Oldtown
Auchlossan
52 53 54 55 56 57
8 09 7 08 6 07 5 06 4 05 3 04 2 03 1 02
107
98

97
85

Scale: 1⅓ inches to 1 mile
0 ¼ ½ mile
0 250m 500m 750m 1 km

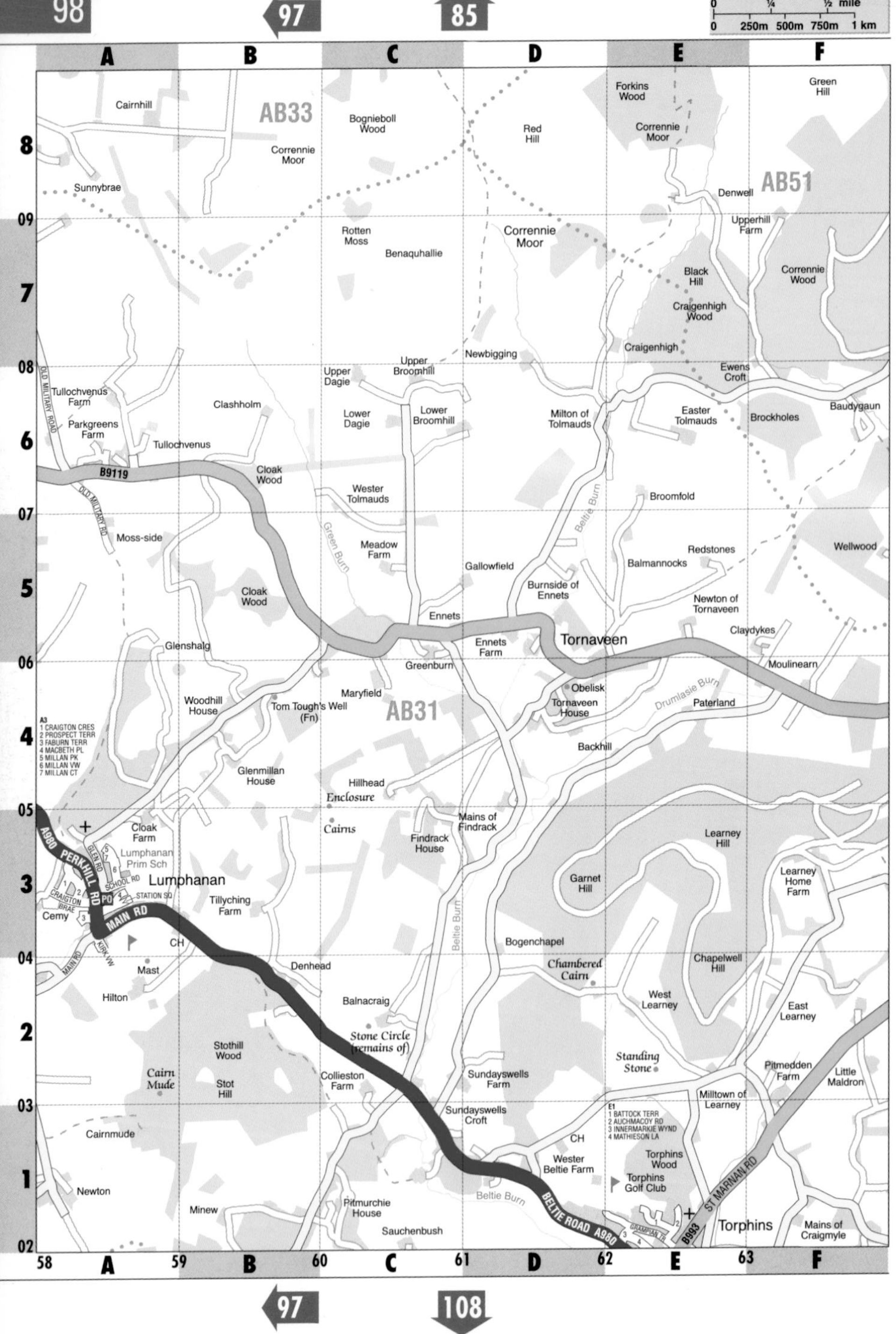

97
108

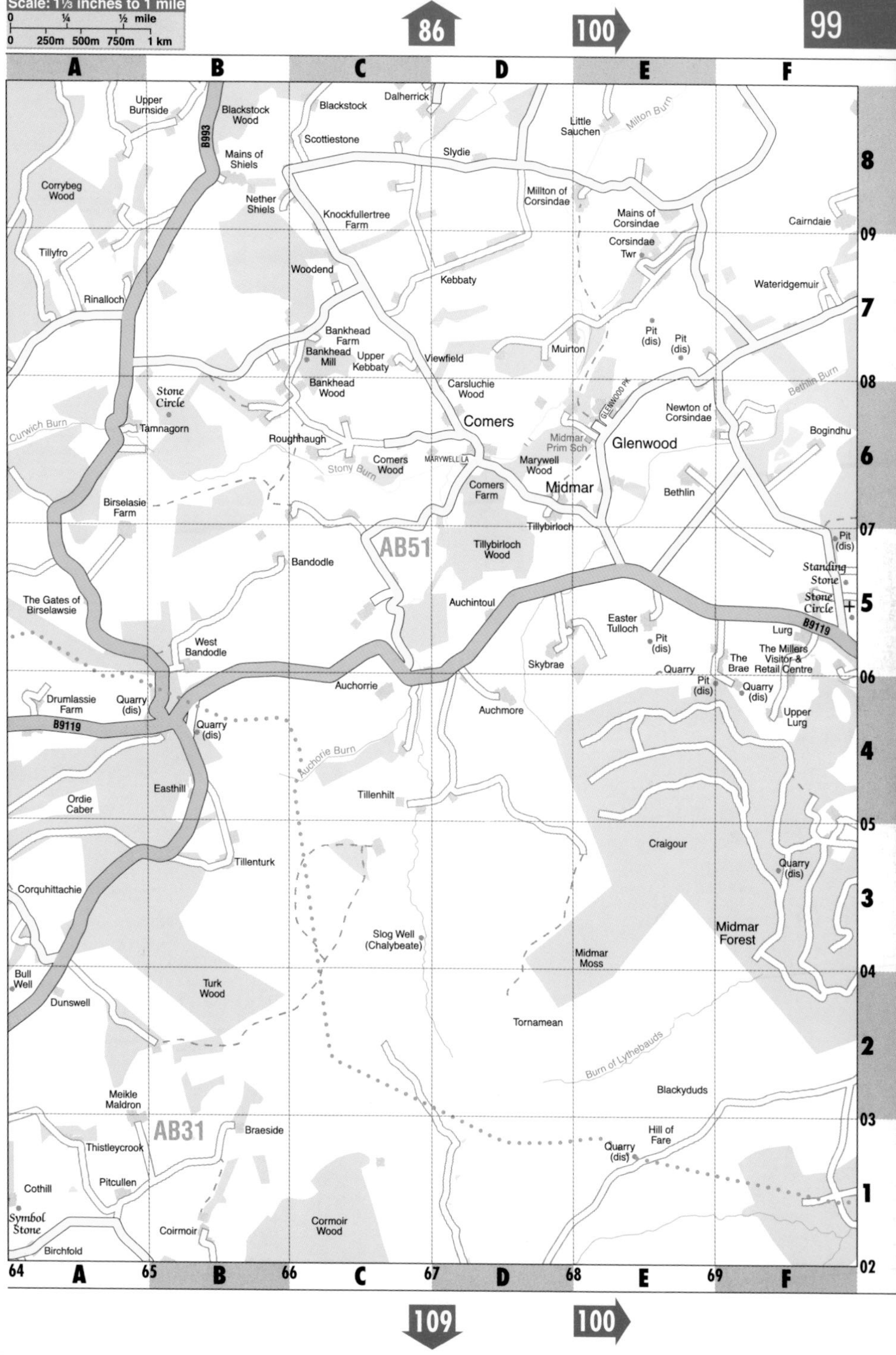
A
B
C
D
E
F
Upper Burnside
Blackstock Wood
Blackstock
Dalherrick
Little Sauchen
Milton Burn
Scottiestone
B993
Mains of Shiels
Slydie
8
Corrybeg Wood
Nether Shiels
Knockfullertree Farm
Millton of Corsindae
Mains of Corsindae
Cairndaie
09
Tillyfro
Corsindae Twr
Woodend
Kebbaty
Wateridgemuir
Rinalloch
7
Bankhead Farm
Pit (dis)
Pit (dis)
Bankhead Mill
Upper Kebbaty
Viewfield
Muirton
Stone Circle
Bankhead Wood
Carsluchie Wood
Glenwood Pk
Newton of Corsindae
Bethlin Burn
08
Curwich Burn
Tamnagorn
Comers
Glenwood
Bogindhu
Roughhaugh
Midmar Prim Sch
Comers Wood
Marywell La
Marywell Wood
6
Stony Burn
Comers Farm
Midmar
Bethlin
Birselasie Farm
Tillybirloch
07
Pit (dis)
AB51
Tillybirloch Wood
Bandodle
Standing Stone
The Gates of Birselawsie
Auchintoul
Stone Circle
5
Easter Tulloch
Lurg
B9119
West Bandodle
Pit (dis)
The Millers Visitor & Retail Centre
Skybrae
The Brae
Quarry
06
Auchorrie
Pit (dis)
Quarry (dis)
Drumlassie Farm
Quarry (dis)
Auchmore
Upper Lurg
B9119
Quarry (dis)
4
Auchorie Burn
Easthill
Tillenhilt
Ordie Caber
05
Craigour
Tillenturk
Quarry (dis)
Corquhittachie
3
Slog Well (Chalybeate)
Midmar Forest
Midmar Moss
Bull Well
04
Turk Wood
Dunswell
Tornamean
2
Burn of Lythebauds
Blackyduds
Meikle Maldron
03
AB31
Braeside
Hill of Fare
Quarry (dis)
Thistleycrook
Cothill
Pitcullen
1
Symbol Stone
Cormoir Wood
Coirmoir
Birchfold
02
64
65
66
67
68
69

99
87

Scale: 1⅓ inches to 1 mile

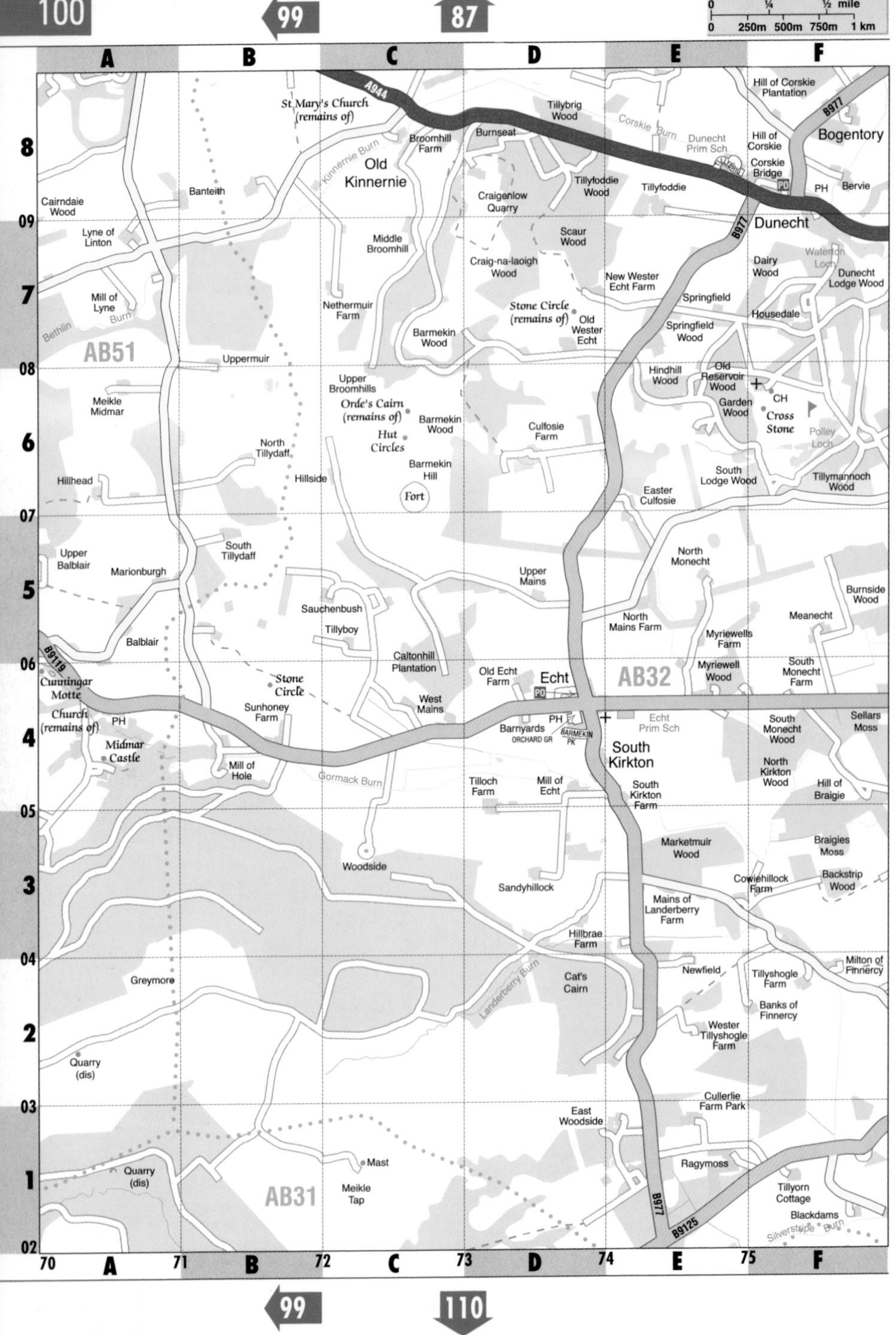

99
110

Scale: 1⅓ inches to 1 mile

0 ¼ ½ mile

0 250m 500m 750m 1 km

88
161

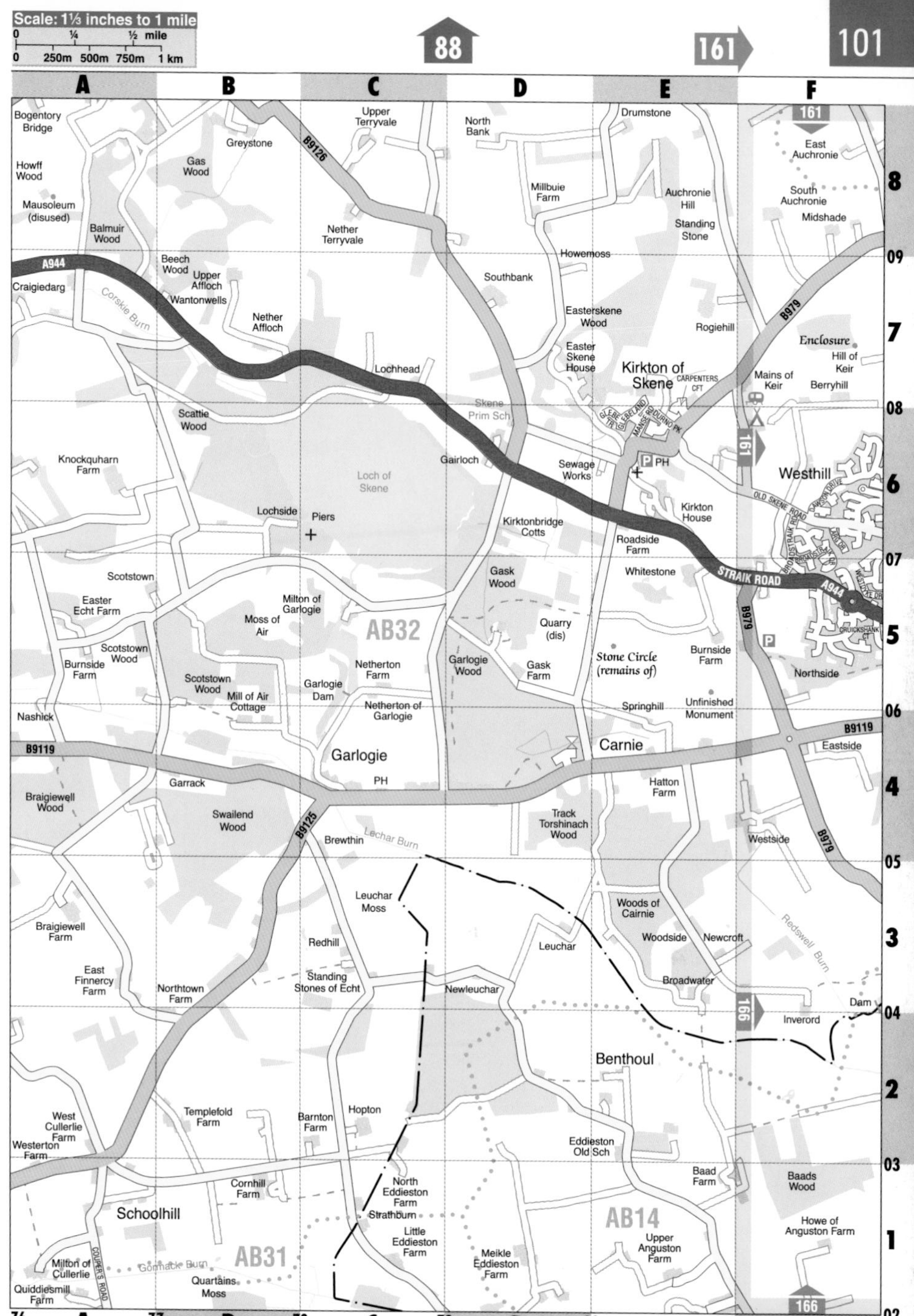

111
166

For full street detail of the highlighted area see pages 161 and 166.

92

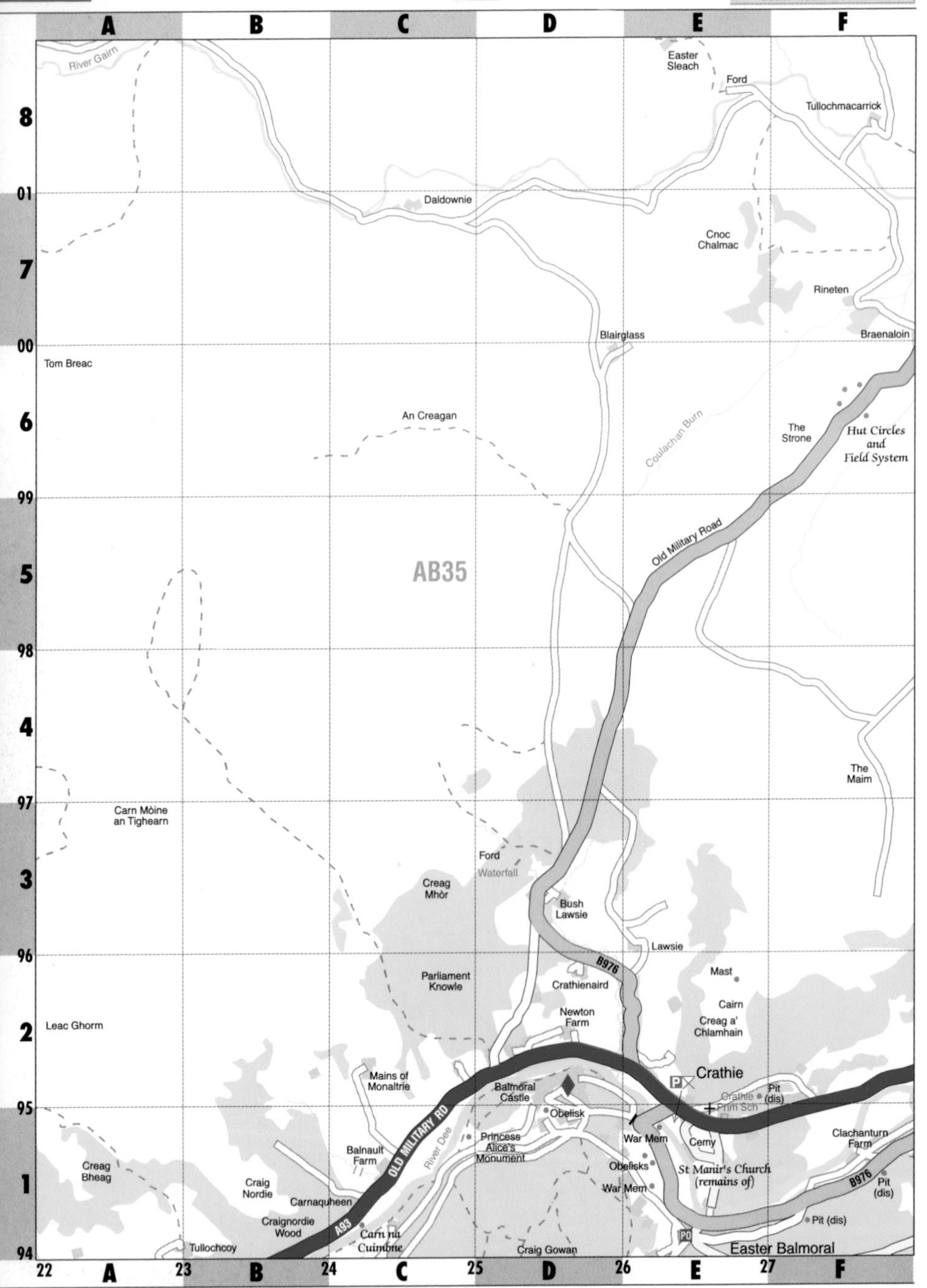

Scale: 1⅓ inches to 1 mile
0 ¼ ½ mile
0 250m 500m 750m 1 km
A B C D E F
8 01 7 00 6 99 5 98 4 97 3 96 2 95 1 94
22 23 24 25 26 27
River Gairn
Easter Sleach
Ford
Tullochmacarrick
Daldownie
Cnoc Chalmac
Rineten
Blairglass
Braenaloin
Tom Breac
An Creagan
Coulachan Burn
The Strone
Hut Circles and Field System
Old Military Road
AB35
The Maim
Carn Mòine an Tighearn
Ford
Waterfall
Creag Mhòr
Bush Lawsie
Lawsie
Parliament Knowle
B976
Crathienaird
Mast
Cairn
Newton Farm
Creag a' Chlamhain
Leac Ghorm
Mains of Monaltrie
Crathie
Balmoral Castle
Pit (dis)
Crathie
Prim Sch
Obelisk
Clachanturn Farm
OLD MILITARY RD
Princess Alice's Monument
War Mem
Cemy
Balnault Farm
River Dee
Obelisks
St Manir's Church (remains of)
Creag Bheag
Craig Nordie
War Mem
B976
Pit (dis)
Carnaquheen
Craignordie Wood
Pit (dis)
A93
Carn na Cuimhne
Tullochcoy
Craig Gowan
Easter Balmoral

115

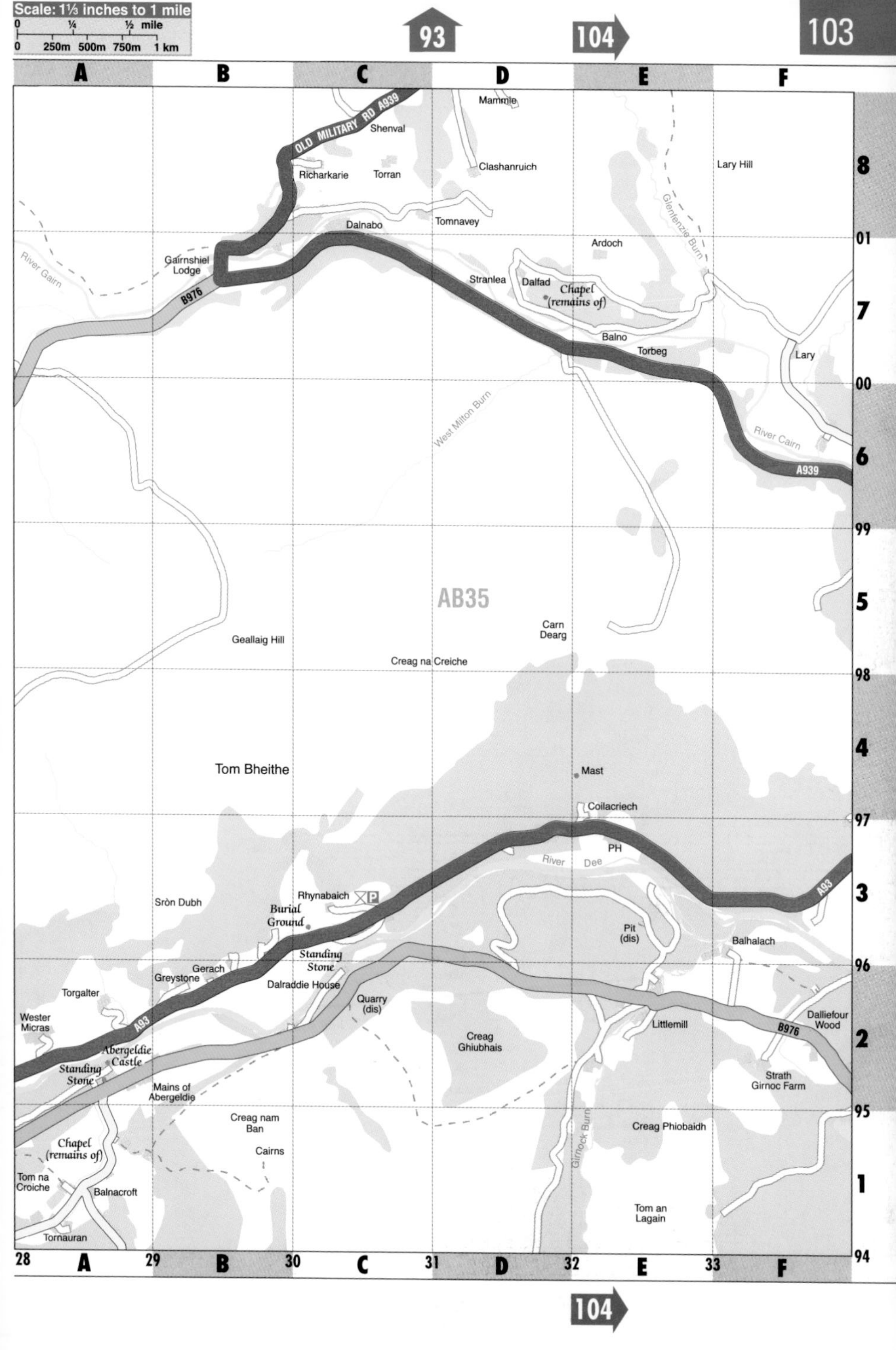

Scale: 1⅓ inches to 1 mile
0 ¼ ½ mile
0 250m 500m 750m 1 km
93
104
A B C D E F
OLD MILITARY RD A939
Mammie
Shenval
Clashanruich
Lary Hill
Richarkarie
Torran
Tomnavey
Dalnabo
Glenfenzie Burn
Ardoch
River Gairn
Gairnshiel Lodge
B976
Stranlea
Dalfad
Chapel (remains of)
Balno
Torbeg
Lary
West Milton Burn
River Cairn
A939
AB35
Carn Dearg
Geallaig Hill
Creag na Creiche
Tom Bheithe
Mast
Coilacriech
PH
River Dee
Rhynabaich
Sròn Dubh
Burial Ground
A93
Pit (dis)
Standing Stone
Balhalach
Gerach
Greystone
Dalraddie House
Torgalter
Quarry (dis)
Dalliefour Wood
Wester Micras
Littlemill
B976
Abergeldie Castle
Standing Stone
Creag Ghiubhais
Mains of Abergeldie
Strath Girnoc Farm
Creag nam Ban
Creag Phiobaidh
Girnock Burn
Chapel (remains of)
Cairns
Tom na Croiche
Balnacroft
Tom an Lagain
Tornauran
28 29 30 31 32 33
8 01 7 00 6 99 5 98 4 97 3 96 2 95 1 94

104

103
94

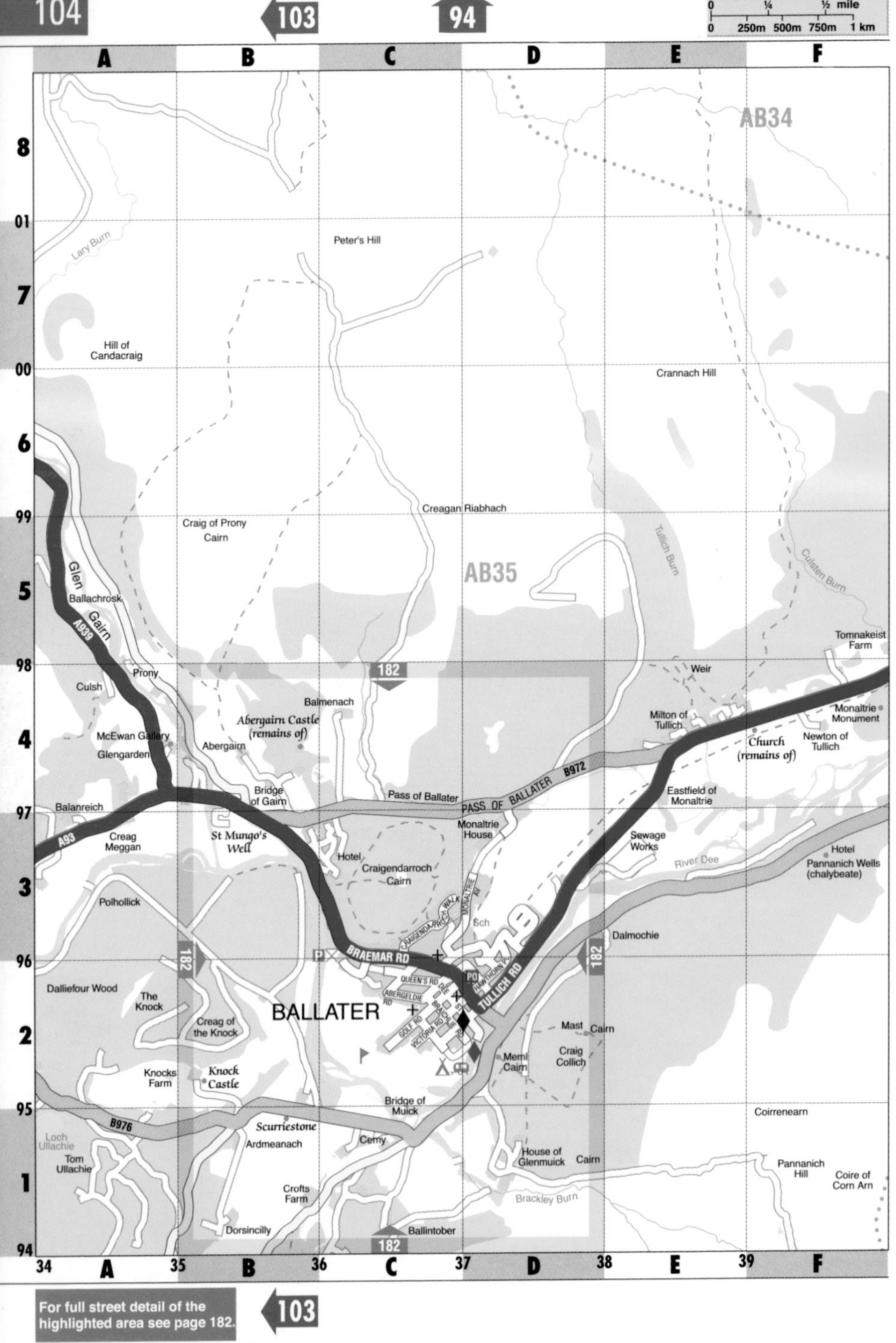

For full street detail of the highlighted area see page 182.
103

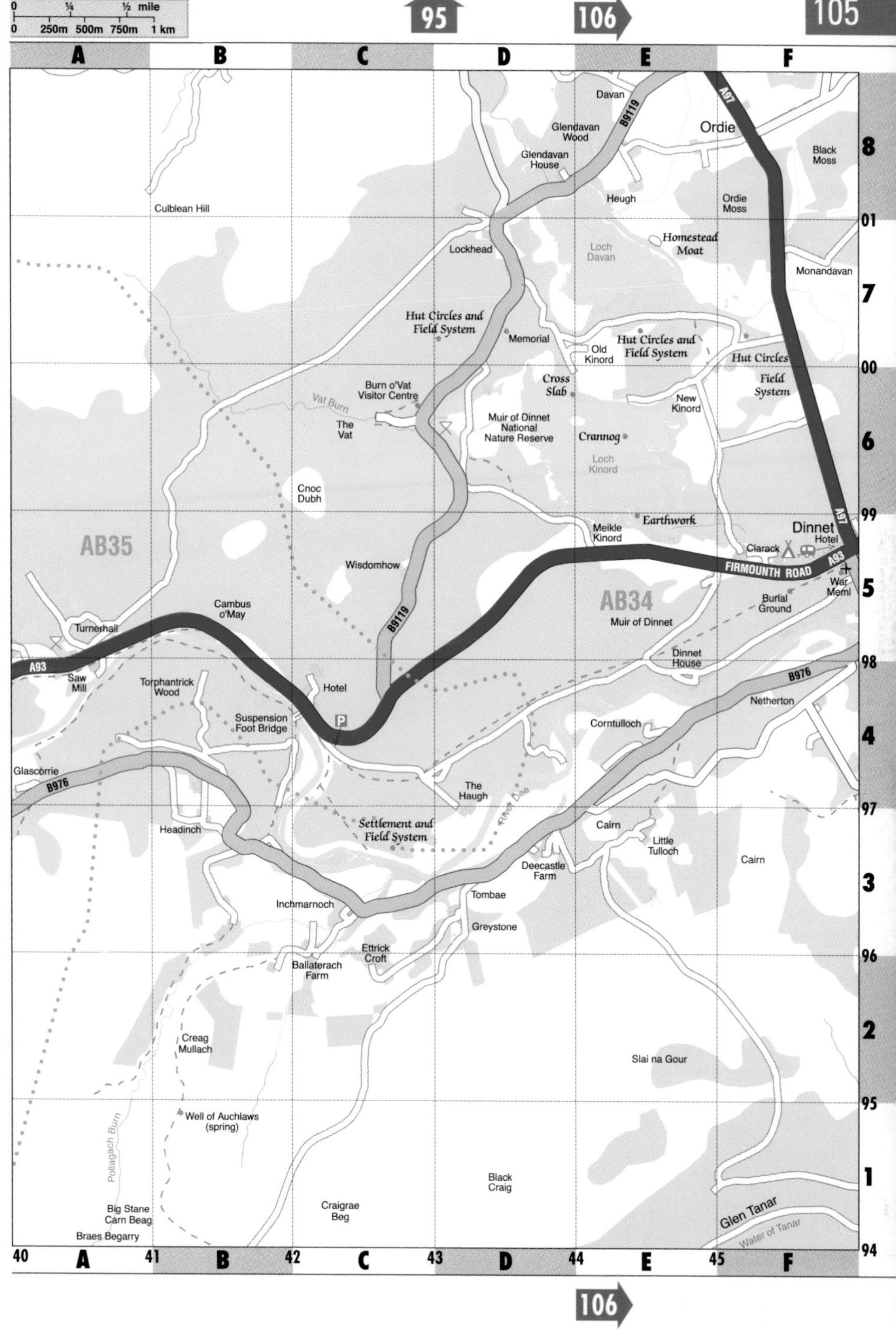

Scale: 1⅓ inches to 1 mile
0 ¼ ½ mile
0 250m 500m 750m 1 km
95
106
Davan
Glendavan Wood
Ordie
Glendavan House
Black Moss
Culblean Hill
Heugh
Ordie Moss
Homestead Moat
Loch Davan
Lockhead
Monandavan
Hut Circles and Field System
Memorial
Old Kinord
Hut Circles and Field System
Hut Circles
Field System
Cross Slab
Burn o'Vat Visitor Centre
Vat Burn
The Vat
Muir of Dinnet National Nature Reserve
New Kinord
Crannog
Loch Kinord
Cnoc Dubh
Meikle Kinord
Earthwork
Dinnet
Hotel
Clarack
AB35
Wisdomhow
FIRMOUNTH ROAD
AB34
War Meml
Burial Ground
Cambus o'May
Muir of Dinnet
Turnerhall
Dinnet House
A93
A97
B9119
B976
Saw Mill
Torphantrick Wood
Hotel
Netherton
Suspension Foot Bridge
Corntulloch
Glascorrie
The Haugh
River Dee
Headinch
Settlement and Field System
Cairn
Little Tulloch
Cairn
Deecastle Farm
Tombae
Inchmarnoch
Greystone
Ettrick Croft
Ballaterach Farm
Creag Mullach
Slai na Gour
Well of Auchlaws (spring)
Pollagach Burn
Black Craig
Big Stane Carn Beag
Craigrae Beg
Glen Tanar
Water of Tanar
Braes Begarry

106

105
96

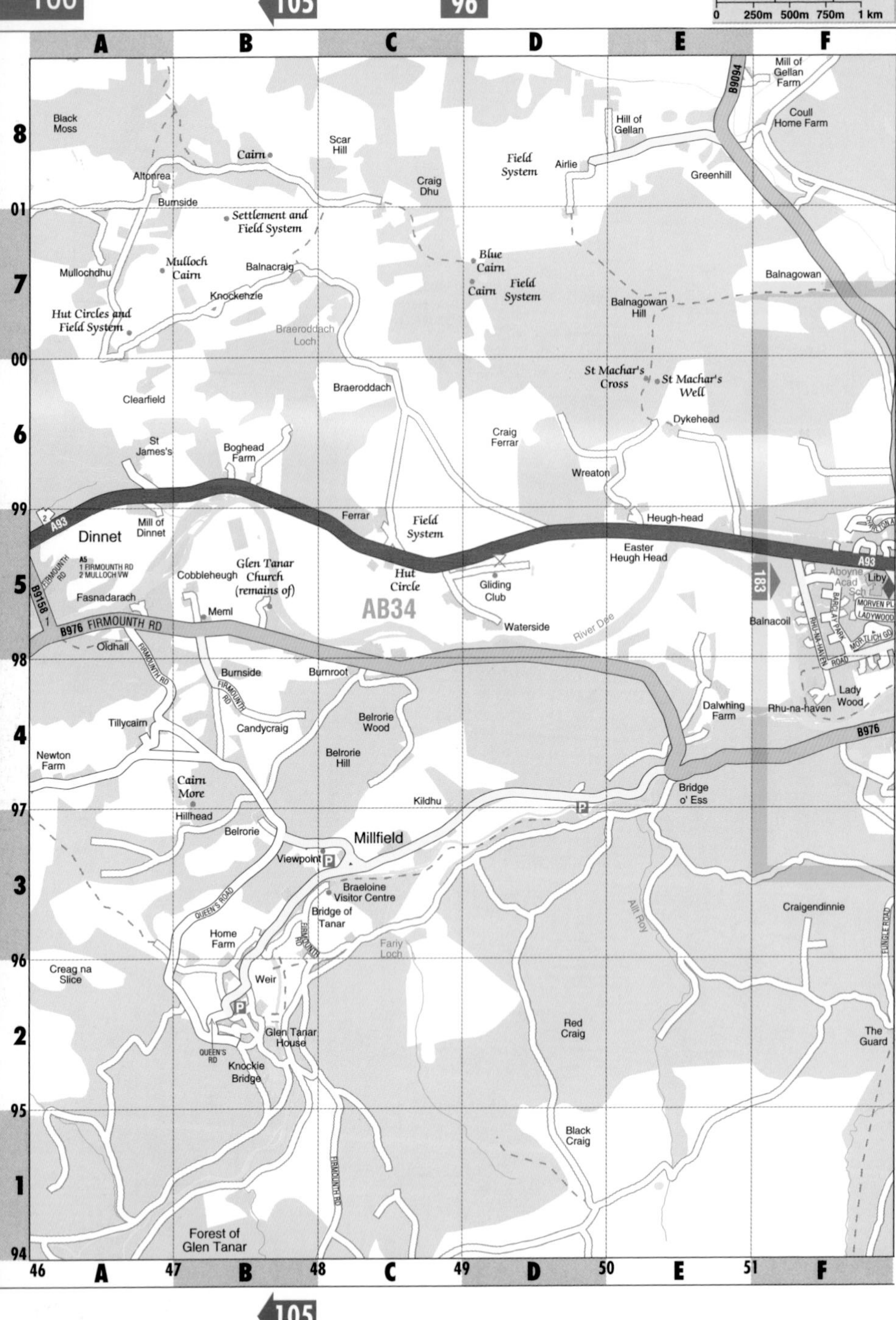
Scale 1⅓ inches to 1 mile
0 ¼ ½ mile
0 250m 500m 750m 1 km
A B C D E F
8 01 7 00 6 99 5 98 4 97 3 96 2 95 1 94
46 47 48 49 50 51
Black Moss
Cairn
Scar Hill
Field System
Airlie
Hill of Gellan
Mill of Gellan Farm
Coull Home Farm
B9094
Altonrea
Burnside
Craig Dhu
Greenhill
Settlement and Field System
Mulloch Cairn
Mullochdhu
Balnacraig
Knockenzie
Blue Cairn
Cairn
Field System
Balnagowan
Balnagowan Hill
Hut Circles and Field System
Braeroddach Loch
St Machar's Cross
St Machar's Well
Clearfield
Braeroddach
Dykehead
Craig Ferrar
St James's
Boghead Farm
Wreaton
Heugh-head
A93
Dinnet
Mill of Dinnet
Ferrar
Field System
Easter Heugh Head
A5
1 FIRMOUNTH RD
2 MULLOCH VW
Glen Tanar Church (remains of)
Cobbleheugh
Hut Circle
Gliding Club
183
Aboyne Acad Sch
Liby
B9158
Fasnadarach
Meml
AB34
MORVEN PL
LADYWOOD
B976 FIRMOUNTH RD
Waterside
River Dee
Balnacoil
BARCLAY PARK
RHU-NA-HAVEN ROAD
MORTLICH GD
Oldhall
FIRMOUNTH RD
Burnside
Burnroot
Lady Wood
Dalwhing Farm
Rhu-na-haven
Belrorie Wood
Tillycairn
Candycraig
B976
Newton Farm
Belrorie Hill
Cairn More
Bridge o' Ess
Kildhu
Hillhead
Belrorie
Millfield
Viewpoint
Braeloine Visitor Centre
QUEEN'S ROAD
Bridge of Tanar
Allt Roy
Craigendinnie
Home Farm
Fariy Loch
FUNGLE ROAD
Creag na Slice
Weir
Red Craig
The Guard
Glen Tanar House
QUEEN'S RD
Knockie Bridge
Black Craig
Forest of Glen Tanar

105

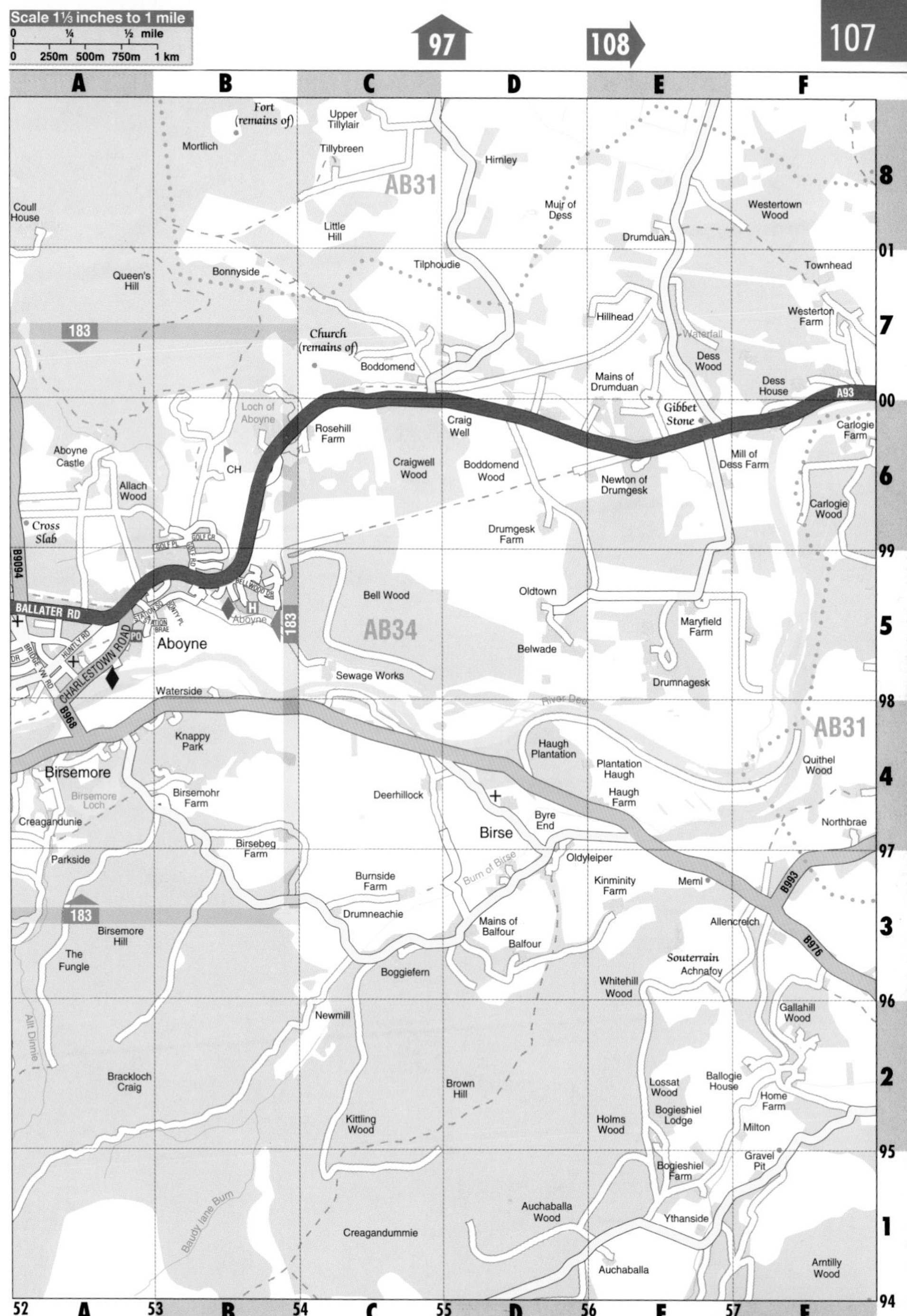

108

For full street detail of the highlighted area see page 183.

107
98

E8
1 EDINGIGHT WYND
2 GROVE TERR
3 ANNESLEY GR
4 INCHLEY TERR
5 ANNESLEY PK
6 FARE VW
7 BREBNER PL
8 KERLOCH CRES
9 VILLAGE FARM CT
10 BRIDGE CRES
11 WILLIAM ST
12 BELTIE RD
13 STATION RD
14 OLD MART RD
15 COWIE WYND
16 MONBODDO RD
17 INCHLEY PL
18 CRAIGOUR AVE
19 KINNAIRDY CL
20 KINNAIRDY TERR

Scale: 1⅓ inches to 1 mile
0 ¼ ½ mile
0 250m 500m 750m 1 km

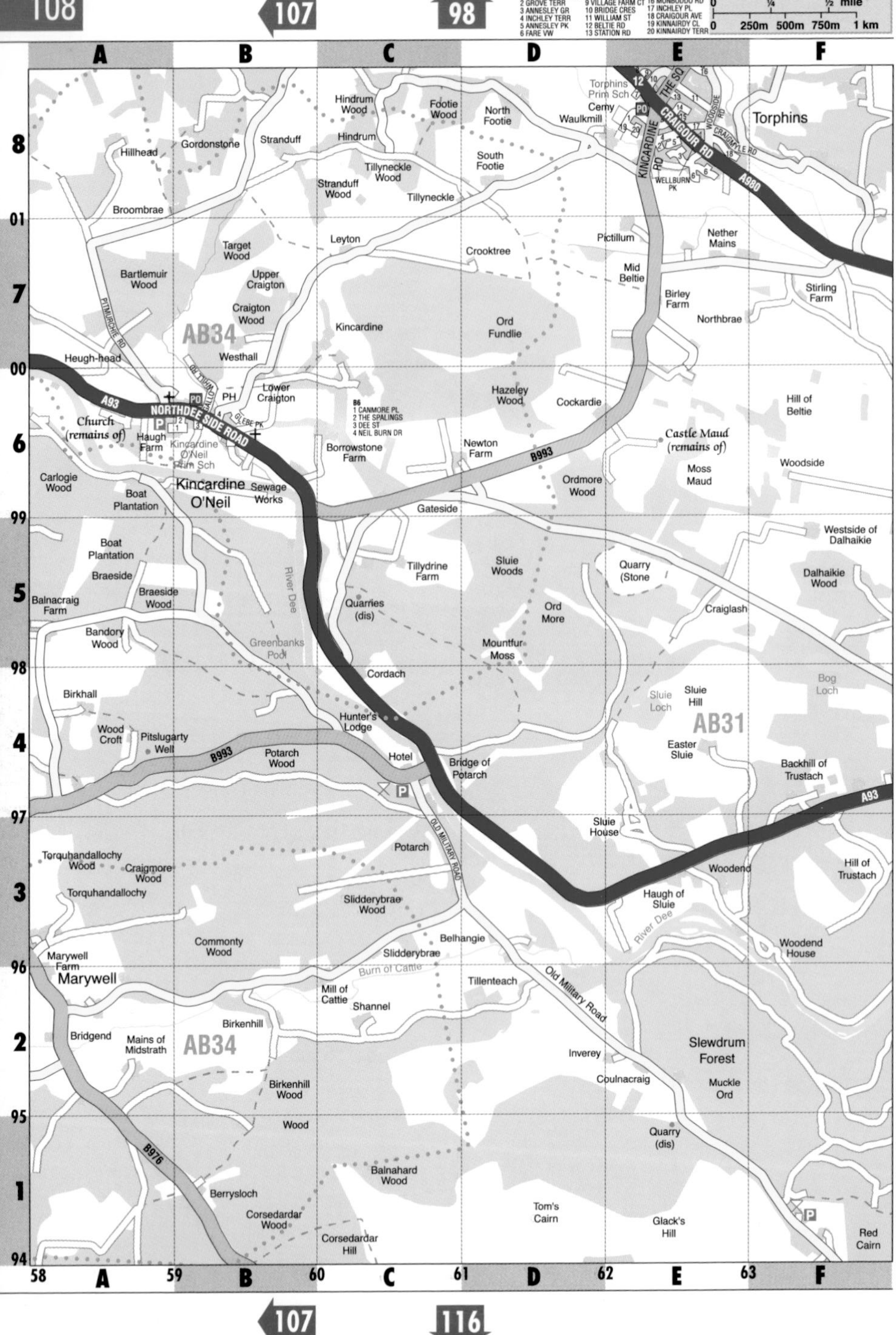

107
116

A B C D E F

Blairhead
Quarry (dis)
Sand & Gravel Pit
Craigrath
Fordie Farm
Blairhead Wood
Hill of Corfeidly
8
Wester Mains
Quarry (dis)
The Skairs
Ferretfold
Quarries (dis)
Knockendash Wood
Quarry (dis)
Slant Ride Covert
Wester Campfield
Campfield House
Scook Covert
Brownhill
01
Craigour Farm
Home Wood
Caterans' Howe Covert
Tillyfaud Wood
Moss-side
Leabank
Corfeidly
Craigbeg
PO
Hill of Kennerty
Burnhead Farm
7
Craigbeg Wood
Milton of Campfield
Greenburn
Cluny Crichton Farm
Dam Wood
Kynoch Plantation
Kennerty Farm
Spy Brae Wood
Craigbeg Wood
High Dam Wood
00
Mains of Easter Beltie
Craignarb
Spy Brae Wood
Standing Stones
Cluny Crichton Castle (remains of)
Bogarn Wood
Water Tower
Larnach Wood
Brockton
Mains of Glassel
Knockings Wood
Hotel
6
Glassel
Mill Wood
Broad Wood
Roadside Belts
Dykehead
Brockton Wood
B977
Corbie Den Wood
99
Broomhill Wood
The Brathens
Balwearie
Mill of Raemoir
Cluny Leys Wood
Marchnear
West Brathens
Brathens
Banchory Research Station
Mill Wood
Mains of Dalhaikie
Bogfish Wood
5
Pittenkerrie
AB31
Bridgend
Brathens Moss
Brathens Wood
Burn of Canny
98
184
Hamlyn's Plantation
Newton of Leys
Lochhead of Leys
RAEMOIR RD
Target Wood
Brathens Wood
Woodhead
Jampots Wood
Aulddeer Wood
Upper Lochton Wood
4
Bridge of Canny
Glencommon Wood
A980
Corsee Wood
BANCHORY
Glencommon Farm
Home Farm
Inchmarlo Golf Course
East Mains
97
UPPER LOCHTON
Waulkmill
Garden Wood
Brathens Wood
QUEENS CT
Inchmarlo
QUEEN'S DR
Glen O'Dee
UPPER ARBEADIE ROAD
Corsee Wood
CH
Clayholes
Reservoirs
H
Trustach Cottage
Burnett Park
3
CORSEE RD
HIGHFIELD AVE
Sports Ground
WOODSIDE RD
River Dee
HILLCROFT RD
Hill of Cairnton
A93
BURNETT RD
ARBEADIE RD
LAWSON AV
WILSON RD
CORSEE HL
MOUNT ST
184
CORSEE ROAD
Blackhall
LAVENDER GR
GRANT RD
96
Gravel Pits
Cairnton House
RAMSAY ROAD
Blackhall Research Station
PO
THE SQUARE
STATION RD
Grove Cott
War Meml
CH
2
Liby
DEE ST
Goauch Wood
Chalybeate Spring
Bridge of Dee
B974
Deebank
Blackhall Forest
Kirkton Muir
95
Goauch Wood
P
Craigloch Wood
Auchattie
1
Hill of Tillylair
Wester Invery Farm
B974
Twr Hill of Goauch
Scolty Wood
Kennel Wood
Tillylair
184
94

64 A 65 B 66 C 67 D 68 E 69 F

For full street detail of the highlighted area see page 184.

109
100

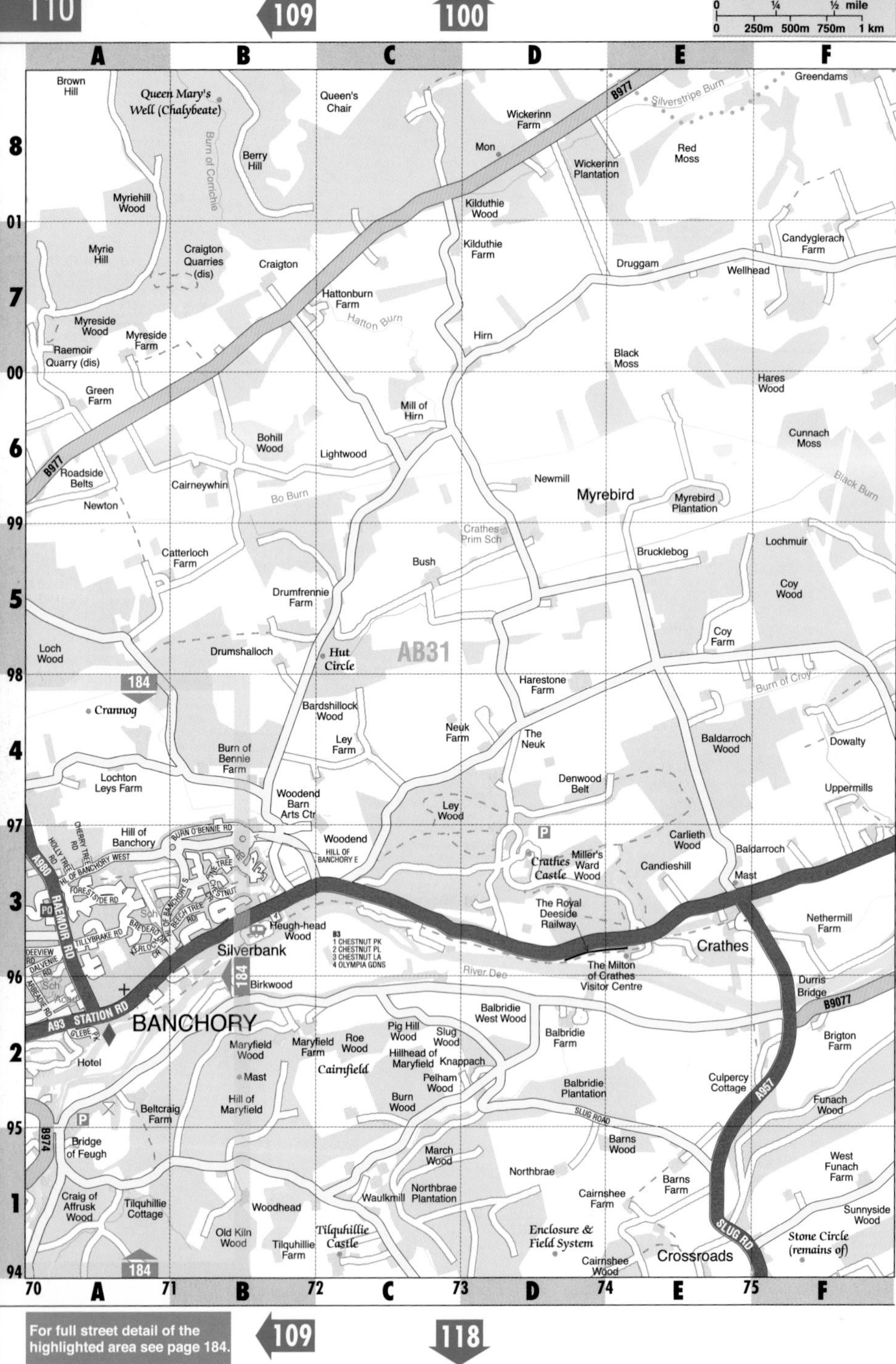

For full street detail of the highlighted area see page 184.
109
118

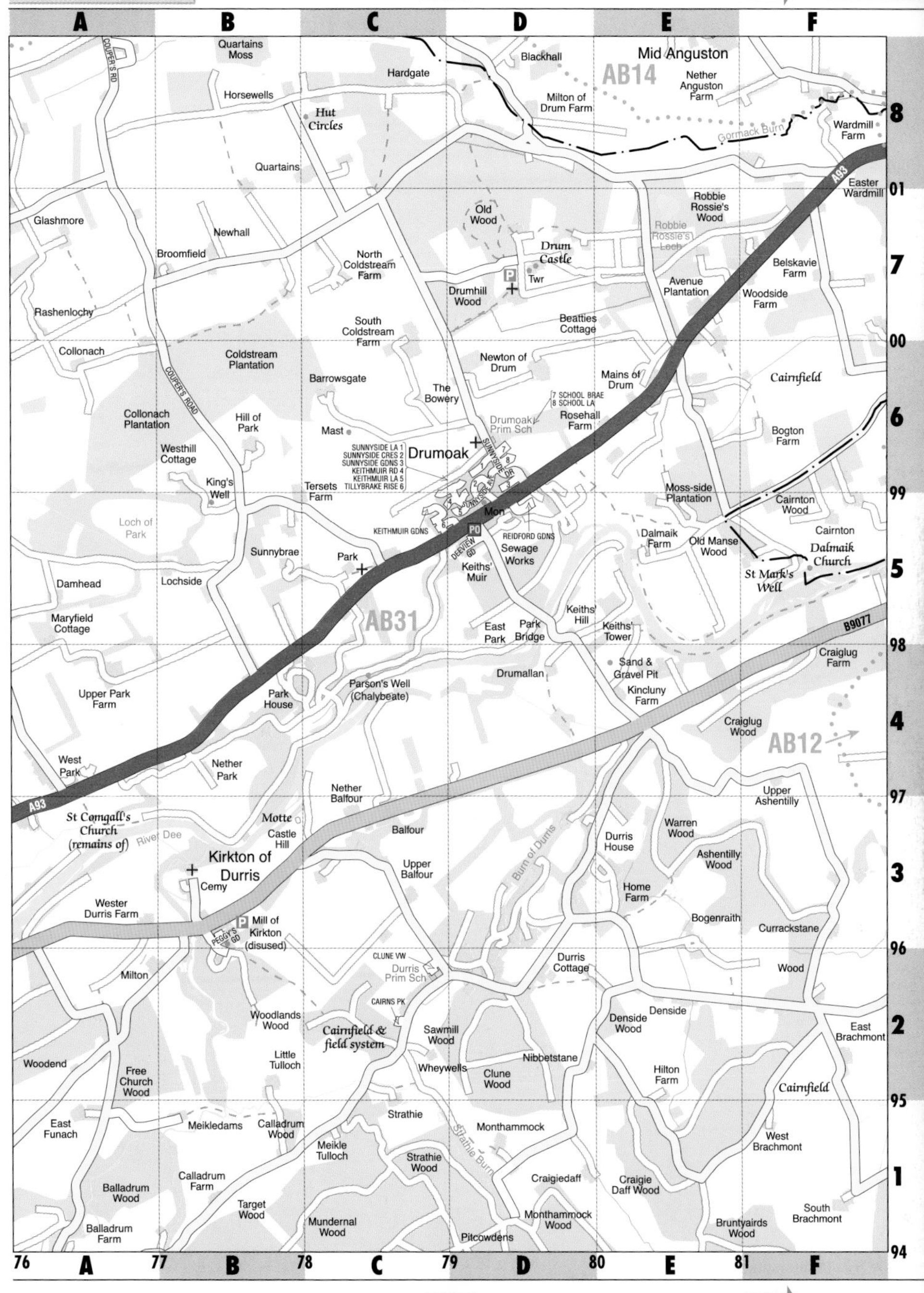
Quartains Moss
Hardgate
Blackhall
Mid Anguston
AB14
Nether Anguston Farm
Horsewells
Hut Circles
Milton of Drum Farm
Wardmill Farm
Gormack Burn
Quartains
A93
Easter Wardmill
Glashmore
Old Wood
Robbie Rossie's Wood
Robbie Rossie's Loch
Newhall
Broomfield
North Coldstream Farm
Drum Castle
Twr
Belskavie Farm
Avenue Plantation
Drumhill Wood
Woodside Farm
Rashenlochy
South Coldstream Farm
Beatties Cottage
Collonach
Coldstream Plantation
Newton of Drum
Mains of Drum
Barrowsgate
The Bowery
Cairnfield
Collonach Plantation
COUPER'S ROAD
Hill of Park
7 SCHOOL BRAE
8 SCHOOL LA
Drumoak Prim Sch
Rosehall Farm
Mast
Bogton Farm
Westhill Cottage
SUNNYSIDE LA 1
SUNNYSIDE CRES 2
SUNNYSIDE GDNS 3
KEITHMUIR RD 4
KEITHMUIR LA 5
TILLYBRAKE RISE 6
Drumoak
SUNNYSIDE DR
King's Well
Tersets Farm
Moss-side Plantation
Cairnton Wood
Mon
Loch of Park
KEITHMUIR GDNS
PO
DEEVIEW GD
REIDFORD GDNS
Dalmaik Farm
Old Manse Wood
Cairnton
Sunnybrae
Park
Sewage Works
Dalmaik Church
Damhead
Lochside
Keiths' Muir
St Mark's Well
Maryfield Cottage
AB31
East Park
Park Bridge
Keiths' Hill
Keiths' Tower
B9077
Craiglug Farm
Drumallan
Sand & Gravel Pit
Upper Park Farm
Parson's Well (Chalybeate)
Park House
Kincluny Farm
Craiglug Wood
AB12
West Park
Nether Park
Nether Balfour
Upper Ashentilly
St Comgall's Church (remains of)
Motte
River Dee
Castle Hill
Balfour
Warren Wood
Durris House
Kirkton of Durris
Burn of Durris
Ashentilly Wood
Upper Balfour
Cemy
Home Farm
Wester Durris Farm
Mill of Kirkton (disused)
Bogenraith
Curracksane
PEGGY'S GD
CLUNE VW
Durris Prim Sch
Durris Cottage
Wood
Milton
CAIRNS PK
Woodlands Wood
Denside
Denside Wood
East Brachmont
Cairnfield & field system
Sawmill Wood
Little Tulloch
Nibbetstane
Woodend
Wheywells
Clune Wood
Hilton Farm
Free Church Wood
Cairnfield
Strathie
East Funach
Meikledams
Calladrum Wood
Monthammock
West Brachmont
Meikle Tulloch
Strathie Burn
Strathie Wood
Calladrum Farm
Craigiedaff
Craigie Daff Wood
Balladrum Wood
Target Wood
Mundernal Wood
Monthammock Wood
Bruntyairds Wood
South Brachmont
Balladrum Farm
Pitcowdens
A B C D E F
8 01 7 00 6 99 5 98 4 97 3 96 2 95 1 94
76 77 78 79 80 81

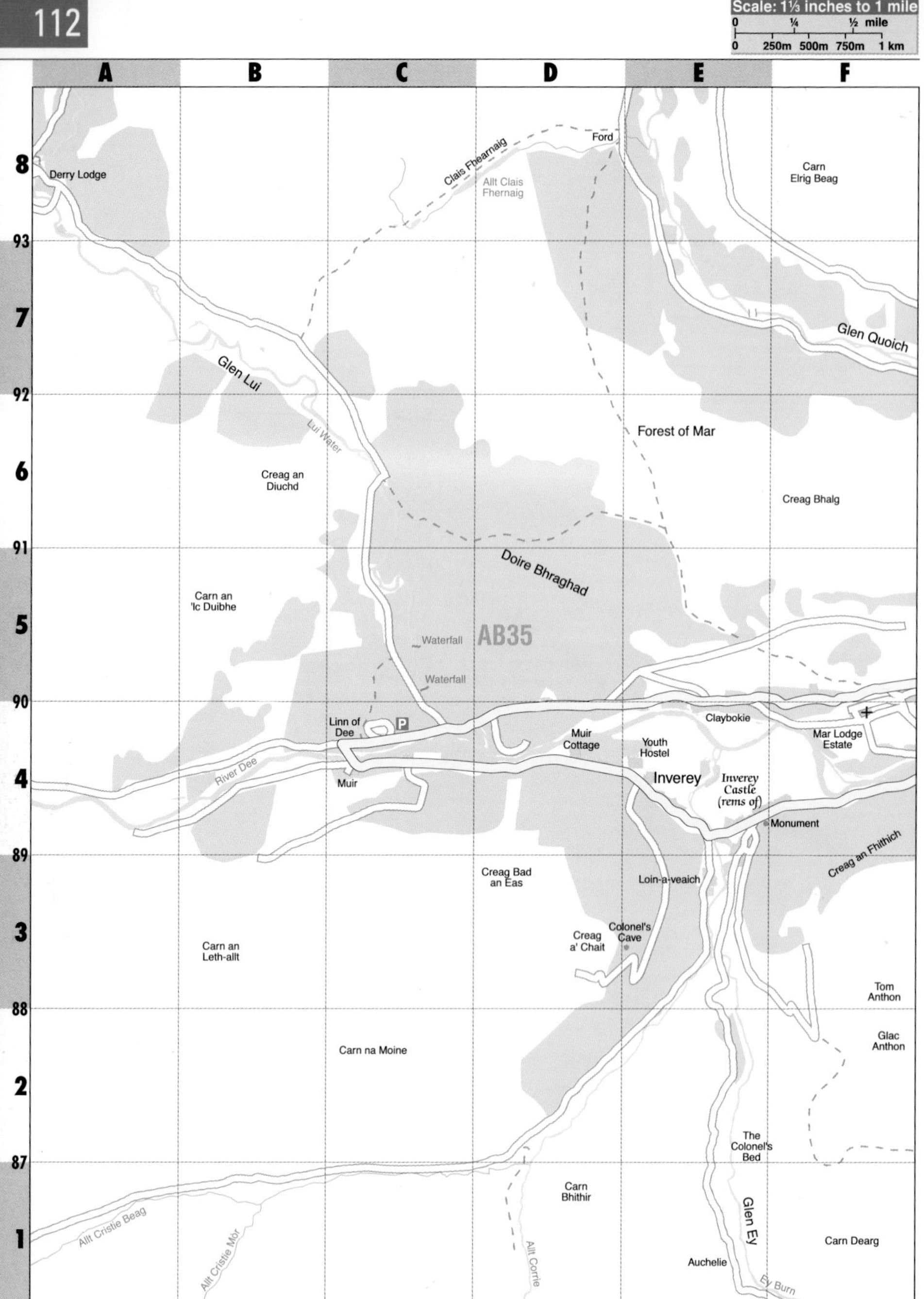

Scale: 1⅓ inches to 1 mile
0 ¼ ½ mile
0 250m 500m 750m 1 km
A
B
C
D
E
F
8
93
7
92
6
91
5
90
4
89
3
88
2
87
1
86
04
05
06
07
08
09
Derry Lodge
Ford
Clais Fhearnaig
Allt Clais Fhernaig
Carn Elrig Beag
Glen Quoich
Glen Lui
Lui Water
Forest of Mar
Creag an Diuchd
Creag Bhalg
Doire Bhraghad
Carn an 'Ic Duibhe
AB35
Waterfall
Waterfall
Linn of Dee
P
Claybokie
Mar Lodge Estate
Muir Cottage
Youth Hostel
River Dee
Muir
Inverey
Inverey Castle (rems of)
Monument
Creag an Fhithich
Creag Bad an Eas
Loin-a-veaich
Colonel's Cave
Creag a' Chait
Carn an Leth-allt
Tom Anthon
Glac Anthon
Carn na Moine
The Colonel's Bed
Carn Bhithir
Glen Ey
Allt Cristie Beag
Allt Cristie Mòr
Allt Corrie
Auchelie
Carn Dearg
Ey Burn

Scale: 1⅓ inches to 1 mile

114

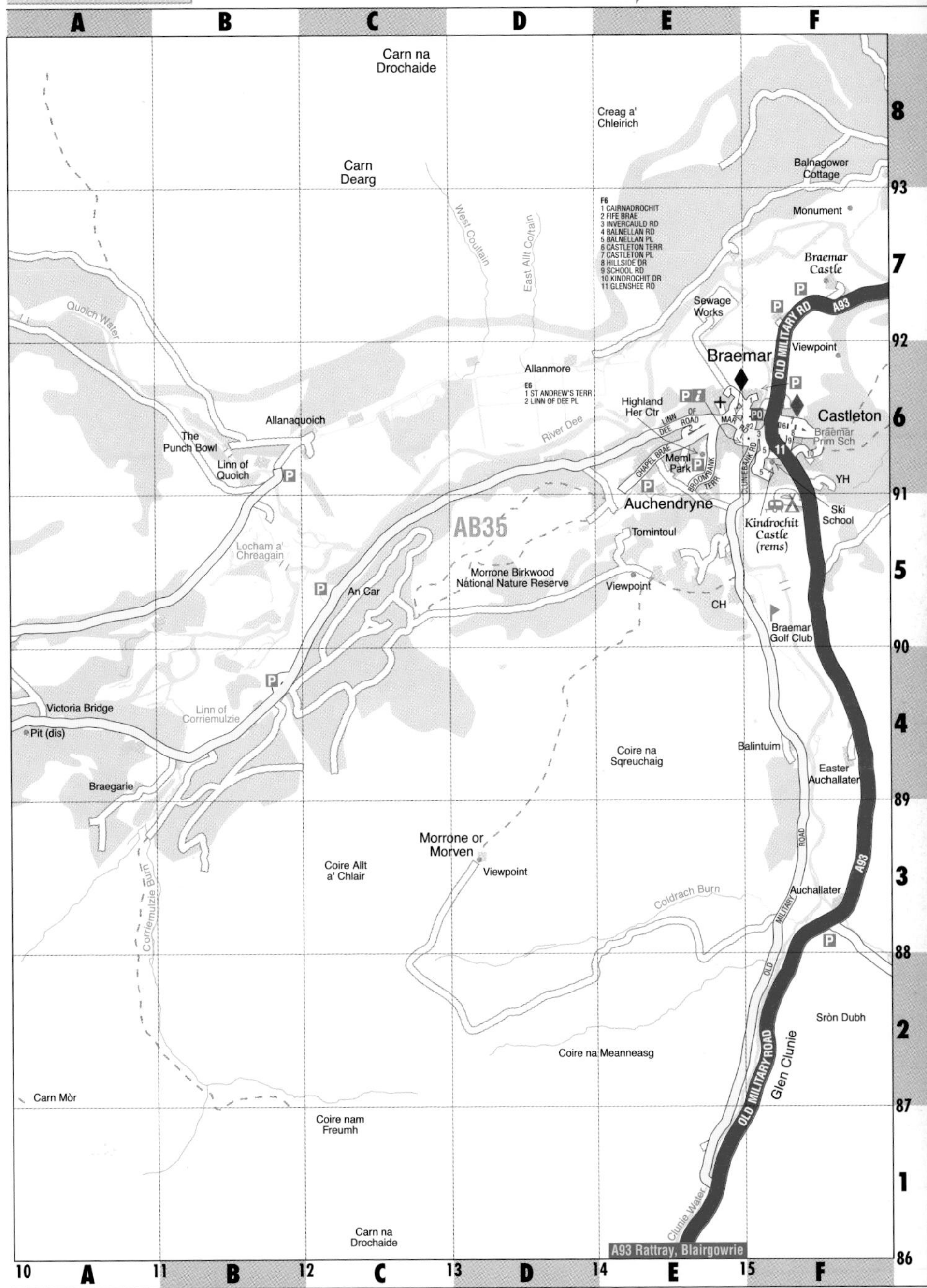

114

113

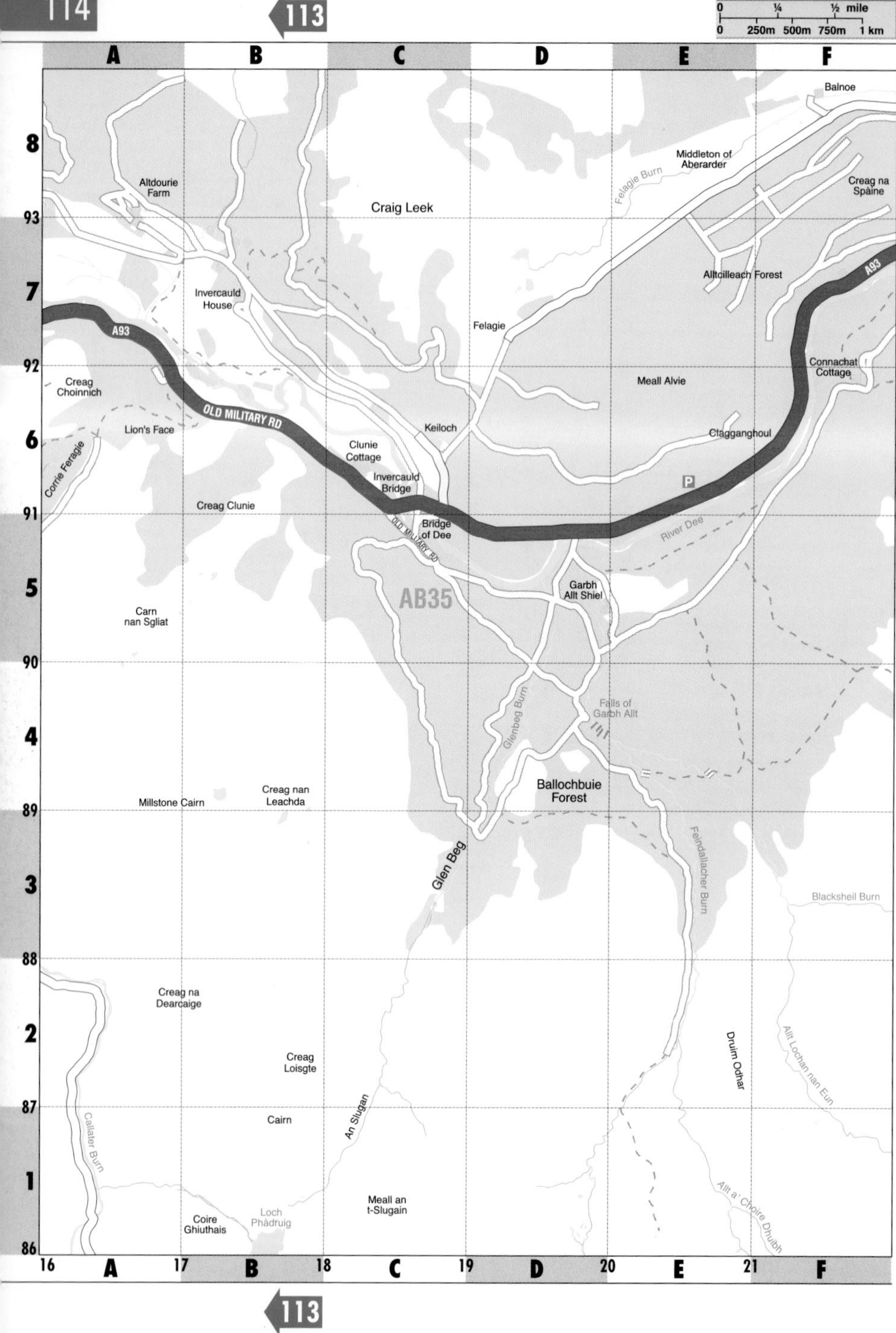

Scale: 1⅓ inches to 1 mile
0 ¼ ½ mile
0 250m 500m 750m 1 km
A B C D E F
8
7
6
5
4
3
2
1
93
92
91
90
89
88
87
86
16 17 18 19 20 21
Balnoe
Middleton of Aberarder
Felagie Burn
Creag na Spàine
Altdourie Farm
Craig Leek
Alltcilleach Forest
A93
Invercauld House
Felagie
Connachat Cottage
Creag Choinnich
Meall Alvie
OLD MILITARY RD
Lion's Face
Keiloch
Clagganghoul
Corrie Feragie
Clunie Cottage
Invercauld Bridge
P
Creag Clunie
Bridge of Dee
River Dee
OLD MILITARY RD
Garbh Allt Shiel
AB35
Carn nan Sgliat
Falls of Garbh Allt
Glenbeg Burn
Ballochbuie Forest
Millstone Cairn
Creag nan Leachda
Glen Beg
Feindallacher Burn
Blacksheil Burn
Creag na Dearcaige
Druim Odhar
Allt Lochan nan Eun
Creag Loisgte
Cairn
An Slugan
Callater Burn
Allt a' Choire Dhuibh
Meall an t-Slugain
Coire Ghiuthais
Loch Phàdruig

113

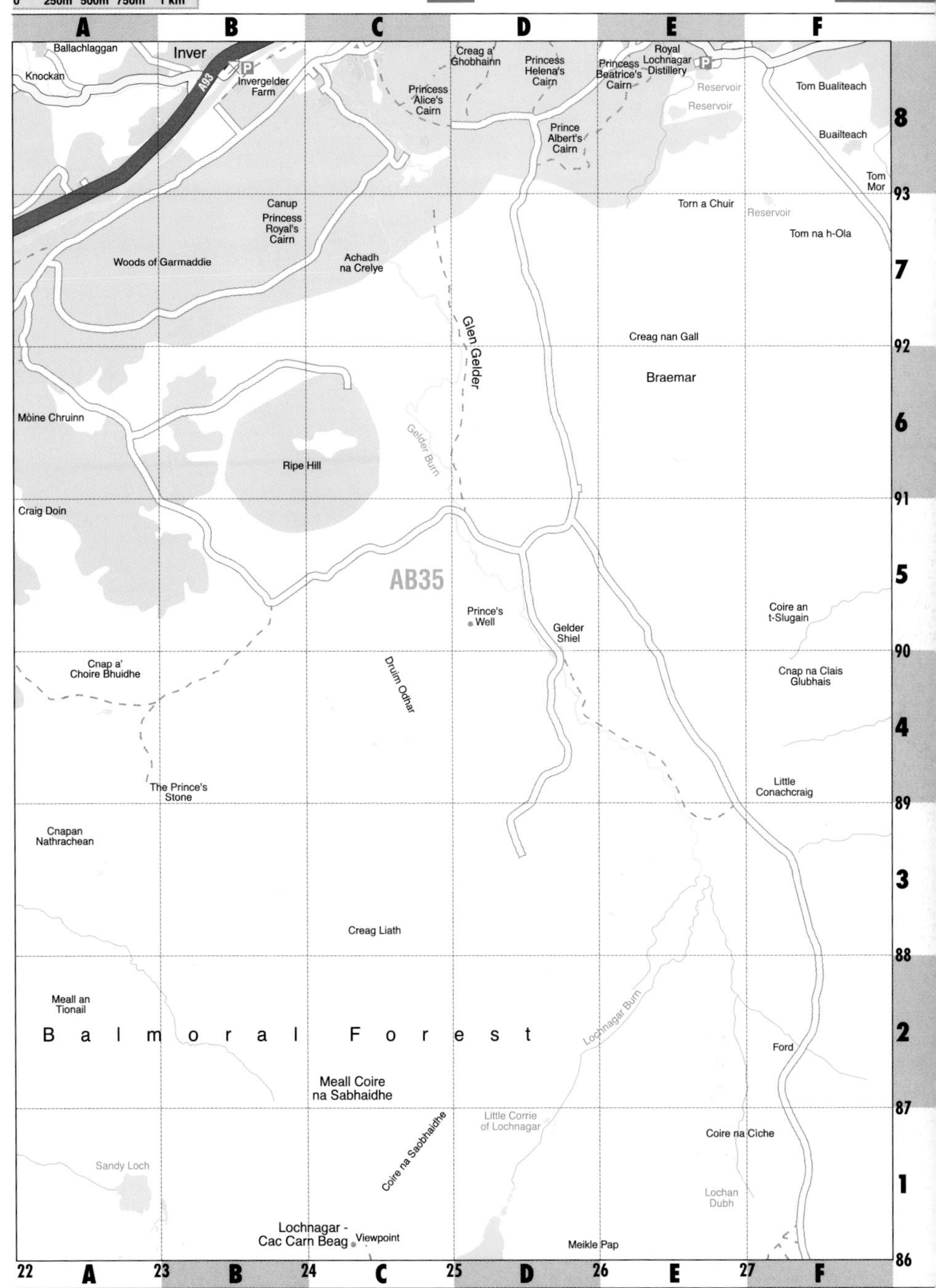
Scale: 1⅓ inches to 1 mile
0 ¼ ½ mile
0 250m 500m 750m 1 km
102
A
B
C
D
E
F
Ballachlaggan
Inver
Knockan
A93
Invergelder Farm
Creag a' Ghobhainn
Princess Alice's Cairn
Princess Helena's Cairn
Princess Beatrice's Cairn
Royal Lochnagar Distillery
Reservoir
Reservoir
Tom Bualiteach
Prince Albert's Cairn
Bualiteach
Tom Mor
Torn a Chuir
Reservoir
Canup
Princess Royal's Cairn
Tom na h-Ola
Woods of Garmaddie
Achadh na Crelye
Glen Gelder
Creag nan Gall
Braemar
Mòine Chruinn
Gelder Burn
Ripe Hill
Craig Doin
AB35
Prince's Well
Coire an t-Slugain
Gelder Shiel
Cnap a' Choire Bhuidhe
Druim Odhar
Cnap na Clais Glubhais
The Prince's Stone
Little Conachcraig
Cnapan Nathrachean
Creag Liath
Meall an Tionail
Balmoral Forest
Lochnagar Burn
Ford
Meall Coire na Sabhaidhe
Little Corrie of Lochnagar
Coire na Saobhaidhe
Coire na Cìche
Sandy Loch
Lochan Dubh
Lochnagar - Cac Carn Beag
Viewpoint
Meikle Pap
8
93
7
92
6
91
5
90
4
89
3
88
2
87
1
86
22
23
24
25
26
27

108

Scale: 1⅓ inches to 1 mile
0 ¼ ½ mile
0 250m 500m 750m 1 km

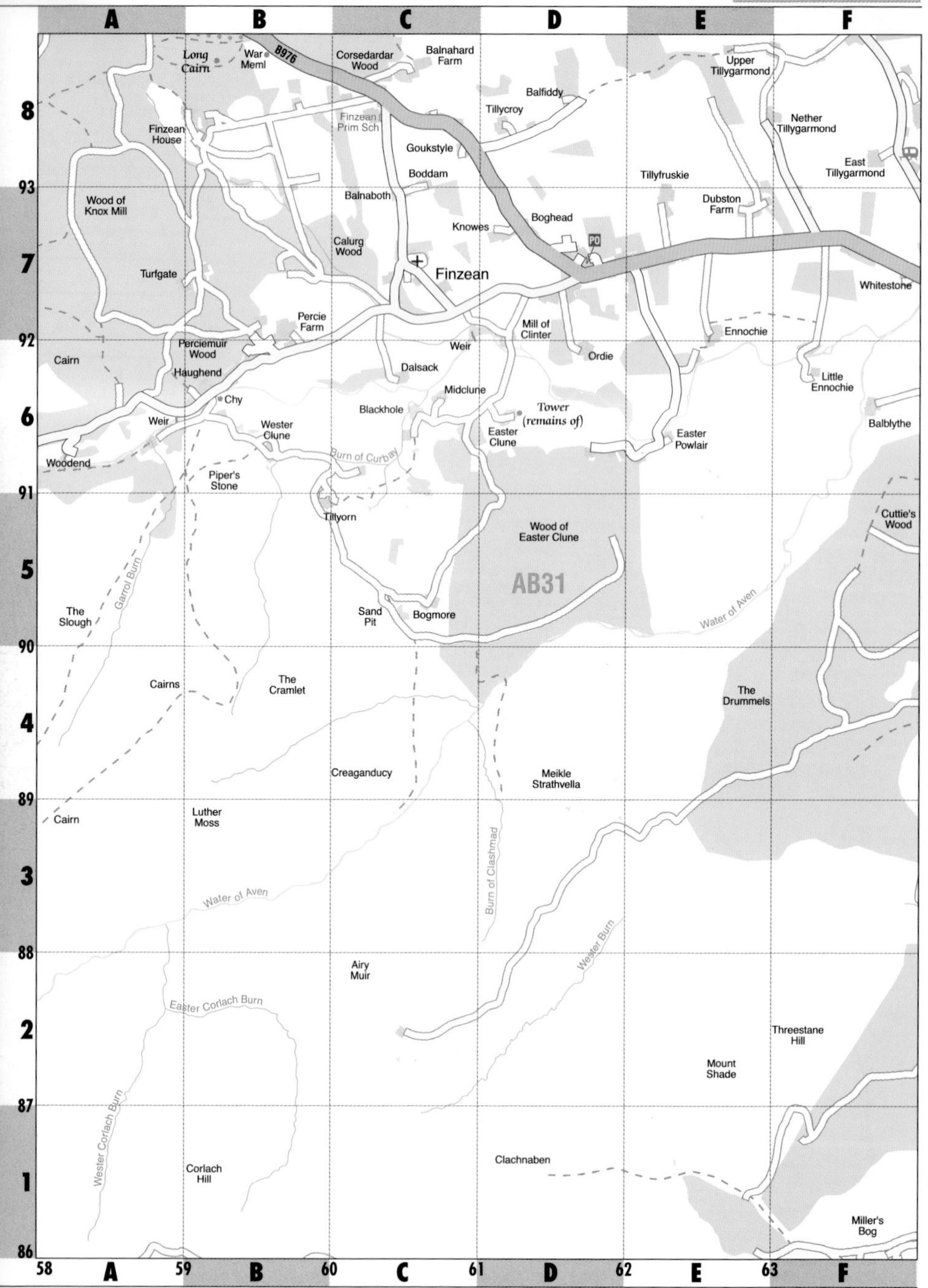

122

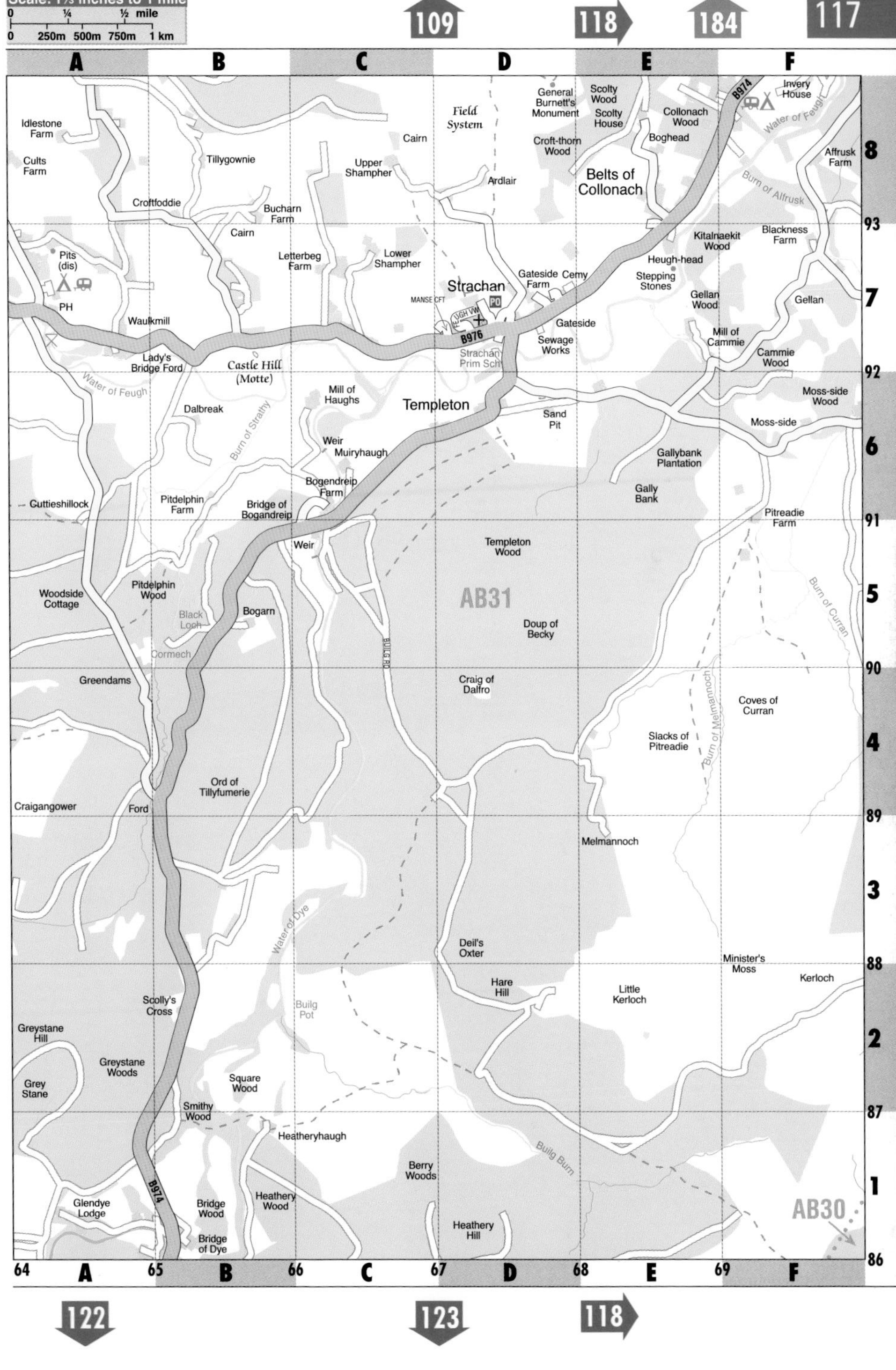

Scale: 1⅓ inches to 1 mile
0 ¼ ½ mile
0 250m 500m 750m 1 km
109
118
184
A B C D E F
Idlestone Farm
Cults Farm
Tillygownie
Croftfoddie
Cairn
Bucharn Farm
Upper Shampher
Cairn
Field System
Ardlair
General Burnett's Monument
Scolty Wood
Scolty House
Croft-thorn Wood
Belts of Collonach
Collonach Wood
Boghead
Invery House
Water of Feugh
Affrusk Farm
Burn of Alfrusk
Blackness Farm
Kitalnaekit Wood
Heugh-head
Stepping Stones
Gellan Wood
Gellan
Mill of Cammie
Cammie Wood
Pits (dis)
PH
Waulkmill
Letterbeg Farm
Lower Shampher
Strachan
MANSE CFT
FEUGH VW
PO
B976
Gateside Farm
Cemy
Gateside
Sewage Works
Strachan Prim Sch
Lady's Bridge Ford
Castle Hill (Motte)
Water of Feugh
Dalbreak
Burn of Strathy
Mill of Haughs
Templeton
Sand Pit
Moss-side Wood
Moss-side
Weir
Muiryhaugh
Bogendreip Farm
Gallybank Plantation
Gally Bank
Cuttieshillock
Pitdelphin Farm
Bridge of Bogandreip
Pitreadie Farm
Weir
Templeton Wood
Woodside Cottage
Pitdelphin Wood
AB31
Burn of Curran
Black Loch
Bogarn
Doup of Becky
BUILG RD
Cormech
Greendams
Craig of Dalfro
Coves of Curran
Slacks of Pitreadie
Burn of Melmannoch
Ord of Tillyfumerie
Craigangower
Ford
Melmannoch
Water of Dye
Deil's Oxter
Minister's Moss
Kerloch
Hare Hill
Little Kerloch
Scolly's Cross
Builg Pot
Greystane Hill
Greystane Woods
Grey Stane
Square Wood
Smithy Wood
Heatheryhaugh
Builg Burn
Berry Woods
B974
Glendye Lodge
Bridge Wood
Heathery Wood
Heathery Hill
Bridge of Dye
AB30
93 92 91 90 89 88 87 86
8 7 6 5 4 3 2 1
64 65 66 67 68 69
122
123
118

184 117 110

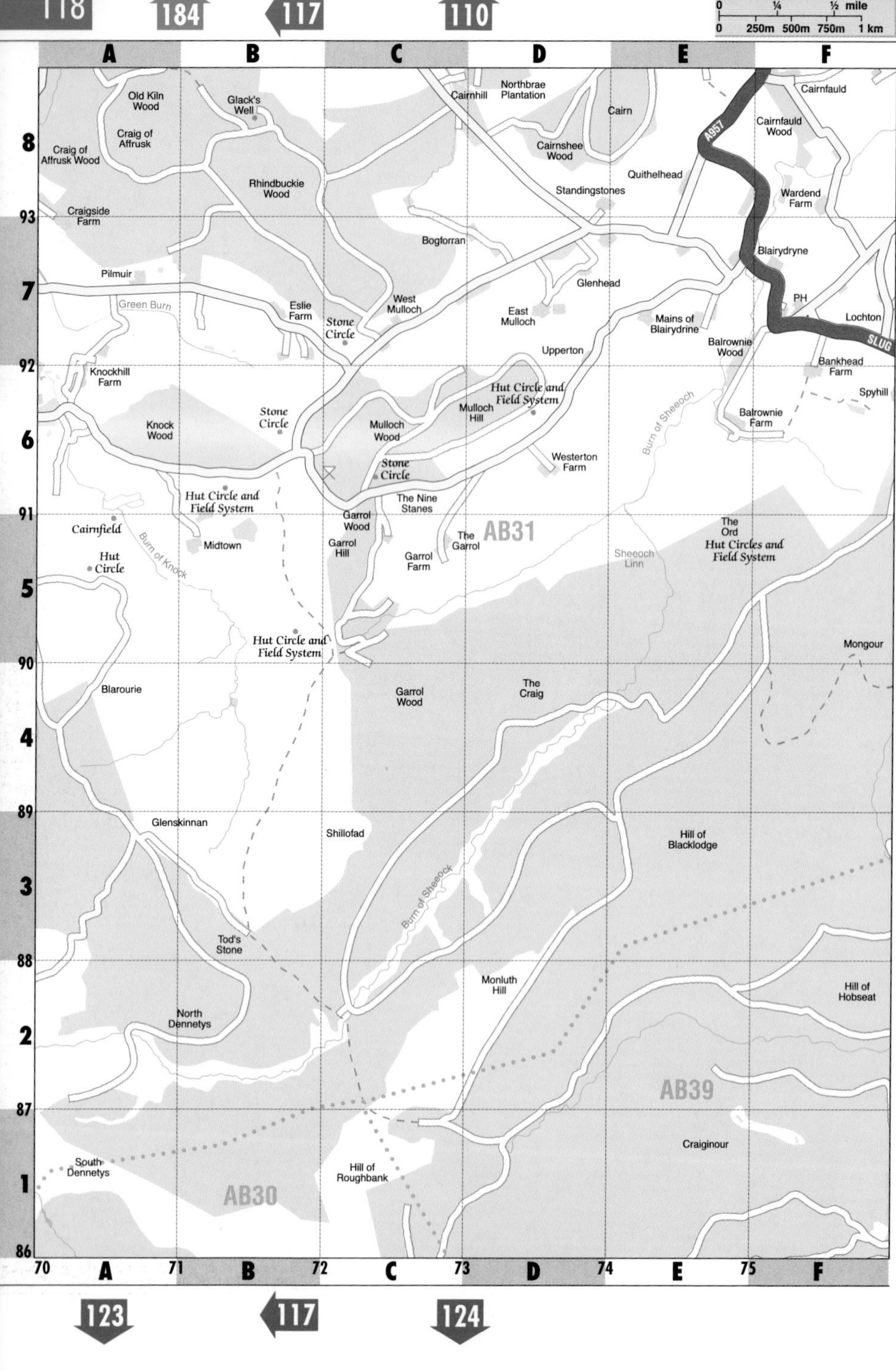

123 117 124

Scale: 1⅓ inches to 1 mile

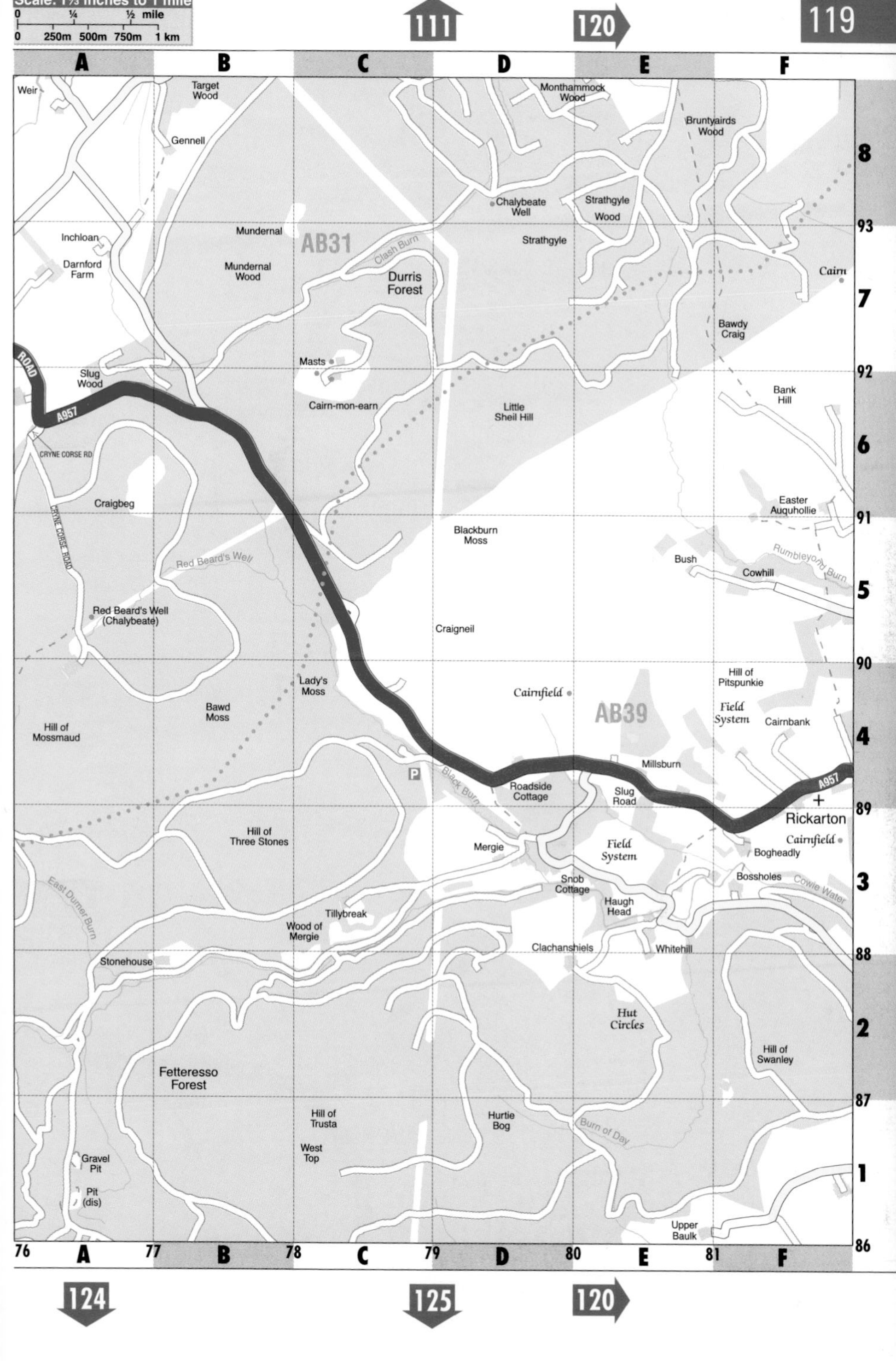

119
177
178

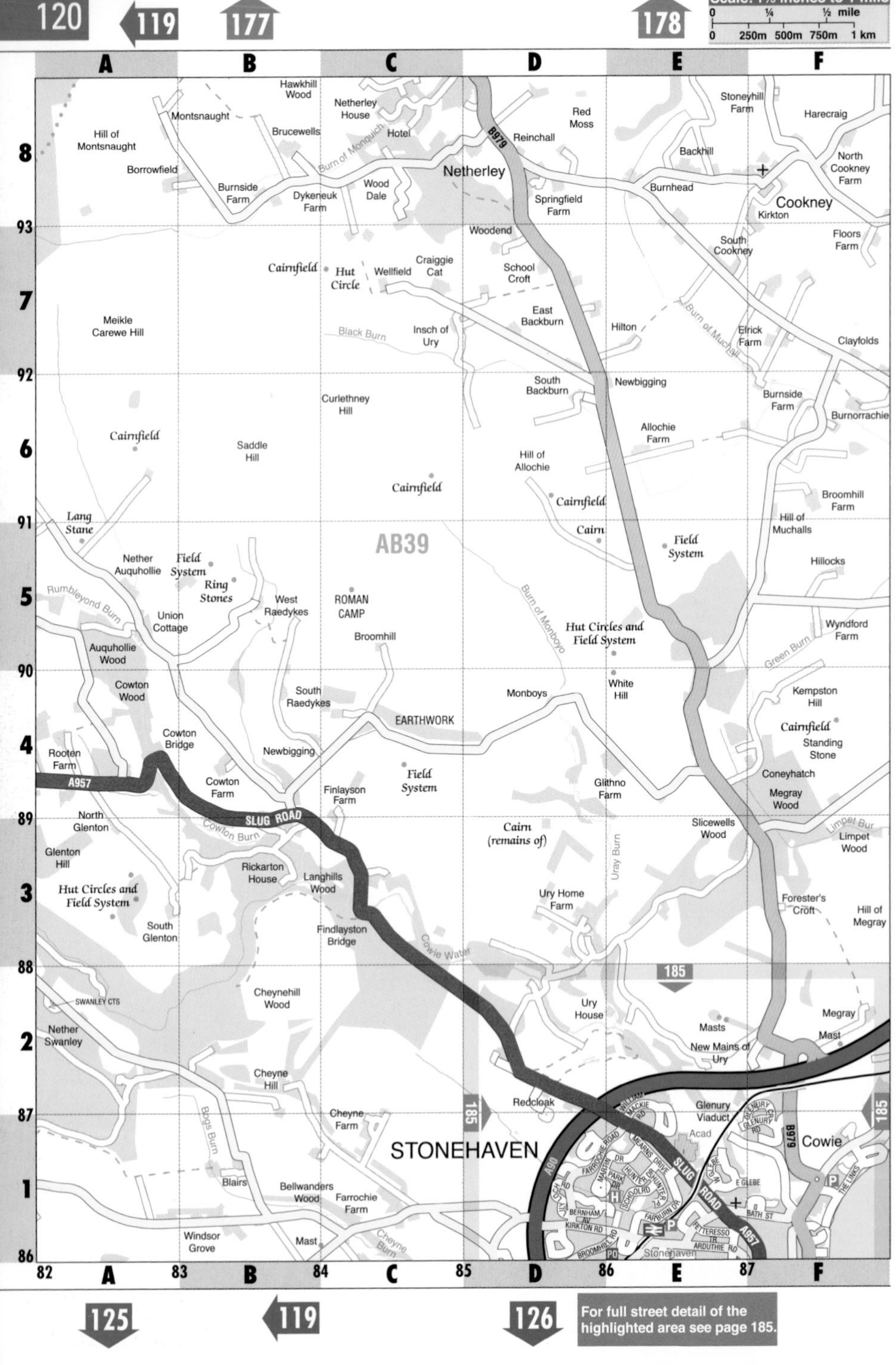

125
119
126
For full street detail of the highlighted area see page 185.

A B C D E F

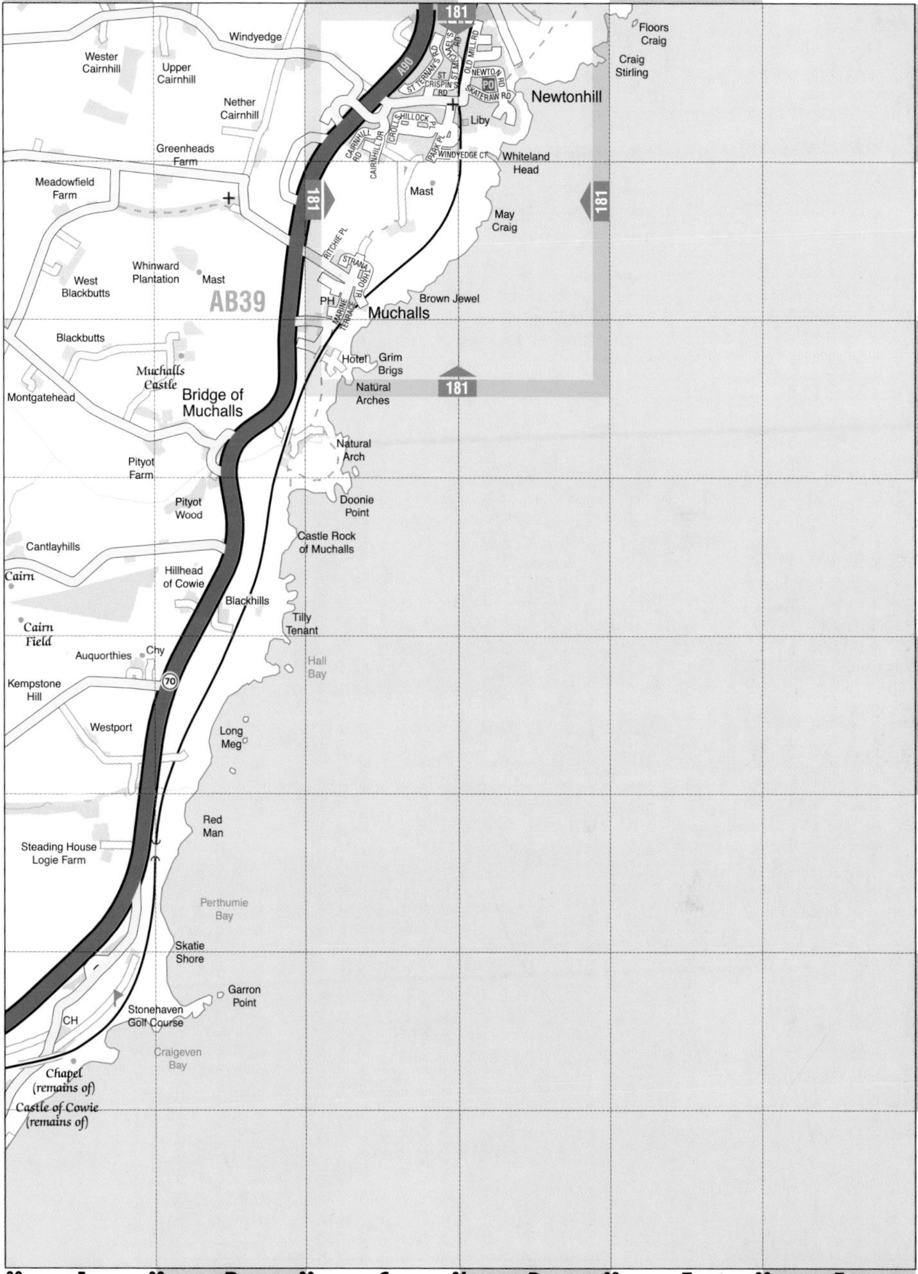

181
Floors Craig
Wester Cairnhill
Upper Cairnhill
Windyedge
A90
ST TERNAN'S RD
ST CRISPIN'S RD
ST MICHAEL'S RD
OLD MILL RD
NEWTON RD
PO
SKATERAW RD
Craig Stirling
Newtonhill
8
Nether Cairnhill
HILLOCK PL
CROLLS
CAIRNHILL RD
CAIRNHILL DR
PARK PL
Liby
WINDYEDGE CT
Greenheads Farm
Whiteland Head
93
Meadowfield Farm
Mast
181
181
May Craig
7
RITCHIE PL
STRANATHRO TR.
Whinward Plantation
Mast
West Blackbutts
AB39
PH
MARINE TERRACE
Brown Jewel
Muchalls
92
Blackbutts
Hotel
Grim Brigs
Muchalls Castle
181
Natural Arches
Montgatehead
Bridge of Muchalls
6
Natural Arch
Pityot Farm
91
Pityot Wood
Doonie Point
Castle Rock of Muchalls
Cantlayhills
5
Cairn
Hillhead of Cowie
Blackhills
Cairn Field
Tilly Tenant
90
Auquorthies
Chy
Hall Bay
Kempstone Hill
70
Westport
4
Long Meg
89
Red Man
Steading House Logie Farm
3
Perthumie Bay
Skatie Shore
88
Garron Point
CH
Stonehaven Golf Course
2
Craigeven Bay
Chapel (remains of)
Castle of Cowie (remains of)
87
1
86

88 A 89 B 90 C 91 D 92 E 93 F

For full street detail of the highlighted area see page 181.

116

Scale: 1⅓ inches to 1 mile
0 ¼ ½ mile
0 250m 500m 750m 1 km

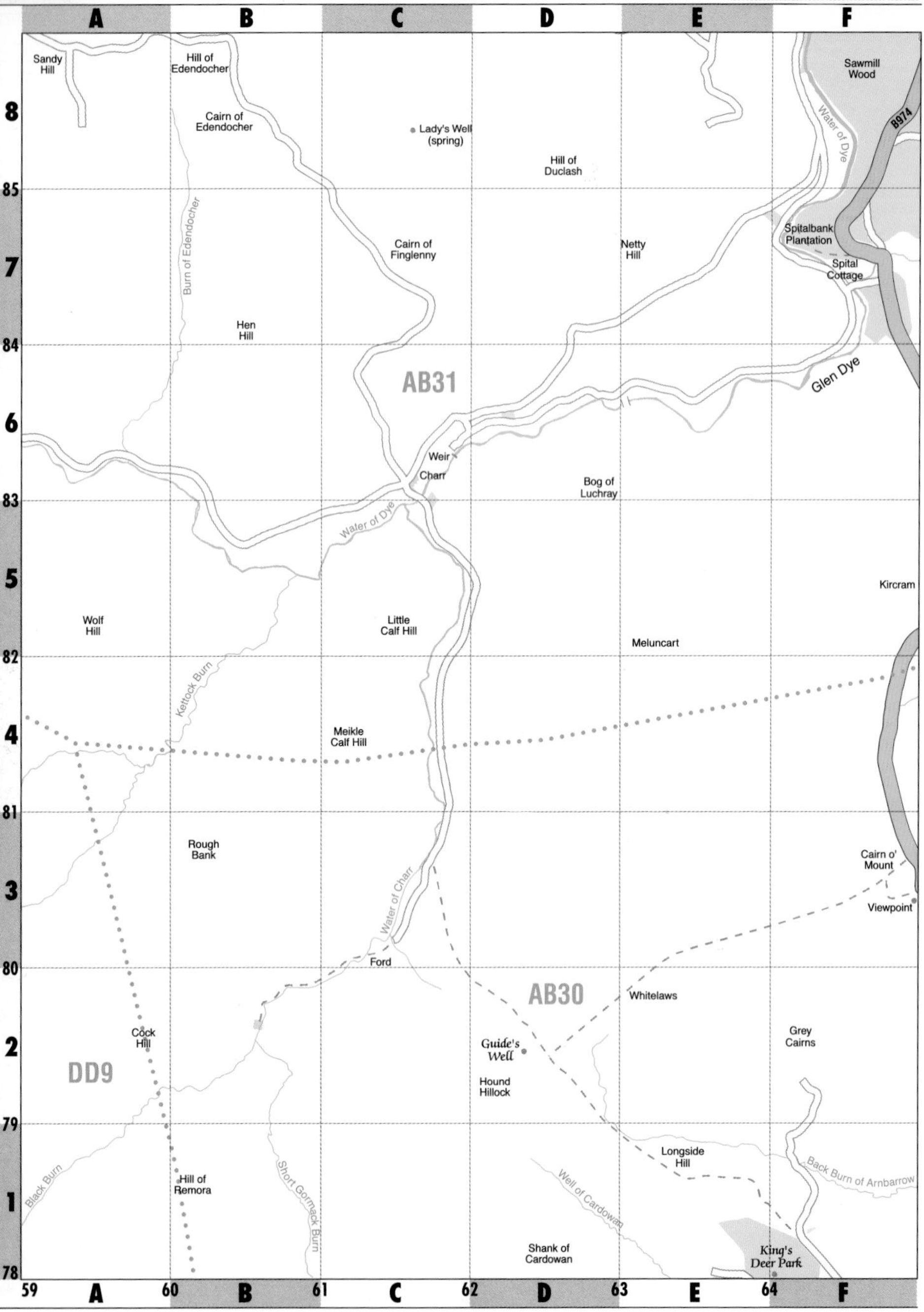

A B C D E F

8
85
7
84
6
83
5
82
4
81
3
80
2
79
1
78

Sandy Hill
Hill of Edendocher
Cairn of Edendocher
Lady's Well (spring)
Hill of Duclash
Sawmill Wood
Water of Dye
B974
Burn of Edendocher
Cairn of Finglenny
Netty Hill
Spitalbank Plantation
Spital Cottage
Hen Hill
AB31
Glen Dye
Weir
Charr
Bog of Luchray
Water of Dye
Kircram
Wolf Hill
Little Calf Hill
Meluncart
Kettock Burn
Meikle Calf Hill
Rough Bank
Cairn o' Mount
Water of Charr
Viewpoint
Ford
AB30
Whitelaws
Cock Hill
Guide's Well
Grey Cairns
DD9
Hound Hillock
Longside Hill
Back Burn of Arnbarrow
Black Burn
Hill of Remora
Short Gormack Burn
Well of Cardowan
Shank of Cardowan
King's Deer Park

59 A 60 B 61 C 62 D 63 E 64 F

127

128

Scale: 1⅓ inches to 1 mile
0 ¼ ½ mile
0 250m 500m 750m 1 km
117
124
118
A B C D E F
White Moss
Bog of Saughs
Tipperweir
The Builg
Bawd Bod
East Burn of Builg
Tire Beggar Hill
Garlot Hill
AB31
Spital Burn
Aikenhead
Bervie Water
Hill of Gothie
Buckies Leys
Goyle Hill
Boy's Hill
Drumtochty Forest
Waird of the Cairn
AB30
Hill of Burnieshag
Thorter Hill
Slack Burn
Hill of Annahar
Castlebank Wood
Ruehill Wood
Drumtochty Castle
Priest's Well
Gardenbank Wood
Colt Moss
Pamphill Burn
Glen of Drumtochty
Redstone Hill
Birnie Burn
Birnie Hill
Loch Hill
Strath Finella
Garrold Wood
St Ringan's Cairn
Bright's Well
Holeglen Wood
Slack Den
Loch Saugh
Bows
Black Hill
Dam
Clatterin' Brig
B974
Drumelzie Wood
Quarry (dis)
Glensaugh Farm
8 85 7 84 6 83 5 82 4 81 3 80 2 79 1 78
65 66 67 68 69 70 71
128
124
129

123 118

Scale: 1⅓ inches to 1 mile

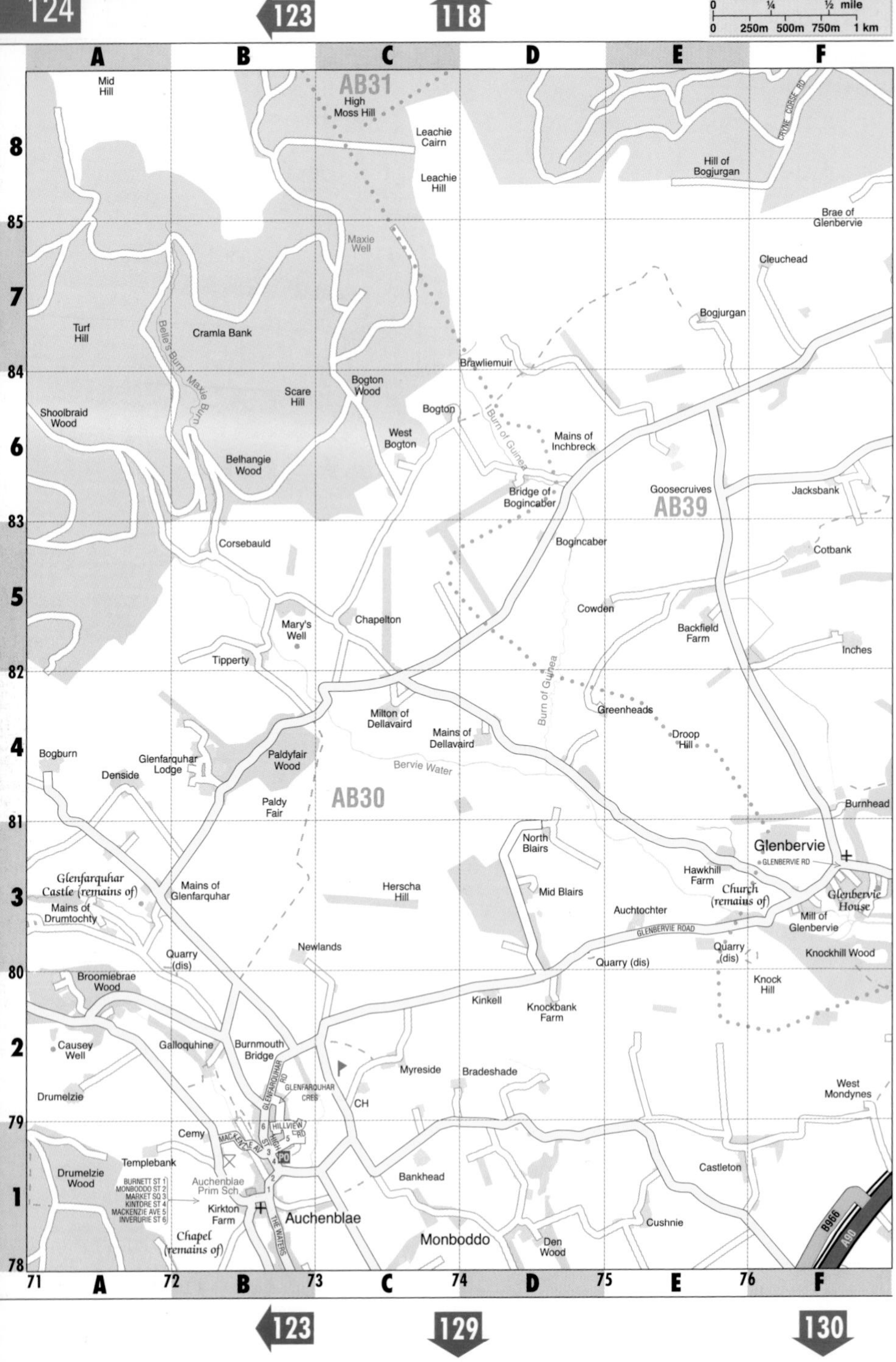

123 129 130

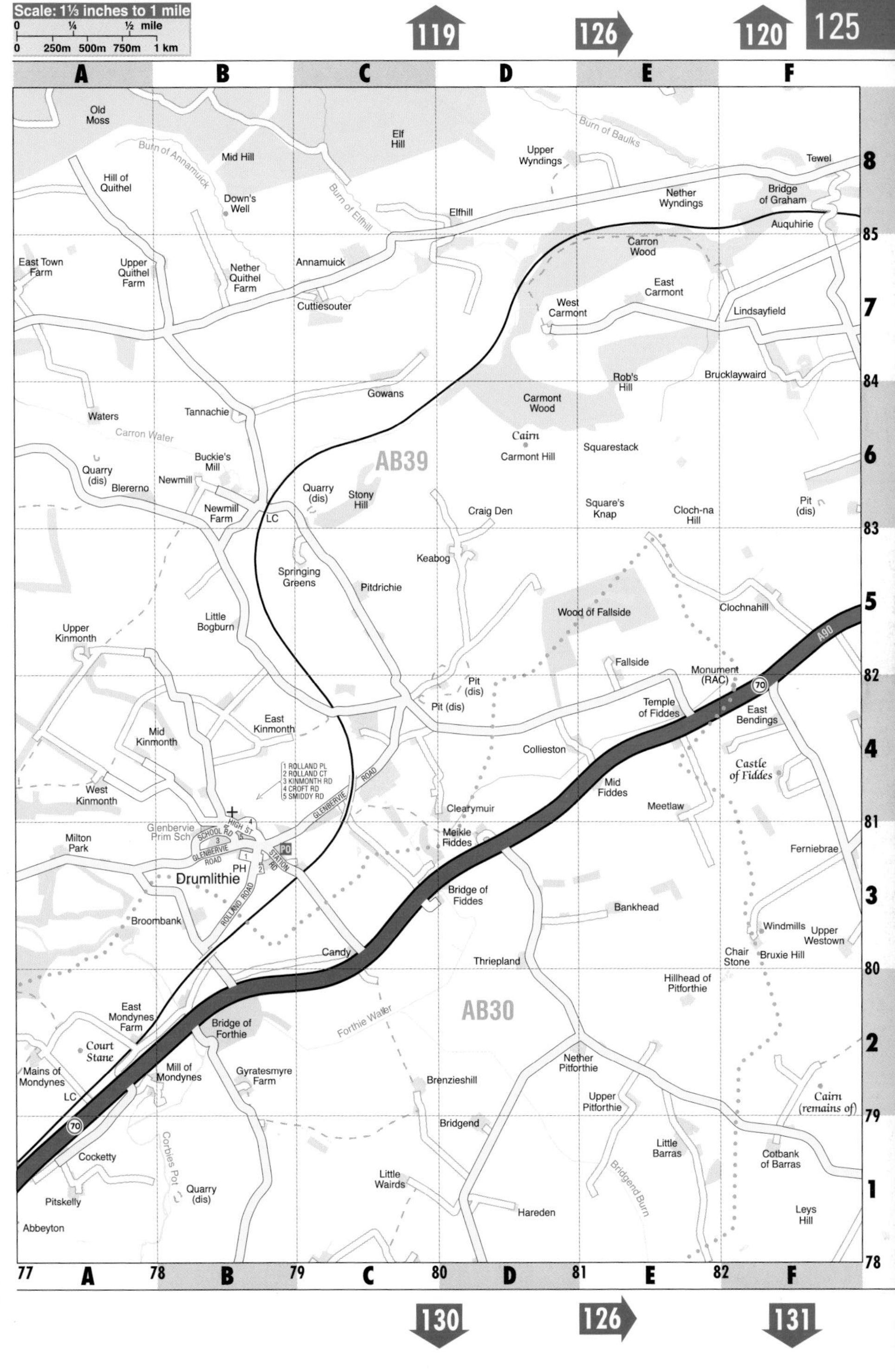
Scale: 1⅓ inches to 1 mile
0 ¼ ½ mile
0 250m 500m 750m 1 km
119
126
120
A
B
C
D
E
F
Old Moss
Elf Hill
Burn of Baulks
Burn of Annamuick
Mid Hill
Upper Wyndings
Tewel
Hill of Quithel
Down's Well
Burn of Elfhill
Nether Wyndings
Bridge of Graham
Elfhill
Auquhirie
East Town Farm
Upper Quithel Farm
Nether Quithel Farm
Annamuick
Carron Wood
Cuttiesouter
West Carmont
East Carmont
Lindsayfield
Gowans
Rob's Hill
Brucklaywaird
Waters
Tannachie
Carmont Wood
Carron Water
Cairn
Carmont Hill
Squarestack
AB39
Buckie's Mill
Quarry (dis)
Blererno
Newmill
Quarry (dis)
Stony Hill
Newmill Farm
LC
Craig Den
Square's Knap
Cloch-na Hill
Pit (dis)
Keabog
Springing Greens
Pitdrichie
Wood of Fallside
Clochnahill
Little Bogburn
Upper Kinmonth
A90
Fallside
Monument (RAC)
Pit (dis)
Pit (dis)
70
Temple of Fiddes
East Bendings
East Kinmonth
Mid Kinmonth
Collieston
1 ROLLAND PL
2 ROLLAND CT
3 KINMONTH RD
4 CROFT RD
5 SMIDDY RD
Castle of Fiddes
West Kinmonth
GLENBERVIE ROAD
Mid Fiddes
Meetlaw
Clearymuir
HIGH ST
Glenbervie Prim Sch
SCHOOL RD
Milton Park
Meikle Fiddes
Ferniebrae
PO
GLENBERVIE ROAD
STATION RD
PH
Drumlithie
Bridge of Fiddes
ROLLAND ROAD
Bankhead
Broombank
Windmills
Upper Westown
Candy
Chair Stone
Bruxie Hill
Thriepland
Hillhead of Pitforthie
AB30
East Mondynes Farm
Bridge of Forthie
Forthie Water
Court Stane
Nether Pitforthie
Mains of Mondynes
Mill of Mondynes
Gyratesmyre Farm
Brenzieshill
Cairn (remains of)
LC
Upper Pitforthie
Corbies Pot
Bridgend
70
Little Barras
Cotbank of Barras
Cocketty
Bridgend Burn
Little Wairds
Quarry (dis)
Pitskelly
Hareden
Leys Hill
Abbeyton
8
85
7
84
6
83
5
82
4
81
3
80
2
79
1
78
77
78
79
80
81
82
130
126
131

125
120
121

Scale 1⅓ inches to 1 mile

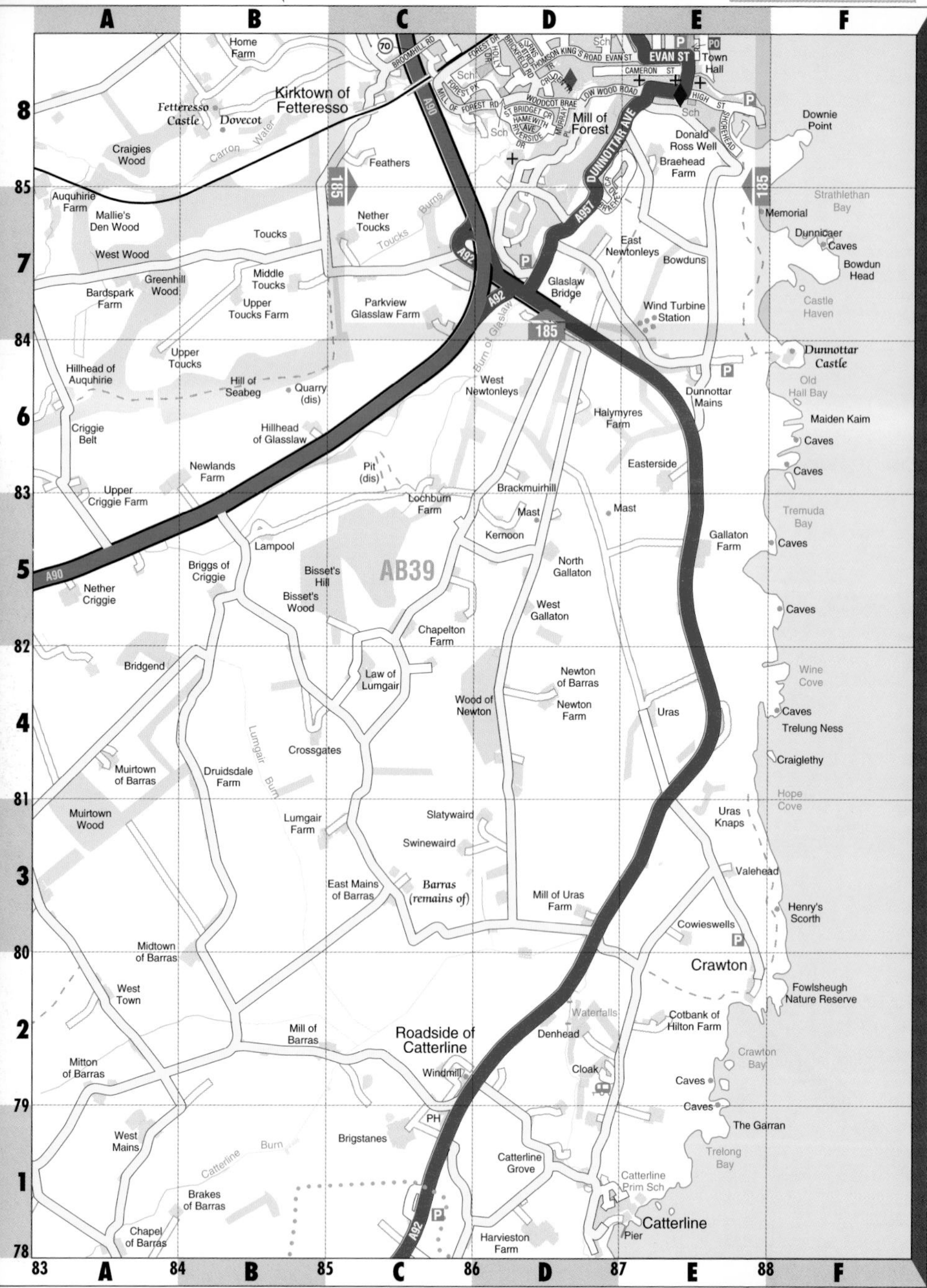

125
131
For full street detail of the highlighted area see page 185.

A B C D E F

8 7 6 5 4 3 2 1

77 76 75 74 73 72 71 70

Sturdy Hill
Slack Pool
Craigancash
Black Goit
Earn Cairn
Maolearn
Burn of Corbrack
Burn of Gonimoch
Burn of Corsheille
Crichie Burn
Brunt Hill
Crichieburn Wood
Herdhill Wood
Herd Hill
Burn of Delalie
Brawlinmuir Wood
Wood of Mon Duff
Bannock Hill
Croftangry Wood
Delalie
Craig of Weston
Saddle Hill
Upper Thainston
Backhows Plantation
Wood of Balnakettle
Nether Thainston
Torrnarock
Auchmull
Mains of Balnakettle
AB30
Manach Hill
Wood of Balfour
Doulie Hill
Mains of Balfour
Burn of Cauldcots
Quarry (dis)
Westerton
Mid Mains of Balfour Farm
Quarry (dis)
Cauldcots Farm
Quarry (dis)
Kirkton of Balfour
Quarries (dis)
Wood of Barna
Gravel Pit
Den of Woodtown
Bonharry
Flatnadriech
Crystal Dairy
Barras Hill Plantation
Balbegno Castle
Hallhill
Rocks of Solitude
DD9
B966
Twr
Thornyhill
Torrnayards
Burn Farm
Cairnton of Balbegno
Round Green Plantation
Green Cairn (Fort)
Tor Hill
Dalbog
Twr
The Neuk
Tillytoghills
Tor Wood
River North Esk
The Burn
Pit (dis)
Little Strath
Serjan Hill
Pit (dis)
Wood of Dalbog
Saltire Wood
Kelpie Bridge
Cave
Drum
Inch of Arnhall
Greendykes
North Disclune Plantation
Gannochy
Gannochy Tower
Well
Bogside
Colt Hill
B966

58 A 59 B 60 C 61 D 62 E 63 F

122
127
123

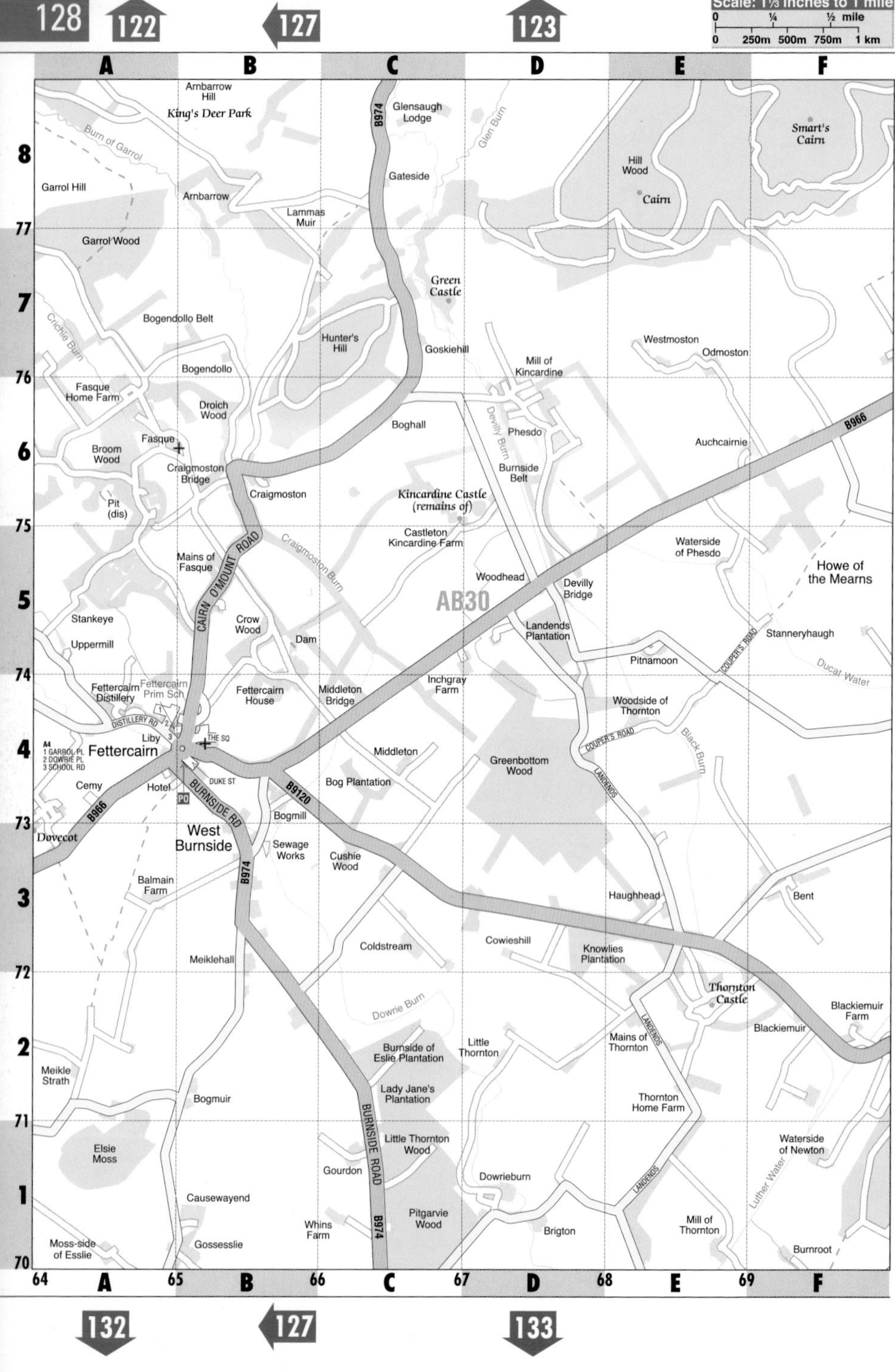

132
127
133

Scale: 1⅓ inches to 1 mile
0 ¼ ½ mile
0 250m 500m 750m 1 km

124
130

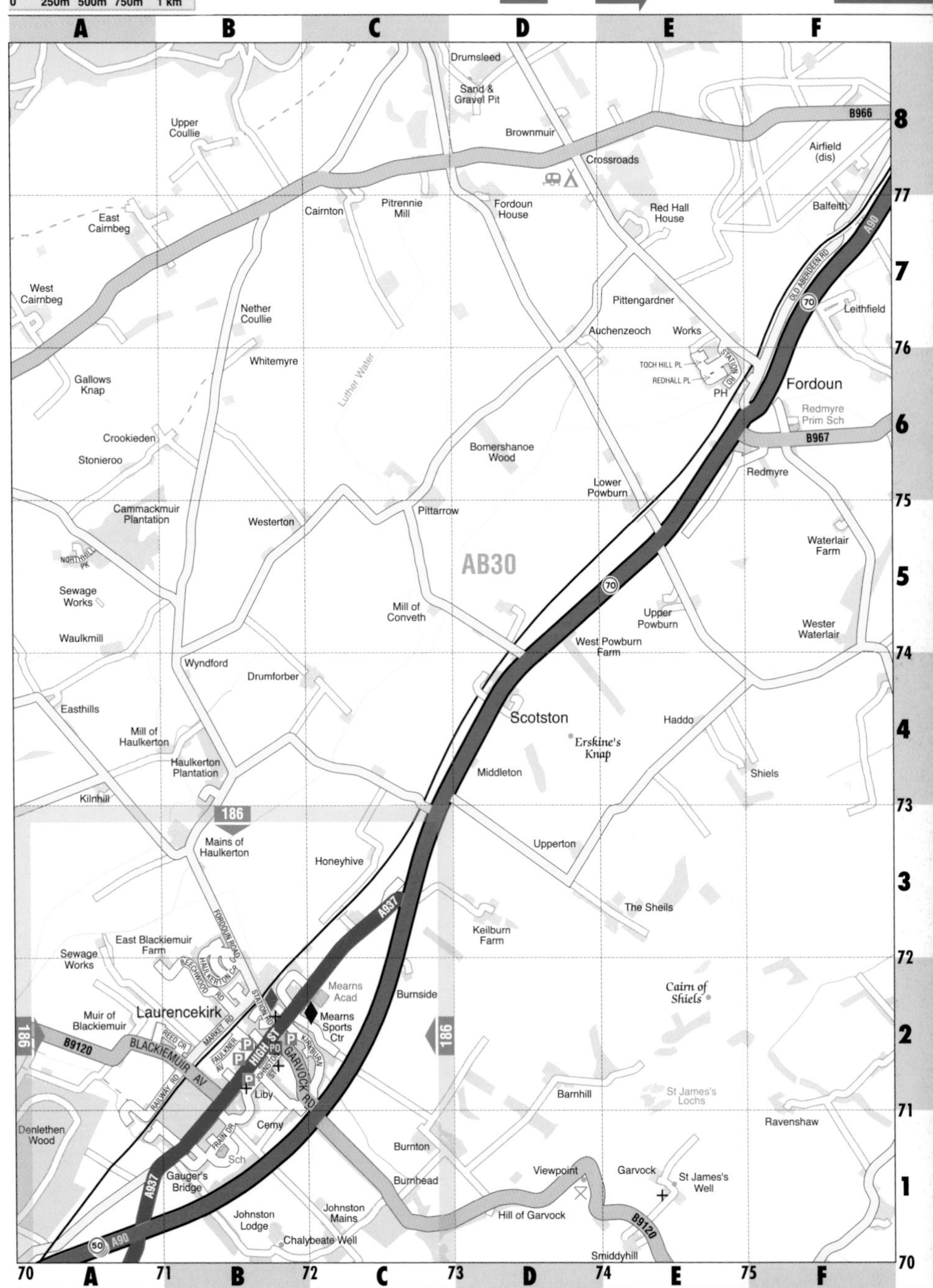

133
134
130
For full street detail of the highlighted area see page 186.

124 129 125
Scale: 1⅓ inches to 1 mile

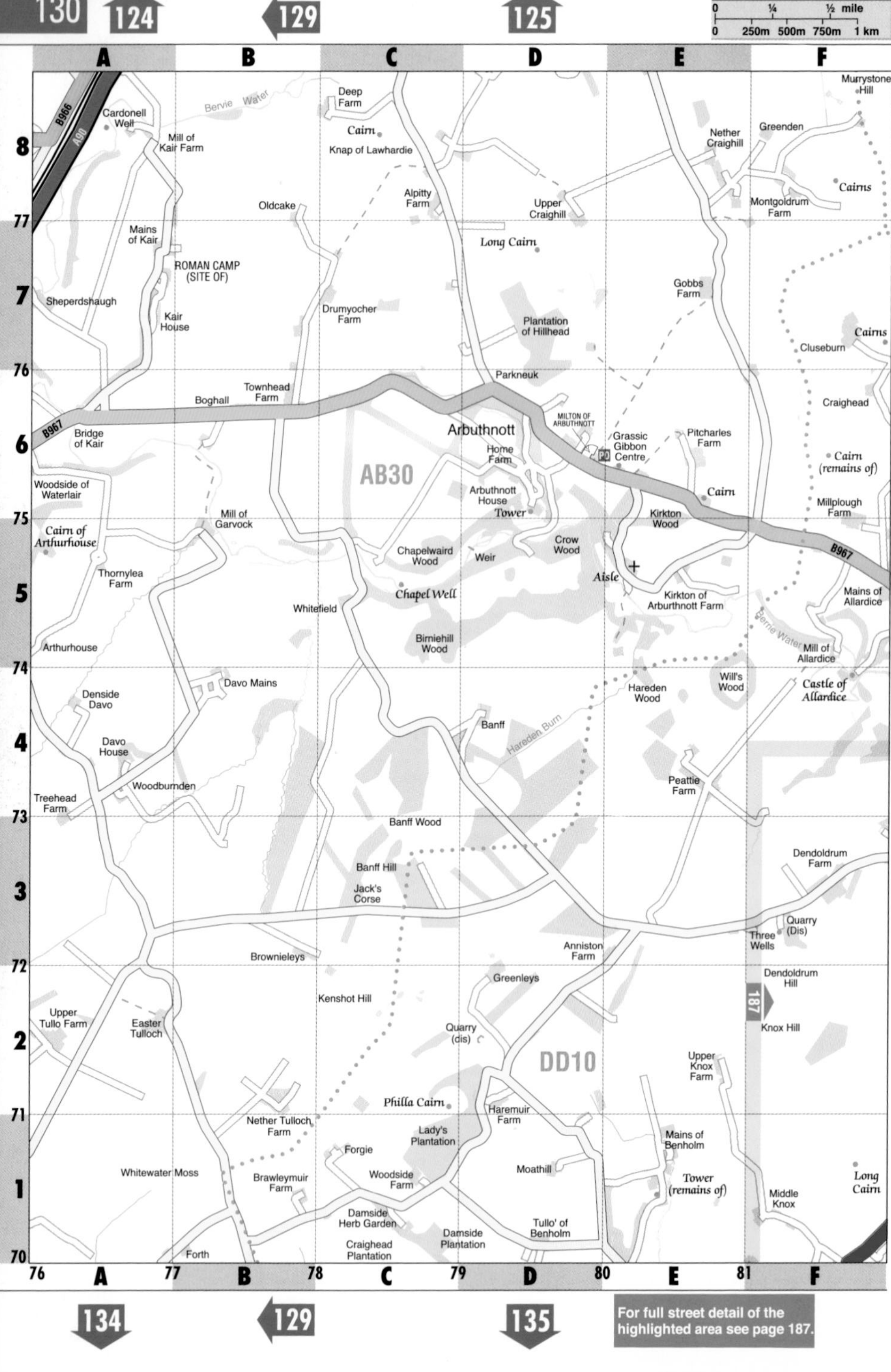

134 129 135

For full street detail of the highlighted area see page 187.

Scale: 1⅓ inches to 1 mile
0 ¼ ½ mile
0 250m 500m 750m 1 km

126

135

For full street detail of the highlighted area see page 187.

127

Scale: 1⅓ inches to 1 mile
0 ¼ ½ mile
0 250m 500m 750m 1 km

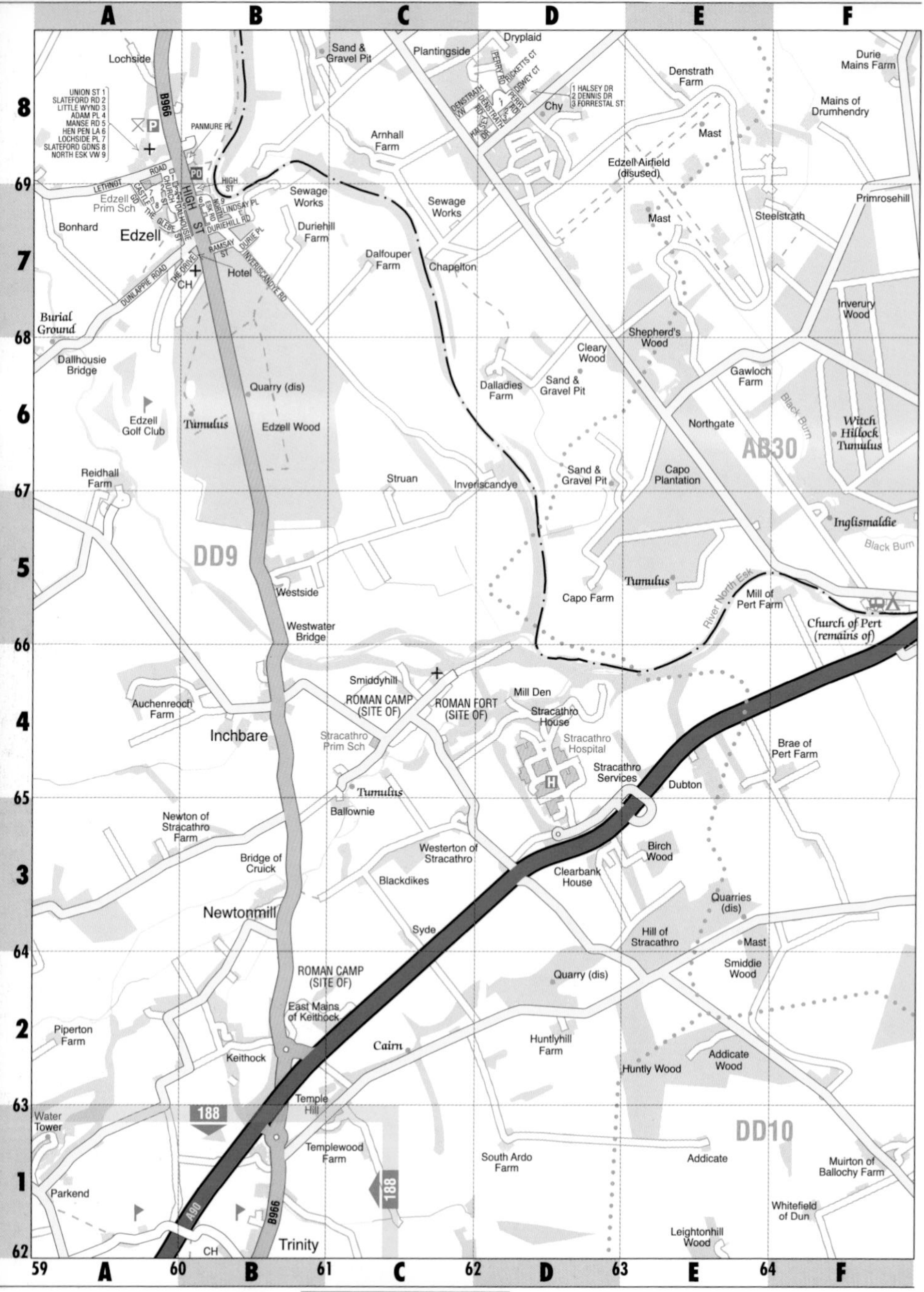

136

For full street detail of the highlighted area see page 188.

137

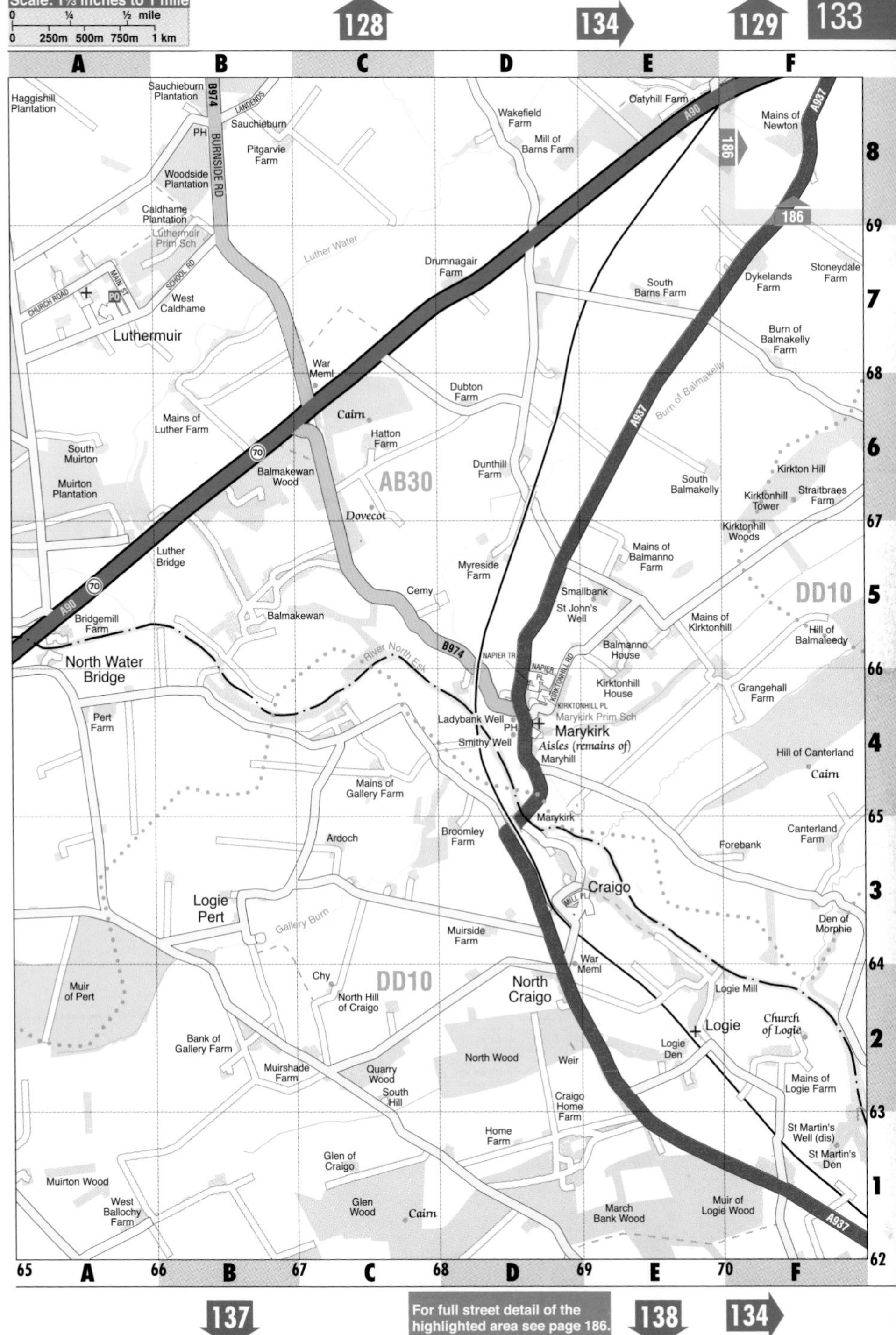

For full street detail of the highlighted area see page 186.

133
129

Scale: 1⅓ inches to 1 mile
0 ¼ ½ mile
0 250m 500m 750m 1 km

A B C D E F

8
69
7
68
6
67
5
66
4
65
3
64
2
63
1
62

Mast
B9120
Longleys
Tower of Johnston (Cairn)
186
AB30
Balhagarty Plantation
East Balhagarty
West Balhagarty
St James's Burn
Garvock Burn
West Bradieston
East Bradieston Farm
South Park of Bradieston
Berryhillock
South Bradieston
Craig of Garvock
Spy Brae
Newlands
Biddrie
Den Finella
Brandshill Wood
Upper Brackenrigg
Chapelfield
Hospital Shields Farm
Totterie
Muirhead
Criggie
Woodstone Hill
Mains of Lauriston
Lauriston Castle
Black Wood
Spittalmyre
Gaupieshaugh
Upper Craighill
DD10
Quarryfield Farm
B9120
A92
Mains of Woodstone
Taylorspark
Mill of Criggie
Lower Craighill Farm
Greystone
Hill Canterland
Home Farm
Bush
PH
Sillycoats
Snadon
West Mathers
Pitbeadlie
AB30
ECCLESGREIG RD
INVERGARRY PK
MANSE LA
Woodston Burn
Nether Woodston
Den of Morphie
ECCLESGREIG RD
HIGHVIEW GR
ARCHER PK
PO
BEACH RD
Church (remains of)
Castle (remains of)
Caves
Hill of Morphie
Lochside
LOCHSIDE ROAD
MORPHIE DR
MERCURY RD
BEACH RD
THE LOCHANS
LONE
MERCURY
St Cyrus Prim Sch
DICKSON WY
St Cyrus
Morphie
Sands of St Cyrus
Scotston of Kirkside
St Cyrus National Nature Reserve
Kirkside
Dannie's Den
Upper Warburton Farm
Visitor Centre
Pathhead
Nether Warburton
Commieston
Mill of Morphie
Stone of Morphie
Waterside Farm
MARYKIRK RD
A937
A92
Lower North Water Bridge
Fisherhills

1 MAYFIELD RD
2 SCOTSTON PL
3 SCOTSTON TERR
4 STATION RD
5 CROFT PL
6 DAVIDSON PL
7 CROFTLANDS
8 CROFT RD
9 OLD STATION SQ
10 SCHOOL WYND

71 A 72 B 73 C 74 D 75 E 76 F

133
138
For full street detail of the highlighted area see page 186.

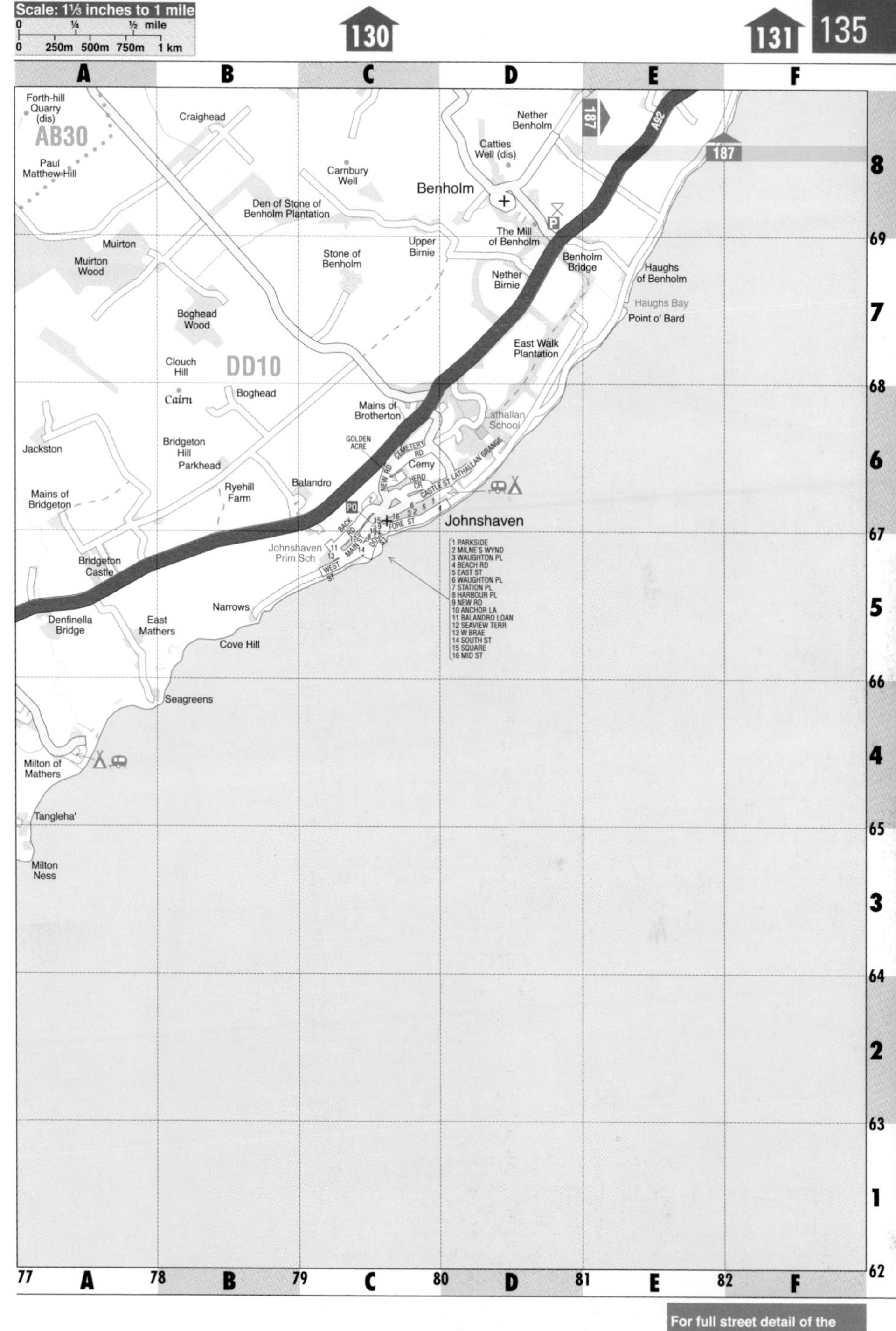

For full street detail of the highlighted area see page 187.

132

Scale: 1⅓ inches to 1 mile

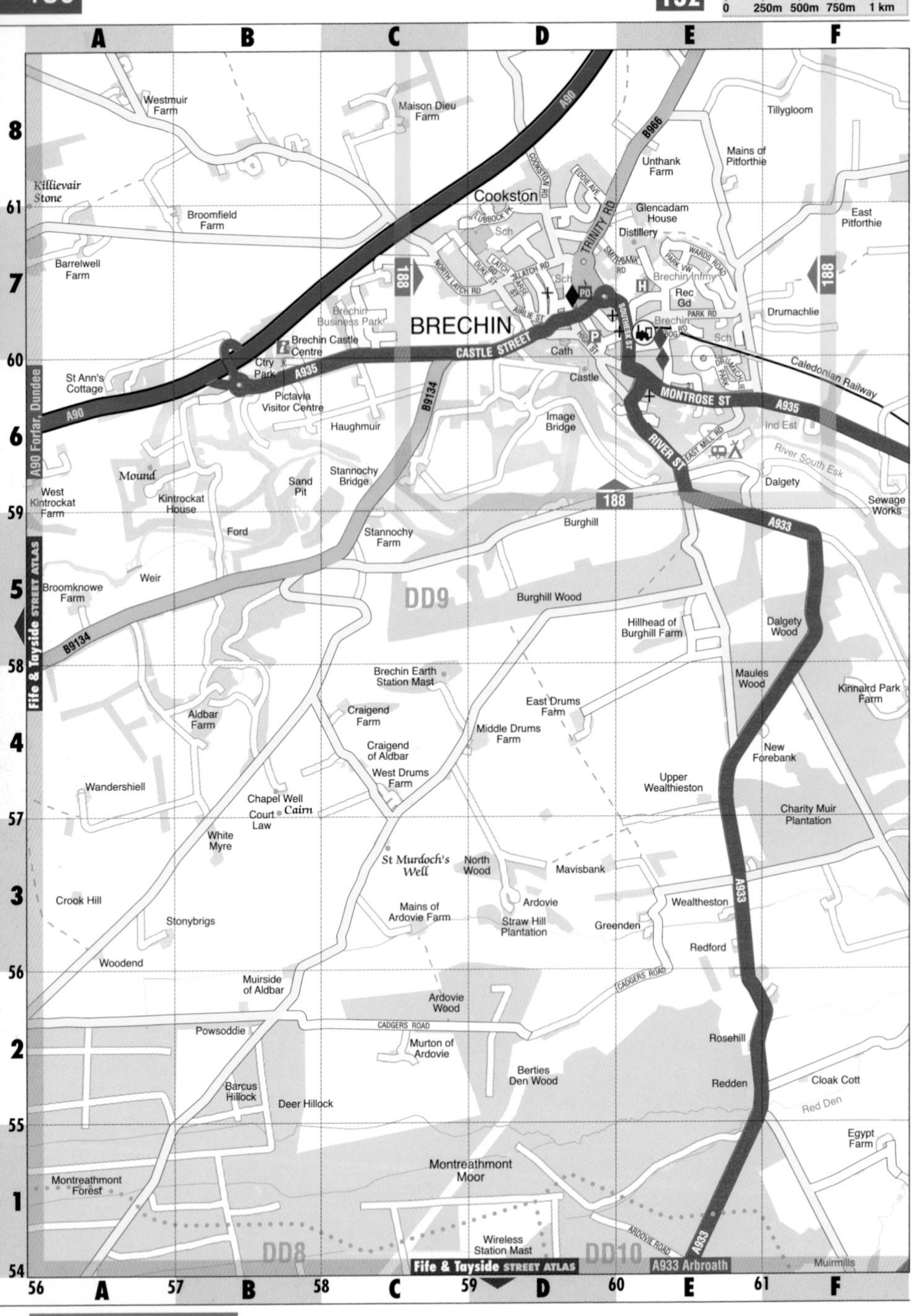

For full street detail of the highlighted area see page 188.

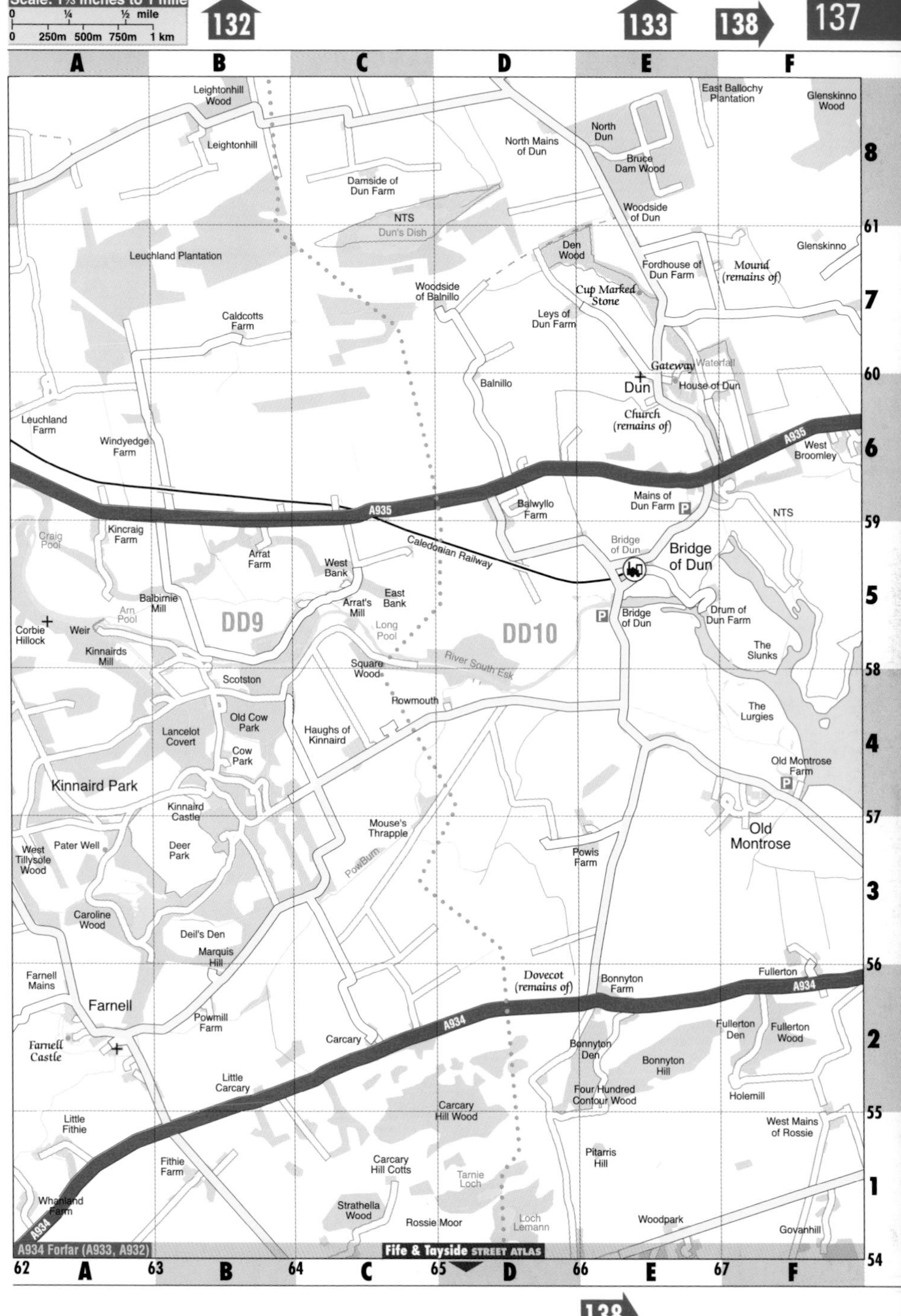
Scale: 1⅓ inches to 1 mile
0 ¼ ½ mile
0 250m 500m 750m 1 km
132
133
138
A
B
C
D
E
F
Leightonhill Wood
Leightonhill
Damside of Dun Farm
NTS
Dun's Dish
North Mains of Dun
North Dun
Bruce Dam Wood
East Ballochy Plantation
Glenskinno Wood
Woodside of Dun
Leuchland Plantation
Den Wood
Glenskinno
Fordhouse of Dun Farm
Mound (remains of)
Woodside of Balnillo
Cup Marked Stone
Caldcotts Farm
Leys of Dun Farm
Gateway
Waterfall
Dun
House of Dun
Balnillo
Church (remains of)
Leuchland Farm
Windyedge Farm
A935
West Broomley
Mains of Dun Farm
Balwyllo Farm
NTS
Kincraig Farm
Craig Pool
Caledonian Railway
Bridge of Dun
Arrat Farm
West Bank
East Bank
Arrat's Mill
Balbirnie Mill
Drum of Dun Farm
Arn Pool
DD9
DD10
Long Pool
Corbie Hillock
Weir
Kinnairds Mill
The Slunks
River South Esk
Square Wood
Scotston
Rowmouth
Old Cow Park
Lancelot Covert
Haughs of Kinnaird
The Lurgies
Cow Park
Old Montrose Farm
Kinnaird Park
Kinnaird Castle
Mouse's Thrapple
Old Montrose
West Tillysole Wood
Pater Well
Deer Park
Pow Burn
Powis Farm
Caroline Wood
Deil's Den
Marquis Hill
Farnell Mains
Dovecot (remains of)
Bonnyton Farm
Fullerton
A934
Farnell
Powmill Farm
Carcary
Fullerton Den
Fullerton Wood
Farnell Castle
Bonnyton Den
Bonnyton Hill
Little Carcary
Four Hundred Contour Wood
Holemill
Carcary Hill Wood
Little Fithie
West Mains of Rossie
Fithie Farm
Carcary Hill Cotts
Pitarris Hill
Tarnie Loch
Whanland Farm
Strathella Wood
Rossie Moor
Loch Lemann
Woodpark
Govanhill
A934 Forfar (A933, A932)
Fife & Tayside STREET ATLAS
8
61
7
60
6
59
5
58
4
57
3
56
2
55
1
54
62
63
64
65
66
67

138

137 133 134

C8
1 MACDIARMID DR
2 HILL RD
3 ROSEMOUNT PL
4 MANSE RD
5 INVERARITY CRES
6 LAMONDFAULD LA
7 CRUICKSHANK PK
8 DICKSON AVE

D8
1 DOWNIE WY
2 HOUGHTON DR

Scale: 1⅓ inches to 1 mile
0 ¼ ½ mile
0 250m 500m 750m 1 km

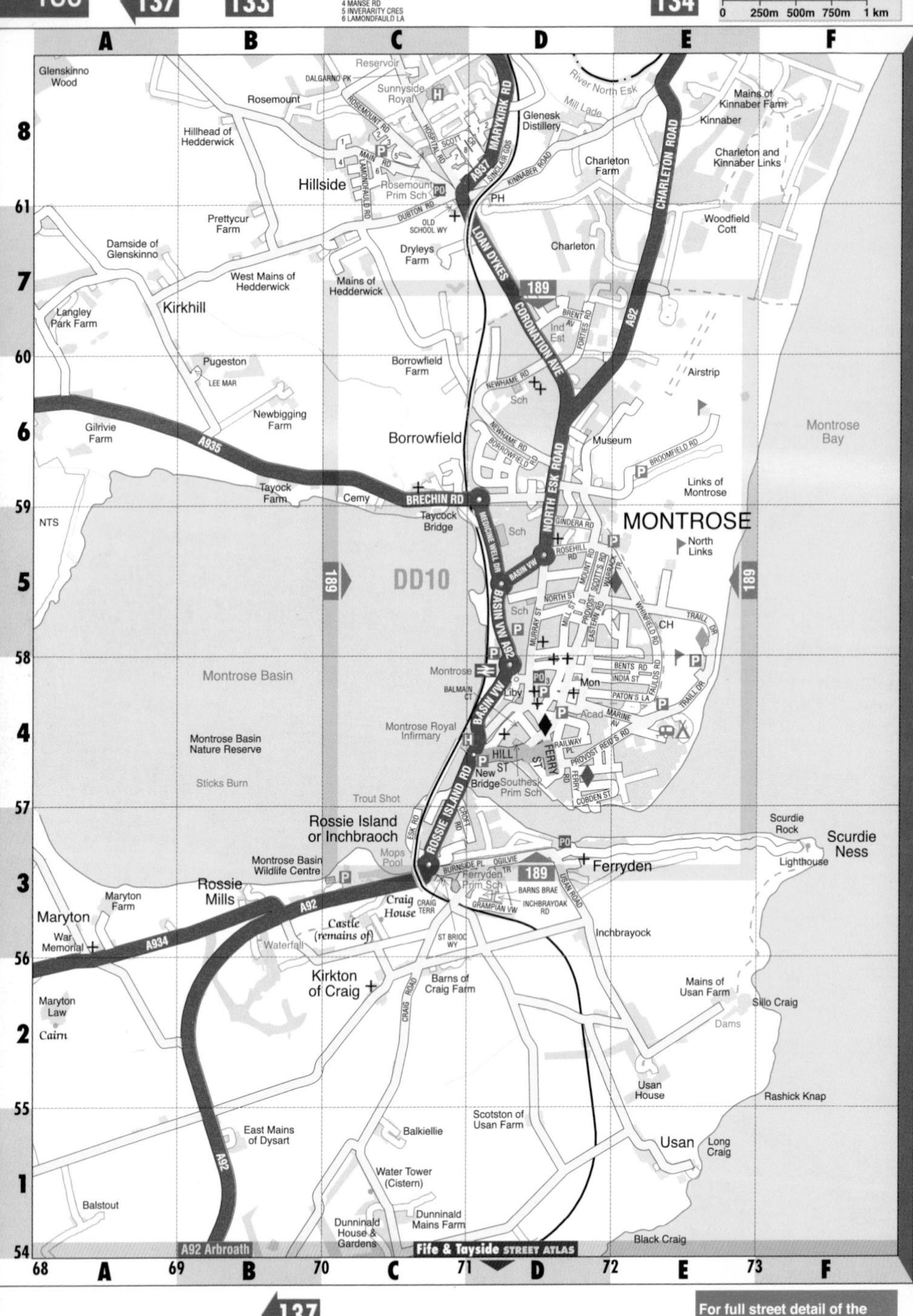

137

For full street detail of the highlighted area see page 189.

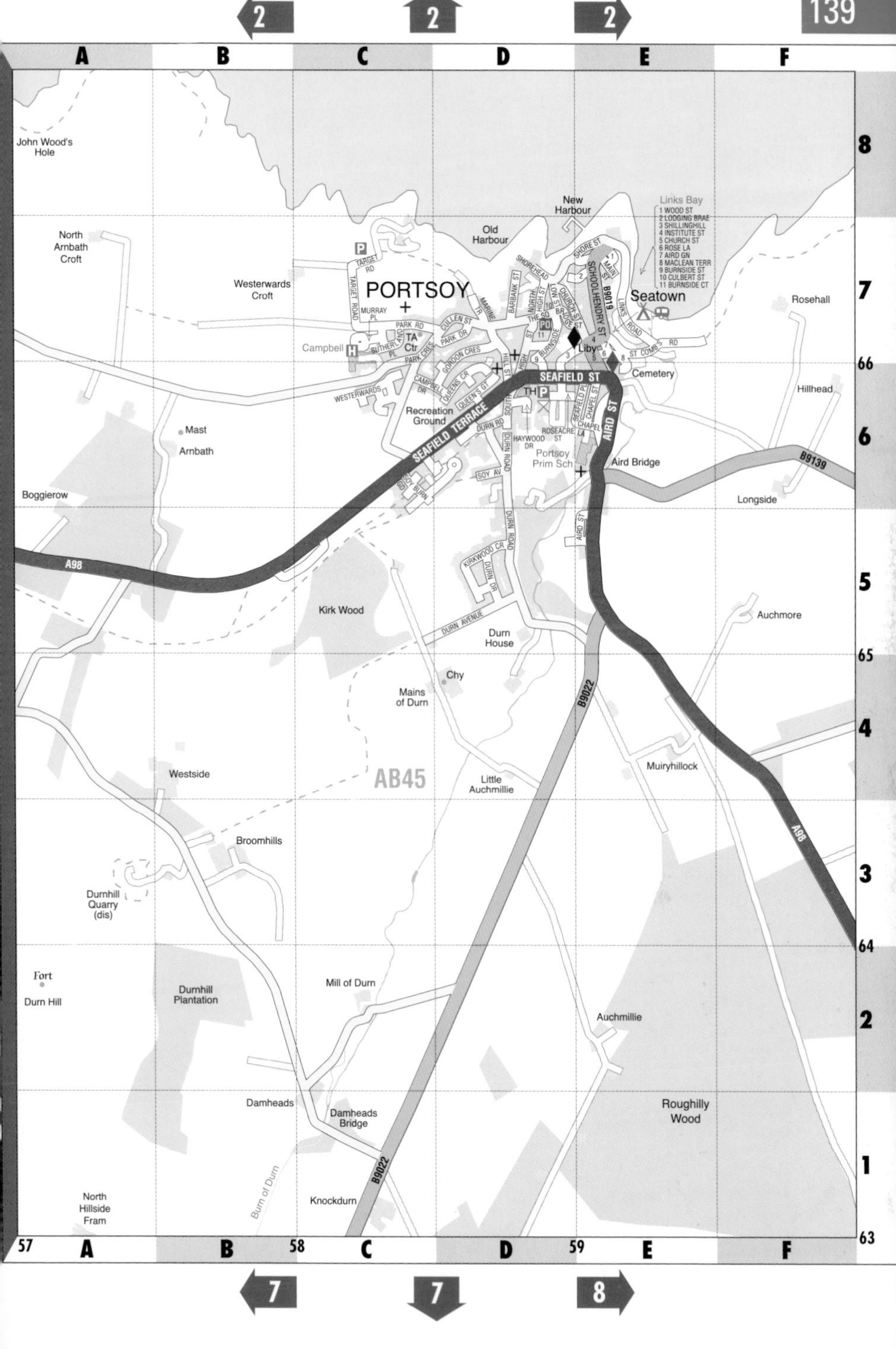
2
2
2
John Wood's Hole
North Arnbath Croft
Westerwards Croft
PORTSOY
Old Harbour
New Harbour
Links Bay
1 WOOD ST
2 LODGING BRAE
3 SHILLINGHILL
4 INSTITUTE ST
5 CHURCH ST
6 ROSE LA
7 AIRD GN
8 MACLEAN TERR
9 BURNSIDE ST
10 CULBERT ST
11 BURNSIDE CT
Seatown
Rosehall
Campbell
TA Ctr
Liby
Cemetery
Hillhead
SEAFIELD ST
SEAFIELD TERRACE
AIRD ST
Recreation Ground
Mast
Arnbath
Portsoy Prim Sch
Aird Bridge
B9139
Longside
Boggierow
A98
Kirk Wood
Durn House
Auchmore
Chy
Mains of Durn
B9022
Muiryhillock
Westside
AB45
Little Auchmillie
Broomhills
Durnhill Quarry (dis)
Fort
Durn Hill
Durnhill Plantation
Mill of Durn
Auchmillie
Damheads
Damheads Bridge
Roughilly Wood
Burn of Durn
Knockdurn
North Hillside Fram
7
7
8

8
9

F6
1 COLDHOME ST
2 REIDHAVEN ST
3 STUART LA
4 STUART ST
5 WHINHILL CRES
6 GALLOWHILL ST
7 KINGSWELL LA
8 SHERIFFS BRAE
9 GEORGE ST
10 CASTLE ST
11 OLD CASTLEGATE

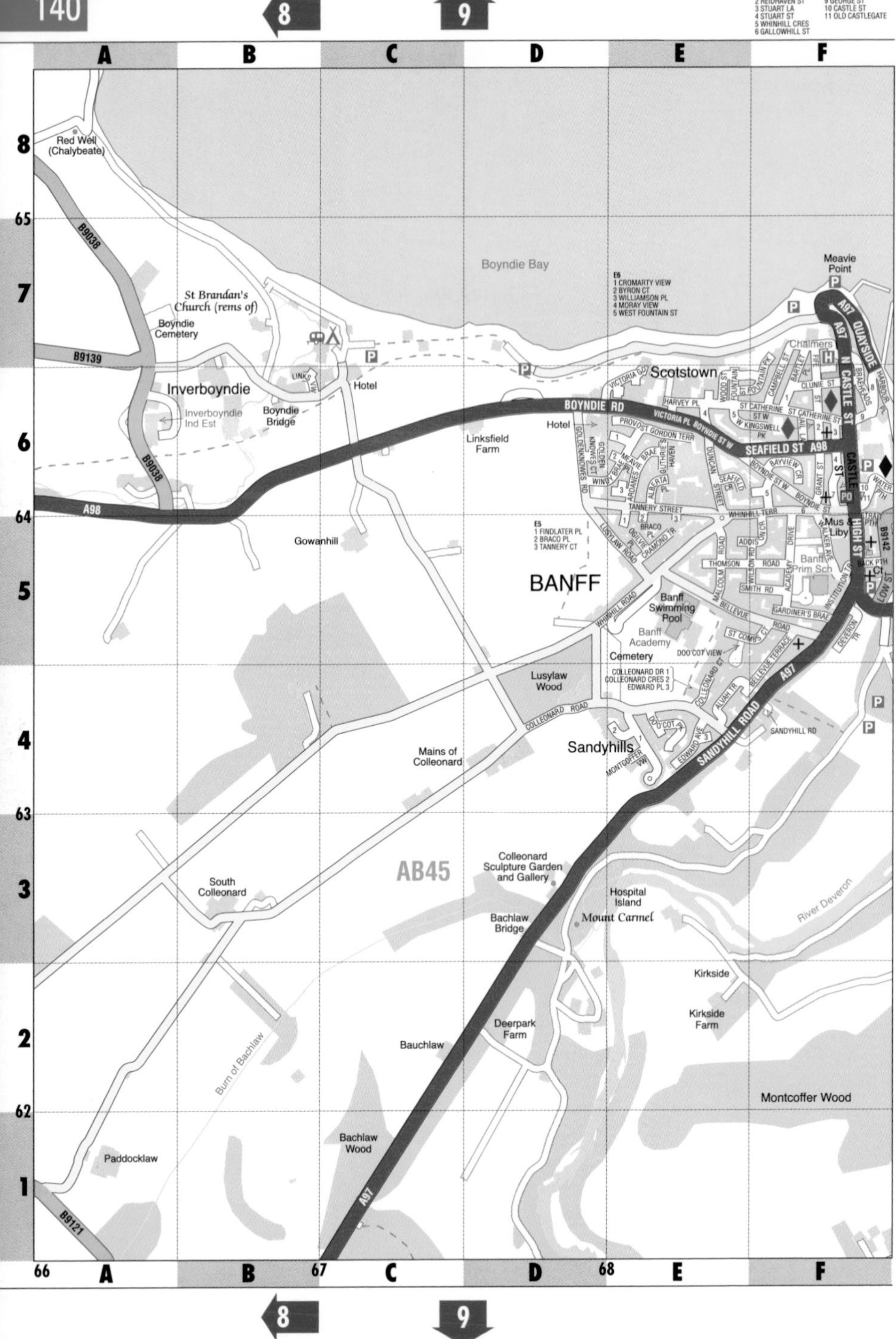

8
9

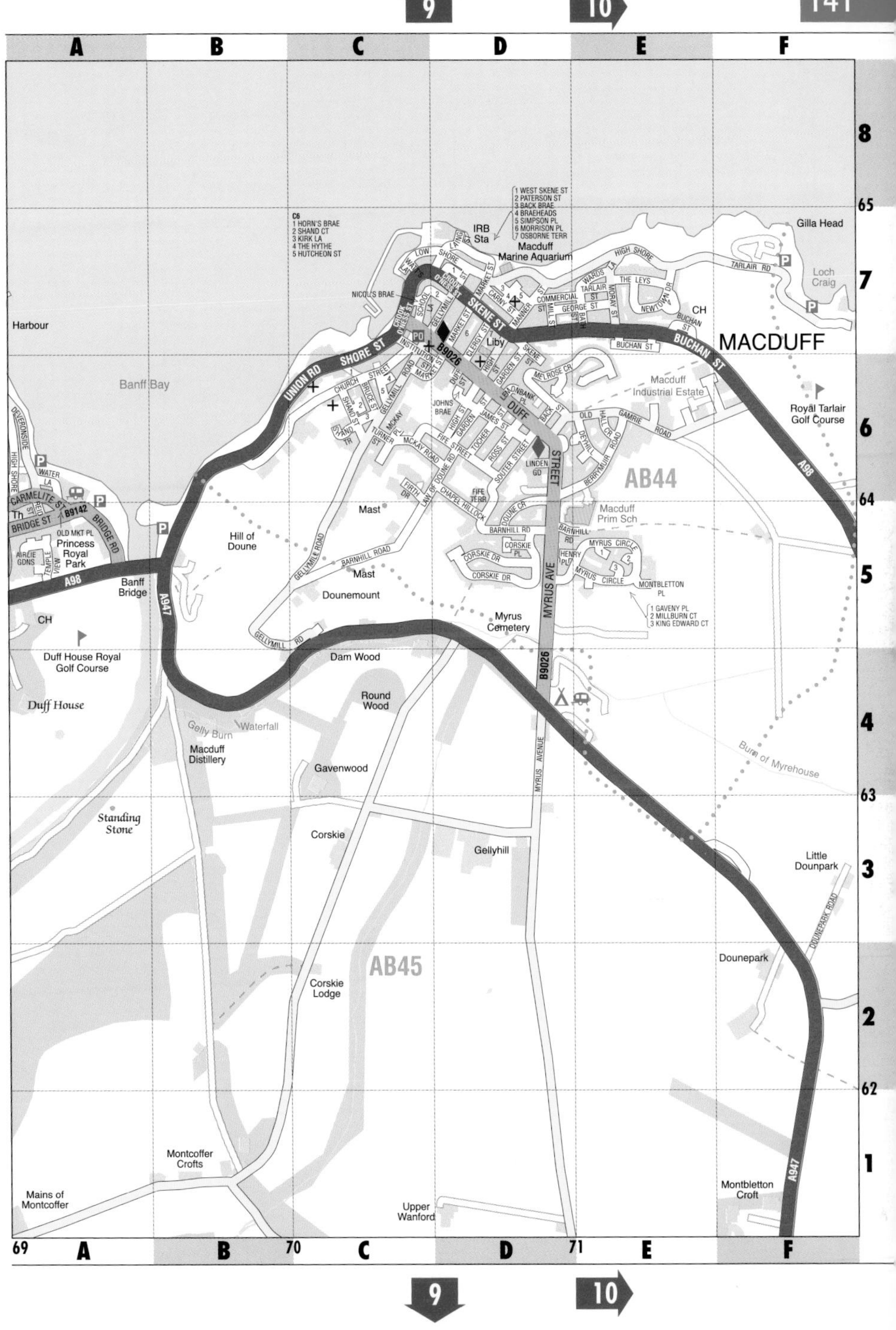
9
10
A
B
C
D
E
F
8
65
7
6
64
5
4
63
3
2
62
1
69
70
71
C6
1 HORN'S BRAE
2 SHAND CT
3 KIRK LA
4 THE HYTHE
5 HUTCHEON ST
1 WEST SKENE ST
2 PATERSON ST
3 BACK BRAE
4 BRAEHEADS
5 SIMPSON PL
6 MORRISON PL
7 OSBORNE TERR
IRB Sta
Macduff Marine Aquarium
Gilla Head
Loch Craig
Harbour
Banff Bay
MACDUFF
Macduff Industrial Estate
Royal Tarlair Golf Course
AB44
Macduff Prim Sch
Hill of Doune
Mast
Banff Bridge
Princess Royal Park
Dounemount
Myrus Cemetery
CH
Duff House Royal Golf Course
Duff House
Dam Wood
Round Wood
Gelly Burn
Waterfall
Macduff Distillery
Gavenwood
Burn of Myrehouse
Standing Stone
Corskie
Gellyhill
Little Dounpark
AB45
Dounepark
Corskie Lodge
Montcoffer Crofts
Mains of Montcoffer
Upper Wanford
Montbletton Croft
1 GAVENY PL
2 MILLBURN CT
3 KING EDWARD CT
MONTBLETTON PL
UNION RD
SHORE ST
SKENE ST
BUCHAN ST
DUFF STREET
MYRUS AVE
MYRUS AVENUE
B9026
A98
A947
B9142
GELLYMILL ROAD
BARNHILL ROAD
CORSKIE DR
MYRUS CIRCLE
GAMRIE ROAD
TARLAIR RD
HIGH SHORE
CARMELITE ST
BRIDGE ST
BRIDGE RD
OLD MKT PL
DOUNEPARK ROAD
Liby
PO

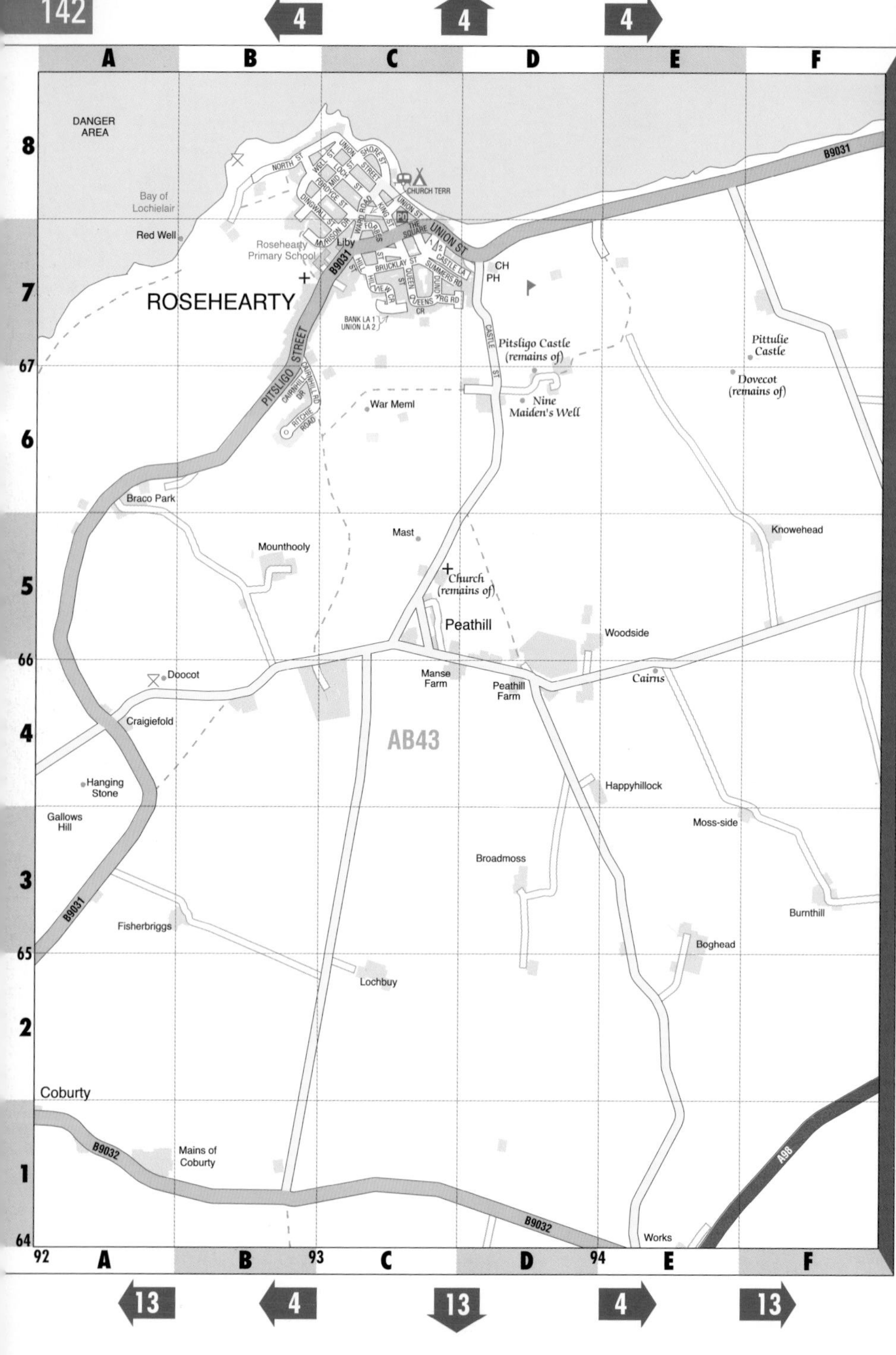

DANGER AREA
NORTH ST
WELL ST
LOCH ST
UNION ST
SHORE ST
STREET
MID ST
FORDYCE ST
DINGWALL ST
MARISON DR
WARD ROAD
KING ST
FORBES
THE SQUARE
UNION ST
CHURCH TERR
Bay of Lochielair
Red Well
Rosehearty Primary School
Liby
ROSEHEARTY
B9031
HILL ST
BRUCKLAY ST
CASTLE LA
SUMMERS RD
HILLVIEW CR
QUEEN ST
QUEENS CR
DUNORG RD
BANK LA 1
UNION LA 2
CH
PH
CASTLE ST
Pitsligo Castle (remains of)
Nine Maiden's Well
Pittulie Castle
Dovecot (remains of)
PITSLIGO STREET
CAIRNHILL DR
CAIRNHILL RD
RITCHIE ROAD
War Meml
Braco Park
Mounthooly
Mast
Church (remains of)
Peathill
Knowehead
Woodside
Doocot
Manse Farm
Peathill Farm
Cairns
Craigiefold
AB43
Hanging Stone
Gallows Hill
Happyhillock
Moss-side
Broadmoss
Burnthill
Fisherbriggs
Boghead
Lochbuy
Coburty
B9032
Mains of Coburty
A98
Works
A B C D E F
8 7 6 5 4 3 2 1
67 66 65 64
92 93 94
4 4 4
13 4 13 4 13

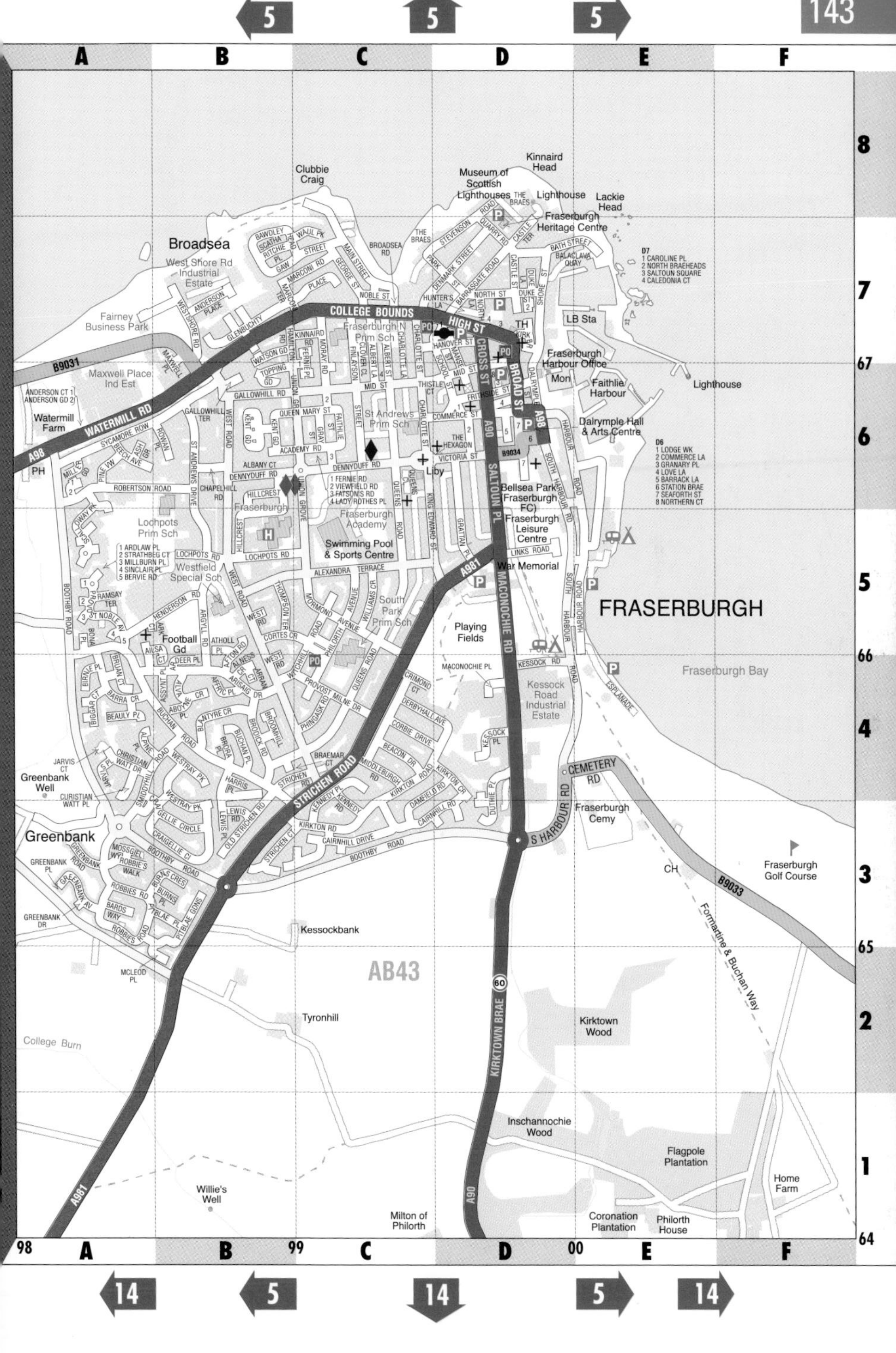

5
5
5
A
B
C
D
E
F
8
7
67
6
5
66
4
3
65
2
1
64
98
99
00
Clubbie Craig
Museum of Scottish Lighthouses
Kinnaird Head
Lighthouse
Lackie Head
Fraserburgh Heritage Centre
Broadsea
West Shore Rd Industrial Estate
Fairney Business Park
Maxwell Place Ind Est
Watermill Farm
COLLEGE BOUNDS
HIGH ST
WATERMILL RD
B9031
A98
PH
LB Sta
TH
Fraserburgh Harbour Office
Mon
Faithlie Harbour
Lighthouse
Dalrymple Hall & Arts Centre
D7
1 CAROLINE PL
2 NORTH BRAEHEADS
3 SALTOUN SQUARE
4 CALEDONIA CT
D6
1 LODGE WK
2 COMMERCE LA
3 GRANARY PL
4 LOVE LA
5 BARRACK LA
6 STATION BRAE
7 SEAFORTH ST
8 NORTHERN CT
Fraserburgh N Prim Sch
St Andrews Prim Sch
Lby
Fraserburgh
Fraserburgh Academy
Swimming Pool & Sports Centre
Lochpots Prim Sch
Westfield Special Sch
1 ARDLAW PL
2 STRATHBEG CT
3 MILLBURN PL
4 SINCLAIR PL
5 BERVIE RD
1 FERNIE RD
2 VIEWFIELD RD
3 FATSON'S RD
4 LADY ROTHES PL
Bellsea Park (Fraserburgh FC)
Fraserburgh Leisure Centre
War Memorial
FRASERBURGH
South Park Prim Sch
Playing Fields
Football Gd
Fraserburgh Bay
Kessock Road Industrial Estate
SALTOUN PL
MACONOCHIE RD
A90
A981
B9034
STRICHEN ROAD
Greenbank Well
Greenbank
CEMETERY RD
Fraserburgh Cemy
S HARBOUR RD
CH
B9033
Fraserburgh Golf Course
Formartine & Buchan Way
Kessockbank
AB43
KIRKTOWN BRAE
60
Tyronhill
College Burn
Kirktown Wood
Inschannochie Wood
Flagpole Plantation
Home Farm
Willie's Well
Milton of Philorth
Coronation Plantation
Philorth House
14
5
14
5
14

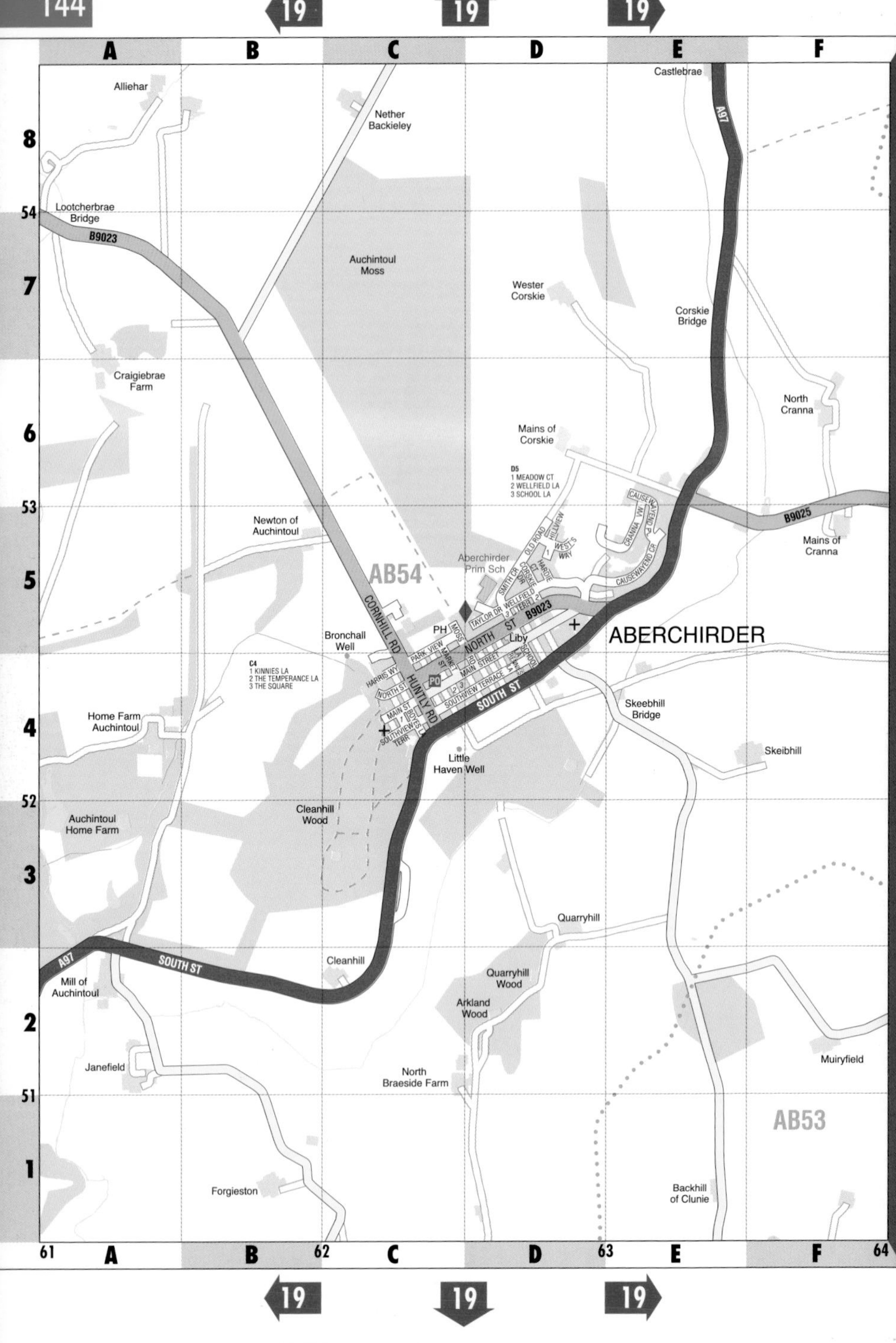
19
19
19
Castlebrae
Alliehar
Nether Backieley
A97
Lootcherbrae Bridge
B9023
Auchintoul Moss
Wester Corskie
Corskie Bridge
Craigiebrae Farm
North Cranna
Mains of Corskie
D5
1 MEADOW CT
2 WELLFIELD LA
3 SCHOOL LA
B9025
Newton of Auchintoul
Mains of Cranna
AB54
Aberchirder Prim Sch
CORNHILL RD
NORTH ST
TAYLOR DR
WELLFIELD TERR
CAUSEWAYEND CR
ABERCHIRDER
Bronchall Well
PH
Liby
C4
1 KINNIES LA
2 THE TEMPERANCE LA
3 THE SQUARE
HARRIS WY
PARK VIEW
MAIN STREET
SOUTHVIEW TERRACE
SOUTH ST
HUNTLY RD
PO
Skeebhill Bridge
Home Farm Auchintoul
Skeibhill
Little Haven Well
Auchintoul Home Farm
Cleanhill Wood
Quarryhill
A97
SOUTH ST
Cleanhill
Mill of Auchintoul
Quarryhill Wood
Arkland Wood
Janefield
Muiryfield
North Braeside Farm
AB53
Forgieston
Backhill of Clunie
A B C D E F
8 7 6 5 4 3 2 1
54 53 52 51
61 62 63 64
19
19
19

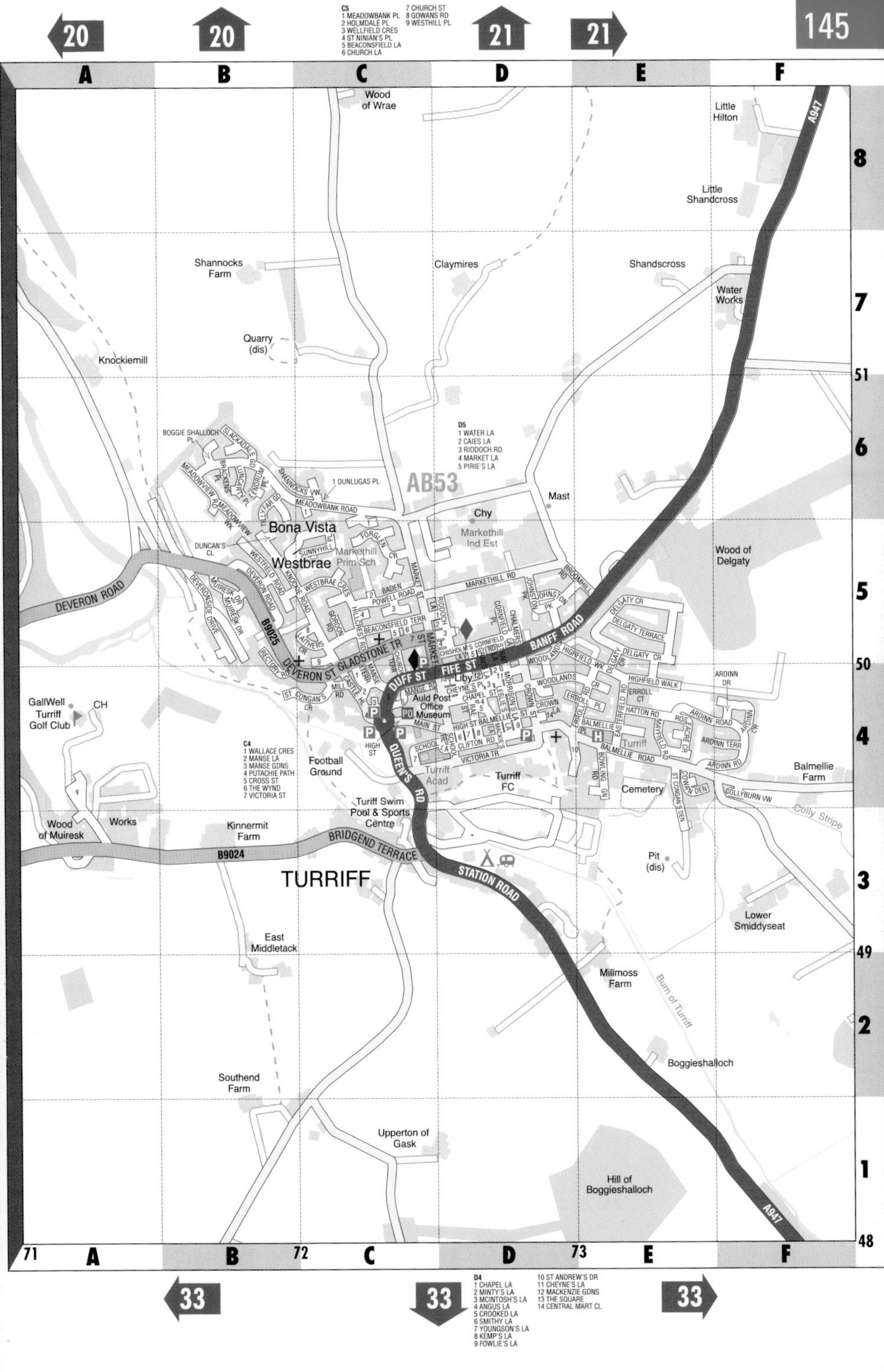

20
20
C5
1 MEADOWBANK PL
2 HOLMDALE PL
3 WELLFIELD CRES
4 ST NINIAN'S PL
5 BEACONSFIELD LA
6 CHURCH LA
7 CHURCH ST
8 GOWANS RD
9 WESTHILL PL
21
21
A
B
C
D
E
F
Wood of Wrae
Little Hilton
A947
8
Little Shandcross
Shannocks Farm
Claymires
Shandscross
Water Works
7
Quarry (dis)
Knockiemill
51
D5
1 WATER LA
2 CAIES LA
3 RIDDOCH RD
4 MARKET LA
5 PIRIE'S LA
BOGGIE SHALLOCH PL
SLACKADALE GD
6
AB53
1 DUNLUGAS PL
Mast
MEADOWBANK ROAD
Chy
Markethill Ind Est
Bona Vista
DUNCAN'S CL
SUNNYHILL
Markethill Prim Sch
Westbrae
Wood of Delgaty
DEVERON ROAD
MARKETHILL RD
BADEN POWELL ROAD
5
BEACONSFIELD TERR
B9025
DELGATY CR
DELGATY TERRACE
DELGATY CR
BANFF ROAD
HIGHFIELD WK
DEVERON ST
GLADSTONE TR
DUFF ST
FIFE ST
Liby
WOODLANDS
HIGHFIELD WALK
ARDINN DR
50
ERROLL CT
GallWell
Turriff Golf Club
CH
ST CONGAN'S CR
Auld Post Office Museum
MANSE RD
CHEYNE'S PL
CHAPEL ST
MAIN ST
HIGH ST
BALMELLIE ST
HATTON RD
ARDINN ROAD
ARDINN TERR
BALMELLIE ROAD
ARDINN RD
4
C4
1 WALLACE CRES
2 MANSE LA
3 MANSE GDNS
4 PUTACHIE PATH
5 CROSS ST
6 THE WYND
7 VICTORIA ST
SCHOOL
CLIFTON RD
VICTORIA TR
HIGH ST
Football Ground
QUEEN'S RD
Turriff Acad
Turriff FC
Turriff
Balmellie Farm
Cemetery
COLLYBURN VW
Colly Stripe
Turriff Swim Pool & Sports Centre
Wood of Muiresk
Works
Kinnermit Farm
BRIDGEND TERRACE
B9024
Pit (dis)
STATION ROAD
TURRIFF
3
Lower Smiddyseat
East Middletack
49
Millmoss Farm
Burn of Turriff
2
Boggieshalloch
Southend Farm
Upperton of Gask
1
Hill of Boggieshalloch
A947
48
71
72
73
33
33
33
D4
1 CHAPEL LA
2 MINTY'S LA
3 MCINTOSH'S LA
4 ANGUS LA
5 CROOKED LA
6 SMITHY LA
7 YOUNGSON'S LA
8 KEMP'S LA
9 FOWLIE'S LA
10 ST ANDREW'S DR
11 CHEYNE'S LA
12 MACKENZIE GDNS
13 THE SQUARE
14 CENTRAL MART CL

37
25
38
Brakeshill
Boghead Farm
Mains of Pitfour
Backhill
Hillhead of Mintlaw
Braeside
Middle Lodge
Balring Farm
Keplahill
Dunshillock
AB42
Recreation Ground
Tait's Well
Mintlaw Station
Hotel
Formantine and Buchan Way
STATION ROAD
LONGSIDE RD
NORTH ST
SOUTH STREET
A952
A950
Mintlaw Academy
Liby
Pitfour School
Mintlaw Prim Sch
Mintlaw
Aden Country Park
Aberdeenshire Farming Museum
Leisure Centre
Nether Aden
Baluss Farm
Mill of Aden
Baluss Bridge
South Ugie Water
Croft of Knock
Easter Knock
Yokieshill
D5
1 OLD SCHOOL
2 THE GREENS
3 BURNSIDE CT
4 BURNSIDE RD
5 SYCAMORE PL
6 HAWTHORN CRES
7 THISTLE GDNS
E5
1 BALUSS VW
E4
1 BAIN GDNS
2 BAIN PL
D4
1 QUARRY PL
C4
1 WOODSIDE PL

A8
1 BROOKSIDE
2 WHITE GATES

B5
1 GADWALL PL
2 EIDER CT
3 MALLARD DR
4 ST MAGNUS PL
5 HAWTHORN RD
6 STRAWBERRY BANK

40
40
40

E5
1 CARTERS CL
2 TOLBOOTHWYND
3 THREADNEEDLE ST
4 NARROW LA
5 THISTLE ST

40
40
40

29 43 30 44

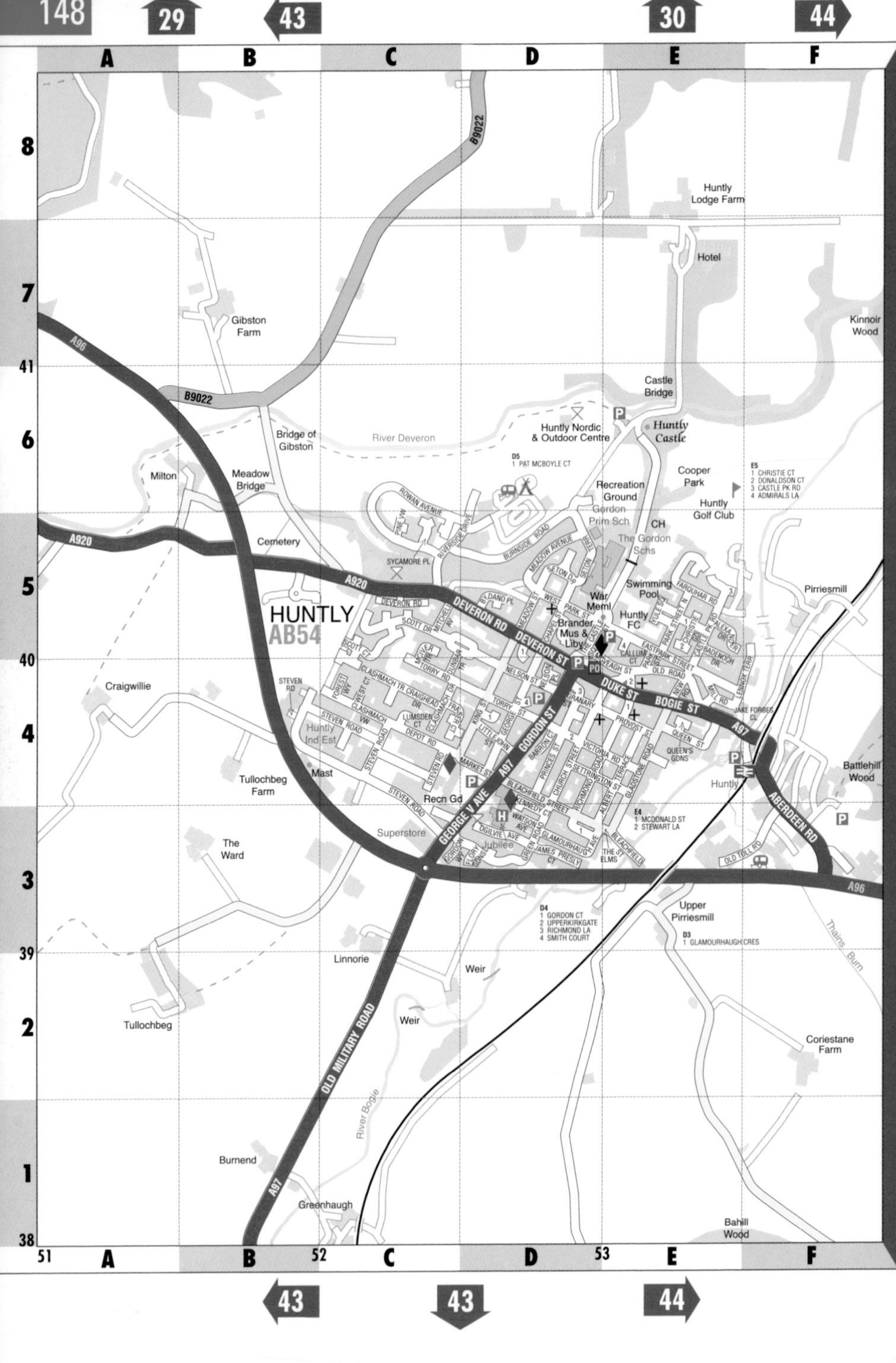

43 43 44

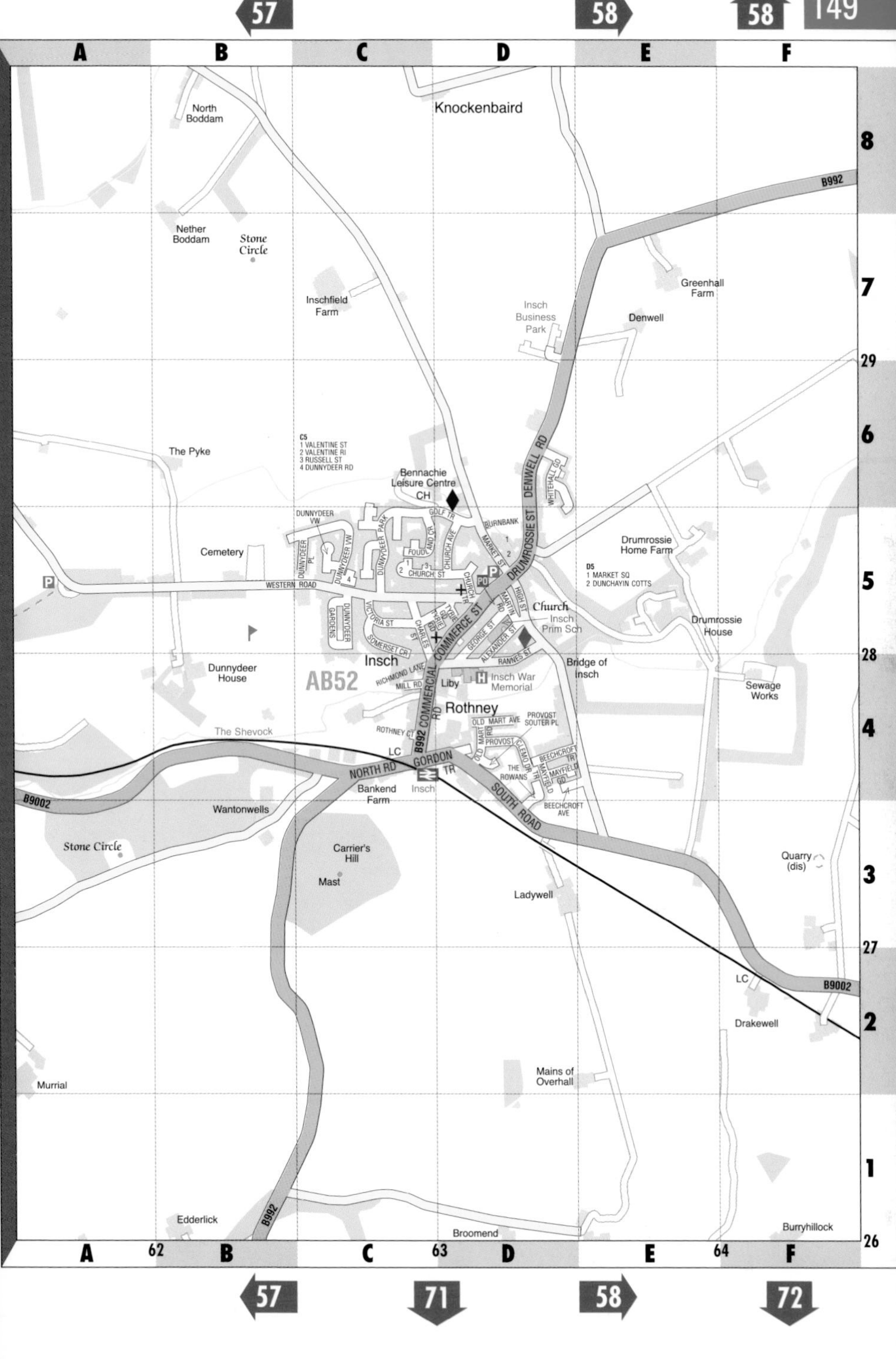
A B C D E F
8 7 29 6 5 28 4 3 27 2 1 26
Knockenbaird
North Boddam
Nether Boddam
Stone Circle
Inschfield Farm
B992
Greenhall Farm
Insch Business Park
Denwell
C5
1 VALENTINE ST
2 VALENTINE RI
3 RUSSELL ST
4 DUNNYDEER RD
The Pyke
Bennachie Leisure Centre
CH
GOLF TR
BURNBANK
DENWELL RD
DRUMROSSIE ST
WHITEHALL GD
DUNNYDEER VW
DUNNYDEER PL
DUNNYDEER PARK
FOUDLAND CR
CHURCH AVE
CHURCH ST
MARKET ST
Cemetery
Drumrossie Home Farm
D5
1 MARKET SQ
2 DUNCHAYIN COTTS
WESTERN ROAD
CHURCH TR
HIGH ST
MARTIN RD
Church
Insch Prim Sch
Drumrossie House
VICTORIA ST
GARDENS
DUNNYDEER
CHARLES ST
COMMERCE ST
GEORGE ST
ALEXANDER ST
SOMERSET CR
RANNES ST
Insch
Dunnydeer House
AB52
RICHMOND LANE
MILL RD
COMMERCIAL RD
B992
Liby
Insch War Memorial
Bridge of Insch
Sewage Works
Rothney
OLD MART AVE
PROVOST SOUTER PL
OLD MART RD
PROVOST CLEMO DR
ROTHNEY CT
The Shevock
LC
NORTH RD
GORDON TR
BEECHCROFT TR
THE ROWANS
MAYFIELD GD
BEECHCROFT AVE
Insch
Bankend Farm
B9002
Wantonwells
SOUTH ROAD
Stone Circle
Carrier's Hill
Mast
Quarry (dis)
Ladywell
LC
B9002
Drakewell
Murrial
Mains of Overhall
Edderlick
B992
Broomend
Burryhillock
62 63 64

60 60 61 61

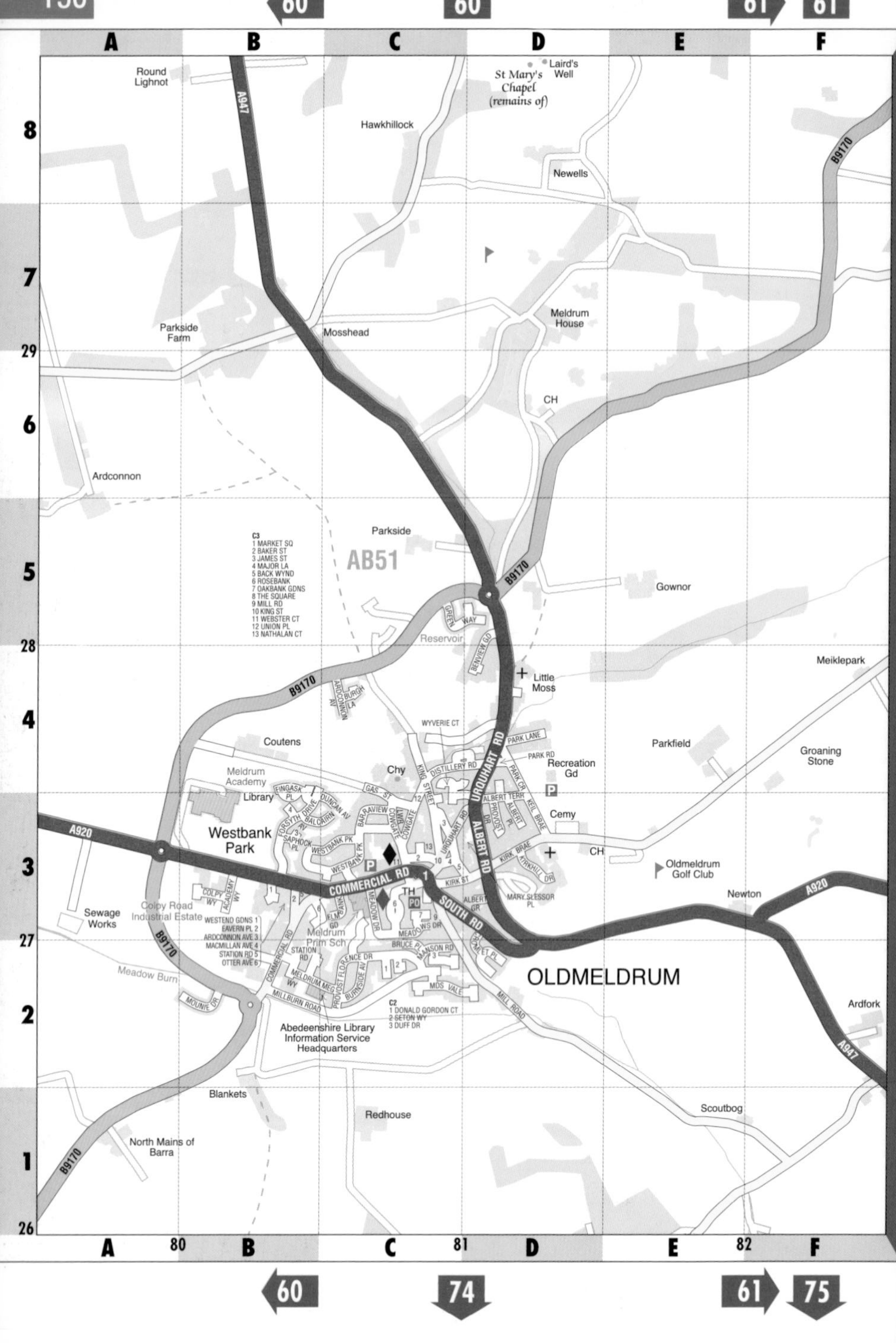

60 74 61 75

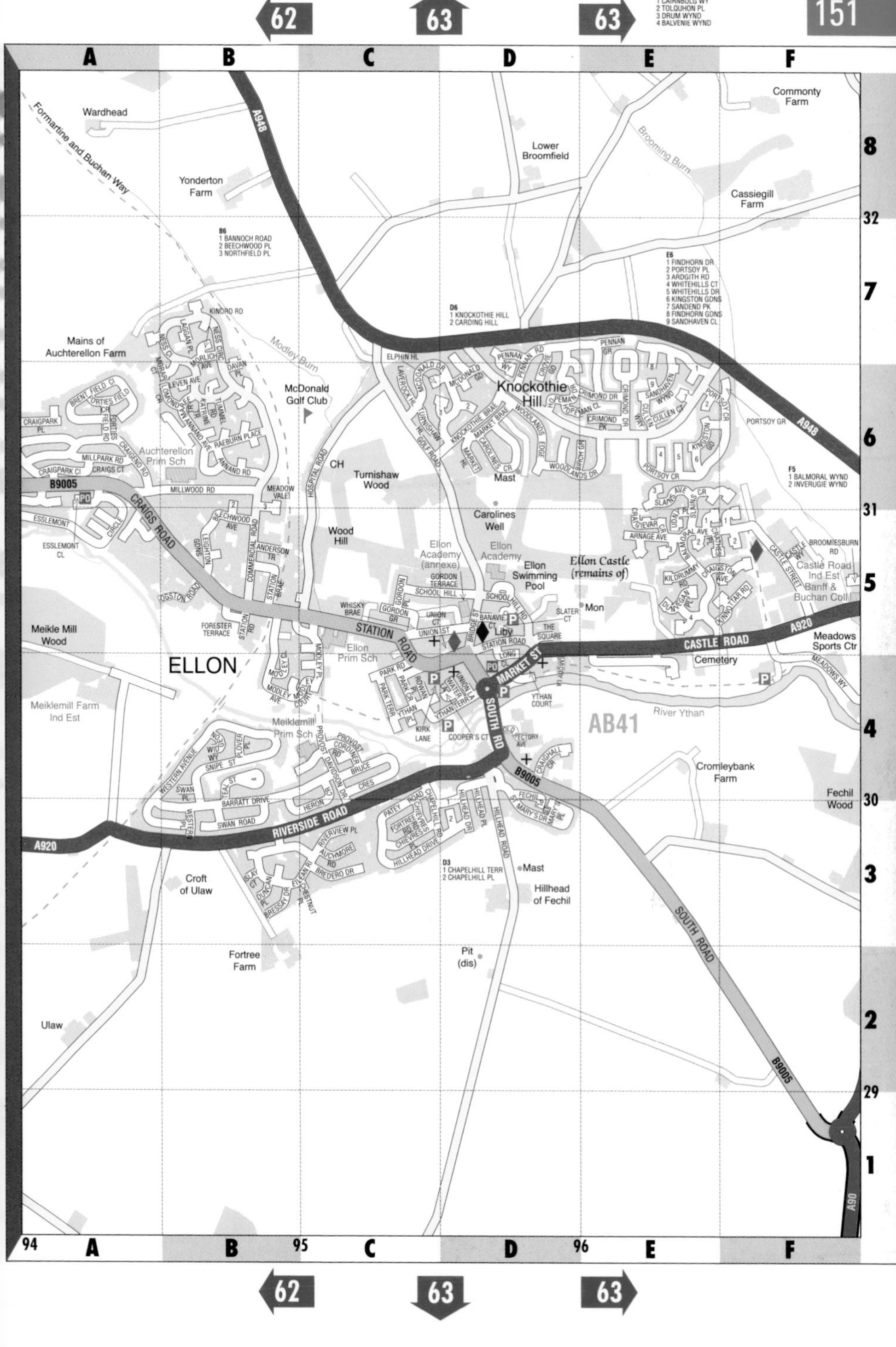
62
63
63
E5
1 CAIRNBULG WY
2 TOLQUHON PL
3 DRUM WYND
4 BALVENIE WYND
Wardhead
Formartine and Buchan Way
A948
Yonderton Farm
Lower Broomfield
Commonty Farm
Brooming Burn
Cassiegill Farm
B6
1 BANNOCH ROAD
2 BEECHWOOD PL
3 NORTHFIELD PL
E6
1 FINDHORN DR
2 PORTSOY PL
3 ARDGITH RD
4 WHITEHILLS CT
5 WHITEHILLS DR
6 KINGSTON GDNS
7 SANDEND PK
8 FINDHORN GDNS
9 SANDHAVEN CL
D6
1 KNOCKOTHIE HILL
2 CARDING HILL
Mains of Auchterellon Farm
Modley Burn
McDonald Golf Club
Knockothie Hill
F5
1 BALMORAL WYND
2 INVERUGIE WYND
Auchterellon Prim Sch
CH
Turnishaw Wood
Mast
Carolines Well
B9005
CRAIGS ROAD
MILLWOOD RD
Wood Hill
Ellon Academy (annexe)
Ellon Academy
Ellon Swimming Pool
Ellon Castle (remains of)
Castle Road Ind Est
Banff & Buchan Coll
Mon
Meikle Mill Wood
STATION ROAD
Liby
CASTLE ROAD
A920
Meadows Sports Ctr
Cemetery
ELLON
Ellon Prim Sch
MARKET ST
SOUTH RD
Meiklemill Farm Ind Est
River Ythan
AB41
Meiklemill Prim Sch
Cromleybank Farm
Fechil Wood
RIVERSIDE ROAD
A920
D3
1 CHAPELHILL TERR
2 CHAPELHILL PL
Mast
Croft of Ulaw
Hillhead of Fechil
SOUTH ROAD
Fortree Farm
Pit (dis)
Ulaw
B9005
A90
A B C D E F
8 32 7 6 31 5 4 30 3 2 29 1
94 95 96

A8
1 CONGLASS GDS
2 CONGLASS WY
3 CRAIGNATHUNDER
4 HUMMEL CRAIG
5 LT OXEN CRAIG

B8
1 MEADOW PL
2 MEADOW RD
3 WHITELEY WELL PL
4 MEARNS CL
5 BRANDSBUTT

C6
1 MARYFIELD PL
2 BENNACHIE AVE
3 BLACKHALL ROAD

73 74 74

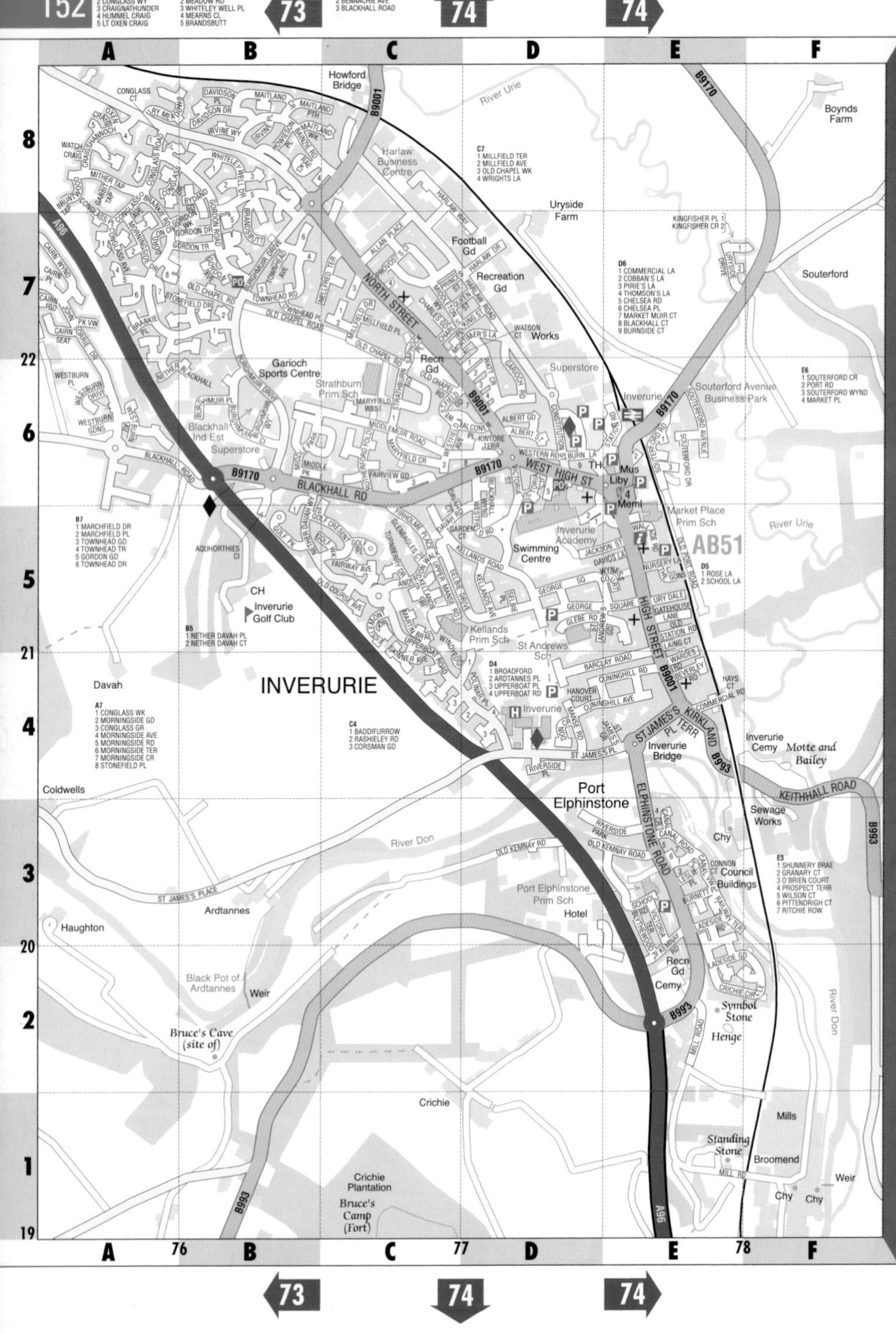

73 74 74

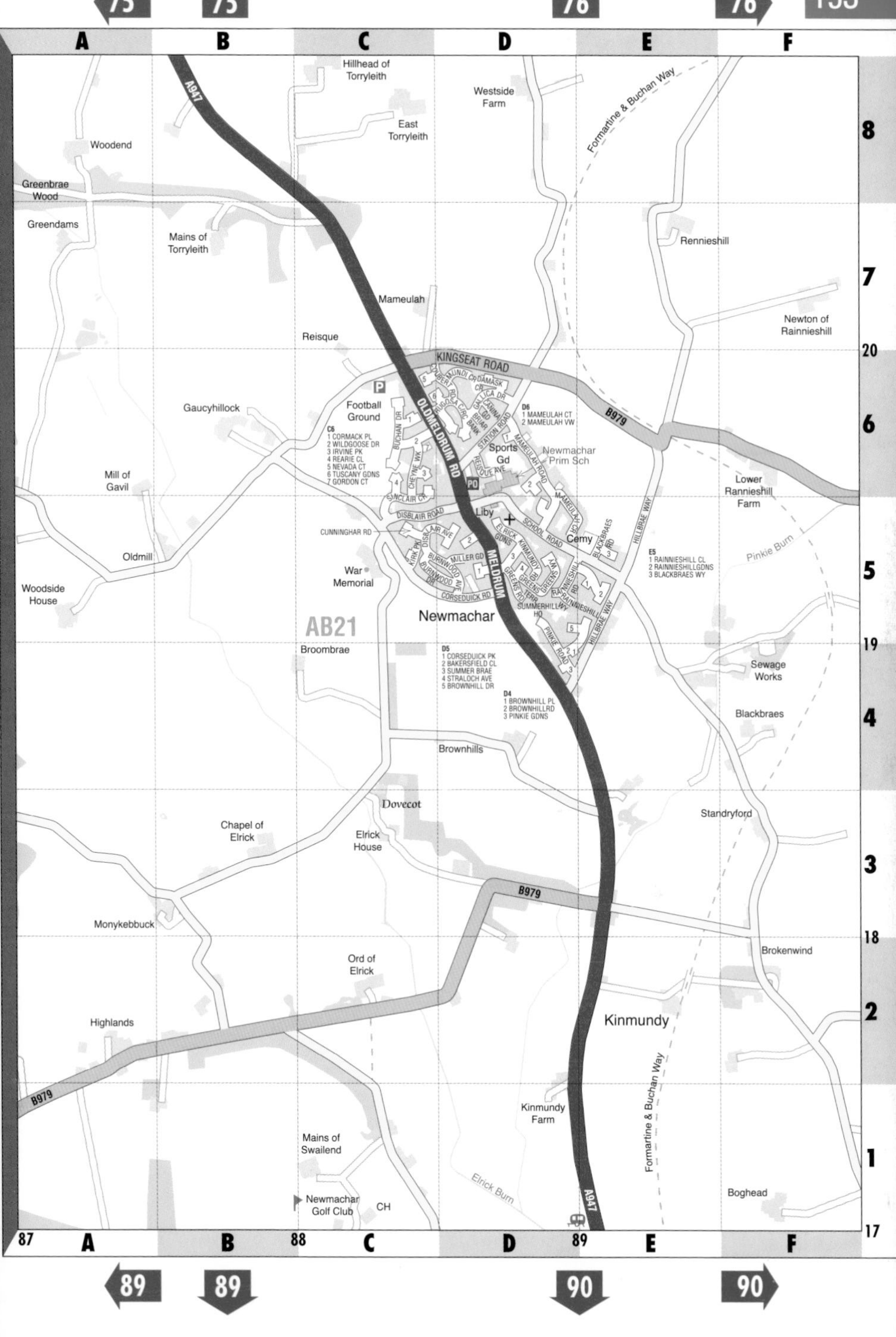
75
75
76
76
A
B
C
D
E
F
8
7
20
6
5
19
4
3
18
2
1
17
87
88
89
Hillhead of Torryleith
Westside Farm
Formartine & Buchan Way
A947
East Torryleith
Woodend
Greenbrae Wood
Greendams
Mains of Torryleith
Rennieshill
Mameulah
Newton of Rainnieshill
Reisque
KINGSEAT ROAD
Football Ground
Gaucyhillock
OLDMELDRUM RD
B979
D6
1 MAMEULAH CT
2 MAMEULAH VW
C6
1 CORMACK PL
2 WILDGOOSE DR
3 IRVINE PK
4 REARIE CL
5 NEVADA CT
6 TUSCANY GDNS
7 GORDON CT
Sports Gd
Newmachar Prim Sch
STATION ROAD
MAMEULAH ROAD
Mill of Gavil
PO
Lower Rannieshill Farm
SINCLAIR CR
DISBLAIR ROAD
Liby
SCHOOL ROAD
CUNNINGHAR RD
Cemy
BLACKBRAES RD
HILLBRAE WAY
Oldmill
MELDRUM
E5
1 RAINNIESHILL CL
2 RAINNIESHILLGDNS
3 BLACKBRAES WY
Pinkie Burn
War Memorial
Woodside House
CORSEDUICK RD
Newmachar
AB21
SUMMERHILL
PINKIE ROAD
Broombrae
D5
1 CORSEDUICK PK
2 BAKERSFIELD CL
3 SUMMER BRAE
4 STRALOCH AVE
5 BROWNHILL DR
Sewage Works
D4
1 BROWNHILL PL
2 BROWNHILLRD
3 PINKIE GDNS
Blackbraes
Brownhills
Dovecot
Standryford
Chapel of Elrick
Elrick House
Monykebbuck
Brokenwind
Ord of Elrick
Highlands
Kinmundy
Kinmundy Farm
Mains of Swailend
Newmachar Golf Club
CH
Elrick Burn
Boghead
89
89
90
90

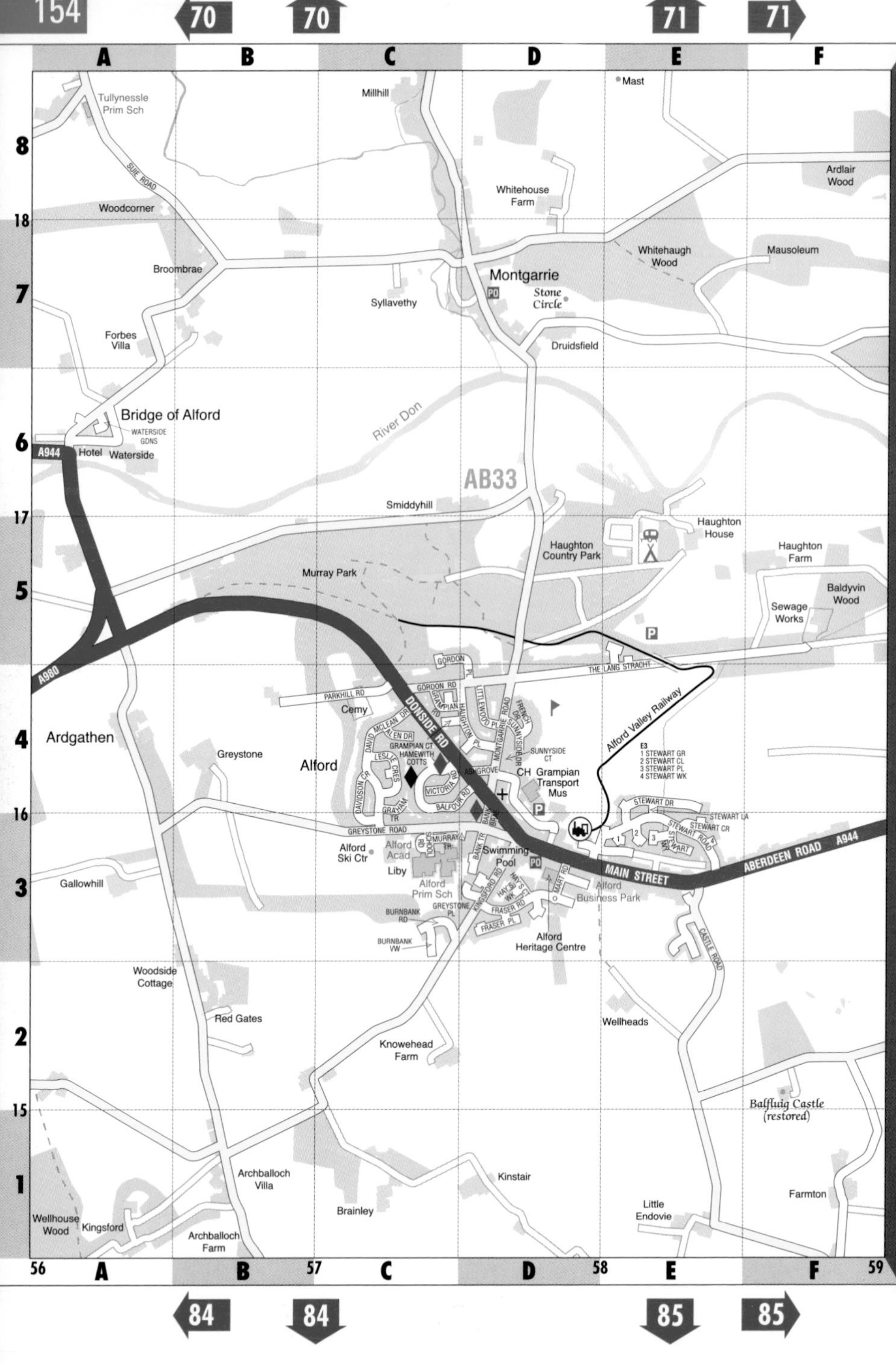

70
70
71
71
A
B
C
D
E
F
Tullynessle Prim Sch
Millhill
Mast
SUIE ROAD
Ardlair Wood
Whitehouse Farm
Woodcorner
Whitehaugh Wood
Mausoleum
Broombrae
Montgarrie
Stone Circle
Syllavethy
Forbes Villa
Druidsfield
River Don
Bridge of Alford
WATERSIDE GDNS
A944
Hotel
Waterside
AB33
Smiddyhill
Haughton House
Haughton Country Park
Haughton Farm
Murray Park
Baldyvin Wood
Sewage Works
A980
THE LANG STRACHT
GORDON PL
GORDON RD
PARKHILL RD
DONSIDE RD
Cemy
Alford Valley Railway
Ardgathen
Greystone
Alford
SUNNYSIDE CT
E3
1 STEWART GR
2 STEWART CL
3 STEWART PL
4 STEWART WK
CH
Grampian Transport Mus
ASHGROVE
VICTORIA RD
BALFOUR RD
GREYSTONE ROAD
STEWART DR
STEWART LA
STEWART CR
STEWART ROAD
Alford Ski Ctr
Alford Acad
Liby
Swimming Pool
MAIN STREET
ABERDEEN ROAD
A944
Gallowhill
Alford Prim Sch
Alford Business Park
BURNBANK RD
BURNBANK VW
GREYSTONE PL
FRASER RD
FRASER PL
Alford Heritage Centre
CASTLE ROAD
Woodside Cottage
Red Gates
Wellheads
Knowehead Farm
Balfluig Castle (restored)
Archballoch Villa
Kinstair
Farmton
Brainley
Little Endovie
Wellhouse Wood
Kingsford
Archballoch Farm
8
18
7
6
17
5
4
16
3
2
15
1
56
57
58
59
84
84
85
85

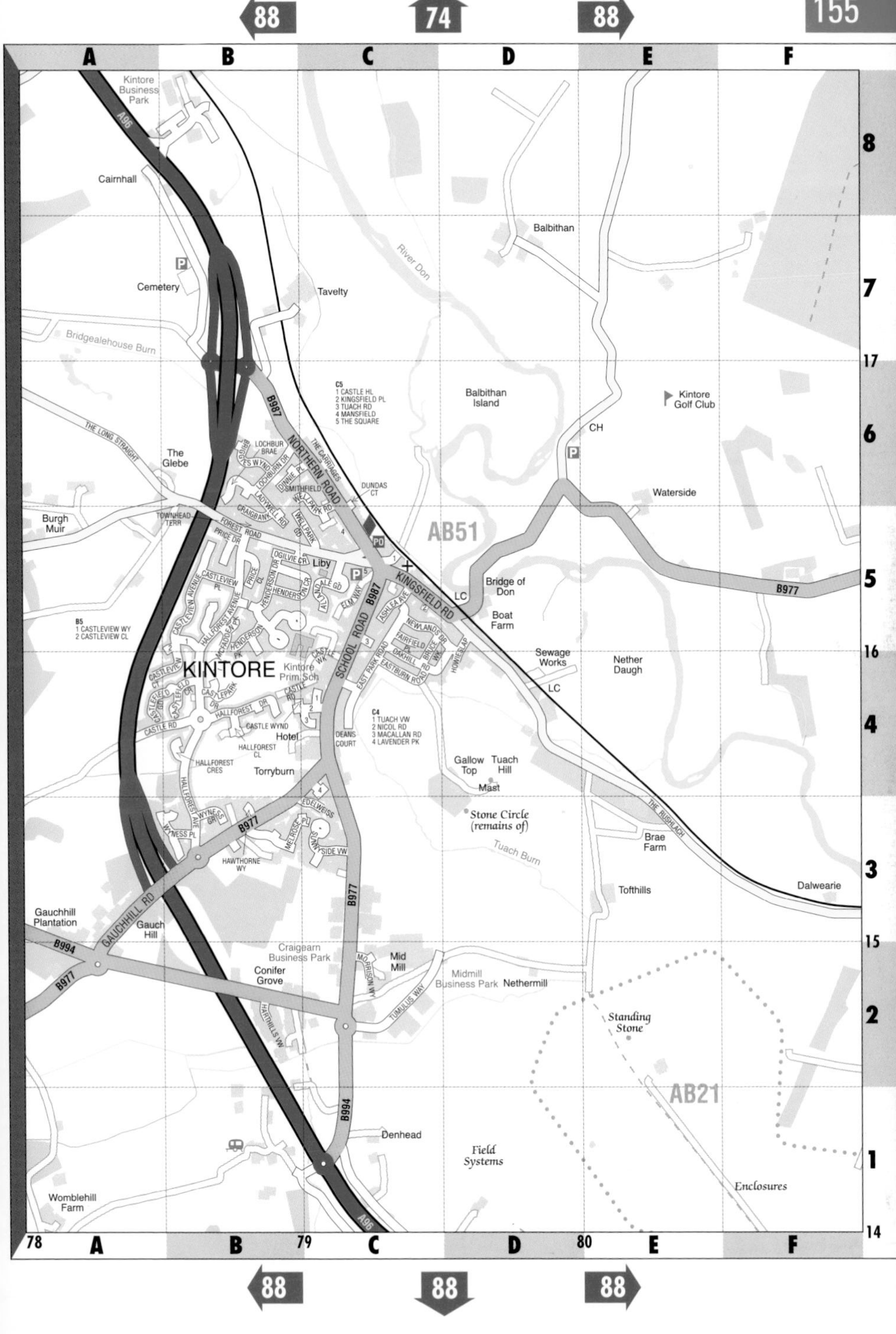

88
74
88
A
B
C
D
E
F
8
7
17
6
5
16
4
3
15
2
1
14
78
79
80
Kintore Business Park
Cairnhall
Cemetery
Tavelty
Balbithan
River Don
Bridgealehouse Burn
Balbithan Island
Kintore Golf Club
CH
The Glebe
Waterside
Burgh Muir
AB51
Liby
Bridge of Don
Boat Farm
LC
B977
KINTORE
Kintore Prim Sch
Sewage Works
Nether Daugh
Hotel
Torryburn
Gallow Top
Tuach Hill
Mast
Stone Circle (remains of)
Tuach Burn
Brae Farm
Tofthills
Dalwearie
Gauchhill Plantation
Gauch Hill
Craigearn Business Park
Conifer Grove
Mid Mill
Midmill Business Park
Nethermill
Standing Stone
AB21
Denhead
Field Systems
Enclosures
Womblehill Farm
A96
B987
B994
NORTHERN ROAD
SCHOOL ROAD
KINGSFIELD RD
GAUCHHILL RD
THE LONG STRAIGHT
THE RUSHLACH
FOREST ROAD
C5
1 CASTLE HL
2 KINGSFIELD PL
3 TUACH RD
4 MANSFIELD
5 THE SQUARE
B5
1 CASTLEVIEW WY
2 CASTLEVIEW CL
C4
1 TUACH VW
2 NICOL RD
3 MACALLAN RD
4 LAVENDER PK
DUNDAS CT
TOWNHEAD TERR
PRICE DR
OGILVIE CR
CASTLE RD
CASTLE WYND
HALLFOREST CL
HALLFOREST CRES
HALLFOREST AVE
HAWTHORNE WY
EDELWEISS
SUNNYSIDE VW
DEANS COURT
EAST PARK ROAD
EASTBURN ROAD
NEWLANDS DR
HARTHILLS VW
MORRISON WY
TUMULUS WAY

88
89

88
161
162

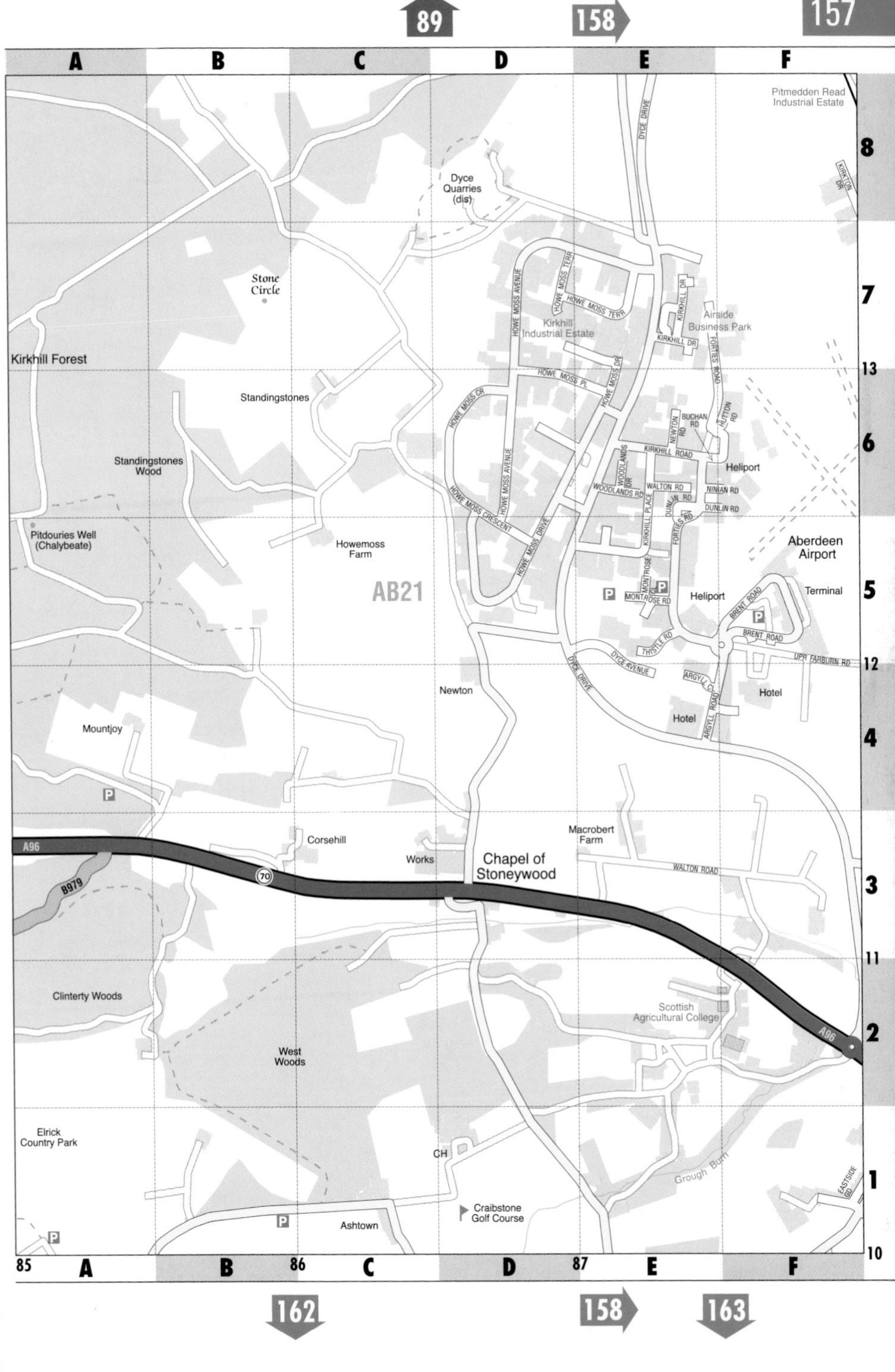
89
158
A
B
C
D
E
F
Pitmedden Read
Industrial Estate
8
KIRKTON DR
DYCE DRIVE
Dyce
Quarries
(dis)
Stone
Circle
7
HOWE MOSS TERR
HOWE MOSS AVENUE
Kirkhill
Industrial Estate
KIRKHILL DR
Airside
Business Park
FORTIES ROAD
Kirkhill Forest
13
HOWE MOSS PL
HOWE MOSS DR
Standingstones
HOWE MOSS CR
BUCHAN RD
NEWTON RD
HUTTON RD
6
KIRKHILL ROAD
Standingstones
Wood
WOODLANDS DR
Heliport
WOODLANDS RD
WALTON RD
NINIAN RD
DUNLIN RD
DUNLIN RD
HOWE MOSS CRESCENT
HOWE MOSS DRIVE
KIRKHILL PLACE
FORTIES RD
Pitdouries Well
(Chalybeate)
Howemoss
Farm
Aberdeen
Airport
AB21
MONTROSE CL
MONTROSE RD
Heliport
BRENT ROAD
Terminal
5
BRENT ROAD
THISTLE RD
DYCE AVENUE
DYCE DRIVE
UPR FARBURN RD
12
ARGYLL CL
Newton
Hotel
ARGYLL ROAD
Hotel
Mountjoy
4
Corsehill
Macrobert
Farm
A96
Works
Chapel of
Stoneywood
WALTON ROAD
B979
70
3
11
Scottish
Agricultural College
Clinterty Woods
A96
2
West
Woods
Elrick
Country Park
CH
Grough Burn
1
EASTSIDE GD
Craibstone
Golf Course
Ashtown
10
85
A
B
86
C
D
87
E
F

162
158
163

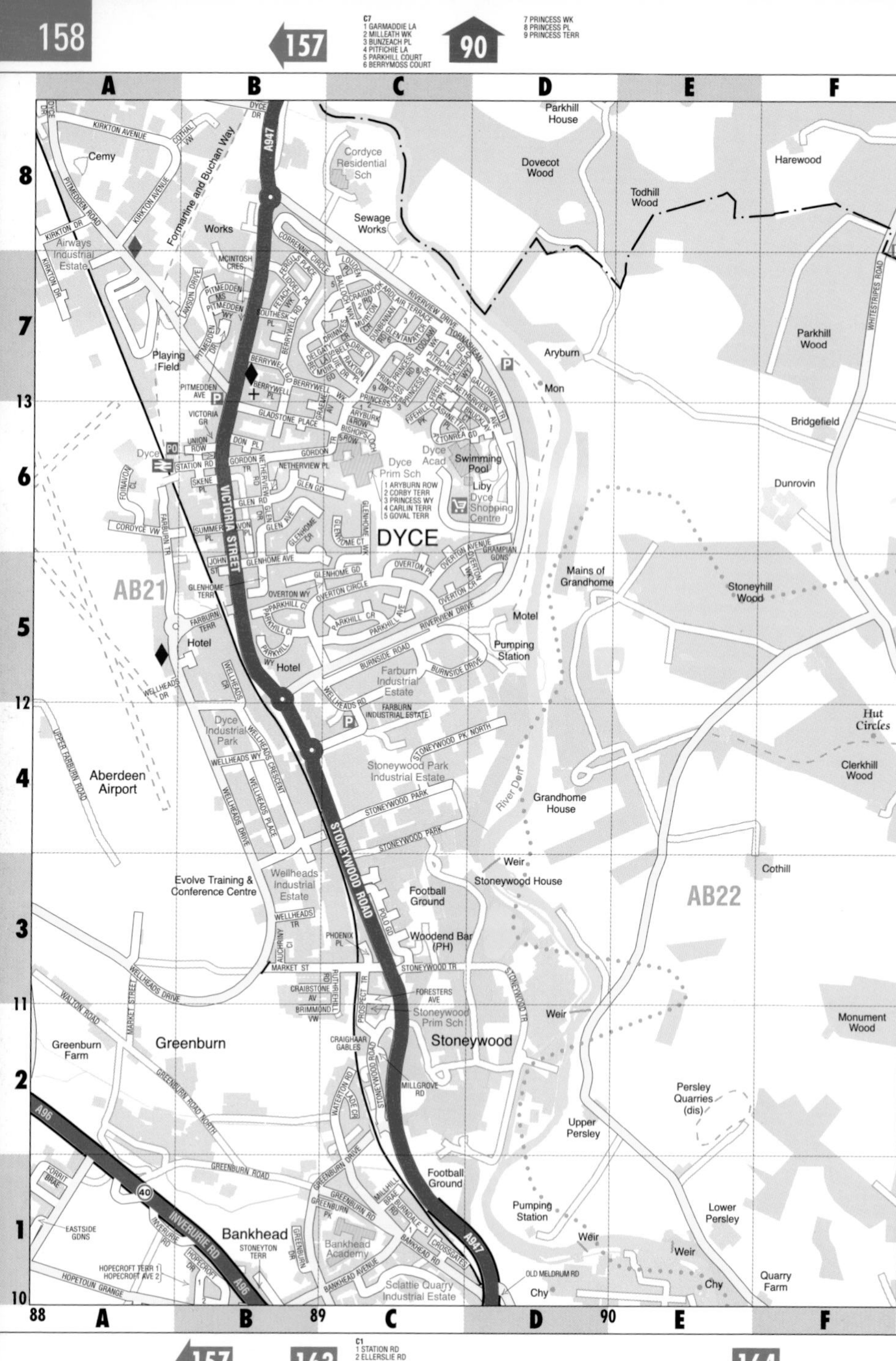
A
B
C
D
E
F
8
7
13
6
5
12
4
3
11
2
1
10
88
89
90
A947
A96
40
Cemy
KIRKTON AVENUE
KIRKTON AVENUE
PITMEDDEN ROAD
KIRKTON DR
KIRKTON DR
Airways Industrial Estate
Formartine and Buchan Way
Works
Cordyce Residential Sch
Sewage Works
Parkhill House
Dovecot Wood
Todhill Wood
Harewood
Parkhill Wood
WHITESTRIPES ROAD
Aryburn
Mon
Bridgefield
Dunrovin
Playing Field
PITMEDDEN AVE
VICTORIA GR
UNION ROW
Dyce
PO
STATION RD
GORDON TR
SKENE PL
GLEN RD
SUMMER PL
JOHN ST
GLENHOME TERR
GLENHOME AVE
CORDYCE VW
FARBURN TR
VICTORIA STREET
CORRENNIE CIRCLE
RIVERVIEW DRIVE
BERRYWELL GD
BERRYWELL WK
GLADSTONE PLACE
NETHERVIEW PL
GLEN GD
GLEN AVE
GLENHOME CR
GLENHOME GD
OVERTON WY
OVERTON CIRCLE
OVERTON PK
OVERTON AVENUE
OVERTON CR
GRAMPIAN GDNS
PARKHILL CI
PARKHILL CR
PARKHILL AVE
PARKHILL WY
RIVERVIEW DRIVE
Dyce Acad
Swimming Pool
Dyce Prim Sch
1 ARYBURN ROW
2 CORBY TERR
3 PRINCESS WY
4 CARLIN TERR
5 GOVAL TERR
Liby
Dyce Shopping Centre
DYCE
AB21
Hotel
Hotel
WELLHEADS DR
WELLHEADS CR
Motel
Pumping Station
BURNSIDE ROAD
BURNSIDE DRIVE
Farburn Industrial Estate
FARBURN INDUSTRIAL ESTATE
WELLHEADS RD
Mains of Grandhome
Stoneyhill Wood
Hut Circles
Clerkhill Wood
UPPER FARBURN ROAD
Aberdeen Airport
Dyce Industrial Park
WELLHEADS WY
WELLHEADS CRESCENT
WELLHEADS PLACE
WELLHEADS DRIVE
STONEYWOOD PK NORTH
Stoneywood Park Industrial Estate
STONEYWOOD PARK
STONEYWOOD PARK
STONEYWOOD ROAD
River Don
Grandhome House
Weir
Stoneywood House
Cothill
AB22
Evolve Training & Conference Centre
Wellheads Industrial Estate
WELLHEADS TR
Football Ground
POLO GD
Woodend Bar (PH)
PHOENIX PL
AUCHRIVY CI
MARKET ST
STONEYWOOD TR
STONEYWOOD TR
CRAIBSTONE AV
BRIMMOND VW
RUTHRIEHILL RD
PROSPECT TR
FORESTERS AVE
Stoneywood Prim Sch
WELLHEADS DRIVE
WALTON ROAD
MARKET STREET
Weir
Monument Wood
Greenburn Farm
Greenburn
CRAIGHAAR GABLES
Stoneywood
MILLGROVE RD
GREENBURN ROAD NORTH
WATERTON RD
LADE CR
STONEYWOOD ROAD
Persley Quarries (dis)
Upper Persley
GREENBURN ROAD
GREENBURN DRIVE
Football Ground
FORRIT BRAE
GREENBURN PK
GREENBURN RD
MILLHILL BRAE
BURNDALE RD
Pumping Station
Lower Persley
EASTSIDE GDNS
INVERURIE RD
INVERURIE RD
Bankhead
STONEYTON TERR
GREENBURN DR
Bankhead Academy
BANKHEAD RD
CROSSGATES
Weir
Weir
HOPECROFT TERR 1
HOPECROFT AVE 2
HOPECROFT DR
HOPETOUN GRANGE
BANKHEAD AVENUE
Sclattie Quarry Industrial Estate
OLD MELDRUM RD
Chy
Chy
Quarry Farm

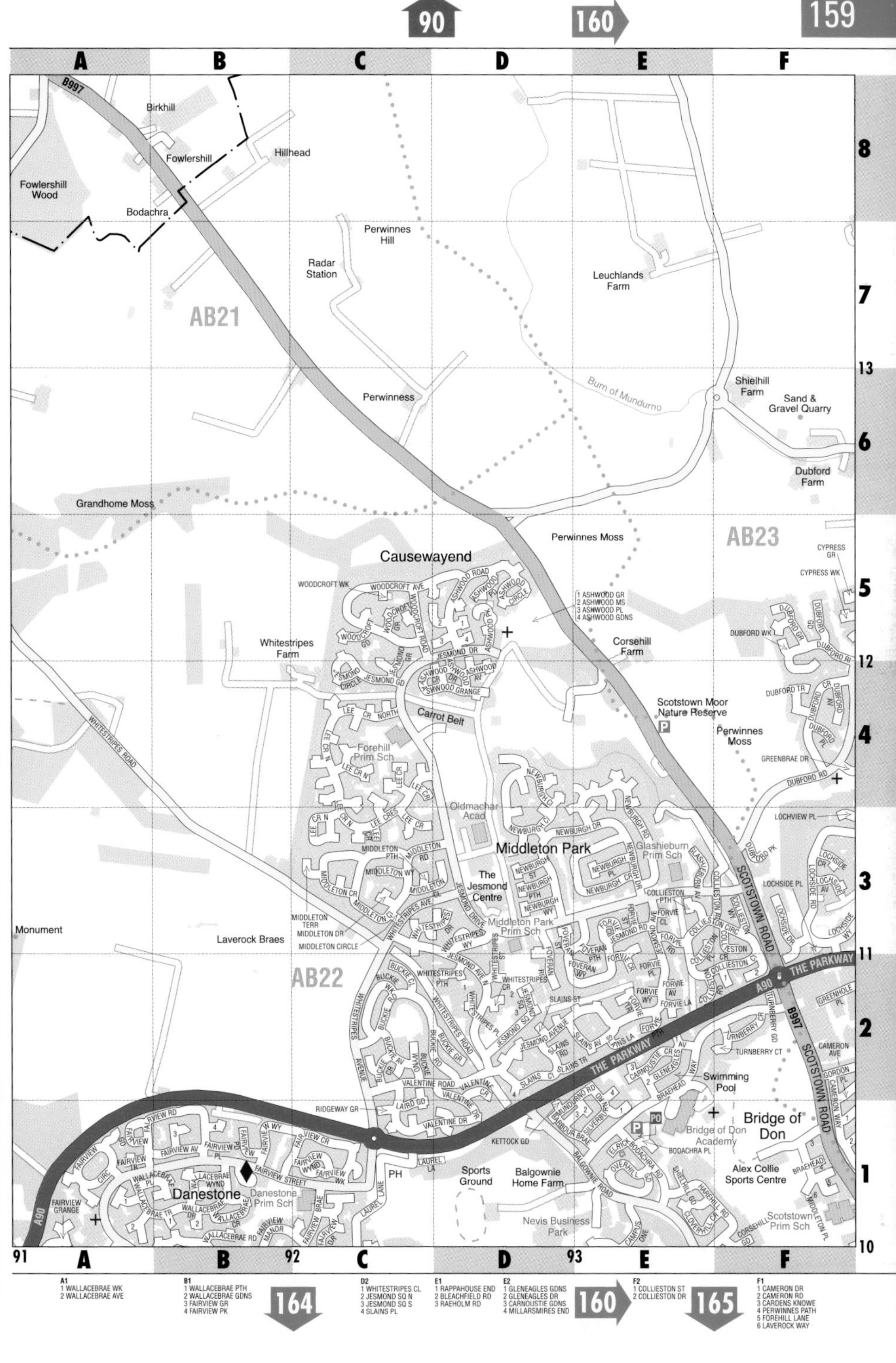
90
160
A
B
C
D
E
F
8
7
13
6
5
12
4
3
11
2
1
10
91
92
93
B997
Birkhill
Fowlershill
Hillhead
Fowlershill Wood
Bodachra
Perwinnes Hill
Radar Station
Leuchlands Farm
AB21
Burn of Mundurno
Shielhill Farm
Sand & Gravel Quarry
Perwinness
Dubford Farm
Grandhome Moss
Perwinnes Moss
AB23
Causewayend
CYPRESS GR
CYPRESS WK
1 ASHWOOD GR
2 ASHWOOD MS
3 ASHWOOD PL
4 ASHWOOD GDNS
WOODCROFT WK
WOODCROFT AVE
WOODCROFT ROAD
Whitestripes Farm
Corsehill Farm
DUBFORD WK
JESMOND DR
ASHWOOD GRANGE
JESMOND GD
DUBFORD TR
Carrot Belt
Scotstown Moor Nature Reserve
Perwinnes Moss
WHITESTRIPES ROAD
Forehill Prim Sch
GREENBRAE DR
DUBFORD RD
Oldmachar Acad
LOCHVIEW PL
NEWBURGH DR
Middleton Park
Glashieburn Prim Sch
The Jesmond Centre
SCOTSTOWN ROAD
LOCHSIDE PL
MIDDLETON TERR
MIDDLETON DR
MIDDLETON CIRCLE
Monument
Laverock Braes
Middleton Park Prim Sch
AB22
THE PARKWAY
A90
GREENHOLE PL
SLAINS ST
TURNBERRY CT
CAMERON AVE
Swimming Pool
RIDGEWAY GR
VALENTINE ROAD
VALENTINE DR
Bridge of Don
Bridge of Don Academy
KETTOCK GD
BODACHRA PL
Danestone
FAIRVIEW STREET
Sports Ground
Balgownie Home Farm
Alex Collie Sports Centre
Danestone Prim Sch
FAIRVIEW GRANGE
PH
Nevis Business Park
Scotstown Prim Sch
WALLACEBRAE RD
CORSEHILL GD
A1
1 WALLACEBRAE WK
2 WALLACEBRAE AVE
B1
1 WALLACEBRAE PTH
2 WALLACEBRAE GDNS
3 FAIRVIEW GR
4 FAIRVIEW PK
164
D2
1 WHITESTRIPES CL
2 JESMOND SQ N
3 JESMOND SQ S
4 SLAINS PL
E1
1 RAPPAHOUSE END
2 BLEACHFIELD RD
3 RAEHOLM RD
E2
1 GLENEAGLES GDNS
2 GLENEAGLES DR
3 CARNOUSTIE GDNS
4 MILLARSMIRES END
160
F2
1 COLLIESTON ST
2 COLLIESTON DR
165
F1
1 CAMERON DR
2 CAMERON RD
3 CARDENS KNOWE
4 PERWINNES PATH
5 FOREHILL LANE
6 LAVEROCK WAY

159 91 91

A1
1 GLASHIEBURN WY
2 CLASHIEKNOWE TERR

159 165 91

88 101 156 162

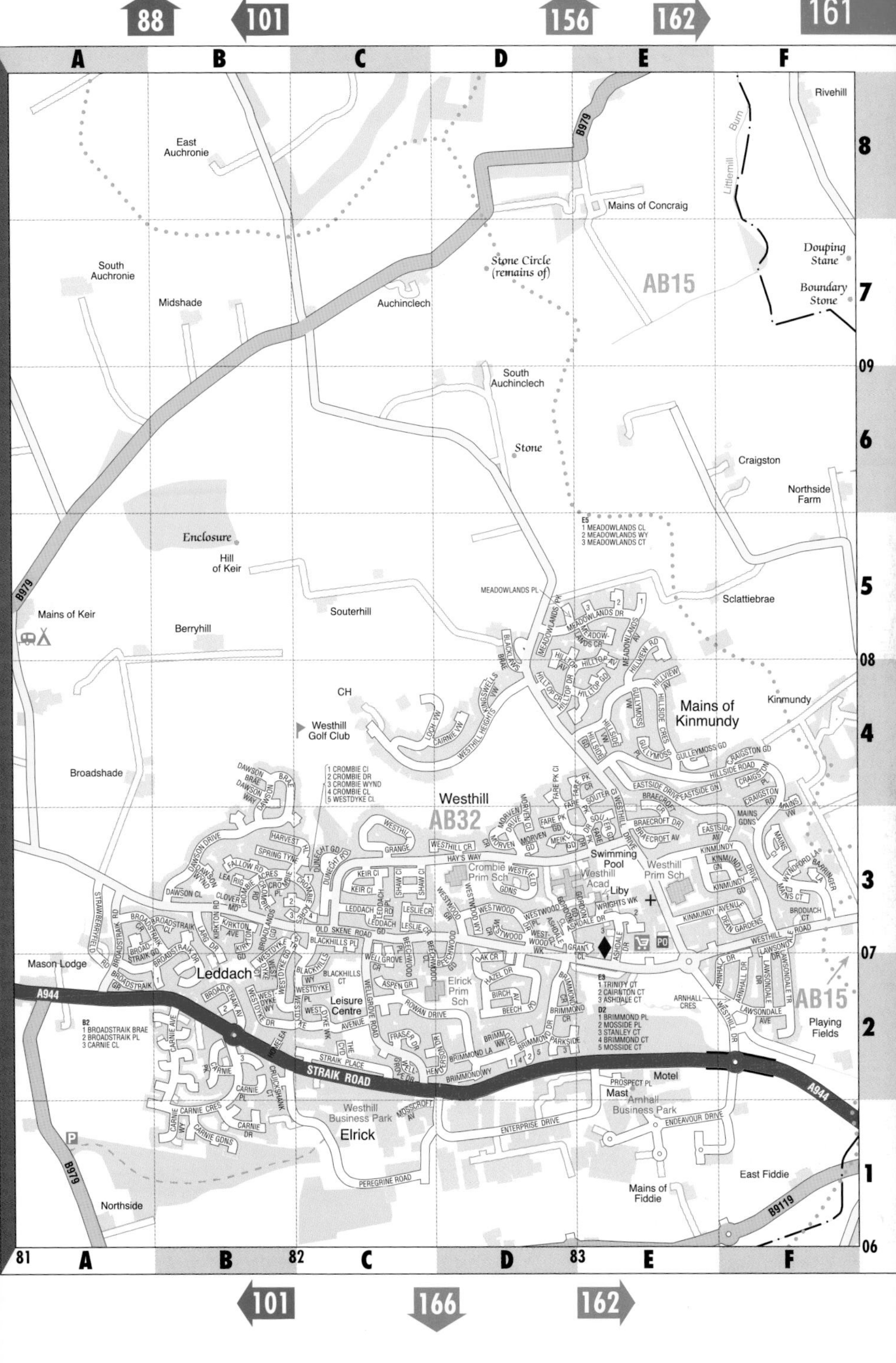

101 166 162

156 161 157

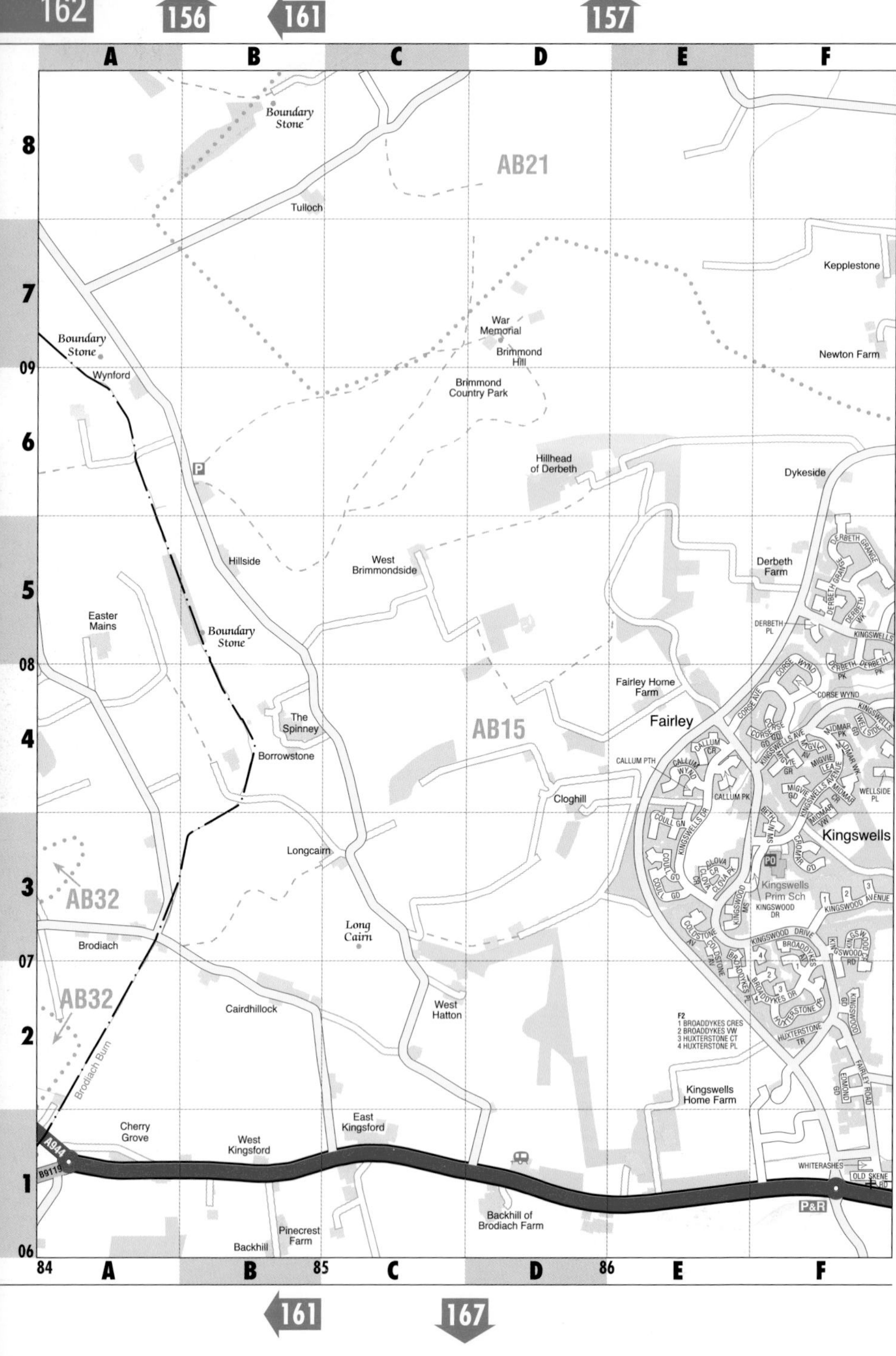

161 167

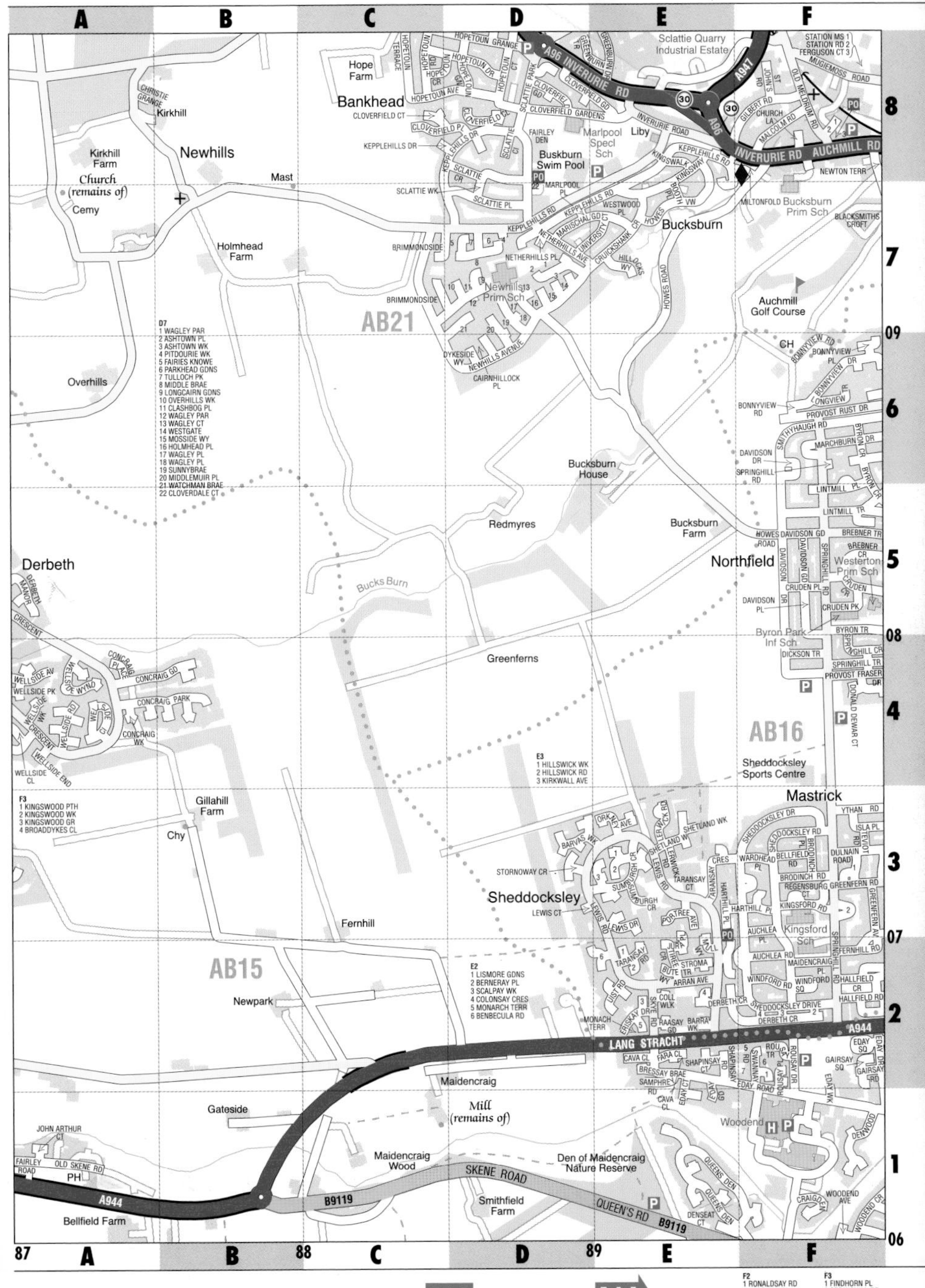
157
158
164
A
B
C
D
E
F
Bankhead
Hope Farm
Kirkhill
Newhills
Kirkhill Farm
Church (remains of)
Cemy
Mast
Holmhead Farm
Overhills
Sclattie Quarry Industrial Estate
Marlpool Specl Sch
Liby
Buskburn Swim Pool
INVERURIE RD
AUCHMILL RD
A96
A947
Bucksburn
Bucksburn Prim Sch
Newhills Prim Sch
AB21
Auchmill Golf Course
Bucksburn House
Redmyres
Bucksburn Farm
Northfield
Derbeth
Bucks Burn
Westerton Prim Sch
Byron Park Inf Sch
Greenferns
AB16
Sheddocksley Sports Centre
Mastrick
Gillahill Farm
Chy
Sheddocksley
Kingsford Sch
Fernhill
AB15
Newpark
LANG STRACHT
A944
Maidencraig
Gateside
Mill (remains of)
Maidencraig Wood
Den of Maidencraig Nature Reserve
SKENE ROAD
QUEEN'S RD
B9119
Smithfield Farm
Woodend
Bellfield Farm
PH
D7
1 WAGLEY PAR
2 ASHTOWN PL
3 ASHTOWN WK
4 PITDOURIE WK
5 FAIRIES KNOWE
6 PARKHEAD GDNS
7 TULLOCH PK
8 MIDDLE BRAE
9 LONGCAIRN GDNS
10 OVERHILLS WK
11 CLASHBOG PL
12 WAGLEY PAR
13 WAGLEY CT
14 WESTGATE
15 MOSSIDE WY
16 HOLMHEAD PL
17 WAGLEY PL
18 WAGLEY PL
19 SUNNYBRAE
20 MIDDLEMUIR PL
21 WATCHMAN BRAE
22 CLOVERDALE CT
E3
1 HILLSWICK WK
2 HILLSWICK RD
3 KIRKWALL AVE
F3
1 KINGSWOOD PTH
2 KINGSWOOD WK
3 KINGSWOOD GR
4 BROADDYKES CL
E2
1 LISMORE GDNS
2 BERNERAY PL
3 SCALPAY WK
4 COLONSAY CRES
5 MONARCH TERR
6 BENBECULA RD
87
88
89
06
07
08
09
168
164
F2
1 RONALDSAY RD
2 CLOGHILL PL
3 BORROWSTONE PL
4 DINBAITH PL
5 SHAPINSAY SQ
6 RONALDSAY SQ
7 SWANNAY SQ
F3
1 FINDHORN PL
2 SPRINGHILL RD

158 163 159

A5
1 WAULKMILL RD
2 WEAVERS ROW

C4
1 STOCKET PAR
2 QUARRYHILL CT
3 PARADISE MS
4 STOCKETHILL WY
5 NURSERY LANE

F6
1 FOUNTVILLE CT
2 CLIFTON CT
3 COWAN PL
4 TANFIELD CT

F7
1 MEADOW CT
2 KING'S CT
3 ELPHINSTONE CT
4 ST MACHAR CT
5 GRANDHOLM CT

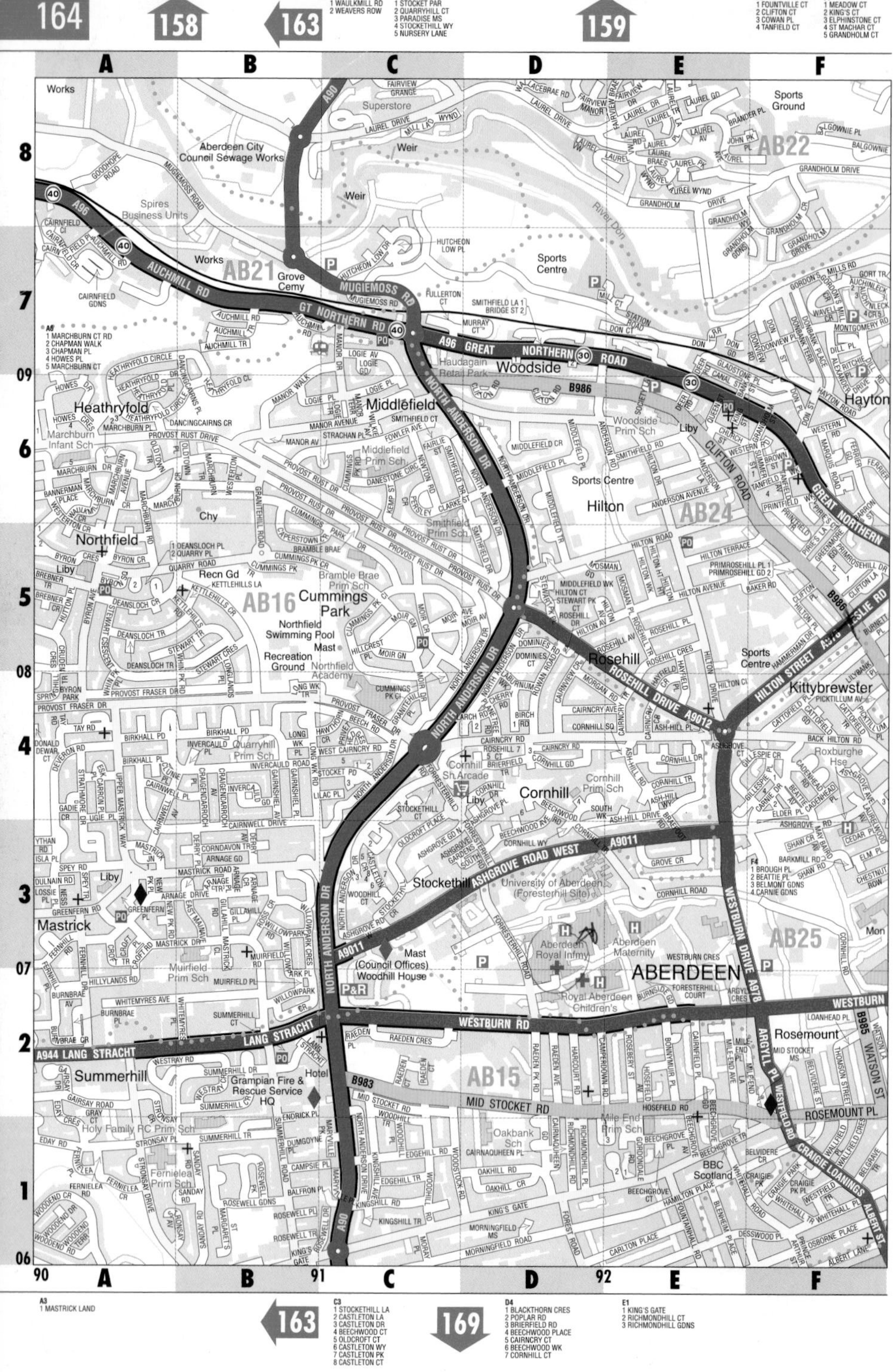

1 2 3 4 5 6 7 8 A B C D E F 90 91 92

A3
1 MASTRICK LAND

163

C3
1 STOCKETHILL LA
2 CASTLETON LA
3 CASTLETON DR
4 BEECHWOOD CT
5 OLDCROFT CT
6 CASTLETON WY
7 CASTLETON PK
8 CASTLETON CT

169

D4
1 BLACKTHORN CRES
2 POPLAR RD
3 BRIERFIELD RD
4 BEECHWOOD PLACE
5 CAIRNCRY CT
6 BEECHWOOD WK
7 CORNHILL CT

E1
1 KING'S GATE
2 RICHMONDHILL CT
3 RICHMONDHILL GDNS

159

160

A6
1 RATTRAY PL
2 KINNAIRD PL
3 DEMPSEY TERR
4 ABERDON CT

B8
1 DAVAN PK
2 KINORD CT
3 STRATHBEG PL
4 TARBOTHILL RD
5 AUCHLOSSAN CT
6 FOWERSHILL GDNS

C4
1 ORCHARD WK
2 THE ORCHARD
3 ST PETER'S GATE
4 HILLHEAD TERR

1 PARK RD CT
2 JACKSON TERR
3 HAWTHORN TERR

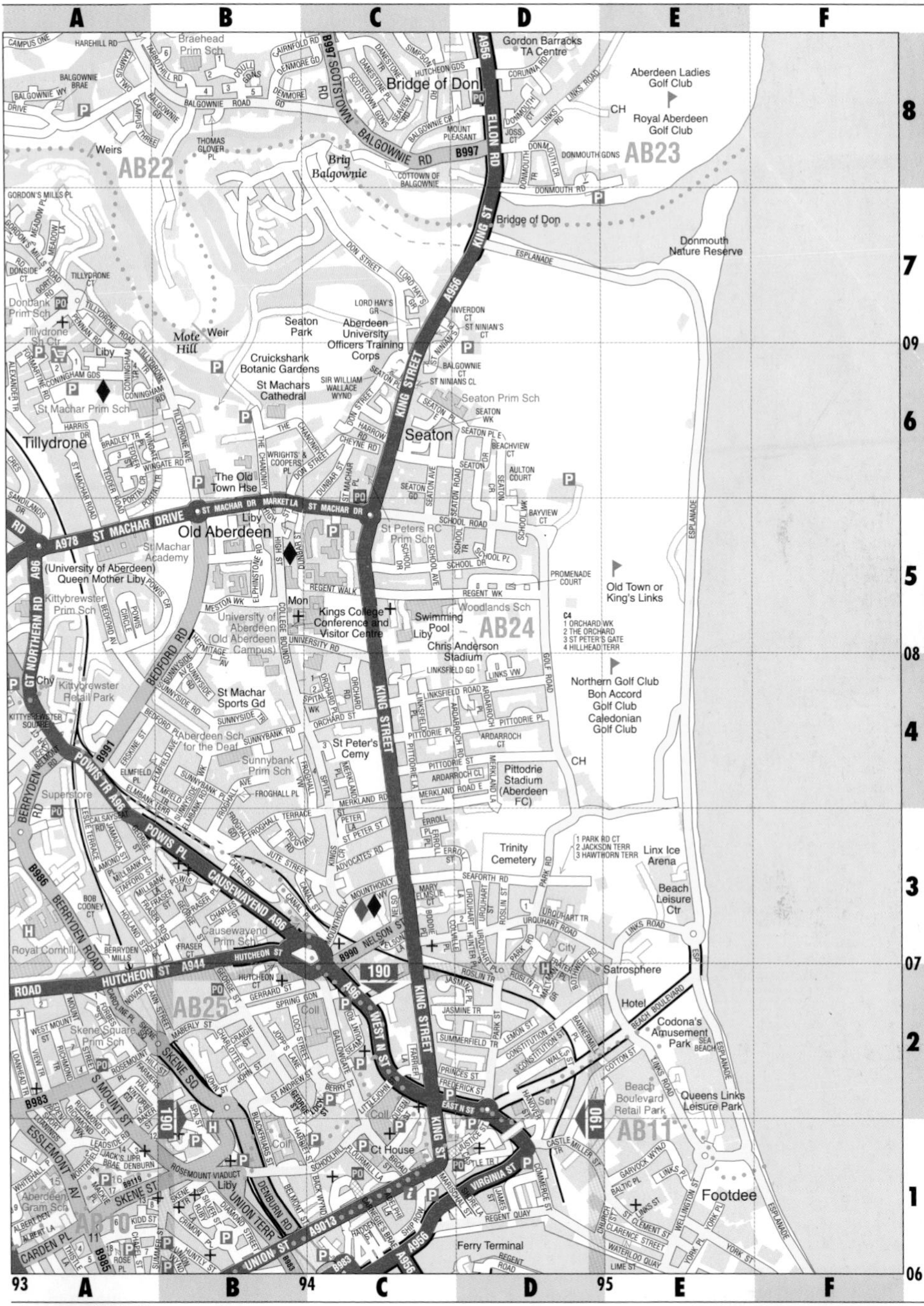

A1
1 GROSVENOR TERR
2 ROSEMOUNT SQ
3 STEVENSON CT
4 PRINCE ALBERT MS
5 MARGARET ST
6 WHITEHOUSE ST
7 LT CHAPEL CT
8 MINISTER LA
9 ALBERT PL
10 GROSVENOR PL
11 ROSE ST
12 GILCOMSTON PK
13 GILCOMSTOUN CT
14 STEVENSON ST
15 Total French Sch
16 Gilcomstoun Prim Sch
17 SKENE PL
18 THISTLE CT

A2
1 ROSEMOUNT TERR
2 WESTBURN CT
3 LOANHEAD WK
4 MOUNTVIEW GDNS
5 BAKER PLACE
6 KINTORE PL
7 RICHMOND CT
8 DONALD PL

For full street detail of the highlighted area see page 190.

101 161

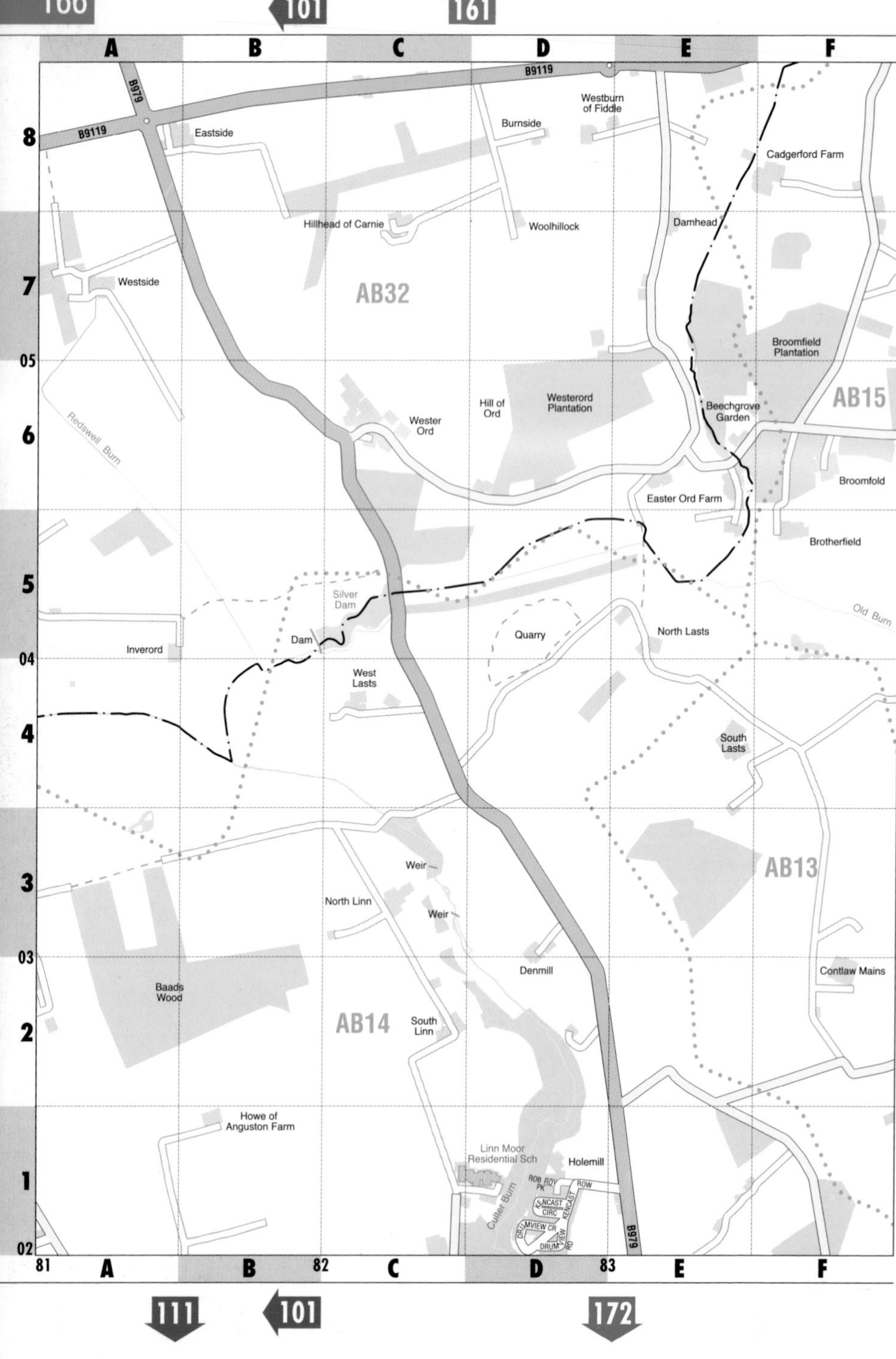

111 101 172

162
168
A
B
C
D
E
F
8
7
05
6
5
04
4
3
03
2
1
02
84
85
86
Upper Kingshill
Auchlea
Kingshill Wood
Kingshill
West Auchlea
Craiglug
Upper Fifeshill
Longside
Nether Fifeshill
Newton of Countesswells Farm
Gairn
Rainbows End
AB15
Gairnhill Wood
Gairnlea
Silverburn Farm
Cup and Ring Marked Stone
P
Westwood
East Brotherfield
Blacktop
Blacktop Farm
Boundary Stone
North Westfield
Foggieton
Beans Hill
Boundary Stone
Westfield
Hilton
Boundary Stone
HILLHEAD ROAD
Upper Beanshill
AB13
Hillhead
CONTLAW ROAD
Hill of Milltimber
Binghill
Nether Contlaw
Stone Circle
Cairn
Head of Wood
CONTLAW RD
MURTLE DEN RD
MURTLE DEN ROAD
Murtle Dam
OLDFOLD PK
OLDFOLD PL
THE MEADOWS
OLDFOLD AV
Nether Beanshill
BINGHILL HEDGES
BINGHILL ROAD
OLDFOLD CR
OLDFOLD DR
OLDFOLD WLK
COLTHILL CR
COLTHILL RD
BINGHILL DR
BINGHILL ROAD NORTH
BINGHILL ROAD W
Oldfold Farm
Milltimber
Tor-na-Dee
H
172
173
168

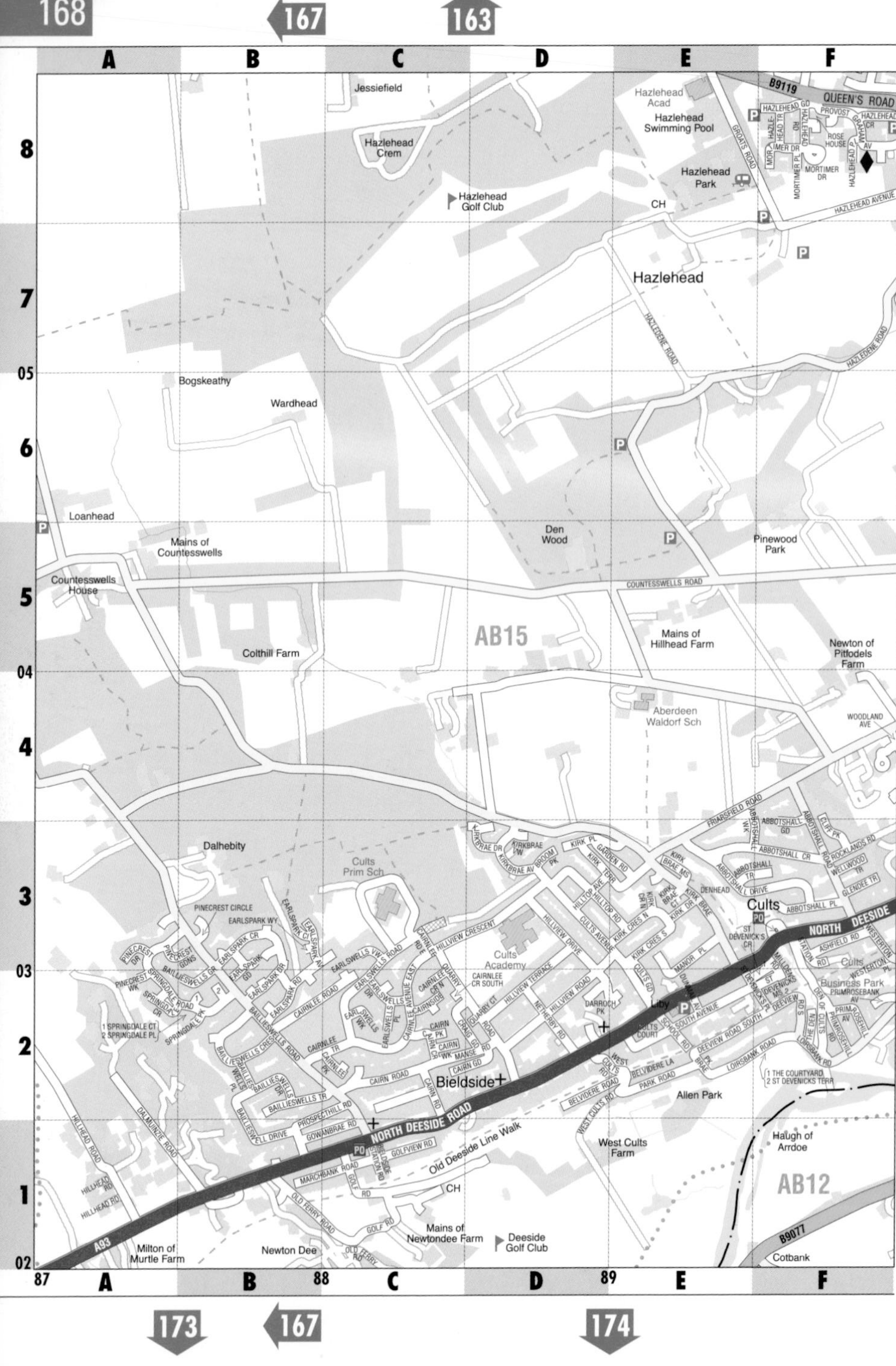
A
B
C
D
E
F
8
7
05
6
5
04
4
3
03
2
1
02
87
88
89
Jessiefield
Hazlehead Crem
Hazlehead Golf Club
Hazlehead Acad
Hazlehead Swimming Pool
Hazlehead Park
B9119
QUEEN'S ROAD
GROATS ROAD
HAZLEHEAD AVENUE
CH
Hazlehead
HAZLEDENE ROAD
Bogskeathy
Wardhead
Loanhead
Mains of Countesswells
Countesswells House
Den Wood
Pinewood Park
COUNTESSWELLS ROAD
AB15
Colthill Farm
Mains of Hillhead Farm
Newton of Pitfodels Farm
Aberdeen Waldorf Sch
WOODLAND AVE
FRIARSFIELD ROAD
Dalhebity
Cults Prim Sch
Cults Academy
Cults
NORTH DEESIDE ROAD
Cults Business Park
Bieldside
Liby
Allen Park
West Cults Farm
Old Deeside Line Walk
Haugh of Arrdoe
AB12
B9077
Cotbank
Mains of Newtondee Farm
Deeside Golf Club
Newton Dee
Milton of Murtle Farm
A93
HILLHEAD ROAD
DALMUINZIE ROAD
OLD FERRY ROAD
GOLF RD
1 SPRINGDALE CT
2 SPRINGDALE PL
1 THE COURTYARD
2 ST DEVENICKS TERR

C7
1 QUEENS HIGHLANDS
2 RUBISLAW SQ
3 RUBISLAW VW
164
170
F7
1 CLAREMONT ST
2 CLAREMONT GDNS
F8
1 CARDEN TERR
2 ALBYN PL
3 GRANTON GDNS
4 ST SWITHIN ROW

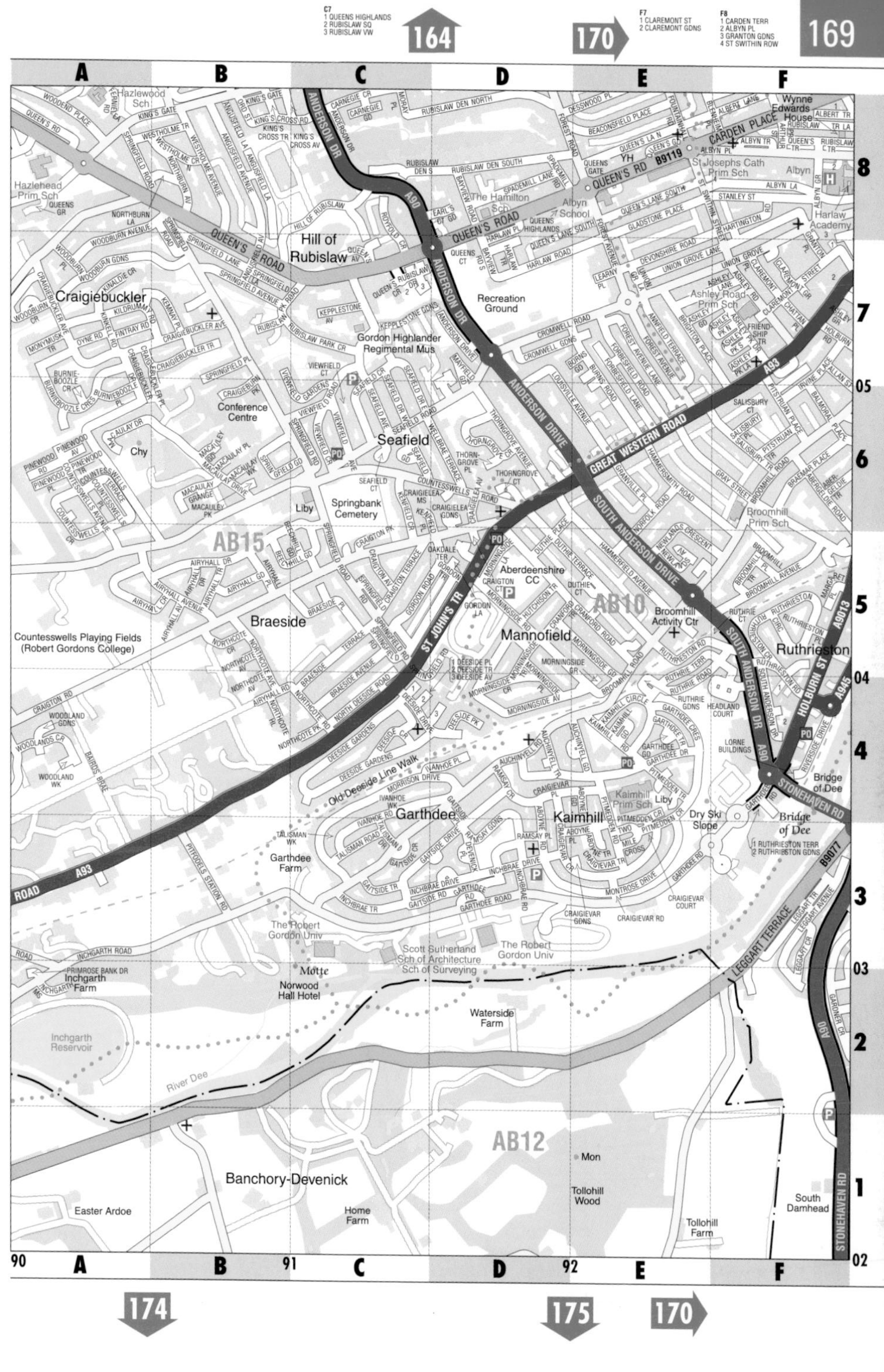

174
175
170

A7
1 FONTHILL GDNS W
2 FONTHILL AVE
3 BROOMHILL MS
4 CUPARSTONE CT
A8
1 UNION GROVE CT
2 STRAWBERRY BANK RD
3 UNION GLEN CT
4 WILLOWGATE CL
5 ASHVALE CT
169
165
A
B
C
D
E
F
8
7
6
5
4
3
2
1
05
04
03
02
93
94
95
Aberdeen
LB Sta
Tidal Harbour
POCRA QUAY
MIDDLE ROW
MARKET ST
COMMERCIAL QUAY
ALBERT QUAY
NORTH ESP E
UNION ST
ALFORD PL
St Margarets Sch for Girls
Bon Accord Baths
WILLOWBANK ROAD
SPRINGBANK TR
HOLBURN ST
A9013
A93
Nellfield Cemetery
Liby
Ferryhill
GT SOUTHERN RD
B9077
AB11
NORTH ESPLANADE WEST
190
SOUTH ESP E
SINCLAIR RD
Victoria Road Prim Sch
VICTORIA ROAD
Torry
Liby
Torry Youth & L Ctr
Walker Road Sch
Torry Acad
HM Prison
WELLINGTON RD
RIVERSIDE DRIVE
A945
Tullos Swim Pool
Balnagask
Tullos Prim Sch
F6
1 LOCHNAGAR RD
2 MORVEN CT
3 BRIMMOND CT
4 GRAMPIAN CT
E6
1 BALNAGASK WK
HOLBURN STREET
Aberdeen Centre for English
Duthie Park
Mon
AB10
Allenvale Cemetery
A945 RIVERSIDE DR
A6
1 BALMORAL GDNS
2 GAIRN CT
River Dee
Works
East Tullos Industrial Estate
Tullos Cairn
Playing Fields
WEST TULLOS RD
B9077 GREAT SOUTHERN ROAD
Craigshaw Business Park
Tullos
Greenbank Business Centre
Chimney
Baron's Cairn
Kincorth Sports Ctr
Kincorth
Abbotswell Prim Sch
AB12
Kirkhill Prim Sch
Kincorth Swimming Pool
Kincorth Academy
Cat Cairn
Beechwood School
Nigg
Kincorth Hill
Altens Centre (Aberdeen College)
HARENESS ROAD
MINTO DRIVE
Masts
Kincorth Quarry
WELLINGTON ROAD
A956
Altens
Altens Industrial Estate
Altens Farm
Playing Fields
SOUTER HEAD ROAD
BURNBANKS VILLAGE
P&R
Hotel
DUGALD BAIRD SQ
175
169
176

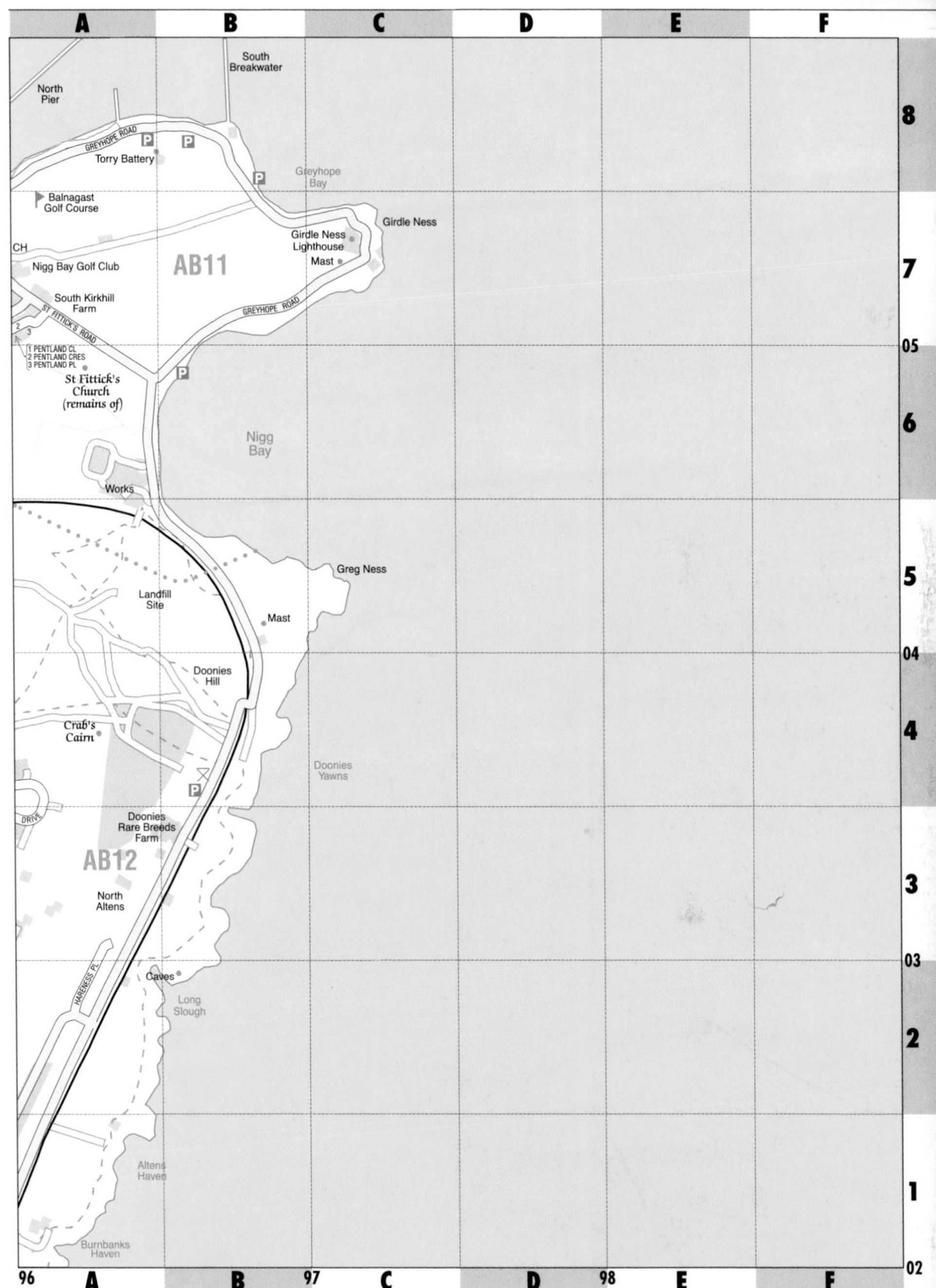
A
B
C
D
E
F
South
Breakwater
North
Pier
GREYHOPE ROAD
Torry Battery
Greyhope
Bay
Balnagast
Golf Course
Girdle Ness
Girdle Ness
Lighthouse
Mast
CH
Nigg Bay Golf Club
AB11
South Kirkhill
Farm
ST FITTICK'S ROAD
GREYHOPE ROAD
1 PENTLAND CL
2 PENTLAND CRES
3 PENTLAND PL
St Fittick's
Church
(remains of)
Nigg
Bay
Works
Greg Ness
Landfill
Site
Mast
Doonies
Hill
Crab's
Cairn
Doonies
Yawns
DRIVE
Doonies
Rare Breeds
Farm
AB12
North
Altens
HARENESS PL
Caves
Long
Slough
Altens
Haven
Burnbanks
Haven
8
7
05
6
5
04
4
3
03
2
1
02
96
97
98

176

111 166 167

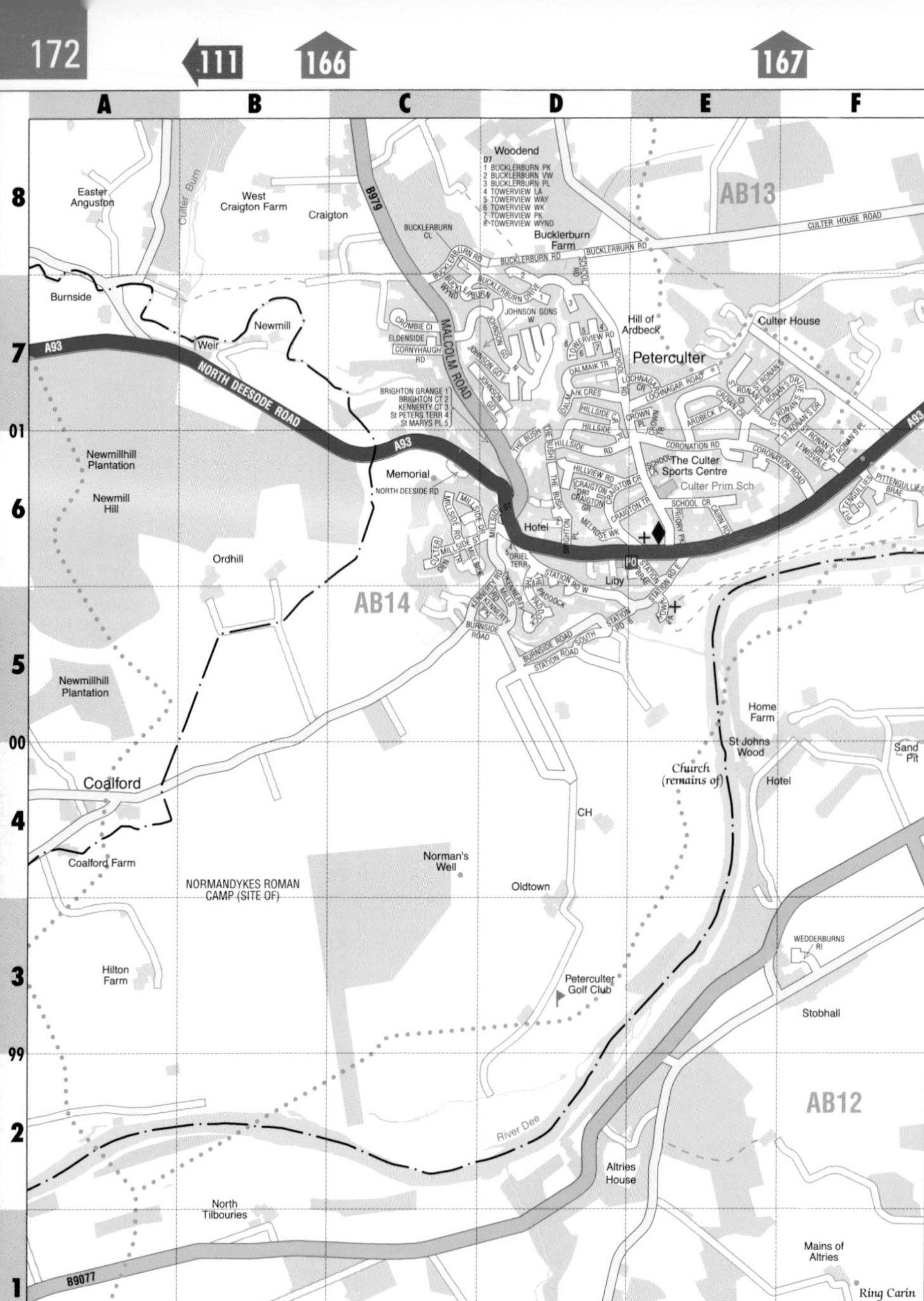

111 177

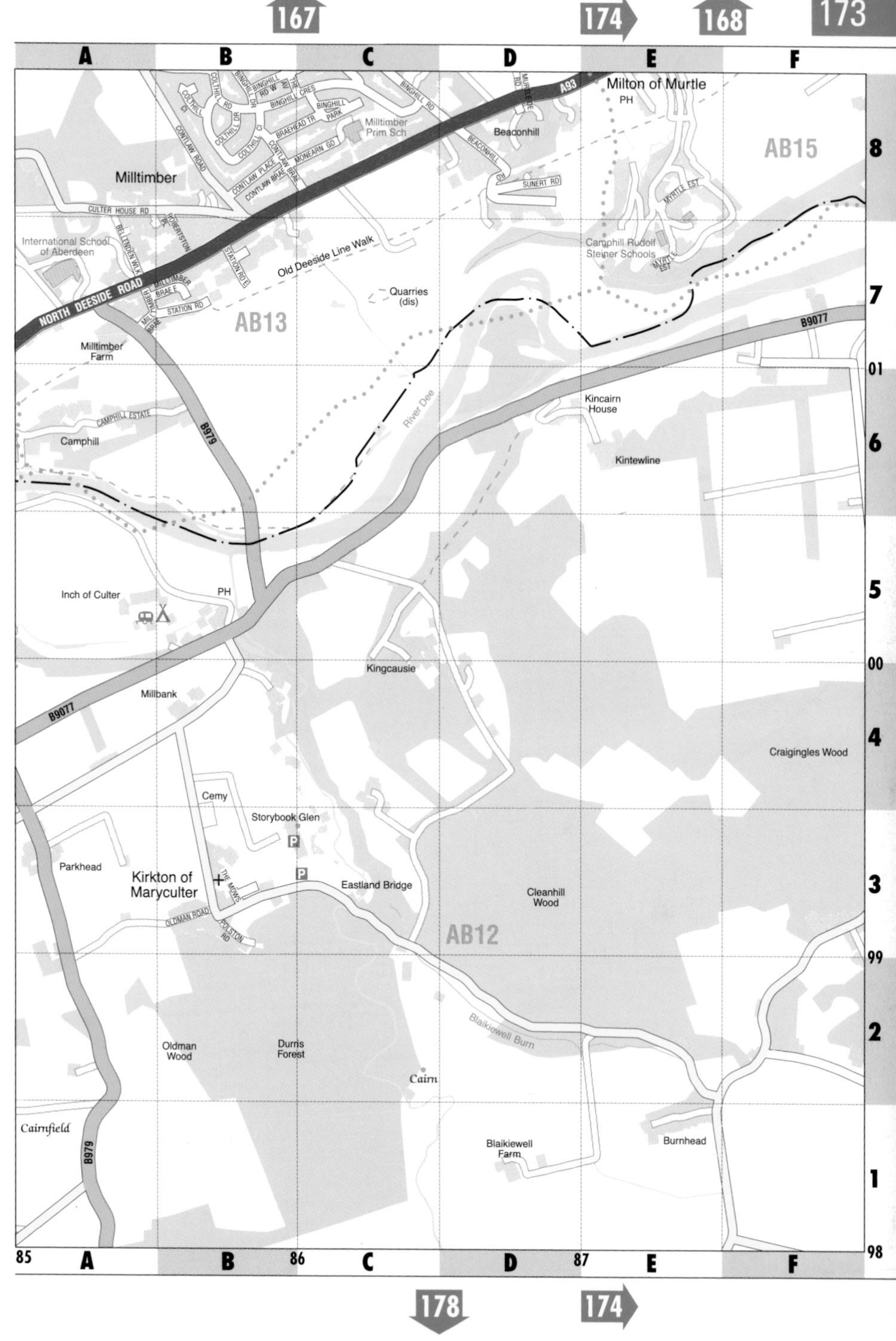
167
174
168
A
B
C
D
E
F
Milton of Murtle
PH
Beaconhill
AB15
Milltimber
Milltimber Prim Sch
International School of Aberdeen
Old Deeside Line Walk
NORTH DEESIDE ROAD
A93
Quarries (dis)
AB13
Milltimber Farm
Camphill Rudolf Steiner Schools
B9077
Kincairn House
River Dee
Camphill
Kintewline
B979
Inch of Culter
PH
Kingcausie
Millbank
Craigingles Wood
Cemy
Storybook Glen
Parkhead
Kirkton of Maryculter
Eastland Bridge
Cleanhill Wood
AB12
Blaikiewell Burn
Oldman Wood
Durris Forest
Cairn
Cairnfield
Blaikiewell Farm
Burnhead
8
7
01
6
5
00
4
3
99
2
1
98
85
86
87
178
174

173
168
169

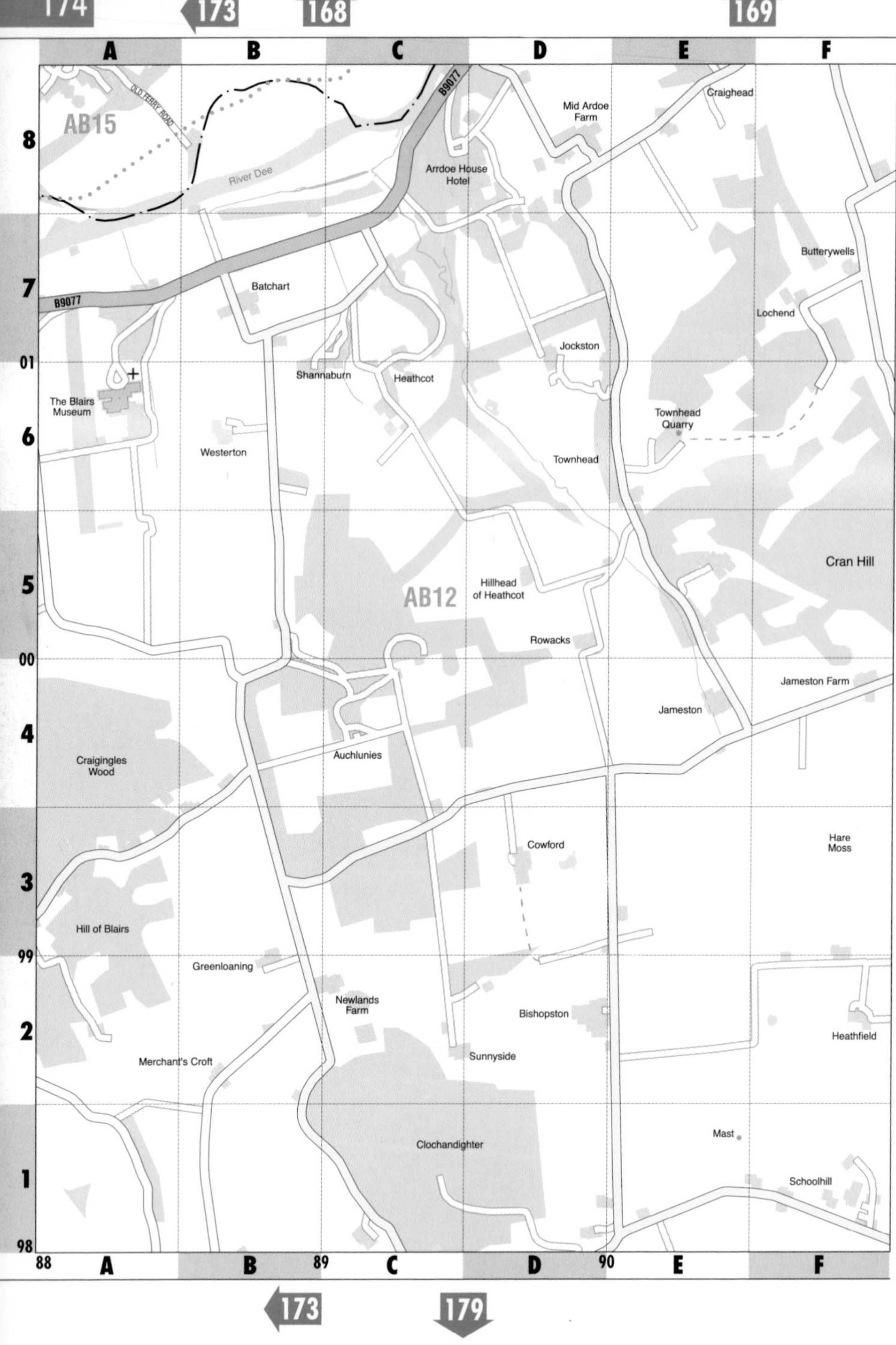

173
179

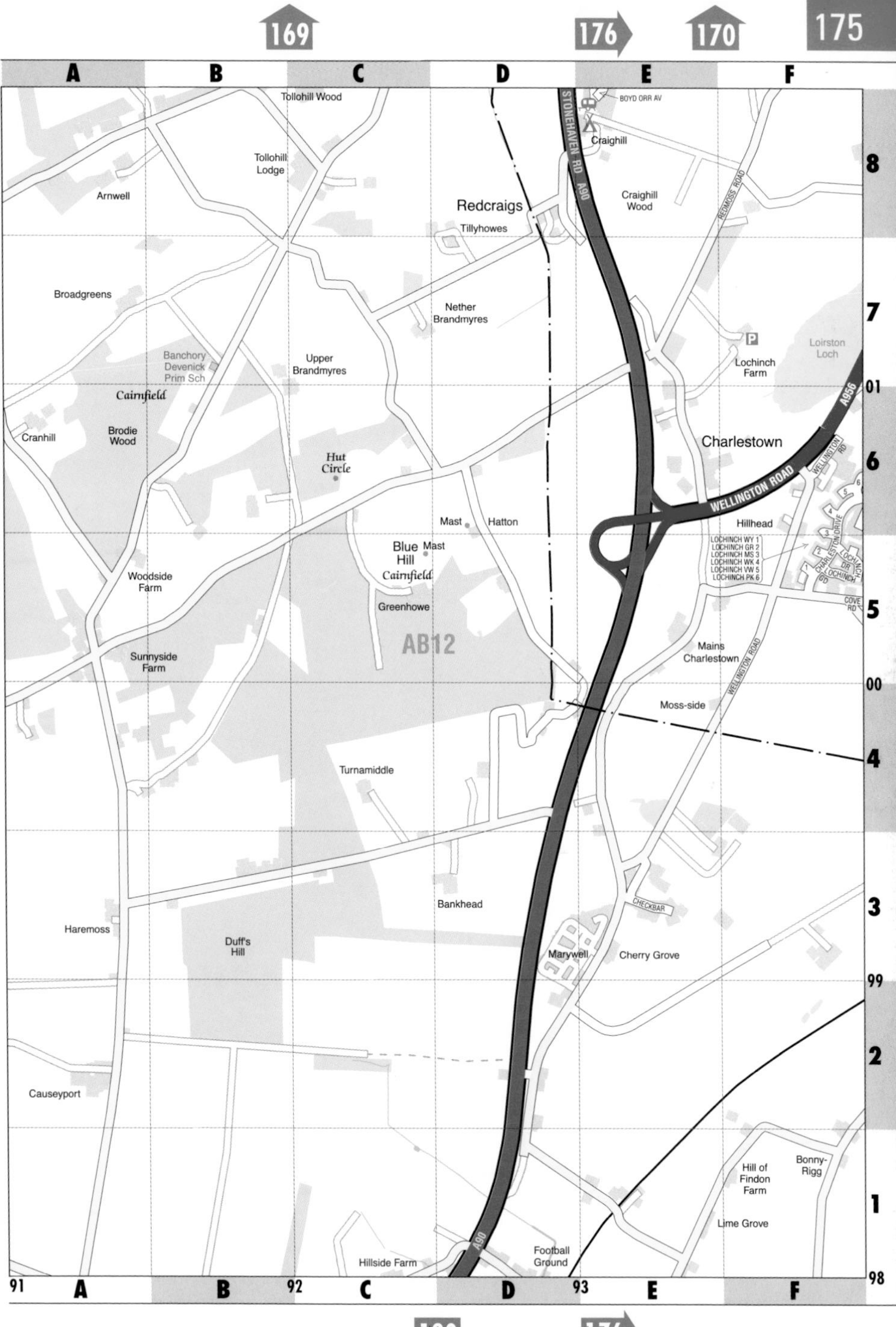
169
176
170
A
B
C
D
E
F
Tollohill Wood
BOYD ORR AV
STONEHAVEN RD A90
Craighill
Tollohill Lodge
Arnwell
Redcraigs
Tillyhowes
Craighill Wood
REDMOSS ROAD
Broadgreens
Nether Brandmyres
Banchory Devenick Prim Sch
Upper Brandmyres
Lochinch Farm
Loirston Loch
Cairnfield
Cranhill
Brodie Wood
Charlestown
A956
Hut Circle
WELLINGTON ROAD
WELLINGTON RD
Mast
Hatton
Hillhead
Blue Hill
Mast
Cairnfield
LOCHINCH WY 1
LOCHINCH GR 2
LOCHINCH MS 3
LOCHINCH WK 4
LOCHINCH VW 5
LOCHINCH PK 6
CHARLESTON DRIVE
LOCHINCH DR
LOCHINCH RD
CHARLESTON GD
Woodside Farm
Greenhowe
COVE RD
AB12
Sunnyside Farm
Mains Charlestown
WELLINGTON ROAD
Moss-side
Turnamiddle
CHECKBAR
Bankhead
Haremoss
Duff's Hill
Marywell
Cherry Grove
Causeyport
Hill of Findon Farm
Bonny-Rigg
Lime Grove
A90
Football Ground
Hillside Farm
8
7
01
6
5
00
4
3
99
2
1
98
91
92
93
180
176

175 170 171

175 181

111 172 178

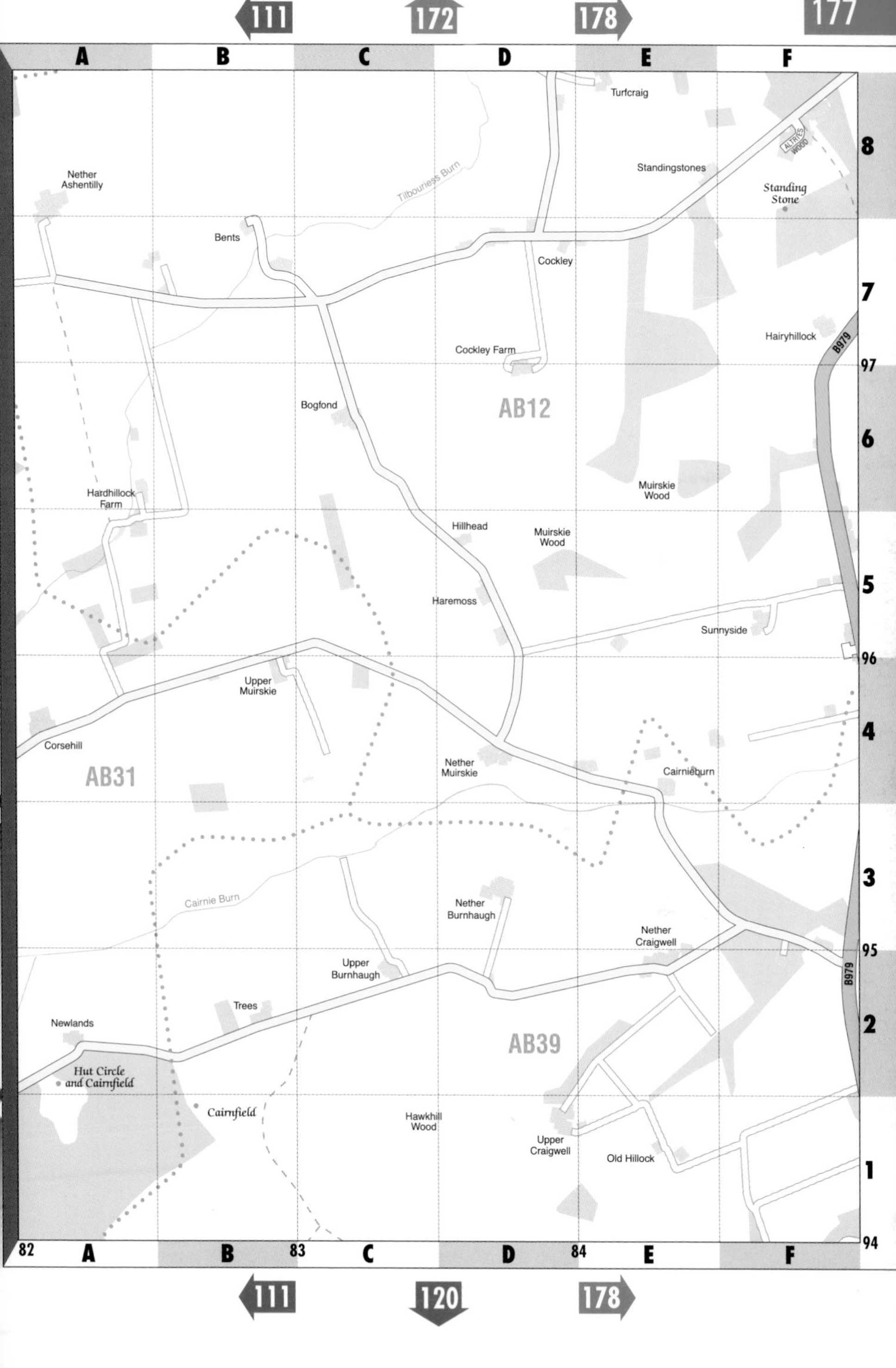

111 120 178

177
173

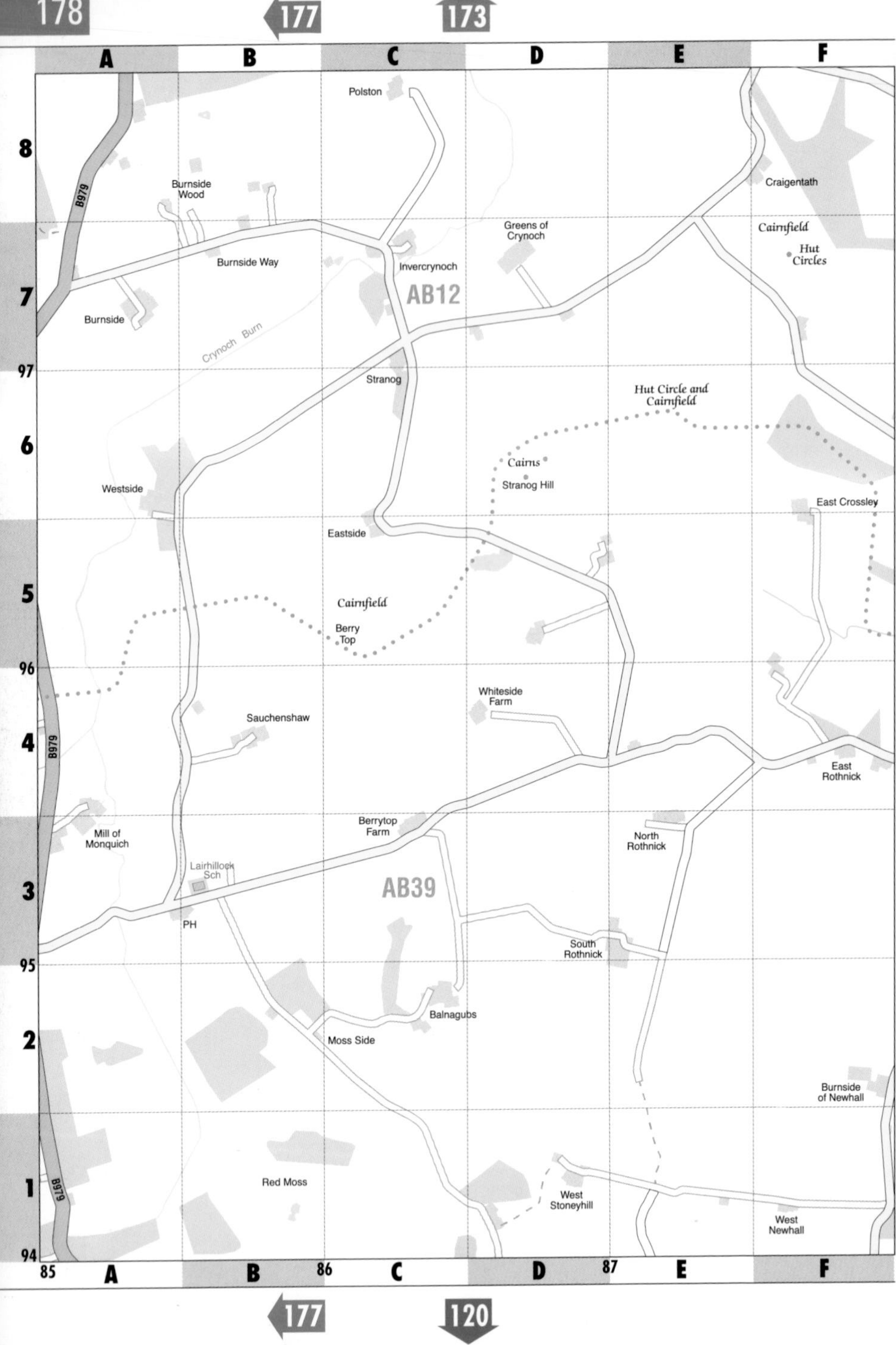

177
120

174
180
A
B
C
D
E
F
Redmyre
AB12
BADENTOY AVENUE
Badentoy Park
BADENTOY PL
BADENTOY CR
BADENTOY WY
Swellhead
Hill of Auchlee
Boswell's Monument
Cairnfield
Cairnwell Hill
Hut Circle
Ring Cairns (remains of)
Auchlee
Cairnwell
Wedderhill
Wedderhill Farm
Hut Circle and Field system
Stone Circle
A90
Shields
Aquhorthies
Stone Circle
Old Bourtreebush
BRUNTLAND RD
Beltcraigs
AB39
Berryhill House
New Bourtreebush
Quoscies
Chapelton
Home Farm
Elsick House
Cammachmore
PH
Gillybrands
Burn of Elsick
ST ANNES CR
ST MICHAEL'S RD
ST JOHN'S WK
Newhall
Newtonhill
Newtonhill Prim Sch
ST MICHAEL'S RD
8
7
97
6
5
96
4
3
95
2
1
94
88
89
90
121
180

179
175

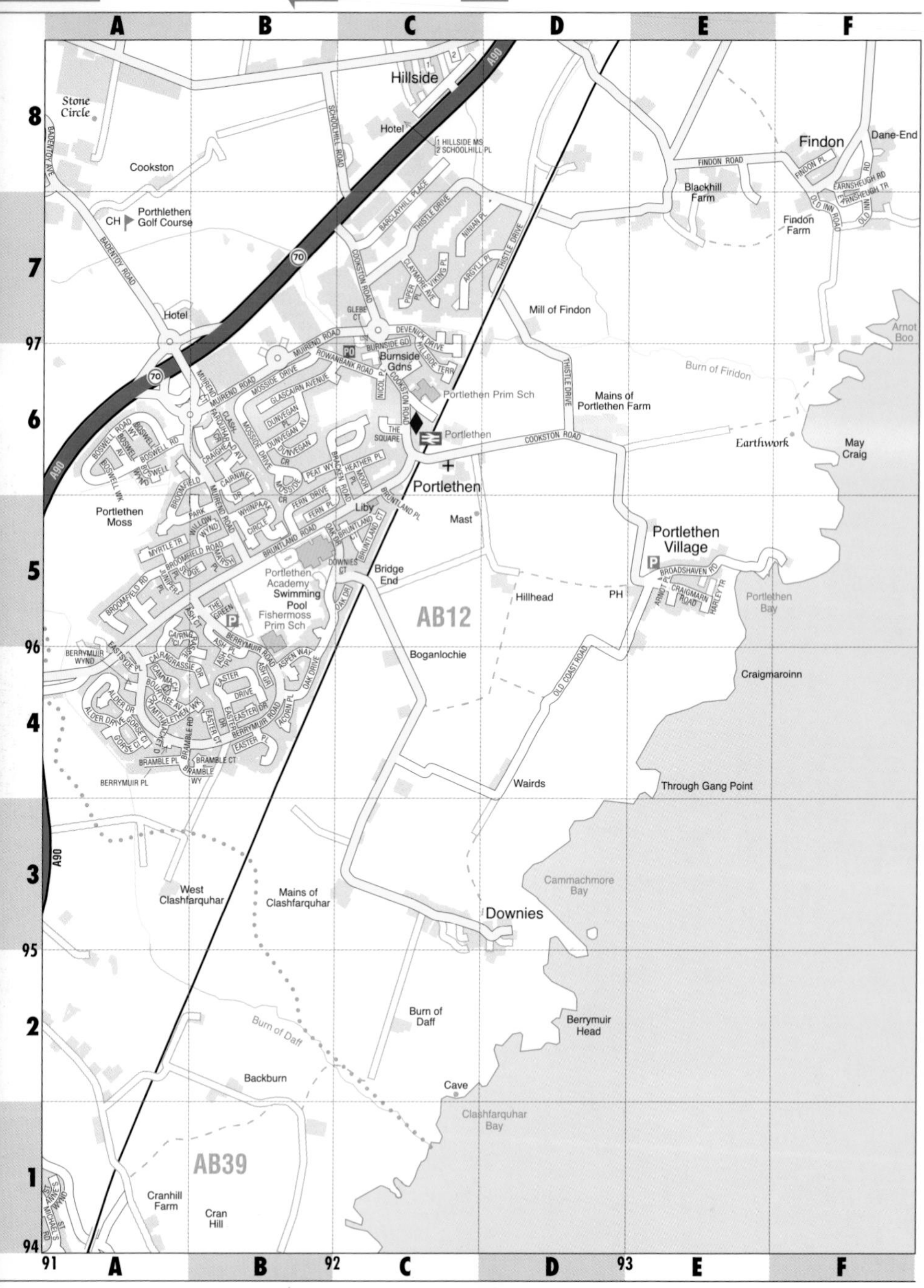

179
121

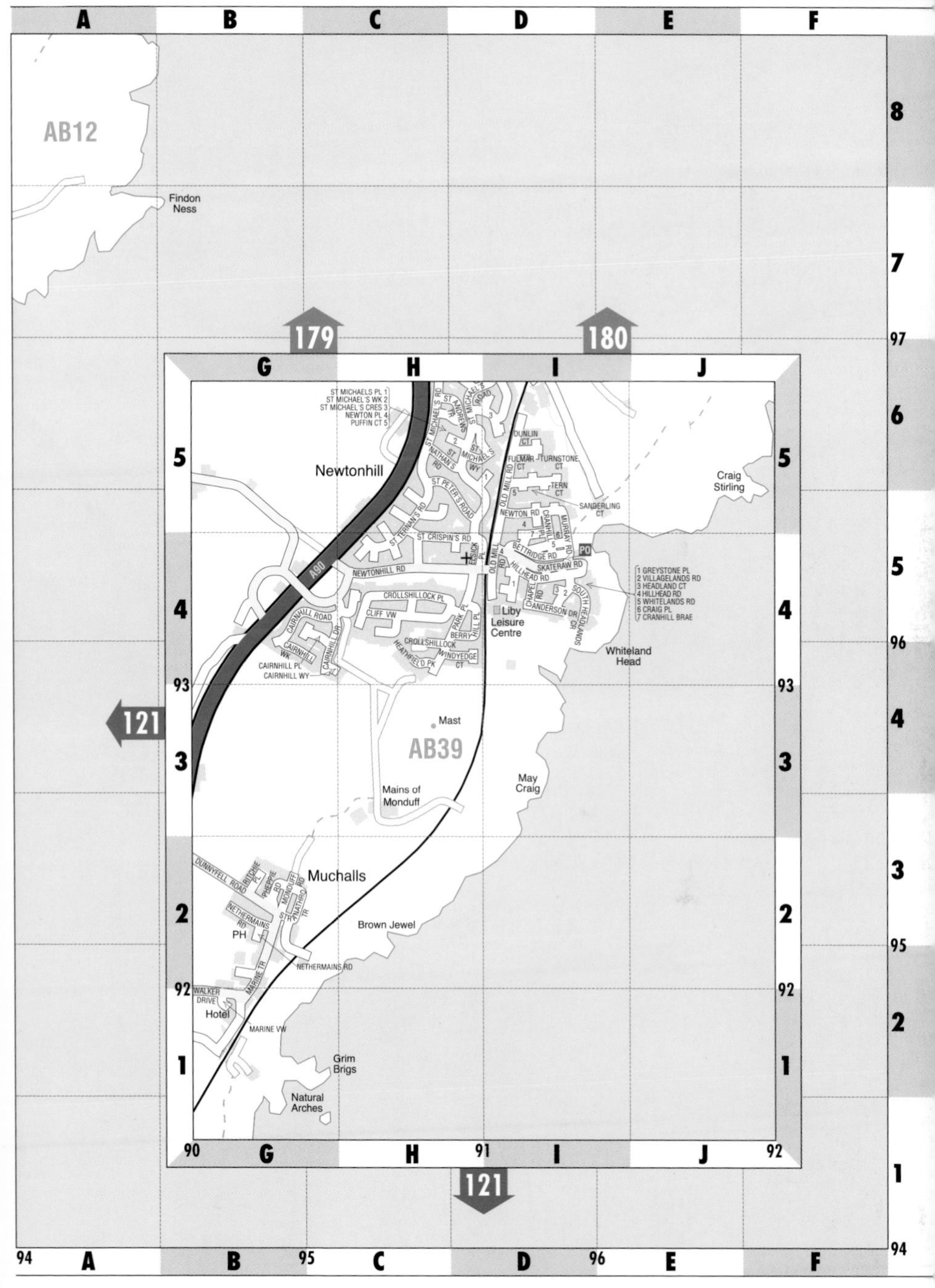
176
A
B
C
D
E
F
8
7
97
6
5
96
4
3
95
2
1
94
94
95
96
AB12
Findon Ness
179
180
G
H
I
J
5
4
93
3
2
92
1
90
91
92
121
Newtonhill
ST MICHAELS PL 1
ST MICHAEL'S WK 2
ST MICHAEL'S CRES 3
NEWTON PL 4
PUFFIN CT 5
DUNLIN CT
FULMAR CT
TURNSTONE CT
TERN CT
SANDERLING CT
NEWTON RD
ST PETER'S ROAD
ST TERNAN'S RD
ST CRISPIN'S RD
BETTRIDGE RD
SKATERAW RD
HILLHEAD RD
NEWTONHILL RD
A90
OLD MILL RD
CRANHILL PL
MURRAY RD
PO
1 GREYSTONE PL
2 VILLAGELANDS RD
3 HEADLAND CT
4 HILLHEAD RD
5 WHITELANDS RD
6 CRAIG PL
7 CRANHILL BRAE
Craig Stirling
CROLLSHILLOCK PL
CLIFF VW
CAIRNHILL ROAD
CAIRNHILL WK
CAIRNHILL PL
CAIRNHILL WY
CAIRNHILL DR
PARK PL
BERRYHILL PL
CROLLSHILLOCK
HEATHFIELD PK
WINDYEDGE CT
Liby Leisure Centre
CHAPEL RD
ANDERSON DR
SOUTH HEADLANDS CR
Whiteland Head
Mast
AB39
Mains of Monduff
May Craig
Muchalls
DUNNYFELL ROAD
RITCHIE PL
PHEPPIE RD
MONDUFF RD
STRANATHRO TR
NETHERMAINS RD
PH
Brown Jewel
NETHERMAINS RD
WALKER DRIVE
MARINE TR
Hotel
MARINE VW
Grim Brigs
Natural Arches

104 104 104

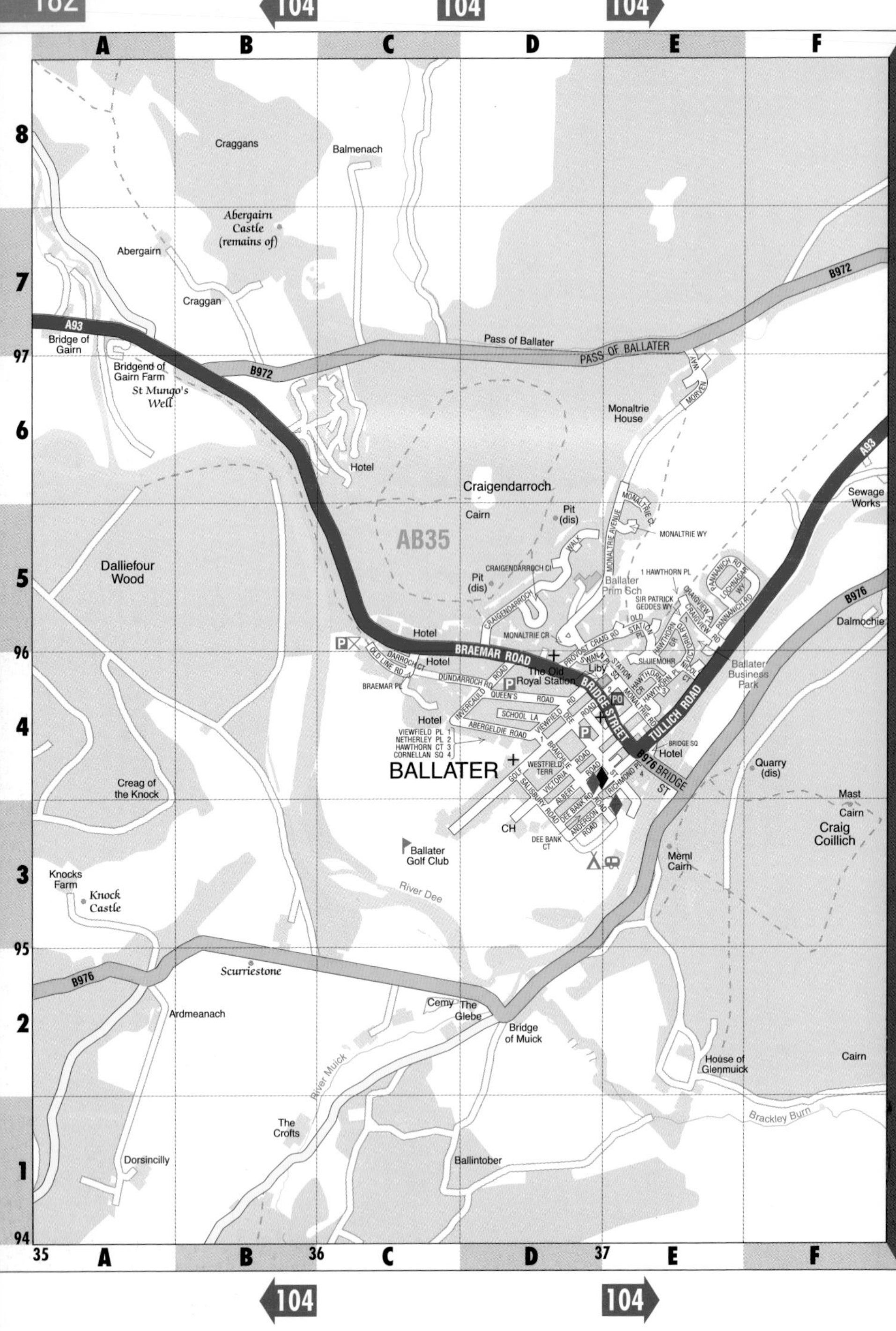

104 104

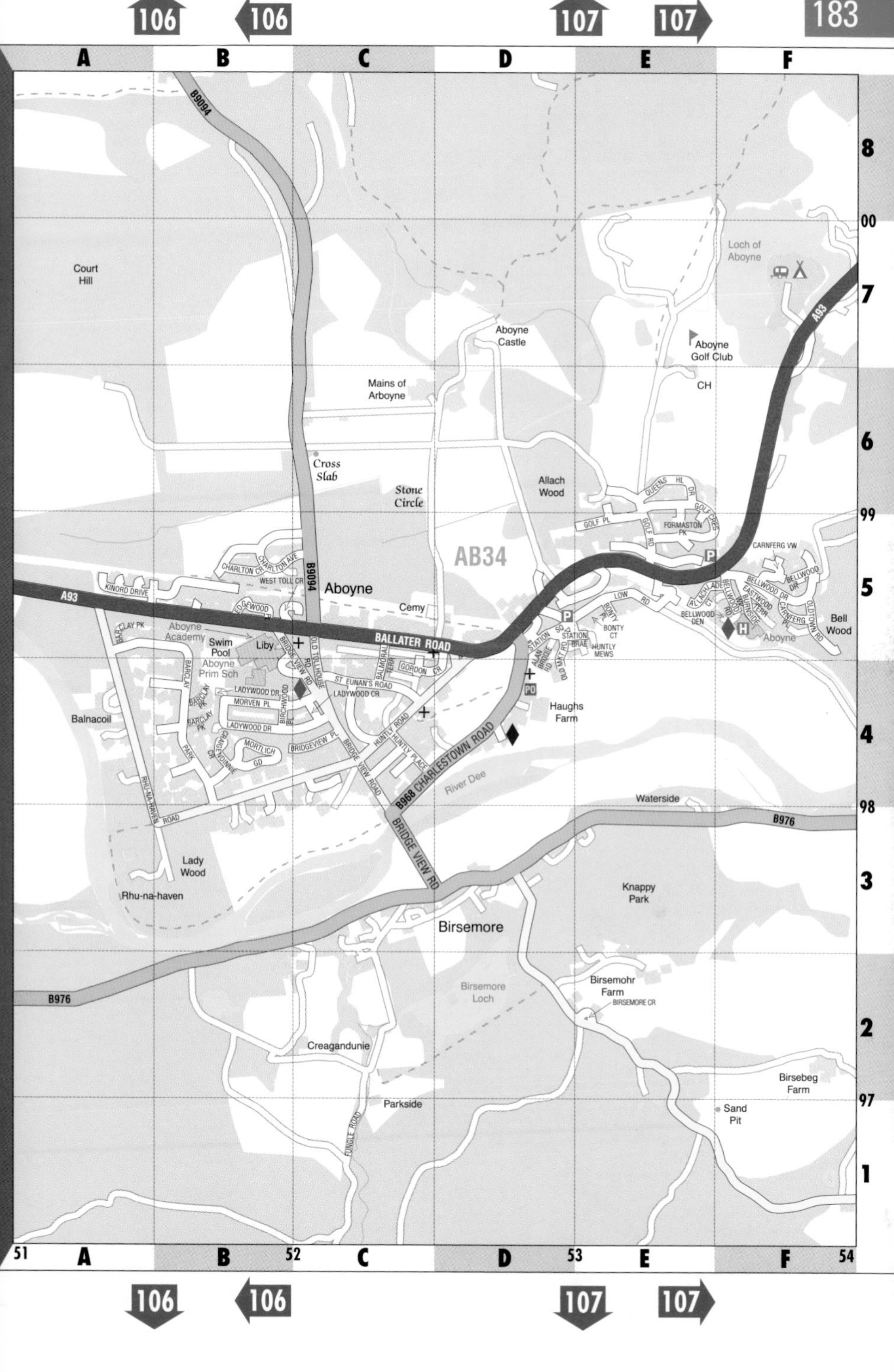

106
106
107
107
A
B
C
D
E
F
8
00
7
6
99
5
4
98
3
2
97
1
51
52
53
54
B9094
Court Hill
Loch of Aboyne
A93
Aboyne Castle
Aboyne Golf Club
CH
Mains of Arboyne
Cross Slab
Stone Circle
Allach Wood
QUEENS HL
DR
GOLF CRES
GOLF PL
FORMASTON PK
GOLF RD
CARNFERG VW
AB34
CHARLTON AVE
CHARLTON CR
WEST TOLL CR
Aboyne
KINORD DRIVE
Cemy
BELLWOOD DR
BELLWOOD
EASTWOOD
CARNFERG PL
OLDTOWN RD
BELLWOOD DEN
Bell Wood
BALLATER ROAD
LOW RD
BONTY PL
BONTY CT
STATION SQ
STATION BRAE
HUNTLY MEWS
BARCLAY PK
Aboyne Academy
Swim Pool
Liby
Aboyne Prim Sch
OLD TOLLHOUSE RD
BRIDGE VIEW RD
BALMORAL TERR
GORDON CR
ST EUNAN'S ROAD
LADYWOOD CR
LADYWOOD DR
MORVEN PL
BIRCHWOOD PL
BARCLAY
Balnacoil
HUNTLY ROAD
HUNTLY PLACE
Haughs Farm
PO
MORTLICH GD
BRIDGEVIEW PL
CRAIGENDINNIE CR
PARK
RHU-NA-HAVEN ROAD
B968 CHARLESTOWN ROAD
River Dee
Waterside
B976
Lady Wood
Rhu-na-haven
Knappy Park
Birsemore
Birsemore Loch
Birsemohr Farm
BIRSEMORE CR
Creagandunie
Birsebeg Farm
Parkside
FUNGLE ROAD
Sand Pit

109 109 110 110

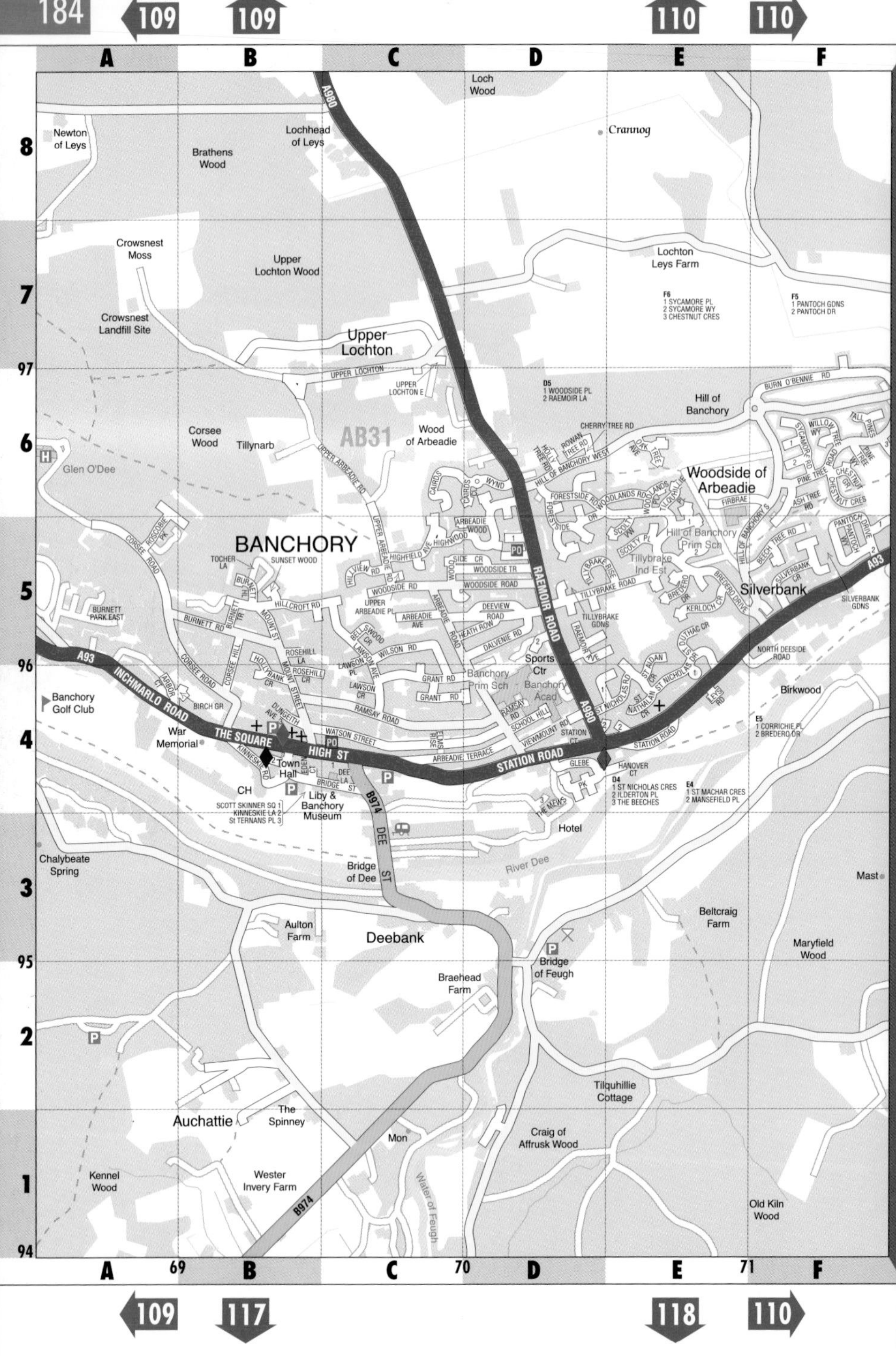

109 117 118 110

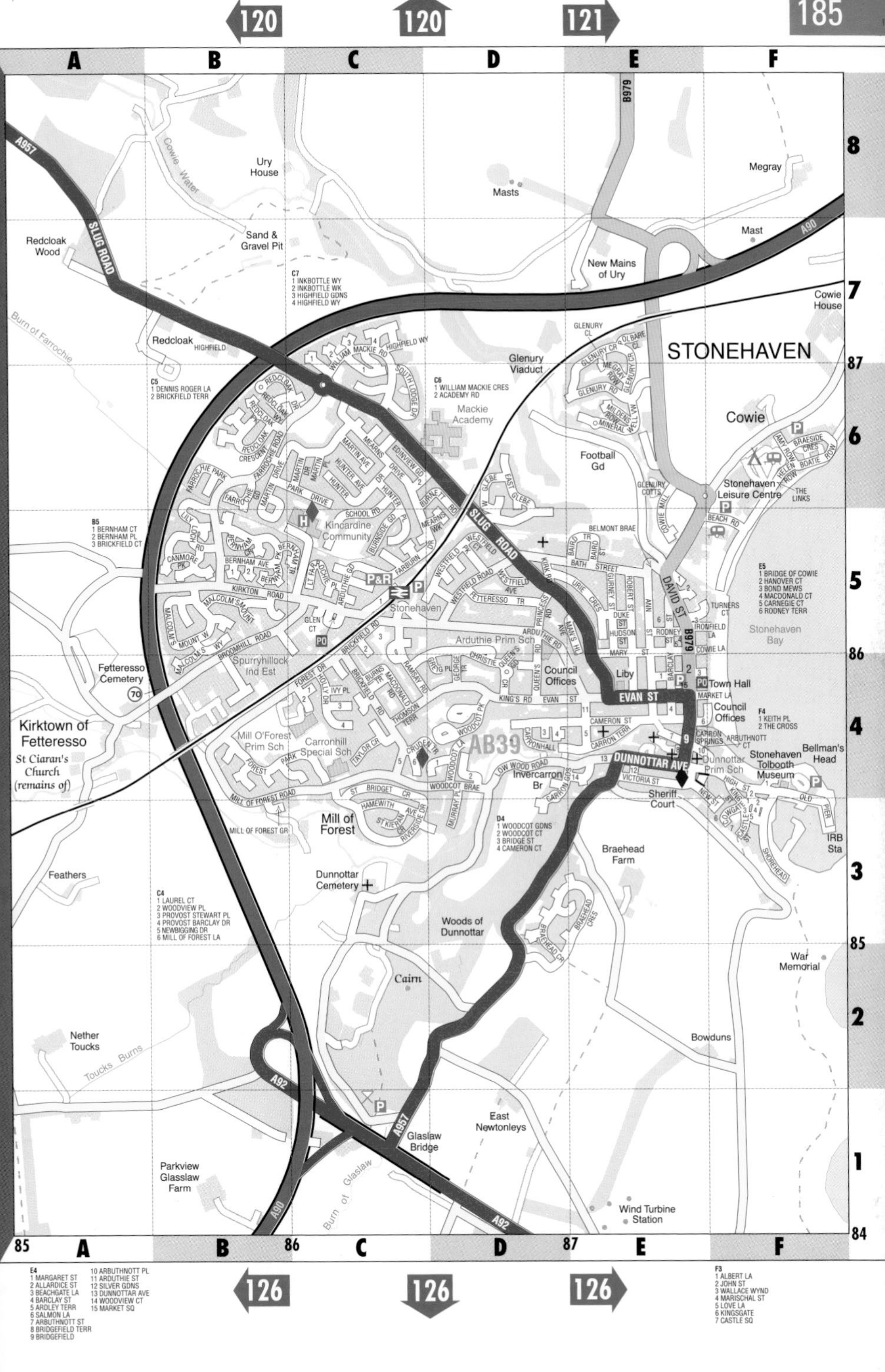
120
120
121
STONEHAVEN
A957
SLUG ROAD
A90
A92
B979
Ury House
Cowie Water
Sand & Gravel Pit
Redcloak Wood
Redcloak
Burn of Farrochie
Masts
Megray
Mast
New Mains of Ury
Cowie House
Glenury Viaduct
Mackie Academy
Cowie
Football Gd
Stonehaven Leisure Centre
THE LINKS
Kincardine Community
Stonehaven
Spurryhillock Ind Est
Arduthie Prim Sch
Council Offices
Liby
Town Hall
Stonehaven Bay
Fetteresso Cemetery
Kirktown of Fetteresso
St Ciaran's Church (remains of)
Mill O'Forest Prim Sch
Carronhill Special Sch
AB39
Invercarron Br
Dunnottar Prim Sch
Stonehaven Tolbooth Museum
Bellman's Head
Sheriff Court
IRB Sta
Mill of Forest
Braehead Farm
Feathers
Dunnottar Cemetery
Woods of Dunnottar
War Memorial
Cairn
Nether Toucks
Toucks Burns
Bowduns
East Newtonleys
Glaslaw Bridge
Parkview Glasslaw Farm
Burn of Glaslaw
Wind Turbine Station
EVAN ST
DUNNOTTAR AVE
DAVID ST
C7
1 INKBOTTLE WY
2 INKBOTTLE WK
3 HIGHFIELD GDNS
4 HIGHFIELD WY
C5
1 DENNIS ROGER LA
2 BRICKFIELD TERR
C6
1 WILLIAM MACKIE CRES
2 ACADEMY RD
B5
1 BERNHAM CT
2 BERNHAM PL
3 BRICKFIELD CT
E5
1 BRIDGE OF COWIE
2 HANOVER CT
3 BOND MEWS
4 MACDONALD CT
5 CARNEGIE CT
6 RODNEY TERR
F4
1 KEITH PL
2 THE CROSS
D4
1 WOODCOT GDNS
2 WOODCOT CT
3 BRIDGE ST
4 CAMERON CT
C4
1 LAUREL CT
2 WOODVIEW PL
3 PROVOST STEWART PL
4 PROVOST BARCLAY DR
5 NEWBIGGING DR
6 MILL OF FOREST LA
85
86
87
84
A
B
C
D
E
F
1
2
3
4
5
6
7
8
126
126
126
E4
1 MARGARET ST
2 ALLARDICE ST
3 BEACHGATE LA
4 BARCLAY ST
5 ARDLEY TERR
6 SALMON LA
7 ARBUTHNOTT ST
8 BRIDGEFIELD TERR
9 BRIDGEFIELD
10 ARBUTHNOTT PL
11 ARDUTHIE ST
12 SILVER GDNS
13 DUNNOTTAR AVE
14 WOODVIEW CT
15 MARKET SQ
F3
1 ALBERT LA
2 JOHN ST
3 WALLACE WYND
4 MARISCHAL ST
5 LOVE LA
6 KINGSGATE
7 CASTLE SQ

128 129 129

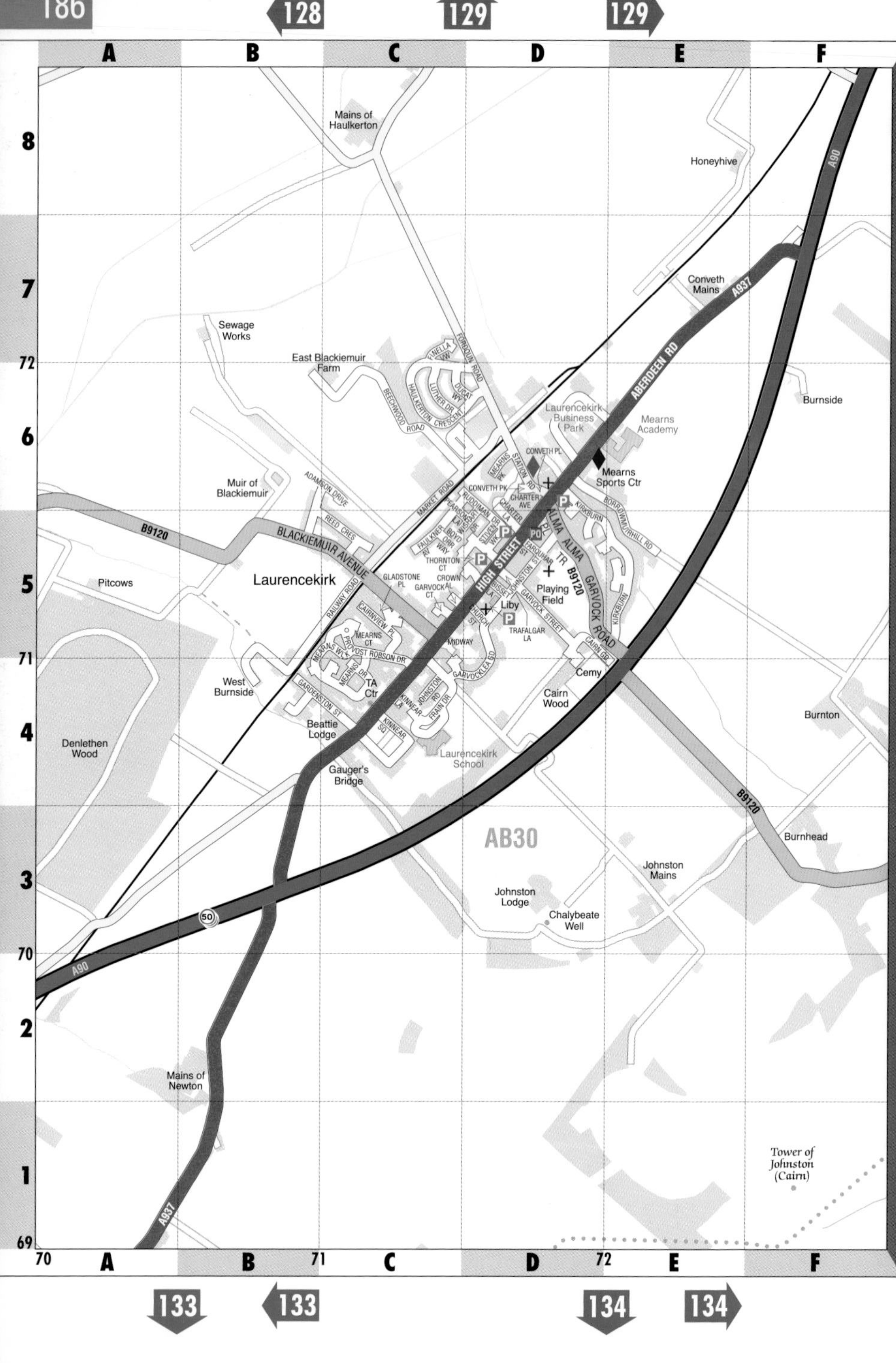

133 133 134 134

130 130 131 131

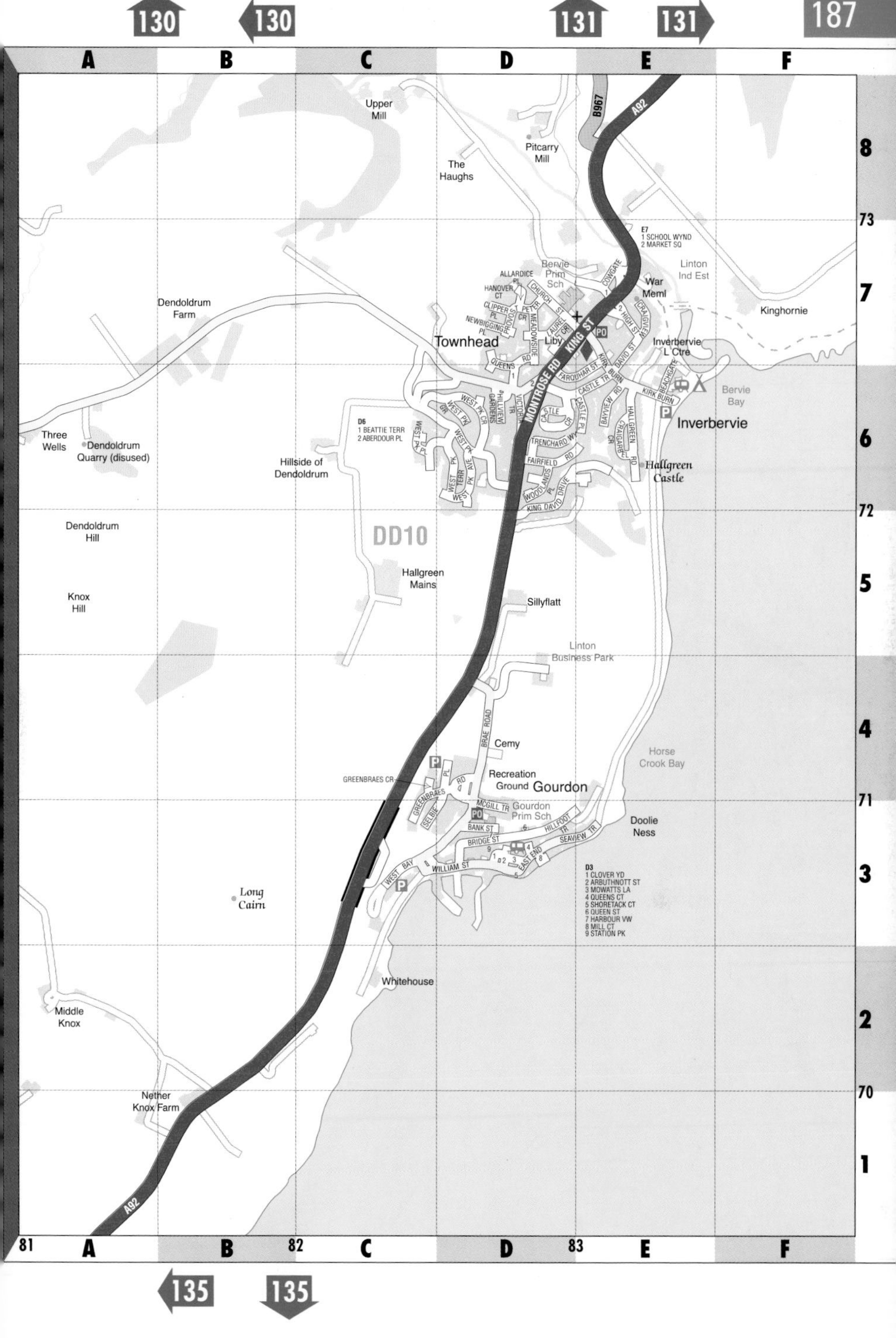

135 135

132 132

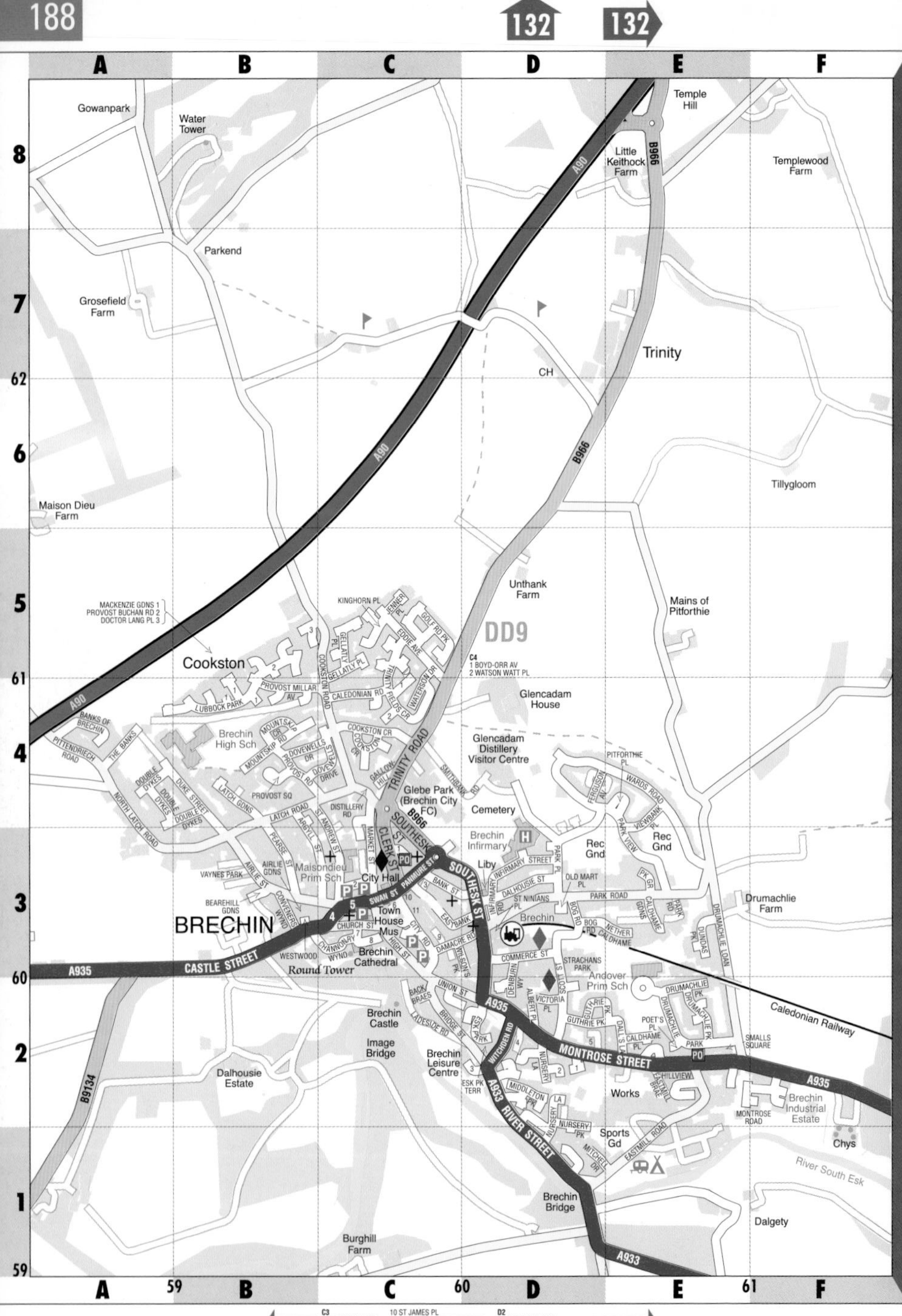

A 59 B C 60 D E 61 F

C3
1 MACGREGOR ST
2 MAISONDIEU LA
3 MARTIN'S LA
4 ST MARY ST
5 ST DAVID ST
6 LIDDLES CL
7 CHURCH LA
8 BISHOP'S CL
9 MATHERS PK
10 ST JAMES PL
11 ANN TERR

D2
1 SOUTHESK TERR
2 KINNAIRD PL
3 MEIKLE MILL
4 UPPER ANDOVER HILL
5 NEWINGTON GDNS

136 136 136

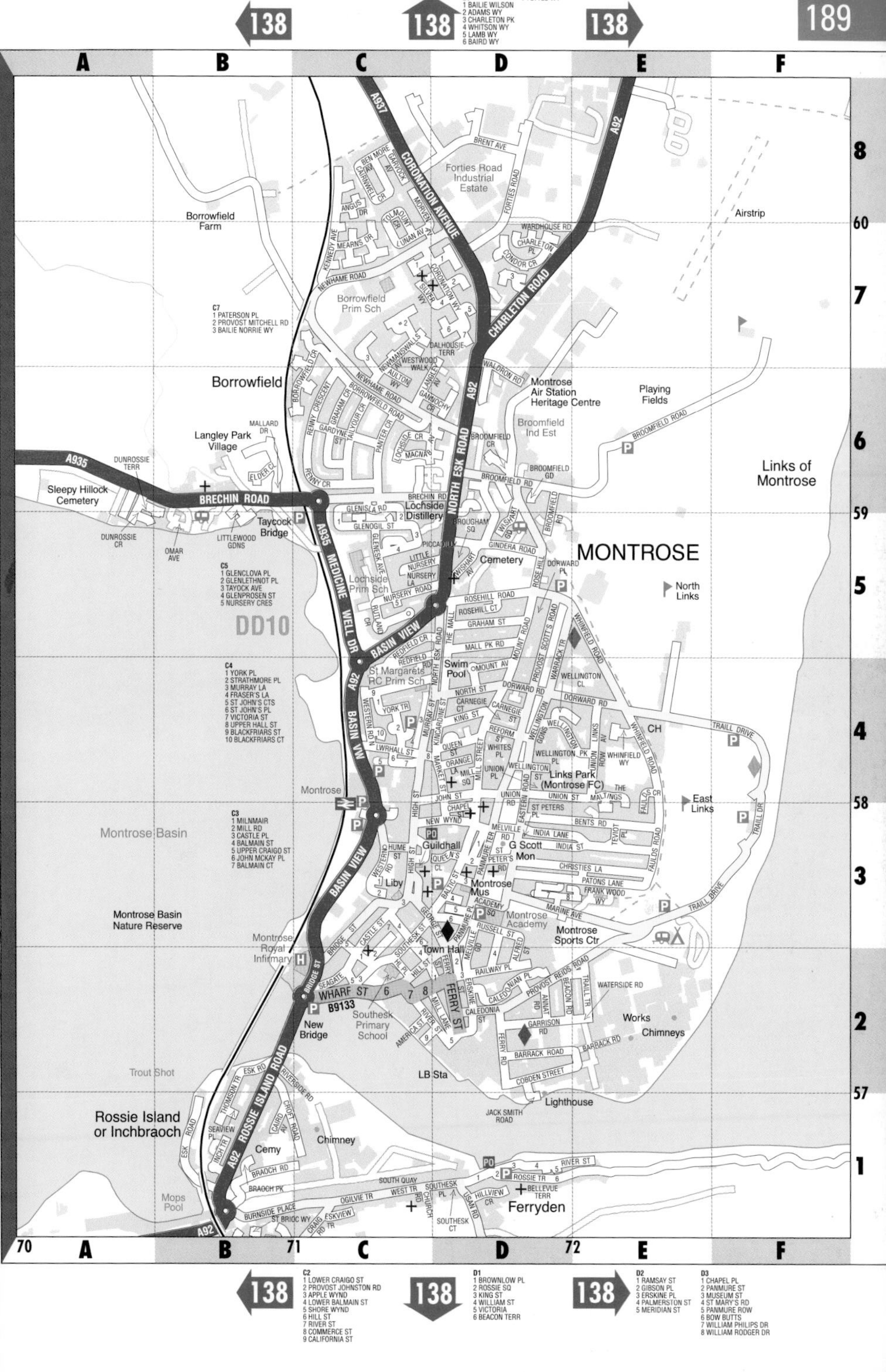
138
138
138
D7
1 BAILIE WILSON
2 ADAMS WY
3 CHARLETON PK
4 WHITSON WY
5 LAMB WY
6 BAIRD WY
7 FETTES WY
A
B
C
D
E
F
8
60
7
6
59
5
4
58
3
2
57
1
A937
A92
BRENT AVE
Forties Road Industrial Estate
FORTIES ROAD
CORONATION AVENUE
BEN MORE AV
GARVOCK AV
CAIRNWELL CR
ANGUS DR
TOLMOUNT CR
MORVEN
Airstrip
Borrowfield Farm
KENNEDY AVE
MEARNS DR
UNAN AV
WARDHOUSE RD
CHARLETON PL
CONDOR CR
NEWHAME ROAD
SILVER
CORONATION WY
CHARLETON ROAD
Borrowfield Prim Sch
C7
1 PATERSON PL
2 PROVOST MITCHELL RD
3 BAILIE NORRIE WY
NEWMANSWALLS AV
WESTWOOD WALK
AULTON WY
DALHOUSIE TERR
LANGLEY AV
GANNOCHY CR
WALDRON RD
Montrose Air Station Heritage Centre
Playing Fields
BROOMFIELD ROAD
Borrowfield
BORROWFIELD CR
NEWHAME ROAD
BORROWFIELD ROAD
RENNY CRESCENT
GRAHAM CR
GARDYNE ST
TAILYOUR CR
PANTER CR
LOCHSIDE CR
MACNAB AV
NORTH ESK ROAD
BROOMFIELD CR
Broomfield Ind Est
BROOMFIELD GD
BROOMFIELD RD
Links of Montrose
MALLARD DR
Langley Park Village
DUNROSSIE TERR
A935
ELDER CL
RENNY CR
Sleepy Hillock Cemetery
BRECHIN ROAD
BRECHIN ROAD
Lochside Distillery
GLENISLA RD
GLENOGIL ST
BROUGHAM SQ
MISPART GD
BROOMFIELD RD
DUNROSSIE CR
OMAR AVE
LITTLEWOOD GDNS
Taycock Bridge
A935 MEDICINE WELL DR
GLENESK AVE
PICCADILLY
LITTLE NURSERY
NURSERY LA
GINDERA ROAD
Cemetery
MONTROSE
C5
1 GLENCLOVA PL
2 GLENLETHNOT PL
3 TAYOCK AVE
4 GLENPROSEN ST
5 NURSERY CRES
Lochside Prim Sch
NURSERY ROAD
WISHART AV
ROSE HILL
DORWARD PL
North Links
DD10
RUTLAND CR
ROSEHILL ROAD
ROSEHILL CT
GRAHAM ST
PROVOST SCOTT'S ROAD
WHINFIELD ROAD
BASIN VIEW
REDFIELD CR
REDFIELD RD
MALL PK RD
THE MALL
MOUNT ROAD
WARRACK TR
Swim Pool
MOUNT AV
St Margaret's RC Prim Sch
C4
1 YORK PL
2 STRATHMORE PL
3 MURRAY LA
4 FRASER'S LA
5 ST JOHN'S CTS
6 ST JOHN'S PL
7 VICTORIA ST
8 UPPER HALL ST
9 BLACKFRIARS ST
10 BLACKFRIARS CT
A92 BASIN VW
NORTH ST
DORWARD RD
WELLINGTON CL
DORWARD RD
CARNEGIE CT
KING ST
CARNEGIE ST
YORK TR
WESTERN RD N
MURRAY ST
KINCARDINE ST
REFORM ST
WHITES PL
WELLINGTON GDNS
WELLINGTON PK
WELLINGTON PL
LINKS AV
UNION ROW
CH
TRAILL DRIVE
WHINFIELD WY
WHINFIELD ROAD
LWRHALL ST
QUEEN ST
ORANGE LA
MILL SQ
MILL STREET
UNION PL
WELLINGTON ST
Links Park (Montrose FC)
THE MALTINGS
FAULDS CR
East Links
Montrose
MARKET ST
HIGH ST
JOHN ST
UNION RD
EASTERN RD
UNION ST
CHAPEL ST
ST PETERS PL
BENTS RD
TRAILL DR
C3
1 MILNMAIR
2 MILL RD
3 CASTLE PL
4 BALMAIN ST
5 UPPER CRAIGO ST
6 JOHN MCKAY PL
7 BALMAIN CT
Montrose Basin
NEW WYND
MELVILLE LA
INDIA LANE
INDIA ST
G Scott Mon
TEVIOT PL
FAULDS ROAD
HUME ST
WESTERN RD
Guildhall
QUEEN'S CL
PANMURE TER
PETER'S ROW
CHRISTIES LA
PATONS LANE
FRANK WOOD WY
Liby
Montrose Mus
BALTIC ST
ACADEMY SQ
Montrose Academy
MARINE AVE
TRAILL DRIVE
Montrose Basin Nature Reserve
GEORGE ST
PANMURE PL
RUSSELL ST
Montrose Sports Ctr
BASIN VIEW
CASTLE ST
BRIDGE ST
SOUTHESK ST
Town Hall
MELVILLE GD
ALFRED ST
Montrose Royal Infirmary
HL PL
HILL ST
FERRY ST
RAILWAY PL
PROVOST REIDS ROAD
TRAILL TR
WATERSIDE RD
BRIDGE ST
SEAGATE
WHARF ST
B9133
ERSKINE ST
CALEDONIAN PL
ANNAT RD
BEACON RD
New Bridge
Southesk Primary School
AMERICA ST
RIVER ST
MILL LANE
FERRY ST
CALEDONIA ST
GARRISON RD
Works
Chimneys
BARRACK ROAD
BARRACK RD
FERRY RD
Trout Shot
ESK RD
RIVERSIDE RD
LB Sta
COBDEN STREET
THOMSON TR
ROSSIE ISLAND ROAD
Lighthouse
JACK SMITH ROAD
Rossie Island or Inchbraoch
SEAVIEW PL
ESK ROAD
CAIRD AV
CROFT ROAD
INCH TR
Chimney
A92
Cemy
BRAOCH RD
RIVER ST
ROSSIE TR
BRAOCH PK
SOUTH QUAY
OGILVIE TR
WEST TR
SOUTHESK PL
USAN RD
HILLVIEW CR
BELLEVUE TERR
Mops Pool
BURNSIDE PLACE
ST BRIOC WY
ESKVIEW
CRAIG RD TR
CHURCH RD
SOUTHESK CT
Ferryden
A92
70
A
B
71
C
D
72
E
F
138
C2
1 LOWER CRAIGO ST
2 PROVOST JOHNSTON RD
3 APPLE WYND
4 LOWER BALMAIN ST
5 SHORE WYND
6 HILL ST
7 RIVER ST
8 COMMERCE ST
9 CALIFORNIA ST
138
D1
1 BROWNLOW PL
2 ROSSIE SQ
3 KING ST
4 WILLIAM ST
5 VICTORIA
6 BEACON TERR
138
D2
1 RAMSAY ST
2 GIBSON PL
3 ERSKINE PL
4 PALMERSTON ST
5 MERIDIAN ST
D3
1 CHAPEL PL
2 PANMURE ST
3 MUSEUM ST
4 ST MARY'S RD
5 PANMURE ROW
6 BOW BUTTS
7 WILLIAM PHILIPS DR
8 WILLIAM RODGER DR

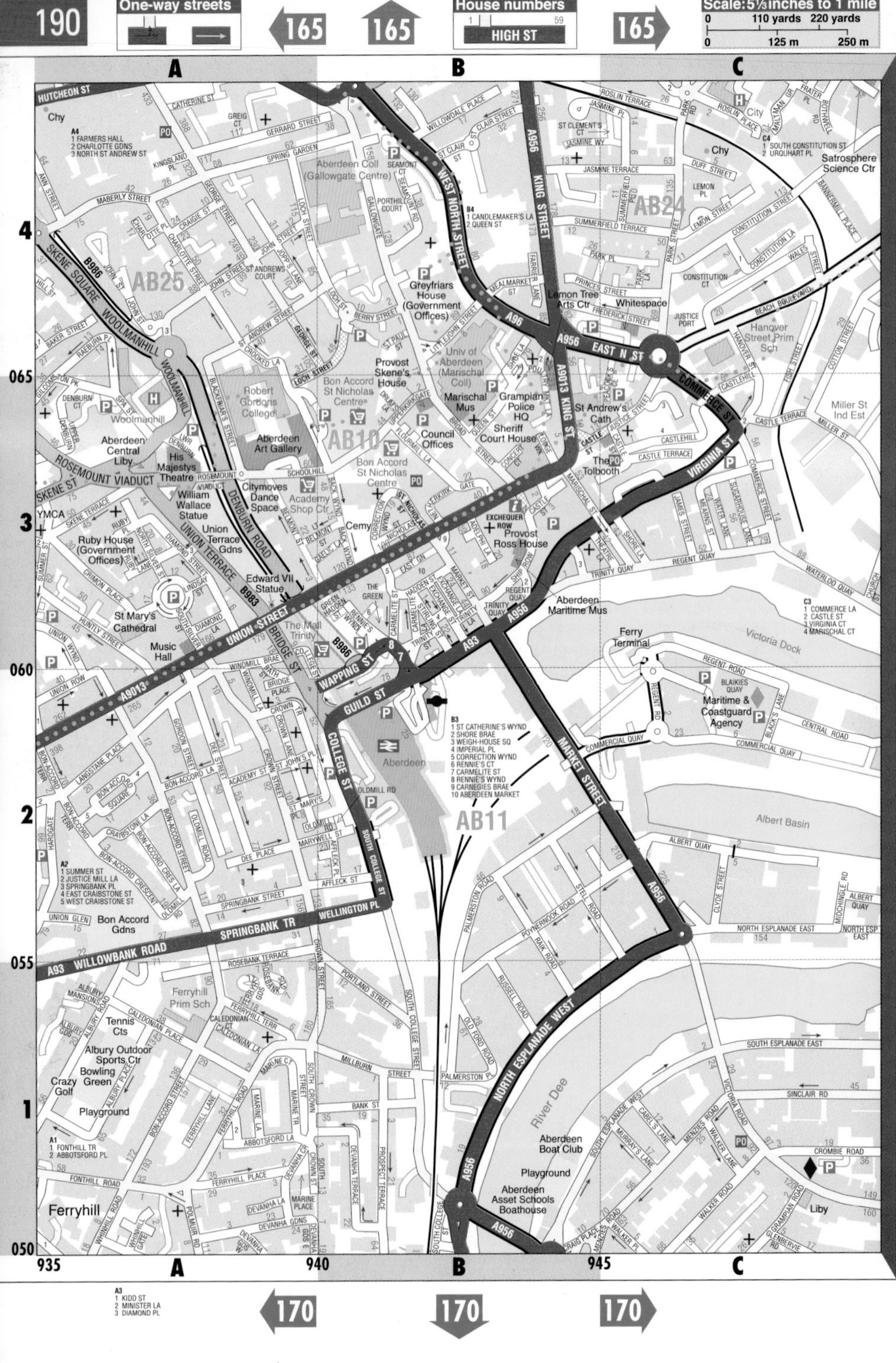
One-way streets
165
165
House numbers
1
59
HIGH ST
165
Scale: 5⅓ inches to 1 mile
0
110 yards
220 yards
0
125 m
250 m
A
B
C
4
065
3
060
2
055
1
050
935
940
945
HUTCHEON ST
CATHERINE ST
GERRARD STREET
SPRING GARDEN
Aberdeen Coll (Gallowgate Centre)
KINGSLAND PL
MABERLY STREET
GEORGE STREET
CHARLOTTE STREET
CRAIGIE ST
JOHN STREET
LOCH STREET
GALLOWGATE
SEAMOUNT RD
PORTHILL COURT
WEST NORTH STREET
KING STREET
WILLOWDALE PLACE
ST CLAIR STREET
ROSLIN TERRACE
JASMINE PL
JASMINE WY
JASMINE TERRACE
ST CLEMENT'S CT
SUMMERFIELD TERRACE
PARK STREET
PARK RD
DUFF STREET
LEMON PL
LEMON STREET
CONSTITUTION ST
CONSTITUTION LA
WALES ST
CONSTITUTION CT
BEACH BOULEVARD
Satrosphere Science Ctr
AB24
AB25
AB10
AB11
A4
1 FARMERS HALL
2 CHARLOTTE GDNS
3 NORTH ST ANDREW ST
B4
1 CANDLEMAKER'S LA
2 QUEEN ST
C4
1 SOUTH CONSTITUTION ST
2 URQUHART PL
SKENE SQUARE
B986
WOOLMANHILL
BAKER STREET
RAEBURN PL
ST ANDREW STREET
CROOKED LA
GEORGE ST
LOCH STREET
BERRY STREET
Greyfriars House (Government Offices)
MEALMARKET ST
FARRIER LANE
Lemon Tree Arts Ctr
Whitespace
PRINCES STREET
FREDERICK STREET
JUSTICE PORT
A96
A956
EAST N ST
Hanover Street Prim Sch
HANOVER STREET
COTTON STREET
Miller St Ind Est
MILLER ST
Woolmanhill
Robert Gordons College
Bon Accord St Nicholas Centre
Provost Skene's House
Univ of Aberdeen (Marischal Coll)
Marischal Mus
Grampian Police HQ
Sheriff Court House
A9013 KING ST
St Andrew's Cath
COMMERCE ST
CASTLEHILL
CASTLE TERRACE
Aberdeen Central Liby
His Majestys Theatre
Aberdeen Art Gallery
Council Offices
BROAD STREET
QUEEN ST
ROSEMOUNT VIADUCT
SKENE ST
DENBURN ROAD
SCHOOLHILL
Citymoves Dance Space
Academy Shop Ctr
Bon Accord St Nicholas Centre
The Tolbooth
CASTLE ST
VIRGINIA ST
William Wallace Statue
Union Terrace Gdns
UNION TERRACE
YMCA
SKENE TERRACE
Ruby House (Government Offices)
Cemy
CORRECTION WYND
ST NICHOLAS ST
EXCHEQUER ROW
Provost Ross House
MARISCHAL ST
SHORE LA
JAMES STREET
WATER LANE
SUGARHOUSE LANE
COMMERCE STREET
REGENT QUAY
WATERLOO QUAY
TRINITY QUAY
Edward VII Statue
B983
CRIMON PLACE
DIAMOND ST
UNION STREET
BRIDGE ST
The Mall Trinity
SHIP ROW
Aberdeen Maritime Mus
Victoria Dock
C3
1 COMMERCE LA
2 CASTLE ST
3 VIRGINIA CT
4 MARISCHAL CT
St Mary's Cathedral
Music Hall
HUNTLY STREET
UNION WYND
A9013
WINDMILL BRAE
WAPPING ST
GUILD ST
A93
Ferry Terminal
REGENT ROAD
BLAIKIES QUAY
Maritime & Coastguard Agency
BLACK'S LANE
CENTRAL ROAD
COMMERCIAL QUAY
UNION ROW
GORDON STREET
CROWN STREET
COLLEGE ST
Aberdeen
OLDMILL RD
MARKET STREET
B3
1 ST CATHERINE'S WYND
2 SHORE BRAE
3 WEIGH-HOUSE SQ
4 IMPERIAL PL
5 CORRECTION WYND
6 RENNIE'S CT
7 CARMELITE ST
8 RENNIE'S WYND
9 CARNEGIES BRAE
10 ABERDEEN MARKET
LANGSTANE PLACE
BON-ACCORD SQUARE
BON-ACCORD ST
BON-ACCORD TERR
CRAIBSTONE LA
BON-ACCORD CRESCENT
DEE STREET
DEE PLACE
SPRINGBANK STREET
MARYWELL ST
AFFLECK ST
SOUTH COLLEGE ST
Albert Basin
ALBERT QUAY
CLYDE STREET
MIDCHINGLE RD
ALBERT QUAY
PALMERSTON ROAD
POYNERNOOK ROAD
STELL ROAD
NORTH ESPLANADE EAST
A2
1 SUMMER ST
2 JUSTICE MILL LA
3 SPRINGBANK PL
4 EAST CRAIBSTONE ST
5 WEST CRAIBSTONE ST
UNION GLEN
Bon Accord Gdns
SPRINGBANK TR
WELLINGTON PL
WILLOWBANK ROAD
ROSEBANK TERRACE
PORTLAND STREET
RUSSELL ROAD
NORTH ESPLANADE WEST
Ferryhill Prim Sch
CALEDONIAN PLACE
FERRYHILL TERR
Tennis Cts
Albury Outdoor Sports Ctr
Bowling Green
Crazy Golf
Playground
MILLBURN STREET
OLD FORD ROAD
PALMERSTON PL
River Dee
SOUTH ESPLANADE EAST
SINCLAIR RD
BANK ST
MARINE LA
FERRYHILL ROAD
BON-ACCORD STREET
ABBOTSFORD LA
DEVANHA TERRACE
PROSPECT TERRACE
Aberdeen Boat Club
Playground
Aberdeen Asset Schools Boathouse
SOUTH ESPLANADE WEST
CAREL'S LANE
MURRAY'S LANE
MENZIES ROAD
WALKER LANE
VICTORIA ROAD
CROMBIE ROAD
Liby
A1
1 FONTHILL TR
2 ABBOTSFORD PL
FONTHILL ROAD
FERRYHILL PLACE
DEVANHA LA
DEVANHA GDNS
MARINE PLACE
Ferryhill
WHINHILL ROAD
POLMUIR RD
CRAIG PLACE
WALKER RD
GRAMPIAN RD
GLENBERVIE RD
A3
1 KIDD ST
2 MINISTER LA
3 DIAMOND PL
170
170
170

Index

Place name May be abbreviated on the map
Location number Present when a number indicates the place's position in a crowded area of mapping
Locality, town or village Shown when more than one place has the same name
Postcode district District for the indexed place
Page and grid square Page number and grid reference for the standard mapping

Cities, towns and villages are listed in CAPITAL LETTERS
Public and commercial buildings are highlighted in magenta
Places of interest are highlighted in blue with a star★

Abbreviations used in the index

Acad	**Academy**	Comm	**Common**	Gd	**Ground**	L	**Leisure**	Prom	**Promenade**
App	**Approach**	Cott	**Cottage**	Gdn	**Garden**	La	**Lane**	Rd	**Road**
Arc	**Arcade**	Cres	**Crescent**	Gn	**Green**	Liby	**Library**	Recn	**Recreation**
Ave	**Avenue**	Cswy	**Causeway**	Gr	**Grove**	Mdw	**Meadow**	Ret	**Retail**
Bglw	**Bungalow**	Ct	**Court**	H	**Hall**	Meml	**Memorial**	Sh	**Shopping**
Bldg	**Building**	Ctr	**Centre**	Ho	**House**	Mkt	**Market**	Sq	**Square**
Bsns, Bus	**Business**	Ctry	**Country**	Hospl	**Hospital**	Mus	**Museum**	St	**Street**
Bvd	**Boulevard**	Cty	**County**	HQ	**Headquarters**	Orch	**Orchard**	Sta	**Station**
Cath	**Cathedral**	Dr	**Drive**	Hts	**Heights**	Pal	**Palace**	Terr	**Terrace**
Cir	**Circus**	Dro	**Drove**	Ind	**Industrial**	Par	**Parade**	TH	**Town Hall**
Cl	**Close**	Ed	**Education**	Inst	**Institute**	Pas	**Passage**	Univ	**University**
Cnr	**Corner**	Emb	**Embankment**	Int	**International**	Pk	**Park**	Wk, Wlk	**Walk**
Coll	**College**	Est	**Estate**	Intc	**Interchange**	Pl	**Place**	Wr	**Water**
Com	**Community**	Ex	**Exhibition**	Junc	**Junction**	Prec	**Precinct**	Yd	**Yard**

Index of towns, villages, streets, hospitals, industrial estates, railway stations, schools, shopping centres, universities and places of interest

A

Aalesund Pl [1] AB42 .... 147 C2
Aalesund Rd AB42 ....147 B2
Abbey Kiln★ AB42 ....37 C7
Abbey La
Aberdeen AB11 ....170 E7
Peterhead AB42...........37 D6
Abbey Pl AB11...........170 E7
Abbey Rd AB11 ....170 F7
Abbey Sq AB11 ....170 E7
Abbey St AB42............37 D6
Abbotsford La AB11..... 190 A1
Abbotsford Pl [2] AB11 .. 190 A1
Abbotshall Cres AB15 ....168 F3
Abbotshall Dr AB15 ......168 E3
Abbotshall Gdns AB15....168 F3
Abbotshall Pl AB15 ......168 F3
Abbotshall Rd AB15......168 F4
Abbotshall Terr AB15.....168 E3
Abbotshall Wlk AB15.....168 E4
Abbots Pl AB12..........170 B4
Abbotswell Cres AB12....170 B4
Abbotswell Dr AB12..... 170 A4
Abbotswell Prim Sch
AB12 .... 170 A3
Abbotswell Rd
Aberdeen AB12 .... 170 C4
Peterhead AB42......... 147 C6
ABERCHIRDER 144 E5
Aberchirder Prim Sch
AB54 .... 144 D5
ABERDEEN...............190 B2
Aberdeen Airport AB21...157 F5
Aberdeen Art Gall★
AB25 .... 190 A3
Aberdeen Coll (Balgownie
Ctr) AB23 .... 160 A1
Aberdeen Coll (Gallowgate
Ctr) AB25 ....190 B4
Aberdeen Ctr for English
AB11 ....170 B6
Aberdeen Ex & Con Ctr
AB23 .... 160 C2
Aberdeen Gram Sch
AB25 .... 165 A1
Aberdeen Maritime Mus★
AB11 ....190 B3
Aberdeen Maternity Hospl
AB25 ....164 E3
Aberdeen Music Hall★
AB10 .... 190 A3
Aberdeen Rd
Aboyne AB34..............96 C3
Alford AB33.............154 F3
Huntly AB54.............148 F4
Laurencekirk AB30 ....186 E6
Aberdeen Royal Infmy
AB25 .... 164 D3
Aberdeen Sch for the Deaf
AB24 ....165 B4
Aberdeenshire Farming
Mus★ AB42 .... 146 A4
Aberdeen Sta AB11 ......190 B2
Aberdeen Terr [2] AB34....96 C3
Aberdeen Waldorf Sch
AB15 ....168 E4
Aberdon Ct [4] AB24..... 165 A6
Aberdour Pl [2] DD10.... 187 D6
Abergeldie Castle★
AB35 .... 103 A2
Abergeldie Rd
Aberdeen AB10 ....169 F6
Ballater AB35 .... 182 D4
Abergeldie Terr AB10 ....169 F6
Abernethy Rd AB42 ..... 147 A4
ABOYNE 183 C5
Aboyne Acad AB34.......183 B5
Aboyne Gdns AB10.......169 E4
Aboyne Hospl AB34 ......183 F5
Aboyne Pl
Aberdeen AB10 .... 169 D3
Fraserburgh AB43........143 B4
Aboyne Prim Sch AB34...183 B4
Aboyne Rd AB10 .... 169 D4
Aboyne Swimming Pool
AB34 ....183 B5
Aboyne Terr AB10........169 E3
Acacia Gr [2] AB42 ...... 147 A5
Academy Gdns AB42 .... 146 C5
Academy Pl AB42....... 147 C5
Academy Rd
Banff AB45..............140 F5
Fraserburgh AB43........143 B6
[2] Stonehaven AB39..... 185 C6
Academy Sq DD10 ...... 189 D3
Academy St AB11....... 190 A2
Academy Way AB51......150 B3
Acad Sh Ctr AB25....... 190 A3
Acorn Pl AB12...........180 B4
Adam Pl DD9 .... 132 A7
Adamson Dr AB30 ....186 B6
Adams Way [2] DD10 .... 189 D7
Adbury Outdoor Sports Ctr
AB11 .... 190 A1
Addison Cres AB45.......140 E5
Adelphi La AB11.........190 B3
Aden Circ AB42......... 146 C5
Aden Cres AB42 ....37 D6
Aden Ctry Pk★ AB42 .... 146 A5
Aden Gdns AB42........ 146 C4
Admirals La [4] AB54 .....148 E5
Advocates' Rd AB24..... 165 C3
Affleck Pl AB11..........190 B2
Affleck St AB11..........190 B2
Affric Pl AB43 ....143 B4
Afton Rd AB43...........143 B4
Ailsa Ct AB43.......... 143 A5
Aird Gn AB45............139 E7
Aird St AB45.............139 E6
Airlie Gdns AB45........ 141 A5
Airlie St DD9 ....188 B3
Airside Bsns Pk AB21 ....157 F7
Airways Ind Est AB21 ... 158 A8
Airyhall Ave AB15........169 B5
Airyhall Cres AB15...... 169 A5
Airyhall Dr AB15.........169 B5
Airyhall Gdns AB15 ......169 B5
Airyhall Pl AB15 ....169 B5
Airyhall Rd AB15.........169 B4
Airyhall Terr AB15........169 B5
Airyhill View [2] AB41......77 F8
Alan Brodie Rd AB34.... 183 D5
Albany Ct AB43..........143 B6
Alberta Pl AB45..........140 E6
Albert Den AB25........ 165 A1
Albert Gdns AB51....... 152 D6
Albert Gr AB51 .... 150 D3
Albert La
Aberdeen AB10 ....164 F1
Fraserburgh AB43....... 143 C7
[1] Stonehaven AB39......185 F3
Albert Pl
[9] Aberdeen AB25 ...... 165 A1
Brechin DD9............ 188 D2
Oldmeldrum AB51 .... 150 D3
Albert Quay AB11....... 190 C2
Albert Rd
Ballater AB35 .... 182 D3
Oldmeldrum AB51 .... 150 D3
Albert St
Aberdeen AB25 ....164 F1
Fraserburgh AB43....... 143 C7
Inverurie AB51 .... 152 D6
Peterhead AB42..........147 F5
Albert Terr
Aberdeen AB10 ....169 F8
[10] Cullen AB56 ....1 B5
Albert Terr *continued*
Huntly AB54.............148 E3
Oldmeldrum AB51 .... 150 D3
Albury Gdns AB11....... 190 A1
Albury Mans AB11 ...... 190 A1
Albury Pl AB11 .... 190 A1
Albury Rd AB11......... 190 A1
Albyn Gr AB10...........169 F8
Albyn La AB10...........169 F8
Albyn Pl [2] AB10 ....169 F8
Albyn Sch AB15..........169 E8
Albyn Terr AB10..........169 F8
Alder Dr AB12 .... 180 A4
Alehousewells Prim Sch
AB51 ....87 C7
Alen Dr AB33 .... 154 C4
Alexander Bell Pl AB43....23 D7
Alexander Cres [5] AB51...87 D7
Alexander Dr
Aberdeen AB24 ....164 F7
Huntly AB54.............148 E5
Alexander St AB52...... 149 D4
Alexander Terr AB24 .... 165 A6
Alexandra Par AB42......147 F6
Alexandra Terr AB43 .... 143 C5
Alex Collie Sports Ctr
AB22 ....159 F1
ALFORD 154 C4
Alford Acad AB33....... 154 C3
Alford Bsns Pk AB33 .....154 E3
Alford Her Ctr★ AB33 ... 154 D3
Alford La AB10.......... 170 A8
Alford Pl AB10.......... 170 A8
Alford Prim Sch AB33... 154 C3
Alford Ski Ctr★ AB33.... 154 C3
Alford Swimming Pool
AB33 .... 154 C3
Alfred St DD10.......... 189 D2
Allachlade Ct AB34 ......183 E5
Allandale Gdns AB51.... 155 C5
Allan Pl AB51........... 152 C7
Allan St AB10............169 F7
Allardice Pl DD10....... 187 D7
Allardice St [2] AB39 .....185 E4
Allathan Pk AB41 ....62 B2
Allenvale Gdns AB10.... 170 A5
Allenvale Rd AB10 ...... 170 A5
Allison Cl AB12..........176 B8
Allochy Pl AB43............15 B7
Allochy Rd AB43...........15 C7
Almanythie Rd [2] AB42 ..147 E6
Alma Pl AB30........... 186 D6
Alma Rd AB23...........160 B1

Aal–ANN

Alma Terr AB30 .... 186 D5
Alness Cres AB43 ....143 B4
Alpine Pl AB43.......... 143 A4
Altdubh Pl [2] AB21 ......156 B6
ALTENS.................170 E1
Altens Ctr (Aberdeen
College) AB12..........170 F2
Altens Farm Rd AB12 ... 170 D3
Altens Ind Est AB12......170 E1
Altonrea Gdns AB21..... 158 C6
Altries Wood AB12.......177 F8
Alva Cres AB43 ....143 B4
Alvah Terr AB45..........140 E4
Alwyn Wind AB42..........27 B3
America St DD10 .... 189 C2
Amy Row AB39 ....185 F6
Anchor La DD10 .... 135 C5
Anderson Ave AB24 ......164 E6
Anderson Ct AB43 ...... 143 A6
Anderson Dr
Aberdeen AB15 .... 169 C8
Huntly AB54..............30 C7
Peterhead AB42...........38 D5
Stonehaven AB39.........181 I4
Anderson Gdns AB43.... 143 A6
Anderson La AB24 ....164 E6
Anderson Pl AB43 ....143 B7
Anderson Rd
Aberdeen AB24 .... 164 D6
Ballater AB35 .... 182 D3
Anderson Terr
Aboyne AB34..............96 B3
Ellon AB41..............151 B5
Anderson Wlk AB51..... 152 C5
Andover Prim Sch DD9...188 E3
Angus Dr DD10 .... 189 C8
Angusfield Ave AB15.....169 B7
Angusfield La AB15 ......169 B8
Angus Gdns AB42..........25 C1
Angus La [4] AB53....... 145 D4
Annand Ave AB41.........151 B6
Annand Rd AB41.........151 B6
Anna Ritchie Sch The
AB42 .... 147 C5
Annat Bank AB12 .... 176 C8
Annat Rd DD10 .... 189 D2
Annesley Gr [3] AB31.....108 E8
Annesley Pk [5] AB31.....108 E8
Annfield Terr AB15.......169 E7
ANNOCHIE................36 F1

Ann St
Aberdeen AB25 190 A4
Stonehaven AB39 185 E5
Anvil Pl AB43 26 C7
Apple Wynd 3 DD10 189 C2
Aquhorthies Circ AB51 152 B5
Aquithie Rd AB51 87 D7
Arbeadie Ave AB31 184 C5
Arbeadie Rd AB31 184 C5
Arbeadie Terr AB31 184 C4
Arbeadie Wood AB31 184 C5
Arbor Ct AB31 184 A4
Arbroath La AB12 170 B3
Arbroath Pl AB12 170 C3
Arbroath Way AB12 170 B3
Arbuthnot Mus* AB42 147 E5
ARBUTHNOTT 130 D6
Arbuthnott Ct AB39 185 F4
Arbuthnot Terr AB42 147 C5
Arbuthnott House* AB30 130 D6
Arbuthnott Pl 10 AB39 185 E4
Arbuthnott St
2 Montrose DD10 187 D3
7 Stonehaven AB39 185 E4
Archaeolink Prehistory Pk* AB52 72 C8
Archer Pk DD10 134 D3
ARDALLIE 51 E5
Ardallie Prim Sch AB42 51 E6
Ardanes Brae AB45 140 E6
Ardarroch Cl AB24 165 C4
Ardarroch Ct AB24 165 D4
Ardarroch Pl AB24 165 D4
Ardarroch Rd AB24 165 C4
Ardbeck Pl AB14 172 E7
Ardconnon Ave AB51 150 C4
Ardeer Pl AB43 143 B4
ARDGATHEN 154 A4
Ardgith Rd 3 AB41 151 E6
Ardinn Cres AB53 145 F4
Ardinn Dr AB53 145 F4
Ardinn Rd AB53 145 E4
Ardinn Terr AB53 145 E4
Ardlair Terr AB21 158 C7
ARDLAWHILL 12 D5
Ardlaw Pl AB43 143 A5
Ardley Terr 5 AB39 185 E4
Ardmachron Dr 2 AB42 53 B3
ARDO 49 B6
Ardovie Rd DD9 136 E1
Ardtannes Pl 2 AB51 152 D4
Arduthie Gdns AB39 185 C5
Arduthie Prim Sch AB39 185 D5
Arduthie Rd AB39 185 D5
Arduthie St AB39 185 E4
Argyll Cl AB21 157 E4
Argyll Cres AB25 164 E2
Argyll Pl
Aberdeen AB25 164 F2
Portlethen AB12 180 C7
Argyll Rd
Aberdeen AB21 157 E4
Fraserburgh AB43 143 B5
Argyll St DD9 188 B4
Arisaig Dr AB43 143 B4
Ark Ct AB43 143 B5
Ark La AB43 5 A4
Armoury La 8 AB42 38 D6
Arnage Ave AB41 151 E5
Arnage Castle* AB41 50 D4
Arnage Cres AB16 164 B3
Arnage Dr AB16 164 A3
Arnage Gdns AB16 164 B3
Arnage Pl AB16 164 B3
Arnage Prim Sch AB41 50 F5
Arnage Terr AB16 164 B3
Arnhall Bsns Pk AB32 161 E1
Arnhall Cres AB32 161 E2
Arnhall Dr AB32 161 F2
Arnot Pl AB12 180 E5
Arn Pl AB43 76 C7
Arran Ave
Aberdeen AB16 163 E2
Peterhead AB42 147 B7
Arran Ct AB43 143 B4
ARTHRATH 51 A3
Artlaw Cres AB42 146 E5
Aryburk Row AB21 158 C6
Aryburn Row AB21 158 C6
Ash Ct AB12 180 A5
Ashdale Cl AB32 161 D3
Ashdale Ct 3 AB32 161 E3
Ashdale Dr AB32 161 E2
Ashfield Rd AB15 168 F3
Ash Gr
Aberdeen AB21 156 B5
Fraserburgh AB43 143 A6
Portlethen AB12 180 B4
Ashgrove AB33 154 D4
Ashgrove Ave AB25 164 F4
Ashgrove Ct AB25 164 E4
Ashgrove Gdns N AB16 164 C3
Ashgrove Gdns S AB16 164 C3
Ashgrove Pl
Aberdeen AB16 164 D3
2 Peterhead AB42 147 B3
Ashgrove Rd AB25 164 F3
Ashgrove Rd W AB16 164 C3
Ash-Hill Dr AB16 164 E3
Ash-Hill Pl AB16 164 E4
Ash-Hill Rd AB16 164 E4
Ash-Hill Way AB16 164 E4
Ashlea Ave AB51 155 C5
Ashley Gdns AB10 169 E7
Ashley Gr AB10 169 F7
Ashley La AB10 169 F7
Ashley Park Dr AB10 169 F7
Ashley Park La AB10 169 F7
Ashley Park N AB10 169 E7
Ashley Park S AB10 169 F7
Ashley Rd AB10 169 F7
Ashley Road Prim Sch AB10 169 F7
Ash Pl AB12 180 B4
Ash Row 8 AB23 91 C8
Ashtown Pl 2 AB21 163 D7
Ashtown Wlk 3 AB21 163 D7
Ash Tree Rd AB31 184 F6
Ashvale Ct 5 AB10 170 A8
Ashvale Pl AB10 170 A8
Ashwood Ave AB22 159 D4
Ashwood Circ AB23 159 D5
Ashwood Cres AB22 159 C4
Ashwood Dr AB22 159 D5
Ashwood Gdns AB22 159 D5
Ashwood Gr AB22 159 D5
Ashwood Grange AB22 159 C4
Ashwood Mews AB22 159 D5
Ashwood Par AB22 159 D5
Ashwood Pk AB22 159 D5
Ashwood Pl AB22 159 D5
Ashwood Rd AB22 159 D5
Asloun Castle (remains of)* AB33 84 C5
Aspen Gr AB32 161 C2
Aspen Way AB12 180 B4
Assynt Pl AB43 143 B4
Atholl Pl AB43 143 B5
Atholl Rise AB41 62 A2
AUCHATTIE 184 B1
AUCHENBLAE 124 B1
Auchenblae Prim Sch AB30 124 B1
AUCHENDRYNE 113 E5
Auchinleck Cres AB24 164 F7
Auchinleck Rd AB24 164 F7
Auchinyell Gdns AB10 169 D4
Auchinyell Rd AB10 169 D4
Auchinyell Terr AB10 169 D4
Auchlea Pl AB16 163 F3
Auchlea Rd AB16 163 F2
Auchlethen Dr 1 AB42 52 C4
AUCHLEVEN 71 E7
Auchlossan Ct 5 AB22 165 B8
Auchmacoy Rd 2 AB31 98 E1
Auchmill Rd AB21 163 F8
Auchmill Terr AB21 164 B7
Auchmore Rd AB41 151 C3
AUCHNAGATT 50 C8
Auchnagatt Prim Sch AB41 50 D8
Auchreddie Road E AB53 36 A5
Auchreddie Road W 1 AB53 36 A5
Auchriny Circ AB21 158 B3
Auchry Rd AB53 22 B1
Auchterellon Prim Sch AB41 151 B6
Auchterless Prim Sch AB53 46 F8
Auldearn Gdns AB12 170 B3
Auldearn Pl AB12 170 B3
Auldearn Rd AB12 170 B3
Auld Kirk Gall The* AB23 91 A6
Auld Post Office Mus* AB53 145 C4
AULDYOCH 46 C8
Aulton Ct AB24 165 D6
Aulton Rd AB42 53 A3
Aulton Way DD10 189 C6
Avenue The
Aberdeen AB13 173 B8
Peterhead AB42 36 E6
Averon Pk AB21 156 A7
Avon Pl AB21 158 B6

B

Back Brae AB44 141 D7
Back Braes DD9 188 C2
Backgate AB42 147 E5
BACKHILL 48 B6
BACKHILL OF FORTRIE 50 F7
Back Hilton Rd AB25 164 F4
Back Path AB45 140 F5
Back Rd DD10 135 C6
Back St
5 Banff AB45 1 F1
Macduff AB44 141 D6
Peterhead AB42 147 E5
Back Wynd
Aberdeen AB25 190 B3
5 Oldmeldrum AB51 150 C3
Baddifurrow 1 AB51 152 C4
Badenoch Dr AB54 148 E4
Baden Powell Rd AB53 145 C5
BADENSCOTH 46 D5
Badentoy Ave AB12 179 F8
Badentoy Cres AB12 179 E8
Badentoy Pk AB12 179 E8
Badentoy Pl AB12 179 F8
Badentoy Rd AB12 180 A7
Badentoy Way AB12 179 E7
Badger Rise AB21 156 B8
Badger View AB21 156 B8
Bailie Norrie Cres 3 DD10 189 C7
Bailie Wilson 1 DD10 189 D7
Baillieswell Dr AB15 168 B2
Baillieswells Cres AB15 168 B2
Baillieswells Dr AB15 168 B2
Baillieswells Gr AB15 168 A2
Baillieswells Pl AB15 168 B2
Baillieswells Rd AB15 168 B2
Baillieswells Terr AB15 168 B2
Bain Cres AB42 146 E4
Bain Dr AB42 146 E4
Bain Gdns 1 AB42 146 E4
Bain Pl 2 AB42 146 E4
Bain Rd AB42 146 E4
Bain Terr AB42 146 E4
Bainzie Rd AB51 152 B8
Baird Rd AB43 24 E6
Bairds Brae AB15 169 A4
Baird St AB39 185 E5
Baird Terr AB39 185 E5
Baird Way 6 DD10 189 D7
Baker Pl 5 AB25 165 A2
Baker Rd AB24 164 F5
Bakersfield Cl 2 AB21 153 D5
Baker St
Aberdeen AB25 190 A4
2 Oldmeldrum AB51 150 C3
Balaclava Quay AB43 143 D7
Balandro Loan DD10 135 C5
Balbegno Castle* AB30 127 F3
Balbithan View 2 AB51 74 F2
Balbrogie Woods 1 AB21 156 A6
Balcairn Ave AB51 150 B3
Balfluig Castle (restored)* AB33 154 F2
Balfour Rd AB33 154 C4
Balfron Pl AB15 164 B1
BALGAVENY 45 F7
Balgownie Brae AB22 165 A8
Balgownie Cres AB23 165 C8
Balgownie Ct AB24 165 C6
Balgownie Dr AB22 164 F8
Balgownie Gdns AB22 165 A8
Balgownie Pl AB22 164 F8
Balgownie Rd AB22 159 D1
Balgownie Way AB22 165 A8
BALLATER 182 C4
Ballater Bsns Pk AB35 182 F4
Ballater Prim Sch AB35 182 E5
Ballater Rd AB34 183 C5
Balloch Way AB21 158 C7
Balmain St 4 DD10 189 C3
BALMEDIE 91 D8
Balmedie Ctry Pk* AB23 91 D8
Balmedie Ctry Pk Visitor Ctr* AB23 77 D1
Balmedie Leisure Ctr AB23 91 C8
Balmedie Prim Sch AB23 91 D8
Balmellie Pl AB53 145 E4
Balmellie Rd AB53 145 E4
Balmellie St AB53 145 D4
Balmoor Ind Est AB42 147 B6
Balmoor Ret Pk AB42 147 B6
Balmoor Stadium (Peterhead FC) AB42 147 C6
Balmoor Terr AB42 147 C6
Balmoral Ave AB41 151 E5
Balmoral Castle* AB35 102 D2
Balmoral Ct AB10 170 A6
Balmoral Gdns 1 AB10 170 A6
Balmoral Pl AB10 169 F6
Balmoral Rd AB10 170 A6
Balmoral Terr AB34 183 C4
Balmoral Wynd 1 AB41 151 F5
Balmuir Wood 4 AB34 96 C3
BALNAGASK 170 F6
Balnagask Ave AB11 170 F6
Balnagask Circ AB11 170 F6
Balnagask Cres
Aberdeen AB11 170 F6
Grange Gardens AB42 147 C5
Balnagask Pl AB11 170 F7
Balnagask Rd AB11 170 D5
Balnagask Wlk 1 AB11 170 E6
Balnagask Wynd AB11 170 F6
Balnellan Pl 5 AB35 113 F6
Balnellan Rd 5 AB35 113 F6
Balquhain Castle (remains of)* AB51 73 D6
BALTHANGIE 22 F2
Baltic Pl
Aberdeen AB11 165 E1
Peterhead AB42 147 F5
Baltic St DD10 189 D3
Baluss Pl AB42 146 E5
Baluss View 1 AB42 146 E5
Balvenie Wynd 4 AB41 151 E5
Banavie Ct AB41 151 D5
BANCHORY 184 B5
Banchory Acad AB31 184 D4
BANCHORY-DEVENICK 169 B1
Banchory Devenick Prim Sch AB12 175 B7
Banchory Mus* AB31 184 C4
Banchory Prim Sch AB31 184 D4
Banchory Sports Ctr & Swimming Pool AB31 184 D5
BANFF 140 D5
Banff Acad AB45 140 E5
Banff & Buchan Coll AB41 151 F5
Banff Prim Sch AB45 140 F5
Banff Rd
New Blyth AB53 22 D5
Turriff AB53 145 D5
Banff Swimming Pool AB45 140 E5
Bank Brae AB33 154 D3
BANKHEAD 163 C8
Bankhead Acad AB21 158 C1
Bankhead Ave AB21 158 C1
Bankhead Rd AB21 158 C1
Bank La
Peterhead AB42 38 D6
Rosehearty AB43 142 C7
Bank Rd AB42 36 E6
Banks of Brechin DD9 188 A4
Bank St
Aberdeen AB11 190 B1
Aberdeen AB24 164 E6
Brechin DD9 188 C3
Montrose DD10 187 D3
Banks The DD9 188 A4
Bank Terr AB33 154 D3
Bannerman Pl AB16 164 A6
Bannermill Pl AB24 190 C4
Bannoch Rd 1 AB41 151 B6
Barbank St AB45 139 D7
Barbour Brae AB22 159 D1
Barclayhill Pl AB12 180 C7
Barclay Pk AB34 183 A5
Barclay Rd AB51 152 D4
Barclay St 4 AB39 185 E4
Barkmill Rd AB25 164 F3
Barleyhill Cl AB51 88 B6
Barmekin Pk AB32 100 D4
Barnhill Rd AB44 141 C5
Barns Brae DD10 138 D2
Barra Castle* AB51 74 D8
Barrack La 5 AB43 143 D6
Barrack Rd DD10 189 D2
Barra Cres AB43 143 A4
Barrasgate Rd AB43 143 D7
Barratt Dr AB41 151 B3
Barraview AB51 150 C3
Barra Wlk AB16 163 E2
Barringer La AB32 161 F3
Barrldykes Way 1 AB52 58 D3
Barron Ct AB54 148 D4
Barron St AB24 164 F6
BARTHOL CHAPEL 48 D1
Barthol Chapel Prim Sch AB51 48 D1
Bartlet Pl AB45 140 F6
Barvas Wlk AB16 163 D3
Basin View DD10 189 C4
Bath St
Aberdeen AB11 190 A3
Fraserburgh AB43 143 D7
Macduff AB44 141 E7
Peterhead AB42 147 E4
Stonehaven AB39 185 E5
Battery Pk 1 AB42 147 F6
Battock Pl AB11 170 D6
Battock Terr 1 AB31 98 E1
Bawdley Head AB43 143 B7
Baxter Ct AB11 170 F7
Baxter Pl AB11 170 F7
Baxter St AB11 170 F7
Baylands Cres AB42 147 C4
Bayview Cres
Banff AB45 140 F6
Peterhead AB42 147 C4
Bayview Ct AB24 165 D5
Bayview Rd
Aberdeen AB15 169 D8
Banff AB45 3 C2
12 Cullen AB56 1 B5
Inverbervie DD10 187 E6
Bayview Rd S AB15 169 D7
Beach Bvd AB11 190 C4
Beach Bvd Ret Pk AB11 165 E2
Beachfield Way 3 AB23 91 C8
Beachgate DD10 187 E6
Beachgate La 3 AB39 185 E4
Beach Leisure Ctr AB24 165 E3
Beach Rd
Johnshaven DD10 135 C6
St Cyrus DD10 134 D3
Stonehaven AB39 185 F5
Beachview Ct AB24 165 D6
Beacon Dr AB43 143 C4
Beaconhill Rd AB13 173 D8
Beacon Rd DD10 189 D2
Beaconsfield La 5 AB53 145 C5
Beaconsfield Pl AB15 169 E8
Beaconsfield Terr AB53 145 C5
Beacon Terr 6 DD10 189 D1
Bearehill Gdns DD9 188 B3
Beattie Ave AB25 164 F4
Beattie Pl 2 AB25 164 F4
Beattie Terr 1 DD10 187 D6
Beauly Pl AB43 143 A4
Bede Way AB41 61 E5
Bedford Ave AB24 165 A5
Bedford Pl AB24 165 B4
Bedford Rd AB24 165 A4
Beech Ave AB43 143 A6
Beech Cl 2 AB41 62 A2
Beechcroft Ave AB52 149 D4
Beechcroft Terr AB52 149 D4
Beech Ct 19 AB51 87 D7
Beeches The
3 Banchory AB31 184 D4
Mintlaw AB42 146 E4
Beechfield AB51 74 E4
Beechgrove Ave AB15 164 E2
Beechgrove Ct AB15 164 E1
Beechgrove Gdn* AB32 166 E6
Beechgrove Gdns AB15 164 E2
Beechgrove Pl AB15 164 E1
Beechgrove Terr AB15 164 E1
Beechhill Gdns AB15 169 B5
Beech Rd
Aberdeen AB16 164 C4
Westhill AB32 161 D2
Beech Tree Rd AB31 184 F5
Beechwood Ave
Aberdeen AB16 164 D3
Ellon AB41 151 B5
Beechwood Cl AB32 161 C3
Beechwood Ct 4 AB16 164 C3
Beechwood Gdns AB32 161 D2
Beechwood Pl
4 Aberdeen AB16 164 D4
2 Ellon AB41 151 B6
Westhill AB32 161 C3
Beechwood Rd
Aberdeen AB16 164 D4
Laurencekirk AB30 186 C6
Beechwood Sch AB12 170 A2
Beechwood Wlk 6 AB16 164 D4
Beldorney Castle* AB54 42 A3
BELFATTON 25 F6
Belgrave Terr AB25 164 F1
Belhaven Rd AB41 62 A2
BELHELVIE 91 B8
BELLABEG 81 B4
Bell Ave AB42 147 C2
Bellenden Wlk AB13 173 A7
Bellevue Rd AB45 140 E5
Bellevue Terr AB45 140 F4
Bellfield Rd
Aberdeen AB16 163 F3
Bridge of Don AB23 160 A1
Bellsea Pk (Fraserburgh FC) AB43 143 D6
Bell's La AB43 5 A4
Bellswood Cres AB31 184 C5
Bell Terr AB42 147 C2
Bellwood Den AB34 183 F5
Bellwood Dr AB34 183 F5
Bellwood Rd AB34 183 F5
Belmont Brae AB39 185 E5
Belmont Gdns 3 AB25 164 F4
Belmont Rd AB25 165 A4
Belmont St AB10 190 A3
Belmuir Gdns AB21 158 B7
BELNACRAIG 81 D7
Belrorie Circ AB21 158 C7
Beltie Rd AB31 98 D1
BELTS OF COLLONACH 117 E8
Belvidere Cres AB15 164 F1
Belvidere La AB15 168 E2
Belvidere Rd AB15 168 D2
Belvidere St AB25 164 F2
Benbecula Rd 6 AB16 163 E2
BENHOLM 135 D8
Ben More Ave DD10 189 C8
Bennachie Ave 2 AB51 152 C6
Bennachie Leisure Ctr AB52 149 C6
Bennachie View 11 AB51 87 D7
BENTHOUL 101 E2
Bents Rd DD10 189 E3
Bents The AB45 1 F3
Benview Gdns AB51 150 D4
Benview Terr AB21 156 B6
BEREFOLD 51 B2
Berefold Cl AB41 51 B2
Berneray Pl 2 AB16 163 E2
Bernham Ave AB39 185 B5
Bernham Cres AB39 185 B5
Bernham Ct 1 AB39 185 B5
Bernham Pk AB39 185 B5
Bernham Pl 2 AB39 185 B5
Bernham Terr AB39 185 B5
Berryden Rd
Aberdeen AB25 165 A3
Peterhead AB42 147 B4
Rosemount AB25 165 A3
BERRYHILLOCK 6 C3
Berryhill Pk AB52 72 D8
Berryhill Pl AB39 181 H4
Berryhill View AB52 72 C8
Berrymoss Ct 6 AB21 158 C7
Berrymuir Pl AB12 180 A4
Berrymuir Rd
Macduff AB44 141 E6
Portlethen AB12 180 B5
Berrymuir Wynd AB12 180 A4
Berry St AB25 190 B4
Berrywell Gdns AB21 158 B7
Berrywell Pl AB21 158 B7
Berrywell Rd AB21 158 B7
Berrywell Wlk AB21 158 B7
Bervie Brow AB12 176 C8
Bervie Prim Sch DD10 187 D7
Bervie Rd AB43 143 A5
Bethany Gdns AB11 170 A7
Bethlin Mews AB15 162 F4
Bettridge Leisure Ctr AB39 181 I4
Bettridge Rd AB39 181 I4
Beverley Rd AB51 152 E4
BIELDSIDE 168 C2
Bieldside Station Rd AB15 168 C1
Biggar Ct AB43 143 A4
Bilbo Gdns AB42 26 E6
Bin Ave AB54 29 C3
Binghill Cres AB13 173 B8
Binghill Dr AB13 167 D1
Binghill Hedges AB13 167 E1
Binghill Pk AB13 173 C8
Binghill Rd AB13 167 E1
Binghill Road N AB13 167 D1
Binghill Road W AB13 167 E1
Binview Rd 6 AB56 1 B4
Binview Terr 7 AB56 1 B4
Birch Ave AB32 161 D2
Birchfield Pl AB12 176 C6
Birch Gr
Banchory AB31 184 B4

Birch Gr *continued*
Ellon AB41 151 E6
Mintlaw AB42 146 D5
Birch Rd AB16 164 D4
Birchwood Pl AB34 183 B4
Birkenhills Croft AB53 33 E4
Birkhall Par AB16 164 A4
Birkhall Pl AB16 164 A4
Birnie Pl
21 Boddam AB42 40 D1
Fraserburgh AB43 143 A4
BIRSE 107 D4
BIRSEMORE 183 D3
Birsemore Cres AB34 183 E2
Bishop Forbes Cres AB21 156 B6
Bishop's Cl 8 DD9 188 C3
Bishopsloch Row AB21 158 C6
Bishop's Manor (remains of)* AB21 90 D5
Bisset La AB30 186 D5
Blackbraes Rd AB21 153 E5
Blackbraes Way 3 AB21 153 E5
BLACKBURN 156 A6
Blackburn Bsns Pk AB21 156 B5
Blackburn Ind Est AB21 156 A6
Blackcraig Rd 3 AB42 53 B3
Blackdog Ind Ctr AB23 91 B5
Blackford Ave AB51 46 F2
Blackfriars Ct 10 DD10 189 C4
Blackfriars St 9 DD10 189 C4
Blackfriar's St AB11 190 A3
Blackhall Cres 6 AB34 96 C3
Blackhall Ct 8 AB51 152 D6
Blackhall Ind Est AB51 152 B6
Blackhall Rd 3 AB51 152 C6
Blackhall Wynd AB51 152 D5
BLACKHILL 26 F7
Blackhills Cres AB42 147 B3
Blackhills Ct AB32 161 C2
Blackhills Pl AB32 161 C3
Blackhill Sta AB51 73 D2
Blackhills Way AB32 161 C2
BLACKHOUSE 147 B7
Blackhouse Circ AB42 147 B7
Blackhouse Ind Est AB42 147 A7
Blackhouse Terr AB42 147 C7
Blackiemuir Ave AB30 186 B5
Blacklaws Brae AB32 161 D5
Blackness Ave AB12 170 E1
Blackness Rd AB12 170 F1
Black's La AB11 190 C2
Blacksmiths Croft AB21 163 F7
Blackthorn Cres 1 AB16 164 D4
BLACKTOP 167 E5
Blaikes Quay AB11 190 C2
BLAIRDAFF 86 F8
Blairs Mus The* AB12 174 A6
Blantyre Cres AB43 143 B4
Blantyre St 8 AB56 1 B5
Bleachfield Rd 2 AB22 159 E1
Bleachfield St AB54 148 D4
Blenheim Pl AB25 164 E1
Bloomfield Ct AB10 170 A6
Bloomfield Pl AB10 170 A7
Bloomfield Rd AB10 170 A6
Blythewood Pl AB51 152 E3
Boat Croft 4 AB51 87 C7
Boatie Row AB39 185 F6
Bob Cooney Ct AB25 165 A3
Bodachra Pl AB22 159 E1
Bodachra Rd AB22 159 E1
BODDAM 40 D1
Boddam Castle (remains of)* AB42 53 F8
Boddam Prim Sch AB42 40 D1
Boddie Pl AB24 165 C3
Bogbeth Rd AB51 87 D6
BOGENTORY 100 F8
Boggie Shalloch Pl AB53 145 B6
Bogie Rd 4 AB54 55 E2
Bogie St AB54 148 E4
BOGNIEBRAE 31 C4
Bog Rd DD9 188 D3
Bogroy Cres AB45 7 D2
BOGTON 20 B2
Bon Accord Baths AB11 170 A8
Bon-Accord Cres AB11 190 A2
Bon-Accord Cres La AB11 190 A2
Bon Accord Gdns* AB11 190 A2
Bon-Accord La AB11 190 A2
Bon-Accord Sq AB11 190 A2
Bon-Accord St AB11 190 A2
Bon Accord-St Nicholas Ctr AB25 190 B3
Bon-Accord Terr AB11 190 A2
Bona Pl AB43 143 A5
BONA VISTA 145 B5
Bond Mews 3 AB39 185 E5
BONNYKELLY 23 B4
Bonnymuir Pl AB15 164 E2
BONNYTON 58 D5
Bonnyton Rd AB41 62 B2
Bonnyview Dr AB16 163 F6
Bonnyview Pl AB21 163 F6
Bonnyview Rd AB21 163 F6
Bonty Ct AB34 183 E5
Bonty Pl AB34 183 E5
Boothby Rd AB43 143 A3
Booth Pl AB21 163 E7
BORROWFIELD 189 B6
Borrowfield Cres DD10 189 C6
Borrowfield Prim Sch DD10 189 C7
Borrowfield Rd DD10 189 C6
Borrowmuirhill Rd AB30 186 D6
Borrowstone Pl 3 AB16 163 F2
Bosies Bank Way 2 AB42 147 A4
Boswell Ave AB12 180 A6
Boswell Rd AB12 180 A6
Boswell Wlk AB12 180 A6
Boswell Wynd AB12 180 A6
Bothwell Rd AB24 190 C4
Bothwell Terr 1 AB41 62 B2
Boultenstone Outdoor Ctr* AB36 82 B2
Bourtree Ave AB12 180 A4
Bow Butts 6 DD10 189 D3
Bowling Gn Rd AB53 145 E4
Bowness Rd 6 AB42 53 A3
Boyd Orr Ave AB12 170 A1
Boyd-Orr Ave DD9 188 C4
Boyd Orr Cl AB12 170 A1
Boyd Orr Pl AB12 170 A1
Boyd Orr Way AB30 186 C5
Boyd Orr Wlk AB12 170 A1
Boyes La AB54 144 C4
BOYNDIE 8 D6
Boyndie Rd AB45 140 D6
Boyndie St AB45 140 F6
Boyndie Street W AB45 140 E6
Boyne Castle (remains of)* AB45 2 F3
Boyne Pl 4 AB45 8 F8
Boyne St AB45 8 F8
Bracken Rd AB12 180 B6
Brackens Pl AB53 145 B6
Bracoden Prim Sch AB45 3 D2
Bracoden Rd AB45 3 C2
Bracoden Terr AB45 3 C2
Braco Pl 2 AB45 140 E5
Bradley Terr AB24 165 A6
Brae Cres AB42 146 D4
Braecroft Ave AB32 161 E3
Braecroft Cres AB32 161 E4
Braecroft Dr AB32 161 E3
Braefoot Rd AB16 164 E4
Braegowan Rd AB45 3 C2
Braehead AB22 159 F1
Braehead Cres
Peterhead AB42 147 B6
Stonehaven AB39 185 D3
Braehead Dr AB42 53 A3
Braehead Pl 13 AB42 38 D6
Braehead Prim Sch AB22 165 B8
Braehead Rd AB42 27 B3
Braeheads
Banff AB45 140 F6
Fraserburgh AB43 15 D6
Macduff AB44 141 D7
Braehead Terr AB13 173 B8
Braehead Way AB22 159 E2
Braeloine Visitor Ctr* AB34 106 C3
BRAEMAR 113 E6
Braemar Castle* AB35 113 F7
Braemar Ct AB43 143 C4
Braemar Pl
Aberdeen AB10 169 F6
Ballater AB35 182 C4
Braemar Prim Sch AB35 113 F6
Braemar Rd AB35 182 C4
Brae Rd DD10 187 D4
BRAESIDE
Aberdeen 169 B5
Ellon 50 A6
Braeside Ave AB15 169 C4
Braeside Cres AB39 185 F6
Braeside Pl AB15 169 C5
Braeside Terr AB15 169 C4
Brae St 16 AB42 40 D1
Braes The AB43 143 D8
Brae The 3 AB53 36 A5
Braichlie Rd AB35 182 D4
Braiklay Ave AB41 61 E5
Bramble Brae AB16 164 B5
Bramble Brae Prim Sch AB16 164 C5
Bramble Ct AB12 180 B4
Bramble Pl AB12 180 A4
Bramble Rd AB12 180 A4
Bramble Way AB12 180 A4
Brander Mus* AB54 148 D5
Brander Pl AB22 164 E8
Brandsbutt AB51 152 B8
Brankie Pl AB51 152 A7
Brankie Rd AB51 152 A8
Braoch Pk DD10 189 B1
Braoch Rd DD10 189 B1
Brebner Cres AB16 163 F5
Brebner Pl 7 AB31 108 E8
Brebner Terr AB16 163 F5
BRECHIN 188 B3
Brechin Bsns Pk DD9 136 B7
Brechin Castle* DD9 188 C2
Brechin Castle Ctr* DD9 136 B6
Brechin Cath DD9 188 C3
Brechin High Sch DD9 188 B4
Brechin Ind Est DD9 188 F2
Brechin Leisure Ctr DD9 188 C2
Brechin Rd DD10 189 B6
Brechin Round Twr* DD9 188 C2
Brechin Sta DD9 188 D3
Breckview 5 AB41 62 B2
Bredero Dr
2 Banchory AB31 184 E5
Ellon AB41 151 C3
Bremner Way 9 AB51 87 D7
Brent Ave DD10 189 D8
Brent Field Circ AB41 151 A6
Brent Rd AB21 157 F5
Bressay Brae AB15 163 E2
Bressay Dr AB41 151 B3
Bressay Way AB42 147 A5
Brewery Rd AB43 24 E5
Briar Bank AB21 153 D6
Briar Gdns AB42 146 D4
Brickfield Ct 3 AB39 185 C5
Brickfield Rd AB39 185 C4
Brickfield Terr 2 AB39 185 C5
BRIDESWELL 44 E6
Bridge Cres 10 AB31 108 E8
Bridgefield 9 AB39 185 E4
Bridgefield Terr 8 AB39 185 E4
Bridge Gdns AB41 77 F7
BRIDGEND 43 D2
Bridgend Cres AB42 52 E4
Bridgend Terr AB53 145 C3
BRIDGE OF ALFORD 154 A6
BRIDGE OF CANNY 109 B4
Bridge of Cowie 1 AB39 185 E5
BRIDGE OF DON 160 B1
Bridge of Don Acad AB22 159 F1
Bridge of Don Swimming Pool AB22 159 E2
BRIDGE OF DUN 138 E5
Bridge of Dun Sta DD10 137 E5
BRIDGE OF MUCHALLS 121 B6
Bridge Pl AB11 190 A2
Bridge Rd
Banff AB45 141 A5
Inverurie AB51 87 C7
Bridge Sq AB35 182 E4
Bridge St
Aberdeen AB11 190 A3
Aboyne AB34 96 C2
Ballater AB35 182 D4
Banchory AB31 184 B4
Banff AB45 141 A5
20 Boddam AB42 40 D1
Brechin DD9 188 C2
Cruden Bay AB42 53 B3
Ellon AB41 151 D5
2 Fordyce AB45 1 F1
Fraserburgh AB43 15 D6
Gourdon DD10 187 D3
Montrose DD10 189 C2
Peterhead AB42 147 F5
Portsoy AB45 139 D7
3 Stonehaven AB39 185 D4
Strichen AB43 24 E5
Turriff AB53 22 E4
Woodside AB24 164 D7
Bridge Terr
14 Newburgh AB41 77 F8
Turriff AB53 22 E4
Bridgeview Pl AB34 183 B4
Bridge View Rd AB34 183 C3
Brierfield Rd 3 AB16 164 D4
Brierfield Terr AB16 164 D4
Briggies Wynd AB51 155 B6
Brighton Ct AB14 172 D6
Brighton Grange AB14 172 D6
Brighton Pl
Aberdeen AB10 169 E7
Peterculter AB14 172 D6
Bright St AB11 170 B6
Brimmond Cres AB32 161 D2
Brimmond Ct
3 Balnagask AB11 170 F6
4 Westhill AB32 161 D2
Brimmond Ctry Pk* AB15 162 D6
Brimmond Dr AB32 161 D2
Brimmond La AB32 161 D2
Brimmond Pl
Aberdeen AB11 170 D6
1 Westhill AB32 161 D2
Brimmondside AB21 163 C7
Brimmond View AB21 158 B2
Brimmond Way AB32 161 D2
Brimmond Wlk AB32 161 D2
Broaddykes Ave AB15 162 F3
Broaddykes Cl 4 AB15 162 F3
Broaddykes Cres 1 AB15 162 F2
Broaddykes Dr AB15 162 F2
Broaddykes Pl AB15 162 E3
Broaddykes View 2 AB15 162 F2
Broadfold Dr AB23 160 A1
Broadfold Rd AB23 160 A1
Broadfold Terr AB23 160 A1
Broadford 1 AB51 152 D4
Broadford Gdns AB21 156 B7
Broadlands Gdns AB32 161 B3
Broad Pl AB42 147 E5
BROADSEA 143 B7
Broadsea Rd AB43 143 C7
Broadshaven Rd AB12 180 E5
Broad St
Aberdeen AB10 190 B3
Fraserburgh AB43 143 D6
4 Peterhead AB42 147 F5
Broadstraik Ave AB32 161 B2
Broadstraik Brae 1 AB32 161 B2
Broadstraik Cl AB32 161 A3
Broadstraik Cres AB32 161 A3
Broadstraik Dr AB32 161 B2
Broadstraik Gdns AB32 161 A2
Broadstraik Gr AB32 161 A2
Broadstraik Pl 2 AB32 161 B2
Broadstraik Rd AB32 161 A2
Brockwood Cres AB21 156 B7
Brockwood Pk AB21 156 B7
Brockwood Pl AB21 156 B7
Brodiach Ct AB32 161 F3
Brodick Rd AB43 143 B4
BRODIESORD 7 D3
Brodinch Pl AB16 163 F3
Brodinch Rd AB16 163 F3
Bronie Cres 7 AB41 62 B2
Bronieside 2 AB41 62 B2
Brooke Cres AB23 160 A3
Brook La AB42 147 F5
Brooklands Ave AB42 40 A6
Brookside 1 AB42 147 A8
Brookwood Cres AB21 156 B7
Broombank Terr AB35 113 E6
Broomfield Cres DD10 189 D6
Broomfield Gdns DD10 189 D6
Broomfield Ind Est DD10 189 D6
Broomfield Pk AB12 180 A5
Broomfield Rd
Montrose DD10 189 D5
Portlethen AB12 180 A5
Broomhill AB43 143 B4
Broomhill Activity Ctr AB10 169 E5
Broomhill Ave AB10 169 F5
Broomhill Cl AB21 76 C1
Broomhill Ct AB21 76 C1
Broomhill Mews 3 AB10 170 A7
Broomhill Pl AB10 169 F5
Broomhill Prim Sch AB10 169 F6
Broomhill Rd
Aberdeen AB10 169 E4
Stonehaven AB39 185 B4
Turriff AB53 145 D5
Broomhill Terr AB10 169 F5
Broomhill Way AB21 76 C1
Broomiesburn Dr AB41 63 D5
Broomiesburn Rd AB41 151 F5
Broom Pk AB15 168 D3
Brora Pl AB43 143 B4
Brough Pl 1 AB25 164 F4
BROWNHILL 36 F1
Brownhill Dr 5 AB21 153 D5
Brownhill Pl 1 AB21 153 D4
Brownhill Rd 2 AB21 153 D4
Brownlow Pl 1 DD10 189 D1
Brown St AB24 164 F6
Bruan Ct AB43 143 A4
Bruce Brae 1 AB42 38 D6
Bruce Cres
Ellon AB41 151 C4
Peterhead AB42 147 A4
Bruce Pl AB51 150 C2
Bruce St AB44 141 C6
Bruce Wlk
Aberdeen AB12 170 C2
Kintore AB51 155 C4
Brucklay Ct
Aberdeen AB21 158 C6
Peterhead AB42 147 B3
Brucklay St AB43 142 C7
Bruinswick Pl AB11 170 B6
Bruntland Ct AB12 180 C5
Bruntland Pl AB12 180 C6
Bruntland Rd
Portlethen AB12 180 B5
Stonehaven AB39 179 F4
Bruntwood Tap AB51 152 A8
Buchanan Gdns AB12 170 B2
Buchanan Pl AB12 170 B3
Buchanan Rd AB12 170 B2
Buchan Dr AB21 153 C6
BUCHANHAVEN 147 C7
Buchanhaven Prim Sch AB42 147 C6
Buchanness Dr 4 AB42 40 D1
Buchanness Pl 15 AB42 40 D1
Buchan Pl
Fraserburgh AB43 143 B4
Peterhead AB42 36 E6
Buchan Rd
Aberdeen AB11 170 F6
Dyce AB21 157 E6
Fraserburgh AB43 143 B4
Buchan St AB44 141 E7
Buchan Terr AB42 147 C5
Buckie Ave AB22 159 C2
Buckie Cl AB22 159 C2
Buckie Cres AB22 159 C2
Buckie Gr AB22 159 D2
Buckie Rd AB22 159 C2
Buckie Wlk AB22 159 C2
Buckie Wynd AB22 159 C2
Bucklerburn Cl AB14 172 C8
Bucklerburn Dr AB14 172 C7
Bucklerburn Pk 1 AB14 172 D7
Bucklerburn Pl 3 AB14 172 D7
Bucklerburn Rd AB14 172 C7
Bucklerburn View 2 AB14 172 D7
Bucklerburn Wynd AB14 172 C7
BUCKSBURN 163 E7
Bucksburn Prim Sch AB21 163 F7
Bucksburn Swimming Pool AB21 163 D8
Builg Rd AB31 117 C5
Bunstane Terr AB12 176 C6
Bunzeach Pl 3 AB21 158 C7
Burgess Dr AB42 38 D5
Burgh La AB51 150 C4
Burghmuir Circ AB51 152 B6
Burghmuir Dr AB51 152 B7
Burghmuir Pl AB51 152 B6
Burghmuir Way AB51 152 B6
Burgh of Rattray (site of)* AB42 16 B4
Burnbank AB52 149 D5
Burnbank Pl AB11 170 F6
Burnbank Rd 2 AB33 154 C3
Burnbanks Village AB12 170 F1
Burnbank Terr AB11 170 F6
Burnbank View AB33 154 C3
Burnbrae Ave AB16 164 A2
Burnbrae Cres AB16 164 A2
Burnbrae Pl AB16 164 A2
Burnbutts Cres AB12 176 C7
Burndale Rd AB21 158 C1
Burnett Hill AB31 184 B5
Burnett Park E AB31 184 A5
Burnett Pl
Aberdeen AB24 164 F5
Inverurie AB51 152 E3
Burnett Rd
Banchory AB31 184 B5
16 Kemnay AB51 87 D7
Stonehaven AB39 185 C6
Burnett St
Laurencekirk AB30 124 B1
Peterhead AB42 37 D5
Burnett Terr AB31 184 B5
Burnhaven Prim Sch AB42 147 D1
BURNHERVIE 73 D2
Burnieboozle Cres AB15 169 A6
Burnieboozle Pl AB15 169 A6
Burn La AB51 152 D6
Burn O'Bennie Rd AB31 184 F6
Burn O'Vat Visitor Ctr* AB34 105 C6
Burns Cres
Fraserburgh AB43 143 B3
St Combs AB43 15 D6
Burns Gdns AB15 169 D7
Burnshangie Rd 7 AB43 24 E6
Burnside AB56 1 B3
BURNSIDE 26 E2
Burnside AB45 139 D7
Burnside Ave AB51 150 C2
Burnside Bsns Pk AB42 147 C1
Burnside Cres AB42 37 D5
Burnside Ct
9 Inverurie AB51 152 D6
3 Mintlaw AB42 146 D5
Portsay AB45 139 D7
Burnside Dr
Bridge of Don AB23 160 A1
Dyce AB21 158 C5
Burnside Gdns
Aberdeen AB25 164 E2
Portlethen AB12 180 C6
Stonehaven AB39 185 C5
Burnside Pl DD10 189 B1
Burnside Rd
Aboyne AB34 96 B3
Dyce AB21 158 C5
Huntly AB54 148 D5
Laurencekirk AB30 128 B4
4 Mintlaw AB42 146 D5
Peterculter AB14 172 C5
Burnside St AB45 139 D7
Burnside Way 2 AB23 91 C8
Burnside Wlk AB34 183 F5
Burns Pl AB43 143 B3
Burns Rd
Aberdeen AB15 169 E7
Peterhead AB42 147 D6
Burns Terr AB39 185 C4
Burnwood Ave AB21 153 C5
Burnwood Dr AB21 153 C5
BUSH 134 F4
Bush The AB14 172 D6
Bute Way AB16 163 E2
Bydand Gdns AB51 152 B8
Bydand Pl
Aberdeen AB23 160 A3
Huntly AB54 148 D5
Byron Ave AB16 164 A5
Byron Cres AB16 163 F6
Byron Ct 2 AB45 140 E6
Byron Park Inf Sch AB16 163 F4
Byron Pk AB16 164 A4
Byron Sq AB16 164 A5
Byron Terr AB16 163 F5

C

Cabel's La AB11 190 C1
Cadenhead Pl AB25 164 F4
Cadenhead Rd AB25 164 F4
Cadgers Rd DD9 136 E2
Cadgers' Rd AB52 58 B8
Caiesdykes Cres
Aberdeen AB12 170 A2
Cove Bay AB12 176 B8
Caiesdykes Dr AB12 170 A2
Caiesdykes Rd AB12 170 A2
Caies La 2 AB53 145 D5
Caird Ave DD10 189 B1
Caird Pl AB43 5 A4
Cairds Cl AB31 184 D6
Cairds Wynd AB31 184 C6
Cairnadrochit 1 AB35 113 F6
Cairnaquheen Gdns AB15 164 D1
Cairnaquheen Pl AB15 164 D1
Cairnbrallan (ruins)* AB54 66 E7

CAIRNBULG 15 B8
Cairnbulg Way 1 AB41 151 E5
Cairncatto Rd AB42 147 D7
Cairn Cres AB15 168 C2
Cairncry Ave AB16 164 D4
Cairncry Cres AB16 164 E4
Cairncry Ct 5 AB16 164 D4
Cairncry Rd AB16 164 D4
Cairncry Terr AB16 164 E4
Cairndenity Pl AB43 15 C7
Cairney Prim Sch AB54 29 C3
Cairnfield Circ AB21 164 A8
Cairnfield Cres AB21 164 A7
Cairnfield Gdns AB21 164 A7
Cairnfield Pl AB21 164 A7
Cairnfold Rd AB22 165 B8
Cairn Gdns
Aberdeen AB15 168 C2
Inverurie AB51 152 A7
Laurencekirk AB30 186 D5
Cairngorm Cres AB12 170 B3
Cairngorm Dr AB12 170 A3
Cairngorm Gdns AB12 170 B3
Cairngorm Pl AB12 170 A3
Cairngorm Rd AB12 170 A3
Cairngrassie Circ AB12 180 A5
Cairngrassie Dr AB12 180 A4
CAIRNHILL 58 C7
Cairnhill Dr
Fraserburgh AB43 143 C3
Rosehearty AB43 142 B6
Stonehaven AB39 181 G4
Cairnhillock Pl AB21 163 D6
Cairnhill Pl AB39 181 G4
Cairnhill Rd
Fraserburgh AB43 143 C3
Newtonhill AB39 181 G4
Rosehearty AB43 142 B6
Cairnhill Way AB39 181 G4
Cairnhill Wlk AB39 181 G4
CAIRNIE 29 D3
Cairnie View AB32 161 C4
Cairnlee Avenue E AB15 168 C2
Cairnlee Crescent N
AB15 168 C2
Cairnlee Crescent S
AB15 168 D2
Cairnlee Pk AB15 168 B2
Cairnlee Rd AB15 168 B2
Cairnlee Road E AB15 168 C3
Cairnlee Terr AB15 168 B2
Cairn O'Mount Rd AB30 128 B4
CAIRNORRIE 49 C8
Cairn Pk AB15 168 C2
Cairn Pl AB51 152 A7
Cairn Rd
Bieldside AB15 168 C2
20 Kemnay AB51 87 D7
Peterculter AB14 172 E6
Cairn Seat AB51 152 A7
Cairnside AB15 168 C2
Cairns Pk AB31 111 C2
Cairntack Rd AB23 91 A8
Cairnton Ct 2 AB32 161 E3
Cairntrodlie AB42 147 C5
Cairnvale Cres AB12 170 A3
Cairnvale Terr AB12 170 A3
Cairn View AB23 91 A8
Cairnview Cres AB16 164 D4
Cairnview Pl AB30 186 C5
Cairnwell Ave AB16 164 A3
Cairnwell Cres DD10 189 C8
Cairnwell Dr
Aberdeen AB16 164 B3
Portlethen AB12 180 B6
Cairnwell Pl AB16 164 A4
Cairn Wlk AB15 168 C2
Cairn Wynd AB51 152 A7
Caldhame Gdns DD9 188 E3
Caldhame Pl DD9 188 E2
Caledonia Ct 4 AB43 143 D7
Caledonian Ct AB11 190 A1
Caledonian La AB11 190 A1
Caledonian Pl
Aberdeen AB11 190 A1
Montrose DD10 189 D2
Caledonian Rd DD9 188 C4
Caledonian Rly* DD9 188 F1
Caledonia St DD10 189 D2
California St 9 DD10 189 C2
Callum Cres AB15 162 E4
Callum Ct AB45 148 E5
Callum Path AB15 162 E4
Callum Pk AB15 162 E4
Callum Wynd AB15 162 E4
Calsayseat Rd AB25 165 A3
Cameron Ave AB23 159 F2
Cameron Ct 4 AB39 185 D4
Cameron Dr 1 AB23 159 F1
Cameron Pk AB51 59 C5
Cameron Pl AB23 160 A1
Cameron Rd 2 AB23 159 F1
Cameron St
Aberdeen AB23 160 A1
Stonehaven AB39 185 E4
Cameron Terr AB23 160 A1
Cameron Way AB23 159 F2
Camiestone Rd AB51 74 B1
Cammach Circ AB12 180 A4
CAMMACHMORE 179 E2
Campbell Dr AB45 139 C6
Campbell Hospl AB45 139 C7
Campbell Pl AB56 1 B5
Campbell St
Banff AB45 140 F6
Campbell St *continued*
1 Cullen AB56 1 B5
Camperdown Rd AB25 164 D2
Camphill Est AB13 173 A6
Camphill Rudolf Steiner
Schools AB15 173 F8
Campsie Pl AB15 164 B1
Campus One AB22 165 A8
Campus Three AB22 165 A8
Campus Two AB22 165 A8
Canal Cres AB51 152 E3
Canal Pl AB24 165 B3
Canal Rd
Aberdeen AB24 165 B3
Inverurie AB51 152 E3
Canal St AB24 164 E7
Canal View AB51 152 E3
Candlemaker's La AB25 190 B4
Canina Gdns AB21 153 D6
Canmore Gdns AB21 76 C1
Canmore Pk AB39 185 B5
Canmore Pl
1 Aboyne AB34 108 B6
Newmachar AB21 76 C1
Cantlay Ct 3 AB42 53 A3
Caperstown Cres AB16 164 B5
Captain Gray Pl 1 AB42 147 A6
Carden Pl AB10 169 E8
Cardens Knowe 3 AB22 159 F1
Carden Terr 1 AB10 169 F8
Carding Hill 2 AB41 151 D6
Carlin Terr AB21 158 C6
Carlton Pl AB15 164 E1
Carmelite La AB11 190 B3
Carmelite St
Aberdeen AB11 190 B3
Banff AB45 141 A5
Carnegie Cres AB15 169 C8
Carnegie Ct 5 AB39 185 E5
Carnegie Gdns AB15 169 C8
Carnegie Inverurie Mus*
AB51 152 E6
Carnegies Brae 9 AB11 190 B3
Carnegie St DD10 189 D4
Carnferg Pl AB34 183 F5
CARNIE 101 E4
Carnie Ave AB32 161 B2
Carnie Cl 2 AB32 161 B2
Carnie Cres AB32 161 B1
Carnie Dr
Aberdeen AB25 164 F4
Elrick AB32 161 B1
Carnie Gdns
Elrick AB32 161 B1
4 Kittybrewster AB25 164 F4
Carnie Pk AB32 161 B2
Carnie Pl AB32 161 B2
Carnie Way AB32 161 B1
Carnoustie Cres AB22 159 E2
Carnoustie Gdns 3
AB22 159 E2
Carny St AB44 141 D7
Caroline Pl
Aberdeen AB25 165 A2
1 Fraserburgh AB43 143 D7
Carolines Cres AB41 151 D6
Carpenters Croft AB32 101 E7
Carriages The AB51 155 C6
Carron Gdns AB39 185 D3
Carronhall AB39 185 D4
Carronhill Specl Sch
AB39 185 C4
Carron Pl AB16 164 A4
Carron Springs AB39 185 E4
Carron Terr AB39 185 E4
Carters Cl
Mintlaw AB42 146 D5
1 Peterhead AB42 147 E5
Cassie Cl AB12 176 B7
Castle Cres DD10 187 D6
Castle Dr
10 Boddam AB42 40 D1
Inverallochy AB43 15 C7
Castlefield Cres AB51 155 B4
Castlefield Gdns AB51 155 A4
Castle Fraser, Gdn & Est*
AB51 87 C3
Castle Gdns DD9 132 A7
Castlehill AB11 190 C3
Castle Hill
1 Kintore AB51 155 C5
Turriff AB53 145 C4
Castlehill Dr AB45 3 C2
Castle Hillock* AB52 71 E7
Castle La
10 Banff AB45 140 F6
4 Fordyce AB45 1 F1
Rosehearty AB43 142 C7
Castle Newe (remains of)*
AB36 81 D3
Castle of Allardice*
DD10 130 F4
Castle of Esslemont (remains
of)* AB41 62 F4
Castle of Fiddes* AB39 125 F4
Castle of Findon (remains
of)* AB45 3 B2
Castle of Hall Forest
(remains)* AB51 88 B6
Castle of King Edward
(remains of)* AB45 21 A7
Castle of Wardhouse*
AB52 57 B3
Castle of Waterton (remains
of)* AB41 63 D5
Castlepark Dr AB51 155 B4
Castle Park Rd 3 AB54 148 E5
Castle Pl
Inverbervie DD10 187 D6
3 Montrose DD10 189 C3
Castle Rd
Alford AB33 154 E3
Cruden Bay AB42 53 B3
Ellon AB41 151 E5
Inverurie AB51 155 B4
Peterhead AB42 36 E7
Castle (remains of) Peel
Ring of Lumphanan*
AB31 97 F2
Castle Road Ind Est
AB41 151 F5
Castle Sq 7 AB39 185 F3
Castle St
Aberdeen AB10 190 B3
Banff AB45 140 F6
Brechin DD9 188 B3
Bridge of Don DD10 135 C6
Ellon AB41 151 F5
Fraserburgh AB43 143 D7
Huntly AB54 148 D5
Montrose DD10 189 C3
Peterhead AB42 147 F4
Stonehaven AB39 185 F3
Woodside AB43 142 D7
Castle Terr
Aberdeen AB11 190 C3
Buckie AB56 1 A5
Fraserburgh AB43 143 D7
Inverbervie DD10 187 E6
Peterhead AB42 36 E6
CASTLETON 113 F6
Castleton Cres AB16 164 C3
Castleton Ct 8 AB16 164 C3
Castleton Dr 3 AB16 164 C3
Castleton La 2 AB16 164 C3
Castleton Pk 7 AB16 164 C3
Castleton Pl 7 AB35 113 F6
Castleton Terr 6 AB35 113 F6
Castleton Way 6 AB16 164 C3
Castleview Ave AB51 155 B5
Castleview Cl 2 AB51 155 B5
Castleview Ct AB51 155 B4
Castleview Pl AB51 155 B5
Castleview Way 1 AB51 155 B5
Castle Way AB41 151 F5
Castle Wlk AB51 155 C4
Castle Wynd AB51 155 B4
Cathay Terr AB56 1 B4
Catherine St AB25 190 A4
CATTERLINE 126 E1
Catterline Prim Sch
AB39 126 E1
Catto Cres
Aberdeen AB12 176 C7
Peterhead AB42 147 C6
Catto Dr AB42 147 C6
Cattofield Gdns AB25 164 F4
Cattofield Pl AB25 164 F4
Cattofield Terr AB25 164 F4
Catto Way AB42 147 B6
CAULDWELLS 22 B7
CAUSEWAYEND 159 C5
Causewayend AB25 165 B3
Causewayend Cres AB54 144 E5
Causewayend Pl AB54 144 E6
Causewayend Prim Sch
AB25 165 B3
Cava Cl AB15 163 E2
Cedar Ave AB42 147 B4
Cedar Ct AB25 165 A4
Cedar Pl AB25 164 F3
Cemetery Rd
Fraserburgh AB43 143 D4
Montrose DD10 135 C6
Central Mart Cl 14 AB53 145 D4
Central Prim Sch AB42 147 E5
Central Rd AB11 190 C2
Centre Point AB23 160 A3
Chalmers Hospl AB45 140 F7
Chalmers La AB53 145 D5
Chalmers Pl AB42 25 C1
Channonry Wynd DD9 188 C3
Chanonry The AB24 165 B6
Chapel Brae
Ballater AB35 113 E6
2 Turriff AB53 22 C1
Chapel Cl AB51 73 B6
CHAPEL HILL 52 E2
Chapel Hillock AB44 141 D6
Chapelhill Pl 2 AB41 151 D3
Chapelhill Rd
Ellon AB41 151 C4
Fraserburgh AB43 143 B6
Chapelhill Terr 1 AB41 151 D3
Chapel La
3 Banff AB45 8 F8
Portsoy AB45 139 E6
1 Turriff AB53 145 D4
CHAPEL OF GARIOCH 73 B7
Chapel of Garioch Prim Sch
AB51 73 C7
CHAPEL OF
STONEYWOOD 157 D3
Chapel Pk 1 AB53 22 C1
Chapel Pl 1 DD10 189 D3
Chapel Rd
Cruden Bay AB42 53 A3
Stonehaven AB39 181 I4
Turriff AB53 22 C1
Chapel St
Aberdeen AB10 165 A1
5 Banff AB45 8 F8
Huntly AB54 148 D5
Montrose DD10 189 D3
Peterhead AB42 147 E5
Chapel St *continued*
Portsoy AB45 139 E6
Turriff AB53 145 D4
Chapelwell Dr 3 AB23 91 D8
Chapelwell Pl 1 AB23 91 D8
Chapelwell Wynd 2
AB23 91 D8
Chapel Wlk AB54 68 F4
Chapman Pl 3 AB16 164 A6
Chapman Wlk 2 AB16 164 A6
Charles Gdns AB51 152 C7
Charles Pl AB51 152 C7
Charles St
Aberdeen AB25 165 B3
Fraserburgh AB43 15 D6
Insch AB52 149 C5
Inverallochy AB43 15 C8
Charleston Ave AB12 176 A6
Charleston Circ AB12 176 A5
Charleston Cres AB12 176 A6
Charleston Dr AB12 175 F6
Charleston Gdns AB12 176 A6
Charleston Gr AB12 176 A5
Charleston Pl AB12 176 A6
Charleston Rd AB12 176 A6
Charleston View AB12 176 A6
Charleston Way AB12 176 A6
CHARLESTOWN 175 F6
Charlestown Rd AB34 183 C4
Charlestown Sch AB12 176 A6
Charlestown Wlk AB12 176 A6
Charleton Pk 3 DD10 189 D7
Charleton Pl DD10 189 D7
Charleton Rd DD10 189 D7
Charlotte Gdns 2 AB25 190 A4
Charlotte La AB43 143 C7
Charlotte Pl AB25 190 A4
Charlotte St
Aberdeen AB25 190 A4
Fraserburgh AB43 143 C6
Peterhead AB42 147 E5
Charlton Ave AB34 183 B5
Charlton Cres AB34 183 B5
Charter Ave AB30 186 D6
Chattan Pl AB10 169 F7
Checkbar AB12 175 E3
Chelsea Pl 6 AB51 152 D6
Chelsea Rd 5 AB51 152 D6
Cherry Gr AB21 156 B5
Cherry Rd AB16 164 D4
Cherry Tree Rd AB31 184 D6
Chestnut Cres AB31 184 F6
Chestnut Gr AB31 184 F6
Chestnut La 3 AB31 110 B3
Chestnut Pk 1 AB31 110 B3
Chestnut Pl
2 Banchory AB31 110 B3
Ellon AB41 151 C3
Chestnut Row AB25 164 F3
Chestnut Wlk AB41 76 C7
Cheves Circ 14 AB42 38 D6
Chevron Cres AB42 147 A5
Cheyne Rd AB24 165 C6
Cheyne's La 11 AB53 145 D4
Cheyne's Pl AB53 145 D4
Cheyne Wlk AB21 153 C6
Chievres Pl AB41 151 C3
Chievres Rd AB41 151 C3
Chisholm's La AB53 145 D5
Chris Anderson Stadium
AB24 165 D5
Christian Watt Dr AB43 143 A4
Christian Watt Pl AB43 143 A4
Christie Cres AB39 185 D4
Christie Ct 1 AB54 148 E5
Christie Gdns AB54 148 E5
Christie Grange AB21 163 A8
Christies La DD10 189 D3
Church Ave
Fraserburgh AB43 26 D7
Insch AB52 149 D5
Church Cres 4 AB53 36 A5
Churchill Dr AB42 147 D7
Church La
Bankhead AB21 163 F8
7 Brechin DD9 188 C3
18 Kemnay AB51 87 D7
Peterhead AB42 38 D6
6 Turriff AB53 145 C5
Church Pl
12 Boddam AB42 40 D1
New Pitsligo AB43 23 D7
Church Rd
Banff AB45 3 C2
Laurencekirk AB30 133 A7
Potterton AB23 91 A6
Church St
Aberdeen AB11 190 C3
Aberdeen AB24 164 E6
Brechin DD9 188 C3
Edzell DD9 132 A8
3 Fordyce AB45 1 F1
Huntly AB54 148 D4
Insch AB52 149 C5
Inverallochy AB43 15 B8
Inverbervie DD10 187 D7
Laurencekirk AB30 186 D5
Macduff AB44 141 C6
New Pitsligo AB43 23 D6
Portsoy AB45 139 D7
St Combs AB43 15 D6
7 Turriff AB53 145 C5
Church Terr
Aberdeen AB21 156 B5
Fraserburgh AB43 142 C8
Insch AB52 149 D5
Turriff AB53 145 C5
Church View 14 AB43 24 E6
City Hospl AB24 190 C4
City Rd DD9 188 C3
Clackriach Castle (remains
of)* AB42 36 F6
Claremont Gdns 2 AB10 169 F7
Claremont Gr AB10 169 F7
Claremont Pl AB10 169 F7
Claremont St 1 AB10 169 F7
Clarence St AB11 165 E1
Clarke St AB16 164 C6
Clark's La AB24 165 C6
Clashbog Pl 11 AB21 163 D7
Clashfarquhar Cres
AB12 180 B6
Clashmach Dr AB54 148 C4
Clashmach Terr AB54 148 C4
Clashmach View AB54 148 C4
Clashnettie Pl AB21 158 C6
Clashrodney Ave AB12 176 A6
Clashrodney Rd AB12 176 B6
Clashrodney Way AB12 176 A6
Clashrodney Wlk AB12 176 A6
CLATT 70 C8
Clatt Prim Sch AB54 56 B1
Claymore Ave
Aberdeen AB23 160 C3
Portlethen AB12 180 C7
Claymore Dr AB23 160 B2
Clergy St AB44 141 D6
CLERKHILL 147 C4
Clerkhill Pl 2 AB42 147 C4
Clerkhill Prim Sch AB42 147 B5
Clerkhill Rd AB42 147 B4
Clerk Maxwell Cres
AB12 170 A1
Clerk St DD9 188 C3
Cleveland Pl AB42 147 D5
Cliff Pk AB15 168 F4
Cliff View AB39 181 H4
Clifton Ct 2 AB24 164 F6
Clifton La AB24 164 F5
Clifton Pl AB24 164 F5
Clifton Rd
Aberdeen AB24 164 D6
Turriff AB53 145 D4
Clinterty Aberdeen Coll
AB21 156 C3
Clinton Cres AB43 23 E6
Clinton Dr AB43 5 A4
Clinton Pl
Fraserburgh AB43 5 A4
2 New Pitsligo AB43 23 E6
Clipper Pl DD10 187 D7
CLOCHCAN 37 A2
Cloghill Pl 2 AB16 163 F2
CLOLA 38 A2
Clova Cres AB15 162 E3
Clova Pk AB15 162 E3
CLOVENSTONE 88 A8
Clover Cl AB43 143 C7
Cloverd le Ct 22 AB21 163 D7
Cloverfield Cl AB21 163 D8
Cloverfield Ct AB21 163 C8
Cloverfield Gdns AB21 163 D8
Cloverfield Pl AB21 163 C8
Cloverhill Cres AB22 159 E1
Cloverhill Rd AB23 160 A1
Clover Mdw AB32 161 B3
Clover Yd 1 DD10 187 D3
Clune View AB31 111 C2
Cluniebank Rd AB35 113 F5
Clunie Pl AB16 164 A4
Clunie St AB45 140 F6
Cluny Crichton Castle
(remains of)* AB31 109 E6
Cluny Prim Sch AB51 86 F2
Clyde St AB11 190 C2
COALFORD 172 A4
Cobban's La 2 AB51 152 D6
Cobden St DD10 189 D2
COBURTY 142 A2
Codona's Amusement Pk*
AB24 165 E2
Coldhome St 1 AB45 140 F6
Coldstone Ave AB15 162 E3
College Bounds
Aberdeen AB24 165 B5
Fraserburgh AB43 143 C7
College St AB11 190 A3
College Wlk AB16 163 E2
Colleonard Cres AB45 140 E4
Colleonard Ct AB45 140 E4
Colleonard Dr AB45 140 E4
Colleonard Rd AB45 140 D4
Colleonard Sculpture Gdn &
Gall* AB45 140 D3
Collieburn Cres AB42 147 C7
COLLIESTON 64 E3
Collieston Ave AB23 159 F3
Collieston Circ AB22 159 E3
Collieston Cres AB23 159 F3
Collieston Dr 2 AB23 159 F2
Collieston Path AB22 159 E3
Collieston Pl AB22 159 E2
Collieston Rd AB22 159 E2
Collieston St 1 AB22 159 F2
Collieston Way AB23 159 F3
Collyburn View AB53 145 F4
Colonsay Cres 4 AB16 163 E2
COLPY 58 A7
Colpy Road Ind Est AB51 150 A3
Colpy Way AB51 150 B3
Colquhonnie Castle (remains
of)* AB36 81 C3
Colsea Rd AB12 176 C6
Colsea Sq 4 AB12 176 C6
Colsea Terr AB12 176 C6
Colthill Circ AB13 173 B8

Colthill Cres AB13 . . . . . . 167 C1
Colthill Dr AB13 . . . . .173 B8
Colthill Rd AB13 . . . . 167 C1
Colville Pl AB24 . . . . 165 C3
COMERS 99 D6
Commerce La
Aberdeen AB11 . . . . 190 C3
2 Fraserburgh AB43 . . . . 143 D6
Commerce St
Aberdeen AB11 . . . . 190 C3
Brechin DD9. . . . . 188 D3
Fraserburgh AB43 . . . . 143 D6
Insch AB52 . . . . 149 D4
8 Montrose DD10 . . . . . . 189 C2
Commercial La 1 AB51 . 152 D6
Commercial Quay AB11 . .190 B2
Commercial Rd
Ellon AB41 . . . . .151 B5
Insch AB52 . . . . 149 C4
Inverurie AB51 . . . . .152 E4
Oldmeldrum AB51 . . . . .150 B2
Commercial St AB44 . . . . 141 D7
Concert Ct AB10. . . . . .190 B3
Concraig Gdns AB15 . . . . 163 A4
Concraig Pk AB15 . . . . . . 163 A4
Concraig Pl AB15 . . . . . . 163 A4
Concraig Wlk AB15 . . . . . 163 A4
Condor Cres DD10 . . . . . . 189 D7
Conference Way AB23. . . .160 B2
Conglass Ave AB51. . . . . . 152 A7
Conglass Ct AB51. . . . . . . 152 A8
Conglass Dr AB51. . . . . . . 152 A8
Conglass Gdns 1 AB51 . 152 A8
Conglass Gr 3 AB51. . . . 152 A7
Conglass Pl AB51. . . . . . . 152 A8
Conglass Rd AB51 . . . . . . 152 A8
Conglass Way 2 AB51 . . 152 A8
Conglass Wlk 1 AB51 . . 152 A7
Coningham Gdns AB24 . . 165 A6
Coningham Rd AB24 . . . . 165 A6
Coningham Terr AB24 . . . 165 A6
Connon Ct AB51 . . . . .152 E3
Constitution Ct AB24. . . . 190 C4
Constitution La AB11. . . . 190 C4
Constitution St
Aberdeen AB24 . . . . 190 C4
Inverurie AB51 . . . . 152 D6
Peterhead AB42. . . . . 147 D5
Contlaw Brae AB13 . . . . . .173 B8
Contlaw Pl AB13. . . . . .173 B8
Contlaw Rd AB13 . . . . 167 A2
Conveners Wynd DD9 . . . .188 B3
Conveth Pk AB30 . . . . 186 D6
Conveth Pl AB30. . . . . 186 D6
Conzie Castle (remains of)*
AB54 . . . . .31 B3
COOKNEY. 120 F8
COOKSTON 188 B5
Cookston Cres DD9 . . . . . 188 C4
Cookston Rd
Aberdeen AB12 . . . . 180 D6
Brechin DD9. . . . . 188 C5
Portlethen AB12 . . . . 180 C6
Cooper's Brae 10 AB42. . . .38 D6
Cooper's Ct AB41 . . . . 151 D4
Copeman Ave AB42 . . . . . .147 B4
Copeman Pl AB42. . . . . . . .147 B4
COPLANDHILL. 147 A6
Coplandhill Cres AB42 . . .147 B6
Coplandhill Pl 1 AB42. . . 147 A5
Coplandhill Rd AB42. . . . .147 B6
Coral Gdns AB42. . . . . 147 A4
Corbie Dr AB43 . . . . 143 C4
Corby Terr AB21 . . . . 158 C6
Cordiner Ct 4 AB42 . . . . .147 E6
Cordyce Residential Sch
AB21 . . . . 158 C8
Cordyce View AB21 . . . . . 158 A6
CORGARFF. 92 F7
Corgarff Castle* AB36 . . . .92 D7
Cormack Pk AB51. . . . . .46 F3
Cormack Pl 1 AB21 . . . . . 153 C6
Cormorant Brae AB12. . . .176 B8
Corndavon Terr AB16. . . . .164 B3
Cornellan Sq AB35. . . . . . .182 E4
Cornfield Pl AB53. . . . . . . 145 D5
Cornfield Rd AB53 . . . . . . 145 D5
CORNHILL
Aberdeen. 164 D4
Banff .7 E1
Cornhill Ct 7 AB16 . . . . . . 164 D4
Cornhill Dr AB16. . . . . 164 D4
Cornhill Gdns AB16 . . . . . 164 D4
Cornhill Prim Sch AB16 . 164 D4
Cornhill Rd
Aberdeen AB25 . . . . .164 E3
Huntly AB54. . . . . 144 C5
Cornhill Sh Arc AB16. . . . 164 D4
Cornhill Sq AB16 . . . . 164 D4
Cornhill Terr AB16 . . . . . . 164 D3
Cornhill Way AB16 . . . . . . 164 D3
Corn Rd AB43 . . . . .15 B7
Cornyhaugh Rd AB14 . . . . 172 C7
Coronation Ave DD10 . . . 189 C8
Coronation Rd AB14 . . . . .172 E6
Coronation Way DD10. . . 189 C7
Correction Wynd 5
AB11 . . . . .190 B3
Corrennie Circ AB21 . . . . .158 B8
Corrichie Pl 1 AB31 . . . . .184 E5
CORSE. 45 A7
Corse Ave AB15. . . . . .162 E4
Corse Castle (remains of)*
AB31 . . . . .97 D6
Corseduick Pk 1 AB21. . 153 D5
Corseduick Rd AB21 . . . . 153 D5
Corsee Hill AB31. . . . . .184 B4
Corsee Rd AB31 . . . . 184 A5
Corse Gdns AB15 . . . . .162 E4
Corsehill Gdns AB22 . . . . .159 F1
Corsekelly Pl AB43. . . . . . . .15 D5
Corse The AB43. . . . . .26 C7
Corse Wynd AB15. . . . . . . .162 F4
Corskie Dr
Aberchirder AB54 . . . . 144 D5
Macduff AB44 . . . . 141 D5
Corskie Pl AB44 . . . . 141 D5
Corsman Gdns 3 AB51 . 152 C4
Cortes Cres AB43 . . . . .143 B5
Corthan Cres AB12. . . . . . .170 B4
Corthan Dr AB12. . . . . 170 C3
Corthan Pl AB12 . . . . .170 B4
Corunna Pl AB23 . . . . .160 B1
Corunna Rd AB23. . . . . . . 165 D8
COTHALL 89 F6
Cothal View AB21 . . . . 158 A8
Cottage Brae AB10. . . . . . 170 A7
Cotton St AB11 . . . . 190 C4
COTTOWN 48 D7
Cottown of Balgownie
AB23 . . . . 165 C8
Coubert Rd AB21 . . . . 153 C6
COULL. 96 F1
Coull Gdns
Aberdeen AB22 . . . . .165 B8
Kingswells AB15 . . . . .162 E3
Coull Gn AB15. . . . . .162 E3
Countesswells Ave AB15 169 A6
Countesswells Cres
AB15 . . . . 169 A6
Countesswells Pl AB15 . . 169 A6
Countesswells Rd AB15 . .168 E5
Countesswells Terr
AB15 . . . . 169 A6
Couper's Rd
Auchenblae AB30. . . . . 124 A1
Banchory AB31 . . . . .111 B6
Laurencekirk AB30 . . . . . . 128 D4
Courtyard The
Cults AB15. . . . . .168 F3
Westhill AB32 . . . . 161 C2
COVE BAY 176 C7
Cove Circ AB12 . . . . 176 C6
Cove Cl AB12 . . . . .176 B6
Cove Cres AB12. . . . . .176 B6
Cove Ct AB12. . . . . 176 C6
Cove Gdns AB12 . . . . 176 C6
Covenanters Dr AB12 . . . .170 B4
Covenanters Row AB12 . 170 A4
Cove Path AB12. . . . . 176 C6
Cove Pl AB12. . . . . 176 C6
Cove Rd AB12 . . . . .175 F5
Cove Way AB12 . . . . .176 B6
Cove Wlk AB12 . . . . .176 B6
Cove Wynd AB12. . . . . .176 B6
Cowan Den AB53 . . . . .145 E4
Cowan Pl 3 AB24 . . . . . . .164 F6
COWBOG 23 B6
Cowgate
Inverbervie DD10 . . . . .187 E7
Oldmeldrum AB51 . . . . 150 C3
Stonehaven AB39. . . . . .185 F3
COWIE. 185 F6
Cowie Cres AB42 . . . . .27 B3
Cowie Gdns 2 AB43 . . . . . .26 C7
Cowie La AB39. . . . . .185 E5
Cowie Mill AB39 . . . . .185 E5
Cowie Wynd 15 AB31. . . . .108 E8
COYNACH. 95 E4
Craibstone Ave AB21. . . . .158 B3
Craibstone La AB11. . . . . . 190 A2
Craigarbel Cres DD10 . . . .187 E6
Craigbank AB51 . . . . .155 B5
CRAIGDAM. 61 C5
Craigden AB15. . . . . .163 F1
CRAIGEARN 87 C5
Craigearn Bsns Pk AB51 .155 B2
Craigellie Circ AB43 . . . . 143 A3
Craigendarroch Ave
AB16 . . . . .164 B4
Craigendarroch Circ
AB35 . . . . 182 D5
Craigendarroch Pl AB16. .164 B4
Craigendarroch Wlk
AB35 . . . . 182 D5
Craigendinnie Cres
AB34 . . . . .183 B4
Craigend Rd AB41 . . . . . . 151 A6
Craigen Terr AB45 . . . . .3 C2
Craigewan Cres AB42. . . . 147 C6
Craig Gdns
Aberdeen AB15 . . . . 168 C2
Blackburn AB21. . . . . 156 C6
Craighaar Gables AB21. . 158 C2
Craighall Cres AB41. . . . . 151 D4
Craighead Ave AB12 . . . . .180 B6
Craighead Dr AB54 . . . . . 148 C4
Craighill Terr 1 AB12. . . . 176 C6
CRAIGIEBUCKLER 169 A7
Craigiebuckler Ave
AB15 . . . . 169 A7
Craigiebuckler Dr AB15 . 169 A7
Craigiebuckler Pl AB15 . 169 A7
Craigiebuckler Terr
AB15 . . . . .169 B7
Craigieburn Pk AB15. . . . .169 B6
Craigielea Ave AB15 . . . . 169 D6
Craigielea Gdns AB15. . . 169 D6
Craigielea Mews AB15 . . 169 D6
Craigie Loanings AB25 . . .164 F1
Craigie Park Pl AB25. . . . .164 F1
Craigie Pk AB25 . . . . .164 F1
Craigie St AB25. . . . . 190 A4
Craigievar Castle* AB33 . .97 E8
Craigievar Cres
Aberdeen AB10 . . . . 169 D3
Craigievar Cres *continued*
Ellon AB41. . . . . .151 E6
Craigievar Ct AB10. . . . . . .169 E3
Craigievar Gdns AB10 . . . 169 D3
Craigievar Pl AB10. . . . . . 169 D4
Craigievar Prim Sch AB33 84 F1
Craigievar Rd AB10 . . . . . .169 E3
Craigievar Terr AB10 . . . . .169 E3
Craig Lea 1 AB51 . . . . .87 C6
Craigmarn Rd AB12 . . . . . .180 E5
Craigmaroinn Gdns
AB12 . . . . .176 B8
Craigmyle Rd AB31 . . . . . .108 E8
Craignabo Rd AB42 . . . . . 147 C3
Craignathunder 3 AB51 152 A8
Craigneen Pl 1 AB45 . . . . . . 8 F8
Craignook Rd AB21 . . . . . 158 C7
CRAIGO. 133 E3
Craigour Ave 18 AB31 . . . .108 E8
Craigour Rd AB31. . . . . . . .108 E8
Craigpark AB12 . . . . 170 D3
Craigpark Circ AB41 . . . . 151 A6
Craigpark Pl AB41 . . . . . . 151 A6
Craig Pl
Aberdeen AB11 . . . . .190 B1
Stonehaven AB39. . . . . .181 I4
Craig Rd DD10. . . . . 189 C1
Craigs Ct AB41 . . . . 151 A6
Craigshannoch AB51 . . . . 152 A8
Craigshannoch Rd AB51. . .59 E3
Craigshaw Bsns Pk
AB12 . . . . 170 D4
Craigshaw Cres AB12 . . . 170 D4
Craigshaw Dr AB12 . . . . . 170 C4
Craigshaw Pl AB12. . . . . . 170 C4
Craigshaw Rd AB12 . . . . . 170 C4
Craigshaw St AB12. . . . . . 170 C3
Craigs Rd AB41 . . . . 151 A6
Craigston Ave AB41 . . . . . .151 E5
Craigston Castle* AB53. . .21 E6
Craigston Gdns AB32 . . . .161 F4
Craigston Pl AB32 . . . . . . .161 F4
Craigston Rd AB32. . . . . . .161 F4
Craigton Ave AB15 . . . . . . 169 C5
Craigton Brae AB31 . . . . . . .98 A3
Craigton Cres
Aberdeen AB14 . . . . 172 D6
1 Banchory AB31. . . . . .98 A3
Craigton Ct AB10 . . . . 169 D5
Craigton Dr AB14 . . . . 172 D6
Craigton Gr AB14 . . . . 172 D6
Craigton Pk AB15. . . . . . . 169 C5
Craigton Rd AB15. . . . . . . 169 A4
Craigton Terr
Aberdeen AB14 . . . . 172 D6
Aberdeen AB15 . . . . 169 C5
Craigview DD10. . . . . .187 E7
Craigview Pl AB35 . . . . . . .182 E5
Craigview Rd AB35. . . . . . .182 E5
Cramond Terr AB45 . . . . . .140 E5
Cranford Rd AB10. . . . . . . .169 E5
Cranford Terr AB10 . . . . . 169 D5
Cranhill Brae AB39. . . . . . .181 I4
Cranhill Pl AB39 . . . . .181 I5
Cranna View
Huntly AB54. . . . . .144 E5
Turriff AB53 . . . . .19 D0
CRATHES 110 E3
Crathes Castle, Gdn & Est*
AB31 . . . . 110 D3
Crathes Pl AB41 . . . . .151 E5
Crathes Prim Sch AB31 . 110 D5
CRATHIE. 102 E2
Crathie Gardens W AB10 170 A5
Crathie Prim Sch AB35. . .102 E2
Crathie Terr AB10. . . . . . . 170 A5
Crawford Pl 2 AB51. . . . . . .47 A2
Crawpeel Rd AB12. . . . . . 170 D1
CRAWTON 126 E2
Crawton Ness AB12. . . . . .176 B8
Creel Ave AB12 . . . . .176 B6
Creel Ct AB12 . . . . .176 B5
Creel Dr AB12 . . . . .176 B6
Creel Gdns AB12. . . . . .176 B6
Creel Pl AB12. . . . . .176 B5
Creel Rd AB12 . . . . 176 A5
Creel Wlk AB12. . . . . .176 B6
Creel Wynd AB12 . . . . .176 B5
Crescent The AB53. . . . . . . .36 A6
Crichie Circ AB51. . . . . . . .152 E2
CRIMOND. 26 D7
Crimond Ct AB43 . . . . 143 C4
Crimond Dr AB41 . . . . .151 E6
Crimond Pk AB41. . . . . . . .151 E6
Crimond Sch AB43. . . . . . . .26 D7
Crimon Pl AB10. . . . . 190 A3
Croftland 4 AB41 . . . . .62 B2
Croftlands DD10 . . . . 134 D3
Croft Pl
Aberdeen AB16 . . . . 164 A3
St Cyrus DD10 . . . . 134 D3
Croft Rd
Aberdeen AB16 . . . . 164 A2
4 Kemnay AB51. . . . . .87 D7
Montrose DD10 . . . . .189 B1
St Cyrus DD10 . . . . 134 D3
Stonehaven AB39. . . . . .125 B3
Croft Terr AB16 . . . . 164 A3
Crollshillock AB39 . . . . . . .181 H4
Crollshillock Pl AB39. . . . 181 H4
Cromar Cres AB34 . . . . .96 B3
Cromar Dr 3 AB34 . . . . .96 C3
Cromar Gdns AB15. . . . . . .162 F3
Cromarty View 1 AB45. . .140 E6
Crombie Acres AB32 . . . . .161 B3
Crombie Castle* AB54. . . .18 E3
Crombie Circ AB14. . . . . . 172 C7
Crombie Cirlce AB32. . . . 161 C3
Crombie Cl AB32. . . . . 161 C3
Crombie Dr AB32 . . . . .161 B3
Crombie Pl
Aberdeen AB11 . . . . .170 E7
Westhill AB32 . . . . .161 B3
Crombie Prim Sch AB32. 161 D3
Crombie Rd
Aberdeen AB11 . . . . 190 C1
Westhill AB32 . . . . .161 B3
Crombie Wynd AB32 . . . . .161 B3
Cromlet Pk AB51 . . . . .48 A1
Cromlet Pl AB51 . . . . 150 D3
Cromwell Gdns AB15. . . . 169 D7
Cromwell Rd AB15 . . . . . . 169 D7
Crooked La
Aberdeen AB25 . . . . 190 A4
1 Peterhead AB42. . . . . . . .147 F5
5 Turriff AB53 . . . . 145 D4
Crookfold Gdns AB23 . . . 160 A1
Crookfold Pl AB23 . . . . . . 160 A1
Crook O'Ness St AB44. . . 141 C7
CROSSBRAE 20 D3
Crossfolds Cres AB42 . . . .147 B6
Crossgates AB21. . . . . 158 C1
CROSS OF JACKSTON 59 F7
CROSSROADS. 110 E1
Crossroads of Braiklay
AB41 . . . . .48 F2
Cross St
Fraserburgh AB43. . . . . . . 143 D7
5 Turriff AB53 . . . . 145 C4
Cross The 2 AB39 . . . . . . .185 F4
CROVIE 3 C3
Crovie Gdns AB41. . . . . . . 151 D6
Crown Alley AB30. . . . . . . 186 C5
Crown Cres AB14 . . . . .172 E7
Crown La
Aberdeen AB11 . . . . 190 A2
Turriff AB53 . . . . 145 D4
Crown Pl AB14. . . . . 172 D7
Crown St
Aberdeen AB11 . . . . 190 A1
Turriff AB53 . . . . 145 D4
Crown Terr
Aberdeen AB11 . . . . 190 A2
Peterculter AB14. . . . . .172 E6
CRUDEN BAY. 53 A3
Cruden Cres AB16 . . . . . . .163 F5
Cruden Pk AB16. . . . . .163 F5
Cruden Pl AB16. . . . . .163 F5
Cruden Terr AB39 . . . . 185 C4
CRUDIE. 22 B8
Crudie Prim Sch AB53 . . . .22 C8
Cruickshank Botanic Gdns*
AB24 . . . . .165 B6
Cruickshank Cres
Aberdeen AB12 . . . . 170 A2
Aberdeen AB21 . . . . .163 E7
Cruickshank Ct AB32. . . . .161 B2
Cruickshank Pk 7 DD10 138 C8
Cryne Corse Rd
Banchory AB31 . . . . 119 A6
Stonehaven AB39. . . . . .124 F8
Culbert St AB45. . . . . 139 D7
CULLEN. 1 B4
Cullen Ct AB41 . . . . .151 E6
Cullen House* AB56. . . . . . . .1 A4
Cullen Prim Sch AB56. . . . . . .1 B4
Cullen St AB45 . . . . 139 D7
Cullen Way AB41 . . . . .151 E6
Cullerlie Farm Pk*
AB32 . . . . .100 E2
Culsh Terr AB53. . . . . .36 A6
Culstruphan Rd AB36 . . . . . .81 E7
CULTERCULLEN 76 E7
Cultercullen Prim Sch
AB41 . . . . .76 E7
Culter Den AB14. . . . . 172 C6
Culter House Rd
Aberdeen AB13 . . . . .173 B7
Milltimber/Aberdeen AB13 172 F8
Culter Prim Sch AB14. . . .172 E6
Culter Sports Ctr The
AB14 . . . . .172 E6
CULTS 168 F3
Cults Acad AB15 . . . . 168 D3
Cults Ave AB15 . . . . 168 D3
Cults Bsns Pk AB15 . . . . . .168 F3
Cults Ct AB15. . . . . .168 E2
Cults Gdns AB15 . . . . .168 E3
Cults Prim Sch AB15 . . . . 168 C3
CUMINESTOWN 22 C1
Cuminestown Rd AB53 . . . .47 E5
CUMMINGS PARK 164 C5
Cummings Park Circ
AB16 . . . . 164 C4
Cummings Park Cres
AB16 . . . . .164 B5
Cummings Park Dr AB16 164 B6
Cummings Park Rd
AB16 . . . . 164 C6
Cummings Park Terr
AB16 . . . . .164 B5
Cuninghill Ave AB51 . . . . 152 D4
Cuninghill Rd AB51 . . . . . 152 D4
Cunninghar Rd AB21. . . . 153 C5
Cuparstone La AB10 . . . . 170 A8
Cuparstone Row AB10 . . 170 A7
Cuperstone Ct 4 AB12. . 170 A7
Curlew Ave 13 AB41. . . . . . .77 F8
CUTTYHILL 26 C1
Cypress Ave AB23. . . . . . . 160 A5
Cypress Gr
Aberdeen AB23 . . . . 160 A5
Middleton Park AB23. . . . . .159 F5
Cypress Wlk AB23 . . . . . . .159 F5

D

Dales Ct AB42 . . . . .147 B4
Dales Ind Est AB42. . . . . . 147 A1
Dales Pk Prim Sch AB42 147 A3
Dales Rd 2 AB42. . . . . 147 C2
Dales View Dr AB42. . . . . . 147 A3
Dales View Pl AB42 . . . . . 147 A3
Dalhousie St
Brechin DD9. . . . . 188 D3
Edzell DD9 . . . . 132 A7
Dall's La DD9. . . . . .188 E2
Dalmaik Cres AB14 . . . . . 172 D7
Dalmaik Terr AB14 . . . . . . 172 D7
Dalmuinzie Rd AB15 . . . . 168 A2
Dalrymple Circ AB21. . . . .156 B6
Dalrymple Hall & Arts Ctr*
AB43 . . . . .143 E6
Dalrymple St AB43. . . . . . 143 D6
Dalvenie Rd AB31. . . . . . . 184 D5
Damacre Rd DD9 . . . . 188 C3
Damask Cres AB21. . . . . . 153 D6
Damfield Rd AB43 . . . . . . 143 C3
Damhead Circ AB42. . . . . .147 B2
Damhead Ind Est AB42. . 147 A1
Damhead Rd AB42 . . . . . . 147 A2
Damhead Way AB42. . . . . .147 B1
Dancingcairns Cres
AB16 . . . . 164 A6
Dancingcairns Pl AB16. . .164 B7
Daneshillock AB45. . . . . . . .20 F8
DANESTONE 159 B1
Danestone Circ AB16. . . . 164 C6
Danestone Pl AB23 . . . . . 165 C8
Danestone Prim Sch
AB22 . . . . .159 B1
Danestone Terr AB23. . . . 165 C8
Darroch Ct AB35. . . . . 182 C4
Darroch Pk AB15 . . . . 168 D2
Daun Wlk 4 AB51 . . . . .87 C6
Davah Ct AB51. . . . . 152 C6
Davah Rd AB51 . . . . 152 C5
Davan Pk 1 AB22 . . . . . . .165 B8
Davan Pl AB41. . . . . .151 B6
David McLean Dr AB33. . 154 C4
Davids La AB51. . . . . 152 D5
Davidson Cres AB33. . . . . 154 C3
Davidson Dr
Aberdeen AB16 . . . . .163 F5
Inverurie AB51 . . . . .152 B8
Mintlaw AB42 . . . . .146 E4
Davidson Gdns AB16 . . . . .163 F5
Davidson Pl
Aberdeen AB16 . . . . .163 F5
Inverurie AB51 . . . . .152 B8
St Cyrus DD10. . . . . 134 D3
David St
Inverbervie DD10 . . . . .187 E6
Stonehaven AB39. . . . . .185 E5
Davies Castle Fort* AB56 . . 6 B7
DAVIOT 59 E3
Daviot Prim Sch AB51. . . . .59 F3
Dawson Brae AB32. . . . . . .161 B4
Dawson Cl AB32 . . . . .161 B3
Dawson Dr AB32. . . . . .161 B3
Dawson Way AB32 . . . . . . .161 B4
Dawson Wynd AB32. . . . . .161 B3
Dean Gdns AB32. . . . . .161 F3
Deans Ct AB51. . . . . 155 C4
Deansloch Cres AB16 . . . 164 A5
Deansloch Pl 1 AB16. . . 164 A5
Deansloch Terr AB16. . . . 164 A5
Deans Well AB21. . . . . .156 B7
DEEBANK 184 C3
Deebank Ct AB35 . . . . 182 D3
Dee Bank Rd AB35. . . . . . 182 D3
Dee La AB31. . . . . 184 C4
Deemount Ave AB11 . . . . 170 C6
Deemount Gdns AB11. . . 170 C6
Deemount Rd AB11 . . . . . .170 B6
Deemount Terr AB11 . . . . .170 B6
Dee Pl AB11. . . . . 190 A2
Deer Abbey (remains of)*
AB42 . . . . .37 D7
Deer Rd
Aberdeen AB24 . . . . .164 E6
Peterhead AB42. . . . . .36 E6
Deer Road E AB42 . . . . .36 E6
Deer Road W AB42 . . . . . . .36 D6
Deeside Ave AB15 . . . . . . 169 D4
Deeside Cres AB15. . . . . . 169 C4
Deeside Dr AB15. . . . . 169 C4
Deeside Gdns AB15. . . . . 169 C4
Deeside Pk AB15 . . . . 169 D4
Deeside Pl AB15 . . . . 169 C4
Deeside Terr AB15 . . . . . . 169 C4
Dee St
Aberdeen AB11 . . . . 190 A2
3 Aboyne AB34 . . . . .108 B6
Ballater AB35 . . . . 182 D4
Banchory AB31 . . . . 184 C3
Deevale Cres AB12. . . . . . 170 A3
Deevale Gdns AB12 . . . . . 170 A3
Deevale Rd AB12 . . . . 170 A3
Deevale Terr AB12 . . . . . . 170 A3
Deeview Gdns AB31. . . . . 111 D5
Deeview Rd AB31. . . . . . . 184 D5
Deeview Road S AB15. . . .168 E2
Delgatie Castle* AB53 . . . .21 D1
Delgaty Cres AB53 . . . . . . .145 E4
Delgaty La AB21 . . . . .158 B7
Delgaty Terr AB53. . . . . . . .145 E5
Dempsey Terr 3 AB24 . . 165 A6

- Denburn Ct AB25 190 A3
- Denburn Rd AB10 190 A3
- Denburn Way DD9 188 D2
- Den Cres AB55 28 D8
- Denhead AB15 168 E3
- DENHEAD
  - Ellon 63 F5
  - Peterhead 25 D3
- Denhead Cres AB23 91 A6
- Denmark St AB43 143 D7
- DENMORE 160 A4
- Denmore Gdns AB22 165 B8
- Denmore Ind Est AB23 160 B4
- Denmore Pl AB23 160 A4
- Denmore Rd AB23 160 A4
- Dennis Dr DD9 132 D8
- Dennis Roger La 1 AB39 185 C5
- Dennyduff Rd AB43 143 B6
- Den of Cults AB15 168 F2
- Den of Maidencraig Nature Reserve* AB15 163 E1
- Denseat Ct AB15 163 E1
- Denstrath Rd DD9 132 D8
- Denstrath View DD9 132 C8
- Den The AB15 168 F2
- Den View AB21 156 A7
- Denview Cres AB23 91 A6
- Denview Rd AB23 91 A6
- Denwell Rd
  - Insch AB52 149 D6
  - Keith AB55 28 D8
- Denwood AB15 163 F1
- Depot Rd AB54 148 C4
- DERBETH 163 A5
- Derbeth Cres AB16 163 E2
- Derbeth Grange AB15 162 F5
- Derbeth Manor AB15 163 A5
- Derbeth Pk AB15 162 F4
- Derbeth Pl AB15 162 F5
- Derbeth Wlk AB15 162 F5
- Derbyhall Ave AB43 143 C4
- Derry Ave AB16 164 B3
- Derry Pl AB16 164 B3
- Desswood Pl AB25 164 E1
- Devanha Cres AB11 190 A1
- Devanha Gardens E AB11 190 A1
- Devanha Gardens W AB11 190 A1
- Devanha Gdns AB11 190 A1
- Devanha La AB11 190 A1
- Devanha Terr AB11 190 B1
- Devanna Gardens S AB11 170 B6
- Devenick Dr AB12 180 C7
- Devenick Pl AB10 169 D3
- Deveron Rd
  - Aberdeen AB16 164 A4
  - Huntly AB54 148 C5
  - Turriff AB53 145 A5
- Deveronside AB45 141 A6
- Deveronside Dr AB53 145 B5
- Deveron St
  - Huntly AB54 148 D5
  - Turriff AB53 145 B5
- Deveron Terr AB45 140 F5
- Devil's Folly AB52 58 B6
- Devonshire Rd AB10 169 E7
- Dewey Ct DD9 132 D8
- Deyhill AB44 141 E6
- Diamond La AB10 190 A3
- Diamond Pl 3 AB10 190 A3
- Diamond St AB10 190 A3
- Dickie Dr
  - 4 Fraserburgh AB43 26 C7
  - Peterhead AB42 147 C7
- Dickson Ave 8 DD10 138 C8
- Dickson Terr AB16 163 F4
- Dickson Way DD10 134 D3
- Dill Pl AB24 164 F7
- Dill Rd AB24 164 F7
- Dinbaith Pl 4 AB16 163 F2
- Dingwall Dr AB42 147 D7
- Dingwall St AB43 142 B8
- DINNET 105 F5
- Dinnie Pl AB51 155 B6
- Disblair Ave AB21 153 C5
- Disblair Rd AB21 153 C5
- Distillery Rd
  - Brechin DD9 188 C4
  - Laurencekirk AB30 128 A4
  - Oldmeldrum AB51 150 C4
- Dock St DD10 135 C5
- Dock Street E AB11 170 E8
- Dock Street W AB11 170 E8
- Doctor Lang Pl DD9 188 B5
- Dominies Ct AB16 164 D5
- Dominies Rd AB24 164 D5
- Donald Ave 6 AB51 87 C6
- Donald Dewar Ct AB16 163 F4
- Donald Gordon Ct 1 AB51 150 C2
- Donaldson Ct 2 AB54 148 E5
- Donbank Pl AB24 164 F7
- Donbank Prim Sch AB24 165 A7
- Donbank Terr AB24 164 F7
- Don Cres AB51 152 D4
- Don Ct AB24 164 E7
- Don Gdns AB24 164 E7
- Donmouth Cres AB23 165 D8
- Donmouth Ct AB23 165 D8
- Donmouth Gdns AB23 165 D8
- Donmouth Nature Reserve* AB24 165 E7
- Donmouth Rd AB23 165 D7
- Donmouth Terr AB23 165 D7
- Don Pl
  - Aberdeen AB24 164 F6
  - Dyce AB21 158 B6
- Donside Ct AB24 165 A7
- Donside Rd AB33 154 C4
- Don St AB24 164 F6
- Don Terr AB24 164 E7
- Donview Gdns 2 AB51 87 C6
- Donview Pl AB24 164 F7
- Donview Rd AB24 164 F7
- Don View Rd 17 AB51 87 D7
- Doo'cot Pk AB45 140 E4
- Doo'cot View AB45 140 E5
- Doolie Ness AB12 176 B8
- Doonies Rare Breeds Farm* AB12 171 A3
- Dorward Rd DD10 189 D4
- Double Dykes DD9 188 A4
- Douglas Cl AB42 147 A7
- Douglas Cres AB42 147 A7
- Doune Cres AB44 141 D5
- Dounepark Rd AB45 141 F2
- Dovewells Dr DD9 188 B4
- DOWNIES 180 D3
- Downies Brae AB11 170 E6
- Downies Ct AB12 180 C5
- Downies Pl AB11 170 E6
- Downie Way
  - 1 Hillside DD10 138 D8
  - 3 Kemnay AB51 87 D7
- Dowrie Pl 2 AB30 128 A4
- DRAKEMYRE 51 A6
- Drinnies Cres AB21 158 C7
- Drinnie's Wood Obsy* AB42 37 D8
- Drive The DD9 132 A7
- Drostan Dr AB42 146 E4
- Drumachlie Loan DD9 188 E2
- Drumachlie Pk DD9 188 E2
- DRUMBLADE 44 E7
- Drumblade Prim Sch AB54 44 D6
- Drum Castle, Gdn & Est* AB31 111 D7
- DRUMDOLLO 44 F5
- Druminnor Castle* AB54 55 F1
- DRUMLIGAIR 90 C7
- DRUMLITHIE 125 B3
- DRUMNAGORRACH 17 E3
- DRUMOAK 111 D6
- Drumoak Prim Sch AB31 111 D6
- Drumrossie St AB52 149 D5
- Drum's La AB25 190 B3
- Drumthwacket Dr AB12 180 A4
- Drumtochty Castle* AB30 123 F3
- Drumview Cres AB14 166 D1
- Drumview Rd AB14 166 D1
- Drum Wynd 3 AB41 151 E5
- DRYMUIR 36 D4
- DUBFORD 3 B1
- Dubford Ave AB23 159 F4
- Dubford Cres AB23 159 F4
- Dubford Gdns AB23 159 F5
- Dubford Gr AB23 159 F5
- Dubford Pk AB23 159 F3
- Dubford Pl AB23 159 F4
- Dubford Rd AB23 159 F4
- Dubford Rise AB23 159 F5
- Dubford Terr AB23 159 F4
- Dubford Wlk AB23 159 F5
- Dubton Rd DD10 138 C7
- Ducat Way AB30 186 C6
- Duff Dr 3 AB51 150 C2
- Duff House* AB45 141 A4
- Duff St
  - Aberdeen AB24 190 C4
  - Macduff AB44 141 D6
  - Turriff AB53 145 C4
- Duff Terr AB45 7 E1
- Dugald Baird Sq AB12 170 A1
- Duke La AB43 143 D7
- Duke St
  - Brechin DD9 188 B4
  - Fraserburgh AB43 143 D7
  - Huntly AB54 148 D4
  - Laurencekirk AB30 128 B4
  - Peterhead AB42 25 C1
  - Stonehaven AB39 185 E5
- Dulnain Rd AB16 163 F3
- Dumgoyne Pl AB15 164 B1
- DUN 138 E6
- Dunbar St AB24 165 C5
- Dunbar Terr AB54 148 C4
- Dunbennan Rd AB21 158 C7
- Duncan Ave AB51 150 C3
- Duncan Cres AB42 147 C6
- Duncan Pl AB41 151 B3
- Duncan Rd AB34 96 B3
- Duncan's Cl AB53 145 B5
- Duncan St AB45 140 E6
- DUNCANSTONE 56 F1
- Dunchavin Cotts 2 AB52 149 D5
- Dundarg Castle (remains of)* AB43 12 F7
- Dundarg Rd AB43 142 C7
- Dundarroch Rd AB35 182 C4
- Dundas Ct AB51 155 C6
- Dundas Pk DD9 188 E3
- Dundas Rd AB43 15 B7
- Dundonnie St 3 AB42 40 D1
- DUNECHT 100 F7
- Dunecht Gdns AB32 161 C3
- Dunecht Prim Sch AB32 100 E8
- Dunecht Rd AB32 161 C3
- Dungeith Ave AB31 184 B4
- Dunlappie Rd DD9 132 A7
- Dunlin Cres AB12 176 B7
- Dunlin Ct AB39 181 I5
- Dunlin Rd
  - Aberdeen AB12 176 B8
  - Aberdeen AB21 157 E5
- Dunlugas Pl 1 AB53 145 C6
- Dunmail Ave AB15 168 E2
- Dunninald House & Gdns* DD10 138 A4
- Dunnottar Ave 13 AB39 185 E4
- Dunnottar Castle* AB39 126 F6
- Dunnottar Prim Sch AB39 185 F4
- Dunnottar Rd AB41 151 E5
- Dunnydeer Gdns AB52 149 C5
- Dunnydeer Pk AB52 149 C5
- Dunnydeer Pl 1 AB52 149 C5
- Dunnydeer View AB52 149 C5
- Dunnyfell Rd AB39 181 G2
- Dunrossie Cres DD10 189 A5
- Dunrossie Terr DD10 189 A6
- DUNSHILLOCK 146 B6
- Dunvegan Ave AB12 180 B6
- Dunvegan Cres AB12 180 B6
- Dunvegan Pl
  - Ellon AB41 151 E5
  - Portlethen AB12 180 B6
- Duriehill Rd DD9 132 B7
- Durie Pl DD9 132 B7
- Durn Ave AB45 139 D5
- Durn Dr AB45 139 D5
- DURNO 59 B3
- Durno Pk AB32 101 E6
- Durn Rd AB45 139 D5
- Durris Prim Sch AB31 111 C2
- Duthie Ct AB10 169 E5
- Duthie Pl
  - Aberdeen AB10 169 D5
  - Fraserburgh AB43 143 D3
- Duthie Rd AB41 61 E5
- Duthie's La AB43 5 A4
- Duthie Terr
  - Aberdeen AB10 169 D5
  - Inverallochy AB43 15 B8
- DYCE 158 C6
- Dyce Acad AB21 158 C6
- Dyce Ave AB21 157 E5
- Dyce Dr AB21 157 E8
- Dyce Ind Pk AB21 158 B4
- Dyce Prim Sch AB21 158 C6
- Dyce Sh Ctr AB21 158 D6
- Dyce Sta AB21 158 A6
- Dyce Swimming Pool AB21 158 C6
- DYKESIDE 33 C2
- Dykeside Way AB21 163 D6

E

- Earl's Court Gdns AB15 169 D8
- Earl's Ct 6 AB42 40 D1
- Earlspark Ave AB15 168 B3
- Earlspark Circ AB15 168 B3
- Earlspark Cres AB15 168 B3
- Earlspark Dr AB15 168 B2
- Earlspark Gdns AB15 168 B2
- Earlspark Rd AB15 168 B2
- Earlspark Way AB15 168 B3
- Earlswells Dr AB15 168 C2
- Earlswells Pl AB15 168 C2
- Earlswells Rd AB15 168 C2
- Earlswells View AB15 168 C2
- Earlswells Wlk AB15 168 C2
- Earn's Heugh Ave AB12 176 B7
- Earn's Heugh Circ AB12 176 B7
- Earn's Heugh Cres AB12 176 B6
- Earn's Heugh Pl AB12 176 B7
- Earnsheugh Rd AB12 180 F8
- Earns Heugh Rd AB12 176 B7
- Earnsheugh Terr AB12 180 F8
- Earns Heugh View AB12 176 B7
- Earns Heugh Way AB12 176 B6
- Earn's Heugh Wlk AB12 176 B7
- Eastbank DD9 188 C3
- Eastburn Rd AB51 155 C4
- East Church St AB45 1 F1
- East Craibstone St 4 AB11 190 A2
- East End DD10 187 D3
- EASTER BALMORAL 102 F1
- Easter Ct AB12 180 B4
- Easter Dr AB12 180 B4
- Easterfield Prim Sch AB53 32 B4
- Easterfield Rd AB53 145 E4
- Eastern Rd DD10 189 D3
- Easter Pl AB12 180 B4
- EASTERTOWN OF AUCHLEUCHRIES 51 F3
- East Glebe AB39 185 D6
- East Gn AB11 190 B3
- East Main Ave AB16 164 B3
- Eastmill Brae DD9 188 E2
- East Mill Rd DD9 188 E1
- East North St
  - Aberdeen AB24 190 B4
  - Peterhead AB42 147 F5
- East Park Rd AB51 155 C4
- Eastpark St AB54 148 E5
- Eastside Ave AB32 161 E3
- Eastside Dr AB32 161 E4
- Eastside Gdns AB21 157 F1
- Eastside Gn AB32 161 E4
- East St
  - Fraserburgh AB43 15 D6
  - Montrose DD10 135 C6
- Eastsyde Pl AB12 180 A5
- East Tullos Ind Est AB12 170 D5
- Eastwood Terr AB34 183 F5
- Eavern Pl 2 AB51 150 B3
- Ecclesgreig Rd DD10 134 C4
- ECHT 100 D4
- Echt Prim Sch AB32 100 E4
- Eday Cres AB15 164 A2
- Eday Ct AB15 163 E1
- Eday Dr AB15 163 F2
- Eday Gdns AB15 163 E1
- Eday Rd AB15 163 E2
- Eday Sq AB15 163 F2
- Eday Wlk AB15 163 F2
- Eddie Ave DD9 188 C5
- Edelweiss AB51 155 C3
- Eden Ct AB31 184 B4
- Eden Dr AB42 147 B5
- Eden Pl AB25 165 A2
- Edge Hill Cres AB23 90 F6
- Edge Hill Gdns AB23 90 F6
- Edgehill Rd AB15 164 C1
- Edgehill Terr AB15 164 C1
- Edgewood Pl AB34 183 B5
- Edindiach Rd AB55 28 D8
- Edingight Wynd 1 AB31 108 E8
- Edinmore Dr AB51 59 E3
- Edinview Gdns AB39 185 C6
- Edmond Gdns AB15 162 F2
- Edmondside 3 AB41 62 B2
- Edward Ave AB45 140 E4
- Edward Pl AB45 140 E4
- EDZELL 132 A7
- Edzell Prim Sch DD9 132 A7
- Eider Ct 2 AB42 147 B5
- Eider Rd AB41 77 F8
- Eigie Ave 4 AB23 91 D8
- Eigie Cl 5 AB23 91 D8
- Eigie Cres AB23 91 C8
- Eigie Pk AB23 91 D8
- Eigie Rd AB23 91 C8
- Eigie View AB23 91 D8
- Eigie Wlk AB23 91 D8
- Eilean Rise AB41 151 B3
- Eldenside AB14 172 C7
- Elder Pl AB25 164 F4
- Elizabeth Cl 13 AB51 87 D7
- Ellerslie Rd AB21 158 C1
- Ellis St AB42 147 E5
- ELLON 151 B4
- Ellon Acad AB41 151 D5
- Ellon Acad (annexe) AB41 151 D5
- Ellon Castle (remains of)* AB41 151 E5
- Ellon Prim Sch AB41 151 C5
- Ellon Rd AB23 160 B1
- Ellon Swimming Pool AB41 151 D5
- Elmbank Gdns AB51 150 B3
- Elmbank Rd AB24 165 B3
- Elmbank Terr AB24 165 A4
- Elmfield Ave AB24 165 B4
- Elmfield Pl AB24 165 A4
- Elmfield Terr AB24 165 B4
- Elm Pl
  - Aberdeen AB25 164 F3
  - 9 Balmedie AB23 91 C8
- Elms Rise AB31 184 C4
- Elms The AB45 148 E3
- Elm Way AB51 155 C5
- Elphin Hill AB41 151 C7
- Elphin St AB43 12 E6
- Elphinstone Ct 3 AB24 164 F7
- Elphinstone Rd
  - Aberdeen AB24 165 B5
  - Inverurie AB51 152 E4
- ELRICK 161 C1
- Elrick Circ AB22 159 E1
- Elrick Ctry Pk* AB21 157 A1
- Elrick Gdns AB21 153 D5
- Elrick Prim Sch AB32 161 D2
- Elsick Pl AB39 181 H4
- Endeavour Dr AB32 161 E1
- Endrick Pl AB15 164 B1
- Enterprise Dr AB32 161 D1
- Eriskay Dr AB16 163 E2
- Erroll Ct AB53 145 E4
- Erroll Pl
  - Aberdeen AB24 165 C3
  - Turriff AB53 145 D4
- Erroll Rd AB53 145 E4
- Erroll St
  - Aberdeen AB24 165 C3
  - Peterhead AB42 147 E5
- Errollston Rd AB42 53 B3
- Erskine Pl 3 DD10 189 D2
- Erskine St
  - Aberdeen AB24 165 A4
  - Montrose DD10 189 D2
- Esk Pk DD9 188 D2
- Esk Pl AB16 164 A4
- Esk Rd DD10 189 B1
- Eskview Terr DD10 189 C1
- Esplanade
  - Aberdeen AB24 165 D7
  - Fraserburgh AB43 143 E4
- Esplanade The AB42 147 F6
- Essie Circ AB42 26 E6
- Essie Rd AB54 55 C3
- Esslemont Ave AB25 165 A1
- Esslemont Circ AB41 151 A5
- Esslemont Cl AB41 151 A6
- Esslemont Dr AB51 152 C5
- Esslemont Sch AB41 62 E4
- Evan St AB39 185 D4
- Exchange La AB11 190 B3
- Exchange St AB11 190 B3
- Exchequer Row AB11 190 B3
- Exhibition Ave AB23 160 B1
- Exploration Dr AB23 160 B2

F

- Faburn Terr 3 AB31 98 A3
- Fairfield Pl AB51 155 C5
- Fairfield Rd DD10 187 D6
- Fairfield Way AB11 170 B6
- Fairies Knowe 5 AB21 163 D7
- Fair Isle Cres AB42 147 A5
- Fairlands AB51 152 A8
- FAIRLEY 162 E4
- Fairley Den AB21 163 D8
- Fairley Rd
  - Aberdeen AB15 163 A1
  - Kingswells AB15 162 F2
- Fairlie St AB16 164 C6
- Fairney Bsns Pk AB43 143 A7
- Fairview Ave AB22 159 B1
- Fairview Brae AB22 164 E8
- Fairview Circ AB22 159 A1
- Fairview Cres AB22 159 C1
- Fairview Dr AB22 164 E8
- Fairview Gdns
  - Aberdeen AB22 159 A1
  - Inverurie AB51 152 C6
- Fairview Gr 3 AB22 159 B1
- Fairview Grange AB22 164 C8
- Fairview Manor AB22 159 B1
- Fairview Par AB22 159 B1
- Fairview Pk 4 AB22 159 B1
- Fairview Pl AB22 159 B1
- Fairview Rd AB22 159 A1
- Fairview St AB22 159 B1
- Fairview Terr AB22 159 A1
- Fairview Way AB22 159 B1
- Fairview Wlk AB22 159 C1
- Fairview Wynd AB22 159 C1
- Fairway Ave AB51 152 C5
- Fairwinds Pl AB42 147 A5
- Faithlie St AB43 143 C6
- Falconer Pl AB51 152 C6
- Falkland Ave AB12 176 C7
- Fallow Rd AB32 161 B3
- Fara Cl AB15 163 E2
- Farburn Dr AB39 185 C5
- Farburn Ind Est AB21 158 C5
- Farburn Terr AB21 158 A6
- Fare Park Circ AB32 161 D4
- Fare Park Cres AB32 161 E4
- Fare Park Dr AB32 161 D3
- Fare Park Gdns AB32 161 D3
- Fare View 6 AB31 108 E8
- Farmers Hall 1 AB25 190 A4
- Farmers' La AB42 147 F5
- FARMTOWN 17 D2
- FARNELL 138 A2
- Farquhar Ave AB11 170 E6
- Farquhar Rd
  - Aberdeen AB11 170 E6
  - Huntly AB54 148 E5
- Farquhar St
  - Inverbervie DD10 187 D6
  - Laurencekirk AB30 186 D5
- Farrier La AB24 190 B4
- Farrochie Gdns AB39 185 B6
- Farrochie Pk AB39 185 B6
- Farrochie Rd AB39 185 B6
- Fassiefern Ave AB23 160 A3
- Fatson's Rd AB43 143 C6
- Faulds Cres
  - Aberdeen AB12 170 B4
  - Montrose DD10 189 E3
- Faulds Gate AB12 170 A4
- Faulds Rd DD10 189 E3
- Faulds Row AB12 170 B3
- Faulds Wynd AB12 170 B3
- Faulkner Ave AB30 186 C5
- Fechil Pl AB41 151 D4
- Fechnie Brae AB21 156 B6
- Fedderate Castle (remains of)* AB42 36 B8
- Ferguson Ave DD9 188 D4
- Ferguson Cres AB42 146 E5
- Ferguson Ct AB21 163 F8
- Ferguson St AB42 25 C1
- Fergus Pl AB21 158 B7
- Fern Dr AB12 180 B5
- Fernhill Dr AB16 164 A3
- Fernhill Pl AB16 164 A3
- Fernhill Rd AB16 163 F2
- Fernie Brae
  - Aberdeen AB11 170 D5
  - Banff AB45 3 B2
- Ferniela Cres AB15 164 A1
- Ferniela Pl AB15 164 A1
- Ferniela Prim Sch AB15 164 A1
- Ferniela Rd AB15 164 A1
- Fernie Pl AB43 143 C7
- Fernie Rd AB43 143 C6
- Fern Pl AB12 180 B5
- Ferrier Cres AB24 164 F6
- Ferrier Gdns AB24 164 F6
- FERRYDEN 189 D1
- Ferryden Prim Sch DD10 138 C3
- FERRYHILL 190 A1
- Ferryhill Gdns AB11 190 A1
- Ferryhill La AB11 190 A1
- Ferryhill Pl AB11 190 A1
- Ferryhill Prim Sch AB11 190 A1

Ferryhill Rd AB11....... 190 A1
Ferryhill Terr AB11...... 190 A1
Ferry Pl AB11............170 E8
Ferry Rd DD10.......... 189 D2
Ferry St DD10.......... 189 D2
Fetach Wlk AB21..........158 B7
FETTERANGUS..........25 D2
Fetterangus Prim Sch
AB42.......................25 C2
FETTERCAIRN.......... 128 A4
Fettercairn Prim Sch
AB30.................... 128 A4
Fetteresso Castle*
AB39.....................126 B8
Fetteresso Terr AB39.... 185 D5
Fetternear House & Bishop's
Pal (remains of)* AB51 .87 C8
Fettes Way 7 DD10.... 189 D7
Feugh View AB31....... 117 D7
Fife Brae 2 AB35........113 F6
Fifehill Pk AB21........ 158 C6
Fife St
Banff AB45..............140 F7
Macduff AB44.......... 141 D6
Turriff AB53............ 145 D4
Fife Terr AB44.......... 141 D6
Findhorn Dr 1 AB41.....151 E6
Findhorn Gdns AB41......151 E6
Findhorn Pl 1 AB16.....163 F3
Findlater Castle (remains
of)* AB45...................1 D5
Findlater Circ AB56........1 B4
Findlater Dr AB56..........1 B4
Findlater Pl 1 AB45.....140 E5
FINDON..................180 F8
Findon Ness AB12...... 176 C8
Findon Pl AB12..........180 F8
Findon Rd AB12.........180 E8
Finella View AB30....... 186 C7
Fingask Pl AB51..........150 B3
Finlayson St AB43...... 143 C7
Finnan Brae AB11........170 F7
FINNYGAUD..............19 A5
Fintray Rd AB15........ 169 A7
FINTRY......................21 D5
Fintry Prim Sch AB53.....21 D5
FINZEAN................ 116 C7
Finzean Prim Sch AB31 . 116 C8
Firbrae AB31............184 E6
Firholme Pl AB51....... 152 C5
Firmounth Rd AB34......105 F5
Firth Dr
Banff AB45...................3 C2
Macduff AB44.......... 141 C6
FISHERFORD..............46 B2
Fisherford Prim Sch
AB51.......................46 A2
Fishermoss Prim Sch
AB12.....................180 B5
Fish St AB11............ 190 C3
Fittick Pl AB12..........176 B7
Fleeman Way 15 AB42.....38 D6
Flory Gdns AB54........ 148 D3
Flourmill La AB10........190 B3
FLUSHING..................38 F5
Foinavon Cl AB21....... 158 A6
Fold The AB21..............75 C7
FOLLA RULE...............59 D8
Fonthill Ave 2 AB11.... 170 A7
Fonthill Ground E AB11 . 170 A6
Fonthill Ground W 1
AB11.................... 170 A7
Fonthill Rd AB11........ 190 A1
Fonthill Terr 1 AB11.... 190 A1
FOOTDEE.................165 E1
Forbesfield La AB15......169 E7
Forbesfield Rd AB15......169 E7
Forbes Pl AB21.............89 C7
Forbes Rd
8 Banff AB45...............8 F8
Fraserburgh AB43...........5 A4
Forbes St
Aberdeen AB25......... 165 A2
Rosehearty AB43........ 142 C7
FORBESTOWN.............81 C3
Forbes View 3 AB41......61 E6
FORDOUN.................129 F6
Fordoun Rd AB30....... 186 C7
FORDYCE.....................1 F1
Fordyce Ave AB53.........36 A6
Fordyce Castle* AB45......1 F1
Fordyce Joiner's Workshop &
Visitor Ctr* AB45..........1 E1
Fordyce Prim Sch AB45....1 F1
Fordyce Rd AB53...........36 A6
Fordyce St AB43.........142 B8
Fordyce Terr AB53.........36 A5
Forehill La 5 AB22.......159 F1
Forehill Prim Sch AB22 . 159 C4
Fore St DD10............ 135 C6
Forest Ave AB15.........169 E7
Forest Ave La AB15......169 E7
Forest Dr AB39......... 185 C4
Foresterhill Ct AB25......164 F2
Foresters Ave AB21..... 158 C3
Forester Terr AB41.......151 B5
Forest Pk AB39..........185 B4
Forest Rd
Aberdeen AB15......... 164 D1
Kintore AB51............155 B5
Forestside Dr AB31..... 184 D6
Forestside Rd AB31..... 184 D6
Forest Way AB54....... 148 C4
Forglen Cres AB53...... 145 C5
FORGUE....................31 D4
Forgue Prim Sch AB54....31 D3
Forgue Rd AB51...........47 A2
Forman Dr AB42........ 147 C4
Formartinedale AB41......76 C7
Formartine Rd AB24.... 165 A6
Formaston Pk AB34.......183 E5
Forrestal St DD9........ 132 D8
Forresterhill Rd AB16.... 164 C4
Forrest Pl 4 AB42....... 147 C4
Forrest Rd AB42........ 147 C4
Forrit Brae AB21........ 158 A1
Forsyth Dr
Aberdeen AB23............91 D8
Oldmeldrum AB51........150 B3
Forsyth Rd AB23............91 D8
Forties Field Cres AB41 . 151 A6
Forties Field Rd AB41... 151 A6
Forties Rd
Aberdeen AB21..........157 E5
Montrose DD10.......... 189 D8
Forties Rd Ind Est DD10. 189 D8
Fortree Rd AB41......... 151 C3
FORTRIE.....................32 C4
Forvie Ave AB22..........159 E2
Forvie Circ AB22..........159 E3
Forvie Cl AB22............159 E3
Forvie Cres AB22.........159 E2
Forvie La AB22...........159 E2
Forvie National Nature
Reserve* AB41..........64 B2
Forvie Path AB22........159 E2
Forvie Pl AB22............159 E2
Forvie Rd AB22...........159 E3
Forvie St AB22............159 E3
Forvie Terr AB22.........159 E2
Forvie Visitor's Ctr*
AB41.......................64 D3
Forvie Way AB22.........159 E2
Foudland Cres AB52.... 149 C5
Fountainhall Rd AB25....164 E1
Fountain Pk AB45.........140 E6
Fountain St AB45.........140 E6
Fountville Ct 1 AB24....164 F6
FOVERAN...................77 D6
Foveran Path AB22......159 E3
Foveran Prim Sch AB41...77 D7
Foveran Rise AB22...... 159 D3
Foveran St AB22........ 159 D3
Foveran Way AB22...... 159 D2
Fowler Ave AB16........ 164 C6
Fowlershill Gdns 6
AB22.....................165 B8
Fowlie's La 9 AB53..... 145 D4
Fowlsheugh Nature
Reserve* AB39.........126 F2
Frain Dr AB30.......... 186 C4
Frank Jack Ct AB42..... 147 C5
FRASERBURGH...........143 E5
Fraserburgh Acad AB43 . 143 C5
Fraserburgh FC AB43... 143 D6
Fraserburgh Her Ctr*
AB43................... 143 D7
Fraserburgh Hospl AB43 .143 B5
Fraserburgh Leisure Ctr
AB43................... 143 D5
Fraserburgh N Prim Sch
AB43................... 143 C7
Fraserburgh Swimming Pool
& Sports Ctr AB43..... 143 C5
Fraser Cres AB43.........15 B7
Fraser Ct
Huntly AB54............ 148 C4
Rosemount AB25.........165 B3
Fraser Dr AB32......... 161 C2
Fraserfield Gdns AB23 .. 160 A1
Fraser Pl
Aberdeen AB25..........165 B3
Alford AB33............ 154 D3
Inverallochy AB43.........15 C8
Kemnay AB51............87 D7
Fraser Rd
Aberdeen AB25......... 165 A3
Alford AB33............ 154 D3
Fraser's La 4 DD10..... 189 C4
Fraser St AB25...........165 B3
Frater Pl AB24.......... 190 C4
Frederick St
Aberdeen AB24..........190 B4
Inverallochy AB43.........15 C7
French Dr AB33......... 154 D4
Friarsfield Rd AB15......168 E3
Friendship Terr AB10.....169 F7
Frithside St AB43....... 143 D6
Froghall Ave AB24.......165 B3
Froghall Gdns AB24......165 B3
Froghall Pl AB24.........165 B4
Froghall Rd AB24........165 B3
Froghall Terr AB24.......165 B3
Froghall View AB24......165 B4
Fullerton Ct AB24....... 164 C7
Fulmar Ct AB39..........181 I5
Fungle Rd AB34......... 183 C1
Fyfe Pk AB51..............87 D7
FYVIE........................47 E5
Fyvie Castle* AB53.......47 E6
Fyvie Prim Sch AB53......47 E5

G

Gadie Cres AB16........ 164 A4
Gadle Braes AB42........147 E6
Gadwall Pl 1 AB42......147 B5
Gaelic La AB10......... 190 A3
Gairn Circ AB10......... 170 A6
Gairn Cres AB10........ 170 A6
Gairn Ct 2 AB10........ 170 A6
Gairn Mews AB10....... 170 A6
Gairn Rd AB10.......... 170 A6
Gairnshiel Ave AB16.....164 B4
Gairnshiel Pl AB16.......164 B4
Gairn Terr AB10......... 170 A6
Gairsay Dr AB15........ 164 A2
Gairsay Rd AB15.........163 F2
Gairsay Sq AB15..........163 F2
Gaitside Cres AB10..... 169 C3
Gaitside Dr AB10....... 169 C3
Gaitside Pl AB10........ 169 D3
Gaitside Rd AB10....... 169 C3
Gaitside Terr AB10..... 169 C3
Gallica Dr AB21......... 153 D6
Gallowgate AB25........190 B4
Gallowhill DD9......... 188 C4
Gallowhill Rd
Aboyne AB34............108 B6
Fraserburgh AB43........143 B6
GALLOWHILLS............26 F2
Gallowhill St 6 AB45....140 F6
Gallowhill Terr
Aberdeen AB21......... 158 D7
Fraserburgh AB43........143 B6
Gamrie Brae AB45..........3 C2
Gannochy Cres DD10.... 189 C6
Garbit Tap AB51........ 152 A8
Garden Cres AB45..........3 C2
Garden Ct AB51......... 152 C5
Garden Pl 4 AB42........53 B3
Garden Rd AB15........ 168 D3
Garden St AB44......... 141 D6
Gardens The AB51.......152 E5
Gardenston St AB30......186 B4
GARDENSTOWN.............3 B2
Gardiner's Brae AB45....140 F5
Gardner Cres AB12.......169 F2
Gardner Dr AB12....... 170 A2
Gardner Rd AB12....... 170 A2
Gardner Wlk AB12...... 170 A2
Gardyne St DD10........ 189 C6
Garioch Rd AB51........ 152 D6
GARIOCHSFORD...........46 B8
GARLOGIE................ 101 C4
Garmaddie La 1 AB21.. 158 C7
GARMOND...................22 C2
Garrison Rd DD10....... 189 D2
Garrol Pl 1 AB30....... 128 A4
GARTHDEE............... 169 D4
Garthdee Cres AB10......169 E4
Garthdee Dr AB10.......169 E4
Garthdee Gdns AB10.....169 E4
Garthdee Rd AB10...... 169 D3
Garthdee Terr AB10......169 E4
GARTLY.....................56 A7
Gartly Prim Sch AB54.....56 A6
Garvock Ave DD10...... 189 C8
Garvock Ct AB30........ 186 C5
Garvocklea Gdns AB30 .. 186 C4
Garvock Rd AB30....... 186 D5
Garvock St AB30........ 186 D5
Garvock Wynd AB11......165 E1
Gas St AB51............. 150 C4
Gatehouse La AB51.......152 E5
Gauchhill Rd AB51...... 155 A3
Gaval Ct 2 AB42..........25 C1
Gaval St AB42.............25 C2
Gaveny Pl AB44...........141 E5
Gaw St AB43..............143 B7
Gean Ct 5 AB23............91 C8
Gean Dr AB21...........156 B5
Geary Pl AB42.......... 147 A5
Gellatly Pl DD9........ 188 C4
Gellymill Rd AB44........141 B5
Gellymill St AB44....... 141 D7
George Garden Ave
AB42................... 147 C7
George Rd AB42........ 147 D6
George Sq AB51........ 152 D5
George St
Aberdeen AB25......... 190 A4
9 Banff AB45............140 F6
Fraserburgh AB43....... 143 C7
Huntly AB54............ 148 D4
Insch AB52.............. 149 D5
Macduff AB44.......... 141 D7
Montrose DD10......... 189 C3
George Terr AB39....... 185 D4
George V Ave AB54...... 148 C3
Gerrard St AB25........ 190 A4
Gerries Yd AB42..........147 F5
Gibson Pl 2 DD10....... 189 D2
Gight Castle* AB41.......48 E6
Gilbert Rd AB21...........163 F8
Gilcomston Stps AB25... 190 A4
Gilcomstoun Ct 13 AB10. 165 A1
Gilcomstoun Prim Sch 16
AB10.................... 165 A1
Gillahill Pl AB16.........164 B3
Gillahill Rd AB16.........164 B3
Gillespie Cres AB25......164 E4
Gillespie Pl AB25........164 F4
Gindera Rd DD10....... 189 D5
Girdleness Rd AB11......170 E5
Girdleness Terr AB11.... 170 D5
Girdlestone Pl AB11......170 E6
Gladstone Pl
Aberdeen AB15..........169 E8
Aberdeen AB24..........164 E7
Dyce AB21...............158 B6
Laurencekirk AB30...... 186 C5
Gladstone Rd
Huntly AB54.............148 E4
Peterhead AB42..........147 F6
Gladstone Terr
New Deer AB53............36 A5
Turriff AB53............ 145 C4
Glamourhaugh Ave
AB54.................... 148 D3
Glamourhaugh Cres 1
AB54.................... 148 D3
Glascairn Ave AB12......180 B6
Glashieburn Ave AB23....159 E3
Glashieburn Prim Sch
AB22.....................159 E3
Glashie Knowe 2 AB23 . 160 A1
Glashie Way 1 AB23.... 160 A1
Glass Prim Sch AB54......42 A6
Glebe Ct AB12.......... 180 C7
Glebefield 12 AB42........38 D6
Glebefield Terr AB42.... 147 C4
Glebeland AB32..........101 E6
Glebe Park Cres 9 AB56...1 B4
Glebe Pk
Aboyne AB34............108 B6
Banchory AB31......... 184 D4
Glebe Pk (Brechin City FC)
DD9..................... 188 C4
Glebe Rd AB51.......... 152 D5
Glebe Terr AB32.........101 E6
Glebe The
Brechin DD9............ 132 A7
2 Kemnay AB51..........87 D6
Glen Ave AB21...........158 B6
GLENBARRY................18 B5
GLENBERVIE.............124 F3
Glenbervie House*
AB39.....................124 F3
Glenbervie Prim Sch
AB39.....................125 B3
Glenbervie Rd
Aberdeen AB11......... 190 C1
Laurencekirk AB30.......124 F3
Stonehaven AB39.........125 B3
Glenbuchat Castle* AB36 .81 F6
Glenbuchty Pl AB43......143 B7
Glenclova Pl 1 DD10... 189 C5
Glen Ct AB39........... 185 C5
Glendale Rd AB42....... 147 C5
Glendee Terr AB15.......168 F3
Glen Dr AB21.............158 B6
Glendronach Distillery
Visitor Ctr* AB54.......31 E3
Gleneagles Ave AB22.....159 E2
Gleneagles Ct AB51..... 152 C5
Gleneagles Dr 2 AB22....159 E2
Gleneagles Gdns 1
AB22.....................159 E2
Glenesk Ave DD10...... 189 C5
Glenfarquhar Castle
(remains of)* AB30... 124 A3
Glenfarquhar Cresent
AB30.....................124 B2
Glenfarquhar Rd AB30...124 B2
Glen Gdns AB21..........158 B6
Glenhome Ave AB21.....158 B5
Glenhome Cres AB21.....158 B6
Glenhome Ct AB21...... 158 C6
Glenhome Gdns AB21....158 B5
Glenhome Terr AB21.....158 B5
Glenhome Wlk AB21.... 158 C6
Glenisla Rd DD10....... 189 C5
GLENKINDIE................82 D5
Glenlethnot Pl 2 DD10 . 189 C5
Glen O'Dee AB31....... 184 A6
Glenogil St DD10....... 189 C5
Glenprosen St 4 DD10.. 189 C5
Glen Rd
Aberdeen AB21..........158 B6
Banchory AB31............98 A3
Glenshee Rd 11 AB35....113 F6
Glentanar Cres AB21.... 158 C7
Glenugie Cres AB42..... 147 C1
Glenugie Dr AB42....... 147 C1
Glenugie Gdns AB42.....147 B1
Glenugie View AB42..... 147 C1
Glenury Cl AB39.........185 E7
Glenury Cotts AB39.......185 E6
Glenury Cres AB39.......185 E6
Glenury Rd AB39.........185 E6
GLENWOOD.................99 E6
Glenwood Pk AB51........99 E6
Golden Acre DD10...... 135 C6
Golden Knowes Ct AB45. 140 D6
Goldenknowes Rd AB45 . 140 D6
Golf Cres
Aboyne AB34............183 E6
Inverurie AB51...........152 B5
Golf Pk
1 Cruden Bay AB42.......53 A3
Inverurie AB51...........152 B5
Golf Pl
Aboyne AB34............183 E5
Inverurie AB51......... 152 C5
Golf Rd
Aberdeen AB15......... 168 C1
Aberdeen AB24......... 165 D4
Aboyne AB34............183 E5
Ballater AB35........... 182 D4
Ellon AB41.............. 151 C6
Peterhead AB42......... 147 C7
Golf Road Pk DD9...... 188 C5
Golf Terr AB52.......... 149 C5
Golfview Cres 3 AB51....87 C6
Golfview Rd AB15....... 168 C1
Golf Wlk AB51............152 B5
Goodhope Rd AB21..... 164 A8
Gordon Ave
Aberdeen AB23......... 160 A1
Boddam AB42..............40 D1
Inverurie AB51...........152 B7
Gordon Cl
11 Boddam AB42..........40 D1
Westhill AB32.......... 161 D3
Gordon Cres
Aboyne AB34........... 183 C4
Inverurie AB51......... 152 A7
Portsoy AB45........... 139 D6
Gordon Ct
1 Huntly AB54......... 148 D4
Gordon Ct *continued*
7 Newmacha AB21..... 153 C6
Gordondale Rd AB15.....164 E1
Gordon Dr AB51........ 152 A7
Gordon Gdns
5 Inverurie AB51........152 B7
Westhill AB32...........161 E3
Gordon Gr AB41........ 151 C5
Gordon Highlanders
Regimental Mus*
AB15................... 169 C7
Gordon La
Aberdeen AB10......... 169 D5
Fraserburgh AB43.........12 E5
Gordon Lennox Cres
AB23................... 160 A3
Gordon Pl
Aberdeen AB23..........159 F2
Alford AB33............ 154 C4
Ellon AB41............. 151 C5
Inverurie AB51..........152 B7
Rothienorman AB51........46 F2
Gordon Prim Sch AB54.. 148 D5
Gordon Rd
Aberdeen AB15......... 169 C5
Alford AB33............ 154 C4
Bridge of Don AB23...... 160 A1
Inverurie AB51..........152 B8
15 Kemnay AB51..........87 D7
Turriff AB53............ 145 C5
Gordon Schools The
AB54.....................148 E5
Gordon's Mills Cres
AB24.....................164 F7
Gordon's Mills Pl AB24.. 165 A7
Gordon's Mills Rd AB24..164 F7
Gordon St
Aberdeen AB11......... 190 A2
13 Boddam AB42..........40 D1
Fraserburgh AB43.........15 D6
Huntly AB54............ 148 D4
GORDONSTOWN
Banff........................18 C7
Inverurie....................46 F5
Gordon Terr
Aberdeen AB15......... 169 D5
Aberdeen AB21..........158 B6
Ellon AB41............. 151 C5
Insch AB52............. 149 D4
Inverurie AB51......... 152 A7
Peterhead AB42......... 147 D7
Gordon Way AB54....... 148 C3
Gordon Wlk AB51........152 B7
Gorse Circ AB12........ 180 A4
Gort Rd AB24........... 165 A7
Gort Terr AB24...........164 F7
Gourdie Pk AB23...........90 F6
GOURDON................ 187 D4
Gourdon Prim Sch DD10 187 D3
Goval Terr AB21........ 158 C6
Gowanbrae Rd AB15.....168 B1
GOWANHILL................15 B6
Gowans Rd 8 AB53..... 145 C5
GOWANWELL...............49 E8
Graeme Ave AB21........158 B6
Graham Cres DD10...... 189 C6
Graham St DD10........ 189 D5
Graham Terr AB33...... 154 C3
Grampian Ct
Alford AB33............ 154 C4
4 Balnagask AB11.......170 F6
Grampian Gdns AB21 .. 158 D6
Grampian Pl AB11...... 170 D6
Grampian Rd
Aberdeen AB11......... 190 C1
Alford AB33............ 154 C4
Grampian Terr AB31.......98 E1
Grampian Transport Mus*
AB33................... 154 D4
Grampian View DD10.... 138 D2
Granary Ct 2 AB51.......152 E3
Granary La AB43.............5 A4
Granary Pl 3 AB43..... 143 D6
Granary St AB54........ 148 D4
Grandholm Cres AB22.....164 F8
Grandholm Ct 5 AB24....164 F7
Grandholm Dr AB22......164 F8
Grandholm Gdns AB22 ...164 E7
Grandholm Gr AB22.......164 F7
Grandholm St AB24.......164 F6
Grandholm Way AB22.....164 E8
GRANGE CROSSROADS...17 A5
GRANGE GARDENS..... 147 C5
Grange Gdns AB42...... 147 C5
Grange Park Pl 1 AB42. .147 B4
Grange Park Rd AB42....147 B4
Grange Rd AB42..........147 B6
Granitehill Pl AB16..... 164 C4
Granitehill Rd AB16......164 B6
Grant Cl AB32.......... 161 D3
Grant Ct AB42............147 E5
Granton Gdns 3 AB10...169 F8
Granton Pl AB10..........169 F8
Grant Rd AB31.......... 184 C4
Grant St
Banff AB45...............140 F6
Buckie AB56.................1 A3
14 Cullen AB56.............1 B5
Granville Pl AB10.........169 E6
Grassic Gibbon Ctr*
AB30.....................130 E6
Grattan Pl AB43........ 143 D5
Gray Ct AB15........... 164 A1
Gray's La AB53......... 145 D5

Gray St
Aberdeen AB10 169 F6
Fraserburgh AB43 143 C6
Great Northern Rd AB24 164 D7
Great Southern Rd AB12 170 A4
Great Stuart St 2 AB42 147 F6
Great Western Rd AB10 169 E6
GREENBANK 143 A3
Greenbank Ave AB43 143 A3
Greenbank Bsns Ctr AB12 170 E4
Greenbank Cres AB12 170 E4
Greenbank Dr AB43 143 A3
Greenbank Pl
Aberdeen AB12 170 D4
Greenbank AB43 143 A3
Greenbank Rd
Aberdeen AB12 170 D4
Greenbank AB43 143 A3
Greenbrae Ave AB23 160 A3
Greenbrae Circ AB23 160 A4
Greenbrae Cres AB23 160 A4
Greenbrae Dr AB23 159 F4
Greenbrae Gardens N AB23 160 A4
Greenbrae Gardens S AB23 160 A4
Greenbrae Pl 3 AB42 147 B4
Greenbrae Prim Sch AB23 160 A3
Greenbraes Cres DD10 187 C4
Greenbraes Rd DD10 187 C3
Greenbrae Wlk AB23 160 A4
GREENBURN 158 A2
Greenburn Dr AB21 158 B1
Greenburn Pk AB21 158 C1
Greenburn Rd AB21 158 B1
Greenburn Road N AB21 158 A2
Greenburn Terr AB21 163 D8
Green Castle* AB30 128 C7
Greenfern Ave AB16 163 F3
Greenfern Pl AB16 164 A3
Greenfern Rd AB16 163 F3
Green Hadden St AB11 190 B3
Greenhill Rd AB42 147 F5
Greenhole Pl AB23 159 F2
Green Mdws AB51 86 F1
Greenmore Gdns AB24 164 F5
Green Rd AB54 148 D3
GREENS 35 A5
Greens Rd AB21 153 D5
Green St AB42 53 B2
Greens Terr AB21 153 D5
Greens The 2 AB42 146 D5
Greens Way AB21 153 D5
Green The
Aberdeen AB11 190 B3
Banff AB45 3 C2
Portlethen AB12 180 B5
Green Way AB51 150 C5
Greenwell Pl AB12 170 F5
Greenwell Rd AB12 170 E5
Gregness Gdns AB11 170 E5
Greig Ct AB25 190 A4
Greig Pl AB39 185 D4
Greyhope Rd AB11 171 A8
Greystone Pl
Alford AB33 154 C3
Stonehaven AB39 181 I4
Greystone Rd AB33 154 C3
Groats Rd AB15 168 E8
Grosvenor Pl 10 AB25 165 A1
Grosvenor Terr 1 AB25 165 A1
Grove Cres AB16 164 E3
Grove Rd AB51 87 D6
Grove Terr 2 AB31 108 E8
Guild St AB11 190 B2
Gulleymoss Gdns AB32 161 E4
Gullymoss Pl AB32 161 E4
Gullymoss View AB32 161 E4
Gurney St AB39 185 E5
Guthrie Pk DD9 188 D2
Guthrie's Haven AB45 140 E6

H

Hacklaw Pl 1 AB42 53 B3
Hadden St AB11 190 B3
Haddo Cres 2 AB41 77 F7
Haddo House* AB41 49 C1
Haddo La AB41 61 E6
Hall Cotts AB55 29 C3
Hall Cres AB44 141 E6
Hallfield Cres AB16 163 F2
Hallfield Rd AB16 163 F2
Hallforest Ave AB51 155 B5
Hallforest Cl AB51 155 B4
Hallforest Cres AB51 155 B4
Hallforest Dr AB51 155 B4
Hallgreen Castle* DD10 187 E6
Hallgreen Rd DD10 187 E6
Halliday Pl AB42 147 A6
HALLMOSS 39 E7
Hall Rd AB42 27 B2
Halsey Dr DD9 132 C8
Hamewith Ave AB39 185 C3
Hamewith Cotts AB33 154 C4
Hamilton Pl AB15 164 E1
Hamilton Rd AB43 143 B7
Hamilton Sch The AB15 169 D8
Hammerfield Ave AB10 169 E5
Hammerman Dr AB24 164 F5
Hammersmith Rd AB10 169 E6
Hanover Ct
Banchory AB31 184 E4
Inverbervie DD10 187 D7
Inverurie AB51 152 D4
2 Stonehaven AB39 185 E5
Hanover St Prim Sch AB11 190 C4
Hanover St
Aberdeen AB11 190 C4
Fraserburgh AB43 143 D7
Peterhead AB42 147 D5
Harbour La AB45 3 B3
Harbour Pl
Banff AB45 140 F6
Montrose DD10 135 C5
Harbour Rd
Banff AB45 3 B2
Fraserburgh AB43 143 D6
Harbour St
Banff AB45 3 B3
1 Boddam AB42 40 D1
Cruden Bay AB42 53 B2
Peterhead AB42 147 F4
Harbour View 7 DD10 187 D3
Harcourt Rd AB15 164 D2
Hardgate AB11 190 A2
Hardgate La AB10 170 A6
Hardie Ct AB54 144 D5
Hareburn Rd AB23 91 C5
Hareburn Terr AB23 91 B5
Harehill Rd AB22 159 E1
Hareness Circ AB12 170 E1
Hareness Pk AB12 170 E2
Hareness Pl AB14 171 A2
Hareness Rd AB12 170 D2
Harestones Stone Circ (remains of) The* AB53 32 C3
Harlaw Acad AB10 169 F8
Harlaw Bsns Ctr AB51 152 C8
Harlaw Dr AB51 152 D7
Harlaw Pl AB15 169 D7
Harlaw Rd
Aberdeen AB15 169 D7
Inverurie AB51 152 D7
Harlaw Terr AB15 169 D7
Harlaw Way AB51 152 C8
Harley Terr AB12 180 E5
Harris Dr AB24 165 A6
Harris Pl AB43 143 B4
Harris Way AB54 144 C4
Harrow Rd AB24 165 C6
Harthill Castle* AB52 72 E8
Harthill Pl AB16 163 E3
Harthills View AB51 155 B2
Hartington Rd AB10 169 F8
Harvest Hill AB32 161 B3
Harvey Pl AB45 140 E6
Hasman Terr 3 AB12 176 C6
HASSIEWELLS 46 A7
HATTON 52 D4
Hatton Castle (remains of)* AB53 33 F5
HATTONCROOK 75 C7
Hatton (Cruden) Prim Sch AB42 52 D4
Hatton Ct 2 AB21 89 B7
Hatton Farm Gdns 2 AB42 52 D4
Hatton Farm Rd AB42 52 C4
HATTON OF FINTRAY 89 C7
Hatton of Fintray Sch AB21 89 C7
Hatton Rd AB53 145 E4
Haudagain Ret Pk AB24 164 C7
HAUGH OF GLASS 42 A6
Haugh Path AB43 12 D6
Haughton Ctry Pk* AB33 154 D5
Haughton Pl AB33 154 C4
Haulkerton Cres AB30 186 C6
Hawthorn Ave AB41 61 F1
Hawthorn Cres
Aberdeen AB16 164 B4
Ballater AB35 182 E4
6 Mintlaw AB42 146 D5
Hawthorn Ct 3 AB35 182 E4
Hawthorne Way AB51 155 B3
Hawthorn Gr AB35 182 E4
Hawthorn Pl AB35 182 E4
Hawthorn Rd 5 AB42 147 B5
Hawthorn Terr AB24 165 D3
Hay Cres AB42 147 D6
Hayfield Cres AB24 164 E4
Hayfield Pl
Aberdeen AB24 164 E5
2 Peterhead AB42 147 A6
Hays Ct AB51 152 E4
Hay's Ct AB33 154 D3
Hay St AB42 53 B3
Hay's Way AB32 161 D3
Hay's Wlk AB33 154 D3
HAYTON 164 F6
Hayton Rd AB24 164 F6
Haywood Dr AB45 139 D6
Hazel Dr AB32 161 D2
Hazledene Rd AB15 168 E7
HAZLEHEAD 168 E7
Hazlehead Acad AB15 168 E8
Hazlehead Ave AB15 168 F8
Hazlehead Cres AB15 168 F8
Hazlehead Gdns AB15 168 F8
Hazlehead Pl AB15 168 F8
Hazlehead Prim Sch AB15 169 A8
Hazlehead Rd AB15 168 F8
Hazlehead Swimming Pool AB15 168 E8
Hazlehead Terr AB15 168 F8
Hazlewood Sch AB15 169 A8
Headland Ct
Aberdeen AB10 169 F4
Stonehaven AB39 181 I4
Heath Dr AB42 147 B3
Heather Pl AB12 180 C6
Heathfield Pk AB39 181 H4
Heath Row AB31 184 C5
HEATHRYFOLD 164 A6
Heathryfold Circ AB16 164 A6
Heathryfold Cl AB16 164 B6
Heathryfold Dr AB16 164 A6
Heathryfold Pl AB16 164 A6
Helen Row AB39 185 F6
Henderson Circ AB42 147 A5
Henderson Cres AB51 155 B5
Henderson Dr
Kintore AB51 155 B5
Westhill AB32 161 C2
Henderson Pk
Kintore AB51 155 B5
Peterhead AB42 147 A5
Henderson Rd AB43 143 B5
Henry La 3 AB42 36 E6
Henry Pl AB44 141 D5
Herd Cres DD10 135 C6
Hermitage Ave AB24 165 B5
Hermit Seat AB52 71 E7
Heron Cres AB41 151 C3
Heron Rd 5 AB51 87 C7
Hetherwick Rd AB12 170 A2
Hexagon The AB43 143 D6
Highfield AB39 185 B7
Highfield Ave AB31 184 C5
Highfield Ct 4 AB39 185 C7
Highfield Gdns 3 AB39 185 C7
Highfield Way AB39 185 C7
Highfield Wlk AB53 145 D5
Highgate Gdns AB11 170 C6
High Gn AB45 3 C2
Highland Her Ctr* AB35 113 E6
High Pen La DD9 132 B7
High Shore AB45 141 A6
High St
Aberdeen AB24 165 B5
Auchenblae AB30 124 B1
Banchory AB31 184 B4
Banff AB45 140 F5
Brechin DD9 188 C3
Cuminestown AB53 22 C1
Edzell DD9 132 B7
Fraserburgh AB43 143 D7
Insch AB52 149 D5
Inverbervie DD10 187 E7
Inverurie AB51 152 E4
Kemnay AB51 87 D7
Laurencekirk AB30 186 D5
Macduff AB44 141 D6
Montrose DD10 189 C3
New Aberdour AB43 12 E5
New Deer AB53 36 A6
New Pitsligo AB43 23 E6
Peterhead AB42 147 D7
Pittulie AB43 4 F4
St Combs AB43 15 D5
Stonehaven AB39 185 F4
Strichen AB43 24 E6
Turriff AB53 145 D4
Highview Gr DD10 134 C3
Highwood AB31 184 C5
Hillbrae Way AB21 153 E4
Hillcrest AB43 143 B5
Hillcrest Pl AB16 164 C5
Hillcrest Rd AB53 145 C5
Hillcroft Rd AB31 184 B5
Hillfoot Terr DD10 187 D3
Hillhead Dr AB41 151 C3
HILLHEAD OF MOUNTBLAIRY 20 C4
Hillhead Pl AB41 151 D4
Hillhead Rd
Aberdeen AB15 167 F3
Crimond AB43 26 E7
Ellon AB41 151 D3
Stonehaven AB39 181 I4
Hillhead Terr AB24 165 C4
Hillocks Way AB21 163 E7
Hill of Banchory E AB31 110 B3
Hill of Banchory Prim Sch AB31 184 E5
Hill of Banchory S AB31 184 E5
Hill of Banchory W AB31 184 D6
HILL OF RUBISLAW 169 C7
Hill of Rubislaw AB15 169 C8
Hill Pl DD10 189 C2
Hill Rd DD10 138 C8
HILLSIDE 138 C8
Hillside
New Pitsligo AB43 23 E6
Pitmedden AB41 62 A2
HILLSIDE 180 C8
Hillside Cres
Aberdeen AB14 172 D7
Westhill AB32 161 E4
Hillside Dr 8 AB35 113 F6
Hillside Gdns AB32 161 E4
Hillside Mews AB12 180 C8
Hillside Pl AB14 172 D7
Hillside Rd
Aberdeen AB14 172 D6
Westhill AB32 161 E4
Hillside Terr AB12 180 C7
Hillside View AB32 161 E4
Hill St
Aberdeen AB25 190 A4
Cruden Bay AB42 53 B2
6 Montrose DD10 189 C2
Hill St *continued*
Peterhead AB42 53 B4
Portsoy AB45 139 D7
Rosehearty AB43 142 C7
Hillswick Rd 3 AB16 163 E3
Hillswick Wlk 1 AB16 163 E3
Hilltop Ave
Aberdeen AB15 168 D3
Westhill AB32 161 D5
Hilltop Cres AB32 161 D4
Hilltop Dr AB32 161 D4
Hilltop Gdns AB32 161 E4
Hilltop Rd AB15 168 D3
Hillview
Aberchirder AB54 144 D5
8 Strichen AB43 24 E6
Hillview Ave AB32 161 E4
Hillview Cres
Aberdeen AB15 168 C3
Montrose DD10 189 D1
Rosehearty AB43 142 C7
Hillview Dr AB15 168 D3
Hillview Gdns DD10 187 D6
Hillview Rd
Aberdeen AB12 170 D4
Banchory AB31 184 C5
Cults AB15 168 D2
Laurencekirk AB30 124 B2
Peterculter AB14 172 D6
Westhill AB32 161 E4
Hillview Terr AB15 168 D2
Hillylands Rd AB16 164 A2
HILTON 164 D6
Hilton Ave AB24 164 D5
Hilton Circ AB24 164 E4
Hilton Ct AB24 164 D5
Hilton Dr AB24 164 E5
Hilton Hts AB24 164 E5
Hilton Pl AB24 164 F5
Hilton Rd AB24 164 E5
Hilton St AB24 164 F4
Hilton Terr AB24 164 E5
Hilton Wlk AB24 164 E5
His Majestys Theatre* AB25 190 A3
Hobshill Pl 5 AB42 52 C4
Holburn Pl AB10 170 A6
Holburn Rd AB10 169 F7
Holburn St AB10 169 F4
Holland Pl AB25 165 A3
Holland St AB25 165 A3
Hollybank Cres AB31 184 B5
Hollybank Pl AB10 170 A7
Holly Dr AB39 185 C4
Holly Tree Rd AB31 184 D6
Holmdale Pl 2 AB53 145 C5
Holmhead Pl 16 AB21 163 D7
Holy Family RC Prim Sch AB15 164 B1
Homelea AB32 161 B2
Hopecroft Ave AB21 158 B1
Hopecroft Dr AB21 158 B1
Hopecroft Terr AB21 158 B1
Hopeman Cl AB41 151 D6
Hopeman Dr AB41 151 D6
Hope St AB42 147 D6
Hopetoun Ave AB21 163 C8
Hopetoun Cres AB21 163 C8
Hopetoun Ct AB21 163 D8
Hopetoun Dr AB21 163 D8
Hopetoun Gn AB21 163 D8
Hopetoun Grange AB21 158 A1
Hopetoun Rd AB21 163 C8
Hopetoun Terr AB21 163 C8
Horn's Brae 1 AB44 141 C6
Hosefield Ave AB15 164 E2
Hosefield Rd AB15 164 E2
Hospital Brae AB43 24 E6
Hospital Rd
Ellon AB41 151 C6
Hillside DD10 138 C8
Houghton Dr 2 DD10 138 D8
House of Dun* DD10 137 E6
House of Monymusk* AB51 86 F6
House of Schivas* AB41 49 F3
Howatt Pk AB43 5 A4
Howburn Ct AB11 170 A7
Howburn Pl AB10 170 A7
Howe Moss Ave AB21 157 D6
Howe Moss Cres AB21 157 D6
Howe Moss Dr AB21 157 D5
Howe Moss Pl AB21 157 D6
Howe Moss Terr AB21 157 D7
HOWE OF TEUCHAR 34 D6
Howes Cres AB16 164 A6
Howes Dr AB16 164 A6
Howes Pl 4 AB16 164 A6
Howes Rd AB16 163 F5
Howes View AB21 163 E7
Howie La AB14 172 E5
Howieslap AB51 155 D4
Howieson Pl AB51 152 B8
Hudson St AB39 185 E5
Hume St DD10 189 C3
Hummel Craig 4 AB51 152 A8
Hunter Ave AB39 185 C6
Hunter Dr AB39 185 C6
Hunter Pl
Aberdeen AB24 165 D3
Stonehaven AB39 185 C6
Hunter's La AB43 143 D7
Hunters Rise AB41 62 B1
HUNTLY 148 B5
Huntly Castle* AB54 148 E6
Huntly Ind Est AB54 148 C4
Huntly Mews AB34 183 E5
Huntly Nordic & Outdoor Ctr* AB54 148 D6
Huntly Pl AB34 183 C4
Huntly Rd
Aberchirder AB54 144 C4
Aboyne AB34 183 C4
Huntly St AB10 190 A3
Huntly Sta AB54 148 E4
Huntly Swimming Pool AB54 148 E5
Hutcheon Ct AB25 165 B3
Hutcheon Gdns AB23 165 C8
Hutcheon Low Dr AB21 164 C7
Hutcheon Low Pl AB21 164 C7
Hutcheon St
Aberdeen AB25 190 A4
5 Macduff AB44 141 C6
Hutchison Terr AB10 169 D5
Hutton Pl AB16 164 A5
Hutton Rd AB21 157 E6
Huxterstone Ct 3 AB15 162 F2
Huxterstone Dr AB15 162 F2
Huxterstone Pl 4 AB15 162 F2
Huxterstone Terr AB15 162 F2
Hythe The 4 AB44 141 C6
HYTHIE 25 F2

I

Ilderton Pl 2 AB31 184 D4
Imperial Pl 4 AB11 190 B3
INCHBARE 132 B4
Inchbrae Dr AB10 169 D3
Inchbrae Rd AB10 169 D3
Inchbrae Terr AB10 169 C3
Inchcumine Dr AB42 27 B3
Inchdrewer Castle (remains of)* AB45 8 F3
Inchgarth Mews AB15 169 A2
Inchgarth Rd AB15 169 A3
Inchgower Terr AB42 27 B3
Inchley Pl 17 AB31 108 E8
Inchley Terr 4 AB31 108 E8
Inchmarlo Rd AB31 184 A4
Inchmore Gdns AB42 53 F8
Inch Rd AB41 65 G4
Inch Terr DD10 189 B1
India La DD10 189 D3
India St DD10 189 D3
Infirmary Rd DD9 188 D3
Infirmary St DD9 188 D3
Ingleside 6 AB41 62 B2
Ingram Wlk AB12 170 C2
Inkbottle Way 1 AB39 185 C7
Inkbottle Wlk 2 AB39 185 C7
Inn Brae AB42 38 D6
INSCH 149 C4
Insch Bsns Pk AB52 149 D7
Insch Prim Sch AB52 149 D5
Insch Sta AB52 149 C4
Insch War Meml Hospl AB52 149 D4
Institute St AB45 139 E7
Institution St AB44 141 C7
Institution Terr AB45 140 F5
International Sch of Aberdeen AB13 173 A7
Intown Rd AB23 160 B2
INVER 115 B8
INVERALLOCHY 15 C8
Inverallochy Castle (remains of)* AB43 15 B5
Inverallochy Prim Sch AB43 15 C7
Inverarity Cres 5 DD10 138 C8
INVERBERVIE 187 E6
Inverbervie L Ctr DD10 187 E7
INVERBOYNDIE 140 B6
Inverboyndie Ind Est AB45 140 B6
Invercauld Gdns AB16 164 B4
Invercauld Pl AB16 164 B4
Invercauld Rd
Aberdeen AB16 164 B4
Ballater AB35 182 C4
3 Braemar AB35 113 F6
Inverdon Ct AB24 165 D7
INVEREY 112 E4
Inverey Castle (remains of)* AB35 112 E4
Invergarry Pk DD10 134 D4
Inveriscandye Rd DD9 132 B7
INVERKEITHNY 31 F6
Invermarkie Wynd 3 AB31 98 E1
INVERNETTIE 147 C2
Invernettie Rd AB42 147 C4
Inverquhomery Rd 4 AB42 38 D6
INVERUGIE 39 E7
Inverugie Castle (remains of)* AB42 39 E7
Inverugie Cotts AB42 147 A6
Inverugie Ct AB42 147 A6
Inverugie Rd AB42 147 A6
Inverugie Wynd 2 AB41 151 F5
INVERURIE 152 B4
Inverurie Acad AB51 152 D5
Inverurie Hospl AB51 152 D4
Inverurie Rd AB21 158 A1
Inverurie St AB30 124 B1
Inverurie Sta AB51 152 E6
Inverurie Swimming Ctr AB51 152 D5
INVERYTHAN 47 D8
Iona Ave AB42 147 B7
Ironfield La AB39 185 F5

Irvine Pk 3 AB21 153 C6
Irvine Pl
Aberdeen AB10 169 F6
3 Fraserburgh AB43 26 C7
Inverurie AB51 152 B8
Irvine Way AB51 152 B8
Isla Pl AB16 163 F3
Islay Ct AB41 151 B3
Ivanhoe Pl AB10 169 C4
Ivanhoe Rd AB10 169 C3
Ivanhoe Wlk AB10 169 C4
Ives Rd AB42 147 E6
Ivy Pl AB39 185 C4

J

Jack's Brae AB25 165 A1
Jackson St AB51 152 D5
Jackson Terr AB24 165 C3
Jail La AB45 140 F6
Jake Forbes Cl AB45 148 E4
Jamaica St
Aberdeen AB25 165 A3
Peterhead AB42 147 F5
James Mitchell Pl AB42 146 E5
James Presly Ct AB54 148 D3
James St
Aberdeen AB11 190 C3
Macduff AB44 141 D6
3 Oldmeldrum AB51 150 C3
Peterhead AB42 147 F5
James Stott Rd AB42 147 A7
Jarvis Ct AB43 143 A4
Jarvis Pl AB43 143 A4
Jasmine Terr AB24 190 B4
Jasmine Way AB24 190 B4
Jenner Pl DD9 188 C5
Jesmond Ave AB22 159 D2
Jesmond Avenue N
AB22 159 D2
Jesmond Circ AB22 159 C4
Jesmond Ctr The AB22 159 D3
Jesmond Dr AB22 159 D5
Jesmond Gdns AB22 159 C4
Jesmond Gr AB22 159 C4
Jesmond Rd AB22 159 E3
Jesmond Sq AB22 159 D2
Jesmond Square N 2
AB22 159 D1
Jesmond Square S 3
AB22 159 D1
John Arthur Ct AB15 163 A1
John Gray Dr 14 AB51 87 D7
John Morrison Cres 1
AB42 36 E6
John Park Pl AB22 164 E8
Johns Brae AB44 141 D6
JOHNSHAVEN 135 D6
Johnshaven Prim Sch
DD10 135 B5
Johnson Gardens E
AB14 172 C7
Johnson Gardens N
AB14 172 D7
Johnson Gardens W
AB14 172 D7
John Sorrie Dr AB51 152 A6
John St
Aberdeen AB25 190 A4
Dyce AB21 158 B5
Montrose DD10 189 D4
2 Stonehaven AB39 185 F3
Johnston Gardens W
AB14 172 D7
Johnston Pk AB53 145 D5
Johnston Rd AB30 186 C4
Johnston St AB30 186 D5
Jopp's La AB25 190 A4
Joss Ct AB23 165 D8
Jubilee Cres AB45 8 F8
Jubilee Hospl AB54 148 D3
Judy's La 3 AB56 1 B4
Juniper Pl AB12 180 A5
Jura Pl AB16 163 E2
Justice Mill Brae AB11 170 A8
Justice Mill La 2 AB11 190 A2
Justice Port AB24 190 C4
Justice St AB10 190 C3
Jute St AB24 165 B3

K

KAIMHILL 169 E3
Kaimhill Circ AB10 169 E4
Kaimhill Gdns AB10 169 E4
Kaimhill Prim Sch AB10 169 E4
Kaimhill Rd AB10 169 E4
Katrine Terr AB41 151 B6
KEIG 71 D2
Keig Prim Sch AB33 71 C2
Keil Brae AB51 150 D3
KEILHILL 9 F2
Keir Circ AB32 161 C3
Keir Hts AB23 91 C8
Keir Rise AB23 91 C8
Keith Ave AB23 91 C8
Keith Cres 12 AB23 91 C8
Keith Gdns
Blackburn AB21 156 B6
1 Fraserburgh AB43 26 D7
Keith Hall* AB51 74 C4
Keithhall Prim Sch AB51 74 D3
Keithhall Rd AB51 152 F3
KEITH INCH 147 F4
Keithleigh Gdns AB41 62 A2
Keithmuir Gdns AB31 111 C5
Keithmuir La AB31 111 D5
Keithmuir Rd AB31 111 D5
Keith Pl 1 AB39 185 F4
Keith St AB42 147 F4
Kellands Ave AB51 152 D5
Kellands Prim Sch AB51 152 D5
Kellands Rd AB51 152 C5
Kellands Rise AB51 152 C5
Kembhill Pk AB51 87 C7
KEMNAY 87 D7
Kemnay Acad AB51 87 D7
Kemnay House* AB51 87 D6
Kemnay Pl AB15 169 B7
Kemnay Prim Sch AB51 87 D6
Kemnay Rd AB51 152 E2
Kemp's La 8 AB53 145 D4
Kemp St AB16 164 C6
Kencast Circ AB14 166 D1
Kencast Row AB14 166 D1
Kendal Rd AB51 87 D7
Kenfield Cres AB15 169 C6
Kenfield Pl AB15 169 C6
Kennedy Ave DD10 189 C7
Kennedy Ct AB54 148 D4
Kennedy Pl AB43 143 C3
Kennedy Rd AB43 143 C4
Kennerty Ct AB14 172 D6
Kennerty Mills Rd AB14 172 D6
Kennerty Pk AB14 172 D5
Kennerty Rd AB14 172 C5
KENNETHMONT 56 B3
Kennethmont Prim Sch
AB54 56 C4
Kent Gdns AB43 143 B6
Kepplehills Dr AB21 163 C8
Kepplehills Rd AB21 163 D7
Kepplestone Ave AB15 169 C7
Kepplestone Gdns AB15 169 C7
Kerloch Cres
Banchory AB31 184 E5
8 Torphins AB31 108 E8
Kerloch Gdns AB11 170 D5
Kerloch Pl AB11 170 C5
Kessock Pl AB43 143 D4
Kessock Rd AB43 143 D4
Kessock Rd Ind Est
AB43 143 D4
Kestrel Rd 10 AB41 77 F8
Kettlehills Cres AB16 164 B5
Kettlehills La AB16 164 B5
Kettlehills Rd AB16 164 A5
Kettock Gdns AB22 159 D1
KIDDSHILL 36 F3
Kidd St 1 AB10 190 A3
KILDRUMMY 83 A8
Kildrummy Castle* AB33 82 F7
Kildrummy Rd
Aberdeen AB15 169 A7
Ellon AB41 151 E5
Kilmarnock Dr 5 AB42 53 A3
Kilsyth Rd AB12 170 C3
Kimberley Ct 5 AB51 47 A2
Kinaldie Cres AB15 169 A7
Kincardine Castle (remains
of)* AB30 128 C6
Kincardine Com Hospl
AB39 185 C5
KINCARDINE O'NEIL 108 B6
Kincardine O'Neil Prim Sch
AB34 108 B6
Kincardine Rd AB31 108 E8
Kincardine St DD10 189 D4
KINCORTH 170 B3
Kincorth Acad AB12 170 B3
Kincorth Circ AB12 170 A3
Kincorth Cres AB12 170 B4
Kincorth Land AB12 170 B3
Kincorth Pl AB12 170 A4
Kincorth Sports Ctr
AB12 170 B4
Kincorth Swimming Pool
AB12 170 B3
Kindrochit Castle (remains
of)* AB35 113 F5
Kindrochit Dr 10 AB35 113 F6
Kinellar Prim Sch AB21 156 B6
King David Dr DD10 187 D5
KING EDWARD 20 F8
King Edward Ct AB44 141 E5
King Edward Prim Sch
AB45 20 F8
King Edward St AB43 143 C6
Kingfisher Cnr AB51 152 E7
Kingfisher Pl AB51 152 E7
Kinghorn Pl DD9 188 C5
King Roberts Pl AB23 160 B1
King Roberts Way AB23 160 B1
Kingscliff Sporting Lodge*
AB41 49 A6
Kings Coll Con & Visitor
Ctr* AB24 165 C5
King's Cross Ave AB15 169 B8
King's Cross Rd AB15 169 B8
King's Cross Terr AB15 169 B8
King's Ct 2 AB24 164 F7
Kingseat Rd AB21 153 D6
Kingsfield Pl 2 AB51 155 C5
Kingsfield Rd
Inverurie AB51 155 C5
Kintore AB51 88 F5
Kingsford Rd
Aberdeen AB16 163 F3
Alford AB33 154 D3
Kingsford Sch AB16 163 F3
Kingsgate 6 AB39 185 F3
King's Gate
Aberdeen AB15 169 A8
1 Rosemount AB15 164 E1
Kingshill Ave AB15 164 C1
Kingshill Rd AB15 164 C1
Kingshill Terr AB15 164 C1
Kingsland Pl AB25 190 A4
King's Rd AB39 185 D4
Kings's Cres AB24 165 C3
King St
Aberdeen AB10 190 B3
Aberdeen AB24 164 E6
Huntly AB54 148 D4
Inverbervie DD10 187 D7
Inverurie AB51 152 D7
3 Montrose DD10 189 D1
10 Oldmeldrum AB51 150 C3
Peterhead AB42 147 D5
Rosehearty AB43 142 C8
Stonehaven AB39 185 F4
Kingston Gdns AB41 151 E6
Kingswalk AB21 163 E8
Kingsway AB21 163 E8
Kingswell La 7 AB45 140 F6
Kingswell Pk AB45 140 F6
KINGSWELLS 162 F3
Kingswells Ave AB15 162 F3
Kingswells Cres AB15 162 F5
Kingswells Dr AB15 162 E3
Kingswells Prim Sch
AB15 162 F3
Kingswells View AB32 161 D4
Kingswood Ave AB15 162 F3
Kingswood Cres AB15 162 F3
Kingswood Dr AB15 162 F3
Kingswood Gdns AB15 162 F3
Kingswood Gr 3 AB15 162 F3
Kingswood Mews AB15 162 E3
Kingswood Path 1 AB15 162 F3
Kingswood Rd AB15 162 F3
Kingswood Wlk 2 AB15 162 F3
Kininmonth Prim Sch
AB42 25 D3
Kinkell Rd AB15 169 A7
Kinloch Rd AB42 27 B2
Kinmohr Rise AB21 156 A7
Kinmonth Rd AB39 125 B3
KINMUCK 75 A2
KINMUNDY 153 E2
Kinmundy Ave AB32 161 E3
Kinmundy Dr
Peterhead AB42 147 B5
Westhill AB32 161 E3
Kinmundy Gdns
Peterhead AB42 147 A4
Westhill AB32 161 E3
Kinmundy Gn AB32 161 E3
Kinmundy Rd
Newmachar AB21 153 D5
Peterhead AB42 147 A4
Kinmundy Wlk AB42 147 B5
Kinnaber Rd DD10 138 D8
Kinnaird Pl
2 Aberdeen AB24 165 A6
2 Brechin DD9 188 D2
Kinnaird Rd AB43 143 C7
Kinnairdy Castle* AB54 31 D8
Kinnairdy Cl 19 AB31 108 E8
Kinnairdy Terr 20 AB31 108 E8
Kinnear La AB30 186 C4
Kinnear Sq AB30 186 C4
KINNEFF 131 D5
Kinneff Prim Sch DD10 131 D7
Kinneskie La AB31 184 B4
Kinneskie Rd AB31 184 B4
Kinnies La 1 AB54 144 C4
Kinord Circ 2 AB22 165 B8
Kinord Dr AB34 183 A5
Kinord Rd AB41 151 B7
KINTORE 155 B4
Kintore Bsns Pk AB51 155 A8
Kintore Gdns AB25 165 A2
Kintore Pl 6 AB25 165 A2
Kintore Prim Sch AB51 155 B4
Kintore St AB30 124 B1
Kintore Terr AB51 152 D6
Kirkbrae 1 AB41 61 E6
Kirk Brae
Aberdeen AB15 168 E3
Fraserburgh AB43 143 D7
Oldmeldrum AB51 150 D3
Kirkbrae Ave AB15 168 D3
Kirk Brae Ct AB15 168 E3
Kirkbrae Dr AB15 168 D3
Kirk Brae Mews AB15 168 E3
Kirkbrae Terr AB53 36 A5
Kirkbrae View AB15 168 D3
Kirkburn AB30 186 D6
Kirk Burn DD10 187 E6
Kirkburn Dr AB42 147 C5
Kirk Crescent N AB15 168 E3
Kirk Crescent S AB15 168 E3
Kirk Dr AB15 168 E3
Kirkgate AB42 37 D6
KIRKHILL 138 A7
Kirkhill AB53 22 D4
Kirkhill Dr
Aberdeen AB21 157 E7
Oldmeldrum AB51 150 D3
Kirkhill Gdns AB23 91 A6
Kirkhill Ind Est AB21 157 D7
Kirkhill Pl
Aberdeen AB11 170 E5
Dyce AB21 157 E5
Kirkhill Prim Sch AB12 170 C3
Kirkhill Rd
Aberdeen AB11 170 D5
Dyce AB21 157 E6
Potterton AB23 91 A6
Kirkhill View AB21 156 B6
Kirkhill Way 1 AB23 91 A6
Kirk La
Ellon AB41 151 C4
3 Macduff AB44 141 C6
4 Tarves AB41 61 E6
Kirkland 3 AB51 87 D6
Kirklands 1 AB41 49 B4
Kirkland Terr AB51 152 E4
Kirk Pk AB21 153 C5
Kirk Pl AB15 168 D3
Kirk Rd AB39 185 D5
Kirk St
Oldmeldrum AB51 150 C3
Peterhead AB42 147 D5
Kirk Terr AB15 168 D3
KIRKTON 72 A8
Kirkton Ave
Aberdeen AB21 158 A8
Westhill AB32 161 B3
Kirkton Cres AB43 143 D4
Kirkton Dr AB21 157 F8
Kirkton Gdns AB32 161 B3
Kirktonhill Pl AB30 133 D4
Kirktonhill Rd AB30 133 D4
KIRKTON OF
AUCHTERLESS 46 F8
KIRKTON OF BOURTIE 74 E7
KIRKTON OF CRAIG 138 C2
KIRKTON OF
CULSALMOND 58 B7
KIRKTON OF DURRIS 111 B3
KIRKTON OF
GLENBUCHAT 81 D6
KIRKTON OF LOGIE
BUCHAN 63 E4
KIRKTON OF
MARYCULTER 173 B3
KIRKTON OF OYNE 72 E8
KIRKTON OF RAYNE 58 F5
KIRKTON OF SKENE 101 E7
KIRKTON OF TOUGH 85 D3
Kirkton Pk
Chapel of Garioch AB51 73 B7
Daviot AB51 59 E2
Kirkton Rd
Fraserburgh AB43 143 C3
Stonehaven AB39 185 B5
Westhill AB32 161 B3
KIRKTOWN
Peterhead 147 D5
St Fergus 27 A2
Kirktown Brae AB43 143 D2
KIRKTOWN OF ALVAH 9 B3
KIRKTOWN OF DESKFORD 6 C4
KIRKTOWN OF
FETTERESSO 185 A4
Kirk View AB31 98 A3
Kirkwall Ave 2 AB16 163 E3
Kirkwood Cres AB45 139 D5
Kitchenhill View AB42 36 E6
KITTYBREWSTER 164 F4
Kittybrewster Prim Sch
AB24 165 A5
Kittybrewster Ret Pk
AB24 165 A4
Kittybrewster Sq AB25 165 A4
KNAVEN 36 A2
KNOCK 18 A3
Knock Ave AB45 8 F8
Knock Castle* AB35 182 A3
KNOCKENBAIRD 149 D8
Knockhall Castle* AB41 63 F1
Knockhall Rd
Ellon AB41 77 F8
6 Newburgh AB41 77 F8
Knockie Rd AB53 145 B5
Knock La 7 AB45 8 F8
Knockothie Brae AB41 151 D6
KNOCKOTHIE HILL 151 D6
Knockothie Hill 1 AB41 151 C6
Knock St
Banff AB45 8 F8
Peterhead AB42 37 D4
Knock View AB42 37 D5
KNOWES OF ELRICK 19 A4

L

Laburnum Gr AB42 147 B4
Laburnum La 11 AB42 38 D6
Laburnum Wlk AB16 164 D4
Ladder Rd The AB36 66 A1
Lade Cres AB21 158 C2
Ladeside Gdns AB51 152 E2
Ladeside Rd
Brechin DD9 188 C2
Inverurie AB51 152 E3
Lady Rothes Pl AB43 143 C6
Ladywell Pl AB11 170 E5
Ladywell Rd AB51 155 B6
Ladywood Cres AB34 183 C4
Ladywood Dr AB34 183 B4
Laggan Pl AB41 151 B7
Laing Ct AB51 152 E5
Laingseat Rd AB23 91 A6
Laing St AB44 141 D7
Laird Gdns AB22 159 C1
Lairds Gr AB21 89 C7
Lairds Pk AB21 89 C7
Laird's Wlk AB42 40 D1
Lairhillock Sch AB39 178 B3
Laithers Cres AB53 145 C5
Lamb Way 5 DD10 189 D7
Lamondfauld La 6
DD10 138 C8
Lamondfauld Rd DD10 138 C8
Lamond Pl AB25 165 A3
Landale Rd AB42 147 D5
Landends
Laurencekirk AB30 128 D4
Luthermuir AB30 133 B8
Lane The AB51 86 F1
Langdykes Cres AB12 176 B8
Langdykes Dr AB12 176 B8
Langdykes Rd AB12 176 B8
Langdykes Way AB12 176 C8
Langley Ave DD10 189 D6
Langley Rd AB42 27 B3
Langstane Pl AB11 190 A2
Lang Stracht AB15 163 E2
Lang Stracht The AB33 154 D4
Larch Rd AB16 164 C4
Larg Dr AB32 161 B3
LARGIE 57 C6
LARGUE 45 D8
Largue Prim Sch AB54 45 D8
Latch Gdns DD9 188 B4
Latch Rd DD9 188 B4
Lathallan Grange DD10 135 D6
Lathallan Sch DD10 135 D6
Laurel Ave AB22 164 E8
Laurel Braes AB22 164 E8
Laurel Cres DD10 187 D7
Laurel Ct 1 AB39 185 C4
Laurel Dr AB22 164 C8
Laurel Gdns AB22 164 E8
Laurel La AB22 159 C1
Laurel Pk AB22 164 E8
Laurel Pl AB22 164 E8
Laurel Rd AB22 164 E8
Laurel Terr
Aberdeen AB22 164 E8
9 Pitmedden AB41 62 B2
Laurel View AB22 164 D8
Laurelwood Ave AB25 164 F4
Laurel Wynd AB22 164 E8
LAURENCEKIRK 186 B5
Laurencekirk Bsns Pk
AB30 186 D6
Laurencekirk Sch AB30 186 D4
Lavender Gr AB31 109 E3
Lavender Pk 4 AB51 155 C4
Laverock Hill AB41 151 C6
Laverock Rd 8 AB41 77 F8
Law of Balgreen* AB45 10 D1
Law of Doune Rd AB44 141 C5
Lawrence Rd AB52 58 A7
Laws Dr AB12 170 A2
Lawson Ave AB31 184 C5
Lawson Cres AB31 184 C4
Lawsondale Ave AB32 161 F2
Lawsondale Dr AB32 161 F2
Lawsondale Terr AB32 161 F3
Lawson Dr AB21 158 A7
Lawson Pl AB31 184 C4
Laws Rd AB12 170 A2
Law The* AB45 3 D4
Leadside Rd AB25 165 A1
Lea Rig AB32 161 B3
Lea Rig Rd AB42 40 A6
Learny Pl AB15 169 E7
Leask Ave AB42 147 C4
Lecht 2090 Ski Ctr*
AB36 79 C3
Lecht Rd AB36 79 C3
LEDDACH 161 B2
Leddach Gdns AB32 161 C3
Leddach Pl AB32 161 C3
Leddach Rd AB32 161 C3
Lee Cres
Aberdeen AB22 159 C3
6 Bridge of Don AB22 159 F1
Lee Crescent N AB22 159 C3
Leeds Terr 2 AB42 25 D5
Lee Mar DD10 138 B6
Leggart Ave AB12 169 F3
Leggart Cres AB12 169 F2
Leggart Terr AB12 169 F2
Leighton Gdns AB41 151 B5
Leith Dr AB53 47 E4
Leith Hall, Gdn & Est*
AB54 56 C4
Lemonbank Pl AB44 141 D6
Lemon Pl AB24 190 C4
Lemon St AB24 190 C4
Lemon Tree Arts Ctr*
AB24 190 B4
Lendrum Pl AB53 145 B6
Lennox Terr AB54 148 E4
LEOCHEL-CUSHNIE 84 B1
Lerwick Rd AB16 163 E3
LESLIE 71 B7
Leslie Cres
Alford AB33 154 C4
Westhill AB32 161 C3
Leslie Pk 2 AB52 58 D3
Leslie Pl
Inverurie AB51 152 E3
5 Kemnay AB51 87 D6
Leslie Rd AB24 164 F5
Leslie's La AB53 145 D4
Leslie Terr AB25 165 A4
LETHENTY 48 C7
Lethen Wlk AB12 180 A4
Lethnot Rd DD9 132 A7
Letter Rd AB32 88 A1
Leven Ave AB41 151 B6
Lewis Ct AB15 163 D3
Lewis Dr AB16 163 E3
Lewis Pl AB43 143 B3
Lewis Rd
Aberdeen AB16 163 E3
Fraserburgh AB43 143 B3

Lewisvale AB14 172 F6
LEYLODGE 88 B4
LEYS 25 E3
Leys Dr 5 AB43 26 C7
Leys Gdns AB21 156 B6
Leys Rd AB31 184 E4
Leys The AB44 141 E7
Leys Way 7 AB51 87 C6
Library Gdns 12 AB43 24 E6
Lickleyhead Castle* AB52 71 F6
Licklyhead Way AB21 158 C7
Liddell Pl AB21 158 B7
Liddles Cl 6 DD9 188 C3
Lilac Gr 1 AB42 147 B3
Lilac Pl AB16 164 B4
Lilybank Pl AB25 164 F4
Lily Loch Rd AB39 185 B5
Lime St AB11 165 E1
Linden Gdns AB44 141 D6
Lindsay Pl DD9 132 B7
Lindsay St AB10 190 A3
Lingbank Terr 1 AB42 147 A4
Links Ave DD10 189 E4
Linksfield Gdns AB24 165 C4
Linksfield Pl AB24 165 C4
Linksfield Rd
Aberdeen AB24 165 C4
3 Peterhead AB42 147 C4
Linksfield Swimming Pool AB24 165 C5
Links Pk (Montrose FC) DD10 189 E4
Links Pl
Aberdeen AB11 165 E1
Cruden Bay AB42 53 A2
Links Rd
Aberdeen AB23 165 D8
Banff AB45 139 E7
Fraserburgh AB43 143 D5
Peterhead AB42 27 B3
Links St AB11 165 E1
Links Terr AB42 147 C5
Links The AB39 185 F6
Links View
Aberdeen AB24 165 D4
Cruden Bay AB42 53 A2
Inverboyndie AB45 140 B6
Peterhead AB42 27 B2
Linn Moor Residential Sch AB14 166 D1
Linn of Dee Pl 2 AB35 113 E6
Linn of Dee Rd AB35 113 E6
LINTMILL 1 B3
Lintmill Brae AB41 63 F5
Lintmill Pl AB16 163 F5
Lintmill Terr AB16 163 F5
Linton Bsns Pk DD10 187 E5
Linton Ind Est DD10 187 E7
Linton The AB51 86 F1
Linx Ice Arena AB24 165 E3
Lismore Gdns 1 AB16 163 E2
Little Belmont St AB10 190 A3
Little Chapel St 7 AB10 165 A1
LITTLE COLLIESTON 64 D4
Little Farrochie Pl AB39 185 C5
Littlejohn St
Aberdeen AB25 190 B4
Huntly AB54 148 D4
Little Nursery DD10 189 C5
Little Oxen Craig 5 AB51 152 A8
Littlewood Pl AB33 154 D4
Little Wynd DD9 132 A7
Loan Dykes DD10 138 D7
Loanhead Pk AB51 59 E3
Loanhead Pl AB25 164 F2
Loanhead Terr AB25 165 A2
Loanhead Wlk 3 AB25 165 A2
Loan The AB45 1 F1
Lochans The DD10 134 C3
Lochburn Brae AB51 155 B6
Lochburn Dr AB51 155 B6
Lochinch Ave AB12 176 C6
Lochinch Dr AB12 175 F5
Lochinch Gdns AB12 175 F5
Lochinch Gr
Charlestown AB12 175 F5
Cove Bay AB12 176 C6
Lochinch Mews AB12 175 F5
Lochinch Pk AB12 175 F6
Lochinch Rd AB12 176 A5
Lochinch View AB12 175 F6
Lochinch Way AB12 175 F5
Lochinch Wlk AB12 175 F6
Loch La AB45 8 F8
Lochnagar Cres AB14 172 D7
Lochnagar Rd
Aberdeen AB14 172 E7
1 Balnagask AB11 170 F6
Lochnagar Way AB35 182 E5
Loch of Strathbeg Nature Reserve* AB43 15 F1
Loch of Strathbeg Visitor Ctr* AB43 15 D1
Lochpots Prim Sch AB43 143 B5
Lochpots Rd AB43 143 B5
LOCHSIDE 134 C3
Lochside Ave AB23 159 F3
Lochside Cres
Aberdeen AB23 159 F3
Montrose DD10 189 C6
Lochside Dr AB23 159 F3
Lochside Pl
Aberdeen AB23 159 F3
Lochside Pl *continued*
Edzell DD9 132 A7
4 Peterhead AB42 147 A4
Lochside Prim Sch DD10 189 C5
Lochside Rd
Aberdeen AB23 159 F3
Montrose DD10 134 C3
Peterhead AB42 147 A4
Lochside Terr AB23 160 A3
Lochside Way AB23 159 F3
Loch St
Aberdeen AB25 190 A3
Banff AB45 8 F8
Rosehearty AB43 142 C8
Loch View
1 Fraserburgh AB43 26 C7
Westhill AB32 161 C4
Lochview Dr AB23 160 A3
Lochview Pl AB23 159 F3
Lochview Way AB23 160 A3
Loch Way 4 AB51 87 D6
Lodge Wlk
Aberdeen AB10 190 B3
1 Fraserburgh AB43 143 D6
Peterhead AB42 147 E4
Lodging Brae AB45 139 E7
LOGIE 133 E2
Logie Ave
Aberdeen AB16 164 C7
11 Cullen AB56 1 B5
Logie Avenue W AB43 26 C8
LOGIE COLDSTONE 95 D3
Logie Coldstone Prim Sch AB34 95 D3
Logie Dr
Buckie AB56 1 B5
Fraserburgh AB43 26 C7
Logie Durno Prim Sch AB51 59 C1
Logie Gdns AB16 164 C7
Logie House* AB51 73 A8
LOGIE PERT 133 B3
Logie Pl AB16 164 B6
Logie Rd
Ellon AB41 63 D2
Fraserburgh AB43 26 D7
Logie Terr AB16 164 C6
Loirsbank Rd AB15 168 E2
Loirston Ave AB12 176 B7
Loirston Cl AB12 176 B7
Loirston Cres AB12 176 C8
Loirston Ct AB12 176 B8
Loirston Manor AB12 176 C7
Loirston Pl
Aberdeen AB11 170 E6
Cove Bay AB12 176 C7
Loirston Prim Sch AB12 176 B7
Loirston Rd AB12 176 C7
Loirston Way AB12 176 B8
Loirston Wlk AB12 176 B8
Lomond Cres AB41 151 B6
Lonach Cres AB54 30 C7
Longate AB42 147 E5
Longcairn Gdns 9 AB21 163 D7
Long Cl AB41 151 D4
LONGHAVEN 53 D6
Longhaven Prim Sch AB42 53 C6
Longlands Pl AB16 164 B5
LONGMANHILL 10 B5
LONGSIDE 38 D6
Longside Rd AB42 146 E5
Longside Sch AB42 38 D5
Long Straight The AB51 155 A6
Longview Terr AB16 163 F6
Long Walk Pl AB16 164 B4
Long Walk Rd AB16 164 B4
Long Walk Terr AB16 164 B4
LONMAY 14 F1
Lord Hay's Gr AB24 165 C7
Lorne Bldgs AB10 169 F4
Lossie Pl AB16 164 A3
Lost Gall The* AB36 80 D6
Louden Pl AB21 158 C7
Louisville Ave AB15 169 D7
Lourin Cl 4 AB52 58 D3
Lovat St AB42 25 D5
Love La
4 Fraserburgh AB43 143 D6
Peterhead AB42 147 E5
5 Stonehaven AB39 185 F3
Lower Balmain St 4 DD10 189 C2
Lower Blantyre St 2 AB56 1 B5
Lower Cowgate AB51 150 C3
Lower Craigo St 1 DD10 189 C2
Lower Denburn AB25 190 A3
Lower Grange AB42 147 B5
Lowerhall St DD10 189 C4
Low Rd AB34 183 E5
Low Shore
Banff AB45 8 F8
Macduff AB44 141 C7
Low St
Banff AB45 140 F5
Fraserburgh AB43 12 E5
New Pitsligo AB43 23 E6
Portsoy AB45 139 D7
Low Wood Rd AB39 185 D4
Lubbock Pk Gdns DD9 188 B4
LUMPHANAN 98 A3
Lumphanan Prim Sch AB31 98 A3
LUMSDEN 69 B5
Lumsden Ct AB45 148 C4
Lumsden Prim Sch AB54 69 B4
Lumsden Way AB23 77 C1
Lunan Ave DD10 189 C7
Luncarty Pl AB53 145 B6
Lusylaw Rd AB45 140 D5
Luther Dr AB30 186 C6
LUTHERMUIR 133 A7
Luthermuir Prim Sch AB30 133 B7
LYNE OF SKENE 88 A1

M

Maberly St AB25 190 A4
MacAllan Rd 3 AB51 155 C4
MacAulay Dr AB15 169 A6
MacAulay Grange AB15 169 B6
MacAulay Pk AB15 169 B6
MacAulay Pl AB15 169 B6
MacAulay Wlk AB15 169 B6
MacAuley Gdns AB15 169 B6
Macbeth Pl 4 AB31 98 A3
McBey Way AB41 77 C6
McCombie Cres 7 AB51 87 D7
MacDiarmid Dr 1 DD10 138 C8
MacDonald Ct 4 AB39 185 E5
McDonald Dr AB41 151 C6
McDonald Gdns AB41 151 D6
MacDonald Rd AB39 185 C4
McDonald St 1 AB54 148 E4
MACDUFF 141 F7
Macduff Ind Est AB44 141 E6
Macduff Marine Aquarium* AB44 141 D7
Macduff Prim Sch AB44 141 E5
McEwan Gall* AB35 104 A4
McFadden Pk AB51 155 B5
McGill Terr DD10 187 D3
McGregor Closet AB42 147 A7
McGregor Cres AB42 147 A7
MacGregor Rd AB43 15 B7
MacGregor St 1 DD9 188 C3
McIntosh Cres AB21 158 B7
McIntosh's La 3 AB53 145 D4
McIver Terr AB54 148 C4
McKay Pl AB44 141 C6
McKay Rd AB44 141 C6
MacKay Rd AB12 170 A2
McKay's Rd AB23 77 A1
Mackenzie Ave AB30 124 B1
Mackenzie Ct AB42 147 C2
Mackenzie Dr AB51 59 E3
Mackenzie Gdns
Brechin DD9 188 B4
12 Turriff AB53 145 D4
Mackie Acad AB39 185 D6
Mackie Ave AB41 61 E6
Mackie Cres AB41 61 E6
Mackie Pl AB25 165 A1
Mackie's La AB53 145 D4
Maclean Terr AB45 139 E7
McLeod Pl AB43 143 A2
Macmillan Ave AB51 150 B3
MacNab Ave DD10 189 C6
Maconochie Pl AB43 143 D4
Maconochie Rd AB43 143 D5
McVeagh St AB54 148 D5
Maggie's Hoosie* AB43 15 C8
Maiden Castle (Fort)* AB51 72 F7
Maidencraig Pl AB16 163 F2
Maiden St AB42 147 E5
Main Rd
Aberdeen AB21 156 B5
Banchory AB31 98 A2
Hillside DD10 138 C8
Mains Circ AB32 161 F3
Mains Ct AB32 161 F3
Mains Gdns AB32 161 F3
MAINS OF KINMUNDY 161 E4
Main St
Aberchirder AB54 144 C4
Alford AB33 154 E3
Banff AB45 3 B2
Cruden Bay AB42 53 B3
Cuminestown AB53 22 B1
Ellon AB41 77 F7
Fraserburgh AB43 143 C7
Fyvie AB53 47 E5
Garmond AB53 22 C3
Hatton AB42 52 C4
Huntly AB54 69 B4
Inverallochy AB43 15 C8
Laurencekirk AB30 133 A7
Longside AB42 38 D6
Montrose DD10 135 C5
New Byth AB53 22 E4
Portsoy AB45 139 E7
Rothienorman AB51 47 A2
Sandhaven AB43 5 A4
Sauchen AB51 87 A1
Turriff AB53 145 C4
Mains View AB32 161 F3
Maisondieu La 2 DD9 188 C3
Maisondieu Prim Sch DD9 188 C3
Maitland Cres AB51 152 B8
Maitland Path AB51 152 B8
Maitland Wlk AB51 152 B8
Major La 4 AB51 150 C3
Malcolm Rd
Aberdeen AB21 163 F8
Banff AB45 140 E5
Peterculter AB14 172 C7
Malcolm's Mount AB39 185 B5
Malcolm's Mount W AB39 185 B5
Malcolm's Way AB39 185 B4
Mallard Ct 12 AB41 77 F8
Mallard Dr 3 AB42 147 B5
Mallard Rd 11 AB41 77 F8
Mall Park Rd DD10 189 D5
Mall The DD10 189 D5
Mall Trinity The AB25 190 A3
Maltings The DD10 189 E4
Maltman Gr AB24 190 C4
Mameulah Cres AB21 153 D5
Mameulah Ct 1 AB21 153 D6
Mameulah Rd AB21 153 D6
Mameulah View 2 AB21 153 D6
Manner St AB44 141 D7
MANNOFIELD 169 D5
Manor Ave AB16 164 B6
Manor Dr AB16 164 C7
Manor Pl AB15 168 E2
Manor Terr AB16 164 C6
Manor Wlk AB16 164 B6
Manse Croft AB31 117 C7
Mansefield 4 AB51 155 C5
Mansefield Pl
Aberdeen AB11 170 E6
2 Banchory AB31 184 E4
2 Fraserburgh AB43 26 D7
Mansefield Rd AB11 170 E6
Manse Gdns 3 AB53 145 C4
Manse La
Aberdeen AB21 89 B7
St Cyprus DD10 134 D4
2 Turriff AB53 145 C4
Manse Pl
Boddam AB42 40 C1
6 Peterhead AB42 52 C4
Manse Rd
Bieldside AB15 168 C2
Brechin DD9 132 B7
4 Hillside DD10 138 C8
Huntly AB54 55 D1
Inverurie AB51 152 D4
Methlick AB41 49 B3
3 Peterhead AB42 52 C4
Potterton AB23 91 A6
Turriff AB53 145 C4
Udney AB41 62 A1
Westhill AB32 101 E6
Manse St
Fraserburgh AB43 143 D7
Peterhead AB42 25 D5
Manse Terr
23 Boddam AB42 40 D1
7 Peterhead AB42 52 C4
Turriff AB53 145 C5
Manse Wlk AB41 61 F5
Man's Hill Ave AB39 185 D5
Manson Rd AB51 150 C2
Maple Pl AB12 176 C6
Marchbank Rd AB15 168 B1
Marchburn Ave AB16 164 A6
Marchburn Cres AB16 164 A6
Marchburn Ct 5 AB16 164 A6
Marchburn Ct Rd 1 AB16 164 A6
Marchburn Dr AB16 163 F6
Marchburn Inf Sch AB16 164 A6
Marchburn Pl AB16 164 A6
Marchburn Rd AB16 164 A6
Marchburn Terr AB16 164 B6
Marchfield Dr 1 AB51 152 B7
Marchfield Pl 2 AB51 152 B7
Marchmont Pl AB12 176 C8
Marchmont St AB12 176 C8
Marconi Rd AB43 143 C7
Marconi Terr AB43 143 B7
Marcus Cres AB21 156 B7
Marcus Dr AB21 156 B7
Marcus Gdns AB21 156 B7
Marcus Rd AB21 156 B6
Maree Terr AB41 151 B6
Margaret Allan Gr AB51 87 A2
Margaret Clyne Ct AB12 170 A3
Margaret Pl AB10 169 F5
Margaret St
5 Aberdeen AB10 165 A1
1 Stonehaven AB39 185 E4
Marine Ave DD10 189 D3
Marine Ct AB11 190 A1
Marine La AB11 190 A1
Marine Pl AB11 190 A1
Marine Terr
Aberdeen AB11 190 A1
Portsoy AB45 139 D7
Stonehaven AB39 181 G1
Marine View AB39 181 G1
Marischal Ct 4 AB11 190 C3
Marischal Gdns AB21 163 D7
Marischal Mus* AB10 190 B3
Marischal St
Aberdeen AB11 190 B3
Peterhead AB42 147 E5
4 Stonehaven AB39 185 F3
Market Brae AB41 151 D6
Market Hill
Ellon AB41 151 D6
3 Peterhead AB42 38 D6
Markethill Ind Est AB53 145 D5
Markethill Prim Sch AB53 145 C5
Markethill Rd AB53 145 D5
Market La
Aberdeen AB24 165 B5
Stonehaven AB39 185 E4
10 Strichen AB43 24 E5
4 Turriff AB53 145 D5
Market Muir Ct 7 AB51 152 D6
Market Pl
4 Inverurie AB51 152 E6
New Pitsligo AB43 23 E6
Market Place Prim Sch AB51 152 E5
Market Rd AB30 186 C5
Market Sq
2 Inverbervie DD10 187 E7
Laurencekirk AB30 124 B1
1 Oldmeldrum AB51 150 C3
15 Stonehaven AB39 185 E4
Market St
Aberchirder AB54 144 C4
Aberdeen AB11 190 B2
Brechin DD9 188 C4
Ellon AB41 151 D4
Greenburn AB21 158 A2
Huntly AB54 148 C4
Insch AB52 149 D5
Macduff AB44 141 C6
Montrose DD10 189 D4
2 Peterhead AB42 36 E6
Turriff AB53 145 C5
Market Stance 7 AB34 96 C3
Market Terr 9 AB43 24 E6
Mar Lodge Est* AB35 112 F4
Marlpool Pl AB21 163 D7
Marlpool Specl Sch AB21 163 D8
MARNOCH 18 F1
Marquis Rd AB24 164 F6
Mar Rd
Ballater AB35 113 E6
Huntly AB54 70 C7
Marsh Pl AB12 180 B5
Martin Ave AB39 185 C6
Martin Brae AB51 152 C5
Martin Dr AB39 185 C6
Martin Pl AB39 185 C6
Martin Rd AB52 149 D5
Martin's La 3 DD9 188 C3
Martin Terr DD10 131 C7
Mart Rd AB33 154 D3
Mary Elmslie Ct AB24 165 C3
Maryfield Cres AB51 152 C6
Maryfield Pl 1 AB51 152 C6
Maryfield W AB51 152 C6
MARYKIRK 133 D4
Marykirk Prim Sch AB30 133 D4
Marykirk Rd DD10 138 D8
Mary Slessor Pl AB51 150 D3
Mary St AB39 185 E4
MARYTON 138 A3
Maryville Pk AB15 164 C1
Maryville Pl AB15 164 C1
MARYWELL 108 A2
Marywell La AB51 99 C6
Marywell St AB11 190 A2
MASTRICK 164 A3
Mastrick Cl AB16 164 B3
Mastrick Dr AB16 164 A3
Mastrick Junc AB16 164 A3
Mastrick Rd AB16 164 B3
Mathers Pk 9 DD9 188 C3
Mathers Pl 1 AB41 77 F8
Mathieson La 4 AB31 98 E1
Matthew Dr AB42 147 A4
Matthews Rd AB12 170 A2
MAUD 36 E7
Maud Hospl AB42 36 E6
Maud Prim Sch AB42 36 E6
Maud Sta Bsns Pk AB42 36 E6
Mavis Bank 7 AB41 77 F8
Maxwell Pl AB43 143 B6
Maxwell Place Ind Est AB43 143 A6
May Baird Ave AB25 164 F3
Mayfield Gdns
Aberdeen AB15 169 D7
Insch AB52 149 D4
Mayfield Rd
St Cyrus DD10 134 D3
Turriff AB53 145 E4
Mayfield Terr AB52 149 D4
Meadow Ave AB54 148 D5
Meadowbank Pl 1 AB53 145 C5
Meadowbank Rd AB53 145 B6
Meadow Croft 1 AB51 74 F2
Meadow Ct
1 Aberchirder AB54 144 D5
1 Danestone AB24 164 F7
Meadow Dr AB51 150 C3
Meadow La AB24 165 A7
Meadowlands Ave AB32 161 E4
Meadowlands Cl 1 AB15 161 E5
Meadowlands Cres AB32 161 E5
Meadowlands Ct 3 AB32 161 E5
Meadowlands Dr AB32 161 D5
Meadowlands Pk AB32 161 D5
Meadowlands Pl AB32 161 D5
Meadowlands Way 2 AB32 161 E5
Meadow Pl
Aberdeen AB24 165 A7
1 Inverurie AB51 152 B8
Meadow Rd
2 Inverurie AB51 152 B8
Turriff AB53 22 C1
Meadows Dr AB51 150 C3
Meadowside DD10 187 D7
Meadows Sports Ctr AB41 151 F5
Meadow St AB54 148 D5
Meadows The
Aberdeen AB13 167 D1
Ellon AB41 63 D5
Kirkton of Maryculter AB12 173 B3
Meadows Vale AB51 150 C2

Meadows Way AB41 151 F4
Meadow Vale AB41 151 B6
Meadowview Rd AB53 145 B6
Meadowview Wlk AB53 145 B6
Mealmarket St AB24 190 B4
Mearns Acad AB30 186 E6
Mearns Cl 4 AB51 152 B8
Mearns Ct AB30 186 C5
Mearns Dr
Laurencekirk AB30 186 C4
Montrose DD10 189 C7
Stonehaven AB39 185 C6
Mearns Pk AB30 186 D6
Mearns Sports Ctr AB30 186 E6
Mearns St AB11 190 C3
Mearns Wlk
Laurencekirk AB30 186 B4
Stonehaven AB39 185 C5
Meavie Pl AB45 140 E6
Medicine Well Dr DD10 189 C5
MEETHILL 147 A4
Meethill Pl AB42 147 B4
Meethill Prim Sch AB42 147 C3
Meethill Rd AB42 147 B5
Megray Row AB39 185 E6
Meikle Gdns AB32 161 D3
Meikle Mill 3 DD9 188 D2
Meiklemill Farm Ind Est AB41 151 A4
Meiklemill Prim Sch AB41 151 B4
MEIKLE WARTLE 59 B6
Meldrum Acad AB51 150 B4
Meldrum Dr AB21 153 D5
Meldrum Meg Way AB51 150 B2
Meldrum Prim Sch AB51 150 C3
Melgum Rd AB34 96 B3
Melrose Cres AB44 141 D6
Melrose Pl AB51 155 B3
Melrose Wlk AB14 172 D6
Melville Gdns DD10 189 D3
Melville Rd DD10 189 D3
MEMSIE 14 A5
Menie Cl 10 AB23 91 C8
Menie Cres 4 AB23 91 C8
Menie House* AB23 77 D3
Menzies Rd AB11 190 B1
Merchants Quay 3 AB42 147 E4
Merchant St AB42 147 E4
Mercury Lone DD10 134 D3
Mercury Terr DD10 134 D3
Meridian St 5 DD10 189 D2
Merkland La AB24 165 D4
Merkland Pl AB24 165 C4
Merkland Rd AB24 165 C4
Merkland Road E AB24 165 C4
Merlin Terr 9 AB41 77 F8
Meston Wlk AB24 165 B5
METHLICK 49 B4
Methlick Prim Sch AB41 49 B4
Methlick Wood AB41 49 B3
Mews The AB31 184 D3
MID ANGUSTON 111 E8
MID ARDLAW 13 E6
Midchingle Rd AB11 190 C2
Middle Brae 8 AB21 163 D7
Middleburgh Rd AB43 143 C4
MIDDLEFIELD 164 C6
Middlefield Cres AB24 164 D6
Middlefield Pl AB24 164 D6
Middlefield Prim Sch AB16 164 C6
Middlefield Terr AB24 164 D6
Middlefield Wlk AB24 164 D5
MIDDLE GRANGE 147 A5
MIDDLEMUIR 24 A7
Middlemuir Pl 20 AB21 163 D7
Middlemuir Rd AB51 152 C6
Middle Pk AB51 152 B6
Middle Row AB11 170 F8
Middleton Circ AB22 159 C3
Middleton Cl AB22 159 C3
Middleton Cres AB22 159 C3
Middleton Dr AB22 159 C3
MIDDLETON PARK 159 D3
Middleton Park Prim Sch AB22 159 D3
Middleton Path AB22 159 C3
Middleton Pk DD9 188 D2
Middleton Pl
Aberdeen AB22 159 F1
Insch AB52 58 D3
Middleton Rd
Aberdeen AB22 159 C3
3 Insch AB52 58 D3
Middleton Terr AB22 159 C3
Middleton Way
Aberdeen AB22 159 C3
Inverurie AB51 152 C7
MIDMAR 99 D6
Midmar Castle* AB51 100 A4
Midmar Cres AB15 162 F4
Midmar Pk AB15 162 F4
Midmar Prim Sch AB51 99 D6
Midmar View AB15 162 F3
Midmar Wlk AB15 162 F4
Midmill Bsns Pk AB51 155 D2
Mid St
Banff AB45 7 E1
Fraserburgh AB43 143 C6
Inverallochy AB43 15 C8
Mid Street AB43 15 D6
Montrose DD10 135 C6
Peterhead AB42 147 D7
Rosehearty AB43 142 C8
Mid Stocket Mews AB25 164 F2
Mid Stocket Rd AB15 164 C2
Midway AB30 186 C5
MIGVIE 95 D5
Migvie Ave AB15 162 F4
Migvie Castle (remains of)* AB34 95 D5
Migvie Gdns AB15 162 F4
Migvie Gr AB15 162 F4
Migvie Lea AB15 162 F4
Mildens Row AB39 185 E6
Mile End AB42 147 C3
Mile-End Ave AB15 164 E2
Mile-End La AB15 164 F2
Mile-End Pl AB15 164 E2
Mile End Pl 2 AB42 147 C3
Mile End Prim Sch AB15 164 E1
Millan Ct 7 AB31 98 A3
Millan Pk 5 AB31 98 A3
Millan View 6 AB31 98 A3
Millarsmires End 4 AB22 159 E2
Millbank La AB25 165 A3
Millbank Pl AB25 165 A3
MILLBRECK 38 A4
Millburn Ave AB43 15 D6
Millburn Ct AB44 141 E5
Millburn Pl AB43 143 A5
Millburn Rd AB51 150 B2
Millburn St AB11 190 B1
Mill Ct
Aberdeen AB24 164 D7
8 Gourdon DD10 187 D3
Millden Rd AB15 168 F3
Milleath Wlk 2 AB21 158 C7
Millend 3 AB41 77 F7
Miller Gdns
Fraserburgh AB43 143 A6
Newmachar AB21 153 D5
Miller St AB11 190 C3
Miller Street Ind Est AB11 190 C3
Millers Visitor & Ret Ctr The* AB51 99 F5
MILLFIELD 106 C3
Millfield Ave 2 AB51 152 C7
Millfield Dr AB51 152 C7
Millfield Pl AB51 152 C7
Millfield Terr 1 AB51 152 C7
Millgrove Rd AB21 158 C2
Millhill Brae AB21 158 C1
Mill La
Montrose DD10 189 C2
Peterhead AB42 37 D4
Mill Lade Wynd AB22 164 C8
Mill of Forest Gr AB39 185 B3
Mill of Forest La 6 AB39 185 C4
Mill of Forest Rd AB39 185 B4
Mill O'Forest Prim Sch AB39 185 B4
Millpark Rd AB41 151 A6
Mill Pk AB42 37 D4
Mill Pl
Aboyne AB34 96 B3
Montrose DD10 133 D3
Mill Rd
Aboyne AB34 96 B3
Huntly AB54 148 E4
Insch AB52 149 C4
Inverurie AB51 152 E1
2 Montrose DD10 189 C3
9 Oldmeldrum AB51 150 C3
Turriff AB53 145 C4
Millside Dr AB14 172 C6
Millside Rd AB14 172 C6
Millside St AB14 172 C6
Millside Terr AB14 172 C6
Mill St
Macduff AB44 141 D7
Montrose DD10 189 D4
Stuartfield AB42 37 D4
Millstone Pl 8 AB51 87 D7
MILLTIMBER 173 A8
Milltimber Brae AB13 173 A7
Milltimber Brae E AB13 173 A7
Milltimber Prim Sch AB13 173 C8
MILLTOWN OF KILDRUMMY 83 A7
MILLTOWN OF ROTHIEMAY 30 D7
Millwood Rd AB41 151 B6
Milnamair 1 DD10 189 C3
Milne's Wynd DD10 135 C6
MILTON 1 B1
Milton Dr AB51 87 C6
Miltonfold AB21 163 F8
Milton of Arbuthnott AB30 130 D6
MILTON OF CAMPFIELD 109 A7
Milton of Crathes Visitor Ctr The* AB31 110 D3
MILTON OF CUSHNIE 84 A2
MILTON OF MURTLE 173 E8
Milton View AB51 87 C6
Mineralwell View AB39 185 E6
Minister La 2 AB10 190 A3
MINTLAW 146 F5
Mintlaw Acad AB42 146 C5
Mintlaw Prim Sch AB42 146 E5
Mintlaw Rd AB42 25 D1
MINTLAW STATION 146 B6
Minto Ave AB12 170 F3
Minto Circ 2 AB51 87 C7
Minto Dr AB12 170 F2
Minto Rd AB12 170 F2
Minty's La 2 AB53 145 D4
Mitchell Ave AB54 148 C5
Mitchell Dr DD9 188 D1
Mitchell Gdns AB21 156 B7
Mitchell Pl AB42 37 D4
Mither Tap AB51 152 A8
Modley Ave AB41 151 B4
Modley Cl AB41 151 B4
Modley Ct AB41 151 B4
Modley Pl AB41 151 C5
Moir Ave AB16 164 C5
Moir Cres AB16 164 C5
Moir Dr AB16 164 C5
Moir Gn AB16 164 C5
Monach Terr AB16 163 E2
Monaltrie Ave AB35 182 E5
Monaltrie Cl AB35 182 E6
Monaltrie Cres AB35 182 D5
Monaltrie Rd AB35 182 E4
Monaltrie Way AB35 182 E5
Monarch Terr 5 AB16 163 E2
MONBODDO 124 C1
Monboddo Rd 16 AB31 108 E8
Monboddo St AB30 124 B1
Monduff Rd AB39 181 G2
Monearn Gdns AB13 173 B8
MONKSHILL 48 B7
Monquhitter Prim Sch AB53 22 C1
Montbletton Pl AB44 141 E5
Montcoffer View AB45 140 E4
Monteach Rd AB41 49 C7
MONTGARRIE 154 D7
Montgarrie Rd AB33 154 D4
Montgomery Rd AB24 164 F7
MONTROSE 189 E5
Montrose Acad DD10 189 D3
Montrose Air Sta Heritage Ctr* DD10 189 D6
Montrose Basin Nature Reserve* DD10 189 A3
Montrose Basin Wildlife Ctr* DD10 138 B3
Montrose Cl AB21 157 E5
Montrose Dr AB10 169 E3
Montrose Mus* DD10 189 D3
Montrose Rd
Aberdeen AB21 157 E5
Inverbervie DD10 187 D6
Montrose Royal Infmy DD10 189 C2
Montrose Sports Ctr DD10 189 E3
Montrose St DD9 188 D2
Montrose Sta DD10 189 C4
Montrose Way AB21 157 E5
Monument Cl AB42 147 C2
MONYMUSK 86 E6
Monymusk Arts Ctr* AB51 86 E5
Monymusk Prim Sch AB51 86 E6
Monymusk Terr AB15 169 A7
Monymusk Walled Gdn* AB51 86 F6
Moor Pl AB12 180 C6
Morar Ct AB41 151 A6
Moray Pl AB15 164 C1
Moray Rd AB43 143 C7
Moray St AB44 141 E7
Moray View 4 AB45 140 E6
Morgan Rd AB24 164 D4
Morlich Ave AB41 151 B6
Mormond Ave AB43 143 C5
Mormond Cres AB42 146 E4
Mormond Pl
Inverallochy AB43 15 B7
Strichen AB43 24 F6
Mormond View 1 AB42 25 D5
Morningfield Mews AB15 164 D1
Morningfield Rd AB15 164 D1
Morningside Ave
Aberdeen AB10 169 D4
4 Inverurie AB51 152 A7
Waterside AB42 40 A6
Morningside Cres
Aberdeen AB10 169 D4
7 Inverurie AB51 152 A7
Morningside Dr AB51 152 A7
Morningside Gdns
Aberdeen AB10 169 E5
2 Inverurie AB51 152 A7
Morningside Gr AB10 169 D5
Morningside La AB10 169 D5
Morningside Pk AB51 152 A8
Morningside Pl AB10 169 D5
Morningside Rd
Aberdeen AB10 169 D5
5 Inverurie AB51 152 A7
Morningside Terr
Aberdeen AB10 169 D4
6 Inverurie AB51 152 A7
Morphie Dr DD10 134 D3
Morrison Ct 1 AB42 36 E7
Morrison Dr AB10 169 C4
Morrison Pl
6 Kemnay AB51 87 D7
Macduff AB44 141 D7
Peterhead AB42 53 A3
Morrison's Croft Cres AB23 160 B1
Morrison's La AB53 145 D4
Morrison Way AB51 155 C2
Morrone Birkwood National Nature Reserve* AB35 113 D5
Mortimer Dr AB15 168 F8
Mortimer Pl AB15 168 F8
Mortimer's La AB51 152 C7
Mortlich Gdns AB34 183 B4
Morven Ave DD10 189 C8
Morven Circ AB32 161 D4
Morven Cres
Peterhead AB42 147 B6
Westhill AB32 161 D3
Morven Ct 2 AB11 170 F6
Morven Dr AB32 161 D3
Morven Gdns AB32 161 D3
Morven Pl
Aberdeen AB11 170 D6
Aboyne AB34 183 B4
Morven View 1 AB34 96 C3
Morven-View Rd AB45 3 C2
Morven Way AB35 182 E6
Mosman Gdns AB24 164 D5
Mosman Pl AB24 164 E5
Mosscroft Ave AB32 161 C1
Mossgiel Way AB43 143 A3
Mosside Cres AB12 180 B6
Mosside Ct 5 AB32 161 D2
Mosside Dr AB12 180 B6
Mosside Pl 2 AB32 161 D2
Mosside Way 15 AB21 163 D7
Moss Rd
Aberchirder AB54 144 C5
Huntly AB54 55 D1
Moss St AB55 28 E7
Mounie Castle* AB51 60 A3
Mounie Dr AB51 150 B2
Mount Ave DD10 189 D4
Mounthooly AB24 165 C3
Mounthooly Way AB24 165 C3
Mount Pleasant AB23 165 D8
Mount Rd DD10 189 D4
Mountskip Cres DD9 188 B4
Mountskip Rd DD9 188 B4
MOUNTSOLIE 13 D2
Mount St
Aberdeen AB25 165 A2
Banchory AB31 184 B5
Mountview Gdns 4 AB25 165 A2
Mowatshill Rd AB42 147 B4
Mowatts La 3 DD10 187 D3
MUCHALLS 181 G2
Muchalls Castle* AB39 121 B6
Mugiemoss Rd AB21 163 F8
Muirend Ct AB12 180 B6
Muirend Rd AB12 180 B6
Muiresk Dr AB53 145 B5
Muirfield Pl AB16 164 B2
Muirfield Prim Sch AB16 164 B2
Muirfield Rd AB16 164 B3
MUIR OF ALFORD 84 C6
Muir of Dinnet National Nature Reserve* AB34 105 D6
MUIR OF FOWLIS 84 D2
MUIR OF KINELLAR 88 E4
Muir Rd AB43 14 B5
Muirs The AB54 55 D2
MUIRTACK 51 D4
Muirton Cres AB21 158 C7
Mulloch View 2 AB34 106 A5
Mull Way AB16 163 E2
Mundi Cres AB21 153 D6
Mundurno Rd AB22 159 D1
Murcar Ind Est AB23 160 A5
Murison Dr AB43 142 B7
Murray Ave 2 AB41 61 E5
Murray Ct AB24 164 D7
Murray La 3 DD10 189 C4
Murray Pl
Portsay AB45 139 C7
Stonehaven AB39 185 D3
Murray Rd AB39 181 I5
Murray's La AB11 190 C1
Murray St DD10 189 C4
Murray Terr
Aberdeen AB11 170 B6
Alford AB33 154 C3
Murtle Den Rd AB13 167 F1
Museum of Farming Life* AB41 62 A3
Museum of Scottish Lighthouses* AB43 143 D8
Museum St 3 DD10 189 D3
MYREBIRD 110 E6
Myrtle Est AB15 173 E7
Myrtle Terr AB12 180 A5
Myrus Ave AB45 141 D4
Myrus Circ AB44 141 E5

N

Napier Pl AB30 133 D4
Napier Terr AB30 133 D5
Narrow La 4 AB42 147 E5
Nathalan Ct 13 AB51 150 C3
Natural Arches & Cliff Stacks* AB42 53 D5
Neil Burn Dr 4 AB34 108 B6
Nellfield Pl AB10 170 A7
Nellfred Terr AB51 152 C7
Nelson Ct AB24 165 C3
Nelson La AB24 165 C3
Nelson Pl AB54 148 D4
Nelson St
Aberdeen AB24 165 C3
Huntly AB54 148 D4
Ness Circ AB41 151 B7
Ness Pl AB16 164 A3
Nether Aden Rd AB42 146 E5
Nether Blackhall AB51 152 A6
NETHERBRAE 11 B2
Netherby Rd AB15 168 D2
Nether Caldhame DD9 188 E3
Nether Davah Ct 2 AB51 152 B5
Nether Davah Pl 1 AB51 152 B5
Nether Davah Way AB51 152 B5
Netherhill La AB42 27 B2
Netherhills Ave AB21 163 D7
Netherhills Pl AB21 163 D7
NETHER KINMUNDY 38 E2
Netherkirkgate AB10 190 B3
NETHERLEY 120 E8
Netherley Pl 2 AB35 182 E4
Nethermains Rd AB39 181 G2
NETHERMUIR 36 C3
Nethermuir Rd AB42 36 D6
Netherview Ave AB21 158 C7
Netherview Pl AB21 158 B6
Netherview Rd AB21 158 B6
Neuk The AB21 156 B7
Nevada Ct 5 AB21 153 C6
Nevis Bsns Pk AB22 159 D1
NEW ABERDOUR 12 E5
New Aberdour Prim Sch AB43 12 E6
Newbigging Dr 5 AB39 185 C4
Newbigging Pl DD10 187 D7
NEWBURGH 77 F8
Newburgh Circ AB22 159 D4
Newburgh Cres AB22 159 E3
Newburgh Dr AB22 159 D3
Newburgh Mathers Prim Sch AB41 77 F8
Newburgh Path AB22 159 D3
Newburgh Pl AB22 159 E3
Newburgh Rd AB22 159 E4
Newburgh St AB22 159 D3
Newburgh Way AB22 159 D3
NEW BYTH 22 D4
NEW DEER 36 A6
New Deer Prim Sch AB53 36 A5
New Gd AB45 3 C3
Newhame Rd DD10 189 C7
NEWHILLS 163 B8
Newhills Ave AB21 163 D6
Newhills Prim Sch AB21 163 D7
Newlands Ave AB10 169 E5
Newlands Cres AB10 169 E5
Newlands Dr AB51 155 C5
Newlands Rd AB42 146 D4
NEW LEEDS 25 D5
NEWMACHAR 153 D5
Newmachar Prim Sch AB21 153 D6
Newmanswalls Ave DD10 189 C6
New Park Pl AB16 164 A3
New Park Rd AB16 164 A3
New Pier Rd AB11 170 F8
NEW PITSLIGO 23 D6
New Pitsligo & St Johns Sch AB43 23 D6
New Rd
Huntly AB54 148 E4
Montrose DD10 135 C6
New St
17 Boddam AB42 40 D1
Peterhead AB42 147 E6
Stonehaven AB39 185 E4
NEWTONHILL 181 H5
Newtonhill Prim Sch AB39 179 F1
Newtonhill Rd AB39 181 H4
NEWTONMILL 132 B3
Newton Pl AB39 181 I5
Newton Rd
Aberdeen AB16 164 C6
Dyce AB21 157 E6
Mintlaw AB42 146 D5
Peterhead AB42 27 B2
Stonehaven AB39 181 I5
Newton Terr AB21 163 F8
Newtown Dr AB44 141 E7
New View Ct 9 AB56 1 B5
New Wynd DD10 189 C3
Nicol Ct AB35 182 E4
Nicol Pl AB12 180 C6
Nicol Rd 2 AB51 155 C4
Nicol's Brae AB44 141 C7
NIGG 170 C2
Nigg Kirk Rd AB12 170 C3
Nigg Way AB12 170 A1
Ninian Pl AB12 180 C7
Ninian Rd AB21 157 E6
NITTANSHEAD 23 C4
Noble St AB43 143 C7
Norfolk Rd AB10 169 E5
North Anderson Dr AB15 164 C2
North Balnagask Rd AB11 170 F7
North Beach Rd AB23 91 C8
North Braeheads 2 AB43 143 D7
Northburn Ave AB15 169 B8
Northburn La AB15 169 A8
North Castle St
Banff AB45 140 F6
13 Cullen AB56 1 B5
Northcote Ave AB15 169 B4
Northcote Cres AB15 169 B5
Northcote Hill AB15 169 B4
Northcote Pk AB15 169 B4
Northcote Rd AB15 169 C4
NORTH CRAIGO 133 D2
North Deeside Rd
Aberdeen AB13 173 A7

North Deeside Rd *continued*
Aboyne AB34 108 A6
Banchory AB31 184 F5
Braeside AB15 169 C4
Peterculter AB14 172 C6
North Deskford St 3 AB56 1 B4
North Donside Rd AB23 160 A1
North East Falconry Ctr* AB54 43 A8
Northern Ct 8 AB43 143 D6
Northern Rd AB51 155 B6
North Esk Rd
Brechin DD9 132 B7
Montrose DD10 189 D4
North Esk View DD9 132 B7
North Esplanade E AB11 190 C2
North Esplanade W AB11 190 B1
NORTHFIELD 164 A5
Northfield Acad AB16 164 C5
Northfield Farm Mus* AB43 12 C2
Northfield Gdns 4 AB42 52 C4
Northfield Pl
Aberdeen AB25 165 A1
3 Ellon AB41 151 B5
Northfield Swimming Pool AB16 164 B5
NORTH FLOBBETS 48 B1
North Grampian Circ AB11 170 D6
North High St AB45 139 D7
Northhill Pk AB30 129 A5
North La
Fraserburgh AB43 143 D7
Peterhead AB42 147 D7
North Latch Rd DD9 188 A4
North Pl AB42 25 C1
NORTH RAYNE 58 F6
North Rd
Insch AB52 149 C4
Peterhead AB42 147 A8
North St Andrew St 3 AB25 190 A4
North Silver St AB10 190 A3
North Sq AB11 170 F8
North St
Aberchirder AB54 144 D4
Fraserburgh AB43 143 D7
Huntly AB54 144 C4
Inverurie AB51 152 C7
Mintlaw AB42 146 D6
Montrose DD10 189 D4
1 Peterhead AB42 147 E6
Rosehearty AB43 142 B8
Strichen AB43 24 E6
NORTH WATER BRIDGE 133 A5
Novar Pl AB25 165 A2
Nursery La
Brechin DD9 188 D1
5 Cornhill AB16 164 C4
Inverurie AB51 152 E5
Nursery Pk DD9 188 D2
Nursery Rd DD10 189 C5

O

Oakbank Gdns 7 AB51 150 C3
Oakbank Sch AB15 164 D1
Oak Cres AB32 161 D2
Oakdale Terr AB15 169 D5
Oak Dr AB12 180 B4
Oakhill Cres AB15 164 D1
Oakhill Rd
Aberdeen AB15 164 D1
Kintore AB51 155 C4
Oak Tree Ave AB31 184 E6
Oak View 6 AB23 91 C8
O'Brien Ct 3 AB51 152 E3
Ogilvie Ave AB54 148 D3
Ogilvie Cres AB51 155 B5
Ogilvie Pk 10 AB56 1 B4
Ogilvie Pl AB45 140 E5
Ogilvie St 2 AB45 8 F8
Ogilvie Terr DD10 189 C1
Ogstonmill 1 AB21 89 B7
Ogston Rd AB41 151 B5
OLD ABERDEEN 165 B5
Old Aberdeen Rd
3 Ellon AB41 61 E5
Laurencekirk AB30 129 F7
Old Castlegate 11 AB45 140 F6
Old Chapel Rd AB51 152 B7
Old Chapel Wlk 3 AB51 152 C7
Old Church Rd
Aberdeen AB11 170 D5
Buckie AB56 1 A4
Old Coast Rd AB12 180 D4
Old Course Ave AB51 152 B5
Oldcroft Ct 5 AB16 164 C3
Oldcroft Pl AB16 164 C3
Oldcroft Terr AB16 164 C3
OLD DEER 37 D6
Old Ferry Rd AB15 168 B1
Oldfold Ave AB13 167 D1
Oldfold Cres AB13 167 D1
Oldfold Dr AB13 167 D1
Oldfold Pk AB13 167 D1
Oldfold Pl AB13 167 D1
Oldfold Wlk AB13 167 D1
Old Ford Rd AB11 190 B1
Old Gamrie Rd AB44 141 E6
Old Inn Rd AB12 180 F7
Old Kemnay Rd AB51 152 D3
OLD KINNERNIE 100 C8
Old Line Rd AB35 182 C5
Oldmachar Acad AB22 159 D3
Oldman Rd AB12 173 B3
Old Market Pl AB45 141 A5
Old Market Rd AB34 183 D4
Old Mart Ave AB52 149 D4
Old Mart Pl DD9 188 D3
Old Mart Rd
14 Banchory AB31 108 E8
Insch AB52 149 D4
OLDMELDRUM 150 D2
Oldmeldrum Rd
Aberdeen AB21 153 C6
Ellon AB41 62 A2
Old Meldrum Rd AB21 158 D1
Old Military Rd
Alford AB33 97 F8
Ballater AB35 113 E1
Banchory AB31 98 A6
Bridgend AB54 43 E3
Crathie AB35 103 C8
Huntley AB45 148 C2
Huntly AB54 56 A7
Old Mill Cres AB23 91 C8
Oldmill Rd AB11 190 A2
Old Mill Rd AB39 181 I4
OLD MONTROSE 138 F3
Old Pier AB39 185 F3
OLD RAYNE 58 D3
Old Rayne Prim Sch AB52 58 D3
Old Rectory Ave AB41 151 D4
Old Road
Aberchirder AB54 144 D5
Balmedie AB23 91 C8
Huntly AB54 148 E4
Old Royal Sta The* AB35 182 D4
Old School 1 AB42 146 D5
Old School Rd AB53 22 D5
Old Skene Rd
Aberdeen AB15 163 A1
Kingswells AB15 162 F1
Westhill AB32 161 C3
Old Station Pl AB35 182 E5
Old Station Rd AB51 152 E5
Old Station Sq DD10 134 D3
Old Strichen Rd AB43 143 B3
Old Tollhouse Rd AB34 183 C5
Old Toll Rd AB54 148 E3
Old Town House The* AB24 165 B5
Oldtown Pl AB16 164 B6
Old Town Rd AB34 183 F5
Oldtown Terr AB16 164 A6
OLD WESTHALL 72 D8
OLDWHAT 23 C2
Olympia Gdns 4 AB31 110 B3
Omar Ave DD10 189 B5
Orange La DD10 189 D4
Orchard Gr
2 Blackburn AB21 156 A6
Ellon AB41 76 C7
3 Peterhead AB42 147 B3
Westhill AB32 100 D4
Orchard Pl AB24 165 C4
Orchard Rd AB24 165 C4
Orchard St AB24 165 C4
Orchard The 2 AB24 165 C4
Orchard Wlk 1 AB24 165 C4
ORDHEAD 86 C1
ORDIE 105 F8
Ordiquhill Prim Sch AB45 18 C7
Ord St AB15 169 B8
Oriel Terr AB14 172 D6
Orkney Ave AB16 163 E3
Osborne Pl AB25 164 F1
Osborne Terr AB44 141 D7
Oscar Pl AB11 170 D6
Oscar Rd AB11 170 D6
OVERBRAE 11 D3
Overhill Gdns AB22 159 E1
Overhills Wlk 10 AB21 163 D7
Overton Ave AB21 158 C5
Overton Circ AB21 158 B5
Overton Cres AB21 158 C5
Overton Pk AB21 158 C5
Overton Way AB21 158 B5
Overton Wlk AB21 158 C6
Oxen Craig AB51 152 A8
OYNE 72 C8
Oyne Prim Sch AB52 72 D8
Oyne Rd AB15 169 A7

P

Paddock The AB14 172 D6
Palmerston Pl AB11 190 B1
Palmerston Rd AB11 190 B2
Palmerston St 4 DD10 189 D2
Panmore Way 2 AB23 91 A6
Panmure Gdns AB23 91 A6
Panmure Pl
Edzell DD9 132 B8
Montrose DD10 189 D3
Panmure Row 5 DD10 189 D3
Panmure St
Brechin DD9 188 C3
2 Montrose DD10 189 D3
Pannanich Rd AB35 182 E5
Panter Cres DD10 189 C6
Pantoch Dr 2 AB31 184 F5
Pantoch Gdns 1 AB31 184 F5
Pantoch Way AB31 184 F5
Paradise Mews 3 AB16 164 C4
Paradise Rd AB51 87 D7
Park Brae AB15 168 E2
Park Cres
Banff AB45 7 E1
Ellon AB41 151 C4
Oldmeldrum AB51 150 D4
Peterhead AB42 36 E6
Portsoy AB45 139 C6
Park Dr
Portsoy AB45 139 D7
Stonehaven AB39 185 C6
Park Gr
Aberdeen AB23 91 A8
Brechin DD9 188 E3
Parkhead Gdns 6 AB21 163 D7
Parkhill AB51 87 D6
Parkhill Ave AB21 158 C5
Parkhill Circ AB21 158 B5
Parkhill Cres AB21 158 C5
Parkhill Ct 5 AB21 158 C7
Parkhill Rd
Alford AB33 154 C4
Peterhead AB42 147 D6
Parkhill Way AB21 158 B5
Park La
Aberdeen AB24 190 C4
Huntly AB54 56 A7
Oldmeldrum AB51 150 D4
3 Peterhead AB42 147 F5
Park Pl
Aberdeen AB24 190 B4
Brechin DD9 188 D3
3 Peterhead AB42 52 D4
Stonehaven AB39 181 H4
Park Rd
Aberdeen AB15 168 E2
Aberdeen AB24 190 C4
Ellon AB41 151 C4
Oldmeldrum AB51 150 D4
Portsoy AB45 139 C7
Park Road Ct AB24 165 D3
Parkside
Montrose DD10 135 C6
Westhill AB32 161 D2
Park St
Aberdeen AB24 190 C4
Fraserburgh AB43 143 C7
Huntly AB54 148 E4
Park Street N AB54 148 E5
Park Terr
Aberdeen AB23 91 A8
Ellon AB41 151 C4
Parkvale 5 AB42 38 D6
Parkview AB42 146 C4
Park View
Aberchirder AB54 144 C4
Brechin DD9 188 E4
Bridge of Don AB23 160 A1
Mintlaw AB42 146 C4
Peterhead AB42 52 D4
Parkway E AB23 160 B2
Parkway The AB22 159 E2
Partan Skelly Ave AB12 176 B7
Partan Skelly Way AB12 176 B7
Pass of Ballater AB35 182 D6
Paterson Pl 1 DD10 189 C7
Paterson St AB44 141 D7
Patey Rd AB41 151 C3
Pat McBoyle Ct 1 AB54 148 D5
Peacock's Cl AB10 190 C3
Pearse St DD9 188 B3
Pearson La AB30 186 C6
PEATHILL 142 C5
Peat Way AB12 180 B6
Peggy's Gdn AB31 111 B3
PENNAN 12 A8
Pennan Gr AB41 151 E7
Pennan Rd
Aberdeen AB24 165 A7
Ellon AB41 151 D6
Pennan Way AB41 151 D7
Penny Pl 3 AB42 147 A5
Pentland Cl AB11 170 F7
Pentland Cres AB11 171 A7
Pentland Pl
Aberdeen AB11 170 F6
Peterhead AB42 147 A6
Pentland Rd AB11 170 F7
Peregrine Rd AB32 161 C1
PERKHILL 97 F4
Perkhill Rd AB31 98 A3
Perry Rd DD9 132 D8
Persley Cres AB16 164 C6
Perwinnes Path 4 AB22 159 F1
Peter Buchan Dr AB42 147 C5
PETERCULTER 172 E7
Petergrange Rd AB42 147 B5
PETERHEAD 147 D4
Peterhead Acad AB42 147 D6
Peterhead Com Hospl AB42 147 D4
Peterhead Leisure Ctr AB42 147 D6
Peterhead Maritime Heritage Ctr* AB42 147 C3
Peterseat Dr AB12 170 F3
Peterwell Rd AB53 47 E4
Peth of Minnonie AB53 48 B3
Pettens Cl AB23 91 D8
Pettens St AB23 91 C8
Pheppie Rd AB39 181 G2
Philorth Ave AB43 143 C4
Phingask Rd AB43 143 C4
Phoenix Pl AB21 158 C3
Picktillum Ave AB25 164 F4
Picktillum Pl AB25 164 F4
Pictavia Ex* DD9 136 B6
Pilot Sq AB11 170 F8
Pinecrest Circ AB15 168 B3
Pinecrest Dr AB15 168 A3
Pinecrest Gdns AB15 168 A3
Pinecrest Wlk AB15 168 A2
Pine Tree Rd AB31 184 F6
Pine Tree Way AB31 184 F6
Pine View
Fraserburgh AB43 143 A6
Huntly AB54 148 C5
Mintlaw AB42 146 D5
Pinewood Ave AB15 169 A6
Pinewood Pl
Aberdeen AB15 169 A6
Cove Bay AB12 176 C7
Peterhead AB42 147 A4
Pinewood Rd AB15 169 A6
Pinewood Terr AB15 169 A6
Pinkie Gdns 3 AB21 153 D4
Pinkie Rd AB21 153 D5
Pintail Pl AB42 147 B5
Piper Pl AB12 180 C7
Pirie's Ct AB24 164 F6
Pirie's La
Aberdeen AB24 164 F5
Fraserburgh AB43 5 A4
3 Inverurie AB51 152 D6
5 Turriff AB53 145 D5
PITBLAE 5 B2
Pitblae Gdns AB43 143 B3
Pitblae Pl AB43 143 A3
PITCAPLE 73 B8
Pitchaidlie Pl 1 AB45 1 F1
Pitdourie Wlk 4 AB21 163 D7
PITFICHIE 86 D7
Pitfichie Castle* AB51 86 D7
Pitfichie La 4 AB21 158 C7
Pitfichie Pl AB21 158 C7
Pitfodels Sta Rd AB15 169 B3
Pitforthie Pl DD9 188 E4
Pitfour Cres 1 AB42 25 C1
Pitfour Ct AB42 147 B4
Pitfour Pl AB42 146 E4
Pitfour Sch AB42 146 C5
Pitlurg Castle* AB55 28 D4
PITMACHIE 58 C3
PITMEDDEN 62 B2
Pitmedden Ave AB21 158 B7
Pitmedden Cres AB10 169 E3
Pitmedden Dr AB21 158 B7
Pitmedden Gdn* AB41 62 A2
Pitmedden Mews AB21 158 B7
Pitmedden Prim Sch AB41 62 B2
Pitmedden Rd
Aberdeen AB10 169 E4
Dyce AB21 158 A8
Overton AB21 89 E5
Pitmedden Road Ind Est AB21 157 F8
Pitmedden Terr AB10 169 E4
Pitmedden Way AB21 158 B7
Pitmunie Pl 3 AB51 87 C7
Pitmurchie Rd AB34 108 A7
Pitsligo Castle (remains of)* AB43 142 D7
Pitsligo St AB43 142 B6
Pitstruan Pl AB10 169 F6
Pitstruan Terr AB10 169 F6
Pittendriech Rd DD9 188 A4
Pittendrigh Ct 6 AB51 152 E3
Pittendrum Gdns AB43 5 A4
Pittengullies Brae AB13 172 F6
Pittengullies Circ AB14 172 F6
Pittodrie La AB24 165 C4
Pittodrie Pl AB24 165 C4
Pittodrie St AB24 165 C4
Pittodrie Stadium (Aberdeen FC) AB24 165 D4
Pittrichie View AB21 75 C7
PITTULIE 4 F4
Pittulie Castle* AB43 142 F7
Place of Tilliefoure* AB51 72 B2
PLAIDY 21 A5
Plane Tree Rd AB16 164 D4
Plane Trees 3 AB53 22 C1
Pleasure Wlk AB42 147 F4
Plover Pl AB41 151 B4
Pocra Quay AB11 170 F8
Poet's Pl DD9 188 E2
Polbare Cl AB39 185 E7
Police La 4 AB43 24 E6
Polinar Pl AB51 152 D4
Polmuir Ave AB11 170 B6
Polmuir Gdns AB11 170 C6
Polmuir Pl AB11 170 B6
Polmuir Rd AB11 190 A1
Polo Gdns AB21 158 C3
Polston Rd AB12 173 B3
Polwarth Rd AB11 170 C6
Pool La AB42 147 F4
Poplar Cres AB42 147 B4
Poplar Rd 2 AB16 164 D4
Portal Cres AB24 165 A5
Portal Terr AB24 165 A5
PORT ELPHINSTONE 152 D4
Port Elphinstone Prim Sch AB51 152 D3
PORT ERROLL 53 B3
Port Erroll Prim Sch AB42 53 B3
Port Henry Pier AB42 147 F5
Port Henry Rd 3 AB42 147 E6
Porthill Ct AB25 190 B4
Portland St AB11 190 B1
PORTLETHEN 180 C6
Portlethen Acad AB12 180 B5
Portlethen Prim Sch AB12 180 C6
Portlethen Sta AB12 180 C6
Portlethen Swimming Pool AB12 180 B5
PORTLETHEN VILLAGE 180 E5
Port Long Rd 15 AB56 1 B5
Port Rd 2 AB51 152 E6
Portree Ave AB16 163 E3
PORTSOY 139 C7
Portsoy Cres AB41 151 E6
Portsoy Gr AB41 151 F6
Portsoy Pl 2 AB41 151 E6
Portsoy Prim Sch AB45 139 D6
POTTERTON 91 A6
Poultry Mkt La AB10 190 B4
Powis Circ AB24 165 A5
Powis Cres AB24 165 A5
Powis La AB25 165 B3
Powis Pl AB24 165 A3
Powis Terr AB24 165 A4
Poynernook Rd AB11 190 B2
Premnay Prim Sch AB52 71 E7
Price Cl AB51 155 B5
Price Dr AB51 155 B5
Primrosebank Ave AB15 168 F2
Primrose Bank Dr AB15 169 A2
Primrosehill Ave AB15 168 F2
Primrosehill Dr AB24 164 F5
Primrosehill Gdns 1 AB24 164 F5
Primrosehill Pl 2 AB24 164 F5
Primrosehill Rd AB15 168 F2
Prince Albert Mews 4 AB10 165 A1
Prince Arthur St AB25 164 F1
Princess Cres AB21 158 C7
Princess Dr AB21 158 C6
Princess Pl 8 AB21 158 C7
Princess Rd
Aberdeen AB21 158 C7
Stonehaven AB39 185 D5
Princes St
Aberdeen AB24 190 B4
Huntly AB54 148 D4
Inverurie AB51 152 C7
Princess Terr 9 AB21 158 C7
Princess Way AB21 158 C6
Princess Wlk 7 AB21 158 C7
Prince St AB42 147 D6
Pringle Ave AB41 61 E5
Printfield Terr AB24 164 F6
Printfield Wlk AB24 164 F6
Priory Pk AB14 172 E6
Privet Hedges AB16 164 C4
Promenade Ct AB24 165 D5
Prospect Ct AB11 170 B6
Prospecthill Rd AB15 168 B1
Prospect Pl AB32 161 E2
Prospect Terr
Aberdeen AB11 190 B1
2 Banchory AB31 98 A3
Dyce AB21 158 C3
4 Inverurie AB51 152 E3
Provost Barclay Dr 4 AB39 185 C4
Provost Buchan Rd DD9 188 B5
Provost Clemo Dr AB52 149 D4
Provost Cordiner Rd AB41 151 C4
Provost Craig Rd AB35 182 D4
Provost Davidson Dr AB41 151 C4
Provost Dr AB51 150 D3
Provost Florence Dr AB51 150 C2
Provost Fraser Dr AB16 163 F4
Provost Gordon Terr AB45 140 E6
Provost Graham Ave AB15 168 F8
Provost Hogg Ct AB11 170 F7
Provost Johnston Rd 2 DD10 189 C2
Provost Millar Ave DD9 188 B4
Provost Milne Dr AB43 143 C4
Provost Mitchell Circ AB23 160 A5
Provost Mitchell Rd 2 DD10 189 C7
Provost Noble Ave AB43 143 A5
Provost Peter Cres DD10 187 D7
Provost Rd DD9 188 B4
Provost Reids Rd DD10 189 D2
Provost Robson Dr AB30 186 C5
Provost Ross House* AB11 190 B3
Provost Rust Dr AB16 163 F6
Provost's Circ AB51 152 C7
Provost Scott's Rd DD10 189 D4
Provost Skene's House* AB25 190 B4
Provost Souter Pl AB52 149 D4
Provost Sq DD9 188 B4
Provost St AB54 148 E4
Provost Stewart Pl 3 AB39 185 C4
Provost Watt Dr AB12 170 B3
Prunier Dr AB42 147 A6
Prunier Pl AB42 147 A6
Puffin Ct AB39 181 I5
Pusey Pl AB42 147 C2
Putachie Path 4 AB53 145 C4

Q

Quarry Ct AB15 . . . . 168 D2
Quarryhill Ct 2 AB16 . . . 164 C4
Quarryhill Prim Sch
AB16 . . . . 164 B4
Quarry Pl
2 Aberdeen AB16 . . . . . . 164 A5
1 Mintlaw AB42 . . . . 146 D4
Quarry Rd
Aberdeen AB15 . . . . 168 C3
Aberdeen AB16 . . . . 164 A5
Fraserburgh AB43 . . . . 143 D7
Mintlaw AB42 . . . . 146 C4
Peterhead AB42 . . . . 52 D4
Quayside AB45 . . . . 140 F7
Queen Mary St AB43 . . . . . 143 B6
Queen's Ave AB15 . . . . . . 169 C7
Queens Cl AB43 . . . . 143 C6
Queen's Cl DD10 . . . . 189 D3
Queens Cres
Portsoy AB45 . . . . 139 D6
Rosehearty AB43 . . . . 142 C7
Queen's Cres
7 Boddam AB42 . . . . 40 D1
Hill of Rubislaw AB15 . . . . 169 C7
Queens Ct
Banchory AB31 . . . . 109 D3
Hill of Rubislaw AB15 . . . . 169 D7
4 Montrose DD10 . . . . . . 187 D3
Queens Den AB15 . . . . 163 E1
Queen's Dr
Banchory AB31 . . . . 109 D3
5 Buckie AB56 . . . . 1 B4
Queens Gate AB15 . . . . 169 E8
Queen's Gate AB45 . . . . . 139 D6
Queens Gdns AB45 . . . . 148 E4
Queen's Gdns
Aberdeen AB15 . . . . 169 E8
Huntly AB54 . . . . 148 E4
Stonehaven AB39 . . . . 185 D5
Queens Gr AB15 . . . . 169 A8
Queens Highlands AB15. 169 D8
Queens Hill Dr AB34 . . . . . 183 E6
Queen's La 8 AB42 . . . . 40 D1
Queen's Lane N AB15 . . . . 169 E8
Queen's Lane S AB15 . . . . 169 D7
Queens Links L Pk AB24 . 165 E2
Queens Rd
Fraserburgh AB43 . . . . 143 C6
Inverbervie DD10 . . . . 187 D7
Queen's Rd
Aberdeen AB15 . . . . 163 E1
Aboyne AB34 . . . . 106 B3
Ballater AB35 . . . . 182 D4
22 Boddam AB42 . . . . 40 D1
Stonehaven AB39 . . . . 185 D4
Turriff AB53 . . . . 145 C4
Queen St
Aberdeen AB10 . . . . 190 B3
Aberdeen AB24 . . . . 164 E6
6 Gourdon DD10 . . . . 187 D3
Huntly AB54 . . . . 148 E4
Inverurie AB51 . . . . 152 C7
Montrose DD10 . . . . 189 D4
Peterhead AB42 . . . . 147 D6
Rosehearty AB43 . . . . 142 C7
Queen's Terr AB10 . . . . 169 F8
Queen's Wlk 9 AB42 . . . . . . 40 D1
QUILQUOX 50 A5

R

Raasay Gdns AB16 . . . . 163 E2
Raasay Rd AB42 . . . . 147 B7
Raeburn Pl
Aberdeen AB25 . . . . 190 A4
Ellon AB41 . . . . 151 B6
Rae Circ AB51 . . . . 152 B8
Raeden Ave AB15 . . . . 164 D2
Raeden Cres AB15 . . . . 164 C2
Raeden Ct AB15 . . . . 164 C2
Raeden Park Rd AB15 . . . 164 D2
Raeden Pl AB15 . . . . 164 C2
Raeholm Rd 3 AB22 . . . . . 159 E1
Raemoir Ave AB31 . . . . 184 D5
Raemoir La 2 AB31 . . . . 184 D5
Raemoir Rd AB31 . . . . 184 D5
Raemoss Rd AB42 . . . . 147 E6
Rae St AB53 . . . . 145 D4
Raik Rd AB11 . . . . 190 B2
Railway Pl DD10 . . . . 189 D2
Railway Rd AB30 . . . . 186 C5
Railway Terr AB51 . . . . 152 E3
Rainnieshill Cl 1 AB21 . . 153 E5
Rainnieshill Gdns 2
AB21 . . . . 153 E5
Rainnieshill Rd AB21 . . . . . 153 E5
Rainnieshill Way AB21 . . 153 D5
Ramsay Cres AB10 . . . . . . 169 D4
Ramsay Gdns AB10 . . . . . 169 D3
Ramsay Pl AB10 . . . . 169 D3
Ramsay Rd
Banchory AB31 . . . . 184 C4
Stonehaven AB39 . . . . 185 C4
Ramsay St
Brechin DD9 . . . . 132 B7
1 Montrose DD10 . . . . . . 189 D2
Ramsay Terr AB43 . . . . 143 A5
Rannes St AB52 . . . . 149 D4
Rappahouse End 1
AB22 . . . . 159 E1
Rashieley Rd 2 AB51 . . . 152 C4
RATHEN 14 E3
Rathen Prim Sch AB43 . . . . 14 E3
Rathen Rd AB43 . . . . 15 B7
Rattray Pl 1 AB24 . . . . . . 165 A6
Rattray Rd AB42 . . . . 147 D7
Ravenscraig Castle*
AB42 . . . . 39 D7
Ravenscraig Rd AB42 . . . 147 C6
Raxton Pl AB21 . . . . 158 C7
Rayne North Prim Sch
AB51 . . . . 58 F6
Rearie Cl 4 AB21 . . . . 153 C6
Rectory Dr 3 AB43 . . . . 24 E6
Rectory Rd AB53 . . . . 145 B5
Redcloak Cres AB39 . . . . . 185 B6
Redcloak Dr AB39 . . . . 185 B6
Redcloak Pk AB39 . . . . 185 B6
Redcloak Way AB39 . . . . . 185 B6
REDCRAIGS 175 D8
Redfield Cres DD10 . . . . . 189 C4
Redfield Rd DD10 . . . . 189 C4
Redhall Pl AB30 . . . . 129 E6
Red Inch Circ 1 AB41 . . . . 77 F7
Redmoss Ave AB12 . . . . . . 170 D2
Redmoss Cres AB12 . . . . . 170 D4
Redmoss Pk AB12 . . . . 170 D2
Redmoss Pl AB12 . . . . 170 C2
Redmoss Rd AB12 . . . . 170 C1
Redmoss Terr AB12 . . . . . 170 D2
Redmoss Wlk AB12 . . . . . . 170 C2
Redmyre Prim Sch AB30 . 129 F6
Redwell Dr 12 AB45 . . . . 8 F8
Redwood Cres AB12 . . . . 176 C6
Reed Cres AB30 . . . . 186 C5
Reform St DD10 . . . . 189 D4
Regensburg Ct AB16 . . . . . 163 F3
Regent Quay AB11 . . . . . . 190 C3
Regent Rd AB11 . . . . 190 C2
Regent Wlk AB24 . . . . 165 C5
Reidfield Pl AB43 . . . . 15 D5
Reidford Gdns AB31 . . . . . 111 D5
Reidhaven Pl 6 AB56 . . . . . . 1 B5
Reidhaven St
Banff AB45 . . . . 8 F8
2 Banff AB45 . . . . 140 F6
7 Cullen AB56 . . . . 1 B4
Reid St AB45 . . . . 141 A5
Reisque Ave AB21 . . . . 153 D6
Rennie's Ct 6 AB11 . . . . . 190 B3
Rennies La AB54 . . . . 144 D4
Rennie's Wynd AB11 . . . . . 190 B3
Renny Cres DD10 . . . . 189 C6
Rhu-na-Haven Rd AB34. 183 A4
RHYNIE 55 D2
Rhynie Prim Sch AB54 . . . . 55 D2
Richmond Ave
3 Huntly AB54 . . . . 55 D2
Peterhead AB42 . . . . 147 A5
Richmond Ct 7 AB25 . . . 165 A2
Richmond Gdns 1 AB54 . . 55 D2
Richmondhill Ct
Aberdeen AB15 . . . . 164 D1
2 Rosemount AB15 . . . . . . 164 E1
Richmondhill Gdns 3
AB15 . . . . 164 E1
Richmondhill Pl AB15 . . . 164 D1
Richmondhill Rd AB15 . . 164 D1
Richmond La
3 Huntly AB54 . . . . 148 D4
Insch AB52 . . . . 149 C4
Richmond Pl AB35 . . . . 182 E4
Richmond Rd AB54 . . . . . 148 D3
Richmond St AB25 . . . . . . 165 A2
Richmond Terr
Aberdeen AB25 . . . . 165 A2
2 Huntly AB54 . . . . 55 D2
Peterhead AB42 . . . . 147 C5
Richmond Wlk AB25 . . . . 165 A2
RICKARTON 119 F3
Ricketts Ct DD9 . . . . 132 D8
Riddoch Ct AB45 . . . . 30 C7
Riddoch La AB53 . . . . 145 D5
Riddoch Rd 3 AB53 . . . . 145 D5
Ridgeway Gr AB22 . . . . . . 159 C1
Riggs The 9 AB42 . . . . 38 D6
Ringway Rd AB42 . . . . 147 A8
Ritchie Pl
Aberdeen AB24 . . . . 164 F7
Stonehaven AB39 . . . . 181 G2
Ritchie Rd AB43 . . . . 142 B6
Ritchie Row 7 AB51 . . . . . 152 E3
Riverside Dr
Aberdeen AB10 . . . . 169 F4
Huntly AB54 . . . . 148 C5
Insch AB52 . . . . 58 D3
Peterhead AB42 . . . . 147 C7
Stonehaven AB39 . . . . 185 C3
Riverside Pk AB51 . . . . 152 D3
Riverside Pl AB51 . . . . 152 D4
Riverside Rd
Ellon AB41 . . . . 151 B3
Inverurie AB51 . . . . 87 C7
Montrose DD10 . . . . 189 B2
Riverside Terr AB10 . . . . . . 170 A5
River St
Brechin DD9 . . . . 188 D2
Montrose DD10 . . . . 189 D1
River View AB42 . . . . 147 A8
Riverview Dr AB21 . . . . 158 C7
Riverview Pl AB41 . . . . 151 C3
ROADSIDE OF
CATTERLINE 126 C2
ROADSIDE OF KINNEFF . 131 C7
ROANHEADS 147 E6
Robbie Cl 11 AB23 . . . . 91 C8
Robbie's Rd AB43 . . . . 143 A3
Robbie's Wlk AB43 . . . . . . 143 A3
Robert Gordons Coll
AB25 . . . . 190 A3
Robert Gordon Univ The
AB10 . . . . 169 C3
Robertson Rd AB43 . . . . . 143 A6
Robert St AB39 . . . . 185 E5
Robertston Pl AB13 . . . . . . 173 B8
Rob Roy Pk AB14 . . . . 166 D1
Rockall Pl AB11 . . . . 170 E6
Rockall Rd AB11 . . . . 170 E6
Rocklands Rd AB15 . . . . . . 168 F3
Rocksley Dr 19 AB42 . . . . . . 40 D1
Roderick Dr AB43 . . . . 5 A4
Rodney St AB39 . . . . 185 E5
Rodney Terr 6 AB39 . . . . . 185 E5
Rolland Ct AB39 . . . . 125 B3
Rolland Pl AB39 . . . . 125 B3
Rolland Rd AB39 . . . . 125 B3
Ronaldsay Rd 1 AB15 . . . 163 F2
Ronaldsay Sq 6 AB15 . . . 163 F2
RORA 26 D1
Roscobie Pk AB31 . . . . . . 184 A5
Roseacre AB45 . . . . 139 D6
Roseacre Cres AB53 . . . . . 145 E4
Rose Ave AB42 . . . . 147 B3
Rosebank 6 AB51 . . . . . . 150 C3
Rosebank Gdns AB11 . . . 190 A1
Rosebank Pl AB11 . . . . . . 170 A7
Rosebank Terr AB11 . . . . . 190 A1
Rosebery St AB25 . . . . 164 E2
ROSEHEARTY 142 B7
Rosehearty Prim Sch
AB43 . . . . 142 B7
ROSEHILL 164 E5
Rose Hill DD10 . . . . 189 D5
Rosehill Ave AB24 . . . . . . 164 D5
Rosehill Cres
Aberdeen AB24 . . . . 164 E5
Banchory AB31 . . . . 184 B4
Rosehill Ct
Cornhill AB16 . . . . 164 D4
Montrose DD10 . . . . 189 D5
Rosehill Dr AB24 . . . . 164 D5
Rosehill La AB31 . . . . 184 B5
Rosehill Pl AB24 . . . . 164 E5
Rosehill Rd DD10 . . . . 189 D5
Rosehill Terr AB24 . . . . 164 E5
Rose House AB15 . . . . 168 F8
Rose La
1 Inverurie AB51 . . . . 152 D5
Portsoy AB45 . . . . 139 E7
ROSEMOUNT 164 F2
Rosemount Pl
Aberdeen AB25 . . . . 164 F1
3 Hillside DD10 . . . . 138 C8
Rosemount Prim Sch
DD10 . . . . 138 C8
Rosemount Rd DD10 . . . . 138 C8
Rosemount Sq 2 AB25 . 165 A1
Rosemount Terr 1
AB25 . . . . 165 A2
Rosemount Viaduct
AB25 . . . . 190 A3
Rose Pl
Aberdeen AB10 . . . . 165 A1
Peterhead AB42 . . . . 147 B3
Rose St
Aberdeen AB10 . . . . 170 A8
2 Peterhead AB42 . . . . 147 F5
Rosewell Dr AB15 . . . . 164 B1
Rosewell Gdns AB15 . . . . . 164 B1
Rosewell Pk AB15 . . . . 164 B1
Rosewell Pl AB15 . . . . 164 B1
Rosewell Terr AB15 . . . . . . 164 B1
Rosewood Ave AB12 . . . . 170 C2
Roslin Pl AB24 . . . . 190 C4
Roslin St AB24 . . . . 165 D3
Roslin Terr AB24 . . . . 190 C4
Ross Cres AB16 . . . . 164 B3
ROSSIE ISLAND OR
INCHBRAOCH 189 A1
Rossie Island Rd DD10 . . . 189 B1
ROSSIE MILLS 138 B3
Rossie Sq 2 DD10 . . . . 189 D1
Rossie Terr DD10 . . . . 189 D1
Ross St AB44 . . . . 141 D6
Rothiemay Prim Sch
AB54 . . . . 30 D7
ROTHIENORMAN 46 F2
Rothienorman Prim Sch
AB51 . . . . 47 A2
ROTHNEY 149 D4
Rothney Ct AB52 . . . . 149 C4
ROUGHPARK 81 A2
Rousay Dr AB15 . . . . 163 F2
Rousay Pl AB15 . . . . 163 F1
Rousay Terr AB15 . . . . 163 F2
Rowan Ave AB54 . . . . 148 C6
Rowanbank 2 AB42 . . . . . 147 B4
Rowanbank Rd AB12 . . . . . 180 B6
Rowan Circ AB42 . . . . 146 D5
Rowan Dr
7 Balmedie AB23 . . . . 91 C8
Westhill AB32 . . . . 161 C2
Rowan Gr AB41 . . . . 76 C7
Rowan Pl
Ellon AB41 . . . . 151 C4
Fraserburgh AB43 . . . . 143 B6
Rowan Rd AB16 . . . . 164 D4
Rowans The AB52 . . . . 149 D4
Rowan Terr 1 AB42 . . . . 52 D4
Rowan Tree Rd AB31 . . . . 184 D6
Row The AB43 . . . . 26 D7
Roxburghe House AB24 . . 164 F3
Royal Aberdeen Childrens
Hospl AB25 . . . . 164 E3
Royal Cornhill Hospl
AB25 . . . . 165 A3
Royal Deeside Rly The*
AB31 . . . . 110 D3
Royal Lochnagar Distillery
Visitor Ctr* AB35 . . . . . . 115 E8
Royfold Cres AB15 . . . . . . 169 C8
Rubislaw Den N AB15 . . . 169 C8
Rubislaw Den S AB15 . . . 169 C8
Rubislaw Dr AB15 . . . . 169 C7
Rubislaw Park Cres
AB15 . . . . 169 B7
Rubislaw Park Rd AB15 . . 169 B7
Rubislaw Pl AB10 . . . . 170 A8
Rubislaw Sq 2 AB15 . . . . 169 C7
Rubislaw Terr AB10 . . . . . . 169 F8
Rubislaw Terrace La
AB10 . . . . 169 F8
Rubislaw View 3 AB15 . . 169 C7
Ruby La AB10 . . . . 190 A3
Ruby Pl AB10 . . . . 190 A3
Ruddiman Dr AB30 . . . . . . 186 D6
Rugosa Circ AB21 . . . . 153 D6
Runcie's La AB43 . . . . 5 A4
Rushlach The AB51 . . . . . . 155 E3
Russell Ct 6 AB43 . . . . 26 C7
Russell Rd AB11 . . . . 190 B1
Russell St
Montrose DD10 . . . . 189 D3
Peterhead AB42 . . . . 37 D6
Rutherford Folds AB51 . . 152 C6
Ruthrie Ct AB10 . . . . 169 F5
Ruthrie Gdns AB10 . . . . 169 E4
Ruthriehill Rd AB21 . . . . . 158 C3
Ruthrie Rd AB10 . . . . 169 E4
RUTHRIESTON 169 F5
Ruthrieston Circ AB10 . . . 169 F5
Ruthrieston Cres AB10 . . . 169 F5
Ruthrieston Gdns AB10 . . . 169 F4
Ruthrieston Pl AB10 . . . . . 169 F5
Ruthrieston Rd AB10 . . . . . 169 E5
Ruthrieston Terr AB10 . . . . 169 F4
Ruthrie Terr AB10 . . . . 169 E4
RUTHVEN 29 E6
Rutland Cres DD10 . . . . . . 189 C5
Ryeland AB41 . . . . 62 A2

S

St Aidan Cres AB31 . . . . . . 184 E4
St Andrews AB51 . . . . 86 E6
St Andrew's Cath AB10 . . 190 C3
St Andrews Ct AB25 . . . . . 190 A4
St Andrews Dr AB43 . . . . . 143 B6
St Andrew's Dr 10 AB53 . 145 D4
St Andrew's Gdns AB51 . 152 D5
St Andrews Prim Sch
AB43 . . . . 143 C6
St Andrews Sch AB51 . . . 152 D5
St Andrew St
Aberdeen AB25 . . . . 190 A4
Brechin DD9 . . . . 188 B4
Peterhead AB42 . . . . 147 E5
St Andrew's Terr AB39 . . . 181 H5
St Andrew's Terr 1
AB35 . . . . 113 E6
St Annes Cres AB39 . . . . . . 179 F1
St Anne's Wynd AB39 . . . 180 A1
St Bridget Cres AB39 . . . . 185 C4
St Brydes Rd 1 AB51 . . . . . 87 D6
St Catherine St AB45 . . . . . 140 F6
St Catherine Street W
AB45 . . . . 140 E6
St Catherine's Wynd 1
AB10 . . . . 190 B3
St Clair Gdns 16 AB41 . . . . . 77 F8
St Clair St AB24 . . . . 190 B4
St Clair Way 4 AB41 . . . . . . 77 F8
St Clair Wynd 3 AB41 . . . . . 77 F8
St Clement's Ct AB24 . . . . 190 B4
St Clement St AB11 . . . . . . 165 E1
ST COMBS 15 C6
St Combs Ct AB45 . . . . 140 E5
St Combs Prim Sch AB43 . . 15 C6
St Comb's Rd AB45 . . . . . . 139 E7
St Congan's Cres AB53 . . . 145 B4
St Congant's Den AB53 . . 145 E4
St Crispin's Rd AB39 . . . . . 181 H4
ST CYRUS 134 D3
St Cyrus National Nature
Reserve Visitor Ctr*
DD10 . . . . 134 D2
St Cyrus Prim Sch DD10 . 134 E3
St David St 5 DD9 . . . . 188 C3
St Devenick's Cres AB15 . 168 E3
St Devenicks Mews
AB15 . . . . 168 F2
St Devenick's Pl AB15 . . . . 168 E3
St Devenicks Terr AB15 . . 168 F2
St Drostans La AB43 . . . . . . 12 E6
St Duthac Cres AB31 . . . . . 184 E5
St Eunan's Rd AB34 . . . . . . 183 C4
ST FERGUS 27 C3
St Fergus Prim Sch AB42 . . 27 B3
St Fittick's Rd AB11 . . . . . 171 A7
St Helena Ct 18 AB42 . . . . . 40 D1
St James's Cres AB51 . . . . 152 E4
St James's Pl AB51 . . . . . 152 A3
St John's Cotts 5 DD10 . 189 C4
St John's Gdns 10 AB51 . . . 87 D7
St John's Pl
Aberdeen AB11 . . . . 190 A2
6 Montrose DD10 . . . . 189 C4
St John's Rd AB21 . . . . 163 F8
St John's Terr AB15 . . . . . . 169 C5
St John's Wlk AB39 . . . . . . 179 F1
St Josephs Cath Prim Sch
AB10 . . . . 169 F8
ST KATHERINES 48 A1
St Kieran Cres AB39 . . . . 185 C3
St Machar Acad AB24 . . . . 165 B5
St Machar Cres 1 AB31 . . 184 E4
St Machar Ct 4 AB22 . . . . 164 F7
St Machar Dr AB24 . . . . . 165 A5
St Machar Pl AB24 . . . . . . 165 C6
St Machar Prim Sch
AB24 . . . . 165 A6
St Machar Rd AB24 . . . . . 165 A6
St Machars Cath AB24 . . . 165 B6
St Magnus Pl 4 AB42 . . . . 147 B5
St Magnus Rd AB43 . . . . 5 A3
St Margaret's Pl AB15 . . . . 164 B1
St Margarets RC Prim Sch
DD10 . . . . 189 C4
St Margarets Sch for Girls
AB10 . . . . 170 A8
St Marnan Rd AB31 . . . . 98 E1
St Marys AB51 . . . . 86 E6
St Mary's Cath AB10 . . . . 190 A3
St Mary's Dr AB41 . . . . . . 151 D4
St Marys Pl AB14 . . . . 172 D6
St Mary's Pl
Aberdeen AB11 . . . . 190 A2
Ellon AB41 . . . . 151 D3
St Mary's Rd 4 DD10 . . . . 189 D3
St Mary St
4 Brechin DD9 . . . . 188 C3
Peterhead AB42 . . . . 147 D5
St Mary Terr 3 AB42 . . . . . . 25 D5
St Michael's Cres AB39 . . 181 I5
St Michaels Pl AB39 . . . . . 181 I5
St Michael's Rd AB39 . . . . 181 H5
St Michael's Way AB39 . . 181 H5
St Michael's Wlk AB39 . . 181 H5
St Nathalan Cres AB31 . . . 184 E4
St Nathan's Rd AB39 . . . . 181 H5
St Nicholas Cres 1
AB31 . . . . 184 D4
St Nicholas Dr AB31 . . . . . 184 E4
St Nicholas La AB10 . . . . . 190 B3
St Nicholas Rd AB31 . . . . 184 D4
St Nicholas St AB10 . . . . . 190 B3
St Ninians AB51 . . . . 86 E6
St Ninians Cl AB24 . . . . . 165 C6
St Ninians Ct AB24 . . . . . 165 C7
St Ninian's Pl
Aberdeen AB24 . . . . 165 C6
4 Turriff AB53 . . . . 145 C5
St Olave Pl 4 AB42 . . . . 53 A3
St Paul St AB25 . . . . 190 B4
St Peter La AB24 . . . . 165 C3
St Peter's Gate 3 AB24. 165 C4
St Peters RC Prim Sch
AB24 . . . . 165 C5
St Peter's Rd
Montrose DD10 . . . . 189 D3
Stonehaven AB39 . . . . 181 H5
St Peter St
Aberdeen AB24 . . . . 165 C3
Peterhead AB42 . . . . 147 E5
St Peters Terr AB14 . . . . . 172 D6
St Ronan's Circ AB14 . . . . 172 E7
St Ronan's Cres AB14 . . . . 172 E7
St Ronan's Dr AB14 . . . . . . 172 E7
St Ronan's Pl AB14 . . . . . . 172 F6
St Swithin Row 4 AB10 . . 169 F8
St Swithin St AB10 . . . . . . 169 E8
St Tarquins Pl 6 AB45 . . . . . 1 F1
St Ternans Pl AB31 . . . . . . 184 B4
St Ternan's Rd AB39 . . . . . 181 H4
Salisbury Ct AB10 . . . . 169 F6
Salisbury Pl AB10 . . . . 169 F6
Salisbury Rd AB35 . . . . . . 182 D4
Salisbury Terr AB10 . . . . . . 169 F6
Salmon La 6 AB39 . . . . . . 185 E4
Saltoun Pl AB43 . . . . 143 D6
Saltoun Sq 3 AB43 . . . . . 143 D7
Samprey Rd AB15 . . . . 163 E1
Sanday Rd AB15 . . . . 164 B1
SANDEND 1 F4
Sandend Pk 7 AB41 . . . . . 151 E6
Sanderling Ct AB39 . . . . . . 181 I5
Sandford Ct 1 AB42 . . . . . 147 C4
SANDFORDHILL 53 D8
Sandford Pl 5 AB42 . . . . . . 40 D1
Sandford Terr AB42 . . . . . 147 C5
SANDHAVEN 5 A4
Sandhaven Cl 9 AB41 . . . 151 E6
Sandhaven Prim Sch AB43 . 5 A4
Sandhaven Wynd AB41 . . . 151 E6
Sandilands Dr AB24 . . . . . 165 A6
Sandyhill Rd AB45 . . . . 140 E4
SANDYHILLS 140 E4
Saphock Pl
Inverurie AB51 . . . . 152 C6
Oldmeldrum AB51 . . . . 150 B3
Satrosphere Science Ctr*
AB24 . . . . 190 C4
SAUCHEN 86 F1
Scalloway Pk AB43 . . . . . . 143 A5
Scalpay Wlk 3 AB16 . . . . . 163 E2
Scatha Ritchie Pl AB43 . . . 143 B7
Schivas Rd AB42 . . . . 147 C4
School Ave AB24 . . . . 165 C5
School Brae
Drumoak AB31 . . . . 111 D6
Fraserburgh AB43 . . . . 23 E6
School Cres
Aberdeen AB14 . . . . 172 E6
5 Newburgh AB41 . . . . 77 F8
School Dr AB24 . . . . 165 C5
Schoolhendry St AB45 . . . 139 E7
Schoolhill AB25 . . . . 190 A3
SCHOOLHILL 101 A1
School Hill
Banchory AB31 . . . . 184 D4
Ellon AB41 . . . . 151 C5
Turriff AB53 . . . . 145 D4

Schoolhill Pl AB12...... 180 C8
Schoolhill Rd
Aberdeen AB12.......... 180 B8
Ellon AB41............. 151 D5
School La
3 Aberchirder AB54..... 144 D5
Ballater AB35.......... 182 D4
Drumoak AB31........... 111 D6
2 Inverurie AB51....... 152 D5
Macduff AB44........... 141 C7
Peterculter AB14....... 172 E6
Turriff AB53........... 145 C4
School Pk 5 AB43........ 24 E6
School Pl
Aberdeen AB24.......... 165 D5
1 New Pitsligo AB43...... 23 E6
School Rd
Aberdeen AB24.......... 165 C5
Aboyne AB34............. 96 C3
Alford AB33............ 154 C3
9 Ballater AB35........ 113 F6
Banchory AB31............ 98 A3
Banff AB45................ 1 F1
9 Banff AB45.............. 8 F8
Cults AB15............. 168 E2
Drumlithie AB39........ 125 B3
Ellon AB41............... 77 F8
Huntly AB54.............. 29 E5
Inverurie AB51......... 152 E3
Kintore AB51........... 155 C4
Kirktown AB42............ 27 B3
3 Laurencekirk AB30.... 128 A4
Laurencekirk AB30...... 133 B7
New Deer AB42............ 36 E6
Newmachar AB21......... 153 D5
Peterculter AB14....... 172 D7
Peterhead AB42......... 147 B3
Stonehaven AB39........ 185 C5
Turriff AB53............. 47 E5
School St
Fraserburgh AB43....... 143 D7
New Pitsligo AB43........ 23 E6
School Terr AB24....... 165 D5
School Wlk AB24........ 165 D5
School Wynd
Inverbervie DD10....... 187 E7
St Cyrus DD10.......... 134 D3
Sclattie Circ AB21...... 163 D8
Sclattie Cres AB21...... 163 D8
Sclattie Pk AB21........ 163 D8
Sclattie Pl AB21........ 163 D7
Sclattie Quarry Ind Est AB21................ 158 C1
Sclattie Wlk AB21....... 163 C7
Scolty Pl AB31.......... 184 E5
Scolty View AB31........ 184 E5
Scotsmill Brae AB21..... 156 B7
Scotsmill Cres AB21..... 156 B8
Scotsmill Den AB21...... 156 B8
Scotsmill Gdns AB21..... 156 B8
Scotsmill View AB21..... 156 B8
SCOTSTON................ 129 D4
Scotston Pl DD10........ 134 D3
Scotston Terr DD10...... 134 D3
SCOTSTOWN............... 140 E6
Scotstown Gdns AB23..... 165 C8
Scotstown Moor Nature Reserve* AB23........ 159 E4
Scotstown Prim Sch AB22................ 159 F1
Scotstown Rd
Aberdeen AB23.......... 159 F3
Peterhead AB42......... 147 B7
Scott Cres DD10......... 138 C8
Scott Ct AB54........... 148 C5
Scott Dr AB54........... 148 C5
Scott Gr AB23............ 91 A8
Scottish Ag Coll AB21.... 157 E2
Scott Skinner Sq AB31... 184 C4
Scott St DD9............ 188 D2
Scott Sutherland Sch of Architecture Sch of Surveying AB10....... 169 D3
Scurdie Ness AB12....... 176 C8
Scylla Dr AB12.......... 176 A6
Scylla Gdns AB12........ 176 B6
Scylla Gr AB12.......... 176 B6
Sea Beach AB24.......... 165 E2
SEAFIELD................ 169 C6
Seafield Ave AB15....... 169 C6
Seafield Cres
Aberdeen AB15.......... 169 C6
Banff AB45............. 140 E6
Seafield Ct AB15........ 169 C6
Seafield Drive E AB15... 169 C7
Seafield Drive W AB15... 169 C7
Seafield Gdns AB15...... 169 C6
Seafield Pl
6 Banff AB45.............. 8 F8
Cullen AB56............... 1 B4
Portsoy AB45........... 139 E6
Seafield Rd
Aberdeen AB15.......... 169 C6
Buckie AB56............... 1 B3
Peterhead AB42......... 147 C4
Seafield St
Banff AB45............. 140 E6
4 Cullen AB56............. 1 B5
Portsoy AB45........... 139 D6
Seafield Terr AB45...... 139 C6
Seaforth Rd AB24........ 165 D3
Seaforth St 7 AB43...... 143 D6
Seagate
Montrose DD10.......... 189 C2
3 Peterhead AB42....... 147 F6
Seal Craig Gdns AB12.... 176 B8
Seamount Ct AB25........ 190 B4
Seamount Rd AB25........ 190 B4
Sea St AB56............... 1 B5
SEATON.................. 165 C6
Seaton Ave AB24......... 165 C5
Seaton Cres AB24........ 165 D6
Seaton Dr AB24.......... 165 D6
Seaton Gdns AB24........ 165 C6
Seaton Pl AB24.......... 165 C6
Seaton Place E AB24..... 165 C6
Seaton Prim Sch AB24.... 165 D6
Seaton Rd AB24.......... 165 D5
Seaton Wlk AB24......... 165 C6
SEATOWN
Banff.................. 139 E7
Buckie.................... 1 A5
Seatown Pl AB43.......... 15 C8
Seaview Ave AB23........ 160 A5
Seaview Circ AB23....... 160 A4
Seaview Cl AB23......... 160 A5
Seaview Cres AB23....... 160 A4
Seaview Dr AB23......... 160 A4
Seaview Gdns AB42....... 147 D1
Seaview Pl
Aberdeen AB23.......... 160 A5
Montrose DD10.......... 189 B1
Seaview Rd
Aberdeen AB23.......... 165 C8
Banff AB45................ 1 F3
24 Boddam AB42........... 40 D1
Peterhead AB42........... 27 B3
Seaview Terr
Cove Bay AB12.......... 176 C6
Gourdon DD10........... 187 D3
Johnshaven DD10........ 135 C5
Sedge Pl AB12........... 180 A5
Selbie Dr AB51.......... 152 C5
Selbie Pl
Inverurie AB51......... 152 D5
Montrose DD10.......... 187 D4
Seton Dr AB54........... 148 D5
Seton Terr
8 Ellon AB41............. 62 B2
Huntly AB54............ 148 D5
Seton Way 2 AB51....... 150 C2
Sett Rd AB21............ 156 B8
Settrington St AB54..... 148 D4
Shand Ct 2 AB44......... 141 C6
Shand St AB44........... 141 C6
Shand Terr AB44......... 141 C6
Shannoch Dr 1 AB51....... 87 D7
Shannocks View AB53..... 145 B6
Shapinsay Ct AB15....... 163 E2
Shapinsay Sq 5 AB15..... 163 F2
Shaw Circ AB32.......... 161 C3
Shaw Cres AB25.......... 164 F3
Shaw Rd AB25............ 164 F3
SHEDDOCKSLEY............ 163 D3
Sheddocksley Dr AB16.... 163 F2
Sheddocksley Rd AB16.... 163 F3
Sheddocksley Sports Ctr AB15................ 163 F4
Shepherd Pl AB12........ 170 A3
Sheriffs Brae 8 AB45.... 140 F6
Sherwood Pl AB53......... 36 A5
Shetland Wlk AB16....... 163 E3
Shieldhill Gdns AB12.... 176 C8
Shielhill Gdns AB22..... 159 E1
Shillinghill AB45....... 139 D7
Shiprow AB42............ 147 F4
Ship Row AB11........... 190 B3
Ship St AB42............ 147 F4
Shoe La AB10............ 190 B4
Shore Brae 2 AB11....... 190 B3
Shorehead
Banff AB45............. 139 D7
Stonehaven AB39........ 185 F3
Shore La AB11........... 190 C3
Shore St
Fraserburgh AB43....... 143 D7
Inverallochy AB43........ 15 C8
Macduff AB44........... 141 C6
Portsoy AB45........... 139 E7
Rosehearty AB43........ 142 C8
Sandhaven AB43............ 5 A4
Shoretack Ct 5 DD10.... 187 D3
Shore Wynd 5 DD10...... 189 C2
Short Loanings AB25..... 165 A2
Shunnery Brae 1 AB51... 152 E3
Sidney Cres 4 AB42....... 52 D4
Sillerton La AB12....... 170 B3
SILVERBANK.............. 184 F5
Silverbank Cres AB31.... 184 F5
Silverbank Gdns AB31.... 184 F5
Silverburn Cres AB23.... 160 A2
Silverburn Pl AB23...... 160 A2
Silverburn Rd AB22...... 159 E1
Silver Gdns 12 AB39..... 185 E4
Silverhillock AB45........ 7 E1
Silver Pitt Gdns 3 AB42 147 A4
Silver Way DD10......... 189 C7
Simpson Ave 1 AB51....... 47 A2
Simpson Pl AB44......... 141 D7
Simpson Rd AB23......... 165 C8
Sims Rd 5 AB54........... 55 D2
Sinclair Cres
Aberdeen AB21.......... 153 C5
Cove Bay AB12.......... 176 C7
Sinclair Gdns DD10...... 138 D8
Sinclair Pl
Aberdeen AB12.......... 176 C7
Fraserburgh AB43....... 143 A5
Sinclair Rd AB11........ 190 C1
Sinclair Terr AB12...... 176 C7
Sir Patrick Geddes Way AB35................ 182 E5
Sir William Wallace Wynd AB24................ 165 C6
Skateraw Rd AB39........ 181 I4
Skelly Rock AB12........ 176 C8
Skelton St AB42......... 147 D6
Skene Pl
Aberdeen AB21.......... 158 B6
17 Rosemount AB25..... 165 A1
Skene Prim Sch AB32..... 101 D6
Skene Rd AB15........... 163 D1
Skene Sq AB25........... 190 A4
Skene Square Prim Sch AB25................ 165 A2
Skene St
Aberdeen AB25.......... 190 A3
Macduff AB44........... 141 D7
Peterhead AB42......... 147 E6
Skene Terr AB10......... 190 A3
Skerry Dr AB42.......... 147 C3
Skerry Pk 14 AB42........ 40 D1
Skinner Ave AB51........ 152 C5
Skinner Rd AB42.......... 38 D6
Skye Rd AB16............ 163 E2
Slackadale Gdns AB53.... 145 B6
Slains Ave
Aberdeen AB22.......... 159 D2
Ellon AB41............. 151 E6
Slains Castle, Old* AB41.. 64 F4
Slains Castle (remains of)* AB42.................. 53 C3
Slains Circ AB22........ 159 D2
Slains Cres AB41........ 151 E5
Slains Ct AB42.......... 147 C3
Slains La AB22.......... 159 E2
Slains Pl 4 AB22........ 159 D1
Slains Prim Sch AB41...... 64 D5
Slains Rd AB22.......... 159 D2
Slains St AB22.......... 159 D2
Slains Terr AB22........ 159 D2
Slateford Rd DD9........ 132 A7
Slater Ct AB41.......... 151 D5
Slatrford Gdns DD9...... 132 A7
Sleigh Cres 6 AB43....... 24 E6
Slessor Dr AB12......... 170 A1
Slessor Rd AB12......... 170 A2
Slug Rd
Banchory AB31.......... 110 D2
Stonehaven AB39........ 185 A7
Sluie Dr AB21........... 158 C7
Sluiemohr AB35.......... 182 E4
Smiddy Field 2 AB41...... 49 B4
Smiddyhill Rd AB43...... 143 A3
Smiddy La AB41.......... 151 D4
Smiddy Pk DD10.......... 131 C7
Smiddy Rd AB39.......... 125 B3
Smithbank Rd DD9........ 188 C4
Smith Cres AB54......... 144 D5
Smith Ct 4 AB45......... 148 D4
Smithfield AB51......... 155 C6
Smithfield Ct AB15...... 164 C6
Smithfield Dr AB16...... 164 D5
Smithfield La AB24...... 164 D7
Smithfield Prim Sch AB16................ 164 C5
Smithfield Rd AB24...... 164 E6
Smith Rd AB45........... 140 E5
Smithyhaugh Rd AB16..... 163 F6
Smithy La
7 Peterhead AB42......... 38 D6
11 Strichen AB43.......... 24 E6
6 Turriff AB53......... 145 D4
Smithy Rd 3 AB51......... 47 A2
Snipe St AB41........... 151 B4
Social Club Rd AB42....... 40 C1
Society La AB24......... 164 E6
Somerset Cres AB52...... 149 C5
Souter Circ AB32........ 161 E4
Souterford Ave AB51..... 152 E6
Souterford Ave Bsns Pk AB51................ 152 E6
Souterford Cres 1 AB51 . 152 E6
Souterford Dr AB51...... 152 E6
Souterford Rd AB51...... 152 E6
Souterford Wynd 3 AB51................ 152 E6
Souter Gdns AB32........ 161 E3
Souter Head Rd AB12..... 170 D1
Souter St AB44........... 141 D6
South Anderson Dr AB10................ 169 E6
South Ave AB15.......... 168 E2
South Castle St 1 AB56.... 1 B4
South Colege St AB11.... 190 B1
South Constitution St 1 AB11................ 190 C4
South Crown St AB11..... 190 A1
South Deskford St 4 AB56. 1 B4
Southesk Pl
Aberdeen AB21.......... 158 B7
Montrose DD10.......... 189 C1
Southesk Prim Sch DD10................ 189 C2
Southesk St
Brechin DD9............ 188 C3
Montrose DD10.......... 189 C2
Southesk Terr 1 DD9..... 188 D2
South Esplande E AB11... 190 C1
South Esplande W AB11... 190 B1
SOUTH FLOBBETS........... 48 B1
South Grampian Circ AB11................ 170 D6
South Harbour Rd AB43... 143 D3
South Headlands Cres AB39................ 181 I4
South High St AB45...... 139 D6
SOUTH KIRKTON........... 100 E4
South La AB42........... 147 D7
South Lodge Dr AB39..... 185 C6
SOUTH LOIRSTON.......... 176 A7
South Mile-End AB10..... 170 A6
South Mount St AB25..... 165 A1
South Park Prim Sch AB43................ 143 C5
South Rd
Ellon AB41............. 151 D4
Insch AB52............. 149 D4
Oldmeldrum AB51........ 150 C3
Peterhead AB42......... 147 C1
South Silver St AB10.... 190 A3
South Sq AB11........... 170 F8
South St
Huntly AB54............ 144 D4
Mintlaw AB42........... 146 E5
Montrose DD10.......... 135 C5
South View Pl AB42...... 147 B2
Southview Terr AB54..... 144 C4
South Wlk AB16.......... 164 D4
Soy Ave AB45............ 139 D6
Soy Burn Gdns AB45...... 139 C6
Spademill La AB15....... 169 D8
Spademill Rd AB15....... 169 D8
Spalings The 2 AB34..... 108 B6
Spark Terr AB12......... 176 C6
Spa St AB25............. 190 A3
Spey Rd AB16............ 164 A3
Spey Terr AB16........... 164 A3
Spires Bsns Units AB21 . 164 A8
Spital AB24............. 165 C4
Spital Wlk AB24......... 165 B4
Spittal The AB42......... 26 D1
Springbank 1 AB42....... 147 C3
Springbank Pl 3 AB11.... 190 A2
Springbank St AB11...... 190 A2
Springbank Terr
Aberdeen AB11.......... 190 A2
Peterhead AB42......... 147 B3
Springdale Cres AB15.... 168 A2
Springdale Ct AB15...... 168 B2
Springdale Pk AB15...... 168 A2
Springdale Pl AB15...... 168 B2
Springdale Rd AB15...... 168 A2
Springfield Ave AB15.... 169 B7
Springfield Gdns
Aberdeen AB15.......... 169 B6
Peterhead AB42........... 36 D7
Springfield La AB15..... 169 B7
Springfield Pl AB15..... 169 B6
Springfield Rd
Aberdeen AB15.......... 169 A8
2 Kemnay AB51............ 87 D7
Spring Gdn AB25......... 190 A4
Springhill Cres AB16.... 163 F5
Springhill Rd 2 AB16.... 163 F3
Springhill Terr
Aberdeen AB16.......... 163 F4
2 Cove Bay AB12........ 176 C6
Spring Tyne AB32........ 161 B3
Springvale Ed Trust AB23................ 160 A4
Spurryhillock Ind Est AB39................ 185 B4
Square DD10............. 135 C6
Square The
3 Aberchirder AB54..... 144 C4
5 Aboyne AB34............ 96 C3
Banchory AB31.......... 184 B4
7 Banff AB45.............. 1 F1
5 Cullen AB56............. 1 B5
Ellon AB41............. 151 D5
Fetterangus AB42......... 25 C1
Fettercairn AB30....... 128 B4
Huntly AB54............ 148 D5
Inverurie AB51........... 86 E6
5 Kintore AB51......... 155 C5
Lumsden AB54............. 69 B5
8 Oldmeldrum AB51..... 150 C3
Portlethen AB12........ 180 C6
Portsoy AB45........... 139 D7
6 Rhynie AB54............ 55 D2
Rosehearty AB43........ 142 C7
Stuartfield AB42......... 37 D4
2 Tarves AB41............ 61 E6
Torphins AB31.......... 108 E8
Turriff AB53............. 22 E5
13 Turriff AB53........ 145 D4
Stable Cl AB51........... 59 E3
Staffa St AB42.......... 147 B7
Stafford St AB25........ 165 A3
Stanley Ct 3 AB32....... 161 D2
Stanley St AB10......... 169 F8
Station Brae
Aberdeen AB14.......... 172 E6
Aboyne AB34............ 183 E5
Ellon AB41............. 151 B5
6 Fraserburgh AB43..... 143 D6
Station Ct AB31.......... 184 D4
Station Mews AB21....... 163 F8
Station Pk 9 DD10....... 187 D3
Station Pl
2 Cruden Bay AB42........ 53 A3
Longside AB42............ 38 E6
Montrose DD10.......... 135 C6
Peterhead AB42......... 147 C5
Station Rd
Aberdeen AB21.......... 163 F8
Banchory AB31.......... 184 D4
Boddam AB42............. 40 C1
Cruden Bay AB42.......... 53 A3
3 Cullen AB56............. 1 B5
Cults AB15............. 168 F3
Dyce AB21.............. 158 A6
Ellon AB41............. 151 B5
Fordoun AB30........... 129 E6
Fraserburgh AB43......... 15 B8
Hatton AB42.............. 52 D4
Insch AB52............... 56 D4
Station Rd *continued*
Inverurie AB51......... 152 E6
Kemnay AB51............. 87 D6
Laurencekirk AB30...... 186 D6
Longside AB42............ 38 D6
2 Maud AB42.............. 36 E7
Milltimber AB13........ 173 B7
Mintlaw AB42........... 146 C5
Newmachar AB21......... 153 D6
Oldmeldrum AB51........ 150 B3
Peterhead AB42......... 147 D5
4 Rothienorman AB51...... 47 A2
St Cyrus DD10.......... 134 D3
Stonehaven AB39........ 125 B3
13 Torphins AB31....... 108 E8
Turriff AB53........... 145 D3
Station Road E
Milltimber AB13........ 173 B7
Peterculter AB14....... 172 E5
Station Road S AB14..... 172 D5
Station Road W AB14..... 172 D6
Station Sq
Aboyne AB34............ 183 D5
Ballater AB35.......... 182 E4
Lumphanan AB31........... 98 A3
Station Terr AB42........ 38 D6
Station Way AB42........ 146 B6
Stell Rd AB11........... 190 B2
Stephen's La 15 AB41..... 77 F8
Steven Rd AB54.......... 148 B4
Stevenson Ct 3 AB25..... 165 A1
Stevenson Rd AB43....... 143 D8
Stevenson St 14 AB25.... 165 A1
Stewart Cl 2 AB33....... 154 E3
Stewart Cotts 2 AB42..... 52 C4
Stewart Cres
Aberdeen AB16.......... 164 B4
Alford AB33............ 154 E3
Stewart Csescent AB16.. 164 A5
Stewart Dr AB33......... 154 E4
Stewart Gr 1 AB33....... 154 E3
Stewart La
Alford AB33............ 154 E3
2 Huntly AB54.......... 148 E4
Stewart Park Ct AB24.... 164 D5
Stewart Park Pl AB24.... 164 D5
Stewart Pl 3 AB33....... 154 E3
Stewart Rd AB33......... 154 E3
Stewart Terr AB16....... 164 A5
Stewart Way AB33........ 154 E3
Stewart Wlk 4 AB33...... 154 E3
STIRLING................. 40 C1
Stirling St AB11......... 190 B3
Stiven Wlk AB30......... 186 D5
STOCKETHILL............. 164 C3
Stockethill Cres AB16... 164 C3
Stockethill Ct AB16...... 164 C4
Stockethill La 1 AB16... 164 C3
Stockethill Way 4 AB16. 164 C4
Stocket Par 1 AB16...... 164 C4
Stonefield Dr AB51...... 152 A7
Stonefield Pl 8 AB51.... 152 A7
STONEHAVEN.............. 185 F7
Stonehaven L Ctr AB39... 185 F6
Stonehaven Rd AB10...... 169 F4
Stonehaven Sta AB39..... 185 C5
Stonehaven Tolbooth Mus* AB39................ 185 F4
Stoneybank Gdns AB53..... 36 A5
Stoneybank Terr 2 AB53... 36 A5
Stoneyhill Terr AB12..... 176 C6
Stoneyton Terr AB21...... 158 B1
STONEYWOOD.............. 158 C2
Stoneywood Park Ind Est AB21................ 158 C4
Stoneywood Park N AB21................ 158 C4
Stoneywood Pk AB21...... 158 C4
Stoneywood Prim Sch AB21................ 158 C2
Stoneywood Rd AB21...... 158 C2
Stoneywood Terr AB21.... 158 C3
Stornoway Cres AB15..... 163 D3
Storybook Glen* AB12.... 173 C3
Stracathro Hospl DD9.... 132 D4
Stracathro Prim Sch DD9................. 132 C4
STRACHAN................ 117 D7
Strachan Pl AB16......... 164 C6
Strachan Prim Sch AB31 117 D7
Strachan's La AB10...... 170 A7
Straik Pl AB32........... 161 C2
Straik Rd AB32........... 161 B2
Strait La AB53........... 145 D5
Strait Path AB45......... 140 F5
Straloch Ave 4 AB21..... 153 D5
Stranathro Terr AB39.... 181 G2
Strathbeg Ct AB43....... 143 A5
Strathbeg Pl 3 AB22..... 165 B8
Strathburn Gdns AB51.... 152 C6
Strathburn Prim Sch AB51................ 152 C6
Strathburn St AB12....... 176 B8
STRATHDON................ 81 B3
Strathdon Sch AB36........ 81 A3
Strathmore Dr AB16...... 164 A4
Strathmore Pl 2 DD10.... 189 C4
Strawberry Bank 6 AB42................ 147 B5
Strawberry Bank Par 2 AB11................ 170 A8
Strawberryfield Rd AB32 161 A3
Street The AB42.......... 26 E1
STRICHEN................. 24 F6
Strichen Ct AB43........ 143 B3
Strichen Prim Sch AB43... 24 F6
Strichen Rd AB43........ 143 C3
Stroma Terr AB16........ 163 E2

Stronsay Ave AB15 164 A1
Stronsay Cres AB15 164 A2
Stronsay Dr AB15 164 A1
Stronsay Pl AB15 164 A1
Stuart Cres 1 AB41 61 E5
STUARTFIELD 37 D5
Stuartfield Prim Sch AB42 37 D4
Stuart La 3 AB45 140 F6
Stuart St 4 AB45 140 F6
Sugarhouse La AB11 190 C3
Suie Rd AB33 154 A8
Sumburgh Cres AB16 163 E3
Summer Brae 3 AB21 153 D5
Summerfield Pl
  Aberdeen AB24 190 C4
  Inverallochy AB43 15 C7
Summerfield Terr
  Aberdeen AB24 190 B4
  Inverallochy AB43 15 C7
Summerfield Wlk AB43 15 C7
SUMMERHILL 164 A2
Summerhill Cres AB15 164 B2
Summerhill Ct AB15 164 B2
Summerhill Dr AB15 164 B2
Summerhill House AB21 153 D5
Summerhill Rd AB15 164 B1
Summerhill Terr AB15 164 B1
Summer Pl AB21 158 B6
Summers Rd AB43 142 C7
Summer St
  Aberdeen AB10 165 A1
  Aberdeen AB24 164 F6
Sunert Rd AB13 173 D8
Sunnybank Cotts AB53 47 E5
Sunnybank Pl AB24 165 B4
Sunnybank Prim Sch AB24 165 B4
Sunnybank Rd AB24 165 B4
Sunnybrae 19 AB21 163 D7
Sunnyhill Pl AB53 145 C5
Sunnyside Ave
  Aberdeen AB24 165 B4
  Banchory AB31 111 D5
Sunnyside Cres AB31 111 D6
Sunnyside Ct AB33 154 D4
Sunnyside Dr
  Alford AB33 154 D4
  Banchory AB31 111 D6
Sunnyside Gdns
  Aberdeen AB24 165 B4
  Banchory AB31 111 D6
Sunnyside La AB31 111 D6
Sunnyside Rd AB24 165 B4
Sunnyside Royal Hospl DD10 138 C8
Sunnyside Terr AB24 165 B4
Sunnyside View AB51 155 C3
Sunnyside Wlk AB24 165 B3
Sunset Wood AB31 184 B5
Sutherland Ave 5 AB42 147 E6
Sutherland Pl AB45 139 C7
Swanley Cotts AB39 120 A2
Swannay Sq 7 AB15 163 F2
Swann Pl AB35 182 D4
Swan Pl AB41 151 B4
Swan Rd AB41 151 B3
Swan St DD9 188 C3
Sycamore Pl
  Aberdeen AB11 170 B6
  1 Banchory AB31 184 F6
  Huntly AB54 148 C5
  5 Mintlaw AB42 146 D5
Sycamore Rd AB31 184 F6
Sycamore Row AB43 143 A6
Sycamore Way 2 AB31 184 F6

T

Tailyour Cres DD10 189 C6
Talisman Dr AB10 169 C3
Talisman Rd AB10 169 C3
Talisman Wlk AB10 169 C3
Tall Pines AB31 184 F6
Tanfield Ave AB24 164 F6
Tanfield Ct 4 AB24 164 F6
Tanfield Wlk AB24 164 F6
Tannery Ct 3 AB45 140 E5
Tannery St AB45 140 E6
Tappie View AB21 156 A6
Taransay Cres AB16 163 E3
Taransay Ct AB16 163 E3
Taransay Rd AB16 163 E2
Tarbothill Rd 4 AB22 165 B8
Target Rd AB45 139 C7
Tarlair Rd AB44 141 F7
Tarlair St AB44 141 E7
TARLAND 96 B3
Tarland Prim Sch AB34 96 C3
TARVES 61 E6
Tarves Prim Sch AB41 61 E5
Taylor Cres
  Peterhead AB42 26 E6
  Stonehaven AB39 185 C4
Taylor Dr AB54 144 D5
Tayock Ave 3 DD10 189 C5
Tay Rd AB16 164 A4
Teal Ct AB42 147 B5
Teal St AB41 151 B4
Tedder Rd AB24 165 A6
Tedder St AB24 165 A6
Temperance La The 2 AB54 144 C4
Temple of Theseus* AB42 37 D7
TEMPLETON 117 D6
Temple View AB45 141 A5
Tern Ct AB39 181 I5
Tern Pl AB23 160 A4
Tern Rd AB12 176 B7
Terpersie Castle* AB33 70 C3
TEUCHAR 34 D8
Teuchar Pk 4 AB53 22 B1
Teuchar Rd AB53 22 B1
Teviot Pl DD10 189 E3
Teviot Rd AB16 163 F3
Thainstone Bsns Ctr AB51 74 B1
Thainstone Ct AB51 74 B1
Theatre La AB11 190 B3
THE POLE OF ITLAW 20 C7
Thistle Ct AB43 143 D6
Thistle Dr AB12 180 D7
Thistle Gdns 7 AB42 146 D5
Thistle La AB10 165 A1
Thistle Pl AB10 170 A8
Thistle Rd AB21 157 E5
Thistle St
  Aberdeen AB10 170 A8
  5 Kirktown AB42 147 E5
Thomas Glover Pl AB22 165 B8
Thompson Terr AB43 143 B5
Thomson Rd AB45 140 E5
Thomson's La 4 AB51 152 D6
Thomson St AB25 164 F2
Thomson Terr
  Montrose DD10 189 B1
  Stonehaven AB39 185 C4
Thores Rd AB42 147 C7
Thorngrove Ave AB15 169 D6
Thorngrove Cres AB15 169 D6
Thorngrove Ct AB15 169 D6
Thorngrove Pl AB15 169 D6
Thornhill Rd AB53 22 C1
THORNROAN 61 E7
Thornton Castle* AB30 128 E2
Thornton Ct AB30 186 C5
Threadneedle St 3 AB42 147 E5
TIFTY 47 F7
Tillybrake Gdns AB31 184 D5
Tillybrake Ind Est AB31 184 E5
Tillybrake Rd AB31 184 D5
Tillybrake Rise
  Banchory AB31 184 D5
  Drumoak AB31 111 C5
Tillybrig AB32 100 E8
Tillycairn Castle (remains of)* AB51 86 C2
TILLYDRONE 165 A6
Tillydrone Ave AB24 165 B6
Tillydrone Ct AB24 165 A7
Tillydrone Rd AB24 165 A7
Tillydrone Sh Ctr AB24 165 A7
Tillydrone Terr AB24 165 A6
Tillyduff Gdns AB43 15 D5
Tillyfar Gdns AB53 145 B5
TILLYFOURIE 86 A3
Tilquhillie Castle* AB31 110 C1
Tilquillie Pl AB31 184 E6
TIPPERTY 63 D1
Tipperty Prim Sch AB41 63 D2
Tiree Cres AB16 163 E2
TOCHER 58 F7
Tocher La AB31 184 B5
Tocher St AB44 141 D6
Toch Hill Pl AB30 129 E6
Tochieneal Cnr AB56 1 B3
Todhead Gdns AB12 176 C8
Todlaw Wlk AB21 158 C7
Tolbooth The* AB11 190 C3
Tolbooth Wynd 2 AB42 147 E5
Tollohill Cres AB12 170 C3
Tollohill Dr AB12 170 B3
Tollohill Gdns AB12 170 C3
Tollohill La AB12 170 B2
Tollohill Pl AB12 170 C3
Tollohill Sq AB12 170 B3
Tolmount Cres DD10 189 C7
Tolquhon Ave AB41 61 E6
Tolquhon Castle (remains of)* AB41 61 F3
Tolquhon Pl 2 AB41 151 E5
Tophead Pl AB42 26 E6
Topping Gdns AB43 143 B6
Tormentil Cres 13 AB23 91 C8
Tornashean Gdns AB21 158 C7
TORNAVEEN 98 D5
TORPHINS 108 F8
Torphins Prim Sch AB31 108 E8
TORRIES 85 D4
TORRY 170 E7
Torry Acad AB11 170 D6
Torry Rd AB54 148 C4
Torry St AB54 148 D4
Torry Youth & Leisure Ctr AB11 170 D6
TORTERSTON 39 B6
Tortorston Dr AB42 39 C5
Tortorston Rd AB42 39 C5
Total French Sch 15 AB25 165 A1
Tough Prim Sch AB33 85 D4
Towerhill AB42 147 C1
Towerhill Pl AB42 147 C2
Towerview La 4 AB14 172 D7
Towerview Pk 7 AB14 172 D7
Towerview Rd AB14 172 D7
Towerview Way 5 AB14 172 D7
Towerview Wlk 6 AB14 172 D7
Towerview Wynd 8 AB14 172 D7
TOWIE 82 D3
Towie Barclay Castle* AB53 33 E2
Towie Castle (remains of)* AB33 82 E3
Towie Prim Sch AB33 82 D3
TOWNHEAD 187 D7
Townhead Ave AB51 152 B7
Townhead Dr 6 AB51 152 B7
Townhead Gdns 3 AB51 152 B7
Townhead Pl AB51 152 B7
Townhead Rd AB51 152 B7
Townhead Terr
  4 Inverurie AB51 152 B7
  Kintore AB51 155 B5
Tradlin Circ AB21 156 A6
Trafalgar La AB30 186 D5
Traill Dr DD10 189 E3
Traill Terr DD10 189 E2
Tree Rd AB41 61 E6
Trenchard Way DD10 187 D6
TRINITY 188 E7
Trinity Ct 1 AB32 161 E3
Trinity Fields Cres DD9 188 C5
Trinity La AB11 190 B3
Trinity Quay AB11 190 B3
Trinity Rd DD9 188 C4
Trinity St AB11 190 B3
Troup House Sch AB45 3 E3
Troup View AB45 3 C2
Tuach Rd 3 AB51 155 C5
Tuach View 1 AB51 155 C4
Tullich Rd AB35 182 E4
Tullochgorum Gdns 2 AB42 38 D6
Tulloch Pk 7 AB21 163 D7
TULLOS 170 D4
Tullos Circ AB11 170 D6
Tullos Cres AB11 170 E6
Tullos House (remains of)* AB51 73 A4
Tullos Pl AB11 170 E6
Tullos Prim Sch AB11 170 F6
Tullos Swimming Pool AB12 170 E6
TULLYNESSLE 70 D2
Tullynessle Prim Sch AB33 154 A8
Tummel Rd AB41 151 B6
Tumulus Way AB51 155 C2
Turfhill Rd AB53 36 A6
Turiff Swimming Pool & Sports Ctr AB53 145 C3
Turin Way AB41 77 C6
Turlundie Terr AB43 23 D7
Turnberry Cres AB22 159 F2
Turnberry Ct AB22 159 F2
Turnberry Dr AB51 152 C5
Turnberry Gdns AB23 159 F2
Turners Ct AB39 185 F5
Turner St AB44 141 C6
Turnishaw Hill AB41 151 C6
Turnstone Ct AB39 181 I5
TURRIFF 145 C3
Turriff Acad AB53 145 D4
Turriff FC AB53 145 D4
Turriff Hospl AB53 145 E4
Tuscany Gdns 6 AB21 153 C6
Two Mile Cross AB10 169 E3
TYRIE 13 C5
Tyrie Gdns AB52 149 D5
Tyrie Prim Sch AB43 13 C5

U

Udny Castle* AB41 62 A1
Udny Gn Prim Sch AB41 62 A1
UDNY GREEN 62 A1
Udny Pl AB41 151 E5
UDNY STATION 76 C7
Ugiebank Pl AB42 147 B7
Ugie Dr AB42 146 E4
Ugie Hospl AB42 147 C7
Ugie Pl AB16 164 A3
Ugie Rd AB42 147 C7
Ugie St AB42 147 E6
Ugie View 1 AB43 24 E6
Uist Rd AB16 163 E2
Union Ct AB41 151 D5
Union Glen AB11 190 A2
Union Glen Ct 3 AB11 170 A8
Union Gr
  Aberdeen AB10 169 F7
  Fraserburgh AB43 143 C6
Union Gr Ct 1 AB10 170 A8
Union Gr La AB10 169 E7
Union La
  Ellon AB41 151 D4
  Rosehearty AB43 142 C7
Union Pl 12 AB51 150 C3
Union Rd
  Macduff AB44 141 C6
  Montrose DD10 189 D4
Union Row
  Aberdeen AB10 190 A2
  Dyce AB21 158 B6
  Montrose DD10 189 E4
Union St
  Aberdeen AB10 190 A3
  Brechin DD9 188 C2
  Edzell DD9 132 A8
  Ellon AB41 151 C5
  Montrose DD10 189 D4
  Peterhead AB42 147 F5
  Rosehearty AB43 142 C7
Union Terr AB10 190 A3
Union Terrace Gdns* AB10 190 A3
Union Wynd AB10 190 A3
University Ct AB21 163 D7
University Rd AB24 165 B5
Univ of Aberdeen (Foresterhill Site) AB24 164 D3
Univ of Aberdeen (Marischal Coll) AB25 190 B4
Univ of Aberdeen (Old Aberdeen Campus) AB24 165 B5
Uphill La 1 AB42 147 E4
Upper Arbeadie Pl AB31 184 C5
Upper Arbeadie Rd AB31 184 B6
Upperboat Pl 3 AB51 152 D4
Upperboat Rd AB51 152 C5
UPPER BODDAM 57 E5
UPPER BOYNDLIE 13 B5
Upper Craigo St 5 DD10 189 C3
Upper Denburn AB25 190 A3
Upper Farburn Rd AB21 157 F5
Upper Hall St 8 DD10 189 C4
Upperkirkgate AB10 190 B3
Upperkirk Gate 2 AB54 148 D4
UPPER LOCHTON 184 C7
Upper Lochton AB31 184 C6
Upper Lochton E AB31 184 C7
Upper Manse Rd AB51 152 C5
Upper Mastrick Way AB16 164 A4
Upperton Ind Est AB42 147 A1
Urie Cres AB39 185 E5
Urievale Rd AB51 59 B1
Urquhart Cres AB42 27 B2
Urquhart La AB24 165 D3
Urquhart Pl 2 AB24 190 C4
Urquhart Rd
  Aberdeen AB24 165 D3
  Oldmeldrum AB51 150 C3
  Peterhead AB42 27 B3
  Turriff AB53 22 E5
Urquhart St AB24 165 D3
Urquhart Terr AB24 165 D3
Ury Dale AB51 152 E5
Ury Mdws AB51 152 A8
Uryside Dr AB51 152 E7
USAN 138 E1
Usan Ness AB12 176 C8
Usan Rd DD10 189 D1

V

Valentine Cres AB22 159 D2
Valentine Dr AB22 159 C1
Valentine Rd AB22 159 C2
Valley Cres AB12 170 C3
Valley Gdns AB12 170 B3
Victoria Cres AB56 1 B5
Victoria Ct AB51 152 D6
Victoria Gdns AB45 140 E6
Victoria Grange AB21 158 B6
Victoria Pl
  Banff AB45 140 E6
  Brechin DD9 188 D2
  Cullen AB56 1 B5
Victoria Rd
  Aberdeen AB11 190 C1
  Alford AB33 154 C4
  Ballater AB35 182 D4
  Huntly AB54 148 D4
  Maud AB42 36 E7
  Peterhead AB42 147 D6
Victoria Road Prim Sch AB11 170 E7
Victoria Sq 5 DD10 189 D1
Victoria St
  Aberdeen AB10 170 A8
  Cullen AB56 1 B5
  Dyce AB21 158 B6
  Fraserburgh AB43 143 D6
  Insch AB52 149 C5
  Inverurie AB51 152 D6
  7 Montrose DD10 189 C4
  Stonehaven AB39 185 E4
  7 Turriff AB53 145 C4
Victoria Terr
  Inverbervie DD10 187 D6
  Inverurie AB51 152 E3
  Kemnay AB51 87 D6
  Turriff AB53 145 D4
Viewbank Pl DD9 188 E3
Viewfield Ave AB15 169 C6
Viewfield Cres AB15 169 C6
Viewfield Ct AB15 169 C7
Viewfield Gdns AB15 169 B7
Viewfield Pl 1 AB35 182 D4
Viewfield Rd
  Aberdeen AB15 169 C6
  Ballater AB35 182 D4
  Fraserburgh AB43 143 C6
View Gdns 2 AB42 40 D1
Viewmount Rd AB31 184 D4
View Terr AB25 165 A2
Viking Pl AB12 180 C7
Village Farm Ct 9 AB31 108 E8
Villagelands Rd AB39 181 I4
Virginia Ct 3 AB11 190 C3
Virginia St AB11 190 C3
Volum St AB42 147 F5

W

Wagley Ct 13 AB21 163 D7
Wagley Par 1 AB21 163 D7
Wagley Pl 17 AB21 163 D7
Waldron Rd DD10 189 D7
Wales St AB11 190 C4
Walker Ave AB45 140 F5
Walker Dr AB39 181 G1
Walker La AB11 190 C1
Walker Pl AB11 190 C1
Walker Rd AB11 190 C1
Walker Road Sch AB11 170 D6
Wallacebrae Ave 2 AB22 159 A1
Wallacebrae Cres AB22 159 B1
Wallacebrae Dr AB22 159 B1
Wallacebrae Gdns 2 AB22 159 B1
Wallacebrae Path 1 AB22 159 B1
Wallacebrae Pl AB22 159 A1
Wallacebrae Rd AB22 159 B1
Wallacebrae Terr AB22 159 A1
Wallacebrae Wlk 1 AB22 159 A1
Wallacebrae Wynd AB22 159 B1
Wallace Cres
  Peterhead AB42 147 A7
  1 Turriff AB53 145 C4
Wallace Rd AB51 152 E5
Wallace St 2 AB42 147 E4
Wallace Way AB42 147 A7
Wallace Wynd 3 AB39 185 F3
Wallfield Cres AB25 164 F1
Wallfield Pl AB25 164 F1
Walton Rd AB21 157 E3
Wapping St AB11 190 B2
Wardes Rd AB51 152 E4
Wardhead Pl AB16 163 F3
Wardhouse Rd DD10 189 D7
Ward Rd AB43 142 C7
Wards La AB44 141 E7
Wards Rd DD9 188 E4
Ward St AB42 53 B3
Ware Rd AB42 147 D7
Warrack Terr DD10 189 D4
Watch Craig AB51 152 A8
Watchman Brae 21 AB21 163 D7
Water La
  Aberdeen AB11 190 C3
  Banff AB45 141 A6
  Ellon AB41 151 D4
  1 Turriff AB53 145 D5
Waterloo Quay AB11 190 C3
Watermill Rd AB43 143 A6
Water Path AB45 140 F6
WATERSIDE 147 A8
Waterside Ct 1 AB51 87 C7
Waterside Gdns AB33 154 A6
Waterside Pl AB42 147 A8
Waterside Rd
  Montrose DD10 189 E2
  Peterhead AB42 147 A8
  Strathdon AB36 81 D2
Waterside Way AB42 147 A7
Waters of Philorth Nature Reserve* AB43 15 A7
Waterson Dr DD9 188 C4
Water St AB43 24 E6
Waters The AB30 124 B1
Waterton Rd AB21 158 C2
Watson Ave AB54 148 D3
Watson Cres AB42 147 A5
Watson Ct AB51 152 D7
Watson Gdns AB43 143 B6
Watson La AB25 164 F2
Watson St
  Aberdeen AB25 164 F2
  Banchory AB31 184 C4
Watson Watt Pl DD9 188 C4
Watt Cres AB51 152 D6
Watt's La AB44 141 C7
Waughton Pl DD10 135 C6
Waulkmill Cres AB16 164 A6
Waulkmill Rd 1 AB16 164 A5
Waul Pk AB43 143 C7
Wavell Cres AB24 164 F7
Waverley Pl AB10 170 A8
Weavers Row 2 AB16 164 A5
Webster Ct 11 AB51 150 C3
Webster Rd AB12 170 A2
Wedderburns Rise AB12 172 F3
Weigh-House Sq 3 AB11 190 B3
Wellbrae AB51 59 E3
Wellbrae Terr
  Aberdeen AB15 169 C6
  Inverurie AB51 59 E2
Wellburn Pk AB31 108 E8
Wellfield Cres 3 AB53 145 C5
Wellfield La 2 AB54 144 D5
Wellfield Terr AB54 144 D5
Wellgrove Cres AB32 161 C2
Wellgrove Dr AB32 161 C2
Wellgrove Rd AB32 161 C2
Wellheads Cres AB21 158 B4
Wellheads Dr AB21 158 A5
Wellheads Ind Est AB21 158 B3
Wellheads Pl AB21 158 B4
Wellheads Rd AB21 158 C5
Wellheads Terr AB21 158 B3
Wellheads Way AB21 158 B4
Wellington Brae AB11 190 B1
Wellington Circ AB12 170 C1
Wellington Pk DD10 189 D4
Wellington Pl AB11 190 B2
Wellington Rd AB12 175 E6
Wellington St
  Aberdeen AB11 165 E1
  Montrose DD10 189 D4

Wellpark AB51 ... 59 E3
Wellpark Gdns AB51 ... 155 C5
Wellpark Rd AB51 ... 155 B6
Wellside Ave AB15 ... 163 A4
Wellside Circ AB15 ... 163 A4
Wellside Cl AB15 ... 163 A4
Wellside End AB15 ... 163 A4
Wellside Gdns AB15 ... 162 F4
Wellside Pk AB15 ... 163 A4
Wellside Pl AB15 ... 162 F4
Wellside Rd AB15 ... 163 A4
Wellside Wlk AB15 ... 163 A4
Wellside Wynd AB15 ... 163 A4
Well St
Peterhead AB42 ... 147 D7
Rosehearty AB43 ... 142 B8
Wellwood Terr AB15 ... 168 F3
WESTBANK PARK ... 150 B3
Westbank Pk AB51 ... 150 B3
West Bay DD10 ... 187 C3
WESTBRAE ... 145 B5
West Brae DD10 ... 135 C5
Westbrae Cres AB53 ... 145 C5
Westburn Ave AB51 ... 152 A6
Westburn Ct 2 AB25 ... 165 A2
Westburn Dr
Aberdeen AB25 ... 164 E3
Inverurie AB51 ... 152 A6
Westburn Gdns AB51 ... 152 A6
Westburn Pl AB51 ... 152 A6
Westburn Rd AB25 ... 164 C2
WEST BURNSIDE ... 128 B3
West Cairncry Rd AB16 ... 164 B4
West Church St AB45 ... 1 F1
West Craibstone St 5
AB11 ... 190 A2
West Ct AB54 ... 148 C4
West Cults Rd AB15 ... 168 D1
Westdyke Ave AB32 ... 161 C2
Westdyke Cl AB32 ... 161 C3
Westdyke Ct AB32 ... 161 B2
Westdyke Dr AB32 ... 161 B2
Westdyke Gdns AB32 ... 161 B2
Westdyke Pl AB32 ... 161 C2
Westdyke Terr AB32 ... 161 B2
Westdyke Way AB32 ... 161 B2
Westdyke Wlk AB32 ... 161 C2
West End AB45 ... 8 F8
Westend Gdns 1 AB51 ... 150 B3
Western Ave AB41 ... 151 B4
Western Pl AB41 ... 151 B3
Western Rd
Aberdeen AB24 ... 164 E6
Insch AB52 ... 149 B5
Inverurie AB51 ... 152 D6
Montrose DD10 ... 189 C3
Western Road N DD10 ... 189 C4
Westerton Cres AB16 ... 164 A6
Westerton Pl
Aberdeen AB16 ... 164 B6
Cults AB15 ... 168 F3
Westerton Prim Sch
AB16 ... 163 F5
Westerton Rd AB15 ... 168 F3
Westerwards AB45 ... 139 C6
Westfield Ave
Inverurie AB51 ... 152 C6
Stonehaven AB39 ... 185 D5
Westfield Ct AB39 ... 185 D5
Westfield Gdns
Inverurie AB51 ... 152 C6
Westhill AB32 ... 161 D3
Westfield Pk AB39 ... 185 D5
Westfield Pl AB42 ... 147 D5
Westfield Rd
Aberdeen AB25 ... 164 F2
Inverurie AB51 ... 152 D6
Stonehaven AB39 ... 185 D5
Turriff AB53 ... 145 B5
Westfield Specl Sch
AB43 ... 143 B5
Westfield Terr
Aberdeen AB25 ... 164 F1
Ballater AB35 ... 182 D4
West Fountain St 5
AB45 ... 140 E6
Westgate 14 AB21 ... 163 D7
West Glebe AB39 ... 185 D6
West Haven Cres AB43 ... 15 B8
West High St AB51 ... 152 D6
WESTHILL ... 161 D4
Westhill Acad AB32 ... 161 E3
Westhill Bsns Pk AB32 ... 161 C1
Westhill Cres AB32 ... 161 C3
Westhill Dr AB32 ... 161 E2
Westhill Grange AB32 ... 161 C3
Westhill Hts AB32 ... 161 D4
Westhill Pl 9 AB53 ... 145 C5
Westhill Prim Sch AB32 ... 161 E3
Westhill Rd AB32 ... 161 F3
Westhill Swimming Pool
AB32 ... 161 E3
Westholme Ave AB15 ... 169 B8
Westholme Cres N AB15 ... 169 B8
Westholme Terr AB15 ... 169 A8
West Mount St AB25 ... 165 A2
West North St AB24 ... 190 B4
West Park Ave DD10 ... 187 D6
West Park Cres DD10 ... 187 D6
West Park Gr DD10 ... 187 D6
West Park Pl DD10 ... 187 C6
West Park St AB54 ... 148 D5
West Park Terr DD10 ... 187 D6
West Pk
Fraserburgh AB43 ... 15 D5
Inverbervie DD10 ... 187 D6
Westray Cres AB15 ... 164 B2
Westray Pk AB43 ... 143 B4
Westray Rd AB15 ... 164 A2
West Rd
Fraserburgh AB43 ... 143 B4
Peterhead AB42 ... 147 C5
Westshore Rd AB43 ... 143 B7
West Shore Rd Ind Est
AB43 ... 143 B7
West Skene St AB44 ... 141 D7
West St
Fraserburgh AB43 ... 15 D6
Montrose DD10 ... 135 C5
Strichen AB43 ... 24 E6
West's Way AB54 ... 144 D5
West Terr DD10 ... 189 C1
West Toll Cres AB34 ... 183 B5
West Tullos Rd AB12 ... 170 B4
Westwood DD9 ... 188 B3
Westwood Cres AB32 ... 161 D3
Westwood Dr AB32 ... 161 D3
Westwood Gr AB32 ... 161 D3
Westwood Pk 3 AB21 ... 156 A6
Westwood Pl
Bankhead AB21 ... 163 E7
Westhill AB32 ... 161 D3
Westwood Way AB32 ... 161 D3
Westwood Wlk AB32 ... 161 D3
Wharf St DD10 ... 189 C2
Wheatland 1 AB41 ... 62 A2
Whinfield Rd DD10 ... 189 E4
Whinfield Way DD10 ... 189 E4
Whinhill Cres 5 AB45 ... 140 F6
Whinhill Gate AB11 ... 190 A1
Whinhill Gdns AB11 ... 170 B6
Whinhill Rd
Aberdeen AB11 ... 190 A1
Banff AB45 ... 140 D5
Whinhill Terr AB45 ... 140 E5
WHINNYFOLD ... 65 B8
Whinpark Circ AB12 ... 180 B5
Whin Park Pl AB16 ... 164 A4
Whin Park Rd AB16 ... 164 B5
Whin Path AB21 ... 156 B7
Whisky Brae AB41 ... 151 C5
Whistleberry Castle (remains of)* DD10 ... 131 E6
WHITECAIRNS ... 76 D1
WHITEFORD ... 59 B1
Whiteford Gdns AB51 ... 59 C1
Whiteford Pl AB51 ... 59 B1
Whiteford Rd AB51 ... 59 B1
White Gates 2 AB42 ... 147 A8
Whitehall Gdns AB52 ... 149 D6
Whitehall Pl AB25 ... 164 F1
Whitehall Rd AB15 ... 164 E1
Whitehall Terr AB25 ... 164 F1
Whitehill Pl AB42 ... 147 B3
WHITEHILLS ... 8 F8
Whitehills Cres AB12 ... 176 B7
Whitehills Ct 4 AB41 ... 151 E6
Whitehills Dr 5 AB41 ... 151 E6
Whitehills Prim Sch AB45 ... 8 F7
Whitehills Rise AB12 ... 176 B6
Whitehills Way AB12 ... 176 A7
Whitehorse Terr 1 AB23 ... 91 C8
WHITEHOUSE ... 85 E5
Whitehouse St 6 AB10 ... 165 A1
Whitelands Rd AB39 ... 181 I4
Whiteley Well Dr AB51 ... 152 B8
Whiteley Well Pl 3
AB51 ... 152 B8
WHITEMYRES ... 59 D5
Whitemyres Ave AB16 ... 164 A2
Whitemyres Pl AB16 ... 164 B2
WHITERASHES ... 75 D6
Whiterashes AB15 ... 162 F1
White Ship Ct 2 AB43 ... 24 E6
Whitespace* AB24 ... 190 C4
WHITESTONES ... 23 A3
Whitestripes Ave AB22 ... 159 C2
Whitestripes Cl 1 AB22 ... 159 D1
Whitestripes Cres AB22 ... 159 D2
Whitestripes Dr AB22 ... 159 C3
Whitestripes Path AB22 ... 159 D2
Whitestripes Pl AB22 ... 159 D2
Whitestripes Rd AB21 ... 158 F7
Whitestripes St AB22 ... 159 D2
Whitestripes Way AB22 ... 159 D3
Whitson Way 4 DD10 ... 189 D7
Widgeon Way AB41 ... 151 B4
Wildgoose Dr 2 AB21 ... 153 C6
Wilkie Ave AB16 ... 164 C6
William Mackie Cres 1
AB39 ... 185 C6
William Mackie Rd AB39 ... 185 C6
Williams Cres AB43 ... 143 C5
Williamson Pl 3 AB45 ... 140 E6
William St
11 Banchory AB31 ... 108 E8
Fraserburgh AB43 ... 15 B8
Montrose DD10 ... 187 C3
4 Montrose DD10 ... 189 D1
Willowbank Rd
Aberdeen AB11 ... 190 A1
Peterhead AB42 ... 147 B3
Willowdale Pl AB24 ... 190 B4
Willowgate Cl 4 AB11 ... 170 A8
Willow Green Gdns
AB21 ... 156 B6
Willowgrove Dr AB21 ... 156 B5
Willowpark Cres AB16 ... 164 B2
Willowpark Pl AB16 ... 164 B3
Willowpark Rd AB16 ... 164 B3
Willow Tree Way AB31 ... 184 F6
Willow Wynd AB12 ... 180 B5
Wilson Cres AB45 ... 8 F8
Wilson Ct 5 AB51 ... 152 E3
Wilson Pl 12 AB51 ... 87 D7
Wilson Rd
Banchory AB31 ... 184 C5
Banff AB45 ... 140 F5
Wilson's Pk DD9 ... 188 C3
Wilson St AB42 ... 147 E6
Windford Rd AB16 ... 163 F2
Windford Sq AB16 ... 163 F2
Windhill St AB42 ... 37 C4
Winding Brae 6 AB42 ... 38 D6
Windmill Brae AB11 ... 190 A2
Windmill Ct AB42 ... 147 E6
Windmill La AB11 ... 190 A2
Windmill Rd AB42 ... 147 A6
Windmill St AB42 ... 147 E6
Windy Brae AB45 ... 140 D6
Windyedge AB51 ... 152 C5
Windyedge Ct AB39 ... 181 H4
Wingate Pl AB24 ... 165 A6
Wingate Rd AB24 ... 165 A6
Wiseman Terr AB42 ... 27 B3
Wishart Ave DD10 ... 189 D5
Wishart Dr AB30 ... 186 D5
Wishart Gdns DD10 ... 189 D5
Witchden Rd DD9 ... 188 D2
Witchhill Rd AB43 ... 143 B4
Woodburn Ave AB15 ... 169 A7
Woodburn Cres AB15 ... 169 A7
Woodburn Gdns AB15 ... 169 A7
Woodburn Pl AB15 ... 169 A7
Woodburn Rd AB21 ... 156 A6
Woodcot Brae AB39 ... 185 D4
Woodcot Ct 2 AB39 ... 185 D4
Woodcot Gdns 1 AB39 ... 185 D4
Woodcot La AB39 ... 185 D4
Woodcot Pk AB39 ... 185 D4
Woodcroft Ave AB22 ... 159 C5
Woodcroft Gdns AB22 ... 159 C5
Woodcroft Gr AB22 ... 159 C5
Woodcroft Rd AB22 ... 159 C5
Woodcroft Wlk AB22 ... 159 C5
Woodend Barn Arts Ctr*
AB31 ... 110 B4
Woodend Cres AB15 ... 163 F1
Woodend Dr AB15 ... 164 A1
Woodend Hospl AB15 ... 163 F1
Woodend Pl AB15 ... 169 A8
Woodend Rd AB15 ... 164 A1
Woodend Terr AB15 ... 164 A1
WOODHEAD ... 48 B5
Woodhill Ct AB16 ... 164 C3
Woodhill Pl AB15 ... 164 C1
Woodhill Rd AB15 ... 164 C1
Woodhill Terr AB15 ... 164 C2
Woodland Ave AB15 ... 168 F4
Woodland Gdns
Aberdeen AB15 ... 169 A4
Inverurie AB51 ... 59 D3
Woodlands AB53 ... 145 D5
Woodlands Cres
Cults AB15 ... 169 A4
Turriff AB53 ... 145 D4
Woodlands Dr
Aberdeen AB21 ... 157 E6
Ellon AB41 ... 151 D6
Woodlands Edge AB41 ... 151 D6
Woodlands Pl
Banchory AB31 ... 184 E6
Inverbervie DD10 ... 187 D6
Woodlands Rd
Aberdeen AB21 ... 157 E6
Banchory AB31 ... 184 D6
Woodlands Sch AB24 ... 165 C5
Woodland Wlk AB15 ... 169 A4
Woodland Wynd AB33 ... 85 C7
Woodlea Gdns AB41 ... 76 C7
Woodlea Gr AB41 ... 76 C7
WOODSIDE ... 164 D7
Woodside Cres
Banchory AB31 ... 184 C5
Mintlaw AB42 ... 146 C4
WOODSIDE OF
ARBEADIE ... 184 E6
Woodside Pl
1 Banchory AB31 ... 184 D5
1 Mintlaw AB42 ... 146 C4
Woodside Prim Sch
AB24 ... 164 E6
Woodside Rd
Aberdeen AB23 ... 160 A3
Banchory AB31 ... 184 C5
Torphins AB31 ... 108 E8
Woodside Terr AB31 ... 184 D5
Wood St
Aberdeen AB11 ... 170 F7
Banff AB45 ... 140 E6
Portsoy AB45 ... 139 E7
Woodstock Rd AB15 ... 164 C1
Woodview Ct 14 AB39 ... 185 E4
Woodview Pl 2 AB39 ... 185 C4
Woolmanhill AB25 ... 190 A4
Woolmanhill Hospl
AB25 ... 190 A3
Wrights' & Coopers' Pl
AB24 ... 165 B6
Wrights La 4 AB51 ... 152 C7
Wrights Wlk AB32 ... 161 E3
Wyndford La AB32 ... 161 F3
Wynd The 6 AB53 ... 145 C4
Wyness Ct AB51 ... 152 D5
Wyness Gr AB51 ... 155 B3
Wyness La AB51 ... 152 E5
Wyness Pl AB51 ... 155 B3
Wynne Edwards House*
AB10 ... 169 F8
Wyverie Ct AB51 ... 150 C4

Y

York Pl
Aberdeen AB11 ... 165 E1
2 Cullen AB56 ... 1 B4
1 Montrose DD10 ... 189 C4
York St
Aberdeen AB11 ... 165 E1
Peterhead AB42 ... 147 D5
York Terr
Kirktown AB42 ... 147 D5
Montrose DD10 ... 189 C4
Youngson's La 7 AB53 ... 145 D4
YTHANBANK ... 50 A1
Ythan Ct AB41 ... 151 D4
Ythan Pl AB41 ... 151 C4
Ythan Rd AB16 ... 163 F3
Ythan Terr AB41 ... 151 C4
YTHANWELLS ... 45 D5
Yule Sq AB54 ... 148 E5